KNIVES
2014

EDITED BY
Joe Kertzman

Published by

Krause Publications, a division of F+W Media, Inc.
700 East State Street • Iola, WI 54990-0001
715-445-2214 • 888-457-2873
www.krausebooks.com

To order books or other products call toll-free 1-800-258-0929
or visit us online at www.shopblade.com

Cover photography by Kris Kandler

ISBN: 0277-0725

ISBN-13: 978-1-4402-3698-3
ISBN-10: 1-4402-3698-4

Cover Design by Sharon Bartsch
Designed by Rachael Wolter
Edited by Corrina Peterson

Printed in the United States of America

Dedication and Acknowledgments

It's high time to acknowledge the collectors of fine knives, as well as accumulators, daily knife users, enthusiasts and anyone who buys blades on a regular basis. If it weren't for you, there would be no industry. That seems obvious, but knives aren't exactly the first things that come to mind when most people think of collections, hobbies or interests, and in a politically correct society, they also aren't the most convenient or positively viewed items to purchase, display or use. As the tagline of several U.S. corporations goes, "We know you have choices of where you spend your money, and want to thank you for choosing us."

The annual *Knives* book is comprised largely of handmade and custom knives, many of them highly embellished, and collectors recognize this and purchase it with that in mind. Some collectors appreciate the artistry of knives and they certainly have many choices of where to spend their money. A collector could purchase oil-on-canvas paintings, sculptures, photography, jewelry, guns, antiques, carvings or a myriad of other aesthetically pleasing items that satisfy their creative nature or need to surround themselves with the finer things in life. They seek out beauty, and choose knives. So again, thank you to those collectors who have chosen our industry. It is truly an honor that you have found beauty in engraved, scrimshawed, carved, sculpted, jewel-inlaid and etched knives.

Most of the blades in this book are built as tools and many are sans any embellishment at all. Gratitude is extended to those who appreciate the utilitarian beauty or simple lines, patterns and designs of fixed blades and folders. It is the form and function to which you gravitate, and there is nothing more gorgeous than that.

The knife community tends to be a tight-knit group, a family that defies all stereotypes. Knifemakers, collectors, knife users and enthusiasts range from artists to businesspeople, hunters, blue-collar workers, doctors, lawyers and everyone in between. This author acknowledges all who have an interest in knives and view them in a positive light.

Many lovers of edged tools and weapons are well-read history buffs and understand the roles that knives, swords and other blades have played in shaping the world we live in. Seekers of knowledge have insight into what has worked in the past, what has failed and how to make the world a better place. They tend to appreciate knives and view them as tools to build a better tomorrow, implements of survival and items to be respected, cared for and maintained. Knives are not implements of destruction or evil like so many would have you believe. This book author acknowledges those who have taken the time to become informed.

I dedicate this book to all of you, as well as to my family and colleagues who have supported and encouraged me over the years, and tried to understand my love for knives and the knife industry. Yes, Mom and Dad, that includes you, my brothers, my sister and their families. My children Danny and Cora, and my wife Tricia, it's you who make my world go round. Jim Schlender, Jamie Wilkinson and Corrina Peterson – thank you for putting your trust in me to create a book people will continue to buy and treasure. I appreciate your commitment to this lowly writer and editor.

Joe Kertzman

Contents

On The Cover

Vivid colors leap off the front cover of *Knives 2014,* and the knives are equally brilliant in hand. Wayne Whittaker's locking-liner folder at far left features a 3.5-inch Robert Eggerling "armadillos"-mosaic-damascus blade and bolsters, a mammoth-tooth handle exuding blue and red hues, file-worked liners, and zirconia (manmade ruby) inlays in the back spacer and thumb stud. To its right is the "Artiste," a fascinating little fixed blade—only 6 inches overall—by Don Cowles showcasing a CPM-154 blade, a Pau de Pernambuco (Brazilian violin-bow wood) handle, a 416 stainless steel guard engraved and gold inlaid by Jim Small, 14k-gold pins and a ruby accent on the ferrule. Half folded at top-right lies a Warren Osborne "Ripcord" model called "Rhinos," parading a Burmese Jadeite handle, a CTS-XHP blade and 416 fittings. Masterful engraving by Tim Adlam, along with inlays of gold, silver and copper, depicts a black rhino on a 24k-gold background on the front bolster, and a Maasai warrior shield on the rear bolster. The reverse side of the knife shows a white rhino and a Swazi warrior's shield. Peter Carey's "Rubicon XL" boasts a Chad Nichols "iguana"-stainless-damascus blade, Gibeon-meteorite bolsters, an ivory-inlaid thumb stud and blue-anodized liners. The pre-ban ivory handle is scrimshawed by Gary Williams in a Viking motif,

the Viking himself with all the character an artist could conjure upon one knife. All are incredible creations by skilled knifemakers and artists.

Introduction

A handshake. It tells so much about a person before a word is even spoken. No one should judge a book by its cover—although the *Knives 2014* book has a fine one at that—but being perceptive, or interested in someone who extends a hand is perfectly natural and good. A knifemaker's hand, now that's a golden glove with stories to tell, isn't it? Generalizations are rarely advised, but one would rightly expect a bladesmith's hands to be rough and dirty, a sign of hard work, with lines where metal met tissue, scarred from cuts, soot embedded under the fingernails. Maybe a few nails are broken from wrestling steel, working a grinder or taking a hammer to an anvil.

Weather also wreaks havoc on a person's hands. Days, weeks and months spent in the shop or smithy prematurely age the skin, killing cells and dulling the nerves. Yet the dedicated craftsman labors on into the wee hours of the night when slumber takes hold of less sturdy stock. The hands build something, a useful tool that must withstand rigors of its own, tough cutting media, sinewy fibers, stubborn plastics and knotty pine. Like the knifemaker, the tool has an eventual job to do. Just as in nature, the materials' circle of life continues.

It's a good metaphor. The bladesmith breathes life into steel, synthetics and natural materials. There is a predestination to build what is useful and necessary. The men and women who choose such a path in life, or are born into it, generally take their craft seriously. There it is, another preconception, but one that is complimentary and backed by fact. It has been this author's experience that knifemakers take great pride in their work. They are a diligent bunch of perfectionists, hand rubbing steel until it shimmers and oiling wood until every grain has a chance to surface.

So what about the fruits of their labor? Turn the pages and look inside. Master craftsmen and women have fashioned some of the finest knives the world over this past year, and hired photographers to capture their work on film or digital pixels, where it has been converted to print and properly attributed.

The question often arises, "How does one make a living building knives?" Another popular query the *Knives* author often receives is: "Don't you eventually run out of things to say about knives?" The answers in order are, "It's not easy," and, "No, never." That which is never easy is often well worth the wait and worth telling. Take a look at the "Trends" and "State Of The Art" sections toward the middle of the book to see the cream of the knifemaking crop that rose to the top of thousands of images submitted for consideration. Like always, the knives themselves helped determine the trends of the era, and decide what common features knifemakers across the globe are including in their designs and patterns.

The "State Of The Art" section is just that, current coverage of the hottest knife embellishments including "Inlays & Etchings," "Stone Infusion," "Whirling-Dervish Damascus," "Non-Prosaic Mosaics," "Full-length Filework" and "Copious Carving." Scrimshaw and engraving get their just due, and "Puzzle Pieces," or knives with several handle pieces put together like jigsaw puzzles, are given prime real estate as well. Handcrafted sheaths round out the artistic offerings and lead into the "Factory Trends" section.

A bank of features in the front of the book include articles and color photos covering switchblades, mauls, art knives, "Blades of the Grand Bazaar," climbing knives and high-carbon steel. Knifemaker Tim Zowada explains "How to Strop a Straight Razor," knife writer Dexter Ewing tells why "Factories Drink from the Custom Maker Well," and American Bladesmith Society master smith Wally Hayes hopes you "Enjoy an Engraving Tutorial."

In all, it's been a busy year in the knife shop, as evidenced by the hands of the maker. They are tough like leather, and convey the character and makeup of the man or woman behind them. That alone is reason to appreciate an extended hand that welcomes you into its world, if only for a time.

Joe Kertzman

2014 WOODEN SWORD AWARD

Some people aren't content to rest on their laurels. They won't rely on past successes for continued fame or recognition. Take knifemakers Michael Vagnino, Jon Christensen, David Lisch and Tom Ferry, for instance. For the past few BLADE Shows, they've shared a booth (usually knifemakers take individual tables at the show, but they pooled their resources and rented booth space), joining forces under the name ACE or Artisans of Cutlery.

I talked to Michael at the show, and he said the group originally formed to show appreciation for the avid knife collector and to further advance the art of making knives. There was an invitation-only show for collectors and knifemakers for a couple years, and in 2013, the ACE group fashioned a bowie and folder for a Custom Knife Collectors Association cancer benefit raffle.

Their initial goal of advancing the art of making knives has come to fruition in the form of innovation. Ferry and Vagnino put their heads together to come up with the Ever Flush spring, a slip-joint split-spring feature in which, unlike traditional pocketknives, the spacer or back spring does not rise above the handle spine when opening and closing the blade. It remains flush with the knife spine, thus the name Ever Flush. The idea evolved from the desire to engrave back bars of slip-joint folders, but that was impossible in the past because slip-joint back springs are heat-treated.

Vagnino has busied himself most recently with "Convertible Lock-Back Push Daggers." Yes, that's correct, he's fashioning handmade knives that convert from a lock-back fixed-blade position to a locked push dagger and back again. The models shown here sport 3.875-inch blades, one in CPM-154 stainless steel and the other in Wootz steel, the former combined with an antique tortoise shell handle and the latter in black-lip

Photos by Hiro Soga (tortoise-shell-handle piece and Eric Eggly of PointSeven Studios

mother-of-pearl. The maker engraved the 416 stainless steel bolsters, and since the push daggers convert to fixed blades, Paul Long sheaths were necessary as fashionable carry options.

For all he has brought to the knifemaking table the past few years; his innovation, talent, all-around good vibes, and for these particularly striking examples of his work, the Knives 2014 Wooden Sword Award goes to Michael Vagnino. Congratulations, Michael, and keep up the good work.

Joe Kertzman

The Decathlete of Big Blades

*A camp knife is a performer, not a relic,
and versatile in form, function and material makeup*

By Roger Pinnock

Baseball, apple pie and the bowie knife—three completely different things with one unifying common element: they are indisputably and famously American. When it comes to the definitive American fixed blade, there is little room for meaningful debate—the bowie rules all. And it's not hard to understand why. It is a blade both steeped in history and shrouded in mystery. The bowie is visually commanding in dimension and design. It is a blade that leapt to the forefront of a nation's cutlery consciousness and has remained there for nearly two centuries.

But what of the bowie's sibling? There is another big blade that has walked through the pages of American history, yet has rarely made history. It has proven every bit as enduring in design, but has endured in comparative obscurity. I speak here of the camp knife—the bowie's less glamorous little brother.

The large field knife is every bit as old and American as the country itself. From the birth of the nation, it is a tool that could be found on the belts of Native Americans and settlers trailblazing the great expanses of the then-unknown West. The term "camp knife," however, is somewhat more contemporary. As best as I can determine, it emerged into to the contemporary cutlery lexicon as used by the man widely regarded as the grandfather of modern bladesmithing, American Bladesmith Society (ABS) co-founder and master smith—Blade Magazine Cutlery Hall of Fame® member Bill Moran.

Among Mr. Moran's many famous designs, to which generations of bladesmiths still pay homage, would be the Rio Grande and Maryland camp knives. Those blades marked a significant milestone in the history of the camp knife for two main reasons. First, while Mr. Moran may not have invented the

The camp knife genre is as old as the nation itself, as this John Cohea knife demonstrates. *(Buddy Thomason photo)*

term "camp knife," he was instrumental in bringing it to prominence. Second, and more significant, he bestowed upon the camp knife aspects of style and desirability that have contributed to its sustained presence in the custom knife market today as both a useful tool and sought-after collectible. The dual aspects of high performance and collector appeal now define the modern camp knife.

In the last 15 years, no single factor has given a greater boost to public awareness of, and affection for, the camp knife than the ABS-sanctioned cutting competitions. While the bowie buyer may engage in wistful imaginings of standing defiantly upon

Wood chips fly as the author puts a Russ Andrews integral camp knife to the test. The results? The piece hit hard and bit deep.

A field-grade camp knife needn't be plain and boring. Premium amboyna burl and an active hamon (blade temper line) enliven this Matt Gregory chopper.

Jerry Fisk, ABS master smith and long-time cutting competition emcee, observes, "The ABS cutting competitions did have an impact on many makers' knives. They should have. They allowed the makers to put their knives up against others so that they could learn where they needed to modify the blades for maximum performance."

Competition Yields Quality

ABS master smith Lin Rhea echoes this sentiment: "I was fortunate to get involved with cutting competitions early in my knifemaking career. That helped me gain a better understanding of the way a knife worked and how the person wielding the knife is supposed to handle it."

So what elements combine to make a good camp knife? Perhaps that question is best answered by first considering the practical uses for such a blade outside of the competitive arena. Fisk has long relied upon the camp knife as an essential field companion. "In my opinion, the camp knife is the most versatile large knife that an outdoorsman can carry," he says. "Similar to a large butcher knife, I use it for chores such as dressing out game, chopping small pieces of firewood, helping prep food and clearing brush when required. A camp knife also serves as a large companion piece while hiking so you do not have to carry an axe. This one knife serves many needs."

Indeed, its varied applications help to distinguish the camp knife from the bowie. As ABS master smith Russ Andrews explains, "The camp knife and bowie

the ramparts of the Alamo, owners of camp knives are seen chopping through two-by-four's, slashing free-hanging rope, and ever a crowd favorite, cutting through rows of water bottles, the latter resulting in an arcing crystalline spray. Seeing what these knives can do in capable hands communicates to the buyer just how well they perform.

Perhaps a more significant factor is the infusion of creative design that has resulted from the cutting competitions. In these competitions, makers take to the public stage with knives they design and build. The educational value of doing so is readily apparent.

Visual excitement dominates master smith Burt Foster's chopper that showcases a laminated blade of stainless steel sandwiching a high-carbon-steel core, a forge-textured finish and fancy burl handle. It's almost enough to disguise what is a simple and serious work knife.

differ in their primary and secondary purposes. The camp knife, being primarily utilitarian, is designed for the tasks involved in breaking trail and in making and maintaining camp. Weapon-related considerations are secondary. The bowie, primarily being a weapon, is less appropriate as a sole utility knife."

That is a sentiment with which Fisk agrees: "The camp knife may not have the 'zing' or historical recognition behind it, but it is more versatile than the bowie."

Designing a knife for versatile field applications can be quite a challenge. For the Olympic decathlete, it is very difficult to excel at not just one sport but many sports. Likewise for the decathlete of big blades, there is no room for failure at any given task. Not surprisingly, the talents of many great knifemakers have combined in the design solution and ultimate performance of the large field knife, and there is great variety within the genre as to blade shape, steel, handle design and materials. The camp knife is second only to the bowie for diversity of

design and materials in a big knife.

Steels run the range from a variety of stainless alloys to several high-carbon steels, including damascus, and even a combination of both, such as stainless-over-carbon laminates. ABS master smith Burt Foster has been a pioneer in the lamination approach, which offers the best of both worlds from a performance standpoint. The high-carbon steel core of the blade forms an edge that stays sharp and is easily re-sharpened, while the stainless outer shell resists environmental impact from use in varied conditions. The striking, high-contrast appearance essentially remains unchanged with use, as the etched carbon core darkens over time, and the stainless shell does what stainless does—resists oxidation.

Diversity Dominates

Apart from consistent reliance upon a large 9- to 11-inch blade, diversity is a dominant feature of the genre. Heavy, broad-blade, cleaver-style chop-

Tight, ladder-pattern damascus, premium fossil-walrus ivory and subtle gold engraving adorn a stout Ron Newton spear-point blade—the camp knife and art knife combined. *(SharpByCoop.com photo)*

Stag and damascus make this Don Hanson III piece a fancier gentleman's camp knife, but 12 inches of sharp steel will definitely get the job done. *(SharpByCoop.com photo)*

pers are quite prevalent, as are lighter and faster upswept blades, stout spear points and everything in between. Each blade's style reflects its intended use. As Russ Andrews explains, "The cleaver has a bit more weight near the tip, which moves the sweet spot close to the point and allows use in close quarters, as between branches. A more pointed type would be better as a large game knife. A blade with 'belly' better accommodates push cuts. Given that the blade will be used primarily for chopping, I believe a properly shaped convex edge is most appropriate. The edge has to have enough mass behind it to ensure resistance to damage, and at the same time be thin enough to bite deep with minimal effort."

Camp knives with single guards are a popular choice, but double guards and guard-less integrals remain quite common. Since an ergonomic handle is a must from a performance standpoint, easily shaped wood or synthetics like Micarta® and G10 are prevalent among field-grade pieces. That said, just as with the bowie, premium natural materials such as stag and ivory are also represented.

Jerry Fisk describes some of the criteria that apply to the crucial aspect of design: "First, in my opinion, the handle must drop at least a quarter-inch to a half-inch below the plane of the edge to give you enough power with the swing. The handle must

have at least one 'pull' for your hand to grip better in the swing (such as a flared butt). Two pulls are even better, such as adding a palm swell. This way, the forward part of the handle also gives your hand something to pull against in a swing."

"The proof of the pudding is in the eating," as our British cousins are fond of saying. The proof of the camp knife is in the chopping, hacking, slashing, slicing, etc. Here we come to one of the defining aspects of the camp knife versus other big blades; it is far more likely to actually see use by the customer, and as a consequence, far more likely to become a source of performance-related feedback for the maker. I have had the opportunity to field test a number of camp knives over the years and continue to be impressed by the capabilities of these large blades, and struck by the impact of variations in design.

My most recent opportunity to put a big camp knife through its paces came on a recent hunting trip in upstate New York, where a large integral camp knife fashioned by Andrews was my chosen field companion. The design of the knife drew inspiration from a number of large Philippine field knives collected by Russ' uncle and passed on down to him. The 10-inch blade featured a gentle re-curved profile, and the African blackwood handle offered enough drop to help generate a powerful cut, as well as

Belgian bladesmith Samuel Lurquin adds some aggressive lines, in high-carbon steel or damascus, to his "Tsavo" camp knife.
(Norbert B. photo)

ergonomic contouring to ensure a comfortable and secure grip through swing and impact.

As a heavy chopper, the knife excelled. Weight, balance and drop all combined to deliver a heavy, powerful blow, allowing the sharp convex edge to bite deeply into large logs and make short one-swing work of smaller branches. Hanging grapevines provided a much tougher test of blade design than rope, and the thick, dense, moist vines cannot be dispatched through power alone. An overly heavy and thick blade will simply bounce off the vine, leaving little impression upon it. A blade too thin and light will cut into the vine, but not deeply. Russ' blade managed the task with ease, however, reflecting the maker's thoughtful design and execution of the piece.

Another strong positive came in the crucial area of handle comfort. I have yet to hear of a knife fight lasting the better part of a day, but clearing a trail can certainly take that long. User comfort over a protracted period is an essential virtue of a good camp knife. A handle that does not assist in blade retention through all aspects of cutting causes the user to grip more tightly, advancing the onset of hand fatigue. Similarly, when vibration is transmit-

ted from the blade through the handle into the user's hand, the task in question becomes longer and less pleasant. The hidden-tang construction and ergonomic contouring of this piece made for a powerful but soft impact, with excellent blade retention and orientation in gloved or bare hand.

The camp knife today remains an established player in the custom knife arena. One indicator of this trend is that it's now an awards category in itself at several knife shows. As Rhea relates, "We now have an award category for 'Best Camp Knife' at the Arkansas Custom Knife Show held in Little Rock. It has been received positively and is getting several entries. We feel the camp knife is a legitimate and separate class of knives, while remaining a close relative to the bowie, a knife for which Arkansas has a strong connection."

While lacking the emotive glamour of the bowie, the camp knife nonetheless plays a strong hand in practical performance, and with the quality and diversity reflected in the custom knife market today it presents a compelling choice for the collector and outdoorsman alike.

Climbing Knives Are Heaven Sent

There aren't many places a knife is more welcomed or needed than on the face of a cliff

By Greg Bean

Something's wrong when a climber reaches for a knife, at least when hanging from a rope on a cliff. It means the knife is needed to free a beginner caught in a belay device, to bring down an injured climber or in the worst case, to recover a body. It wouldn't be for opening packages, slicing up dinner, skinning game or cutting fishing line, although perhaps to cut rope.

Typically, a climber carries a one-hand-opening folder when he gets vertical, possibly one with an assisted opener, a lanyard hole or ring for a carabiner and a serrated blade that locks closed. Cutting through rope is quick work with a serrated edge, and that's a primary use for climbers. One-hand opening pays for itself when one of the climber's hands is needed to keep the rope locked into a safety device. Lose that rope hand and there's trouble.

An assisted-opening knife hanging from a climbing harness and in contact with a cliff, trees, rope or gear could result in an open blade dangling around a climber's crotch, so a lock is a welcome safety feature. A lanyard hole or loop allows the climber to safely tether the knife to his or her gear because a dropped knife would be a hazard to anyone below the climber's position.

Rock climbing is first and foremost an adrenaline high—it's a way to feel as if a person is in a life or death situation, competing against the cliff with victory achieved through skill, conditioning and tenacity. It's a safe way to "live on the edge." When all goes right it's safe, yet the experienced climber prepares for the small margin of error or equipment failure.

"Top-rope climbing," or "top roping," is the safety-first way to get the adrenaline. The climber is tied onto a rope that stretches from the climber to

The author's climbing knife is a Buck Redpoint one-hand-opening, semi-serrated folder that locks open and closed, and includes a lanyard loop for a tether, with the metal loop also doubling as a bottle opener. All the bases are covered.

an anchor at the top of the cliff or rock, and back to a belayer on the ground. The belayer takes up slack as the climber ascends, keeps the rope taut if he or she falls, and controls the person's fate when they descend. It's wise to be nice to your belayer. The rope is a safety net, limiting falls to a few feet. Climbing injuries here are similar to those an can athlete expect from any sport—temporary bruises and scrapes that give a climber the chance to sound reckless when telling stories at work. The risks of sport climbing are no greater than a weekend football or basketball game. Injuries are a risk but not a danger. But for those who want more, the opportunities are out there to up the amperage.

"Lead climbing" is one of the riskier undertakings. The lead climber does not have a rope positioned above that will hold them if they fall. They fix anchors in place as they go up, then clip into each anchor. As long as a climber is below the anchor they can only fall a short distance. When the anchor is below the climber they will fall twice the distance to the already-placed anchor plus the stretch of the rope. Lead climbing calls for an experienced and confident climber, as the falls can be spectacular events, with the greatest chance of serious injury.

Hair Trimmer

The standard belay device, the ATC (Air Traffic Control), is a simple tool essential to climbing. It has no moving parts except the rope that passes through it, yet the ATC controls the rope and therefore, the climber. It is used for climbing and rappelling and will be found wherever climbers and cliffs cross paths. The ATC is a magnet for long hair, however.

Getting hair caught in a belay device sounds like a scenario from *The Three Stooges,* but it does happen. Bec Baxter, an associate at the outdoors sporting goods chain REI, learned the hard way to keep her hair pulled back when rappelling. Halfway down a cliff her hair caught in the ATC device and she was stuck. Fortunately, she didn't have to learn the hard way to carry a knife and was able to cut herself free. The story may sound funny, but it could have had a painful ending.

At Smith Rock State Park a climber crosses an open-air traverse from the main body of a massif to the pinnacle Monkeyface. As dramatic as this looks, it is one of the easier ways to get to the top.

Climbers call their gear their rack, which leads to some smirks in mixed adult company, but any gun shooter recognizes the term.

In a shoulder harness, mountaineer Craig Gianelli carries an A.G. Russell Sting with a forged 1050 dagger-shaped blade and indexing dimples on the handle. It was originally designed in the 1970's as a reaction to poorly designed boot knives available at the time. It is now offered by CRKT.

Chad Jones, an engineer and lead climber, freed a first-time rappeller who became stuck when her hair was caught in her ATC. An engineer, Chad is geared towards planning and prevention, and has never had a problem on any climbs he's led. He has learned that being prepared includes helping the unprepared. The tangled climber was with an inexperienced leader that was clueless about what to do. Chad rigged a rope at the top of the cliff and rappelled down to free the stranded girl. He had to borrow a knife to get her free, but now he's a believer and doesn't start a climb without a knife. Chad has since followed up the experience with training for climbing rescues and an intensive three-day wilderness first aid course.

Rappelling is a parallel activity to climbing, but most climbers rappel don't think of it as the main course. It is more of a way to get from point A to point B, when A is at the top and B is at the bottom. Rappelling has a skill set and risks all its own, though. The rope isn't a safety net, but instead more like the main rail of an amusement park ride.

Backup protection for rappelling is provided via a small cord rigged between the climber's harness and the rappel rope, that is secured by a sliding knot called a prussic knot.

The climber slides the prussic knot down the rope with them as they descend. If something goes wrong, the knot pulls taught on the rappel rope and arrests the descent. Releasing the tension on the prussic knot releases its grip, and the climber keeps descending. If the climber doesn't work the prussic knot correctly they will experience an unplanned stop. If the climber is below an overhang then they are left dangling without an easy way to take the tension off the prussic knot.

Rappelling down a cliff that has a waterfall is one of the more esoteric of roped events. Also called

Kelly Sewell goes for the classic Leatherman as part of her gear, tethered to her harness and taped for identification. All her gear has a stripe of pink tape to mark it as hers.

Upper Cuts

Katerina McHugh, a nurse practitioner and wilderness first responder keeps a multi-tool as part of her climbing gear. The multi-tool's scissors are used to cut tape for climbers' hands, which is standard practice for "crack climbing." Cracks are vertical fissures a climber wedges some part of his or her body into to gain a hold. They are equal parts problem and solution. Ascending a crack may be the only way to get up a surface that looks like glass. The classic move, jamming, is to insert the hand and flex the fingers as if to make a fist. If a climber can make a fist, he or she wedges it into a narrow spot for a hold.

More often, the climber flexes their hand, pressing the back of the hand against one surface and the fingers and palm against another surface. By applying enough force, they create a wedge that will get them a little further up the crack. Reaching up with the other hand, they do the same thing. Eventually they reach the top or to a place where there are more user-friendly rock features. Eventually they will also shreds their hands, making the tape a necessity.

Watching Katerina prepare climbers at the New River Gorge in West Virginia, famous for its crack-laden cliffs, was like watching a trainer tape a boxer's hands before a fight. Getting a climber ready was a methodical process with many pieces of tape and many cuts required before the task was complete.

Alberto Beani is the most experienced climber I've ever met and has been a mentor to more climbers than he'll ever remember. He's also taken part in more rescues than he cares to remember. From Biella, Italy, he started climbing when he was 12 years old, and is approaching his 50th year as a climber. Biella is between Milan and Turin in northern Italy and within sight of the Italian Alps where he learned to climb. Alberto is always equipped with a knife and believes it is indispensable. In Italy he became involved with search and rescue as a member of the "Soccorso Alpino Italiano," the Alpine Search and Rescue.

"You slash the tether quickly or you lose the climber," Alberto says, punctuating his story with a quick slashing movement of his hand, shown with the conviction that comes from having made the move to save a climber. His liveliest stories are the ones about helicopters evacuating climbers, hikers and mountaineers.

A typical rescue starts when a climber makes a mistake that strands them on a cliff with disabling injuries that won't allow them to complete the climb or descend the rock. Once the search and rescue

cascading, it is beautiful to watch and exciting to experience. Besides the usual challenges of manipulating the rope and dealing with a rock structure, the climber gets soaked, often on slippery rock.

At Big Bradley Falls in the Blue Ridge Mountains near Saluda, North Carolina, Craig Gianelli freed a couple of rappellers who had stuck prussic knots, once requiring a self-rescue because he himself was caught with the same problem. He positioned himself below a dangling climber, held in place by his backup prussic knot, and the climber stood on his shoulders to get enough slack to release her knot so she could complete the rappel. Craig was then swinging free and his prussic knot had become hopelessly tight from holding the weight of two climbers. He tied a second cord for protection and cut the first free. Being prepared with a backup prussic cord and a knife, along with a cool head and a plan, gave a couple of climbers a funny story instead of a nightmare to tell around the campfire.

Craig, a classic mountaineering adrenaline junkie, is an exception to the "climbers carry folders" rule and prefers fixed-blade knives. He carries a double-edged A.G. Russell Sting dagger that clips into the sheath to hold and release the knife. He transfers the knife from his climbing harness to his pack when hiking, and to his person when he moves away from his pack.

Alberto Beani of Biella, Italy shows the knife he always has with him when outdoors—an Ozark Trail one-hand-opening folder with a plain-edge 440 stainless steel blade and a wood handle. He considers one-hand opening essential.

personnel locate the injured climber they anchor him securely and perform what first aid they can. The rescue helicopter approaches at the closest safe distance and lowers a crewmember on a cable, with a stretcher if the terrain allows it. The cable is fastened to the climber's harness and the safety line is cut as the helicopter rises. Once away from the cliff, a winch raises the climber to the helicopter.

"You don't have time to untie a knot or loosen a carabiner. When the helicopter goes, it goes," Alberto says, making the slashing movement again just in case I missed it the first time. He's worked rescues at altitudes as high as 15,000 feet, where the air is so thin only small copters can fly.

While in the U.S., Alberto took part in the rescue of a climber who was leading and took a fall of about 40 feet before the rope caught him. He swung into the cliff hard enough to break his climbing helmet, crack his skull, lose an eye and sustain a severe brain injury. Alberto was climbing on the same mountain outside of Charlotte, North Carolina, and was called for help. Alberto reached the injured climber and attached himself to a fixed rope dropped from above, then positioned himself under the climber and became a human stretcher. Cutting the climber loose was the only way to release him from the fixed rope, and with only one hand available to do the cutting, Alberto's one-hand-opening folder was an essential part of the rescue.

Any climber will tell you, when a knife is for rescue or repair, they hope it's never opened. But when it is needed, it must be "at the ready." Lives and limbs may depend on it.

Voila! There's an Art Knife

It's not quite so easy, but Lloyd Hale has been making the craft look that way for 45 years

By Don Guild

It's 3 a.m. dark. Wide awake, he stares at the ceiling. In vivid detail, a distinct art knife bounces around in his head. Next morning, he hotfoots it to his shop and starts grinding steel. No drawing. No scaled outline. No color yet. The knife's details gestate from a bar of steel, to the file work, to the application of inlays, to the final polishing. Voila! What an intertwined complexity, made up of five or more organic materials and 78-150 separately worked steel parts, to illustrate the intuitive, innovative talent knifemaker Lloyd Hale has in spades.

In 1977, the demand for Hale knives reportedly produced the longest backorder waiting period up until that time in knifemaking history—five years—and his knives sold for $75 apiece.

Out of nowhere, in 1981, a monumental event changed Hale's life and career. He says, "While helping Gil Hibben turn out a couple of knives in Louisville, Kentucky, a Mr. Owsley Brown Frazier contacted me. He was heir and CEO of Brown-Forman, the largest U.S. distillery that produced Jack Daniel's, Old Forester, Early Times and Southern Comfort. He asked if I'd work full time and create a one-of-a-kind collection for him. Each knife had to be unique and make him smile. If and when we parted, he promised he'd eventually sell the knives, and then we'd split the profit 50/50.

"He bought, below market price, each knife as I made it," Hale continues. "But the pressure was enormous because to hang on to my originality, it meant I couldn't look at knife magazines, talk to other knifemakers or let them see what I made. So I literally disappeared from the knifemaking world for 23 years. He got his knife collection. He left me with empty promises."

Hale couldn't refuse the offer Frazier made in 1981, for it afforded him the opportunity to completely vanish from the prior conflict he'd stirred up in The Knifemakers' Guild, where he'd spoken too loudly about the makers who put their own name on a knife when they had used helpers in their shops to craft the knives.

Hale says, "It hit the fan in 1988, when Mr. Frazier's wife got wind of his buying a farm—a place for me to live and make his knives. She threatened him with a massive divorce suit, 'if that guy doesn't get

A large Lloyd Hale sub-hilt fighter, the blade and fittings are 440C stainless steel complemented by nickel silver bezels and handle inlays of gold-lip pearl, silver mother-of-pearl and abalone. The overall length: 14 inches.

his sorry ass out of Kentucky.'"
In 2002, Frazier was about to
open his Louisville museum,
and declared his knife collection
complete. By then Lloyd had made
him about 350 knives, and today
most of them reside in The Frazier
Historical Arms Museum.

"When my job ended with Mr.
Frazier, he gave me $10,000 cash,
a new pickup truck, and told me
to, 'Go somewhere and hide out
until my wife cools off.' She never
cooled off," Hale explains. "By
2008, I had pissed him off also,
so all the agreements we'd made
back in 1981 never came through.
He never sold the knives I had
made to give me my share. Very
sad! But I can't complain; it was
quite a ride while it lasted. I'm too
old to worry about it.

The image of knifemaker Lloyd Hale in his shop holding one of his impressive bowies is courtesy of David Darom, and was first published in his book *The World Of Art Knives* **in 2010.**

Yowie! The Kid's Face Lit Up

"But we did have some good
times, especially one in 1981, when I built Mr.
Frazier my massive sculpture project 'Sword in the
Stone' featured at 'Bittners 2' (his upscale antique,
interior design, architectural and furniture store
in Louisville). Prominently on view at the store's
grand opening, a three-foot stone had a very large
and ornate sword stuck fast into it," Hale details.
"As people crowded around it, Mr. Frazier and I both
noticed a boy of 12 years old watching a burly man,
who tried to free the embedded sword. This tempted
the young boy, who then went over and tugged and
tugged at the sword's handle with all his might.
Owsley Frazier, standing a short distance from the
crowd, then flipped an electric switch that released
the sword. Yowie! The kid's face lit up like a neon
sign when the evil stone gave up the sword he held.
The boy's puzzled look pleased Mr. Frazier no end."

Soon after Hale was cut loose he got a computer,
learned how to navigate through Google, and looked
up "Lloyd Hale knives" to see if his old knives were
still being bought. Wow! They were. That search led
him to Ed Wormser, Walter Hoffman and myself, Don
Guild, who told him we'd buy every knife he made.

Hale says, "Just doing good work in my shop, and
giving the knives I make the best chance of being
loved, is quite enough for me now."

Of Hale's shop, author and long-time knifemaker
Bud Lang tells this story, "As I viewed a couple of
Lloyd's hollow-ground, mirror-polished blades, I noticed a very sharp line between the flats and hollow-
grinds. I realized for him to achieve that sharp edge
meant he was polishing the blades 'edge up,' I told
him he was insane, and he asked, 'Why?' So I pointed
out his sharply polished edges and mentioned that
blades could catch in the buffing wheel. He said that
he'd had a couple of blades 'get away' from him, and
at least once he'd gotten stabbed. So I asked him why
he did it this way, and his answer was plain. 'I think
most good knifemakers polish and grind their blades
edge up. I know Loveless and Dowell do.'"

Hale reflecting on his colorful past says, "My
knifemaking's been a fun run for 44 years. Around
'72 or '73, I added file work to my big bowie blades,
even though it was frowned on by other makers. I've
had my ups and downs, but who hasn't? I learned
long ago never to settle on one line of knives. You get
in a rut and stay there, doing the same three or four
styles over and over, just because there's a buyer out
there waiting and wanting. In the mid '70s, magazine
articles scared me off. Whenever a magazine showed
one of my knives, and 50 or 60 people wanted one just
like it, I found that my fire went out when I repeated
the same knife. It was just another boring job.

The gorgeous gut-hook skinner exhibits white and gold-lip mother-of-pearl, red coral and abalone, along with 440C stainless steel fittings and a finely file-worked blade. *(SharpByCoop.com photo)*

"The first time a man looked at my work and said, 'Oh you're an artist,' I didn't know for sure, but I thought I'd been insulted. Now I know what I make is art, and each new creation lives in my head for a month, 24 hours a day, until it's completed," Hale remarks. "Then it's shipped off and I wait for comments from the new owner. After the adoption is successful I start over again. All remnants of the old knife must be swept away. It's out with the old and in with the new, yet lessons learned are stored for future recall. Then it's time to start over from scratch and design something totally different.

On Top of the World

"Now, when I'm in the shop, I feel I'm on top of the world. My knife shop is the only place I can express myself without saying the wrong thing. My machines can't hear me, although they have tried to kill me several times. They've set me on fire, thrown unfinished blades at me, ground my flesh, tried to electrocute me and stopped working for no reason. But they still seem to love me."

And Lloyd loves his shop and the time he spends there. But sometimes the shop doesn't love Lloyd, because more than once it's struck back. As he smilingly relates, "One day I was grinding a bowie blade while sitting on a padded bar stool with a back rest. I get less tired that way when I grind. Lost in the moment, I dropped the blade. Still perched on the bar stool, I bent down to pick it up. My shoulder came in contact with the fast-spinning 60-grit belt. I jerked to get clear of the grinding belt, lost my balance backward, and my right foot came up and kicked over the 5-gallon water bucket I used to cool off blades. The bar stool continued its backward travel, and the blade in my hand went flying, as the back of my head came in contact with my steel workbench. I hit the floor, in a blaze of stars and pain in my shoulder, just as 5 gallons of water joined me. I lay there in all that mess thankful no one was there to see my classic pratfall."

One of a few U.S. knifemakers in the late '60s, Lloyd relates how he got started: "In 1967, I was watching this guy shoot a 90-pound draw Howard Hill longbow while wearing buckskin clothes and a knife. Later I find out it was a Case Bowie. He gives me a few archery pointers and said, 'I read in the paper you built a guitar for The Mamas and The Papas. Could you make me a bowie knife?' I said, 'Sure.' Truth was, I didn't know what a bowie knife was, so I had to go to the library and research it. This led me to learn about Jim Bowie and Bo Randall, so I wrote Mr. Randall, who answered my letter, and his stag-handled Randall #3 became a huge inspiration for me. I worked at Alcan in their forging and extrusion plant, and lucky me, they had a metallurgy lab where I could ask the right questions about tool steel and heat-treating. So I made the bowie for Don Brown and was bit by the knifemaking bug. That knife is in Mr. Frazier's collection at his museum.

"When I made my first knife I felt like I was home," he surmises. "It's hard to explain how I knew I'd found what I was destined to do. I just knew. In 1969, my wife squalled and balled when I told her I was quitting my job and going full-time as a knifemaker. We made $40 that first December. I sold one hunting knife."

Hale says, "I was influenced by the 19th-century classic English bowie knives, the large German knives with roping and acorns, and the pre-1920s stag-horns. My first file work was around 1970. One diehard purist hunter would

Rope-style twisted sterling silver wire wraps around the fluted ebony handle of a 440C art dagger. As per Lloyd Hale's style, handle inlays help enliven the piece. *(SharpByCoop.com photo)*

Sometimes it's not the fact that Lloyd Hale is known to inlay white and gold mother-of-pearl, as well as abalone, but the way they're inlaid into the handle and frame of a knife, in this case a 440C sub-hilt fighter. *(SharpByCoop.com photo)*

Lloyd Hale shows his brother Sam the Frazier Historical Arms Museum. The centerpiece is the infamous ivory-handled "Sword in the Stone" that Owsley Brown Frazier loved so much.

have no part of it and asked, 'You ain't one of them California faggots, are you boy?'

"In 1973, my wife and I heard of Springdale, Arkansas, a town that had good schools where they let kids go to their neighborhood school rather than be bussed. So we moved there. At the time A.G. Russell helped a lot of us new knifemakers get known through his company that, by then, made the Morseth knife. He asked me if I would help him out. So I made his Morseth knife part time, and made my own knives full time—two totally different types of knife.

"In 1969, I met Hans Tanner, editor for Guns & Ammo magazine," Hale remembers. "My knifemaking skills had advanced to the point where they wanted to do a profile on me. A young Bud Lang, former editor of Knives Illustrated, wrote the article. This exposure helped my knifemaking career take off."

In summation Hale says, "I think, as in any profession, being looked upon as a master of my craft is a great honor, and becoming a master of what I call man's true oldest profession is twice humbling. Knives can be traced back to cavemen and have shaped man's history of conquest up to today's modern world."

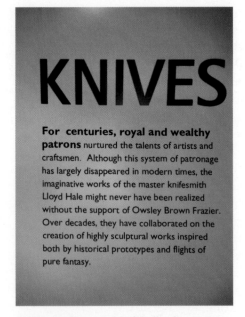

KNIVES

For centuries, royal and wealthy patrons nurtured the talents of artists and craftsmen. Although this system of patronage has largely disappeared in modern times, the imaginative works of the master knifesmith Lloyd Hale might never have been realized without the support of Owsley Brown Frazier. Over decades, they have collaborated on the creation of highly sculptural works inspired both by historical prototypes and flights of pure fantasy.

A sign explains the knife display at the Frazier Historical Arms Museum.

Fueling the Switchblade Obsession!

The author takes you on a journey of one-hand-opening knife discovery, collecting and obsessing

By Michael Janich

My fascination with one-hand-opening knives began late in the spring of 5th grade. The heat and humidity of the Chicago summer arrived early that year, and afternoons in the classroom were pretty uncomfortable. To help pass the time as we counted the days till summer, my teacher would end each day by turning off the lights and reading the novel *The Outsiders* to us. While some kids would put their heads down on their desks and nap, I was captivated by the story and the switchblade knives described in it. Based on the vivid descriptions in the story, I drew pictures of switchblades and dreamed of having one of my own.

Without having any ready sources to buy a real switchblade that summer I did the next best thing: I bought a novelty switchblade comb and a cheap pocketknife, and managed to swap the blade for the comb. It worked briefly before the blade went airborne, but thanks to those few satisfying "snaps"–I was hooked.

The following summer, I helped my dad renovate a friend's apartment in southern Illinois. Located above a bar and dance hall, it was packed with antiques—including a vintage but broken Shur-Snap

The author's obsession with one-hand openers is clear in this progression of his personal carry knives over the past 30-plus years. From bottom up: a Gerber Folding Sportsman II with "Flicket" attachment, a first-generation Spyderco Endura, a Benchmade Model 68 Bali-Song™, an Emerson Raven (hand-ground prototype), his Masters of Defense Tempest, Spyderco Yojimbo, BlackHawk Blades Be-Wharned and his current Spyderco Yojimbo2.

While living in Hong Kong the author traveled regularly to the Philippines, using the opportunity to expand his collection of traditional Filipino butterfly knives.

The author's fascination with butterfly knives also included modern expressions of the design, such as these from Spyderco (color anodized piece), Benchmade (below the Spyderco) and Darrel Ralph. Note that the Benchmade blades are marked as prototypes.

fishtail switchblade. After doing my fair share to help out, I talked the owner into letting me have it.

Back home, I carefully disassembled the knife and fixed the problem. Then I proudly carried, used, broke and fixed that knife for about a year before the kick spring finally gave out. Disappointed but not discouraged, I set my sights on finding a suitable replacement and learning everything that I could about switchblades and other one-handed knives.

High school, its underground economy and the dynamics of the knife industry in the 1970s combined to support my addiction. On the automatic front, I managed to add several classic Italian switchblades to my collection. I also discovered *Soldier of Fortune* magazine and the writings of David E. Steele, which collectively fueled my interest in other types of one-handed folders and switchblade alternatives. Based on Steele's recommendations, my first true defensive carry knife was a Gerber Folding Sportsman II equipped with a "Flicket"—one of

several add-on devices sold back then that allowed a knife blade to be thumbed open. Carried in my back pocket in the days before pocket clips, it gave me quick, one-handed deployment to support my burgeoning interest in edged-weapons tactics.

The prosperity afforded by a summer job and two well-stocked local gun shops prompted the next chapter in my one-hand-opener journey. Again, thanks to Steele, I discovered the fun of a classic Barry Wood folder in the form of a Powder River production model. Fascinated by the German paratrooper out-the-front (OTF) gravity knife shown in Steele's book, *Secrets of Modern Knife Fighting,* I had my first taste of the OTF concept with the unique Benchmark Diamondback and its manual Rolox™ mechanism. Enthralled by the concept of a gravity knife as a side opener, I added a first-production Gerber Paul Knife featuring Paul Poehlmann's revolutionary lock design. Push the button, swing the handle and you've got instant gratification.

Right after high school I enlisted in the U.S. Army. While studying Chinese-Mandarin at the Defense Language Institute, I saw *The Big Brawl* starring Jackie Chan and got a glimpse of a butterfly knife. Once again, I was obsessed and couldn't wait to get my hands on one. As an Army private I couldn't afford one of the Bali-Song, Inc. (the progenitor of Benchmade) knives from the movie, so when I was home on leave I decided to make my own. Using the blade from a Pro-Thro throwing knife, some brass from the hobby shop, and a few pieces of black Micarta®, I successfully made my first butterfly knife.

Alone with that Knife

I spent countless hours with that knife learning and refining opening and manipulation techniques. As I earned rank (and more money) and production butterfly knives became readily available, my collection grew by leaps and bounds. Among them was a Bali-Song, Inc. Model 68 that replaced my well-worn Gerber FSII and served as my daily carry knife for most of my nine years of military service.

I left the Army and accepted a position with the Defense Intelligence Agency (DIA) at the U.S. Consulate in Hong Kong. Around that time I also discovered some uniquely different folding knives with round holes in the blades allowing easy one-handed opening, clips for convenient carry at the top of the pocket, and serrated edges that cut with a vengeance. Made by Spyderco of Golden, Colo., those revolutionary knives literally defined the modern tactical folder and popularized the concept of the one-hand opener. Although my Model 68 Bali-Song stayed in my back pocket, my right-front pocket became home to a first-generation Spyderco Endura Lightweight with an integral pocket clip.

As an Intelligence Officer for DIA, I was required to travel to the Philippines four to six times a year, as well as frequent trips to my team's head office in Bangkok. Every trip to Manila included shopping in the Ermita district to search for traditional handmade butterfly knives, in addition to barongs, krises and other Filipino big blades. Similarly, my visits to Bangkok involved prowling the stalls of street vendors to pick up all forms of Asian-made switchblades including the newly released double-action, out-the-front autos. These power-out/power-in OTFs were cheaply made, but tremendous fun. And at street prices of less than $20 each, I couldn't resist. Thanks to these opportunities—and the benefits of a diplomatic passport—my collection of one-hand-openers swelled.

In the early 1990s, I began writing articles for knife magazines and worked hard to provide insightful reviews of a wide range of custom and production knives, many of which were one-hand openers. Over time, the editors of those publications came to appreciate my obsession with one-handers and I became the "go-to" reviewer for high-speed folders. My passion for Bali-Songs led to reviews of Benchmade's iconic Model 42 and a host of prototype variants of that model. Later on I had the honor of reviewing Darrel Ralph's Venturi butterfly knife and subsequent generations of his work, which I still regard as the pinnacle of the breed.

Several years later I began publicly teaching my approach to edged-weapon self-defense and established Martial Blade Concepts (MBC). MBC is a modern, legally defensible system of knife tactics that focuses heavily on methods of getting everyday-carry folders into action quickly and decisively. That aspect of MBC taught me a lot about the finer points of knife carry and deployment—especially the nuances of tip-up versus tip-down carry, the advantages and disadvantages of various carry positions, and the leverages and mechanics of one-hand folders.

It also enabled me to earn the friendship and respect of other personal-defense instructors, knifemakers and designers; like the late Col. Rex

Out-the-fronts are a special breed of one-hand-opening folders. From left to right are a WWII-era Nazi Paratrooper gravity knife, two modern German gravity knives with plastic handle scales, a power-out auto, an inexpensive double-action (power-out/power-in) auto, a Masters Of Defense Triton auto with dagger blade, a Masters Of Defense prototype Triton with a tanto-style blade, and two inexpensive double-action out-the-front autos.

Applegate, James Keating, Kelly Worden, Kelly McCann, Allen Elishewitz, Ernest Emerson and Bram Frank. Through those friendships I learned a lot and also got an inside peek at some landmark developments in one-hand folders—like some of Emerson's very first "Wave" openers. Hands down the fastest-opening folders ever developed, they feature an integral hook on the back of the blade that snags the pocket as the knife is drawn, swiftly and automatically opening the blade. Too cool to pass up, they quickly found their way into my collection.

In 1997 I was offered the opportunity to be one of the inaugural designers of the Masters of Defense (MOD) knife company—then a partnership with Microtech. The process of designing a knife for commercial production motivated me to take a hard look at all of the one-hand openers in my collection and analyze the mechanics of their operation. My initial design—the R.O.C.K. (Ramp-Opening Combat Knife) used a convex ramp on the back of the blade as a thumb lever. The company's engineers decided

Some one-hand folders are even more special than others. Of the author's most prized possessions are, from top to bottom: THE original prototype of the Applegate-Fairbairn folder–which was a collaboration between Bill Harsey and Butch Vallotton, Mike Snody's one-of-a-kind original Yojimbo model, and an exquisite flipper-style handmade folder by Allen Elishewitz.

The culmination of the author's obsession with one-handed openers is his patented Jani-Song design. Like a butterfly knife, it has two handles, but one is nested within the other, and the "safe" handle is on the outside. The handles and blade pivot on a common pin, providing butterfly-knife-like flipping action without the fear of getting cut.

that a concave ramp was better, but unfortunately that replicated the function of the Emerson Opener, so it was replaced with conventional thumb studs. On the positive side, my Tempest design (as it was ultimately known) was a graduate course for me in the mechanics of one-handed manual openers. It also represented my full-fledged entry into the cutlery industry and led to my first S.H.O.T. (Shooting Hunting Outdoor Trade) Show and my first BLADE Show.

Whetting the Blade Appetite

Since the Tempest was also produced as an automatic, it whetted my appetite for the state-of-the-art autos that were emerging at that time. Soon, top-of-the-line autos by Microtech, Combat Elite, Paragon, Randall King and others joined my collection of traditional Italian switchblades.

Despite my intense passion for knives and knife training, up until 2004 my involvement in the cutlery industry was only an avocation. That all changed when Jim Ray, the founder of MOD, sold the company to BlackHawk Products Group and offered me a position as director of product development. I left my previous dream job (video production manager for Paladin Press) and accepted the position with BlackHawk, jumping into the knife and tactical markets with both feet.

With the benefit of Ray's tutelage, I ultimately became the brand manager of both MOD and Black-Hawk Blades—BlackHawk's imported knife line. In that capacity I had the opportunity to design and bring to market a number of different knife projects.

Not surprisingly, most were one-hand-opening folders, automatics and an assisted opener (yes, I like those too). But as gratifying as those projects were, I still felt something was missing—the ultimate one-hand-opening knife. And since it didn't exist, I decided to try to invent it.

I began with the concept of the butterfly knife, since it is the most versatile and flamboyant of all one-handed folders. Unfortunately, it is also one of the most skill-dependent folders and one of the least forgiving of mistakes. Typical single-edged butterfly knives have two handles; the "safe" handle, into which the unsharp-ened back of the blade folds, and the "free" or "bite" handle, into which the sharp edge folds. As long as you hold the safe handle, only the other handle or the spine of the blade can contact your hand. Grasp the "bite" handle, however, and you are vulnerable to the edge.

In my mind, the perfect one-handed knife would be a butterfly knife that literally made it impossible to grasp the "bite" handle and would be easier to learn to manipulate than the traditional version. After many hours of daydreaming, countless sketches and numerous models, I had my epiphany. Instead of two handles side by side, I placed one handle inside the other and the blade within the inner handle. I also eliminated one of the pivot pins so all three parts rotated on a single pivot. This design literally put the "safe" handle on the outside of the knife and the "bite" handle on the inside, making it impossible to grasp the wrong handle. An ambidextrous sliding latch completed the package, creating a knife that was as fast and flashy as a butterfly knife, but almost as easy to use as a push-button auto. I dubbed it the "Jani-Song."

The revolutionary design of the Jani-Song easily earned it a utility patent, but unfortunately only about 40 of them were ever manufactured. In 2009 BlackHawk eliminated my position, but I was fortunate to find a home with the pioneers of the manual one-hand-opening knife, Spyderco. I bought the Jani-Song patent from BlackHawk and sold it to Spyderco with the hope and confidence that they will someday bring the design to its full potential.

In the meantime, I continue to live the dream. I work for the company that basically invented the modern one-hand tactical folder and have the privilege of using and promoting their products every day. I teach defensive knife tactics around the world and help others learn and appreciate the life-saving advantages of one-hand openers. Throughout the process my appreciation for one-handed knives—as well as my collection—continues to grow.

Enjoy an Engraving Tutorial

Knifemaker Wally Hayes is thankful to those who taught him to engrave and wants to share his knowledge

Shown are the author's engraving tools and workspace.

By Wally Hayes, ABS master smith

People like Yves Baril, Adone Pozzobon and David Riccardo have helped me tremendously on my journey into knife engraving. Without their help I would not have progressed very far in the craft, and it is my pleasure to share what I have learned from them so that others may also benefit.

Twenty years ago I was fortunate enough to meet Yves, who worked at the Canadian Bank Note Co. in Ottawa, Ontario for 43 years. While employed there he engraved 146 stamps and numerous bank notes, including 11 stamps for the United States. I took lessons from Yves and would go over to his place Monday nights to learn the fascinating craft of engraving.

Early on, even with Yves' help, I encountered the problem of trying to cut modern stainless steel materials with regular high-speed gravers. The tips kept breaking, causing me to slide the graver across my work and make a mess of it. As a bank note engraver, Yves did not engrave with a heel on his graver. I was trying to cut long lines without a heel, pushing the graver by hand, and it was extremely difficult to control the tool in that manner. Another problem was that my drawing skill was not up to par and an engraving is only as good as its design. Because of these problems I stopped engraving, even though I loved the art of "cutting steel."

Fast forward to 2006. I was making folders and decided to get back into engraving, so I began researching as much as I could on the Internet including visiting many online engraving forums. I called Adone, an accomplished and respected engraver, and talked with him quite a bit. Renewed with modern tools and equipment, as well as design and transfer methods, my passion for engraving resurfaced stronger than ever.

So now I would like to share what I have learned with people that want to learn the craft of engraving.

Tools of the Trade

The tools now available for an engraver help make the art form easier and faster to learn. Yet, while the correct tools speed up the learning curve, you still have to put in the time practicing. I use a GRS Graver Max (http://www.grstools.com) and Steve Lindsay's Sharpening System (http://airgraver.com/sharpening.htm). I also use Lindsay's new Carbalt™ gravers, and have found that GRS cobalt gravers work well too. I employ a high-speed air rotary tool connected to my Graver Max for removing background, as well as a cheap rotary tool from the hardware store. Some type of magnification is necessary and I've found that an old stereoscope suits my needs just fine. I also use an old ball vise, comprising the last of the major tools, along with assorted gravers, punches, files, burnishers and a scraper.

With the advent of Photoshop 7 and Corel-DRAW—a computerized vector graphics editor developed by the Corel Corporation—you can draw a shape on a tablet personal computer, move it around, stretch it, shrink it, layer over top of it, copy scroll parts, and move them to fit into the space you need engraved. I can also create a mirror image of the design for printing. Plus, I have an entire library of Dover Design copyright-free books, and I use these to help with what I want to engrave.

Now I can draw dragons and fish well enough freehand, and just started learning scrollwork with the help of Ron Smith's book *Drawing & Understanding Scroll Designs,* and a lot of help from Riccardo. Drawing scrolls freehand is time consuming, but with Photoshop you can draw and shape your scrolls to produce a design in much less time. Now I can print the design with an inexpensive laser printer and transfer that picture onto the steel. Regardless of how you get your design you don't have to let your ability or lack of drawing skills stop you from engraving. There is plenty of clip art available to get you started.

The Design Transfer

There are also many options for transferring a design onto steel. If you happen to be a skilled artist, you can paint your steel with a light, thin coat of white water paint, then draw the design onto the steel with a pencil. You can also use Sam Alfano's Transfer Wax, dab a coat on the surface and draw on the wax using a pencil. Then you can lightly scribe your design onto the steel. Yves initially taught me to scribe acetate and rub modeling clay on the acetate. I would then burnish the acetate on the steel, scribe the layout and cut the design.

These methods work, but there is an easier way to transfer a design onto steel—utilizing Tom White's Transfer Magic, available on eBay for $10. With this solution you can transfer a drawing from artist's films, which are clear plastic sheets, onto your steel, or print a design on paper via laser printer and transfer it from the paper to the steel. Although I use paper, clear plastic is better because you can actually burnish the ink onto the steel.

First, I put a thin coat of Transfer Magic onto the steel with a cotton swab and allow it to dry. Then I lay the drawing

The dragon design is printed out and ready to be applied to the steel handle slab.

ink-side down onto the steel. I tape this down with masking tape, load up two cotton swabs with nail polish remover and roll the cotton swabs gently across the drawing. Next, I dip two fresh cotton swabs in water and dab them on the paper to soak it. I then take my finger and gently rub it across the paper, and the paper comes off in little pieces. The drawing is now transferred onto the steel. To illustrate this article I chose one of my favorite dragonheads, but the method described herein is great for any design or lettering.

Now we're ready to start engraving the outline of our design. I use a 3/32" square Lindsay Tungsten Carbide "Carbalt" graver sharpened with the Lindsay Universal Sharpening Jig. With a small heel on the graver, I won't dig into the steel too much and it is easier for me to control. Power-assisted engraving is the way to go to save time, increase the learning curve and achieve deep cuts in one even pass. It may take me several passes to engrave scrolls and curves, but I outlined the dragon illustrated for this story in one pass.

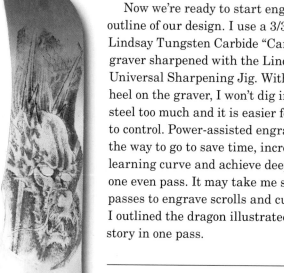

The design is transferred onto the steel.

Here the author has started to cut the outline of the dragon.

The outline is cut, so author and knifemaker Wally Hayes has begun to shade the image.

The shading has been completed, and the knife handle is ready for gold wire inlay in the shape of a lightning bolt.

After I cut the outline, I started shading the dragon. Light lines, dots or a combination of both work for shading. On this dragon, I used many dots. I sharpened a separate 3/32" graver down to a small point using a Lindsay Detailing Sharpening Jig, but did not put a heel on the graver this time. Instead, I pushed the tip of the graver into the steel and popped it out, making one small, diamond-shape dot.

You can spend as many hours as you want shading or creating the whole engraving with dots. It is a lot of fun, and with practice you can achieve an array of shades and tones. As I worked, I filled in the engraving with flat-black model paint. This showed me how dark my overall engraving was.

Wire Inlay & Engraving

I decided to add a gold lightning bolt to my design, and will detail here how I created the embellishment. First, I drew a lightning bolt onto the steel using a fine Sharpie™ marker. Next, I cut the line with my sharpened detailing graver. Generally, the cut should be as wide as the diameter of the wire to be inlaid, and the depth of the cut itself half the diameter of the wire. For this example I used 0.5mm, 23-karat rose gold. Then I took an old high-speed steel graver knife and undercut the sides of my channel. I re-sharpened this tool often while I used it. The tip had to stay very small as to not scratch the other side of the channel as I undercut the groove.

Next, I undercut a small amount of metal on each side of the channel. Then I took a small brass punch and dulled the end with 60-grit sandpaper. I placed the gold wire in the groove and held it down with the brass punch, gave it a good tap with a small hammer, and continued to move along holding and tapping until I got to the end of the channel. Then I tapped over the entire length again to make sure it was well seated.

After that it was time to trim off the excess gold with a slightly rounded flat chisel. In this step, I wanted to round off the corners of the chisel so they didn't dig into the surface. Then I sanded the gold with sandpaper until it was flush and shiny. In this case, I used a block of flat steel as backing for the sandpaper.

There are many ways to texture the background on an engraving. I used a ball burr, about 1/8" in diameter, and textured the entire surface of the plate around the dragonhead and lightning bolt. Most people that engrave knives fill in the engraved

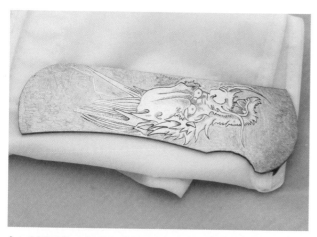

A gold lighting bolt is inlaid into the knife handle.

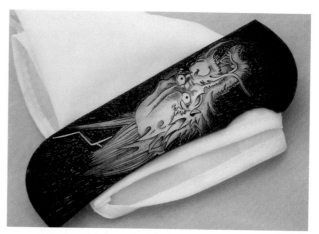

The folder scale is blued and polished.

The folder is finished and on its way to a new home. Let's hope they like dragons!

cuts with flat-black paint. On this example I used O-1 tool steel so I could "cold blue" the whole surface. I cleaned the surface with acetone, put bluing on it with a cotton swab until the whole surface turned black, then dipped the entire handle in cold water. I placed the knife handle in a mix of baking soda and water, removed it and dried it with paper towel.

In this instance, I used 2000-5000 grit sandpaper to highlight the dragon and gold lightning bolt. Using a burnishing tool, I gently rubbed the gold lightning bolt to give it a high sheen. Because I used high-carbon steel on the handle, I warmed up the steel with a heat gun and put a coat of beeswax on it to protect it from rusting.

Finally, I assembled the engraved knife, and it was teatime!

Shopping Mauls?
We've Got You Covered

When the author tested a selection of mauls and axes, it changed from boring chore to fun exercise

By *Roderick T. Halvorsen*

For many people facing crushing home heating costs during the current down-turned economy, the opportunity exists to fire up the woodstove, fireplace insert or wood furnace to supplement or replace more expensive fuels. For those folks, the renewable resource of wood is readily available and can be inexpensive. Power splitters are an option for some, but excellent hand tools can get the job done with surprising speed and efficiency.

Such work involves the use of two basic types of splitters—the maul and the axe. The maul offers heavy-head construction and a sturdy poll for direct splitting and driving of the steel wedge, the wedge being a separate study in its own right. The splitting axe features a thinner blade, less eye support and a lighter poll, all making for a handier tool designed for splitting smaller pieces of wood. Instead of focusing on readily available hardware store splitting tools, I assembled a selection of less common varieties. The results of my testing caused me to reclassify wood splitting from being a boring chore to that of a fun exercise and hobby!

I found no "bests" or "worsts" among the blades tested. All 12 have convex edge grinds with the exception of the Leveraxe, which sports a modified chisel grind. Since wood is such a variable substance, each maul or axe user should evaluate their tooling needs with an eye toward what is best for the wood they intend to split. This likely requires some experimentation with tools. Further, homeowners may find that with the acquisition of two or three separate mauls and/or axes, their chore becomes easier and more enjoyable. Indeed, an investment of $200-$300 would easily assemble a battery of cutting tools that would last indefinitely, yet each year help save on the heating bill and provide vigorous physical workouts, as well.

Clockwise on the "clock," starting at 1 o'clock just right of top center, the dandy dozen are: (1) Biber Classic; (2) Stihl PA 80; (3) Stihl PA 50; (4) Fiskars X27 Super Splitting Axe; (5) Gerber Splitting Axe II; (6) Wetterlings Splitting Maul; (7) Bavarian Splitting Axe; (8) Helko Tomahawk; (9) Helko Vario 2000; (10) Vipukirves Leveraxe; (11) Gränsfors Bruks Splitting Axe; and (12) Gränsfors Bruks Splitting Maul. The diversity of blade shapes, poll thicknesses and attachment of heads to hafts can easily be seen.

Here on the ranch we burn mostly Douglas fir and Ponderosa pine. Trees are selected for their poor merchantability. They are girdled, left to stand and dry somewhat, then felled, bucked and split dry. To give myself an idea of what the tools were capable of and how they handled, I chose a still-green Ponderosa pine. Springy, knotty and sometimes spongy, this wet "P-pine" was the perfect candidate to challenge all the blades. At 111 feet tall, it provided about two cords of wood, with rounds (round or unsplit sections

Poll types indicate some can be used for driving wedges, some not. From top to bottom are the: (1) Biber Classic; (2) Stihl PA 80; (3) Stihl PA 50; (4) Fiskars X27 Super Splitting Axe; (5) Gerber Splitting Axe II; (6) Wetterlings Splitting Maul; (7) Bavarian Splitting Axe; (8) Helko Tomahawk; (9) Helko Vario 2000; (10) Vipukirves Leveraxe; (11) Gränsfors Bruks Splitting Axe; and (12) Gränsfors Bruks Splitting Maul.

Using what the author calls a "splitting tire," he says the Vipukirves Leveraxe made quick work of the large "round" of wood within it.

of log) up to 30 inches in diameter, enough to give each blade a good workout.

Every splitter I put to work deserves a look-see by prospective wood burners.

First I used the Biber Classic by Mueller. This large splitting axe features a 4-pound head, a 4-inch wide face, a 30-inch long handle and an overall weight of 6.25 pounds. It is hand-forged in Austria, and without a doubt it represents an Old World look that would have fit into the hands of the Woodsman in the Grimm's fairy tale. In my hands I found it to be a good splitting axe. Blade configuration with integral side "wedges" (wedge-shaped raised faces on the head) allows good lateral energy transfer for breaking rounds apart, and easy withdrawal of the blade from the wood when knots prevent complete separation. There is a unique feel to this axe that makes it a joy to use. I also found it somewhat useful for limbing logs.

The STIHL PA 80 Splitting Maul was next up to bat, and though we normally think of STIHL as the maker of chainsaws and other fine power tools, the company also sells a fine line of hand tools, with the heavy PA 80 being a sterling example of them. With a 6.6-pound, drop-forged head of C60 steel and an extra-long, 33 inch hickory handle, the wide, heavy poll made wedge-driving a cinch. The other side of the blade, with a wide, straight swell to provide good lateral drive, performed equally well. On the bottom of the edge is a little tooth that makes the maul an effective "hookeroon" (tool for moving small logs and firewood) of sorts for righting, rolling and positioning rounds in preparation for striking—a handy feature!

As with the PA 80, the STIHL PA 50 Splitting Axe with oversized neck and drop-forged head is made by the famous Ochsenkopf (Oxhead) Company in Germany. With a 29.5-inch ash shaft and

Safety calls for good eye protection, boots and gloves. In addition, a string wrapped around a dry round of wood makes for a handy package for carry to the campsite or hearth.

Not all rounds, or sections of log, are big ones, and they don't always pan out to be of even length. Here with the help of a tire, the Gränsfors Bruks Splitting Maul makes short work and easy handling of some odds and ends.

4.4-pound head, it combines good splitting performance on smaller rounds and performed adequately on some chopping chores. This one conjures up the category of "survival splitting axe" for backcountry use. Light hammering can be accomplished using the stout poll, with chopping and splitting being accomplished employing the sharp side.

Optimum Blade Geometry

When the Finnish Fiskars Company says their comparatively lightweight X27 Super Splitting Axe with a 4-pound head possesses optimum blade geometry, they are not kidding. This one keeps up with the heavies! With its 36-inch, "stronger-than-steel" DuraFrame™ handle extending the swing radius outward, blade speed is extremely fast and the head sinks deeply into both wet and dry wood. The side wedges on the head then go to work efficiently separating the material. This is an excellent tool!

Made by Fiskars and available through Gerber Legendary Knives and its Gerber Gear line, the Splitting Axe II sports a 3.4-inch, Teflon™-coated head that measures 55 HRC on the Rockwell hardness scale, boasting the same efficient head design as the previous axe. It is interesting to note that the head-in-haft method used to secure handle and blade is of ancient origin, going back thousands of years.

Applying modern technology, the head is combined with the synthetic handle, a mating that results in a secure, permanent grip on the blade with all the advantages synthetic offers in weather resistance, shock absorbency and general toughness. The Fiskars and Gerber axes also slip inside ingeniously designed carry and hanging scabbards for safe storage and transport. These would also be superb dual-purpose axe/splitters while carried sky high in a bush plane or with backcountry camping gear.

Hand-forged in Storvik, Sweden, the American hickory-handle Wetterlings Splitting Maul, at 32 inches long and with a weight of 8.5 pounds, is of classic Scandinavian design, sporting a slight central ridge running the length of the blade. This improves both splitting and withdrawing from the wood. Made from Swedish carbon steel, the final Rockwell hardness of the edge is 56-58 HRC. I found the edge design of this one excellent for dry wood, but it tended to bounce on wet wood, a common characteristic of some American-style mauls. Balance was perfect for hammering wedges.

The 4.5-pound, handmade Bavarian Splitting Axe is forged by a small, family blacksmithing firm and exudes the same rustic charm as the previously described Biber model. The head on the Bavarian axe is fitted with a 24-inch American hickory handle conformed to a comfortable and ergonomic shape. Best suited to the smaller rounds, naturally, this model simply floats in the hands and fits neatly into what might be called the "kitchen axe" category, highly suitable for splitting kindling or for the smaller rounds commonly used to feed a cook stove or cottage hearth. It also looks so charming it seems well suited to adorning that hearth after heating it! I did find it to be the only tool tested that had a handle that loosened somewhat after use.

Specialized Splitters

The German company Helko dates back to 1844. Their axes and hatchets meet stringent German DIN manufacturing standards (DIN 7287, 7294, 7295, 5131 and 5132). Helko states that their axes are then safety proofed with edge hardness held between 47-56 HRC up to 30 millimeters from the cutting edge. Helko, unlike some makers who prefer to use a water quench, asserts their oil quench to be superior in minimizing the potential for quench cracking.

The Helko Tomahawk, with a fiberglass polyamide composition handle and Scandinavian-style, 3.5-pound head, has an overall length of 31.5 inches. This axe yet again demonstrates that shape and design really do contribute to superior performance. The "re-curved" handle feels a bit odd at first, until one starts striking wood. Plus, the two-screw blade attachment allows use of different blades, an ingenious and deservedly patented design!

This latter option makes all heads and handles interchangeable between the Tomahawk and Helko Vario 2000 series, though the two types require separate screw sets. Obviously, these are specialized splitters sans hammer polls and should not be used for driving wedges.

Big brother to the Tomahawk is the Vario 2000 Heavy Log Splitter with an overall length of 35.4 inches, a weighty 5.1-pounds, wedge-shaped head and hickory handle designed for heavy use. With the steel bracket and overstrike protector, the head remains secure on the haft, but if it should loosen, it is easily tightened with the provided wrench. This axe provided efficient splitting of the thickest rounds.

The most unusual splitter tested was the fascinating Finnish-made Vipukirves Leveraxe. With a

The wide variety of blade shapes is impressive. In the left column, from top to bottom, lie the: (1) Biber Classic; (2) Stihl PA 80; (3) Stihl PA 50; (4) Fiskars X27 Super Splitting Axe; (5) Gerber Splitting Axe II; and (6) Wetterlings Splitting Maul. In the right column, from top down, sit the: (7) Bavarian Splitting Axe; (8) Helko Tomahawk; (9) Helko Vario 2000; (10) Vipukirves Leveraxe; (11) Gränsfors Bruks Splitting Axe; and (12) Gränsfors Bruks Splitting Maul.

uniquely designed, cast-steel, 4-pound, 2-ounce head, this is no mere splitting axe but more of a firewood "processor!" Reviewing the videos on the company website led me to wonder if it would be difficult to use, but when the axe arrived I found it was easily wielded, and most importantly, works exactly as demonstrated. The long, 35.5-inch birch handle provides excellent control and energy transfer for this truly amazing tool.

I challenged the axe with many difficult pieces of wood and found it to work well on all. In practice, one

Handle length makes for handling differences. Longer normally allows greater head speed, striking velocity, penetration of the wood, and consequently, better splitting characteristics. But sometimes the shorter-hafted models' handiness is safer and more effective, especially on kindling and the intentional splitting of thin strips.

and 27-inch hickory haft is heavy enough for many home firewood chores and handy for splitting kindling. I found it capable of splitting heavy dry rounds and edge splitting of wetter wood. It has an edge fine enough for some bucking and is far superior to any hatchet or felling axe for breaking up thick rounds.

The Gränsfors Bruks Splitting Maul (a.k.a "Hammer-Poll Axe") features a 5½-pound head, 2½-inch face and 31-inch handle, and I found it effective on all types of wood. For splitting of wet and dry wood, it was a handy and efficient tool, biting deeply and splitting wet wood delightfully well. It also blended well with my physique and strength perfectly, a point that should be touched on in regards to the selection of splitting tools. Splitting work is strenuous, and can be quite dangerous, so choice of the maul or axe should be done with care.

Initially, I doubted that I could learn much more than I already knew about a chore as mundane as splitting wood. But now, after a couple cords split with this dandy dozen, I find these blades have taught me many lessons that will make my future efforts far more effective and enjoyable to boot!

CONTACTS:

Bailey's (Fiskars Axe), POB 550, Laytonville, CA 95454 707-984-6133 or 800-322-4539, www.baileysonline. com; **Garrett Wade** (Wetterlings Maul and Bavarian Axe), 5389 E. Provident Dr., Cincinnati OH 45246 800-221-2942, www.garrettwade.com; **Gerber Legendary Blades**, 14200 S.W. 72nd Ave., Portland, OR 97224 www.gerbergear.com; **Helko North America**, 9215 Santa Fe Springs Rd., Santa Fe Springs, CA 90670 562-946-6668, www.helkonorthamerica.com, info@ helkonorthamerica.com; **Smoky Mountain Knife Works** (Gransfors Bruks Splitting Axe), 2320 Winfield Dunn Pkwy., POB 4430, Sevierville, TN 37864 800-251-9306, www.smkw.com; **STIHL Northwest**, 215 Hamilton Rd. N, POB 999, Chehalis, WA 98532 360-748-869; **Traditional Woodworker** (Biber Classic), 885 E. Collins Blvd., Ste. 104, Richardson, TX 75081 800-509-0081 or 972-437-0081, info@ traditionalwoodworker.com; Vipukirves Leveraxe, Heikki Kärnä, Gumbontie 139, 01120 Västerskog, Sipoo, Finland, Tel. +358 9 877 9152, vipukirves@elisanet. fi; **Wisemen Trading and Supply** (Gransfors Bruks Splitting Maul), 8971 Lentzville Rd., Athens, AL 35614 888-891-8411, www.wisementrading.com

simply places a round inside a splitting tire (a rubber tire is a useful aid to all splitting) and commences striking the upright wood about 1½-2 inches inside the outer diameter of the round while walking around the log in clockwise fashion. Slabs of wood simply pour off the sides. The chopped wood flies off with speed and velocity too, so it is highly advised that for safety sake, rounds are contained in the splitting tire. A Leveraxe was certain to be included in my wood-splitting battery.

Two Gränsfors Bruks splitters were hand-forged, hardened and tempered by the Swedish company to a Rockwell hardness of 57 HRC. Each features a steel handle collar for protection of the haft and a roughed grip for secure retention by the stationary hand. The Large Splitting Axe, with 3.5-pound head, 3-inch face

Blades of the Grand Bazaar

Some exotic trips are worth the while, particularly one to the "Secret Lane Of Steel"

By James Morgan Ayres
© All photos MLAyres

Hidden deep within the Grand Bazaar of Istanbul, Turkey is the Secret Lane of Steel. This narrow corridor houses an Aladdin's treasure of jeweled daggers with damascus blades actually forged in Damascus, Syria. There are yatagans, both long and short; swords once used by mounted Janissaries and bearing the nicks and scars of battle; ivory-handled Ottoman fighting knives with sweeping blades and engraved silver sheaths; court lady's dirks; Chinese sleeve daggers; sword canes; scimitars; 100-year-old folding knives and straight razors.

Many of these marvels from the past can be purchased for the price of a modern factory knife. Others might cost as much as a new flat-screen television. But prices are flexible and subject to discussion. To view or purchase any of the treasures, you must first find your way to the Secret Lane of Steel, concealed in a maze of passageways in an almost forgotten corner of this sprawling complex and known only to the cognoscenti.

The Grand Bazaar was built by the order of a Sultan in the 15th century, when Istanbul was Constantinople. Before it was Constantinople the city was named Byzantium, and for over 2,000 years prior to that known to the world simply as "The City." The Grand Bazaar lies within the still-standing walls of this ancient city. During my visits to Istanbul I spend as much time in the Bazaar as I can manage, and after many visits I still find it fascinating. Recently I overheard a woman in a tour group say to a companion, "It's a tourist trap. Everything's overpriced. Bargain to get the prices down. Be careful. Watch for pickpockets."

Well of course it's a tourist trap, being at the end of the Silk Road it has been a tourist trap for over 500 years. No doubt the famous tourist Marco Polo

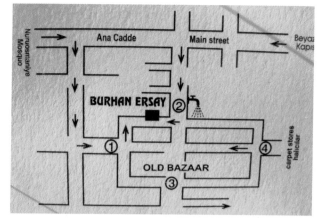

The map shows the way to Burhan Ersay's shop in the Grand Bazaar.

would have shopped here if he had passed through a little later. But the Grand Bazaar is also an important shopping center for local people, an amazing resource for the knowledgeable shopper, and a delight, a wonder, a cornucopia of goods and an enchanting diversion with vast and endless halls. There are 61 covered walkways, uncounted miles of narrow passageways and lanes, over 4,000 shops, dozens of coffee and tea shops, restaurants, cafés, kebab houses, a score of water fountains—some crafted of marble—and a dozen or so shops specializing in antique blades.

Of these, the tiny shop of Burhan Ersay is my favorite. Burhan is a genial man with the air of a scholar rather than a merchant. He and his establishment have been open for business and purveying antique blades since 1968. There are many cheap reproductions for the tourist market on sale around Istanbul. You'll find none of these in Burhan's. He does have some excellent reproductions, which only the most educated eye could pick out. But Burhan will tell you exactly which items in his stock are antiques and which are reproductions. He values his reputation as

Of the treasures on display in the tiny shop of Burhan Ersay is a Turkish folding yatagan with a sheep horn handle and a convex-ground carbon steel blade.

an honest dealer in antiques, is knowledgeable about edged weapons and tools, and won't lead you astray.

To find Burhan's magical treasure trove—he also has amber and coral jewelry, icons and bric-a-brac from the centuries—you must wend your way through the major passages, down small walkways and finally into the Secret Lane of Steel. It's easy to get lost, so I'll give you a map to show you the way. You'll need it. Think of it as a treasure map.

Seductive Riches

While making your way through the Grand Bazaar you must take great care to not be distracted and seduced by the riches on display. Along these ancient corridors there are mountains of gold jewelry; a pasha's wealth of silks; crystals; emeralds and diamonds; leather jackets and shoes with turned-up toes; handmade leather luggage with pick-proof locks; Turkish carpets—even flying carpets, the dealers say; Byzantine gold coins; an icon of St. Joseph painted by a Greek artist in 1510; Turkish Delight—a candy created for a Sultan; sandalwood; frankincense and myrrh; musk; rosewater; perfumes; colored lanterns; porcelain vases; samovars and copper pots for Turkish coffee; underwear; umbrellas; lacy linen handkerchiefs; silver cigarette cases; pocket watches and sword canes from the 19th century. Hold firm to your purpose or you might blow your budget before finding the Secret Lane of Steel.

Once you reach your goal you'll find knives and swords like those I discovered during my most recent visit. The first one that caught my eye was a Kindjal, a double-edged, long straight knife or short sword. The design of the Kindjal goes back to ancient Greece and its use has been widespread throughout the Caucasus for all of history. This one had a 16-inch blade of forged and layered steel, a sheep horn handle, and a silver hilt and pommel. Burhan

Burhan Ersay shows off a selection of antique Kindjals, daggers and other exotic knives.

informed me that this one was forged in the mid-19th century in Circassia. Deep fullers on both sides of the blade aided the balance, as did the distal taper.

Unlike many modern long knives designed for combat, which are thick, heavy and more suited for chopping than quick thrust and cut, the Kindjal was light and fast. Balanced just forward of the guard it seemed like an extension of my arm, a weapon refined over centuries.

During the 19th century, armed with long cavalry yatagans and Kindjals, Caucasian guerilla fighters defeated tsarist armies in deadly close-quarter combat, battle after battle. Even today, razor-sharp Kindjals, many of them hundreds of years old, are carried and used in the mountains of the Caucasus, and represent the fighting spirit of mountain warriors who could not be defeated by tsarist or modern Russian armies.

The next blade I handled was slender and no more than 10 inches overall, a poniard with a needle-sharp damascus blade, fossil ivory handle and carved silver decoration. The small dagger was light and radiated fierce purpose. I asked Burhan if it had been a lady's sleeve dagger. He told me that it was called a "Sis," and that far from being a lady's dagger, it was the last weapon of a fighting man. The Sis was designed to be small, slender and light, to be easily concealed and carried at all times in a boot or sleeve, yet strong and tough enough to parry a sword. With its triangular cross section, the Sis could reportedly pierce chain mail. It was a last-ditch weapon for Janissaries and other soldiers who would fight to the death rather than surrender.

In one of the glass cases I noticed a knife that was similar to a contemporary hunter, albeit with a 6-inch damascus blade, camel bone handle scales, a forged lion's head pommel and file work on the spine. In response to my inquisitive look, Burhan told me this was a reproduction of an 18th century utility/hunting knife, made in Damascus only a few years ago. Burhan is always careful to point out which of his knives are reproductions and which are antiques, a testament to his integrity because the reproductions in his shop could fool all but the most expertly informed.

Bristly-Boar Skinner

Burhan had used this particular knife on his frequent hunts for wild boar in the Northern Anatolian Mountains near the Black Sea. He showed me some photos of a recent hunt. I've hunted boar on three continents, but I had never seen a boar this huge. The critter was the size of a Volkswagen Beetle. From experience I know how tough bristly boar skin is and how quickly it can dull an edge. Burhan said this damascus blade had been used to dress out and break down two boars, and for other camp jobs,

---

Displayed are two exceptionally fine 19th-century kindjals with sheaths from Circassia.

A Jambiya-style Ottoman dagger features a camel bone handle, a ribbed damascus blade, and an ornamented hilt and pommel.

gold-washed, silver-chased, engraved and embossed blades with ornate sheaths decorated to match the knives they protect. There are knives with deeply curved damascus blades, like short scimitars, but with ribs running down the center of the steel, sometimes known as Jambiyas. Some feature handles of jade, lapis and other precious stones. There are also a few more common knives.

From the work-a-day world, there is an interesting collection of European and Middle Eastern folding knives, including the all-purpose folding yatagans with sheep-horn handles and forged high-carbon-steel blades. The folders have been used in this part of the world for time out of mind, and are still the everyman's daily tools for pruning grape vines and olive trees, slicing cold melon on a hot summer afternoon and splitting kindling for wood burning stoves. Last year I spent some time in the Taurus Mountains with the Yurok nomads, who still migrate with the seasons (and their goats) and keep to the old ways. They use these simple but elegant friction folders for everything from slicing goat cheese, which is their primary source of income, to killing and butchering goats to be roasted over open fires.

Whether you seek an antique Kindjal from Circassia, a Janissaries' Sis, or a folding yatagan, you can find it in the Secret Lane of Steel. But remember, the Grand Bazaar is a place to get happily lost, and to be drawn into shops by seductive merchants who have learned their trade from generations of master merchants before them, merchants who have served local people and explorers for centuries. To engage with a merchant of the Grand Bazaar is to take part in a play—sometimes a drama, perhaps a comedy, occasionally a tragedy—a play that has been running before Shakespeare's work was first performed.

Soft voices, cajoling, draw you in. Merchants more courteous than any diplomat invite you for tea and to sit, rest, take your time and take the merchant's time. He has nothing more important in his life than to talk with you and while away the hours. If by chance you happen to buy something, he will give you the best price possible and make sure the item you purchase is the very best of its kind. If you do not buy, he will be devastated, but will recover, place his hand over his heart, and will swear that you will always be welcome in his humble shop, whether you buy or not. Here's the thing—he means it. Return in a month or a year and he will remember you, welcome you with a smile, ask about your family, send for tea, talk with you and pass the time. Maybe one

without being sharpened. The blade was still sharp enough to shave hair from my arm.

I asked if the damascus steel for this blade was actually forged in Damascus, or if the steel was imported from India. In ancient times much damascus steel was forged from billets of Wootz steel from India. Burhan was not sure about the origin of raw steel billets, but he was confident that the blade and many of these blades, both antique and reproductions, were forged in Damascus in local workshops. He has personally visited Damascus workshops, and there has been active and continuous trade between blade merchants in Istanbul and the same workshops in Damascus for generations.

Burhan's shop contains a king's ransom of

A display case houses an assortment of Burhan Ersay's wares.

Another display showcases a Chinese sleeve dagger, an Ottoman yatagan with gold-chased sheath and Jambiya-style daggers.

day you will become a customer. If not, you will still be welcome, always.

If you stick to the map and find your way through the maze of passageways and enticements to the Secret Lane of Steel, and to Burhan's hidden treasure trove, he will order tea for you and happily spend hours showing you his wares and discussing them with you. His shop is a wonder. He is a gentleman. Of course, there are hustlers in the Grand Bazaar. Beware of the kebab stands outside at the entrances. The food is good, but the prices triple if you sit at a table. There are no pickpockets. The Grand Bazaar is well policed. But do bargain, gently, politely.

Factories Drink from the Custom Maker Well

Consulting known and respected makers, companies tap into sources of creative knife design

By Dexter Ewing
All photos by Dexter Ewing

The Kershaw Cryo is a Rick Hinderer frame-lock folder that features his patented Lock-Bar Stabilizer™, Speed Safe™ assisted opener and four-way pocket clip.

New knives resulting from collaborations between manufacturers and custom knifemakers reflect a forward-thinking mindset. They are polished and refined, adding a sense of style along with a generous helping of utility. After all, a knife is a tool first and foremost regardless of its design. Today, nearly every major knife company enlists the talents of one or more custom knifemakers, particularly well-known respected makers.

Such collaborative efforts result in a maker's design at a price and delivery schedule that everyone can appreciate. When the design prowess of an accomplished knifemaker is coupled with top production capabilities and high-end blade and handle materials, the result is a mass-produced knife that has the indelible thumbprint of a maker.

KAI USA, parent company of Kershaw and Zero Tolerance knives, has employed the work of custom knifemakers since the late 1990s, initially working with Ken Onion, and later with Grant and Gavin Hawk, R.J. Martin, Tim Galyean, and most recently Rick Hinderer. Hinderer's designs have shown up under both corporate banners in the form of the Kershaw Cryo and the Zero Tolerance ZT0550.

"Designed by Rick Hinderer, the 0550 blends rugged, overbuilt construction with great ergonomics," says Jim McNair, design engineer for KAI USA. Featuring a 3.5-inch CPM-S35VN modified-clip-point blade, the titanium frame-lock folder is engineered to withstand rugged use. "(S35VN) is a third-generation powder-metallurgical steel formulated to offer increased toughness over S30V, yet to retain ease of machining and polishing," McNair explains. He adds that it is clean steel that resists edge chipping, wear and corrosion.

"The 0550 ensures a secure grip through an ergonomic, contoured handle, as well as a textured G-10 front handle scale," McNair says. "The back is titanium and features a super-secure frame lock with Hinderer's patented Lock-Bar Stabilizer™ to prevent over-flexing of the lock."

The Kershaw Cryo is another Hinderer frame-lock design that is on the opposite end of the spectrum from the ZT0550 in several ways. It is a bang-for-the-buck piece that offers anyone a well-designed knife without prying open the wallet too wide! "With Hinderer knives difficult to obtain, Kershaw is proud to be able to create a Rick Hinderer design at a price almost everyone can afford," says Thomas Welk, Kai USA's director of sales and marketing. But don't be too quick to discount the inexpensive knife as without features. The Cryo sports a myriad of amenities from the SpeedSafe™ assisted-opening device to a sturdy frame lock, and like the ZT0550, a Lock-Bar Stabilizer. "The knife features our new deep-carry pocket

Russ Kommer's expertise in designing hunting knives comes through in the CRKT Free Range series, with two blade styles and fixed or folding variants.

clip and the handle is drilled for tip-up, tip-down, left- or right-handed carry," McNair informs.

Wilderness Engineering

Columbia River Knife & Tool's Free Range family of hunting knives encompasses both fixed-blade and folding knife models, each designed by Russ Kommer. A knifemaker hailing from Fargo, North Dakota, Kommer has an extensive background as a hunter and hunting guide in the Alaskan wilderness. His Free Range models pair ergonomic, dual-molded handle scales with efficient clip-point or drop-point skinner blades in fixed-blade or lock-back-folder configurations.

Doug Flagg, vice president of sales and marketing for Columbia River Knife & Tool (CRKT), says, "The Free Range designed by Russ Kommer offers the benefits of a custom knife at the value of a mass-produced knife." Flagg goes on to cite key elements of the knife design. The double-injection-molded

handle—a soft, tactile rubber grip—is married with 8Cr13MoV blade steel for edge holding and ease of sharpening in the field, and each fixed-blade sheath includes an accessory pocket for storing a sharpener or other survival supplies.

Kommer extensively field tests all the knives manufactured by CRKT. "Russ spent 185 days in the field last year!" Flagg relates. The Free Range is offered in two fixed-blade and two folder versions, including options with drop-point, gut-hook and clip-point blades. The folders sport 3.75-inch blades and ambidextrous thumb studs for ease of opening, while the non-folding models come in 4.25-inch blades and nice ballistic-nylon belt sheaths with snap closures.

Pro-Tech's Spindrift tactical fixed blade showcases the manufacturing excellence of the company coupled with the design prowess of custom maker Allen Elishewitz. "The Spindrift is a thoughtfully designed and well-built, medium-size fixed blade," says Dave

Case and Tony Bose teamed up for the Lanny's Clip, a stout, clip-point folder that comes in a limited edition and five handle choices.

Wattenberg, president of Pro-Tech Knives. "Fashioned from 154CM blade steel and a precision-machined G-10 handle, all wrapped up in a custom Kydex® sheath, it's a super package." The blade measures a little over 5 inches and is ground from Crucible 154CM stainless, a "workhorse blade material," according to Wattenberg. The drop-point blade shape allows for adept use in utility and tactical applications.

Elishewitz doesn't taper the blade toward the tip, but instead takes the full thickness of the steel nearly all the way to the tip for strength should the knife be used for prying. The ergonomic, G-10 handle is three-dimensionally milled for an aggressive surface texture. "There is approximately 40 minutes of machining per pair of Spindrift handle scales!" exclaims Wattenberg.

A tough and stylish knife just under a foot in length, each Spindrift comes with molded-Kydex sheath from Scott's Sheaths in Colorado, including a Blade-Tech TekLok™ for ease of carry in a variety of configurations. There are currently four variations of the Spindrift available, varying in handle material and blade finishes. "I feel like the project pushed

us out of our normal comfort zone because it's such a strong fixed blade, and we are mostly known for auto folders," says Wattenberg. "It's given me a lot of enthusiasm to move on other fixed-blade projects, and we have several in the pipeline already."

Standing Aesthetically Apart

Mantis Knives always has something interesting in the pipeline, and aesthetically, its knives stand out from others in the industry. Take for instance the MSR series of friction folders designed in conjunction with custom maker Warren Thomas. Says Jared West, president of Mantis Knives, "Warren Thomas is probably the most innovative knife designer and maker in the world. Just look at his stuff! It's sweet! The designs are minimal in nature, super-simple."

Super simple is what you get. "The best part of the MSR friction folder series is the blend of old design and new technology," West explains. Like a traditional straight razor, the tang of the friction folder extends for ease of opening one-handed. When open, the extended tang lies flat against the spine where the user's hand naturally secures the tang and holds the folder open. The hand is essentially the lock.

The MSR friction folder features a 2.5-inch, modified-drop-point AUS-8 stainless blade, and a choice of a white or black G-10 handle, the latter grooved for further hand purchase. The "J" shape of the handle ensures a proper grip, and when the blade is open it forms a prominent choil between it and the handle for choking up during detail work.

"At first glance, the handle shape is odd, but when you grab it in a forward or reverse grip, it's a perfect fit," West explains. Two large bicycle-chain ringbolts hold everything together. "No one else on the planet makes knives like Warren does," West declares. "It's Mantis' desire to bring his work into a price range that the everyman can afford. Otherwise, when you're buying Warren's custom work, you're easily paying $600-$1,100 a knife."

The Spyderco Pingo is the result of a rather unique collaboration—a "three-way call"—between Spyderco and renowned Danish knifemakers Jens Anso and Jesper Voxnaes. The Danish makers conceived and designed the Pingo. "It is a unique knife, especially for Spyderco because of its purpose," begins founder Sal Glesser. "The purpose drove the design. A number of years ago Denmark changed its laws in regards to what knives are permitted to be carried on a daily basis."

Current Danish laws call for a blade no longer than 2.75 inches, no blade lock, and two-handed opening like a slip-joint folder. At the 2011 IWA trade show, Glesser met with Voxnaes and Anso, who presented the idea of designing and mass-producing a Spyderco folder that is in compliance with their country's knife laws. During the 2011 BLADE Show, the duo presented a prototype to the company of what would later become the Pingo.

The knife sports a Bohler Uddeholm N690Co stainless steel blade, known for superior edge holding and corrosion resistance, in a sheepsfoot style that Anso often incorporates into his designs. "The curved edge works in a variety of applications," Glesser comments, " and we used the

The Mantis MSR friction folders exude Warren Thomas's fresh take on old-school design, and showcase updated materials. Handle choices include black grooved G-10, white textured G-10 and carbon fiber. Blades are AUS-8 stainless.

trademark Spyderco hole in the blade for identity only.

"The blade does not lock open but is what we call a 'notch joint,'" he expounds. "It is a kind of slip joint, yet it enlists a hammer similar to a lock-back folder that, rather than locking, slips out of the notch when closing the blade." A lightly checkered Zytel® handle sports a Spyderco wire pocket clip for ambidextrous tip-up carry. "Pingo," according to the Danish makers, is the nickname of the present heir to the throne of Denmark.

Even though it was designed to meet Denmark's strict knife laws, the Pingo has global appeal with its stylish looks, highly useful curved edge, sheepsfoot blade and handy size. It makes a great everyday carry knife for anyone looking for a compact working folder.

Faithful Reproduction

The Case Lanny's Clip slip-joint folder is a faithful a reproduction of custom knifemaker Tony Bose's original design. "Case and Tony Bose have collaborated to produce four models for our standard catalog—the TB39 Sowbelly, TB110 Saddlehorn, TB117 Sway Back Jack and TB546 BackPocket®," says Fred Feightner, consumer marketing and communications manager for W.R. Case & Sons. Once a year, Case and Bose select a particular design that requires more attention to detail in terms of fit and finish than a standard production Case knife.

"We think the Lanny's Clip is as close to a custom piece as any modern factory knife," Feightner remarks. Amenities include precisely milled steel liners, smooth blade action, a fine fit and finish between the handle spine, liners and back spring, satin-finished, fluted steel bolsters, a premium 154CM stainless steel blade and a pinned handle shield.

"We're proud to be producing knives in our own factory that showcase premium features and built-in quality that rivals some of those found in the high-end custom market," says Feightner. The Lanny's Clip comes in five handle options, including limited editions of antique peach-seed jigged bone, chestnut peach-seed jigged bone, ebony, abalone and stag.

"Tony has influenced many of our production processes," Feightner states. "Simply put, he has made Case a better knife manufacturer." This is evident in such collaborative pieces as the Lanny's Clip. In fact, time and again the maker/manufacturer dynamic proves mutually beneficial for all involved.

"When we work with Rick Hinderer, the process is a true collaboration. We learn from each other," McNair stresses. "Rick appreciates the fact that we're able make those knives on a production scale and still retain the quality to which he strives."

"Mr. Elishewitz is a real pleasure to work with—he's straightforward and we tend to see things the same way," Wattenberg notes. "His designs combine the best in ergonomics and aesthetics, and I'm proud to have his name and designs associated with our brand."

West enthuses, "Warren teaches us something new in each knife collaboration we do with him. Overall, he has influenced nearly every knife that we've created since we began working with him."

CRKT's pairing with Russ Kommer to date has resulted in quite a few highly useful fixed blades and folding hunters. "Working with Russ is a dream," states Doug Flagg. "He is demanding on quality but also understands that mass production is different from custom knives."

Though primarily known for auto-opening folders, Pro-Tech already has amassed a small but diverse line of fixed blades such as the Spindrift, designed by Allen Elishewitz.

How to Strop a Straight Razor

It might be time to lather up and put the old straight razor to work on those whiskers

By Tim Zowada

This razor, made by the author, features a damascus blade, ivory-inlaid tang and ivory handle scales.

The last decade has shown several changes in the knife industry. One of the most surprising is how straight razors have regained popularity. While going through the daily ritual of preparing for work, the straight razor user has the chance to turn a routine task into an enjoyable hobby. They are not only rewarded with a better shave, but they also have a solid skill set and understanding of what it takes to keep razors and knives keen.

Unlike modern razors, straight razors are made for a lifetime of use. That means the razor will require a bit of maintenance. Most straight razor blades are fashioned from high-carbon steel, and will rust if not cared for. Even the best razors will dull in time and require sharpening. While sharpening a razor isn't difficult, it is a skill that has been mostly lost with the passing of time.

Sharpening a straight razor is a daily routine, and it is accomplished on a leather razor strop. Before shaving, a quick session on the strop is usually performed while whiskers are being conditioned by the first lathering. By the time the stropping is complete, the whiskers have been softened and are ready for shaving. Proper stropping will keep a razor sharp for months. One Japanese *tamahagane* razor (a blade forged from iron ore extracted from iron-rich sand) was reputed to have given over 1,000 shaves before requiring sharpening on stones. When the strop will no longer keep the razor shaving smoothly, it is time to take it to a stone, or have it honed by a professional.

With the increase in the popularity of straight razor shaving, there are now several craftsmen offering honing services for an average rate of $20-$25 per razor. For the person who only has one razor, or is not interested in learning the techniques, these services provide a good value. For those who like to tinker and are after the very best shave possible, learning to hone can be an enjoyable option.

Honing a razor is different from honing a knife. A razor should have an extremely smooth, polished edge. With the exception of Shechita, sushi and other specialized knives, most blade edges work better with fine micro-teeth on the cutting edge.

The reason for the difference in edge finish is due to how each tool performs the cut. Most knives cut with a slicing or sawing motion. If the material being cut is fibrous, slicing with a micro-tooth edge makes things easier. Razors remove hair by shearing. The

These tools will cover any regular honing situation, short of a damaged edge. At top from left are a 7 Diopter Opti-Visor, electrical tape and water. At center displayed from left to right are a lapping plate, a 4,000-grit Norton water stone, an 8,000-grit Norton water stone, an Escher finishing hone and a balsawood bench hone. At bottom is a hanging leather strop.

whisker is held in place by the skin and since it is so small, there isn't enough room for a sawing action to take place. For this reason, and because the cutting edge is in contact with skin, the smoothest possible edge is desired.

Unlike knives, the manufacturer sets the angle of the razor's edge. A razor is laid flat on the hone or strop for sharpening, and thus it is easy to keep the edge angle constant. The spine of the razor acts like a honing guide. Most straight razor honing bevels fall in the 14- to 18-degree range. But don't worry about the angles, the razor manufacturer will make sure they are correct during production. The only time the angle becomes a serious factor is with worn or abused razors.

Tools

This list covers all routine sharpening. Damage repair requires additional tools.

1. 4,000-grit water stone. The Norton hones are great. Naniwa, King, Shapton and others make quality hones as well.
2. 8,000-grit water stone
3. Finishing stone. This could be an Escher, Belgian Coticule, 12,000-grit Chinese water stone or similar ultra-fine hone.
4. Balsawood bench hone. This is optional, but a good idea.
5. Hanging leather strop—Horsehide, Latigo, English Bridle and even Vegan (synthetic) strops are available.

6. Electrical tape
7. Water
8. Protective oil— mineral oil, or Ballistol
9. Electrical tape

When a hone is new it should be lapped to assure flatness. As received from the manufacturers, all hones need to be lapped. After the initial flattening, the primary purpose of lapping is to keep the abrasive fresh on the surface of the stone. Abrasive surfaces will clog and glaze so lapping assures you are working on a good surface. It is standard practice to lap 4,000- and 8,000-grit water stones after sharpening two or three razors. Finish hones are touched up after sharpening about every 10 razors.

To lap a hone you can use either lapping plates designed for that purpose, or regular 400-grit silicon carbide sandpaper clamped to a flat surface. Diamond Machining Technology (DMT) diamond plates also work well as lapping plates. A DMT D8C works well on everything except finish hones. Milling grooves in the surface of the D8C helps to break the surface tension of the water. For lapping finish hones that are 10,000-grit and above, it is preferable to use 2,000-grit silicon carbide sandpaper.

Lapping is simple. Draw a grid on the surface of the hone with a pencil. Keeping the surface of the lapping plate or sandpaper wet with water, work the hone against the lapping surface in a figure-eight pattern. When the pencil marks are gone, the lapping is finished.

Electrical tape is used to protect the spine of the razor while sharpening on the bench hones. This does two things: it protects the blade spine from being scratched by the hone, and allows for tinkering with the edge angle while on the hone. Most traditionalists scoff at the use of tape. Others like it, especially for protecting the etching on a damascus blade. Both perspectives are valid, try it and decide for yourself.

Almost all razor hones are water hones so be sure they are always wet with water during use. To begin honing, lay the razor down on one end of the hone with the blade facing toward the middle. Both the spine and cutting edge of the blade should be resting on the surface of the hone. The blade is simply slid across the hone to the other end. After reaching the opposite end of the hone, roll the blade over its spine. The blade is then slid back to the other end of the hone. This constitutes one pass.

To be sure the tip of the razor is sharpened use an X-pattern. The blade travels in the shape of the

Illustrated are, in order, the beginning of both the standard and X-pattern honing strokes, the finish of the standard honing stroke, and the finish of the X-pattern stroke.

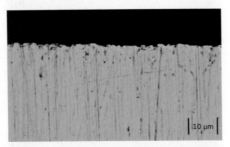

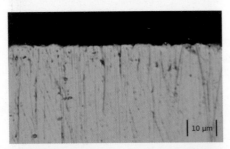

letter X relative to the surface of the hone. Start with the blade in the same position as the regular stroke. The difference is, while the blade is being slid across the hone, it is also pulled diagonally across the stone. This leaves only the tip of the blade and end of the spine in contact with the hone at the end of the stroke. Flip the blade over the spine and do the same motion on the other side of the blade, but going in the opposite direction. Experience will lead to a combination of regular and X-pattern strokes that will cover the edge evenly.

Spine On Hone

The easiest way to get the hang of flipping the blade is to remember the spine of the blade should be in contact with the hone at all times. It is important not to press down on the blade while honing or stropping. Razor edges are thin and flexible. It is quite easy to deform the edge and change the honing angle if down pressure is used. It is amazing, but the weight of the razor is sufficient to get the job done.

A balsa hone is used just like the regular hone, except the blade is pulled away from the edge. If the blade were to be pushed in the direction of the edge, it would cut into the balsa. Charged with 0.5-micron chromium oxide paste, the balsa hone starts the final polishing of the edge. Charge the surface with the paste and wipe off the excess with a paper towel. The paste should just fill the pores of the balsa and not be a thick coating on the surface of the wood.

For a hanging strop, pull the strop tight, not allowing it to sag. Pull the blade towards you, away from the edge. Flip the blade over its spine and push it back to the top. No down pressure should be used. The blade should gently slide across the surface of the strop. Do not rock the blade up on its edge. The spine of the razor should be in contact with the strop at all times.

The following is a fairly common step-by-step procedure for the complete honing of a straight razor. Other razor practitioners will have different perspectives and procedures, but this is a good place to start. If the razor is damascus or tamahagane, start off with one layer of electrical tape covering the spine of the razor. This protects the damascus patterning.

If the edge only needs a minor touch-up, you can start with the finish hone. See step 3 below. The way to think of the finish stone is that it is for polishing only. If any metal removal needs to be done, or if there are any little chips or nicks on the edge at all, start with a 4,000-grit stone. The 8,000-grit hone is only for removing 4,000-grit scratches, and the 12,000-grit hone is only for removing the 8,000-grit scratches and so on.

Shown are close-up images of a razor edge, in order: 1. After touched up with a 4,000-grit hone, and the edge is still coarse and ragged; 2. Upon sharpening with an 8,000-grit hone, and the edge is smoothed a bit; 3. After the Escher finishing hone has polished the honing bevel; 4. The angle has been kicked up a little to help remove the micro-teeth; 5. The edge has been taken to a balsa hone treated with 0.5-micron chromium oxide to remove the remainder of the micro-teeth and smooth the edge; 6. Here is the stropped, finished edge.

Shown is a Tim Zowada straight razor with a smelted tamahagane blade and mammoth-ivory grip.

1. Start with a 4,000-grit Norton stone using one layer of tape and 10 strokes, or whatever it takes to remove all visible chipping. A good rule of thumb is if a nick can't be seen with a 7 Diopter Opti-Visor, don't worry about it.

2. Progress to an 8,000-grit Norton stone using one layer of tape and 20 strokes. Remove all visible 4,000-grit scratches. It is easy to see problem areas at this level of polish. If any are found, don't try to take them out with the 8,000-grit stone. Drop back to 4,000 grit until things are cleaned up.

3. Next use a 12,000-grit Escher, or Chinese hone with one layer of tape and 20 strokes. By this point the polish is so fine a microscope is required to see what is going on.

3a. Optional: Here I like to add two additional layers of tape, for a total of three. This increases the angle by almost two degrees, making it easier to get a smooth edge with the final honing. Use 20 light, additional strokes with the Escher/Chinese 12,000-grit hone. This is not considered the traditional way of doing things, but it works well. Otherwise skip to step 4 and stay with one layer of tape.

4. Employ a balsawood bench hone with chromium oxide paste for extra smoothness, and use 25 strokes. Remember to pull away from the edge. If you opted for step 3a, leave three layers of tape.

5. Take the edge to a hanging strop treated with chromium oxide paste. Don't use any tape and hone for 20 strokes.

6. Take the edge to a hanging strop, but perform 50 strokes on clean horsehide, English bridle or Latigo. Apply no tape here.

For daily pre-shave honing only do steps 4 and 5. Some will do only step 5.

Step 3a can be a little confusing. The purpose is to remove the serrations, or saw-teeth left from the 4,000-grit stone. Kicking up the angle by a couple degrees, in combination with a fine stone, will knock off these serrations. That is the only purpose—to remove the saw-like serrations from the edge.

The bench hone work is only a good set-up for the stropping. It is the final stropping that really defines the quality of the shave. Chromium oxide smooths and polishes the edge, resulting in a more comfortable shave. Once a little experience is gained the entire routine takes no more than about 15 minutes. Be sure to coat the blade with a protective coat of oil when finished.

The very best test for a razor is to shave with it on properly prepared whiskers. This has been a lot of explanation for what is actually a simple task. One hundred years ago, everyone that shaved used a straight razor, and most users sharpened their own. Give it a try. You will see that shaving with straights and honing your own is a wonderful way to turn a daily chore in to an engaging, rewarding experience.

Bob Dozier uses D2 blade steel almost exclusively and is largely responsible for its popularity today. This is the knifemaker's DK-5 model, a hidden-tang tour de force in a stacked-exotic-wood handle.

The High Carbon Diet

Twenty years into the modern steel revolution, and old is new again!

By Pat Covert

Sometimes when you reinvent the wheel it only rides better on a smooth road. The advent of the modern tactical knife movement in the early 1990s spawned a technological revolution in cutlery never before seen in its entire history. ATS-34 was the king of stainless steels at the time, but soon the begetting began to newer, greater iterations like BG-42, Stellite™, Talonite™, CPM-S30VN, H-1 and the list goes on. Ironically, some of these so-called new blade steels had been around for years, and in the case of cobalt-based Stellite, over 100 years. But sometimes newer isn't necessarily better.

Welcome to the 2010s where non-stainless blade steels are not only making a comeback, they're achieving cult status for several good reasons. From a military standpoint two factors have weighed in to sway this "retro-fit" mindset. First off, many of our troops can't afford the high-dollar price tag that comes with several of the new exotic steels. High-carbon steels are much more affordable in this regard. Secondly, to troops in the field a knife is just another tool in a loaded bag of gear. So in their minds the cost-to-benefit ratio isn't worth it. The same is true for the average outdoorsman. Most of these users don't live and breathe steel like we avid knife aficionados.

Some custom knifemakers like John Greco, Bob Dozier and Daniel Winkler never did jump on the high-dollar-steel bandwagon. Greco and Dozier chose to make affordable, hard-use knives for their customers, and Winkler transitioned from being primarily a maker of primitive or pioneer-style knives, to a supplier of highly specialized custom knives for military personnel stationed overseas. These knifemakers and others like them represent a core of craftsmen who believe high-carbon, non-stainless steels will serve their customers quite well, thank you, and tout their benefits. You'll often hear such alloys referred to as "tool" or "spring" steels, and sometimes the term "high-carbon, low-alloy" steels is used. There are exceptions to the low-alloy content, such as D2, which has only 1 percent less chromium than stainless steels.

On the manufacturing side, KA-BAR has been supplying standard-issue knives with high-carbon-steel blades to our troops for decades. Heeding a call for more affordable battle blades, newer companies like TOPS Knives jumped into the tactical knife market with modern, state-of-the-art designs incorporating basic 1095 steel. One example of this is the Wolfhawk, produced in collaboration with Battle Blades, which includes an innovative Picatinny or MIL-STD-1913 (a bracket used on some firearms to provide a standardized mounting platform) rail-

Daniel Winkler became involved with military/tactical knives after many years of making primitive or pioneer-style pieces. His high-carbon, full-tang Spike model features a glass-breaker pommel and is available in a cord-wrapped or synthetic handle.

mount sheath. It is the first of its type. The Wolfhawk is available in a clip-point or tanto-style blade with a choice of an injection-molded or cord-wrapped handle. The Battle Blades sheath is also M.O.L.L.E. compatible, or can be converted for neck-knife wear.

Jeff Randall, co-founder of ESEE Knives and Randall Adventure Training, tells Knives 2014, "Obviously, price per pound, the 1095 high-carbon steel we use is less expensive, not to mention it doesn't need to be sent out to be atmospherically heat treated as some steels do. Consequently, the customer gets a great product that's tough and holds an edge without paying the higher prices of exotic steel coupled with higher heat-treat costs."

Field Friendly

A second key reason high-carbon blade steel is enjoying renewed popularity is because it doesn't require a special sharpener. Most of the hi-tech steels are harder than a common Arkansas stone and therefore require special diamond and ceramic sharpeners to restore an edge. Lose your special sharpening stone in the field and you're stuck with a dull knife. High-carbon steels can be sharpened on

any quality hone or stone, and if you get in a pinch, a rock will do.

In the 40 years that he's been making knives, Winkler has forged most of the blades for his primitive knives and historically accurate reproduction pieces, marketing them to re-enactors, bowie collectors and other knife enthusiasts. That changed when he started receiving requests for tactical and military knives to be used in the Middle East conflicts. It also affected the way he fashioned knives for such markets. "I have been making knives since the late 1970s and would guess at least 99 percent have been from what might be termed simple carbon steels. I recommend these steels because of the ease of the heat-treating, performance and 'forge-ability' of the grades," Winkler notes. "Often the higher and more complex steel grades cause problems in these areas."

"I forge the blades of all 'Daniel Winkler Hand Forged' knives and 'Hawks' (tomahawks)," Winkler continues. "The 'Winkler Knives II' (tactical and military) pieces are fashioned using the stock-removal method of blade making. Because of my experience using these steels over the past 30 years, I feel comfortable with the material. I do use some CPM steels and some of the high-shock-resistant grades for specialty products, but most of my knives and axes have 5160, 52100 or 1084 blades. Often, depending on the grade of the more complex steels and the heat-treating, the user may spend a lot of time sharpening the first time taking a knife to a stone, until the final bevel angles are uniform to the user's method. Simply put, carbon steels are easier to sharpen and take less time."

Other popular forging steels include, but are not limited to, O1, A2, 1075, 1095, 1084, and of course, the ever-exquisite damascus forge-welded steels.

Greco states, "High-carbon steels, like the 8670 I use, are generally found to be much easier to sharpen than stainless steel blades. The reason is that non-high-carbon stainless steel blades require more extensive heat-treating procedures, including in some cases sub-zero quenches, just to become hard enough to hold a cutting edge that won't curl over when used."

Randall speaks specifically about 1095 steel, saying, "Carborundum (silicon carbide) or diamond hones work exceptionally well for keeping a good edge on 1095. A keen edge is also easily acquired by stropping on a quality piece of leather combined with some grinding compound. 1095 blade steel

its high chromium content, the surface of D2 doesn't require a special coating, only light occasional maintenance. For these reasons many knife users feel the "almost stainless" is the perfect blade steel.

Even though D2 is considerably less expensive than the top-dollar exotic blade steels, Dozier, who has been using it since 1989, doesn't think price is an issue. "Cost doesn't enter into my philosophy of knifemaking. I don't consider price at all. I choose the best materials available for my customers. I like to use D2 because of the edge retention. It's tough steel, and it's easy to heat treat. And due to its high chromium content, D2 is extremely corrosion resistant," he says.

As for sharpening, Dozier states, "I use a diamond stone because it's quicker, but you can also sharpen it on an Arkansas or carborundum stone. You can even sharpen it on a rock if you have to, it just takes more time."

Perhaps the biggest issue with high-carbon steel is that it tends to oxidize much quicker than stainless when exposed to the elements. A couple of pros indicated, interestingly, that some of their customers liked the natural patina found on weathered carbon steel. Greco lends, "There are, to my knowledge, only two ways to finish any knife blade. The first is to leave it 'as ground' or polished, that is, bare steel

lends itself to creating a convex edge, which a lot of users put on the blades once they receive our knives."

The "Almost Stainless"

Knifemaker Bob Dozier is largely responsible for the cult-like following of D2 steel. It is a high-carbon steel just one percent shy of the chromium content necessary to classify it as a stainless steel. Indeed, some refer to D2 as "semi-stainless." D2's high chromium content gives it excellent corrosion resistance and edge retention, yet the blade steel is practically as easy to sharpen as high-carbon steels. Because of

Knifemaker Kenny Teague makes hard-use, down-to-earth knives, and chooses D2 steel to keep his prices in line. At top is the knifemaker's KT-3 Medium Hunter, and below it the KT-8 Utility.

The D2 tool steel blade of the Benchmade Adamas folder (top) is noncoated, while the fixed-blade version of the knife sports a "Desert Sand Coating" to enhance corrosion resistance and to give it a camouflage look for our soldiers stationed in the arid Middle East.

exposed to the environment, or to coat the blade with some substance to seal and protect it from the elements. Either way works for me. With some of my personal knives, the joy of seeing a patina develop over time and through extensive use is a sign of character."

"The coated blades—our G-1 coating, powder-coated or blued blades—will require less attention over time and do offer a great deal of protection," he adds, "especially in harsh environments. There is really no more of a trick to maintaining your high-carbon-steel knife than any other tool: keep it dry, apply a light coat of oil from time to time, and just enjoy it."

Winkler offers his customers a choice of two blade coatings to keep the oxidizing bugs away. "For the 'Winkler Knives II' products I offer either a Caswell black-oxide finish or a KG Gun coat," he says. "Personally I prefer the Caswell, as I use my own equipment, and the finish is going to wear off anyway with time and use. The Caswell wears more naturally."

TOPS Knives was on the ground floor of manufacturing modern military/tactical knives using high-carbon steel. The Wolfhawk, a collaborative effort with Battle Blades, showcases the first Picatinny-adaptable sheath.

Iron in Your Diet

Randall echoes Greco's remarks and adds a little insight of his own. "We powder coat our knives, but many of our customers remove the coating and allow the blade to form a patina. The bottom line to us is we make using knives, so we don't concern ourselves with finish that much. Toughness, flexibility, edge holding, cutting efficiency and ergonomics in the

Many serious collectors prefer high-carbon steel simply because it is closer to the blade steel of traditional knives. Shown is Steve Hill's Rio Grande Bowie in hand-forged 01 blade steel and a stag handle.

cut are the most important aspects of a using knife. True, 1095 or any high-carbon steel will rust if not cared for, but we still consider it one of the best working steels there is. A little iron rust in your diet is probably good for you anyway."

The adage of "what is old is new again" applies to high-carbon steel quite well. It is by far the most widely used knife steel across the globe, and as Jeff Randall relates, "I would guess that carbon steel knives are some of the oldest known cutting tools there are outside of stone and bronze. I do know it has been the chosen steel for knives for hundreds of years, and continues to be very popular in Third World countries where the populace still relies on a

cutting edge to carve out their everyday survival. So, that in itself is reason enough for us to base our modern knives on such steel."

Randall's "if it ain't broke, don't fix it" mantra is one appreciated more and more by serious knife users. For historic collectors and re-enactors who desire a degree of authenticity, high-carbon steels are the way to go. Modern, state-of-the-art exotic steels do offer distinct advantages in their own right, and the knife buyer should weigh these against the pros and cons of high-carbon steel. But for the average user on a budget, or one desiring the ease of field sharpening, the high-carbon diet will satisfy the appetite quite well!

TRENDS

There aren't many dull, boring or mundane trends, and for good reason. Knifemakers embrace the old saying, "Change is constant." The "same old, same old" never catches on with a new generation. Knife craftsmen strive for fascinating and innovative ways of blade building, and collectors seek out the rare and unusual. Eventually knifemakers find something modern that is not only aesthetic and utilitarian, but it also catches on with other artists. That's the start of a trend. Or a new mechanism is invented, a smoother pivot, a sturdier lock or a more favorable sheath.

You get the idea—trends are born out of creative thinking and design capabilities, and not from copying old patterns without any tweaking, improving or thinking outside of the box. Sure, some trends have staying power. In this book alone, "Bowies by Many Names," "Heavy D-Guards," fighters, boot knives, chute knives, daggers, hunters, tactical folders, fixed blades and pocketknives are covered in the "Trends" section. Yet, they are not your everyday, run-of-the-mill bowies, hunters, fighters and folders. They are modern renditions, new takes on old patterns, or if exacting replicas, then using state-of-the-art materials.

There are many new trends to take in, like dimpled or sculpted titanium-handle folders, "lightning strike" carbon-fiber grips, state-of-the-art Santoku-style cutlery, modern takes on tacticals, "Molar Knife Caps," the "Tusk at Hand" and "Dedicated Folders of Fashion." After all, this is the "Trends" section, not some boring rehash of what's been done before in knives.

Bowies By Many Names

A name. It is not only a direct reflection of the person or object it represents, but also an identity, a personal handle. If a gentleman named "Stephen" wants to be called "Steve," he can rightly expect others to address him as such. Similarly, if an American Indian prefers the term "Native American," or if a knifemaker bestows the name "Bowtie Bowie" on his bowie knife because it has a bowtie-shaped guard, it seems only fitting to trust their good judgment.

The American bowie is arguably one of the most recognizable knife forms born out of the New World. Each bowie knife is a version of that which Col. James Bowie carried at the Sandbar Fight and the Alamo. It is a knifemaker's representation of a knife described in text as one carried by Bowie. There is a general form and features, like a straight blade similar to a butcher's knife with or without a slight clip point, that identify it as a bowie. Yet, there are so many variations, one almost has to name the bowies to keep them straight. And that's exactly what innovative makers have done.

Considering each model started as a bar or billet of steel that a knifemaker handcrafted, forged or shaped, beveled, honed, hand fit, finished and assembled, it really becomes one of their babies. And what's the first thing bestowed upon a baby? A name. It becomes part of the infant's identity, a personal reflection of its very being, its handle. And that's why we have Bowies By Many Names. You got that, Chuck?

▲ **JASON KNIGHT:** A 10-inch damascus blade, stainless steel guard, dyed tiger-maple handle and Paul Long sheath distinguish the "Founders Bowie." *(SharpByCoop.com photo)*

◄ **TERRY VANDEVENTER:** Of take-down construction, the knife named "California Bowie" sports a 6⅜-inch damascus blade, damascus fittings and a mammoth-ivory handle. *(Ward photo)*

▶ **RALPH TURNBULL:** The "No. 5 Coffin Handle Bowie" is named such for the coffin-shaped African-blackwood handle with nickel silver wrap, and because it's a bowie knife.

► **JERRY FISK:** Of the "Southwest Bowie" ilk, the long, 17-inch model parades a damascus blade, an engraved pommel and ferrule, and a stag handle. *(Ward photo)*

► **BEN SEWARD:** The ironwood handle of the "Red River Bowie" is inviting, but the 10⅜-inch 5160 blade—a bit intimidating. *(Ward photo)*

▲ **BRUCE BOHRMANN:** Simply named "The Alamo," the short and sweet 7-inch bowie boasts a mesquite-burl grip. *(BladeGallery.com photo)*

▲ **TAD LYNCH:** Make mine a "Turkey Mt. Bowie" with a 9.5-inch W2 blade, wavy temper line and Turkish walnut handle. *(Ward photo)*

▲ **DAN PIERGALLINI:** An eagle-head pommel leads to an ivory handle carved to resemble a wing and feathers, and a guard that continues the bird motif. The "Eagle" bowie/camp knife also enlists a "buffalo skinner" blade style. *(Hoffman photo)*

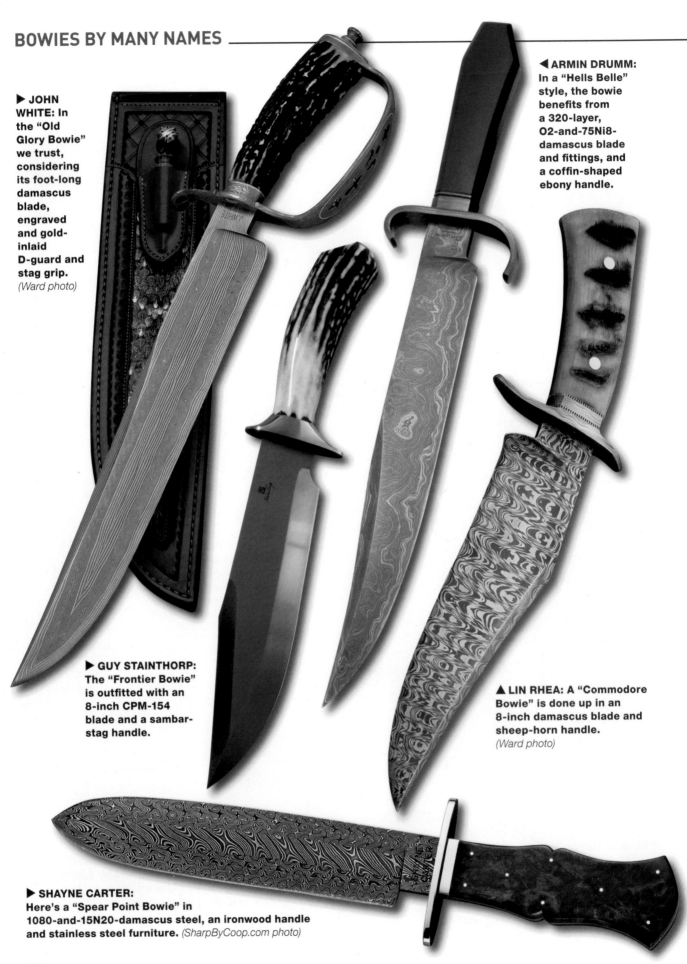

▶ **JOHN WHITE:** In the "Old Glory Bowie" we trust, considering its foot-long damascus blade, engraved and gold-inlaid D-guard and stag grip. *(Ward photo)*

◀ **ARMIN DRUMM:** In a "Hells Belle" style, the bowie benefits from a 320-layer, O2-and-75Ni8-damascus blade and fittings, and a coffin-shaped ebony handle.

▶ **GUY STAINTHORP:** The "Frontier Bowie" is outfitted with an 8-inch CPM-154 blade and a sambar-stag handle.

▲ **LIN RHEA:** A "Commodore Bowie" is done up in an 8-inch damascus blade and sheep-horn handle. *(Ward photo)*

▶ **SHAYNE CARTER:** Here's a "Spear Point Bowie" in 1080-and-15N20-damascus steel, an ironwood handle and stainless steel furniture. *(SharpByCoop.com photo)*

▶SHIVA KI: Taking liberties with the bowie pattern is all part of the game, and considering the Japanese-style take-down curly maple handle with silk wrap, S-guard and double-clay-tempered damascus blade, the maker made solid choices for the "Spirit Bowie."

◀BILL LUCKETT: A "Battle Bowie" charges forth in a double-hollow-ground, 10-inch CPM-154 stainless steel blade, an ironwood handle, and stainless steel fittings set off by black and brass spacers.

▲STEVEN TEDFORD: The "Survival Bowie" relies on a 9-inch freehand-ground, ATS-34 stainless steel blade, an Ontario moose-horn handle, copper lanyard tube and five hidden pins.

▶MIKE TYRE: The "Cowboy Bowie" is rustled up in walnut, bronze and 52100 ball-bearing steel. *(Ward photo)*

▶DAVID CRAWFORD: Certainly a sporting affair, the "Sporting Bowie" exhibits a 9.25-inch 1075 high-carbon-steel blade, a 416 stainless steel "clamshell" guard, ebony handle and recessed escutcheons. *(SharpByCoop.com photo)*

STEVE JANIK: A lonely sort, the "Vigilante Bowie" works discreetly in stag, damascus and a swordfish-bill-inlaid pommel. *(Ward photo)*

▶ **J. NEILSON:** Reigning over the battlefield is the "Warlord Bowie" done up in damascus, amber stag and mokumé. *(Ward photo)*

▲ **BRUCE BUMP:** A ladder-pattern-damascus blade, Jere Davidson engraving and a pre-ban bark-ivory handle define "The Mayhem Bowie." *(SharpByCoop.com photo)*

▲ **JOHN COHEA:** The "Bear Jaw Bowie" has just that for a handle—a bear jaw—protected by a wrap-around wrought iron guard, as well as a 10-inch, copper-washed damascus blade. *(Ward photo)*

Heavy D-Guards

▲ **KYLE ROYER:** Twisted wire spirals over a blackwood handle, protected by a gun-blued D-guard and 14 inches of damascus bade. *(Ward photo)*

▶ **GARY MULKEY:** The 1084-and-15N20 damascus wends its way along the bowie, D-touring around the blackwood handle. *(Ward photo)*

▶ **MICHAEL RUTH JR.:** Pre-ban ivory and 21 inches of 1084-and-15N20 damascus, as well as a D-guard, make up the presentation Naval cutlass. *(PointSeven photo)*

▶ **DAVID LISCH:** The D-guard bowie encompasses ancient ivory and modern damascus, the latter giving the blade a feather-like appearance. *(SharpByCoop.com photo)*

▲ **JOHN WHITE:** Of takedown construction, the D-guard bowie showcases a walrus ivory dog-bone-shaped grip with domed pins, a rectangular damascus handle shield and a 10.25-inch damascus blade. *(PointSeven photo)*

An Ultimate Fighting Force

◄ **DAVID LISCH:** The 15N20-and-1080 damascus pattern works its way down the 10.25-inch blade of a single-ring fighter. *(SharpByCoop.com photo)*

▶ **ALAN HUTCHINSON:** Stag and steel are kept in their respective corners by a bronze guard. *(Ward photo)*

◄ **ALFREDO KEHIAYAN:** The full-integral fighter is forged from SAE 9260, then satin finished and given a handle of vegetable fibers laminated with resins.

◄ **ERIK FRITZ:** The fighter contends for the championship in an eight-bar "Twisted-W's"-pattern damascus blade steadied by a walnut-burl handle. *(PointSeven photo)*

▲ **RAMON CHAVEZ:** Practically impenetrable black linen Micarta® anchors the "RCK 13" fighter in a CPM-D2 blade. *(SharpByCoop.com photo)*

▲ **RALPH RICHARDS:**
Wrap your fingers around the ironwood handle of the "Crazy Horse Blood Brother" and hang on for dear life. *(Ward photo)*

▶ **ANDREW TAKACH:**
A "Turkish-twist" damascus blade, stag handle, fire-blackened 1018 guard and threaded "skull crusher" pommel nut prep a fighter for battle. *(SharpByCoop.com photo)*

▶ **KYLE ROYER:**
Walrus ivory and damascus provide the one-two punch for a 16.5-inch fighter. *(Ward photo)*

▲ **BILL LUCKETT:**
A fighter to its double-hollow-ground CPM-154 steel core, the "Tac III Fighter" also sports a G-10 handle with a black-Micarta core and satin-finished 304 stainless steel fittings.

◀ **WILLIAM WELLING:** The flat-ground 1095 blade and Micarta® handle of the "Menace Fighter" take full advantage the maker's own Up-Armored "ACU Skull Pattern" DuraCoat™.

▶ **LUCAS LANCE:** Stag and burl might make odd bedfellows, but not on this 9.5-inch ATS-34 fighter.

◀ **BRUCE BINGENHEIMER:** Damascus and ironwood span the 14-5/8 inches of a fixed-blade fighter. *(SharpByCoop.com photo)*

▶ **KEVIN CASEY:** Let the line running down the center of the damascus blade show you the way to the oval damascus guard, bronze spacer and fossilized-walrus handle. *(SharpByCoop.com photo)*

▶ **KEVIN KLEIN:** There's woolly mammoth tusk inlaid or set into the pommel of the "Watchful Owl," and a magnificent damascus pattern forged into the blade and bolsters. African blackwood brings it all together. *(SharpByCoop.com photo)*

▶ **ROBERT FLYNT:** The fighter is in fine form, parading its 9-inch CPM-154 blade, double guard, file-worked nickel-silver spacers and pommel, and stabilized and dyed waterbuck-horn handle.

▶ **JOE MALLOY:** Fashioned for a collector of guns and knives, the canvas-Micarta handle of the fighter also becomes the grip of the gun-shaped sheath. The gun-blued A2 high-carbon steel blade bends and reaches, doesn't it? *(Hoffman photo)*

▶ **RON NEWTON:** Too pretty to fight, but not incapable, the integral model enlists a Turkish-damascus blade and a 24k-gold-inlaid bolster, the latter literally interconnecting with an ebony handle. *(Ward photo)*

▼ **BEN SEWARD:** Buckeye burl is figured just right for the fight. *(Ward photo)*

▶ **LIN RHEA:** Damascus dizzies up enemy forces while the flawless ivory puts a spell on them. *(Ward photo)*

▼ **ALLEN ELISHEWITZ:** A double-aged stainless steel front bolster has a thumb-print-style indent, book-ended on either side by a 7-inch CTS-XHP blade and ironwood handle scales.

Work That Walrus!

Cut! Ok, now smooth it down, shape it, shape it, and there. Now attach it, shine it up, and work that walrus! Girl, look at that walrus. Girl, look at that walrus. It works out!

Ok, enough with the fashion and music references. I couldn't help it, but think about that one. Who on earth would have thought walrus tusk or oosik (that's a petrified walrus penis bone for any of you wondering, and no, it's no joke) would become the next hot handle material in custom knives? It's not as if walruses are pretty. They're not hot. And the ancient walrus—the particular species from which knifemakers seek the tusk—is old and ugly! But the tusk, oh that tusk, or the bone for that matter, with its aged patina, hued exterior and solid interior. That's the stuff an aesthetically superior knife handle is made from.

There's something Mother Nature can do to an animal tusk or bone that no human, not even the most skilled painter, sculptor, engraver or scrimshaw artist, can master. The blues, greens, browns, yellows and beiges emitted are remarkable. They're a painter's palette in a perfectly preserved, calcified package, and that's something a hardcore craftsman can get excited about. So don't slow that walrus wagon down. Keep it moving, harvest that tusk through the permafrost, thaw it, shine it up and work it, yeah, work that walrus!

▶ **ANDERS HOGSTROM: The "Smatchet" hunting/fighting dagger features a "mill head"-damascus blade with an offset grind, giving the user two edges to work with for slicing and chopping, a bronze guard with copper spacer, and a top-notch walrus-tusk handle.** *(SharpByCoop.com photo)*

◀ **DOUG CAMPBELL: The integral camp knife sports a primitive-style, hammer-forged 5160 blade with as much character as the fossil walrus grip. The knife is delivered in a Robin Severe sheath.** *(SharpByCoop. com photo)*

◀ **KEVIN D. CROSS: Browner than the average ancient walrus tusk, the handle of the damascus bowie works wonderfully as it is. Randy Haas is credited for the damascus, and the knife comes with a Paul Long sheath.** *(Hoffman photo)*

▶ **TAD LYNCH:** The damascus gent's fighter works the fossil walrus to its advantage. *(Ward photo)*

▶ **MIKE CRADDOCK:** Blue and brown streaks run across the beige fossil-walrus handle of a "feather"-pattern-damascus bowie. *(SharpByCoop.com photo)*

◀ **DON HANSON III:** Walrus ivory and wavy damascus make up the 7⅜-inch bowie. *(SharpByCoop.com photo)*

▼ **GLEN MIKOLAJCZYK:** Naturally colored walrus ivory is teamed with an "X"-pattern damascus blade for a winning combination. *(Cory Martin Imaging)*

▲ **BILL BUXTON:** The fighter forges ahead in a 9.5-inch damascus blade and an ancient walrus handle. *(Ward photo)*

◀ **DAVID MIRABILE:** A carbon-fiber wrap is an innovative addition to an ancient-walrus-ivory grip, accompanied by a damascus blade and stainless steel guard. *(SharpByCoop.com photo)*

▶ **SCOTT ROUSH:** You couldn't replicate the artifact-walrus ivory of the "Migration Cutter" if you tried, and the shipwreck-wrought-iron guard and 19-inch W2 blade aren't bad, either. *(SharpByCoop.com photo)*

◀ **BRUCE BINGENHEIMER:** While the walrus ivory is handsome, the clay-quenched W2 blade makes some waves of its own, and the "W's"-pattern damascus guard, spacer and pommel cap top it all off. *(SharpByCoop.com photo)*

▶ **DILLON HORTON:** Even 12-year-old Dillon Horton knows a good thing when he sees it, incorporating fossil-walrus ivory into the handle half of his ladder-pattern-damascus bowie that also features a meteorite guard, and "Superconductor" and silver spacers. *(SharpByCoop.com photo)*

▼ **ROB HUDSON:** An 8-inch trailing-point fixed blade is made up of CPM-154 stainless steel, walrus ivory and engraving by Jere Davidson.

▶ **GARY HOUSE:** The handle is walrus ivory, the spacer from the interior of the walrus tusk, and the blade all patterned up and prettified. *(PointSeven photo)*

◀ **BILL BURKE:** He clay-and-water quenched the blade, fire-etched the wrought-iron guard and allowed the fossilized walrus ivory to speak for itself. *(PointSeven photo)*

▶ **MIKE MALOSH:** The end of the ancient-walrus handle is as endearing as the exterior of the beastly tusk, and the bowie blade stands guard over the entire works. *(Ward photo)*

◀ **JOHN WHITE:** Colorful walrus ivory shares billing with an equally winsome 4.5-inch damascus blade. *(Ward photo)*

◀ **RONALD WELLING:** For his 18.5-inch bowie, Ronald combined a 5160 blade, bronze fittings and a walrus handle. *(Ward photo)*

Dedicated Folders of Fashion

▶ **ANDERS HEDLUND:** 18k-gold dots and pins embellish the heat-colored Devin Thomas damascus blade and checkered black-lip-pearl handle of the "Ruby Princess," thus named for the ruby inlays on the engraved handle medallion. It also sports Ettore Gianferrari mosaic-damascus bolsters.

◀ **JIM TURECEK:** It's just a guess, but perhaps the antique-walrus ivory is the inspiration behind the "Arctic White" name for the W1-and-203-damascus folder.

▲ **CHICCHI YONEYAMA:** A pair of gent's folders parades damascus blades with laminated steel edges, stainless steel bolsters, and ironwood and mammoth-ivory handles. *(SharpByCoop.com photo)*

▲ **JIMMY CHIN:** An auto folder leaves a rainbow hue of titanium and black-lip mother-of-pearl in its damascus wake. The back spacer is fully engraved and inlaid. *(Ward photo)*

▶ **DOC HAGEN:** The button-release stiletto sports a presentation-grade black-lip-pearl grip, damascus bolsters and a polished CPM-154 blade. *(Custom Knife Gallery Of Colorado photo)*

◀ **LEONARDO FRIZZI:** From the tip of the Bertie Rietveld "nebula"-pattern damascus blade to the 18k-gold bale, this one is a winner. The Alabama Damascus of the handle is carved away to reveal antique tortoise shell.

◀ **GRACE HORNE:** The brass-and-copper Mokumé handle is a pleasing sort, properly paired with an RWL-34 blade. *(PointSeven photo)*

◀ **PETER CAREY:** The "Cayman" flipper folder features a Chad Nichols "blackout"-pattern stainless-damascus blade, a Timascus handle, pivot ring and back spacers, and zirconium bolsters and pocket clip. *(Mitchell Cohen, Prairie Digital Inc. photo)*

▲ **ERIC OCHS:** The handle is green-spruce cone from Ankrom Exotics with a thin G-10 backing. The hammered copper bolsters and "scramble"-pattern Chad Nichols stainless-damascus blade need no backing.

Dedicated Folders of Fashion

▶ **RICHARD TESARIK:** The Pavel Sevecek damascus and mother-of-pearl are the black and white of the fancy folder.

◀ **GAIL LUNN:** A sterling silver "belt buckle" and Macassar-ebony "belt" embellish the "Buckle Up" damascus dress folder. *(Hoffman photo)*

◀ **RONALD BEST:** There's an Art Deco feel to the carved frame of the folding Damasteel dagger with black-lip-pearl handle inlays. *(SharpByCoop.com photo)*

◀ **MICHAEL WALKER:** The blue honeycomb-patterned handle is sweet, and the Damasteel blade of the tactical LinerLock® is sharp as all get out. *(SharpByCoop.com photo)*

▲ **R.B. JOHNSON:** The bolster-release auto benefits from a naturally colored mammoth-ivory handle, mosaic damascus bolsters and a random-pattern-damascus blade. *(Cory Martin Imaging)*

▲ **BARRY GALLAGHER:** The auto folder perfectly blends the golden hues of Mokumé with the ivory handle and restless damascus blade. *(Cory Martin Imaging)*

▲ **ED BRANDSEY:** Elephant ivory and snakewood could only be secured with gold-plated screws. A faceted Burmese ruby is mounted in a 14k-gold thumb stud. *(Cory Martin Imaging)*

▲ **HOWARD HITCHMOUGH:** Gold buttons and screws enhance the Damasteel folder with white pearl handle and rope file work along the back spacer. *(PointSeven photo)*

▼ **MARCELLO GARAU:** The heat-colored "starburst"-pattern bolsters blend seamlessly into the ancient tortoise shell handle of the damascus locking-liner folder. *(Francesco Pachi photo)*

▲ **CLIFF PARKER:** The maker's first non-damascus folder is fashioned from a 1095 blade, a titanium frame and stag handle scales. *(Hoffman photo)*

Hilts, Boots & Chutes

Show him some love. There's obviously a lot of love left to go around for the late, great R.W. "Bob" Loveless. The knife patterns he created and popularized are seemingly emulated more today than ever, and the master has been gone three years now, but not forgot. Never forgotten, not in the knife industry he won't be anyway. He contributed too much, influenced too many people and unleashed an incomprehensible amount of innovations. Such would include sub-hilt fighters (the "hilts" in the headline of this section), boot knives and chute knives. And these seem to be the most popular patterns copied today.

It is not just one or two "clinging-on" knifemakers creating their own renditions of popular Loveless patterns, either, but a wide variety of artisans contributing versions and visions of the master's work. So it's a trend, a wave of people creating similar objects and selling them to collectors who gobble them up like candy.

Beauty may be in short supply at times, but it is never remaindered or left unappreciated. Beauty doesn't end up in the bargain bin. And that's exactly what Bob Loveless-style knives are, beautiful, gorgeous, inspired and comely. The lines are sexy, the handles hot and the materials magnificent. The knives the makers are fashioning—the hilts, boots and chutes—are the mayonnaise, lettuce and tomato of the knife industry, and that's worth setting out the fine China for, don't you agree?

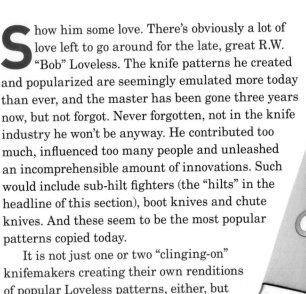

◀ **BOB LOVELESS:** Let's start with one from the master himself—a single-hilt fighter, special ordered by a CIA agent, and exhibiting Bob's Lawndale, California logo, a full, tapered tang and some Loveless bolts. *(SharpByCoop.com photo)*

◀ **JOHN YOUNG:** The maker's prototype of a "Mini Chute" parades a 3-inch CPM-154 blade, red liners and an amber-stag handle. *(SharpByCoop.com photo)*

▲ **ALAIN DESAULNIERS:** A pair of sub-hilt fighters do it double-guard style in stainless steel, ironwood and maroon Micarta®. *(SharpByCoop.com photo)*

▼**ALAIN DESAULNIERS:** One sub-hilt fighter in Micarta, a chute knife donning mammoth ivory, and a couple double-ground CPM-154 blades do all the damage. *(SharpByCoop.com photo)*

◄**RON NEWTON:** Integral Loveless-style "New York Special" knives exhibit damascus blades, hilts and sub-hilts that connect seamlessly with ebony and ironwood grips. *(Ward photo)*

◄**DAVID SHARP:** Fashioned from actual Bob Loveless shop patterns and dimensions, the chute knife exhibits a 4.35-inch, double-ground CPM-154 blade, and just like Loveless would have liked it, a green-canvas-Micarta handle with red liners. *(SharpByCoop.com photo)*

▼**STEVEN R. JOHNSON:** Enter the Big Bear in an 8.75-inch, double-ground CTS-XHP blade (a first for the maker), a mammoth-bark-ivory handle and red liners. *(Hoffman photo)*

▶ **KUNIHIKO TAMATSU:** Boot knives in black linen Micarta, ironwood and ATS-34 blade steel belong in a class all their own, yet belong to one popularized by Loveless. *(PointSeven photo)*

◀ **CHAD NELL:** Mother-of-pearl is a sweet handle choice for a CPM-154 sub-hilt fighter. *(SharpByCoop.com photo)*

▶ **CHARLES VESTAL:** The Loveless-style boot knife is one of 15 knives for members of the Custom Knife Collectors Association, and includes a 4.75-inch CPM-154 blade, a 416 stainless steel guard and a stabilized-curly-koa handle. *(SharpByCoop.com photo)*

▶ **CHAD NELL:** Amber stag complements the red liners along the tapered tang of a sub-hilt fighter. *(SharpByCoop.com photo)*

▶ **LLOYD HALE:** Though the maker says the grind is "all wrong" to be a chute knife, it does reflect design elements of a Bob Loveless piece, yet in the end it is "all Lloyd" in pearl and abalone inlays complementing an ironwood handle. *(SharpByCoop.com photo)*

Dimpled, Sculpted, Grooved and Glass Beaded

◄ PETER RASSENTI: There are enough grooves on the titanium handle to get a good grip before cutting with the CPM-S90V blade. *(PointSeven photo)*

▲ WILLIAM WELLING: The all-purpose Up-Armored Wood Craft knife coordinates a "Dark Earth Cerakote™"-coated 1095 blade with a sculpted-tan-Micarta handle and flared brass rivets.

▲ GUY STAINTHORP: Sculpted black Micarta® eases the eye into the "Hakkapella" Damasteel blade of the boot knife.

▲ BEN TENDICK: The maker knapped and textured the handle of the stonewashed, integral "B.P.K." (Bombproof Knife.)

◄ ALLEN ELISHEWITZ: Guilloché decorative engraving on the titanium bolsters leads into a machined, stippled and anodized zirconium handle. The frame-lock folder boasts a Chad Nichols San Mai 420 blade with an A2 core.

◄ **JERRY MCCLURE:** The walrus-ivory handle of the 16.5-inch, ball-bearing-damascus bowie features Art Deco carving and gold leaf overlay. *(SharpByCoop.com photo)*

▲ **TIM BRITTON:** The titanium handle of the flat-ground CPM-S35VN flipper folder is "groovilicious." *(SharpByCoop.com photo)*

▶ **BRIAN TIGHE:** The maker offers his "Tighe Coon" flipper folder in a plain or "paint splatter"-anodized-titanium handle, each version fluted to complement the machine-lined stainless steel or damascus blade. The knife features Glenn Klecker's NIRK locking mechanism. *(PointSeven photo)*

▶ **BILL COYE:** Get a load of the groovy G-10 handle, black and tan, and the big CPM-154 blade. *(PointSeven photo)*

▲ **JOSH SMITH:** Carved black-lip pearl plays counterpart to a hot-blued mosaic-damascus blade and bolsters. *(Cory Martin Imaging)*

▼ **JAMES SCROGGS:**
The textured handle of the two-finger CPM-154 neck knife was accomplished using a ball-end cutter on a rotary tool.

► **LUCAS BURNLEY:** Here's a new take on titanium knife handle frames—wood-grain-pattern carving—and the "viral"-finished CPM-154 blade is equally innovative.
(PointSeven photo)

► **ROD OLSON:**
The button-lock flipper folder has a grooved titanium body and a 2-inch Damasteel blade.
(PointSeven photo)

▼ **DAN RAFN:** A "Vinland" Damasteel dagger sashays its mother-of-pearl handle, 16 yellow sapphires and dimpled silver and gold handle frame.
(Jette Schulz photo)

► **SERGE PANCHENKO:**
The "Arion" CPM-S35VN locking-liner folder features textured and antiqued copper handle scales.

▼ **ERIC OCHS:** The bronze-anodized titanium LinerLock® folder integrates hand-hammered bolsters, a CPM-S30V blade, "lightning-strike"-carbon-fiber handle scales and Sally Martin mosaic pins.

Daggers on Display

▶ **WAYNE HENSLEY:** Nothing spells class like a pearl-handle dagger with guard and pommel engraving. *(Hoffman photo)*

▶ **VINCE EVANS:** One twist-damascus dagger with carved pommel and quillion guard, some fossil-walrus-ivory in the hand—places to go and people to see, or fortresses to breach. *(PointSeven photo)*

▶ **STEVEN RAPP:** Pinned perfectly is the carved mastodon-ivory handle of a 154CM ring dagger. *(PointSeven photo)*

▼ **ANDERS HOGSTROM:** The maker forged the run-out twist-damascus blade, made up of random and mosaic steels, adding a snakewood handle and copper fittings.

▶ **PAUL BRACH:** The 5160 quillion dagger flaunts a fluted-ebony handle with twisted-wire inlay. *(PointSeven photo)*

▶ **RON NEWTON:** Pre-ban ivory bulges on one end, damascus delivers a blow on the other, and gold inlays enliven the guard. *(Ward photo)*

▶ **BERTIE RIETVELD:** The maker's signature "dragonskin"-damascus blade in brilliant colors is combined with an octagonal Picasso-marble handle and a Stanhope-logo lens. *(SharpByCoop.com photo)*

▶ **LIN RHEA:** The "Heart Afire Dagger" will send your heart aflutter, palpitating like the damascus blade and soothed only by the pre-ban-ivory handle. *(Ward photo)*

◀ **JERRY LAIRSON SR.:** In case there are services later, the damascus dagger displays a sterling silver cross on its mammoth-ivory grip. *(Ward photo)*

▶ **JEFF HAINES:** The Romanesque dagger comes complete with a 512-layer damascus blade, guard and pommel, blood groove and mammoth-ivory grip. *(Cory Martin Imaging)*

▲ **MIKE O'BRIEN:** A leaf-shaped, hollow-ground CPM-154 blade narrows at the waist, as does the amboyna-burl handle. *(BladeGallery.com photo)*

▼ **SHAYNE CARTER:** Done dagger style is a damascus piece in a nickel-silver guard and mastodon-ivory grip. *(SharpByCoop.com photo)*

◀◀▲ **STEVE JOHNSON:** More a double-edged stiletto than a dagger, the V-42-style piece, similar to the famous Fairbairn-Sykes military knife, sports an ivory handle, pointed pommel and thumb-print ferrule above the guard. *(SharpByCoop.com photo)*

▼ **REINHARD TSCHAGER:** The jewel-knife dagger is delivered in a Chad Nichols damascus blade, mammoth-ivory handle, and gold pins and lanyard ring.

Bronzed Bodies

▶ **MARK NEVLING:** The bronze bolsters of a damascus folder call out like a beacon against a dark night sky. *(Ward photo)*

◀ **VAN BARNETT:** Inspired by the book of the same name written by H.G. Wells, the "Time Machine" includes working gears turned by running your fingers along the glass case, irises in the bolster area that open and close, and gears on the damascus blade that mesh and rotate. Everything is brass, copper, bronze and steel, and there are lots of tiny rivets throughout the handle. *(PointSeven photo)*

▼ **PETER MARTIN:** Part of a growing trend of "steam punk" (industrial, steam-powered, sci-fi) knives, the locking-liner folder is done up in mosaic damascus, bronze, copper and stainless steel. *(Cory Martin Imaging)*

▶ **ALLEN ELISHEWITZ:** Dimpled bronze bolsters mark the halfway point between "lightning strike" carbon-fiber handle scales and a "Takefu" laminated stainless steel blade with a VG-10 core.

▼ **THINUS HERBST:** A bronze guard and pommel give the N690 sword an aged and ageless feel, though the grooved handle is shiny stainless steel.

You've Been Lightning Struck

Of all the "Trends" in knives, material trends are some of the most fascinating to track. It shouldn't be surprising that knifemaking materials often determine what is popular or unpopular in handmade knives. Knifemakers tend to use what's readily available, inexpensive, utilitarian and aesthetic. It has to be a workable material, not too difficult to cut, grind, machine, groove, sand or chamfer, and non-toxic, or at least pose no health risks if facemasks or exhaust filtration systems are used in the shop.

Perhaps the most popular current handle material for flipper folders, tactical knives, gent's knives and other high-tech fixed blades and folders is "lightning-strike" carbon fiber. Gold-colored wires weave their way through the carbon-fiber handle material like static electricity from a lightning strike.

When asked about "lightning strike" carbon fiber during an interview for BLADE® Magazine, knifemaker Lance Abernathy of Sniper Bladeworks said, "Carbon fiber, especially lightning-strike carbon fiber, is requested quite a bit. Carbon fiber has always been a popular material, and with the addition of copper, it makes it sexy, giving it color, depth, layers and cool factor. Plus, anything from the aerospace industry is cool. Lightning-strike carbon fiber is where hi-tech meets bad ass."

▶ DAVID SHARP: A Loveless "Hideout" pattern combines a double-hollow-ground CPM-S35VN blade and a lightning-strike carbon-fiber handle. (SharpByCoop.com photo)

▲ BRIAN FELLHOELTER: The "FTR" frame-lock folder combines three of the most popular knifemaking materials used today—a Chad Nichols damascus blade, "superconductor" bolsters and a lightning-strike carbon-fiber handle. The knife is a Fellhoelter/Horton collaboration. (SharpByCoop.com photo)

▲ DANIEL ERICKSON: A pattern borrowed from the original knife carried by Ezra Meeker, founder of Puyallop, Washington, the folder sports a 1080-and-15N20-damascus blade and a lightning-strike carbon-fiber handle. The original sported a brass handle with a high-carbon-steel blade.

▶ **GREG LIGHTFOOT:** Lightning only struck the bolster of the "Darcon" flipper folder, designed by Joel Pirela. The handle itself is standard carbon fiber, and the flats of the CPM-S35VN blade are hammer finished for a textured look.

▲ **RALPH TURNBULL:** A lock-back folder seamlessly blends damascus and lightning-strike carbon fiber.

▶ **SCOT MATSUOKA:** The flipper folder is a smart combination of titanium, CPM-154 blade steel and lightning-strike carbon fiber. *(SharpByCoop.com photo)*

◀ **JERRY MOEN:** At only 1.3 ounces, "The Feather," designed in collaboration with Lloyd McConnell, is all lightning-strike carbon fiber and XHP Carpenter steel. "The fact you can put this knife in your pocket and forget you're carrying it is my favorite characteristic," Moen states. *(PointSeven photo)*

The Tusk At Hand

▼ **STEVE NOLTE:** Here's mammoth ivory cut in a cross-grain manner for the grip of a drop-point hunter that also features an Alabama-damascus blade, herringbone spacers, mosaic pins, and guard and pommel engraving by Eric Nelson. *(Ward photo)*

▶ **MICHAEL RUTH JR.:** Chocolate-brown mammoth ivory makes its move on an otherwise all-damascus sub-hilt fighter. *(SharpByCoop.com photo)*

▶ **KEVIN CASEY:** The Siberian mammoth ivory is the blue type, similar to the anodized titanium liners, but unlike the damascus blade and meteorite bolsters. *(SharpByCoop.com photo)*

◀ **DON HANSON III:** The blue, brown and beige Siberian-mammoth-ivory handle scales color coordinate well with the mosaic damascus and titanium of a folding dress dagger. *(SharpByCoop.com photo)*

▲ **INGEMAR NORDELL:** The full tang of an "Orient twist"-Damasteel blade is sandwiched between mammoth-ivory handle slabs.

▶ **TERRY VANDEVENTER:** A teardrop-shaped mammoth-ivory handle slides easily into the hand, as the "feather"-damascus blade and clamshell-style guard grab more of the attention. *(Ward photo)*

▶ **RUSS ANDREWS:** A damascus combat/chute knife breaches the fortress anchored by a pre-ban elephant-ivory handle. *(SharpByCoop.com photo)*

▶ **MIKE TYRE:** Feather-pattern damascus and mammoth ivory work their magic on the "Agaue Dress Folder." *(Ward photo)*

▼ **TONY HUGHES:** Mammoth ivory and damascus are a match made in bowie knife heaven. *(SharpByCoop.com photo)*

▼ **MIKE CRADDOCK:** Mammoth ivory is chocolaty sweet on a slightly upswept, Persian-style damascus fixed blade. *(SharpByCoop.com photo)*

▶ **SAL MANARO:** The maker was in no hurry when he fashioned the "Rush" folder, masterfully matching up Devin Thomas damascus, mammoth ivory and titanium. *(SharpByCoop.com photo)*

◀ **CLIFF PARKER:** The "Warren Cliff" model is a long, sleek damascus folder outfitted in mammoth ivory. *(Ward photo)*

▲ **CHAD NELL:** Mammoth ivory makes a lasting impression on a CPM-154 sub-hilt fighter. *(SharpByCoop.com photo)*

▲ **DOUG ASHBY:** The ATS-34 skinner goes to work in mammoth-ivory handle scales and a guard engraved by J.R. French. *(Dave McDearmont photo)*

▼ **JOHN YOUNG:** The mammoth ivory had to be cut to match the tapered tang of the double-hollow-ground CPM-154 boot knife, and was done so beautifully. *(SharpByCoop.com photo)*

▶ **DAN RAFN:** The deer hunter hits the woods in RWL-34 blade steel, 416 stainless steel bolsters and pins, and a mammoth-ivory handle. *(Jette Schulz photo)*

▶ **BRET DOWELL:** Dale Harwood engraved the areas around the mammoth ivory, while Bret built the fine slip-joint folder. *(Ward photo)*

▶ **CRAIG STEKETEE:** The ivory definitely gives more than it takes away from the overall look of the damascus bowie. *(Ward photo)*

▶ **HARVEY DEAN:** A bowtie shield is centered on the mammoth-ivory grip of a damascus folder with gold-inlaid bolsters. *(PointSeven photo)*

▲ **CURT ERICKSON:** The knifemaking/engraving duo of Curt and his wife Julie Warenski-Erickson team up again, this time on a dynamic dagger showcasing an ancient ivory grip, and a golden guard and pins. *(SharpByCoop.com photo)*

Class "A" Hunters

It is generally accepted that the knife is man's oldest tool. Assuming that a hunting knife could truly be man's oldest knife, it would therefore be the most ancient of the oldest tools, the elder statesman, the wise man and ancestor of all knives and edged weapons. How? Well, skinning or cutting meat for food could conceivably have been the task at hand the first prehistoric man who chipped a rock into an edge was trying to accomplish. If so, then the hunter is the oldest knife pattern. No one will ever know unless Neanderthal Number 1 emerges from the permafrost or desert sands, wakes or thaws and starts talking.

It is safe to assume, however, that the hunting knife is one of the oldest tools ever known to man. Prehistoric people needed to eat. They had big molars and incisors. They likely ate both meat and vegetables, and they needed to kill, butcher and prepare their meat, and that required a sharp tool. It could be the first knife was used to cut a loincloth or stab an intruder, but again, where did they get the loincloth, and what was the intruder after? Meat? You see ... a lot of it goes back to hunting.

Regardless, the hunting knives being made in 2013 are a bit more advanced than those of prehistoric man, as the pattern has been perfected over millions of years. Some of the knives are downright good looking, and that's more than can be said for Og, Son of Fire. These are a different class of hunters, Class "A" Hunters to be exact, and they're taking the 21st century by storm, or at least the hunting and collecting segments who care about such things as man's oldest tool and how it was put to use.

▶ **LARRY COX: The wide 1080 blade shows enough belly for skinning and dressing, and speaking of which, the ironwood handle is more than just window dressing, isn't it?**
(Ward photo)

▲ **THOMAS HASLINGER: An elegant hunting knife with a San Mai damascus blade, the solid-damascus bolsters are dovetailed and invisibly fastened, while pebbled Sambar stag makes the handle pop.**

▼ **DAVID SHARP: Dyed and stabilized sycamore certainly makes an impression on a Bob Loveless-style CPM-154 drop-point hunter.**
(SharpByCoop.com photo)

▼ **RICHARD VAN DIJK: There's something about this stag-handle damascus hunter that exudes tradition. Maybe it's the brass bolster and pommel with aged patina, but methinks it's more than that.**

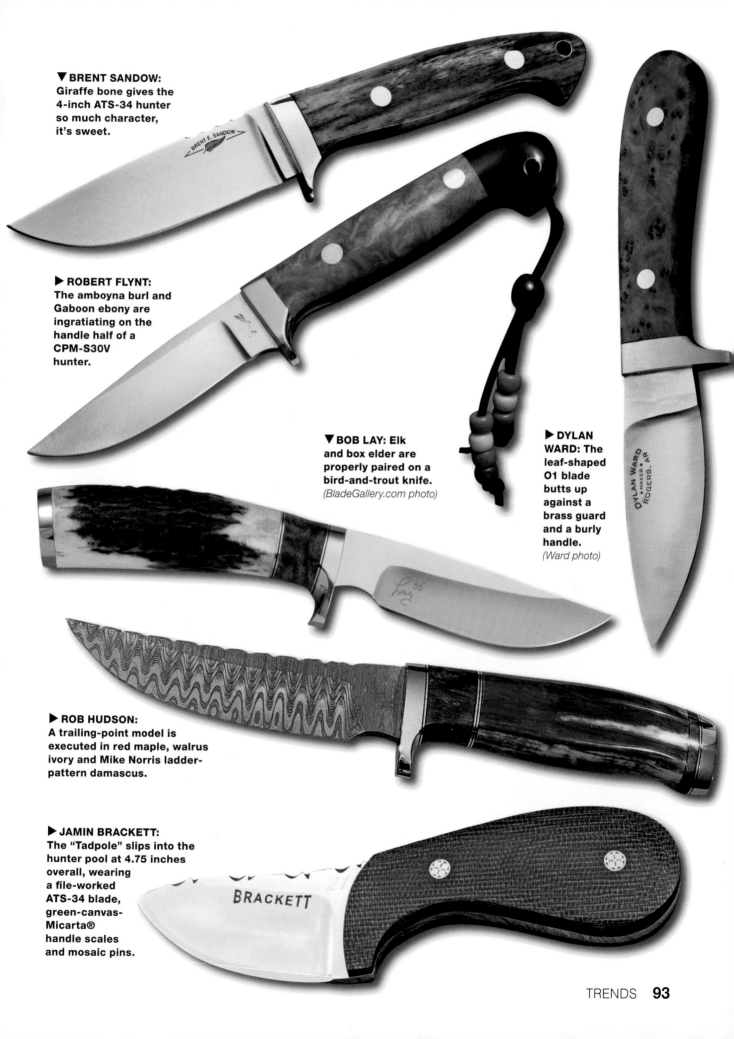

▼ **BRENT SANDOW:** Giraffe bone gives the 4-inch ATS-34 hunter so much character, it's sweet.

▶ **ROBERT FLYNT:** The amboyna burl and Gaboon ebony are ingratiating on the handle half of a CPM-S30V hunter.

▼ **BOB LAY:** Elk and box elder are properly paired on a bird-and-trout knife. *(BladeGallery.com photo)*

▶ **DYLAN WARD:** The leaf-shaped O1 blade butts up against a brass guard and a burly handle. *(Ward photo)*

▶ **ROB HUDSON:** A trailing-point model is executed in red maple, walrus ivory and Mike Norris ladder-pattern damascus.

▶ **JAMIN BRACKETT:** The "Tadpole" slips into the hunter pool at 4.75 inches overall, wearing a file-worked ATS-34 blade, green-canvas-Micarta® handle scales and mosaic pins.

Class "A" Hunters

▶ **ANSSI RUUSUVUORI:** As the Turkish walnut slips into your hand, the differentially heat-treated 1080 steel gives you a glint that makes you smile.

▶ **PEKKA TUOMINEN:** Like all good puukkos should, it sports a birch-bark handle and a Scandi-ground RWL-34 blade.

◀ **BRUCE BOHRMANN:** The grains of cherry wood drift their way over to the smooth lines of a 4.25-inch skinning blade. *(BladeGallery.com photo)*

▼ **DANIEL WINKLER:** Given a frontier flavor via the smoothing of stag and crimping of copper, the damascus hunter howls like a wolf, doesn't it? *(BladeGallery.com photo)*

▲ **STEVEN TEDFORD:** The Ontario deer horn bends beautifully, and so does the ATS-34 blade for that matter. The maker says it's the knife he's wanted to make all his life.

▶ **GUY STAINTHORP:** A pair of field dressing knives is prepared in desert ironwood handles, RWL-34 blades and mosaic pins.

▼ **RON ROSENBAUGH:** The bone is jigged, the flats flinted and a-hunting we will go.

▶ **R.W. WILSON:** A stainless-damascus hunter is outfitted in a brass guard and pommel sandwiching Micarta spacers and a camel-bone handle.
(Cory Martin Imaging)

▲ **RICK SMITH:** The ergonomic skinner works in rounded rosewood handle scales, a 5.5-inch O1 tool steel blade, nickel-silver guard and star-mosaic pins.

▶ **DAN DUGDALE:** A place for the palm, a place for the finger, and now if we find a place to use the 2.5-inch 440C blade, we'll be cooking with Crisco.
(SharpByCoop.com photo)

Class "A" Hunters

▶ **ROBERT APPLEBY JR.:** The whitetail-tine tip gives the William Scagel-style "Fishtail Hunter" its name, but it is the 1095 blade that dives right in. *(Ward photo)*

◀ **PAUL LUSK:** Stag, red spacers, CPM-154 steel and some file work make up the "Little River Pocket Skinner." *(Ward photo)*

▼ **MICHAEL MOONEY:** The classic drop-point hunter has a 4.25-inch CPM-S30V blade with thumb notches on the spine, dovetailed 416 stainless steel bolsters and amber-dyed Sambar stag handle scales.

▶ **J.R. REEVES:** The "Buckshot Skinner" is released in a streaked water-buffalo-horn handle, stainless guard and "buckshot-bird's-eye"-damascus blade.

▲ **TIMOTHY STEINGASS:** The full-tang hunter with Micarta handle is built like a tank. *(Ward photo)*

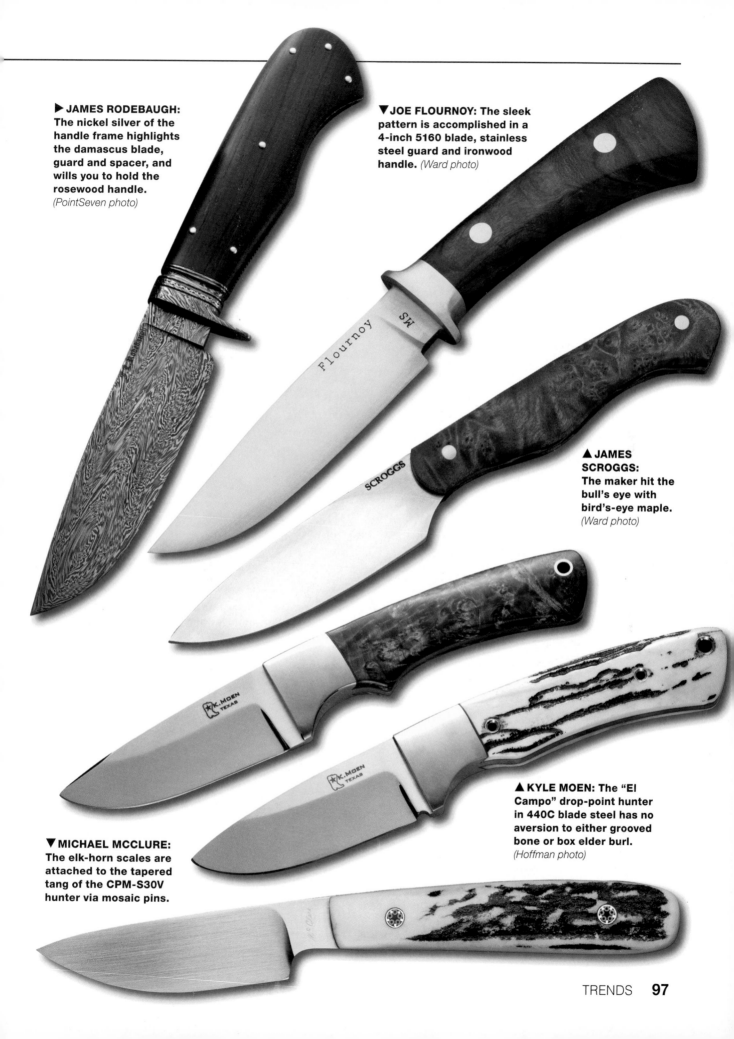

▶ **JAMES RODEBAUGH:** The nickel silver of the handle frame highlights the damascus blade, guard and spacer, and wills you to hold the rosewood handle. *(PointSeven photo)*

▼ **JOE FLOURNOY:** The sleek pattern is accomplished in a 4-inch 5160 blade, stainless steel guard and ironwood handle. *(Ward photo)*

▲ **JAMES SCROGGS:** The maker hit the bull's eye with bird's-eye maple. *(Ward photo)*

▲ **KYLE MOEN:** The "El Campo" drop-point hunter in 440C blade steel has no aversion to either grooved bone or box elder burl. *(Hoffman photo)*

▼ **MICHAEL McCLURE:** The elk-horn scales are attached to the tapered tang of the CPM-S30V hunter via mosaic pins.

▶ **BILL KIRKES:** The dark stag with only a little amber peeking out is accompanied by a wide 5160 blade and a stainless steel buttcap carved to emulate the grooves of the stag itself. *(Ward photo)*

▲ **JERRY MOEN:** One was so gorgeous, he made two, then three, all in ivory, and with stainless steel bolsters engraved and gold inlaid by Nathan Dickinson. *(PointSeven photo)*

▼ **JAMES R. LUCIE:** A William Scagel-style small skinner is hand forged from 1084 steel and styled just so.

▲ **LIN RHEA:** Looks like the sheep gave up its horn for a good cause. *(Ward photo)*

◄ **KUNIHIKO TAMATSU:** A gut-hook skinner and semi-skinner share features, including rounded and finger-grooved African-blackwood handles and 4-inch CPM-S30V blades. *(PointSeven photo)*

◄ **BENONI BULLARD:** His hunter/utility knife looks nice in a 5.5-inch 5160 blade and palm-swelling stag handle. *(Ward photo)*

► **JACK JONES:** Patterned after a Randall Model 20 Yukon Skinner, the hunter does its predecessor justice in a 4.5-inch CPM-154, trailing-point blade, a nickel-silver guard and Sambar stag handle. *(Hoffman photo)*

▲ **KEVIN D. CROSS:** A small hunter leaves a large impression in CPM-S35VN steel, a brass guard and a spalted-ash grip. *(Hoffman photo)*

A, B, C's of Burl

Once again we're back to wood, reverting to nature and relying on what the earth provides. It's funny, no matter how far society has advanced, how fast technology has developed or how connected computers have made us, the world has yet to improve upon the beauty and utility of burl. And the knife itself has never been replaced.

Tools are still necessary. Building things is not out of favor or fashion. In fact, caught up in the whirlwind of the 21st century is a movement toward organic, self-sufficiency and living ready. Knifemakers have never closed their eyes to their surroundings, but instead, like conservationists, they embrace the natural world, take only what they need, leave the rest as they found it and repair what has been damaged.

There are such things as renewable resources and wood happens to be one of them, burly wood, highly-figured wood, with grains, grooves, knots and notches. It cannot be replicated, at least not yet, and the atmosphere weathers wood and gives it character. Try that in an environmentally controlled furnace, with a programmable CNC machine or on a production line. You can't stamp out ash, manufacture bog oak or engineer curly maple. And that's just the A, B, C's of burl.

▼ STEVE MILLER: If you wore a pattern like that of the black palm, people would stare at you, too.

◄ JULIUS MOJZIS: The carved steel weasel emerges from a forest of coconut palm wood.

▼ BILL KENNEDY JR.: Mosaic pins dot the stabilized mineral redwood of the finely crafted 440C fixed blade.
(PointSeven photo)

▼ MICHAEL OLIVE: Spalted maple lends tiger stripes to a 1095 blade.

▲ SEAN O'HARE: The maker's "Finback" model relies on a 3.5-inch CPM-154 blade, dovetailed stainless steel bolsters and a stabilized-amboyna-burl handle.

▶ **RAY KIRK:** As the grains of maple burn themselves into your consciousness, drink in the 6-inch 52100 blade with rough-finished spine and integral bolster. *(Ward photo)*

▶ **ANSSI RUUSUVUORI:** The puukko knife follows a natural form, incorporating oak burl, nickel silver and a hand-forged, heat-treated 1080 steel blade.

▼ **GARTH HINDMARCH:** The full-tang 440C hunter is outfitted in afzelia lay.

JOHN COHEA: The ringed maple haft of the pipe tomahawk, as with the 5160 head, and copper, rawhide and mammoth-ivory fittings, harkens back to an age of pure tranquility and occasional wartime turbulence. *(Ward photo)*

◄ DAVID SHARP: Dyed and stabilized sycamore sets off a Loveless-style drop-point hunter executed in CPM-154 blade steel and a full-height hollow grind. *(SharpByCoop.com photo)*

▼ SAMUEL LURQUIN: Stabilized koa wood kicks the "Hurak Fighter" into high gear, led forward by a damascus blade and gun-blued guard. *(SharpByCoop.com photo)*

◄ BILL LUCKETT: The "Pit Viper" extends an 8-inch CPM-154 stinger and a Masur-birch body dyed black.

▼ BILL POST: Thank goodness the "Delta post oak" wasn't permanently relegated to being a fence post, as it's much appreciated as the grip of a D2 fighter with brass pins. *(Ward photo)*

▲ BUTCH SHEELY: The pristine pipe tomahawk is finely furnished in a wrought 1095 head, curly maple haft, a bowl forged from a rifle barrel, and a poured-pewter band and mouthpiece. *(PointSeven photo)*

▶ **RICHARD VAN DIJK:** Sterling silver fittings cap the bocote-wood handle on each side, and help set off a 50-layer damascus blade of the executive knife.

◀ **JERRY HOSSOM:** The "Retribution Scout" forges ahead in a CPM-3V blade and California-buckeye-burl handle. *(SharpByCoop.com photo)*

▶ **BURT FOSTER:** Two laminated-steel fighters fare better than one, fashionably adorned in curly-koa-wood grips. *(SharpByCoop.com photo)*

▶ **RIK PALM:** Patterned after a prehistoric belt dagger the maker once saw, he carved the guard from stacked cow bone to look like wrapped rawhide, gave it an antiqued patina, fashioned a handle from golden fiddleback wood and forged a 1084-and-15N20-damascus blade to shape.

▶ **KEVIN D. CROSS:** White cedar and walnut share billing on a bird-and-trout knife. *(Hoffman photo)*

▼ **DAVID C. LEMOINE:** A Damasteel blade sets the bar high for the snakewood handle of a hidden-tang hunter. *(Hoffman photo)*

▶ **J.R. REEVES:** Pattern development involves that of California buckeye burl and "raindrop buckshot" damascus.

◀ **ROBERT FLYNT:** The stabilized curly redwood handle was finished until it shined, and the Brad Vice ladder-pattern-damascus blade wasn't ignored, either.

▲ **RON ROSENBAUGH:** A "Modified Nessmuk" model makes use of a stabilized lacewood handle, Corby rivets, a thong tube, and a clay-hardened and differentially heat-treated 1095 high-carbon-steel blade.

► **CHAD HARDING:** He dyed and rubbed the curly maple until it shone with the same brilliance as the W1 tool steel blade.
(SharpByCoop.com photo)

► **CONNER MCGHEE:** Assisted by his father, E. Scott McGhee, the 9-year-old Conner fashioned "The Blue Buddha" in a flat-ground 1084 blade and dyed-curly-maple handle.
(SharpByCoop.com photo)

◄ **STUART BRANSON:** Aged white oak gives the "Relic Oak Fighter" its name, married with a W2 blade, wispy temper line and chainsaw-bar guard.
(SharpByCoop.com photo)

▲ **TAD LYNCH:** There's nothing wrong and everything right with an "Integral Light Fighter" in W2 blade steel and a stabilized koa grip.
(Ward photo)

▲ **LUCAS LANCE:** The scale from heat-treating was left on the ATS-34 blade of the bowie for an aged patina, matching it up nicely with a spalted-maple grip, and turned-bronze guard and butt.

▲ ROB HUDSON: Reddish-brown maple spacers bookend the maple-burl handle of a clip-point fixed blade.

▼ KEVIN LESSWING: Once you wrap your mind around the tiger-maple handle, look at the way the maker engraved the guard and pommel of the W1 drop-point hunter. *(SharpByCoop.com photo)*

▼ ALLEN NEWBERRY: The Brut-de-Forge Sword is decked out in 19 inches of file-marked 5160 steel and curly maple of the sticky sweet variety. *(Ward photo)*

► PEKKA TUOMINEN: Calling it an "ancient-style women's puukko knife," the maker did it up in a curly-birch handle, brass bolsters and a 155CrV3 blade, the latter referred to as "Silversteel."

▲ MICHAEL MOONEY: A Japanese vegetable knife, the *nikiri bocho* employs a very thin edge of CPM-S30V steel and a traditional, octagonal handle of oak and African blackwood.

▶ **MICHAEL DEIBERT:** The not quite big, yet not small "mid-Bowie" gains favor in a palm-swelling, spalted-maple grip, a 1095 blade and blued mild-steel fittings. *(PointSeven photo)*

▼ **PAUL LUSK:** Creatively combining blue resin with buckeye burl, and using it for the handle of an Alabama-damascus gent's folder proved a stroke of genius. *(Ward photo)*

▲ **LIN RHEA:** The bowie is paraded out in swirled and burled ironwood, as well as an 11.5-inch 1095 blade. *(Ward photo)*

▼ **MICHAEL RUTH JR.:** Catch the Damascus fighter by its curly-koa grip and admire it for a spell. *(Ward photo)*

▼ **BILL BEHNKE:** Stabilized curly maple, damascus in feather and ladder patterns, and mosaic pins combine to lend character to a medium hunter.

▼ **JAMES "RICK" LUCAS:** The maker used local spalted maple burl for the grip of a damascus fixed blade, adhering it with a mosaic pin and marrying it up to a wrought-iron guard and a walrus-ivory buttcap.

Global Arming

◀ **SERGE PANCHENKO:** Everything is antiqued on the African dagger, including the W1 blade and copper handle.

◀ **DOUGLAS STICE:** Calling it a fast, durable, Westernized tanto design, the maker's "Rakurai" is executed nicely in an Alabama Damascus blade, and a cord-wrapped, maroon stingray-skin handle.

▲ **KIKU MATSUDA:** The Japanese knifemaker takes a successful crack at a Nepalese kukuri that combines a foot-long, compound-ground, acid-finished OU-31 semi-stainless steel blade, and a carved-canvas-Micarta® grip. *(BladeGallery.com photo)*

▼ **DAVID MIRABILE:** The smoking-hot San Mai steel tanto is delivered in mokumé fittings and a cord-wrapped carbon-fiber handle and sheath. *(SharpByCoop.com photo)*

▲ **KEVIN HARVEY:** "Magnetism" mosaic damascus thrusts forward on a *main-gauche* (French for "left hand") parrying dagger that also sports a silver-wire-wrapped, hippo-tooth handle and a bronze pommel engraved in floral scroll. *(BladeGallery.com photo)*

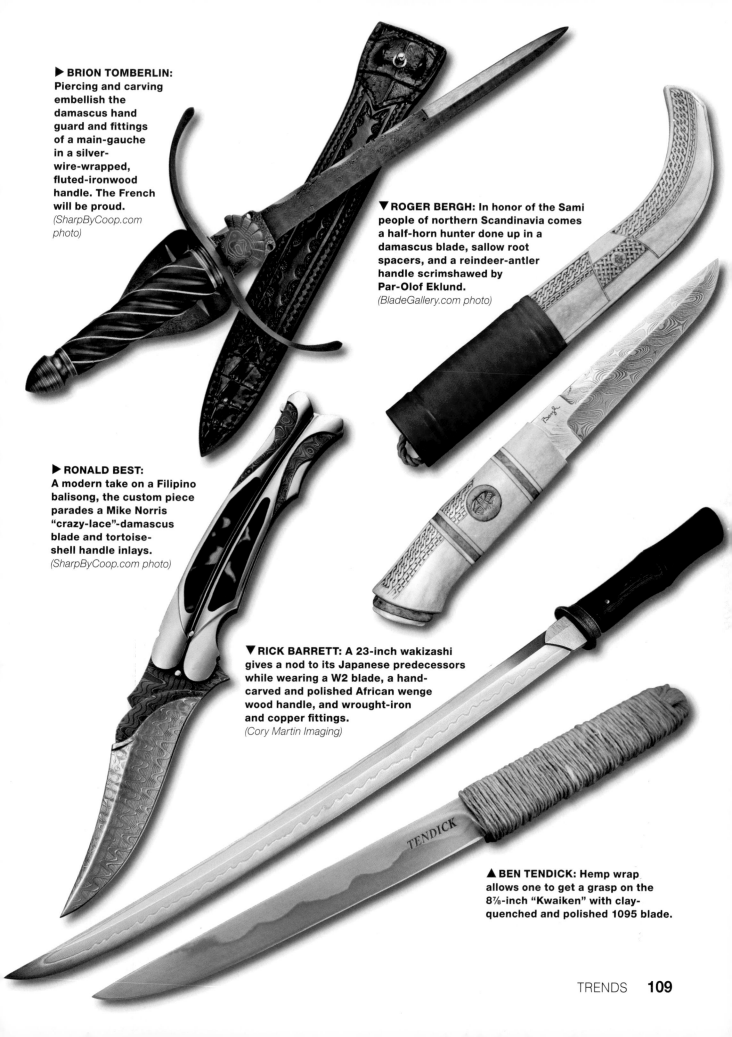

▶ **BRION TOMBERLIN:** Piercing and carving embellish the damascus hand guard and fittings of a main-gauche in a silver-wire-wrapped, fluted-ironwood handle. The French will be proud. *(SharpByCoop.com photo)*

▼ **ROGER BERGH:** In honor of the Sami people of northern Scandinavia comes a half-horn hunter done up in a damascus blade, sallow root spacers, and a reindeer-antler handle scrimshawed by Par-Olof Eklund. *(BladeGallery.com photo)*

▶ **RONALD BEST:** A modern take on a Filipino balisong, the custom piece parades a Mike Norris "crazy-lace"-damascus blade and tortoise-shell handle inlays. *(SharpByCoop.com photo)*

▼ **RICK BARRETT:** A 23-inch wakizashi gives a nod to its Japanese predecessors while wearing a W2 blade, a hand-carved and polished African wenge wood handle, and wrought-iron and copper fittings. *(Cory Martin Imaging)*

▲ **BEN TENDICK:** Hemp wrap allows one to get a grasp on the 8⅞-inch "Kwaiken" with clay-quenched and polished 1095 blade.

▼ANDERS HOGSTROM: The "Sculpted Persian" flexes its 10-inch Mill Head Damascus blade, bronze guard, copper spacer and top-notch walrus-ivory handle. *(SharpByCoop.com photo)*

▼DAVID GOLDBERG: The "Chishio Tokage" (Blood Dragon) katana boasts a 28.5-inch *tamahagane* (sand iron steel) blade with a folded-iron core, hand-carved sterling silver fittings in a "dragon in the waves" motif, and a magnolia wood hilt covered in lacquered stingray skin and wrapped in black calf's leather. With a magnolia *saya* (case), it reportedly sold for $30,000. *(PointSeven photo)*

▼ERIC DOBRATZ: The tanto blade is over 1,400 layers of 1095-and-1035-damascus steel married up with a *shibuichi*—silver and copper—blade collar, a file-worked copper washer, and a fiddleback koa wood handle and sheath.

◄RAY RYBAR: The "23rd Psalm Blade" is fittingly outfitted in an olive wood and ancient-sheep-horn ("The lord is my shepherd; I shall not want.") handle, a 14-inch, blued mosaic-damascus blade, and Brazilian gold and silver carved fittings. *(SharpByCoop.com photo)*

▼THINUS HERBST: The cinquedea (Italian short sword) sports true-to-the-pattern grooves along an N690 stainless steel blade, a giraffe-bone handle and carved bronze fittings.

▶ **INGEMAR NORDELL:** An "Odin's Eye" Damasteel blade starts off the Finnish puukko belt knife, finished off in bronze fittings, a desert-ironwood handle and a red-gold matrix liner.

▶ **J.D. SMITH:** A "Spanish Tinge" dress folder parades a 4⅜-inch 15N20-and-1084-damascus blade, mokumé gane bolsters, a file-worked back spacer and a gold-lip-pearl handle. *(SharpByCoop.com photo)*

◀ **VINCE EVANS:** A Viking sword showcases a 32-inch, composite-damascus blade, a 22k-gold-inlaid guard and pommel, twisted-silver-wire fittings, and a walrus-ivory hilt. *(PointSeven photo)*

◀ **"INDIAN GEORGE" REBELLO:** The damascus fixed-blade fighter embraces an African theme, hence the ivory and water-buffalo-horn spacers, and springbok-horn handle. *(SharpByCoop.com photo)*

▼ **RICHARD VAN DIJK:** Any Saxon worth his salt would take pride in the three-bar-damascus Seax with an iron spine and 100-layer edge, a carved-elm-burl handle, cow-horn bolster, and copper ring and fittings.

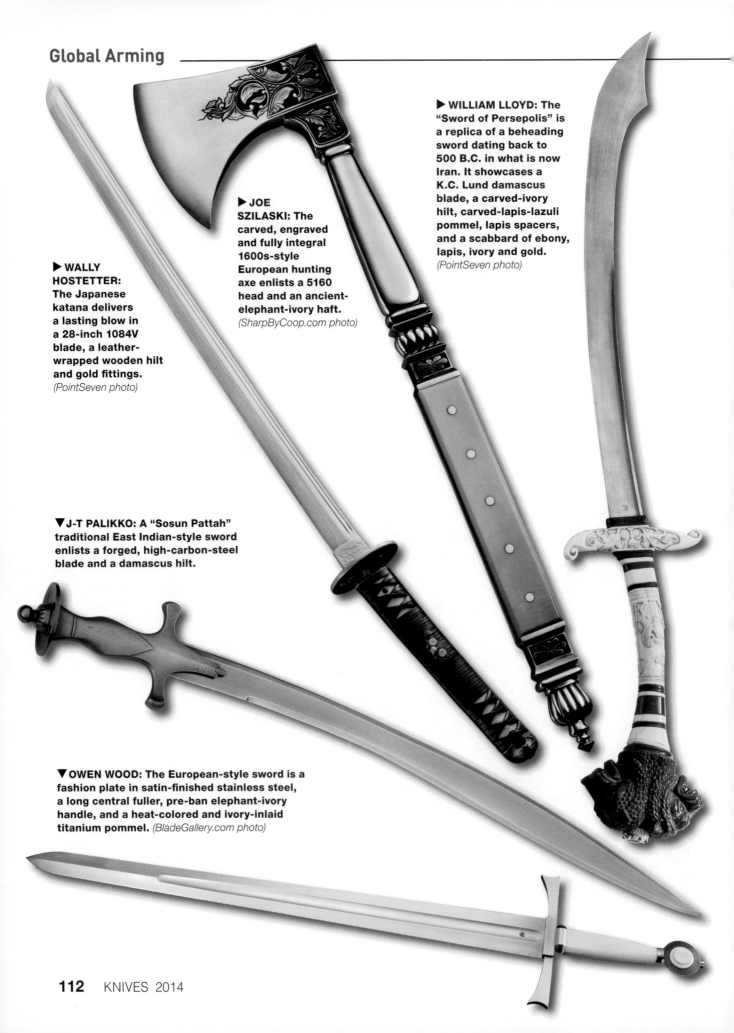

► **WILLIAM LLOYD:** The "Sword of Persepolis" is a replica of a beheading sword dating back to 500 B.C. in what is now Iran. It showcases a K.C. Lund damascus blade, a carved-ivory hilt, carved-lapis-lazuli pommel, lapis spacers, and a scabbard of ebony, lapis, ivory and gold. *(PointSeven photo)*

► **JOE SZILASKI:** The carved, engraved and fully integral 1600s-style European hunting axe enlists a 5160 head and an ancient-elephant-ivory haft. *(SharpByCoop.com photo)*

► **WALLY HOSTETTER:** The Japanese katana delivers a lasting blow in a 28-inch 1084V blade, a leather-wrapped wooden hilt and gold fittings. *(PointSeven photo)*

▼**J-T PALIKKO:** A "Sosun Pattah" traditional East Indian-style sword enlists a forged, high-carbon-steel blade and a damascus hilt.

▼**OWEN WOOD:** The European-style sword is a fashion plate in satin-finished stainless steel, a long central fuller, pre-ban elephant-ivory handle, and a heat-colored and ivory-inlaid titanium pommel. *(BladeGallery.com photo)*

◀ PEKKA TUOMINEN: A sizeable leukku would survive a Scandinavian winter in 12C27 blade steel, a carbon-fiber handle and a Kydex® sheath.

▼ KONSTANTINOS ZAFEIRIADIS: Greek in origin, the kopis sashays its 1,124-layer damascus blade, bronze guard and eagle-head-style curved wood pommel.

▼ NESTOR LORENZO RHO: An Argentine "Criollo" sports an engraved 420C stainless steel blade, a crown stag handle and a walrus-ivory spacer. *(Federico Koch photo)*

▶ DWIGHT TOWELL: A fully engraved Mediterranean bowie is delightfully delivered in an African-blackwood handle with 24k-gold and abalone inlays.

▲ JOT SINGH KHALSA: A ceremonial sword carried by baptized Sikhs, this kirpan is executed in a long, sweeping Devin Thomas damascus blade, a Pietersite (South African mineral) handle and Tim Adlam guard, pommel and sheath engraving. *(SharpByCoop.com photo)*

Molar Knife Caps

Well, they're not melting, that's for sure. The mammoth-tooth knife handles—or molar knife caps—on this and the facing page might not be piping hot, but they're fresh from the permafrost from which they emerged. And emerge they did, intact and full of character, color and contrast. Apparently while the northern lights danced across the night skies for centuries on end, some of that brilliance sank down to earth and soaked into the old ivories of woolly mammoths.

Nothing can beat mammoth tooth for adding a high-class, natural look to a knife grip. It doesn't shrink or swell over time. It's as hard as, well, a mammoth tooth, cool to the touch, easy on the eye and quite like lapidary work when it comes to cutting, smoothing and rounding it out. There aren't too many rough edges that will dig into the palm of a hand, and no slivers or blisters resulting from hard use.

Do people really use these knives anyway, you might ask? Do you use your teeth to chomp food? Even if they're purchased as collectibles, it is this *Knives* book editor's hope that the collectors at least slice a thread or two, or open a box before relegating the blades to the display case. After all, the mammoth teeth have been buried for long enough. Let the little molar knife caps breathe, take in some fresh air and live a little. They're too cool to ever melt away into obscurity anyway.

▲ **CHAD NELL:** For his 100th knife, the maker splurged on red-hued mammoth tooth and a length of CPM-154 steel. *(SharpByCoop.com photo)*

▶ **LARRY HOSTETLER:** The maker chose a nice slab of grayish, not garish, mammoth tooth to match up with a subtle damascus pattern and some classy bolster engraving by Sheila Hostetler. *(PointSeven photo)*

◀ **PAUL JARVIS:** Carved nickel silver, nickel damascus and mammoth tooth alternate moves on an art dagger. *(PointSeven photo)*

► **JERRY MOEN:** We could be so lucky to live long enough for our molars to turn as green as the mammoth tooth of a Carpenter steel drop-point hunter. Nathan Dickinson worked his engraving magic on the pretty piece. *(Hoffman photo)*

▼ **RICHARD TESARIK:** He had to carve the Pavel Sevecek damascus blade and bolsters just to vie for attention against the mammoth-tooth handle scales.

▼ **FRANK NIRO:** While the Rob Calcinore mosaic-damascus blade displays the colors of the rainbow, the Randy Haas Jr. mosaic-damascus bolsters give off a gold hue, and the mammoth-tooth handle is green, blue, brown and beige all over. *(Custom Knife Gallery of Colorado photo)*

► **MARK KNAPP:** The combination of mammoth tooth, musk ox horn and mokumé works magically on a damascus drop-point hunter. *(SharpByCoop.com photo)*

► **PETE TRUNCALI:** Mammoth tooth is like the ketchup and mustard on a hotdog of a lockback folder, complete with bolster engraving by Tony Pitts. *(Ward photo)*

Bowie Bloodlines

▶ **ALEX DANIELS:** A Woodhead and Hartley reproduction, a lion rests on the coffin-shaped pommel, while an ivory handle, oval shield and a 5⅝-inch blade fill up the rest of the scenery.

▶ **JAMES BATSON:** Engraved German silver fittings highlight the maker's interpretation of an antique bowie produced for Wolfe and Clark of New York. A walnut handle and 9-inch high-carbon-steel blade complete the piece. *(PointSeven photo)*

◀ **JERRY VAN EIZENGA:** The Confederate bowie is aged to look the part, and features a walnut handle and 18.75-inch 5160 blade. *(PointSeven photo)*

▲ **DOUGLAS NOREN:** A repro of a rare, circa-1835 American bowie, the piece showcases a silver-mounted hilt, silver quillons, a chain knuckle guard, carved-ivory handle, a 13.75-inch 5160 blade with a Spanish notch and a sharpened swedge along the spine. *(PointSeven photo)*

▼ **GARY MULKEY:** In the style of Sheffield maker William Butcher, the bowie sports a blackwood handle, a W2 blade with a Spanish notch and a rectangular shield. *(Ward photo)*

Wup, Wup, Wuppa Santoku Style

▶ **GLEN MIKOLAJCZYK:** Dyed camel bone is the palpable counterpart to a hand-forged, 360-layer 1095-and-15N20 random-pattern damascus blade of a Santoku kitchen knife. *(Cory Martin Imaging)*

▲ **ED SCHEMPP:** Of the one-hand-opening, folding Santoku variety, the ATS-34 stainless steel piece is properly outfitted in a maroon-Micarta® handle. *(PointSeven photo)*

▲ **STUART BARKER:** The "Toxic Santoku" is named after the "toxic green" and orange G-10 handle seeping into a flat-ground, belt-finished O1 blade treated to a forced patina through exposure to mustard and lemon juice. Lap that puppy up.

▶ **KEITH BAGLEY:** The folding cleaver borrows elements from a Santoku style, but remains its own entity in a damascus blade and flame-colored, grooved titanium handle. *(Hoffman photo)*

▼ **ERIC DOBRATZ:** You could cut up some kale and a few other veggies using the 1087 kitchen blade with discernable *hamon* (temper line), and a handle of buffalo horn and curly satinwood.

Hot Temper Lines

There's not much of a market for handmade hammers or saws. It's pretty difficult to obtain a custom drill, disc sander or air compressor. Try a Google search for a hand-fashioned nail gun or pipe wrench. Yet not only are handmade knives a commodity, but knifemakers are known to differentially temper blades to obtain *hamons*, or temper lines. The lines result from etching blades after they have been clay coated and tempered to achieve soft spines and hard edges. Temper lines mark the divisions between soft and hard.

Japanese sword smiths are often credited with achieving wispy and smoky temper lines as a result of clay coating and differentially tempering their blades. It was important for Samurai swordsmen to be able to trust their edges, for them not to chip, to cut, and to remain sharp for long periods of time, and equally imperative that the blades did not break because they were too hard. Sword smiths figured out how to achieve soft spines and hard edges, pretty ingenious, really, and now modern blade smiths practice and improve upon the methodology.

These are custom tools, hand fashioned in exacting detail, with impeccable fitting and finishing, everything aligned, materials married, precision, custom handwork. The blade temper lines are marks of quality, the makers' marks, hot little temper lines permanently etched in steel and undeniable in their appeal.

◄ **ROBERT GARDNER:** The temper line of a W2 blade does a dance from tip to stag grip. *(PointSeven photo)*

▲ **ANDREW TAKACH:** The forged 1095 blade of the fighter features a hand-polished hamon, and is complemented by a clamshell-style damascus guard and a fossilized-walrus-oosic handle. *(SharpByCoop.com photo)*

▲ **ALLEN NEWBERRY:** The camp cutlass design is unusual enough, but add on the differentially tempered 1095 blade and ironwood handle, and it's a one-of-a-kind piece. *(Ward photo)*

◀ **ERIC DOBRATZ:** A W2 bowie blade has a cloudy temper line reminiscent of an active afternoon sky, conjoined to a stabilized-maple-burl handle by way of a wrought-iron guard and stainless steel ferrules.

◀ **STEVE RANDALL:** A clay-quenched W2 blade displays an active hamon, while the bowie itself boasts a mild-steel guard and desert-ironwood handle. *(SharpByCoop.com photo)*

▲ **TIMOTHY STEINGASS:** The battle bowie is readied in a 10-inch W2 blade, ironwood handle, stainless steel fittings and a smokescreen of a temper line. *(Ward photo)*

▼ **BILL BURKE:** Are the lines of the laminated stainless steel blade with high-carbon-steel cutting edge more to your liking, or those of the musk ox-horn grip or mokumé-gane bolster? *(BladeGallery.com photo)*

▶ **MICHAEL MOONEY:** The Japanese slicing knife has an 11-inch, clay-hardened W2 tool steel blade with a complex hamon. The handle is a marlinspike of a pale jade color, and nickel-silver fittings complete the pretty package.

Modern Takes on Tacticals

The one area where knives have most noticeably advanced is in the tactical arena. The exact minute someone says that there's nothing new in knives, or everything's been done before, a flipper folder sells somewhere around the world. They're that popular. Or an assisted-opening folder surprises someone with its speed, and that person pulls out his or her pocketbook on the spot. A multi-ground, swedge-ground or tanto fixed blade or folder moves off a store shelf, a cord-wrapped neck knife finds its proper place concealed under a policeman's uniform, a frame-lock folder working off a ball-bearing pivot system is clipped to an enthusiast's pants pocket, or a double-action auto is triggered by nudging a knife bolster.

There's more. Lightning-strike carbon fiber finds favor with the tactical crowd, as does "super-conductor" material, Digi-Camo™ or colored G-10, titanium, meteorite and grooved Micarta®. From a technological standpoint, tactical folders and fixed blades seem to be the testing grounds. It shouldn't be surprising, especially considering how our military, police and EMTs rely on those knives and require solid, handy, reliable and not overly expensive pieces. Tactical fixed blades and folders are where the tires hit the pavement, and the modern takes on tacticals are proving to be revved up and ready to go.

▶ MARCUS CLINCO: A cord-wrapped, integral 1095 fixed blade is bead blasted and black oxide coated.

▼ SEAN O'HARE: Black and tan G-10 partner up like dark beer and pale ale, but never weighing down a CPM-154 folder.

▲ STAN WILSON: The "Tac 1" tanto is done up in gun-blued O1 blade steel, a carbon-fiber handle, and a titanium frame and liners.
(Hoffman photo)

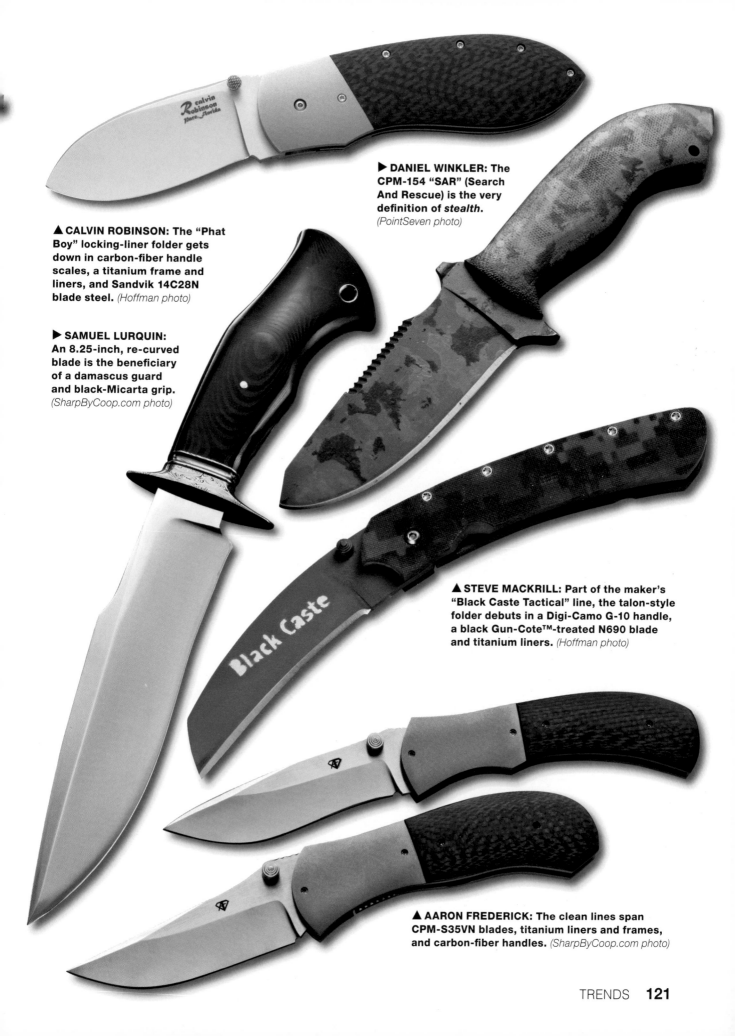

▲ **CALVIN ROBINSON:** The "Phat Boy" locking-liner folder gets down in carbon-fiber handle scales, a titanium frame and liners, and Sandvik 14C28N blade steel. *(Hoffman photo)*

▶ **DANIEL WINKLER:** The CPM-154 "SAR" (Search And Rescue) is the very definition of *stealth*. *(PointSeven photo)*

▶ **SAMUEL LURQUIN:** An 8.25-inch, re-curved blade is the beneficiary of a damascus guard and black-Micarta grip. *(SharpByCoop.com photo)*

▲ **STEVE MACKRILL:** Part of the maker's "Black Caste Tactical" line, the talon-style folder debuts in a Digi-Camo G-10 handle, a black Gun-Cote™-treated N690 blade and titanium liners. *(Hoffman photo)*

▲ **AARON FREDERICK:** The clean lines span CPM-S35VN blades, titanium liners and frames, and carbon-fiber handles. *(SharpByCoop.com photo)*

Modern Takes on Tacticals

▲ JOHN CHASE: An acutely curved 5-inch D2 blade extends from a brass guard, red spacer and black-Micarta grip.

▲ KEITH OUYE: If you like your tactical folders dressed up, then the "Gryphon" should suffice via Bruce Shaw gold inlay and engraving on a 6AL-4V-titanium frame, as well as an ATS-34 blade, jeweled liners and a low-riding pocket clip. *(SharpByCoop.com photo)*

▼ JOHN BARKER: Carbon fiber and Chad Nichols "sweep" damascus lend character to a pair of shapely black-and-grey tactical folders in titanium bolsters. *(PointSeven photo)*

◄ LUCAS BURNLEY: A master of disguises, the "Kwaiken" flipper folder changes in and out of damascus, noncoated and coated blades, and natural, carbon-fiber and grooved-titanium handles. *(PointSeven photo)*

▶ **ANDRE THORBURN:** The flipper folder has all the amenities—a satin-finished Bohler N690 blade, black G-10 handle, Ikoma Korth Bearing System, and titanium liners, pivot and belt clip.

▼ **ALLEN ELISHEWITZ:** Mokumé bolsters and sculpted-ironwood handle scales proved a match made in flipper-folder heaven. The "Takefu" stainless steel blade is laminated with a VG-10 core.

▲ **ERIC OCHS:** The honeycomb appearance of the Composite Craft C-Tek™ handle scales is enhanced by dimpled titanium bolsters and a satin-finished CPM-S30V blade.

◀ **PHILIP BOOTH:** In a moment of inspiration, the maker added a stainless steel stripe between carbon-fiber handle sections of the ball-bearing flipper folder, complete with a Mike Norris stainless-damascus blade.
(SharpByCoop.com photo)

▲ **TOM FERRY:** The "Tango Foxtrot Knives" are paraded out in D2 blades, and carbon-fiber and G-10 handles.
(SharpByCoop.com photo)

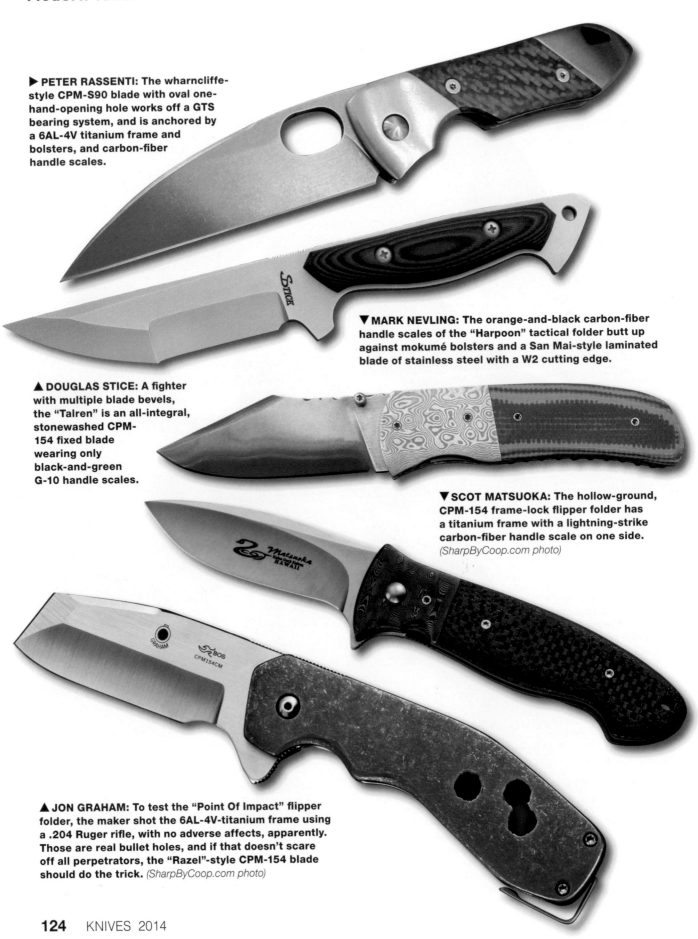

▶ **PETER RASSENTI:** The wharncliffe-style CPM-S90 blade with oval one-hand-opening hole works off a GTS bearing system, and is anchored by a 6AL-4V titanium frame and bolsters, and carbon-fiber handle scales.

▼ **MARK NEVLING:** The orange-and-black carbon-fiber handle scales of the "Harpoon" tactical folder butt up against mokumé bolsters and a San Mai-style laminated blade of stainless steel with a W2 cutting edge.

▲ **DOUGLAS STICE:** A fighter with multiple blade bevels, the "Talren" is an all-integral, stonewashed CPM-154 fixed blade wearing only black-and-green G-10 handle scales.

▼ **SCOT MATSUOKA:** The hollow-ground, CPM-154 frame-lock flipper folder has a titanium frame with a lightning-strike carbon-fiber handle scale on one side. *(SharpByCoop.com photo)*

▲ **JON GRAHAM:** To test the "Point Of Impact" flipper folder, the maker shot the 6AL-4V-titanium frame using a .204 Ruger rifle, with no adverse affects, apparently. Those are real bullet holes, and if that doesn't scare off all perpetrators, the "Razel"-style CPM-154 blade should do the trick. *(SharpByCoop.com photo)*

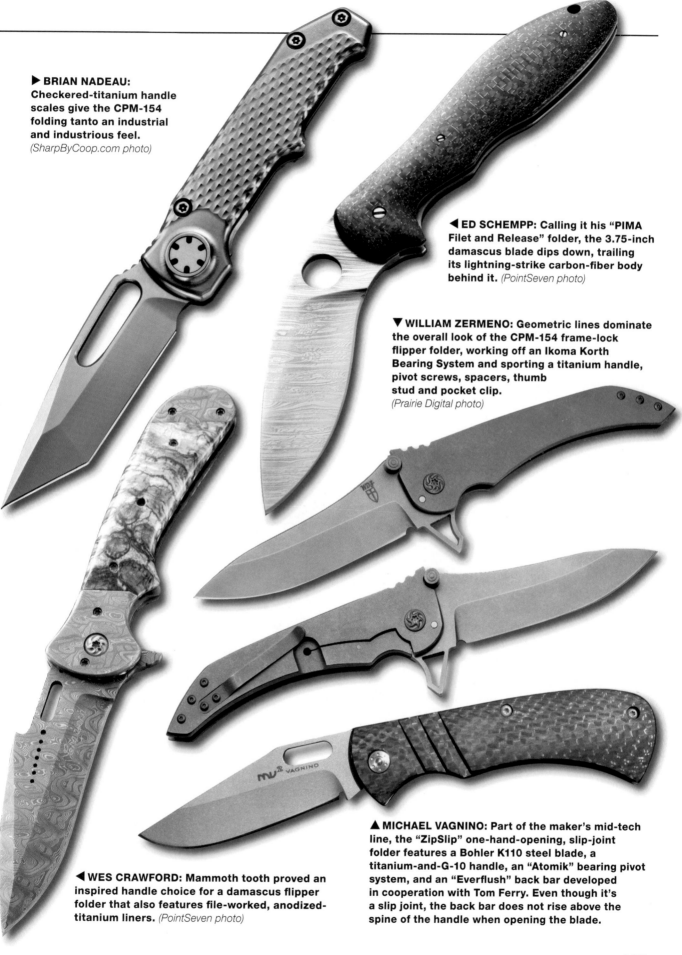

► **BRIAN NADEAU:** Checkered-titanium handle scales give the CPM-154 folding tanto an industrial and industrious feel. *(SharpByCoop.com photo)*

◄ **ED SCHEMPP:** Calling it his "PIMA Filet and Release" folder, the 3.75-inch damascus blade dips down, trailing its lightning-strike carbon-fiber body behind it. *(PointSeven photo)*

▼ **WILLIAM ZERMENO:** Geometric lines dominate the overall look of the CPM-154 frame-lock flipper folder, working off an Ikoma Korth Bearing System and sporting a titanium handle, pivot screws, spacers, thumb stud and pocket clip. *(Prairie Digital photo)*

◄ **WES CRAWFORD:** Mammoth tooth proved an inspired handle choice for a damascus flipper folder that also features file-worked, anodized-titanium liners. *(PointSeven photo)*

▲ **MICHAEL VAGNINO:** Part of the maker's mid-tech line, the "ZipSlip" one-hand-opening, slip-joint folder features a Bohler K110 steel blade, a titanium-and-G-10 handle, an "Atomik" bearing pivot system, and an "Everflush" back bar developed in cooperation with Tom Ferry. Even though it's a slip joint, the back bar does not rise above the spine of the handle when opening the blade.

Pick a Peck of Pocketknife Patterns

There are plenty of patterns to choose from, and that's the overwhelming reason why knifemakers continue to fashion traditional pocketknives in a day and age when fast-opening, high-tech folders have exploded onto the scene. It's nice to have choices. One motorcycle enthusiast drools over a 178-horsepower, four-stroke Kawasaki Ninja ZX-12R that does a top speed of 185.8 miles per hour, and another biker can't believe his luck hopping onto a Harley-Davidson Softail Deluxe in "old school" paint.

Think of this peck of pocketknife patterns as the Harleys of the knife industry, even though their ride might not be as fast or smooth, they embody the retro cool factor. Just as one bike collector is more apt to gravitate toward the Softail than the Ninja, an established group of knife enthusiasts favor the highly fit and finished multi-blade folders of world-famous makers over flipper folders in G-10 handles, meteorite bolsters and Teflon™ bushings.

Like the Kawasaki that's a life-changing, possibly threatening adrenaline rush to ride, an assisted-opening folder looks great clipped to a pocket, plus has the "wow" factor in spades when it's flicked open with a resounding "snap!" Similar to the Harley, however, with its mean growl and wicked look and feel, the pocketknives featured herein are loud and proud in their own right. They capture an attentive audience of knife lovers longing for the days when apples were peeled with jackknives, and whittling on the porch with Grandpa was a favorite pastime akin to baseball, hotdogs, apple pie and, well, Harleys.

▶ TOM PLOPPERT: Elephant ivory gives an already clean CPM-154 saddlehorn pocketknife a pristine look and feel. *(SharpByCoop.com photo)*

▲ T.R. OVEREYNDER: It's easy to like the "M-34 Big Jack" in Carpenter CTS-XHP steel, antique Remington bone and an acorn handle shield. *(Hoffman photo)*

▼ CRAIG BREWER: A congress pattern, slip-joint folder is flawlessly executed in hand-rubbed, satin-finished CPM-154 blade steel, 416 stainless steel liners and bolsters, and golden-root-colored Culpepper & Company jigged bone handle scales.

▼ **ROBERT MERZ:** Brown picked bone busts a move on a 154CM lock-back folder displaying a stainless steel handle shield. *(Ward photo)*

▲ **JOEL CHAMBLIN:** The Sheffield folding dirk parades carved stainless steel bolsters, black-lip mother-of-pearl handle scales and ATS-34 blade steel. *(Ward photo)*

▶ **RICK BROWNE:** Carved bolsters, a gold shield and mother-of-pearl handle scales lend style and panache to a fancy folding dirk. *(Ward photo)*

▲ **CALVIN ROBINSON:** In a Hen & Rooster sowbelly stockman pattern, the folder takes full advantage of Sambar stag and 14C28N blade steel. *(Hoffman photo)*

▶ **STANLEY BUZEK:** Say hello to the swayback jack in jigged bone and sweet CPM-154 steel. *(Ward photo)*

Pick a Peck of Pocketknife Patterns

► **HARVELL PRICE:** The amber-color horn handle has enough character to carry the wharncliffe folder by itself, with each natural groove a haven of hand purchase. *(PointSeven photo)*

◄ **TOM PLOPPERT:** A three-blade CPM-154 "diamond edge cattle knife" in jigged bone is ready for the roundup. *(PointSeven photo)*

► **JOHNNY STOUT:** Long nail nicks assist in opening the clip-point and spay blades, while linen Micarta® and file-worked liners add character to the piece. *(SharpByCoop. com photo)*

▲ **YOSHIO SAKAUCHI:** A horseman's knife exhibits a mother-of-pearl handle, and gold bolsters and shield, packing a baker's dozen of steel implements into a small space. *(PointSeven photo)*

► **JIM DUNLAP:** The saddlehorn folder sits up straight in file-worked ATS-34 stainless steel and ivory. *(Ward photo)*

► **GARY CROWDER:** Ready for the trousers pocket is a three-blade stockman of the stag and steel type. *(Ward photo)*

▼ **STANLEY BUZEK:** There's nothing ordinary about the standard trapper in jigged amber bone and CPM-154 blade steel. *(Ward photo)*

▲ **DAVID TABER:** With each model in ATS-34 steel and springs, at top-left is a dogleg jackknife featuring a spear-point blade, long-pull nail nick, bollock shield and green-canvas-Micarta handle, while to its lower right lies a "Lanny's Clip" (a Tony Bose design) pocketknife in bark elephant ivory. *(PointSeven photo)*

► **JOHN PERRY:** Not your standard two-blade congress, this one comes alive in "squirrel fur"-pattern damascus and antique tortoise shell, the latter with a gold-leaf underlay. *(Ward photo)*

▲ **TOM OVEREYNDER:** Nothing but 18k-gold would do to embellish antique Remington bone on this quality two-blade folder. *(PointSeven photo)*

▶ **JERALD NICKELS:** Bolster engraving highlights a two-blade trapper donning ivory and stainless steel. *(Ward photo)*

▼ **DOC HAGEN:** The "Lanny's Clip" pattern ala Tony Bose is gaining attention, and rightly so considering this rendition in amber jigged bone, a bomb shield, fluted 416 stainless steel bolsters and a satin-finished CPM-154 blade. *(Custom Knife Gallery Of Colorado photo)*

▲ **RICHARD ROGERS:** An eight-blade barrel knife in ivory and eight liners must have been a bear to accomplish, but we're all better for having witnessed it. *(PointSeven photo)*

▲ **CRAIG BREWER:** Of the sowbelly trapper inclination, the two-blade pocketknife exhibits stag handle slabs, an oval shield, and 416 stainless steel liners and bolsters.

▲ **CALVIN ROBINSON:** Jigged bone "gets jiggy wit' it" on a two-blade trapper of the Sandvik 14C28N steel kind. *(Hoffman photo)*

STATE OF THE ART

When thinking of the talent, one can't help but be impressed. A carpenter works with wood, a mason in concrete and a tool-and-die maker with plastic, metal dies and steel. A knifemaker—especially a modern custom knifemaker or blade smith—forges steel; grinds blade billets or pattern-welds damascus; inlays silver and gold wire; sets precious stones; creates bezels; stitches and stamps leather sheaths; carves wood, natural handle material or metal; engraves; pierces; scrimshaws ivory; files stainless and high-carbon steels; and pieces together a myriad of materials.

One knifemaker might not perform all duties, but many do, and if you talk to them, the makers brush it aside as if it doesn't take a creative genius to do such work. These are the chosen few. Theirs is not a predestined lot in life, but a lifelong field of endeavor.

The artistic talent of the modern maker is off the steel charts! These guys might not have been born with a brush in their hands, but they certainly have creativity in spades. Most perform impressive handiwork, fashioning knives with tight fits and finishes, and few, if any blemishes, no gaps, sharp edges, comfortable handles and sturdy guards. They toil in shops until their work gleams under hooded lights, and they're satisfied with their own results. Only then does an appreciative public have the opportunity to view the final products. It's the State Of Art in knives and it has no legitimate critics.

Whirling-Dervish Damascus

I t's a great visual, isn't it? A sect of mystic Islamic dancers who have been taught to love everything, spastically spinning, dancing and whirling, round and round, until they become dizzy and enter a prophetic state. In studying and getting lost in the damascus patterns within the "Whirling-Dervish Damascus" chapter, one can visualize the Dervishes who continue to practice their 800-year-old ceremonial tradition of Sufi whirling.

In fact, if you gaze at the damascus long enough, you may just become dizzy and enter a prophetic state of your own, realizing new knife and steel forms, envisioning models never experienced by mankind, conceptualizing stylistic lines that lead to patterns undiscovered in this or any universe. You may become a great innovator of pattern-welded steel and join the ranks of master smiths who have come before you. Minions will stoop before your scepter and swear allegiance to your tips, your dies and wares. You'll forge whirling-dervish damascus, and the tradition will continue for hundreds of years, spastically spinning out of control, whirling, round and round, until the end of time.

▲ RODRIGO SFREDDO: A "keyhole integral" is done up in damascus and ebony—smoothed, rounded, honed and polished nice—for the touch, feel and slice. *(SharpByCoop.com photo)*

▲ JOHN WHITE: Feather damascus tickles the edge and spine of a fine fixed blade dressed in walrus ivory. *(PointSeven photo)*

▲ GARY HOUSE: "Blossom and lace" damascus is an excellent steel arrangement on a dagger with a fluted mammoth-ivory handle wrapped in twisted silver wire. *(PointSeven photo)*

▼ LARRY COX: English walnut makes up the traditional end of a bowie that's bedazzling in 15N20, 1080 and 5160 damascus. *(Ward photo)*

▼JIM TURECEK: The maker's "Eleuthera Dream" automatic folder features a damascus pattern that's as cool as The Bahamas' breezes.

▼JERRY MCCLURE: A cold drink would go well with the "cracked ice" damascus bowie featuring an elephant-ivory grip and pommel engraving by Suzanne Williams. *(SharpByCoop.com photo)*

▲ BILL BUXTON: "W's-pattern" damascus waves splash across the blade of a sub-hilt fighter anchored by pre-ban elephant ivory. *(SharpByCoop.com photo)*

▶J. NEILSON: It took quarter-inch 52100 ball bearings, 1084 high-carbon powder steel and a talented blade smith to create the powerful damascus pattern of a stag-handle bowie.

SHAYNE CARTER: The stakes are high in this game of horseshoes. *(SharpByCoop.com photo)*

STATE OF THE ART **133**

▶ **STUART BARKER:** The rounded handle of a fully integral Damasteel knife leads into a flat-ground, drop-point blade, and all is polished and shined.

▲ **MICHAEL RUTH JR.:** It would take a ladder to climb to the heights of patterning that a damascus Southwest bowie reaches. *(SharpByCoop.com photo)*

▶ **TERRY VANDEVENTER:** Feather damascus splays out for the cutting edge of a utility hunter, while blue mammoth ivory puts a solid hold on the piece. *(Ward photo)*

▲ **ANDRE THORBURN:** Hot-blued Ettore Gianferrari damascus acts as the pinstripes on a golden suit of armor.

▲ **TOMMY MCNABB:** A coffin-handle bowie lays a damascus blade out for a viewing.

▲ **EMIL BUCHARSKY:** The aptly named "Eclipse" folder sends grooved damascus shooting for the other side of the sun. *(BladeGallery.com photo)*

▶ **PETER CAREY:** Brilliantly colored Timascus challenges "Intrepid" damascus to a steely flipper folder standoff. *(Mitchell Cohen, Prairie Digital image)*

▼ **RONNIE PACKARD:** Ten inches of Chad Nichols damascus makes a lasting impression on a walrus-ivory-handled bowie. *(SharpByCoop.com photo)*

▶ **JERRY FISK:** It took a three-sided clamshell guard to protect the fingers from the 11.25-inch damascus blade, and fossil walrus ivory holds it all in place. *(SharpByCoop.com photo)*

▼ **MARCELLO GARAU:** An Italian "Murex Variation No. 3" folder is a tasty little number in abalone inlays and a double-feather-pattern damascus blade with a twist-damascus edge. *(Francesco Pachi photo)*

Whirling-Dervish Damascus

▶ **DON HANSON III:** While ancient ivory fills the grip, damascus dances its way to the tip. *(SharpByCoop.com photo)*

▶ **NICK WHEELER:** Tiger maple and damascus lay tracks on a fixed-blade fighter. *(SharpByCoop.com photo)*

▶ **DAVID LISCH:** "Fighting dragons" overtake a world of whirled damascus. *(SharpByCoop.com photo)*

◀ **ED SCHEMPP:** The pattern of "The Broken Feather" is unbroken. *(PointSeven photo)*

◀ **R.W. WILSON:** Stag, brass and giraffe bone usually have it covered when it comes to prettying up a fighting knife, but in this case the stainless damascus holds its own. *(Cory Martin Imaging)*

▶ **PETER MARTIN:** Blued random-pattern damascus wends its way around the blade, guard and pommel of a dagger that is also wrapped up in sterling silver wire. *(Cory Martin Imaging)*

▲ **REINHARD TSCHAGER:** Devin Thomas damascus is highlighted by gold inlays and pins, Velerio Peli engraving and an amazing blue-coral handle.

▶ **JAMES COOK:** Not even inspired guard and pommel engraving can completely distract one's attention away from the 8.7-inch damascus blade of the Southwest bowie. *(Ward photo)*

▶ **STEVE MYERS:** You don't have to have a nervous disorder or shifty eyes to appreciate the pattern of the 10-inch 1080-and-15N20 damascus blade of the clip-point bowie in nickel-silver furniture and a Sambar stag handle. *(Hoffman photo)*

▶ **RON NEWTON:** The Turkish damascus blade of an integral Persian model locks itself onto the hand-checkered, carved-ironwood grip. *(Ward photo)*

▶ **MACE VITALE:** Akin to snow-capped mountain peaks, five-layer composite damascus rises and falls along the blade of a flat-ground fighter, and silver wire zigzags its way across the maple handle. *(SharpByCoop.com photo)*

▲ **NORMAN SANDOW:** A damascus blade ducks into a giraffe-bone handle when the folder is closed via the tiger-eye-inlaid thumb stud.

► **CLIFF PARKER:** Butterflies, faces, pinwheels, flowers and checkers are but a few forms forged into the damascus blade and bolsters of a mammoth-ivory-handle folder. *(PointSeven photo)*

◄ **KEVIN CASEY:** Feather damascus and pearl prove a winning combination. *(SharpByCoop.com photo)*

◄ **DANIEL WARREN:** Maple and damascus share whirling-dervish duties on a utility hunter. *(PointSeven photo)*

▼ **JIMMY CHIN:** Damascus dazzles the crowd, while ironwood kicks back and waits for a hand. *(Ward photo)*

▲ **RALPH RICHARDS:** The "Sitting Bull Lakota" knife does a damascus ghost dance. *(Ward photo)*

Inlays & Etchings

You arrive home from work, enter the house wanting nothing but dinner and a drink, and your wife says, "A package arrived for you, dear." Oh, man, it's the knife you've been waiting for, the handmade piece that's been six months in the making, the one with the damascus blade and ironwood handle. It's one of the reasons you've been working so hard in the first place.

You reach in your pocket, fumbling for your own folding knife, cut the tape, open the box, unroll the bubble wrap, and there it is, gleaming. But there's more, more than what you bargained for, additional embellishment, an extra little something. The knife is inlaid with wire, and gorgeously inlaid at that. It's the perfect highlight to an already incredible handmade piece of art.

Could it be a mistake? Was this knife meant for you? It's what you ordered. The size, style and materials are the same. There's just extra workmanship, a finishing touch if you will, that speaks to the quality, high standards and character of the maker, of so many knifemakers around the world. They aren't satisfied with the status quo, and that's why you love knives, enjoy the industry and prize your own personal knife collection.

Thanks for the inlays and etchings, makers. We know it's one more step in a painstaking knifemaking process, but you surely have outdone yourselves … again.

E. JAY HENDRICKSON: A large, upswept damascus fixed blade is the beneficiary of a curly maple handle and sheath enlivened by silver-wire inlay. *(SharpByCoop.com photo)*

▶ **S.R. JOHNSON:** Whether it's burnished gold or gilded pearl, the handle and bolster handiwork of Barry Lee Hands is incomparable. *(SharpByCoop.com photo)*

▲ **GAIL LUNN:** A sterling-silver-wire design adorns the ebony handle of a "Treasure Within" folder that also parades a damascus blade, nine sapphires on the spine, a sapphire-inlaid thumb stud and file-worked titanium liners. *(Hoffman photo)*

◄ **ALLEN NEWBERRY:** A couple pocket cutlasses sport cherry-burl handles and copper-etched 1095 blades. *(Ward photo)*

▼ **JOE KEESLAR:** Carved and engraved German silver, as well as silver wire, embellish the curly maple handle, buttcap and ferrule of a 1075 Southwest bowie, including the maker's 50th-year silver medallion. *(SharpByCoop.com photo)*

▼ **KEN DURHAM:** The maker pinned four sides of the blackwood handle of his Spanish notch bowie in chain and vine patterns, adding silver fittings and a coral cabochon pommel inlay. *(Ward photo)*

▲ **LARRY NEWTON:** Only 24k-gold inlays would suffice for a pair of folding damascus daggers in tortoise-shell handles. *(PointSeven photo)*

▲ **JAMES COOK:** The Four Horsemen of the Apocalypse are permanently etched into the damascus blade of a mammoth-ivory-handle "Famine" knife that's part of the master smith's "From the End of Time" set. *(Ward photo)*

Stone Infusion

▶ SCOTT SAWBY: For his art nouveau-style "Murrelet" (north Pacific sea bird) folding dagger, the maker combined an agate-handle inlay with Marian Sawby gold inlay, engraving in a hibiscus and butterfly motif, and a CPM-154 blade.

▶ ROBERT FLYNT: Reconstituted turquoise fabulously fills the space between a crown stag handle, stainless steel guard and Brad Vice twist-damascus blade.

◀ MICHAEL PELLEGRIN: The tiger-eye-in-hematite (tiger iron) inlays of the Damasteel folder were so pretty, Nathan Dickinson engraved all around them. (SharpByCoop.com photo)

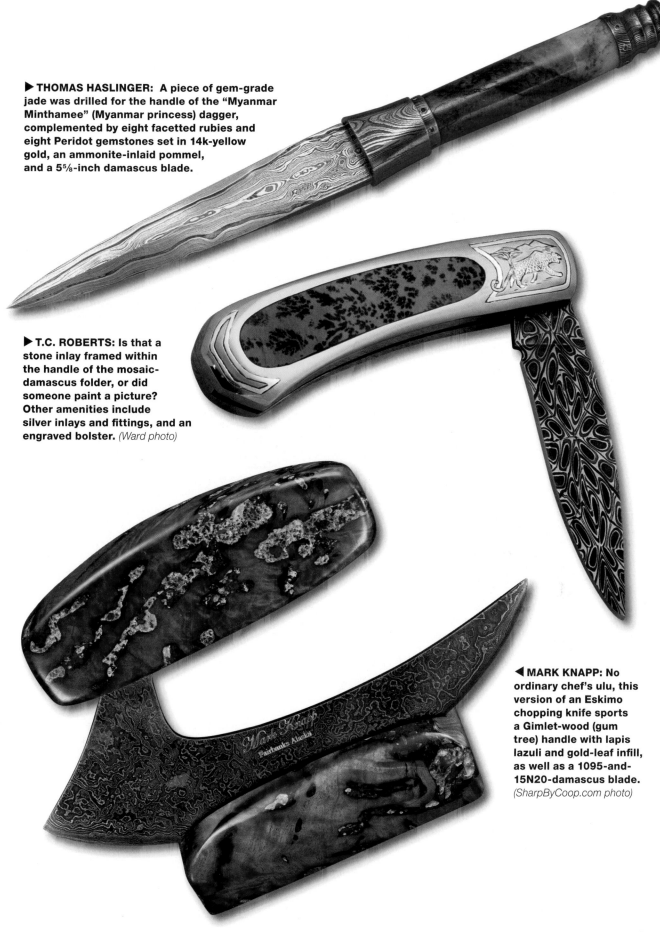

▶ **THOMAS HASLINGER:** A piece of gem-grade jade was drilled for the handle of the "Myanmar Minthamee" (Myanmar princess) dagger, complemented by eight facetted rubies and eight Peridot gemstones set in 14k-yellow gold, an ammonite-inlaid pommel, and a 5⅝-inch damascus blade.

▶ **T.C. ROBERTS:** Is that a stone inlay framed within the handle of the mosaic-damascus folder, or did someone paint a picture? Other amenities include silver inlays and fittings, and an engraved bolster. *(Ward photo)*

◀ **MARK KNAPP:** No ordinary chef's ulu, this version of an Eskimo chopping knife sports a Gimlet-wood (gum tree) handle with lapis lazuli and gold-leaf infill, as well as a 1095-and-15N20-damascus blade. *(SharpByCoop.com photo)*

Non-Prosaic Mosaics

▶ **DAVID LEMOINE:** A spidery blade smith wove a web of sharp desire for a giraffe-bone-handle, locking-liner folder. Doug Ponzio is the smith credited for the damascus. *(Ward photo)*

▼ **SANDRO BOECK:** An African javali (wild boar) graces the bolster of a mosaic-damascus hunter in a warthog-tusk handle. *(SharpByCoop.com photo)*

▶ **SHANE TAYLOR:** I'm sensing a theme here considering the "mosaic-dice"-damascus blade, engraving of a royal flush on the ferrule and carved card suits incorporated into the walrus-ivory handle. *(PointSeven photo)*

◀ **TOBBE LUNDSTROM:** A multi-bar, mosaic-damascus blade and handle shield forged by Mattias Styrefors do more than hint at the origins of the engraved ivory handle. *(BladeGallery.com photo)*

▼ **MARK NEVLING:** "Radials"-pattern damascus emulates starbursts across the blade of a knife in a fossil-walrus-ivory handle, Mokumé bolsters and an alligator-skin-inlaid leather sheath.

▶ **KYLE ROYER:** Winner of the "Best Bowie" award at the 2012 Arkansas Custom Knife Show, it's no wonder considering the mosaic-damascus blade, checkered-pearl handle, gold wire inlays and clamshell-style guard. *(Ward photo)*

▼ **SHAWN MCINTYRE:** Shapes akin to puffer fish, tumbleweeds or billowy cotton, whatever your slant may be, reveal themselves in the mosaic-damascus blade of a big bowie wearing a fossil-walrus-ivory handle. *(SharpByCoop.com photo)*

▼ **ANDERS HEDLUND:** Sweden's own Johan Gustafsson forged the mosaic-damascus blade and bolster bar stock, which proved a perfect complement to a mammoth-ivory handle with black-lip-pearl inlays, 18k-gold pins and an engraved medallion.

◀ **STEVE HILL:** Named for the femme fatale in a Jimi Hendrix song, the "Dolly Dagger" features a Robert Eggerling "Spirograph"-pattern-mosaic-damascus blade and bolsters, a mammoth-ivory handle, a sapphire-inlaid thumb stud, and three carved skulls and 52 carved bones along the back spacer.

STATE OF THE ART   **145**

▶ **MARVIN SOLOMON:** The wide mosaic-damascus blade justifiably monopolizes a fixed-blade skinner in an ironwood grip. *(Ward photo)*

▶ **R.B. JOHNSON:** Between a twist-pattern-damascus blade and a manta-ray-skin handle lie bolsters of powdered-mosaic-damascus steel. *(Cory Martin Imaging)*

▶ **REINHARD TSCHAGER:** Now do you believe in unicorns? They're permanently immortalized within the Johan Gustafsson mosaic-damascus blade, and accompanied by a file-worked-rose gold ring and a fossil-walrus-ivory handle.

▶ **CLIFF PARKER:** Since the handle is narwhal tusk, it seemed a fitting subject for the mosaic-damascus bolsters of a dress folder. *(SharpByCoop.com photo)*

▶ **NICO PELZER:** The group effort on a gent's folder includes heat-blued "linked chains"-mosaic-damascus bolsters by Ettore Gianferarri, a Freek Morsner twist-damascus blade and black-lip-pearl handle scales. *(BladeGallery.com photo)*

▲ **RON NEWTON:** Someone needs to king the "China Checkerboard"-mosaic-damascus blade of the "Shi-Li Chinese Folder" with green mammoth-ivory handle scales and 24k-gold fittings. *(Ward photo)*

▶ **DON HANSON III:** "Monster"-mosaic damascus is the inspiration for the "Monster Clack" name given to the tactical folder, and inspiring it is! Walrus ivory makes up the handle end, and get a load of that double-ground W2 blade with smoky temper line! *(SharpByCoop.com photo)*

▶ **RAY RYBAR:** Look close enough, and you can clearly see the words "Semper Fidelis" and "I will never leave thee nor forsake thee" forged into the mosaic-damascus blade of a bronze-handle dagger. Incredible! *(PointSeven photo)*

▶ **MIKE TYRE:** Niter-blued, mosaic-damascus bolsters accessorize a damascus folder in a mammoth-ivory grip. *(PointSeven photo)*

◀ **CALVIN NICHOLS:** The damascus master mixes up a blued mosaic batch for the blade and bolsters of a fancy fixed blade that also comes with diamond inlays and a white-bone handle. *(PointSeven photo)*

STATE OF THE ART   **147**

Sheath Whizzes

Not even sheaths are the same anymore. But before you lose your mind completely, go off the deep end and into a tirade about how the world was a thousand times better in the good old days when we walked to school 10 miles in three feet of snow, and ate ham bones and applesauce for lunch, the changes in sheaths might be a good thing.

They've become works of art in many ways, and the methods of building them refined and perfected. They are no longer simple leather slip, belt or snap sheaths with some stamping, stitching or inlay. Many come with engraved conchos, wire-inlaid wood exteriors, beads, fringes, carvings and even mosaic-damascus overlays.

Mosaic-damascus overlays, you may ask? Yes, there's one example of such herein—a sheath by Tobbe Lundstrom and the damascus forged by Mattias Styrefors. The two combined are proven sheath whizzes, and so you see, the changes in sheaths aren't necessarily a bad thing. No reason to rant.

▶ E. JAY HENDRICKSON: The master smith is known for his wire-inlaid wood knife handles, here expanding his craft to the sheath for a fluted-ivory-handle damascus dagger. *(SharpByCoop.com photo)*

▶ KENNY ROWE: The sheath maker didn't stop at carving and engraving the leather, but added engraved conchos, and it's a sweet combo. *(Ward photo)*

▲ JOHN COHEA: A gorgeous pouch sheath for a friction folder parades leather, wood, beadwork, fringe and horsehair tassels. When the friction folder is folded and in the sheath, the wrought-iron tang sticks out for easy extraction of the knife when needed. *(SharpByCoop.com photo)*

▼**ARPAD BOJTOS:** A faun and nymph are carved in mammoth ivory for the buffalo-horn sheath fashioned for an integral knife of the same theme. Engraved silver and gold are a nice touch. *(PointSeven photo)*

◄**LARRY PARSONS:** A snakeskin-inlaid, stamped and stitched leather snap sheath holds a single-guard fixed blade securely. *(Ward photo)*

►**TOBBE LUNDSTROM:** Mosaic-damascus posts engraved by Mattias Styrefors embellish a length of belt sheath also showcasing embossed rawhide leather dyed and sewn by hand.

►**J.P. JONES:** A basket-weave leather sheath is a nice addition to any knife package.

The Whaler's Art

Not all seafaring men were salty sailors with permanent squints, mean dispositions and hot tempers. There were artists among the seasoned crews, but even they would have held their own against shady shipmates, ruffians or pirating bands. Meantime, there were long periods of lulling waves, endless horizons, burning sun and cold ocean sprays. To pass the time a few of the more artistically inclined engraved, carved and scrimshawed the bones, muscle and teeth of sperm whales, or the tusks of walruses if one happened to cross within their coordinates.

Imagine traversing the Pacific in the mid-1700s, pricking pigment into whale teeth for endless hours until a masterpiece revealed itself just beneath the ivory surface. It was a hobby back then, and still is today to some, though modern scrimshanders have elevated it to fine art, the kind only a select few can achieve with breathtaking results.

When gazing at the masterworks pinpricked into the ivory pores one tiny dot at a time, even the sea spray can't draw your attention away. These are masterpieces permanently engraved in bone and ivory, and there's not a painter, sculptor or carver in the world who wouldn't stop to take notice. It's a whaler's art, yet there's never been a bigger trophy fish harpooned in maritime history.

▲ **DR. PETER JENSEN:** The orange hue of the fossil walrus ivory begged for tiger scrim, while the Johan Gustafsson damascus blade proved the perfect choice for a Reinhard Tschager art knife.

▶ **PANJA POJIEW:** Sensuous subject matter is scrimshawed in ivory on one Suchat Jangtanong knife, and engraved in steel on the other, each with blued Robert Calcinore damascus blades. *(SharpByCoop.com photo)*

◀ **LINDA KARST STONE:** Incredibly detailed "Icy Waters" scrimshaw invigorates the fossil walrus tusk, making it come to life. What a study in characters and wildlife! *(PointSeven photo)*

LINDA KARST STONE: An elephant herd is immortalized in walrus ivory, highlighted by Bruce Shaw engraving, and trumpeted by the damascus blade of a D'Alton Holder hunter. *(PointSeven photo)*

LINDA KARST STONE: There's always room for a leopard on a handmade D'Alton Holder damascus knife. Bruce Shaw engraved the guard. *(PointSeven photo)*

KURTZ MILLER: Whether quail or trout is your sport, there's one scrimshawed in ivory on a Robert P. Smith bird-and-trout knife with a Mike Norris stainless-damascus blade and sculpted finger guard. *(Ward photo)*

BOB HERGERT: The Japanese Yakuza gang comes to life on the antique-elephant-ivory handle of a Chuck Gedraitis slip-joint folder featuring Mike Sakmar's tri-color Mokumé for the bolsters, and a differentially heat-treated 1095 tanto blade. *(SharpByCoop.com photo)*

◀ **RIKARD PERMAN:** A scrimmed walrus-ivory handle and a bronze guard anchor the impressive 13-inch "droplet"-pattern damascus blade of an Anders Hogstrom art knife.

▲ **ED BRANDSEY:** The great wolf spirit is captured in mammoth ivory, its paws permanently engraved by Joe Szopa for the bolsters of a "Rainy Lake Hunter" in an Alabama Damascus blade. *(Cory Martin Imaging)*

▶ **LEE BERG:** Whether it's Old Man Winter, a Greek god or another fantastical figure, the face in ivory is a nice counterpart to the Albert May damascus blade of a bowie. Ebony, purple-heart-wood and silver spacers frame the figure. *(Ward photo)*

DAVID SEMONES: A red-eyed dragon guards the damascus blade of a Lowell Bray custom knife. *(Hoffman photo)*

► **LORI RISTINEN:** An "elephant toenail"-style Peter Martin bolster-release auto with a mosaic-damascus blade parades pachyderm scrimshaw in elephant ivory, showing the front and back of the elephant on the front and back of the handle. *(Cory Martin Imaging)*

► **LINDA KARST STONE:** The Civil War scene on an all-integral Edmund Davidson sub-hilt fighter encompasses images of Jefferson Davis, President Abraham Lincoln and Ulysses S. Grant. Jere Davidson worked his engraving magic on every flat piece of steel, and many of the rounded ones. *(PointSeven photos)*

► **GARY "GARBO" WILLIAMS:** If the scrimshaw of a Lee Gene Baskett folder doesn't make you howl at the moon, the damascus blade, or gold inlay and Bulino-style engraving by Paul Markow, should do the trick. *(PointSeven photo)*

LINDA KARST STONE: The subjects on the elephant-ivory handle of an Ed Lary Norwegian-style knife are taken from a tomb in Jelling, Norway. The sheath has a Viking portrayed on one side and Thor's six-legged horse, and Ravens, Muggin and Uggen on the other side. The latter three characters kept Thor apprised of what mortals were doing. *(Cory Martin Imaging)*

▲ **GARY "GARBO" WILLIAMS:** A Confederate soldier poses stoically for his portrait on a Dennis Friedly fighter, also featuring a Robert Eggerling damascus blade and gold nuggets inlaid on the ferrule.

GARY "GARBO" WILLIAMS: You've gotta love the hairstyle, from head to chin, of a beaded warrior on an 8.5-inch Dennis Friedly fighter.

LINDA KARST STONE: A Native American and a bald eagle each do their own rain dances on Jerry Moen's hot-blued Alabama Damascus folder. *(PointSeven photo)*

PANJA POJIEW: Her candle burned out long before the flame that fired the blued-damascus blade ever did. Robert Calcinore is credited for the mosaic damascus of a Suchat Jangtanong folder. *(SharpByCoop.com photo)*

STEPHEN MACKRILL: A battle cross and saluting soldier are the scrimshawed subjects of the hippo-tooth handle and sheath on the "Remember" fighter. Mammoth tooth makes up the knife's pommel and ferrule, as well as the throat and tip of the sheath. *(Hoffman photo)*

Full-Length File Work

TONY DAUGHTERY: File work spans most of the spine of a 14.25-inch ATS-34 blade and extends onto the curved "S"-guard. *(PointSeven photo)*

TIMOTHY POTIER: Not even crown stag could upstage the vine file work comely creeping all along the lengthy blade. *(PointSeven photo)*

▲▶ **JEFF HEBEISEN:** The first third of the CPM-154 blade and entire tapered tang are file worked and accented by gorgeous maple burl handle scales.

Copious Carving

There are so many beautiful ironies in the carving of knives. First off, you carve *with* knives, but also it's not just carving. In "copiously carving" knives the steel is sculpted, precious metals engraved, the blades etched, and facets smoothed or dimpled. The embellishing technique involved in carving and sculpting a knife medium employs not just carving tools, or wood chisels and whittlers, but hand files, burrs, sandpaper, needles, engravers and grinders. Then the elbow grease is applied with liberal amounts of polishing compound and oil. The flats, grooves and corners are sanded until the funny bone is not so funny anymore.

There again, it's not that simple. One can't just go about carving knives willy-nilly with no rhyme or reason. Utilitarian tools must perform tasks, and with knives that would involve cutting. To cut or chop with a knife for long periods of time, the handle, guard and ferrule must be comfortable. Sure, there are knives in the "State Of The Art" section of the *Knives 2014* book that are just that—art and display pieces—but most are also fashioned primarily for use. That, my friends, is the final irony in the carving of knives.

◄ **LOYD MCCONNELL:** The carved-ivory handle slips beneath a textured gold guard and before an ATS-34 blade. A watermelon-tourmaline inset is the finishing touch. *(PointSeven photo)*

▲▶ **DONALD VOGT:** The blade is carved Rob Thomas "herringbone" damascus, the handle of the carved-ivory variety, and the guard and pommel cut, filed and carved damascus, with leaves draping over the guard. A gold ring containing 22 rubies lies between the guard and handle. *(Rudolph Lopez photo)*

▶ **LOGAN PEARCE:** Could the same tools have been used to carve the giraffe-bone handle as the damascus blade? It's doubtful, but the "Frost" fixed blade deserved all the tools and attention it got. *(Ward photo)*

▶ **WOLFGANG LOERCHNER:** Carving out the integral fixed-blade dagger from half-inch 440C stock was one accomplishment, and carved gold, pearl and other media were quite another, including the engraving work of Julie Warenski. *(SharpByCoop.com photo)*

LARRY FUEGEN: The handle is plume agate harvested from the Bloody Basin of Arizona and cradled by a carved 14k-gold wrap, which is partly why it's a gentleman's dress bowie, in damascus no less. *(PointSeven photo)*

ARPAD BOJTOS: The maker integrated stainless steel for the human figures and titanium for the monsters, with silver and gold mixed in. Regardless, it's a Damasteel masterwork if there ever was one.

▲ RICHARD TESARIK:
The Damasteel blade and bolsters, and jet handle of
the folding dagger are equal parts copious carving.

▶ JIM TURECEK: Sometimes a name
just fits, as is the case with the "Sea
Wing" folder in a carved tiger-
coral handle and wavy-
damascus blade.

▶ E. JAY HENDRICKSON: Carved
maple leaves decorate the
maple grip and sheath of a
long damascus fixed blade.
(SharpByCoop.com photo)

WILLIAM LLOYD: Carved elephant-
ivory gargoyles and dragons with
garnet eyes make up the handles
of friction folders that also sport
Two Finger Knife damascus
blades. The knives are
versions of a 12th-century
Norse folding knife found
in an archeological dig
in York, England.
(PointSeven photo)

▲ STEVE SCHWARZER: As a goblin emerges
from the crown stag grip of a damascus folder,
the carving tools are laid upon the workbench
to be picked up another day. *(PointSeven photo)*

◄ **DENNIS FRIEDLY:** The horse-head-pommel dagger is exquisitely executed with the help of engraver Gil Rudolph and carver Stan Hawkins.

▶ **MARDI MESHEJIAN:** Among the many amenities are carved *shibuichi* (silver and copper) flowers along the basket hilt of a 1080-and-15N20-damascus sword, as well as an ebony hilt. *(PointSeven photo)*

▶ **J.D. SMITH:** Carved blackwood anchors a 32-inch 1084-and-15N20-damascus hunting sword, also with a sculpted silver guard and pommel. *(SharpByCoop.com photo)*

▶ **DON FOGG and MURAD SAYEN:** Carved fossil ivory, an engraved gold guard, carved pommel, textured silver collars and gold pins highlight the damascus Viking dagger. *(PointSeven photo)*

▶ **JON CHRISTENSEN:** A "feathered bamboo leaves" theme is repeated from the damascus spear-point tip to the carved-ivory grip. *(SharpByCoop.com photo)*

Copious Carving

◄ **JULIUS MOJZIS:** Meerkats nearly smile upon the carved-mammoth-ivory handle of a drop-point damascus fixed blade. Mr. Lasky is credited for forging the damascus, wherein a scorpion is carved into the bolster area.

◄ **RON BEST:** The carved grip of the damascus dress auto folder is like layers of golden goodness just waiting to be peeled away. *(SharpByCoop.com photo)*

▶ **JEFFREY CORNWELL:** The carved and sculpted "Angel Hair" model is Robert Eggerling damascus with 24k-gold flashing. *(SharpByCoop.com photo)*

▶ **DANIEL STEPHAN:** Carving extends from the elk handle in an oak leaf motif to the O1 blade and even the carved silver handle pins. Gold and rubies are inlaid into the blade spine. *(PointSeven photo)*

▼ **LEONARDO FRIZZI:** A little carbon-damascus fish swims from the pommel of the "Salmon River" lockback folder up the carved-titanium handle scales that, in turn, drip down over an ocean of black-lip pearl.

▶ **TERRY LEE RENNER:** The feather-damascus "Natchez" push dagger, forged by Randy Haas Jr., boasts a carved bark-mammoth-ivory grip and a silver-brazed bronze frame. *(SharpByCoop.com photo)*

◀ **GARY ROOT:** The red of the stag just before the eagle head (carved by Paul Grussenmeyer) is repeated in the rust-colored patina of the Ray Rybar damascus blade. The oval guard is Bob Eggerling damascus. *(Kris Kandler photo)*

▲ **JERRY MCCLURE:** There's not an Alaskan salmon stream with colors prettier than those of the blued ball-bearing-damascus fighter blade, nor a polar bear with more character than the Brian Kahuli carved whale-tooth handle. *(SharpByCoop.com photo)*

◀ **LARRY PRIDGEN:** The apocalypse is happening here and now on the carved-antler handle of a damascus short sword. *(PointSeven photo)*

▼ **RIK PALM:** The "Horse" was carved and textured with needle files, chisels and ball burrs, and features a hickory handle wrapped in beaver-tail leather. Real horsehair was employed for the mane.

▼ **ALFREDO KEHIAYAN:** Though the handle looks carved, it's natural gazelle horn, but the silver caps, now that's another story—they're carved and adorned in 40 karats of rubies.

Puzzle Pieces

▶ **ALEX DANIELS:** Pieces of pearl fit together, divided classically by gold wire, like the prettiest puzzle in the toy store.

▶ **R.B. JOHNSON:** A "sunfish"-pattern pocketknife features mosaic-damascus bolsters and mammoth-ivory grip fragments put together in a mosaic style to match. *(Cory Martin Imaging)*

▶ **DAVID LEMOINE:** A solid stainless steel cross is nothing less than a blessing on a CPM-S30V and ironwood big-game hunter. *(Ward photo)*

◀ **JIMMY CHIN:** The tightly patterned clip-point damascus blade interlocks snugly onto an ironwood handle. *(Ward photo)*

▲ **GAIL LUNN:** Red stars add sparkle to the pearl handle and ATS-34 blade of a lock-back folder. *(Hoffman photo)*

▲ **PETER MARTIN:** A checkerboard of black, gold and white pearl is secured with 14k-gold-plated screws, butted up against mosaic-damascus bolsters and paraded before a hot-blued damascus blade. *(Cory Martin Imaging)*

▼ **TOM LEWIS:** Red and yellow heartwood splay out in a mosaic style for the handle of a drop-point hunter, creatively combined with a cable-damascus blade and mosaic pins.

◀ **STEVE JERNIGAN:** Afghanistan lapis lazuli pools like pure lake water on a stainless steel handle frame. *(PointSeven photo)*

▶ **JOE OLSON:** The maker has found a niche in enamel knife handle inlays, a method used masterfully here to depict a client's favorite guitar players Eric Clapton, Jimi Hendrix, Duane Allman, Stevie Ray Vaughan and Peter Green. The guard is sculpted into the form of a guitar, and the 10-inch composite-bar damascus blade is a piece of art itself. *(SharpByCoop.com photo)*

▲ **RON NEWTON:** Damascus clasps onto checkered ironwood and won't let go. *(Ward photo)*

▼ **KEN STEIGERWALT:** Plying pearl like a wizard, the different types are precisely inlaid for effect on a clip-point art folder. *(SharpByCoop.com photo)*

From Under the OptiVisor

You know it's a cool job when you get to wear headgear. You see them at knife shows around the world. They tend to be a quiet type, magnifiers strapped to their heads and small but powerful lamps pointing toward their work. They guide handheld gravers across steel using precise, controlled movements. As a show attendee you barely have the nerve to breathe, much less speak, as to not disturb the artists.

Their work is mesmerizing, and to watch an artist create a masterpiece is an honor and thrill. From behind the OptiVisors, they engrave pictures in steel, scrolls, lines, human figures, flora and fauna. Of all things to bring to life, steel has to be the most difficult. The imagination it takes to transform shiny, grey metal into seemingly living, breathing subject matter is mind numbing. And to do it realistically is astonishing.

Beauty might be in the eye of the beholder, but once a person has beheld the engraved knives on this and the following seven pages, beauty can hardly escape them. The knives are exquisite, the workmanship top notch, and all achieved with hand tools from under the OptiVisor. Enjoy. I know anyone who has seen the engravers hard at work certainly felt a chill or two.

▲ **JERE DAVIDSON:** "Goliath" is a good name for the exquisitely engraved Edmund Davidson integral dagger, stretching 20 ⅛ inches overall, and featuring Linda Karst Stone scrimshaw in ivory of a mountain man and Native American. (*PointSeven photo*)

▶ **BRIAN HOCHSTRAT:** A Warren Osborne folding dagger takes on a gladiator theme, art nouveau-style scrollwork, a Mike Norris stainless-damascus blade, and antique tortoise shell and 19k-rose-gold inlays.

▲ **C.J. CAI:** A fox sniffs out grapes in the tranquil setting of green jade and stainless steel that a Rick Genovese folder provides. (*SharpByCoop.com photo*)

▼ **GORDON ALCORN:** Bolster engraving adds so much to a John Doyle 1080-steel hunter in African blackwood. *(BladeGallery.com photo)*

◀ **DAVE RICCARDO:** The Les Voorhies flipper folder features a Devin Thomas damascus blade and one hellacious engraved titanium handle. *(SharpByCoop.com photo)*

▶ **LISA TOMLIN:** A "Shanghai Doll" stares invitingly out from the titanium handle frame of a Keith Ouye "herringbone"-damascus flipper folder. *(SharpByCoop.com photo)*

◀ **JODY MULLER:** Calling all knights, presenting King Arthur, engraved in steel, adorned in gold, overlooking ivory and located near damascus. *(SharpByCoop.com)*

▲ **MARIAN SAWBY:** Engraved and gold-inlaid bitterroot flowers take root on the bolsters of a Scott Sawby wharncliffe folder in black jade and Mike Norris damascus.

► **MEL FASSIO:** Bark-mammoth ivory crackles, and the bolster and blade engraving pops!

▼ **JULIEN MARSHAL:** An engraved gift opens itself on the front bolster of an André Thorburn flipper folder that also shows off a Damasteel blade, an IKBS (Ikoma Korth Bearing System) and fossil-walrus-ivory handle scales. *(SharpByCoop. com photo)*

▲ **ANDERS HEDLUND:** An engraved medallion lies within a circle of pearl at the center of the grip, and engraving frames the black-lip-pearl handle inlays of a locking-liner folder. Devin Thomas forged the damascus blade, while Soderfors Smedja of Sweden did the handle steel honors. Gold pins vie for attention.

► **BARRY LEE HANDS:** Gorgeous gold leaf and vine engraving covers a Joe Kious "Pocket Locket" folder that also boasts a carat of diamonds and sapphires. *(SharpByCoop.com photo)*

▼ **THINUS HERBST:** Animal forms emerge from the zoomorphic engraving of a "Sountaka Sword" (modeled after an Iron Age sword owned by a noble female warrior) in N690 blade steel and a bronze handle with integral guard and pommel.

► **NATHAN DICKINSON:** Sporting a Mike Norris stainless damascus blade and a black-lip-pearl handle, the Calvin Robinson folder wouldn't have been complete without gold-inlaid and engraved bolsters. *(Hoffman photo)*

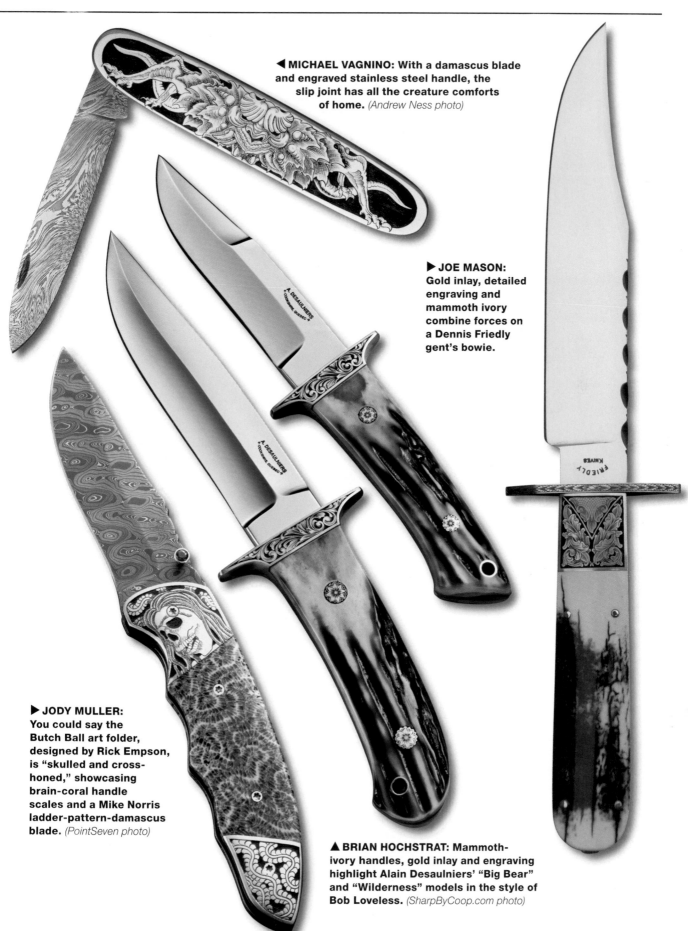

◀ **MICHAEL VAGNINO:** With a damascus blade and engraved stainless steel handle, the slip joint has all the creature comforts of home. *(Andrew Ness photo)*

▶ **JOE MASON:** Gold inlay, detailed engraving and mammoth ivory combine forces on a Dennis Friedly gent's bowie.

▶ **JODY MULLER:** You could say the Butch Ball art folder, designed by Rick Empson, is "skulled and cross-honed," showcasing brain-coral handle scales and a Mike Norris ladder-pattern-damascus blade. *(PointSeven photo)*

▲ **BRIAN HOCHSTRAT:** Mammoth-ivory handles, gold inlay and engraving highlight Alain Desaulniers' "Big Bear" and "Wilderness" models in the style of **Bob Loveless.** *(SharpByCoop.com photo)*

▶ **TOM FERRY:** Engraving turns a damascus fighter into a "skull-ery blade." *(SharpByCoop.com photo)*

◀ **JERE DAVIDSON:** Engraving caps off a Doug Ashby Persian dagger in snakewood handle scales. *(Dave McDearmont photo)*

▶ **JULIE WARENSKI-ERICKSON:** A Steven Rapp 154CM bowie dons a "dog bone"-style, mammoth-ivory handle attached to a full tang with domed pins, and exhibiting an engraved and gold-inlaid shield and ferrule. *(Hoffman photo)*

▶ **JOE MASON:** The large Bill Ruple double-blade trapper in "feather"-pattern damascus and stag allowed plenty of room for gold-leaf-style engraving. *(PointSeven photo)*

◀▼ **LUCA BRASCHI:** A gangster and nude dame come to life on the handle of Leonardo Frizzi's "Goodfellows" locking-liner folder in a "rose"-pattern damascus blade.

◀ **BRIAN HOCHSTRAT:** Art nouveau scroll rises over a 22k-gold background and contrasts beautifully with the premium Edwards black-jade handle of a T.R. Overeynder folder. *(SharpByCoop.com photo)*

▶ **WALLY HAYES:** This must be what it felt like to open King Tut's tomb. *(SharpByCoop.com photo)*

▶ **TONEY PITTS:** A hummingbird and flowers flit across the bolsters of a Pete Truncali folder in high-carbon damascus and mammoth ivory. *(Ward photo)*

C.J. CAI: The leopard is gold, the pearl black and the Steve Hoel folder brilliant. *(SharpByCoop.com photo)*

◄ DAVID RICCARDO: One of Les George's **FM1** knife models with a Mike Norris damascus blade was turned into a Mayan "Prophecy" knife depicting what some believe is the inside of an ancient spaceship during takeoff with a Mayan king at the controls. Other engraved subjects include a Mayan calendar in a circle at the rear bolster, pyramids, assorted heads of snake gods, and two human heads facing each other. *(SharpByCoop.com photo)*

▶ BRIAN HOCHSTRAT: A Bruce Bump black-powder pistol/folder packs a powerful punch, and a whole lot more into its damascus and pre-ban-ivory frame, including engraving of a seahorse and sea lion in raised 14k gold. *(Ward photo)*

▶ MICHAEL HENNINGSSON: An incredibly detailed 3" x 1" Bulino-style engraved scene depicts the Mayan calendar on the handle of a stainless-damascus art folder.

▶ GIL RUDOLPH: Scroll, leaf and gold floral engraving grabs your attention on a Dennis Friedly California ring dagger with a fossil-ivory handle, which itself would be nice to grab. *(PointSeven photo)*

▶ **STEVE DUNN:** Damascus and engraving double-team a sub-hilt fighter secured in stag. *(SharpByCoop.com photo)*

▼ **RON NEWTON:** A damascus boot knife gains from engraving, and gold and a black-lip-pearl inlay. *(Ward photo)*

◀ **DWIGHT TOWELL:** Floral and leaf engraving surrounds the jasper handle inlay of the folding art dagger.

◀ **RICARDO VELARDE:** Where the engraving stops, the natural handle material begins, then stops, then begins again. *(PointSeven photo)*

▶ **JULIE WARENSKI-ERICKSON:** A Curt Erickson damascus dagger has anything but a sinister demeanor after gold inlay and engraving. *(SharpByCoop.com photo)*

▼ **ANDREW OVALLES:** The bronze handle of a Chuck Gedraitis folder is engraved in a winsome Dia De Los Muertos (Day Of The Dead) theme, and accompanied by a Chad Nichols damascus blade. *(SharpByCoop. com photo)*

STATE OF THE ART **171**

Pierced Arrows

▶ **GLEN MIKOLAJCZYK:** Heart shapes are pierced through the damascus head of a pipe tomahawk hafted in carved tiger maple and trailing a horsehair lanyard, trade beads and feathers. *(Cory Martin Imaging)*

▶ **RON APPLETON:** Stylistic piercing, sculpting and carving enhances the titanium frame of an "Advanced IQ Innova" folder in a D2 blade. *(SharpByCoop.com photo)*

TOSHIAKI MICHINAKA: In the style of W.W. Cronk's "Ace Of Spades," a pierced ATS-34 blade is all there in spades, and curvaceous enough to distract the dealer.

▼ **PHILIP BOOTH:** The "Hotrod Flipper," or pierced arrow, sports a racy Doug Ponzio damascus blade, a titanium handle anodized with ghost flames, and heat color on the wheels. *(SharpByCoop.com photo)*

▼ **DONALD BELL:** The theme of the carved and sculpted 14k-gold over a silver handle is continued onto the pierced and carved Hank Knickmeyer damascus blade. A circle of green Tsavorite garnets embellishes the front bolster. *(SharpByCoop.com photo)*

FACTORY TRENDS

I t's a phenomenal American success story, the fact that factory knife companies not only still exist, but continue to thrive after having experienced a harsh economic downturn in a time when automation and stamped-out parts eclipsed handcraftsmanship and ingenuity. Manufacturers had to adapt. Some took their business offshore having knife parts, blades and handles made or assembled overseas, taking advantage of cheap labor and low business costs. Others remained staunchly on the home front, holding prices steady or raising them, but marketing quality, craftsmanship and the advantage of being "Made In the USA."

Regardless of how companies survived, they improved. Blade steels are stainless and tough; pivots, bushings and bearings are smooth, quick and strong; handles are comfortable and clean; and knives themselves are lightweight, sturdy and impervious to corrosives and the environment. Folders are easy to open, lightning fast, and can be clipped onto pants pockets, gear or clothing. Some are one-hand openers with spring-assisted mechanisms, and others are "flipper folders" that pop open with a finger or thumb pressing an extended flipper mechanism.

Knife companies did the job, did it better and gave the consumers more options. That's where the state of Factory Trends currently resides, and it's trending upward.

Telling the History of America ...
"One Knife at a Time"

Early advertising collectibles include pocketknives exhibiting fascinating period artwork

By Richard D. White

The popular television show *American Pickers* has sparked a renewed interest in the quest for valuable antique finds. While the thrill of the hunt is often more exciting than the actual find, the discovery of a hidden treasure trove can be the cherry on top of the antiques pursuit. The weekly introduction to the television show sets the tone for the series and for this feature article, with Mike Wolfe and Frank Fritz "telling the history of America, one piece at a time."

Advertising items provide special insight into the history of the United States, with slogans, logos and corporate images embossed, stamped, painted or designed right into the products themselves. Even the handle of the humble pocketknife was fair game for companies wanting to tout their products. Once as common in a person's pocket as the cell phone is today, a knife was considered a "never leave home without it" item.

For many companies, the pocketknife proved the perfect advertising giveaway. While most product giveaways such as fans, calendars and pens were designed to be useful, those who received a well-made pocketknife were particularly proud to not only possess, but also employ the indispensable edged implement. Perhaps more than any other gift that bore the name, address and slogan of the advertiser, the pocketknife played an essential role as a problem solver in the daily life of the customer. Whether it

Over 100 years old, the "O. Stader, Germany" knife that advertised Hires Root Beer is extremely rare to find in any condition. Deep handle etching highlights a butler dressed in a three-piece suit and standing in front of several frosty mugs of Hires Root Beer one side of the grip, and a small child with upraised hand on the other. Between her shoes is the slogan "Drink Hires."

Striking graphics and bold wording define the pocketknife that was given to customers who purchased a Metropolitan Life Insurance policy. It is desirable to any advertising collector because of its accurate representation of the actual New York City landmark. The detail is accurate down to the clock located between the 25th and 27th floors.

be to open a package, cut a length of string or plug of tobacco, clean a dirty fingernail, cut an apple or remove a splinter of wood from the palm, and hundreds of other small, daily tasks, the pocketknife proved the ideal solution to the task at hand.

The heyday of advertising appears to be from the late 1890s to the Great Depression, a time when some of the most significant inventions and products were developed for the consumer. It was also a time when there was some disposable income to spread around town.

One of the earliest advertising knives touted a drink well known to American consumers. The pharmacist Charles Elmer Hires, after sampling a refreshing beverage on his honeymoon in 1875, created his own recipe and eventually developed Hires Root Beer. An entrepreneurial spirit allowed him to develop the drink that he debuted at the 1876 Philadelphia Centennial Exposition. His pharmaceutical background came in handy for formulating a beverage that he advertised would "purify the blood" and make "rosy cheeks" of its users.

By the 1890s, Hires sold packs of root beer concentrate to soda fountain owners who mixed his pre-packaged concentrate with water, and served the resulting drink from their dispensers. In addition, Hires sold his root beer in small tinted bottles to grocery stores.

The advertising knife that features Hires Root Beer is unique for several reasons. First is the embossing—a deeply-etched pebble background highlights two figures, one on each side of the knife handle. The first is what looks like a butler dressed in a three-piece suit and standing in front of several frosty mugs of Hires Root Beer. With a hand on his hip and a smile on his face, he exudes satisfaction as he ponders the three mugs before him.

The reverse side of the advertising knife is even more interesting—the figure of a small child with one upraised, pointing hand, and her other hand cradling a large foaming mug of root beer. Between her shoes is the slogan "Drink Hires." This small figure, with her chunky cheeks and curled hair, is the same girl showcased on several Hires Root Beer advertising postcards. Marketed as a drink that would give children rosy cheeks, she is the manifestation of the slogan.

Watch Fob Folder

Made by "O. Stader, Germany," the folder sports four blades and a bail for watch-fob carry. With its shiny foreground, matte background and perimeter floral and scroll design, the advertising knife would have been worn prominently on a watch chain hanging below the vest pocket of some important citizen. The knife was in all probability given away to merchants, loyal customers and employees who helped Hires build an empire based on this popular soft drink.

A pocketknife that features the Metropolitan Life Insurance Building is highly sought after by advertising knife collectors. Constructed in New York City in 1909, Metropolitan Life Insurance was housed, as the knife indicates, in the "highest building in the world." This record height was short lived, however, as the Woolworths Building erected in New York four years later stood slightly higher. Such information is extremely useful in dating the manufacture of the stand-alone advertising knife, in this case from 1909-1913.

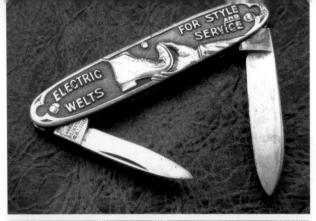

The P.F. Kirkendall & Co. advertising knife features a fancy scrolled company logo set above a pebbled background on one side of the handle, and a hand testing the flexibility of a shoe on the other side.

Another way to date old advertising knives is to look at the tang of the master blade where the name of the company is stamped. The Metropolitan Life Insurance Building knife is stamped "A Kastor & Bros., Warranted Cutlery," and the back of the master blade indicates "Germany." A (Adolph) Kastor was a famous German knife company that manufactured and exported knives to the United States.

The Metropolitan Life Insurance Building, located at 5 Madison Avenue in New York City, was the world headquarters for the insurance company until 2005. It is currently owned by Marriott International, which plans to turn it into a major New York hotel.

In addition to its outstanding building depiction, the pocketknife showcases many embellishments commonly found on the best and most desirable advertising knives of the period. Each end of the handle is decorated with "fleur-de-lis" and scrollwork, adding greatly to the attractiveness and desirability of the special piece.

The Industrial Revolution of the 1890s acted as a springboard for hundreds of American companies that took advantage of innovative scientific develop-

ments. The Goodyear Tire and Rubber Co. was just one of the newly formed entities. Its invention, the vulcanization of rubber, allowed it to produce tires from imported raw rubber. Vulcanization is a chemical process that converts rubber into a more durable product by adding sulfur, curatives and accelerators, making it less sticky, and with superior mechanical properties ideally suited for a long-lasting tire.

Even with the economic depression of 1893 affecting the overall business climate in the United States, Charles Goodyear forecast that the bicycle craze and newly developed automobile would provide potential business opportunities beyond the wildest expectations of those with a more limited vision. Although lacking substantial capital, but with this vision in mind, Goodyear incorporated the Goodyear Tire and Rubber Co. in 1898. He experienced almost instant success as thousands of people purchased his rubber bicycle tires, inner tubes, and later, automobile tires.

By 1916, Goodyear's forward thinking allowed him to build upon his earlier successes to grow the business into the largest tire company in the world. Over the last 75 years, Goodyear has expanded its product line to not only include tires, but also plastics, synthetic rubber, chemicals, hoses, conveyor belts, adhesives and various sealants. Although it took over a half century for the company to reach its $1 billion-per-year sales goal, annual sales now exceed $20 billion. That's not bad for a man who started a company with less than $100,000.

Fancy Figural Knife

Collectors scramble for the Goodyear Tire advertising knife primarily because it touts a well-known product and falls under the category of a figural knife. Its unusual oval shape and unmistakable tire motif make it attractive to figural and advertising knife collectors. The metal-handle knife was made by the E. Bonsmann Cutlery Co. of Solingen, Germany. Bonsmann was one of many outstanding German knife companies producing superb and highly detailed knives, many of which were exported to the United States during the 1890s.

Founded in the 1880s and located in Omaha, Neb., the F.P. Kirkendall Boot Co. became known in the American West as a leading shoe manufacturer specializing in cowboy boots. The style known as the "Challenger" was a well-known boot with rather simple stitch patterns and a square toe designed to be worn with spurs—a necessity for the working cowboy. Kirkendall also made outstanding custom cowboy boots with beautiful inlay patterns and classic designs. All of the boots had tapered heels, as one historian stated, that were "made to hold a stirrup." In addition, the F. P. Kirkendall Co. sold soft-sole shoes for infants, women's felt slippers, children's gold metal shoes and many other styles.

An ornate F.P. Kirkendall knife depicts a hand holding on to the toe of a boot, and bending it up at an abrupt angle. The ad enveloping the image touts "Electric Welts For Style And Service." Although somewhat abstract, the "electric welt" is a process that allows a shoe to be resoled many times, thus adding greatly to its longevity. Like many early advertising knives, this one has an aluminum handle with extremely detailed lettering, visuals and background. Manufactured by United Cutlery Co. of Germany, from 1901-1920, the unique graphics and outstanding detail work place the pocketknife squarely as the centerpiece of any advertising collection.

An article on advertising knives would not be complete without including a pocketknife given away to customers during the Great Depression. One particular piece produced for the Boyles Brothers Co., a clothing and furnishings outfit, includes the catchy slogan "Money's Worth Or Money Back … A Knife With Every Suit." It seems to sum up the economic situation of the United States during the 1930s. Times were tough, and money was almost non-existent. Thousands of companies went out of business during this time period, causing an unemployment figure of 25 percent. The enticement, according to this rare advertising knife, was to offer

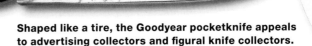

Shaped like a tire, the Goodyear pocketknife appeals to advertising collectors and figural knife collectors.

each person who purchased a suit a free knife.

Today, the incentive sounds ridiculous—nobody would actually purchase a whole suit just to get a knife. During the Depression, however, pocketknives were constant companions to most workers and would have been useful and gracious gifts for people lucky enough to be able to afford a new suit of clothes.

Plus, it was the first advertising knife I purchased. The slogan printed on the handle along with the circumstances by which it was to be given away speaks loudly to an important historical time period in the country, and volumes about why we collect items with a historical past.

Individuals who own pocketknives always find uses for them, making the edged collectibles ideal advertising giveaways. Most of the advertising knives manufactured in the last 40 years have plastic handles with silk screen advertising. Although some of them have collector value, the number of cheaply made examples diminishes their overall worth to collectors.

Those with metal handles, however, have a strong collector following, especially the early examples that advertised products or companies no longer in existence. The best examples exhibit embossing or fancy scrollwork on the ends of the handles, and are generally made by German cutlery companies. These are certainly the most valuable and most sought after. In a slow antique market, the fancy, metal-handle pocketknives have continued to hold their value, and are being purchased at surprising prices.

This small advertising knife says a lot about the U.S. economy during the Great Depression, as well as how important the pocketknife was to the average man.

Black Blades Abound

◄ Ken Onion's "Redemption" model offered by CRKT incorporates a 9.5-inch, black powder-coated O1 tool steel blade and a contoured G-10 handle. It includes a nylon sheath with a thermal-plastic insert.

▲ The Buck "Reaper" full-tang survival knife comes in a 6.75-inch, re-curved blade of 420HC stainless steel with a black-traction coating, a textured "Viper Snakeskin" handle and a single guard.

► In addition to its 4.75-inch, black 1095 high-carbon-steel blade, the removable Micarta handle of the ESEE Knives "Laser Strike" houses a fire-starting flint and tinder tabs.

◄ Designed by Greg Lightfoot, the black flipper blade of the Hand Tech Made Knives "Bullwhip" is combined with a 3D-machined handle of a "reverse fish scale" design to provide a non-slip grip.

▼ In a limited edition of 100 pieces, the Pro-Tech "TR-4.65" combines a black blade with a "splash anodized" handle and a sterling silver skull. It is based on the artwork of Bruce Shaw.

►Gerber's "Downrange Tomahawk" cuts through walls and rope, smashes hinges, doorknobs and locking devices, and breaches with a pry bar leveraged via the cutaway handle in the black axe head.

► The TOPS Knives "HKT," designed by C. Despins, offers up a distinctive 4-inch blade of black-traction-coated 1095 steel and a black-linen-Micarta® handle.

▼ The Famars USA "Azione SRT (Survival Rescue Tactical)" sports a black 154CM stainless steel blade to complement its textured rubber handle.

▼ The KA-BAR "Zombie Zomstro" looks the part in a black-powder-coated SK5 high-carbon-steel blade and a bright green synthetic handle.

▲ Kershaw's "LoneRock Folder" features a black-coated 8Cr13MoV blade and a glass-filled-nylon "K-Texture" handle with multiple grip options.

It's a Flip Fest

▶ In its bright orange, glass-filled-nylon handle, tungsten carbide window breaker, seat belt cutter and flipper mechanism, the CRKT M-16-14ZER makes for an ideal EMT knife. The fact that Kit Carson designed it is icing on the cake.

▲ Anthony Marfione and Mick Strider teamed up on the design of the Microtech "D.O.C." flipper folder in a multi-ground, drop-point CPM-S35VN blade and a dot-textured, carbon-fiber handle.

▼ ▶ An extended flipper mechanism offsets the upward curve of an 8Cr14 blade on HallMark Cutlery's "Spiraling Demise," designed by Sean Kendrick for the "Bad Blood" line.

▼ Designed by R.J. Martin, the Kershaw "1985ST RJI" combines a SpeedSafe™ assist mechanism with a flipper at the base of the 8Cr13MoV stainless steel blade.

Collector Corner

▶ With the recent sale of the Queen factory, its 2011 and 2012 knives—particularly the "QN-19ACSB 4⊠-inch Trapper" in "honey amber"-stag-bone handle scales and a D2 blade—could be possible investments for the gambling collector.

▲ German knives like the Eye Brand "Yellow Handle Lockback Sodbuster," with hammer-forged steel blade, are popular collectibles.

▶ Most collectors agree that stag-handle trappers like the Case XX Rancher are likely to hold or increase their value in years to come. *(photo courtesy of Knives Plus)*

▲ Discontinued knives, such as the Spyderco "C135GP Perrin PPT," designed by Fred Perrin, can be excellent investments.

Knives Marketplace

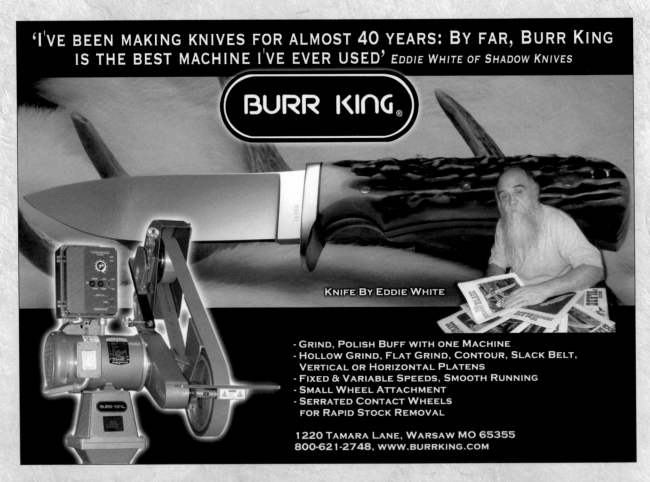

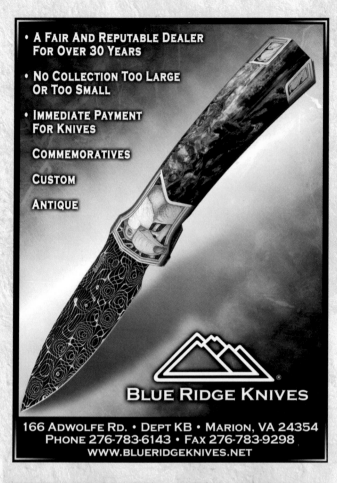
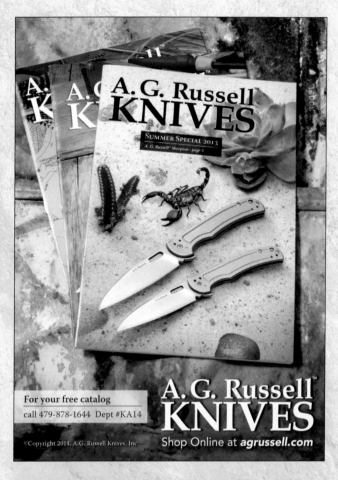
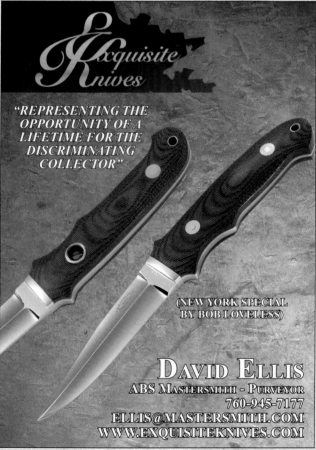

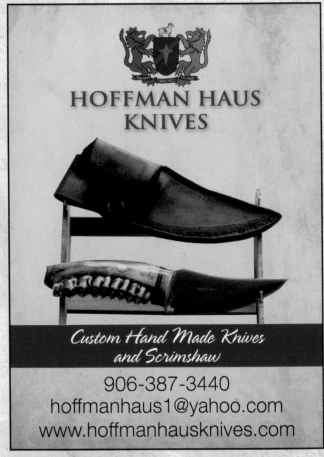

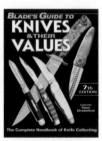

Retain your edge

UDDEHOLM PM STEEL FOR KNIVES

What is the best knife in the world? We all have different preferences, handling techniques and areas of use. No matter how and when you will use your knife, the blade steel is probably the single most important thing to consider. Uddeholm's superclean powder metallurgical steel grades are used in some of the toughest knives available on the market – knives that are put to extreme use in the hands of professionals. With Uddeholm Vanax or Elmax, a knife manufacturer can produce a blade that stays sharp, no matter what. Retain your edge – go for a better steel for your blade.

Happy Anniversary

Jerry Busse Full-Time Knifemaker

Busse Combat Knife Co.

Swamp Rat Knife Works

Let's Party!

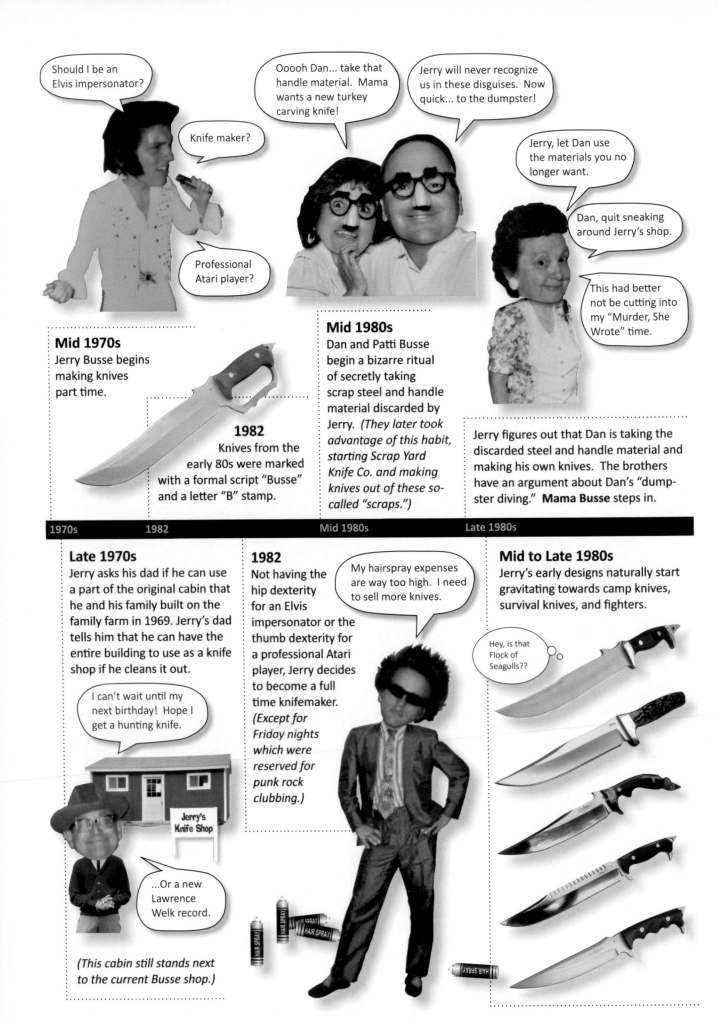

Should I be an Elvis impersonator?

Knife maker?

Professional Atari player?

Ooooh Dan... take that handle material. Mama wants a new turkey carving knife!

Jerry will never recognize us in these disguises. Now quick... to the dumpster!

Jerry, let Dan use the materials you no longer want.

Dan, quit sneaking around Jerry's shop.

This had better not be cutting into my "Murder, She Wrote" time.

Mid 1970s
Jerry Busse begins making knives part time.

1982
Knives from the early 80s were marked with a formal script "Busse" and a letter "B" stamp.

Mid 1980s
Dan and Patti Busse begin a bizarre ritual of secretly taking scrap steel and handle material discarded by Jerry. *(They later took advantage of this habit, starting Scrap Yard Knife Co. and making knives out of these so-called "scraps.")*

Jerry figures out that Dan is taking the discarded steel and handle material and making his own knives. The brothers have an argument about Dan's "dumpster diving." **Mama Busse** steps in.

| 1970s | 1982 | Mid 1980s | Late 1980s |

Late 1970s
Jerry asks his dad if he can use a part of the original cabin that he and his family built on the family farm in 1969. Jerry's dad tells him that he can have the entire building to use as a knife shop if he cleans it out.

I can't wait until my next birthday! Hope I get a hunting knife.

...Or a new Lawrence Welk record.

Jerry's Knife Shop

(This cabin still stands next to the current Busse shop.)

1982
Not having the hip dexterity for an Elvis impersonator or the thumb dexterity for a professional Atari player, Jerry decides to become a full time knifemaker. *(Except for Friday nights which were reserved for punk rock clubbing.)*

My hairspray expenses are way too high. I need to sell more knives.

HAIR SPRAY

Mid to Late 1980s
Jerry's early designs naturally start gravitating towards camp knives, survival knives, and fighters.

Hey, is that Flock of Seagulls??

Hmmm... she obviously likes guys with giant heads who carry swords. I'm so in!

Man, I just love a good marching band rendition of Ice Ice Baby! The tuba solo really brought it home!

Boy, Jerry really knows how to rope 'em in.

1991
Jerry spots Jennifer baton twirling at a Michigan State football game.

Late 1990s
After a hand injury, Jerry consults with an orthopedic surgeon and redesigns all of the "straight handle" knives to be ergonomically correct. The new line becomes known as the "ergo" series.

straight handle

ergo handle

1999
While the current norm in the knife industry was "performance videos" Jerry began a practice of performing "live demonstrations" at trade shows around the country. Prior to the 1999 Blade Show Jerry released a series of ads challenging the industry's other makers and manufacturers to a live challenge in front of an audience. Sadly, there were no takers, so Jerry went on to perform a live "demonstration" by cutting 2,771 pieces of 1" hemp rope with the same section of the blade of a Busse Basic #9 *(the Basics were the "affordable" line.)* Jerry ran out of rope before the knife even thought about dulling. Viewers were amazed that the knife could still shave and cut paper.

| 1990s | | 1995 | Mid to Late 1990s | 1999 |

1992
Jerry and Jennifer tie the knot.

1995
Invention of INFI™ steel.

Jerry awakens from a strange dream with the formula for a super steel, an accompanying heat treatment protocol, a freshly burned brand on the back of his hand, and the lack of ability to focus when confronted with shiny objects, jingling keys, or beef jerky.

This has got to be the dumbest pose for a wedding pic EVER! Oh well, at least no one's ever gonna see it.

Busse Combat is born only months after the honeymoon! Busybodies begin to question when the company was conceived.

Hey Macarena!

BUSSE KNIVES ARE OUT OF THIS WORLD

Now THAT was one realistic dream.

V, Mo, Cr, C ... Where are these letters coming from?

How do I now know all the moves to the Macarena?

INFInity- from Latin infinitas, which can be translated as "unboundedness." Derived from the Greek word apeiros, meaning "endless."

Mmmmmm... beef jerky.

2003

The first Busse "Hog Induction" takes place.

By the powers vested in me, I dub thee...

When do I get the beer?

Hogs, rats, & dogs... what about crickets?

Early 2000s

Once again, Jerry tries through ads, personal invitations, and even taunting trade show booth signs to get other makers or manufacturers to agree to "live performance challenges," competing head to head against a Busse knife.

Yawn

Chirp

Sadly, there was no response except for the crickets.

2002

Swamp Rat Knife Works born.

After years of hearing Jerry complain that Busse Combat has no competition, Jennifer Busse decides to help him out by becoming his nearest competition and starting Swamp Rat Knife Works. Swamp Rat knives quickly become the closest competitors Busse knives have ever encountered.

Each year at Blade Show and other knife shows across the country, all Busse, Swamp Rat, and Scrap Yard customers attending the show are invited to attend dinner and a party hosted by Jerry. New members are inducted during a private ceremony in which they receive their new "hog name." Swamp Rat "rats" and Scrap Yard "dogs" are also inducted. Customers compete in games and contests to win valuable prizes.

2006

The stork visits Jerry.

Buh.. Buh... Busse!

2000s	2002	2003	Mid 2000s	2006	2009	2012

Early 2000s

Busse starts offering models known as "variants" available through the custom shop. Standard models are modified and outfitted with unique grinds, handle materials, and blade coatings.

talon hole

2003

The "talon hole" becomes an official registered trademark of Busse Combat, 15 years after making its first appearance on a Busse knife.

2006

Scrap Yard Knife Co. born.

After years of hearing Jennifer complain that Swamp Rat has no competition, Dan Busse decides to help her out by becoming her nearest competition and starting Scrap Yard Knife Co. Scrap Yard knives quickly become the closest competitors Swamp Rat knives have ever encountered.

Burp

2009

The stork visits Jerry again ...and again...

2012

...and again.

Let's party, daddy!

DIRECTORY

custom knifemakers

A

ABEGG, ARNIE,
5992 Kenwick Cr, Huntington Beach, CA 92648, Phone: 714-848-5697

ABERNATHY, LANCE,
Sniper Bladeworks, 15477 N.W. 123rd St., Platte City, MO 64079, Phone: 816-585-1595, lanceabernathy@sbcglobal.net; Web: www.sniperbladeworks.com
Specialties: Tactical frame-lock and locking-liner folding knives.

ACCAWI, FUAD,
131 Bethel Rd, Clinton, TN 37716, Phone: 865-414-4836, gaccawi@comcast.net; Web: www.acremetalworks.com
Specialties: I create one of a kind pieces from small working knives to performance blades and swords. Patterns: Styles include, and not limited to hunters, Bowies, daggers, swords, folders and camp knives. Technical: I forge primarily 5160, produces own Damascus and does own heat treating. Prices: $150 to $3000. Remarks: I am a full-time bladesmith. I enjoy producing Persian and historically influenced work. Mark: My mark is an eight sided Middle Eastern star with initials in the center.

ACKERSON, ROBIN E,
119 W Smith St, Buchanan, MI 49107, Phone: 616-695-2911

ADAMS, JIM,
1648 Camille Way, Cordova, TN 38016, Phone: 901-326-0441, jim@JimAdamsKnives.com Web: www.jimadamsknives.com
Specialties: Fixed blades in classic design. Patterns: Hunters, fighters, and Bowies. Technical: Grinds Damascus, O1, others as requested. Prices: Starting at $150. Remarks: Full-time maker. Mark: J. Adams, Cordova, TN.

ADAMS, LES,
6413 NW 200 St, Hialeah, FL 33015, Phone: 305-625-1699
Specialties: Working straight knives of his design. Patterns: Fighters, tactical folders, law enforcing autos. Technical: Grinds ATS-34, 440C and D2. Prices: $100 to $500. Remarks: Part-time maker; first knife sold in 1989. Mark: First initial, last name, Custom Knives.

ADAMS, WILLIAM D,
PO Box 439, 405 Century Farms Rd, Burton, TX 77835, Phone: 979-289-0212, Fax: 979-289-6272, wd4adams@broadwaves.net
Specialties: Hunter scalpels and utility knives of his design. Patterns: Hunters and utility/camp knives. Technical: Grinds 1095, 440C and 440V. Uses stabilized wood and other stabilized materials. Prices: $100 to $200. Remarks: Part-time maker; first knife sold in 1994. Mark: Last name in script.

ADDISON, KYLE A,
588 Atkins Trail, Hazel, KY 42049-8629, Phone: 270-492-8120, kylest2@yahoo.com
Specialties: Hand forged blades including Bowies, fighters and hunters. Patterns: Custom leather sheaths. Technical: Forges 5160, 1084, and his own Damascus. Prices: $175 to $1500. Remarks: Part-time maker, first knife sold in 1996. ABS member. Mark: First and middle initial, last name under "Trident" with knife and hammer.

ADKINS, RICHARD L,
138 California Ct, Mission Viejo, CA 92692-4079

AIDA, YOSHIHITO,
26-7 Narimasu 2-chome, Itabashi-ku, Tokyo, JAPAN 175-0094, Phone: 81-3-3939-0052, Fax: 81-3-3939-0058, Web: http://riverside-land.com/
Specialties: High-tech working straight knives and folders of his design. Patterns: Bowies, lockbacks, hunters, fighters, fishing knives, boots. Technical: Grinds CV-134, ATS-34; buys Damascus; works in traditional Japanese fashion for some handles and sheaths. Prices: $700 to $1200; some higher. Remarks: Full-time maker; first knife sold in 1978. Mark: Initial logo and Riverside West.

ALBERT, STEFAN,
U Lucenecka 434/4, Filakovo 98604, SLOVAKIA, albert@albertknives.com Web: www.albertknives.com
Specialties: Art Knives, Miniatures, Scrimshaw, Bulino. Prices: From USD $500 to USD $25000. Mark: Albert

ALCORN, DOUGLAS A.,
14687 Fordney Rd., Chesaning, MI 48616, Phone: 989-845-6712, fortalcornknives@centurytel.net
Specialties: Gentleman style and presentation knives. Patterns: Hunters, miniatures, and military type fixed blade knives and axes. Technical: Blades are stock removal and forged using best quality stainless, carbon, and damascus steels. Handle materials are burls, ivory, pearl, leather and other exotics. Prices: $300 and up. Motto: Simple, Rugged, Elegant, Handcrafted Remarks: Knife maker since 1989 and full time since 1999, Knife Makers Guild (voting member), member of the Bladesmith Society. Mark: D.A. Alcorn (Loveless style mark), Maker, Chesaning, MI.

ALDERMAN, ROBERT,
2655 Jewel Lake Rd., Sagle, ID 83860, Phone: 208-263-5996
Specialties: Classic and traditional working straight knives in standard patterns or to customer specs and his design; period pieces. Patterns: Bowies, fighters, hunters and utility/camp knives. Technical: Casts, forges and grinds 1084; forges and grinds L6 and O1. Prefers an old appearance. Prices: $100 to $350; some to $700. Remarks: Full-time maker; first knife sold in 1975. Doing business as Trackers Forge. Knife-making school. Two-week course for beginners; covers forging, stock removal, hardening, tempering, case making. All materials supplied; $1250. Mark: Deer track.

ALEXANDER, DARREL,
Box 381, Ten Sleep, WY 82442, Phone: 307-366-2699, dalexwyo@tctwest.net
Specialties: Traditional working straight knives. Patterns: Hunters, boots and fishing knives. Technical: Grinds D2, 440C, ATS-34 and 154CM. Prices: $75 to $120; some to $250. Remarks: Full-time maker; first knife sold in 1983. Mark: Name, city, state.

ALEXANDER, EUGENE,
Box 540, Ganado, TX 77962-0540, Phone: 512-771-3727

ALEXANDER,, Oleg, and Cossack Blades,
15460 Stapleton Way, Wellington, FL 33414, Phone: 443-676-6111, Web: www.cossackblades.com
Technical: All knives are made from hand-forged Damascus (3-4 types of steel are used to create the Damascus) and have a HRC of 60-62. Handle materials are all natural, including various types of wood, horn, bone and leather. Embellishments include the use of precious metals and stones, including gold, silver, diamonds, rubies, sapphires and other unique materials. All knives include hand-made leather sheaths, and some models include wooden presentation boxes and display stands. Prices: $395 to over $10,000, depending on design and materials used. Remarks: Full-time maker, first knife sold in 1993. Mark: Rectangle enclosing a stylized Cyrillic letter "O" overlapping a stylized Cyrillic "K."

ALLEN, MIKE "WHISKERS",
12745 Fontenot Acres Rd, Malakoff, TX 75148, Phone: 903-489-1026, whiskersknives@aol.com; Web: www.whiskersknives.com
Specialties: Working and collector-quality lockbacks, liner locks, automatic folders and assisted openers of his own proprietary mechanisms. Patterns: Folders and fixed blades. Technical: Makes Damascus, 440C and ATS-34, engraves. Prices: $200 and up. Remarks: Full-time maker since 1984. Mark: Whiskers and month and year.

ALLRED, BRUCE F,
1764 N. Alder, Layton, UT 84041, Phone: 801-825-4612, allredbf@msn.com
Specialties: Custom hunting and utility knives. Patterns: Custom designs that include a unique grind line, thumb and mosaic pins. Technical: ATS-34, 154CM and 440C. Remarks: The handle material includes but not limited to Micarta (in various colors), natural woods and reconstituted stone.

ALLRED, ELVAN,
31 Spring Terrace Court, St. Charles, MO 63303, Phone: 636-936-8871, allredknives@yahoo.com; Web: www.allredcustomknives.com
Specialties: Innovative sculpted folding knives designed by Elvan's son Scott that are mostly one of a kind. Patterns: Mostly folders but some high-end straight knives. Technical: ATS-34 SS, 440C SS, stainless Damascus, S30V, 154cm; inlays are mostly natural materials such as pearl, coral, ivory, jade, lapis, and other precious stone. Prices: $500 to $4000, some higher. Remarks: Started making knives in the shop of Dr. Fred Carter in the early 1990s. Full-time maker since 2006, first knife sold in 1993. Take some orders but work mainly on one-of-a-kind art knives. Mark: Small oval with signature Eallred in the center and handmade above.

ALVERSON, TIM (R.V.),
622 Homestead St., Moscow, ID 83843, Phone: 208-874-2277, alvie35@yahoo.com Web: cwknives.blogspot.com
Specialties: Fancy working knives to customer specs; other types on request. Patterns: Bowies, daggers, folders and miniatures. Technical: Grinds 440C, ATS-34; buys some Damascus. Prices: Start at $100. Remarks: Full-time maker; first knife sold in 1981. Mark: R.V.A. around rosebud.

AMERI, MAURO,
Via Riaello No. 20, Trensasco St Olcese, Genova, ITALY 16010, Phone: 010-8357077, mauroameri@gmail.com
Specialties: Working and using knives of his design. Patterns: Hunters, Bowies and utility/camp knives. Technical: Grinds 440C, ATS-34 and 154CM. Handles in wood or Micarta; offers sheaths. Prices: $200 to $1200. Remarks: Spare-time maker; first knife sold in 1982. Mark: Last name, city.

AMMONS, DAVID C,
6225 N. Tucson Mtn. Dr, Tucson, AZ 85743, Phone: 520-307-3585
Specialties: Will build to suit. Patterns: Yours or his. Prices: $250 to $2000. Mark: AMMONS.

AMOS, CHRIS,
PO Box 1519, Riverton, WY 82501, Phone: 520-271-9752, caknives@yahoo.com
Specialties: HEPK (High Endurance Performance Knives). Patterns: Hunters, fighters, bowies and camp knives. Technical: Hand-forged, high rate of reduction 52100 and 5160 steel. Prices: $150 to $1,500. Remarks: Part-time maker since 1997, full time since 2012. Coach/instructor at Ed Fowler's Knifemaking School. Mark: Early mark: CAK stamped; current mark: Amos on right side.

AMOUREUX, A W,
PO Box 776, Northport, WA 99157, Phone: 509-732-6292
Specialties: Heavy-duty working straight knives. Patterns: Bowies, fighters, camp knives and hunters for world-wide use. Technical: Grinds 440C, ATS-34 and 154CM. Prices: $80 to $2000. Remarks: Full-time maker; first knife sold in 1974. Mark: ALSTAR.

ANDERS, DAVID,
157 Barnes Dr, Center Ridge, AR 72027, Phone: 501-893-2294
Specialties: Working straight knives of his design. Patterns: Bowies, fighters and hunters. Technical: Forges 5160, 1080 and Damascus. Prices: $225 to $3200. Remarks: Part-time maker; first knife sold in 1988. Doing business as Anders Knives. Mark: Last name/MS.

ANDERS, JEROME,
14560 SW 37th St, Miramar, FL 33027, Phone: 305-613-2990, web:www.andersknives.com
Specialties: Case handles and pin work. Patterns: Layered and mosaic steel. Prices: $275 and up. Remarks: All his knives are truly one-of-a-kind. Mark: J. Anders in half moon.

ANDERSEN, HENRIK LEFOLII,
Jagtvej 8, Groenholt, Fredensborg, DENMARK 3480, Phone: 0011-45-48483026
Specialties: Hunters and matched pairs for the serious hunter. Technical: Grinds A2; uses materials native to Scandinavia. Prices: Start at $250. Remarks: Part-time maker; first knife sold in 1985. Mark: Initials with arrow.

ANDERSEN, KARL B.,
20200 TimberLodge Rd., Warba, MN 55793, Phone: 218-398-4270, Karl@andersenforge.com Web: www.andersenforge.com
Specialties: Hunters, Bowies, Fighters, Camp knives forged from high carbon tool steels and Andersen Forge Damascus. Technical: All types of materials used. Exotic inlay materials and silver wire embellishments utilized. Prices: Starting at $450 and up. Remarks: Full-time maker. ABS Journeyman Smith. All knives sole authorship. Andersen Forge was instrumental in paving the way for take-down knife construction to be more recognized and broadly accepted in knife making today. Mark: Andersen in script on obverse. J.S. on either side, depending on knife.

ANDERSON, GARY D,
2816 Reservoir Rd, Spring Grove, PA 17362-9802, Phone: 717-229-2665
Specialties: From working knives to collectors quality blades, some folders. Patterns: Traditional and classic designs; customer patterns welcome. Technical: Forges Damascus carbon and stainless steels. Offers silver inlay, mokume, filework, checkering. Prices: $250 and up. Remarks: Part-time maker; first knife sold in 1985. Some engraving, scrimshaw and stone work. Mark: GAND, MS.

ANDERSON, MARK ALAN,
1176 Poplar St, Denver, CO 80220, mcantdrive95@comcast.net; Web: www.malancustomknives.com
Specialties: Stilettos. Automatics of several varieties and release mechanisms. Patterns: Drop point hunters, sub hilt fighters & drop point camp knives. Technical: Almost all my blades are hollow ground. Prices: $200 to $1800. Remarks: Focusing on fixed blade hunting, skinning & fighting knives now. Mark: Dragon head.

ANDERSON, MEL,
29505 P 50 Rd, Hotchkiss, CO 81419-8203, Phone: 970-872-4882, Fax: 970-872-4882, artnedge@tds.net, melsscratchyhand@aol.com; Web: www.scratchyhand.com
Specialties: Full-size, miniature and one-of-a-kind straight knives and folders of his design. Patterns: Tantos, Bowies, daggers, fighters, hunters and pressure folders. Technical: Grinds 440C, 5160, D2, 1095. Prices: Start at $175. Remarks: Knifemaker and sculptor, full-time maker; first knife sold in 1987. Mark: Scratchy Hand.

ANDERSON, TOM,
955 Canal Rd. Extd., Manchester, PA 17345, Phone: 717-266-6475, andersontech1@comcast.net Web: artistryintitanium.com
Specialties: Battle maces and war hammers.

ANDREWS, ERIC,
132 Halbert Street, Grand Ledge, MI 48837, Phone: 517-627-7304
Specialties: Traditional working and using straight knives of his design. Patterns: Full-tang hunters, skinners and utility knives. Technical: Forges carbon steel; heat-treats. All knives come with sheath; most handles are of wood. Prices: $80 to $160. Remarks: Part-time maker; first knife sold in 1990. Doing business as The Tinkers Bench.

ANDREWS, RUSS,
PO Box 7732, Sugar Creek, MO 64054, Phone: 816-252-3344, russandrews@sbcglobal.net; Web:wwwrussandrewsknives.com
Specialties: Hand forged bowies & hunters. Mark: E. R. Andrews II. ERAII.

ANGELL, JON,
22516 East C R1474, Hawthorne, FL 32640, Phone: 352-475-5380, syrjon@aol.com

ANKROM, W.E.,
14 Marquette Dr, Cody, WY 82414, Phone: 307-587-3017, weankrom@hotmail.com
Specialties: Best quality folding knives of his design. Bowies, fighters, chute knives, boots and hunters. Patterns: Lock backs, liner locks, single high art. Technical: ATS-34 commercial Damascus, CPM 154 steel. Prices: $500 and up. Remarks: Full-time maker; first knife sold in 1975. Mark: Name or name, city, state.

ANSO, JENS,
GL. Skanderborgvej 116, Sporup, DENMARK 8472, Phone: 45 86968826, info@ansoknives.com; Web: www.ansoknives.com
Specialties: Working knives of his own design. Patterns: Balisongs, swords, folders, drop-points, sheepsfoots, hawkbill, tanto, recurve. Technical: Grinds RWL-34 Damasteel S30V, CPM 154CM. Handrubbed or beadblasted finish. Prices: $400 to $1200, some up to $3500. Remarks: Full-time maker since January 2002. First knife sold 1997. Doing business as ANSOKNIVES. Mark: ANSO and/or ANSO with logo.

APELT, STACY E,
8076 Moose Ave, Norfolk, VA 23518, Phone: 757-583-5872, sapelt@cox.net
Specialties: Exotic wood and burls, ivories, Bowies, custom made knives to order. Patterns: Bowies, hunters, fillet, professional cutlery and Japanese style blades and swords. Technical: Hand forging, stock removal, scrimshaw, carbon, stainless and Damascus steels. Prices: $65 to $5000. Remarks: Professional Goldsmith. Mark: Stacy E. Apelt - Norfolk VA.

APLIN, SPENCER,
5151 County Rd. 469, Brazoria, TX 77422, Phone: 979-964-4448, spenceraplin@aol.com; Web: www.stacustomknives.com
Specialties: Custom skinners, fillets, bowies and kitchen knives. Technical: Stainless steel powder metals, stainless damascus. Handles include stabilized woods, various ivory and Micarta. Guard and butt-cap materials are brass, copper, nickel silver and Mokume. Prices: $250 and up. Remarks: First knife sold in 1989. Knives made to order only, nothing is pre-made. All blades are hand drawn, then cut from sheet stock. No two are exactly the same. Mark: Signature and date completed.

APPLEBY, ROBERT,
746 Municipal Rd, Shickshinny, PA 18655, Phone: 570-864-0879, applebyknives@yahoo.com; Web: www.applebyknives.com
Specialties: Working using straight knives and folders of his own and popular and historical designs. Patterns: Variety of straight knives and folders. Technical: Hand forged or grinds O1, 1084, 5160, 440C, ATS-34, commercial Damascus, makes own sheaths. Prices: Starting at $75. Remarks: Part-time maker, first knife sold in 1995. Mark: APPLEBY over SHICKSHINNY, PA.

APPLETON, RON,
315 Glenn St, Bluff Dale, TX 76433, Phone: 254-728-3039, ron@helovesher.com or ronappleton@hotmail.com; Web: http://community.webshots.com/user/angelic574
Specialties: One-of-a-kind folding knives. Patterns: Unique folding multi-locks and high-tech patterns. Technical: All parts machined, D2, S7, 416, 440C, 6A14V et.al. Prices: Start at $12000. Remarks: Full-time maker; first knife sold in 1996. Mark: Initials with anvil or initials within arrowhead, signed and dated. Usually only shows at the Art Knife Invitational every 2 years in San Diego, CA.

ARBUCKLE, JAMES M,
114 Jonathan Jct, Yorktown, VA 23693, Phone: 757-867-9578, a_r_buckle@hotmail.com
Specialties: One-of-a-kind of his design; working knives. Patterns: Mostly chef's knives and hunters. Technical: Forged and stock removal blades using exotic hardwoods, natural materials, Micarta and stabilized woods. Forge 5160 and 1084; stock removal D2, ATS-34, 440C and 154CM. Makes own pattern welded steel. Prices: $195 to $700. Remarks: Forge, grind, heat-treat, finish and embellish all knives himself. Does own leatherwork. Part-time maker. ABS Journeyman smith 2007; ASM member. Mark: J. Arbuckle or J. ARBUCKLE MAKER.

ARCHER, RAY AND TERRI,
4207 South 28 St., Omaha, NE 68107, Phone: 402-505-3084, archerrt@cox.net Web: www.archersknives.com
Specialties: Basic high-finish working knives. Patterns: Hunters, skinners camp knives. Technical: Flat grinds various steels like 440C, ATS-34 and CPM-S30V. Prices: $75 to $500. Remarks: Full-time maker. Makes own sheaths; first knife sold 1994. Mark: Last name over knives.

ARDWIN, COREY,
4700 North Cedar, North Little Rock, AR 72116, Phone: 501-791-0301, Fax: 501-791-2974, Boog@hotmail.com

ARM-KO KNIVES,
PO Box 76280, Marble Ray, KZN, SOUTH AFRICA 4035, Phone: 27 31 5771451, arm-koknives.co.za; Web: www.arm-koknives.co.za
Specialties: They will make what your fastidious taste desires. Be it cool collector or tenacious tactical with handles of mother-of-pearl, fossil & local ivories. Exotic dye/stabilized burls, giraffe bone, horns, carbon fiber, g10, and titanium etc. Technical: Via stock removal, grinding Damasteel, carbon & mosaic. Damascus, ATS-34, N690, 440A, 440B, 12C27, RWL34 and high carbon EN8, 5160 all heat treated in house. Prices: From $200 and up. Remarks: Father a part-time maker for well over 10 years and member of Knifemakers Guild in SA. Son full-time maker over 3 years. Mark: Logo of initials A R M and H A R M "Edged Tools."

ARMS, ERIC,
11153 7 Mile Road, Tustin, MI 49688, Phone: 231-829-3726, ericarms@netonecom.net
Specialties: Working hunters, high performance straight knives. Patterns: Variety of hunters, scagel style, Ed Fowler design and drop point. Technical: Forge 52100, 5160, 1084 hand grind, heat treat, natural handle, stag horn, elk, big horn, flat grind, convex, all leather sheath work. Prices: Starting at $150 Remarks: Part-time maker Mark: Eric Arms

ARNOLD, JOE,
47 Patience Cres, London, ON, CANADA N6E 2K7, Phone: 519-686-2623, arnoldknivesandforge@bell.net
Specialties: Traditional working and using straight knives of his design and to customer specs. Patterns: Fighters, hunters and Bowies. Technical: Grinds 440C, ATS-34, 5160, and Forges 1084-1085 Prices: $75 to $500; some to $2500. Remarks: Full-time maker; first knife sold in 1988. Mark: Last name, country.

ARROWOOD, DALE,
556 Lassetter Rd, Sharpsburg, GA 30277, Phone: 404-253-9672
Specialties: Fancy and traditional straight knives of his design and to customer specs. Patterns: Bowies, fighters and hunters. Technical: Grinds ATS-34 and 440C; forges high-carbon steel. Engraves and scrimshaws. Prices: $125 to $200; some to $245. Remarks: Part-time maker; first knife sold in 1989. Mark: Anvil with an arrow through it; Old English "Arrowood Knives."

ASHBY, DOUGLAS,
10123 Deermont Trail, Dallas, TX 75243, Phone: 214-929-7531, doug@ashbycustomknives.com Web: ashbycustomknives.com
Specialties: Traditional and fancy straight knives and folders of his design or to customer specs. Patterns: Skinners, hunters, utility/camp knives, locking liner folders. Technical: Grinds ATS-34, commercial Damascus, and other steels on request. Prices: $125 to $1000. Remarks: Part-time maker; first knife sold in 1990. Mark: Name, city.

ASHWORTH, BOYD,
1510 Bullard Place, Powder Springs, GA 30127, Phone: 770-422-9826, boydashworth@comcast.net; Web: www.boydashworthknives.com
Specialties: Turtle folders. Fancy Damascus locking folders. Patterns: Fighters, hunters and gents. Technical: Forges own Damascus; offers filework; uses exotic handle materials. Prices: $500 to $2500. Remarks: Part-time maker; first knife sold in 1993. Mark: Last name.

ATHEY, STEVE,
3153 Danube Way, Riverside, CA 92503, Phone: 951-850-8612, stevelonnie@yahoo.com
Specialties: Stock removal. Patterns: Hunters & Bowies. Prices: $100 to $500. Remarks: Part-time maker. Mark: Last name with number on blade.

ATKINSON, DICK,
General Delivery, Wausau, FL 32463, Phone: 850-638-8524
Specialties: Working straight knives and folders of his design; some fancy. Patterns: Hunters, fighters, boots; locking folders in interframes. Technical: Grinds A2, 440C and 154CM. Likes filework. Prices: $85 to $300; some exceptional knives. Remarks: Full-time maker; first knife sold in 1977. Mark: Name, city, state.

AYARRAGARAY, CRISTIAN L.,
Buenos Aires 250, Parana, Entre Rios, ARGENTINA 3100, Phone: 043-231753
Specialties: Traditional working straight knives of his design. Patterns: Fishing and hunting knives. Technical: Grinds and forges carbon steel. Uses native Argentine woods and deer antler. Prices: $150 to $250; some to $400. Remarks: Full-time maker; first knife sold in 1980. Mark: Last name, signature.

B

BAARTMAN, GEORGE,
PO Box 1116, Bela-Bela, LP, SOUTH AFRICA 0480, Phone: 27 14 736 4036, Fax: 086 636 3408, thabathipa@gmail.com
Specialties: Fancy and working LinerLock® folders of own design and to customers specs. Specialize in pattern filework on liners. Patterns: LinerLock® folders. Technical: Grinds 12C27, ATS-34, and Damascus, prefer working with stainless damasteel. Hollow grinds to hand-rubbed and polished satin finish. Enjoys working with mammoth, warthog tusk and pearls. Prices: Folders from $380 to $1000. Remarks: Part-time maker. Member of the Knifemakers Guild of South Africa since 1993. Mark: BAARTMAN.

BACHE-WIIG, TOM,
N-5966, Eivindvik, NORWAY, Phone: 475-778-4290, Fax: 475-778-1099, tom.bache-wiig@enivest.net; Web: tombachewiig.com
Specialties: High-art and working knives of his design. Patterns: Hunters, utility knives, hatchets, axes and art knives. Technical: Grinds Uddeholm Elmax, powder metallurgy tool stainless steel. Handles made of rear burls of Nordic woods stabilized with vacuum/high-pressure technique. Prices: $430 to $900; some to $2300. Remarks: Part-time maker; first knife sold 1988. Mark: Etched name and eagle head.

BACON, DAVID R.,
906 136th St E, Bradenton, FL 34202-9694, Phone: 813-996-4289

BAGLEY, R. KEITH,
OLD PINE FORGE, 4415 Hope Acres Dr, White Plains, MD 20695, Phone: 301-932-0990, keithbagley14@verizon.net; Web: www.oldpineforge.com
Specialties: Technical: Use ATS-34, 5160, O1, 1085 and 1095. Patterns: Ladder-wave lightning bolt. Prices: $275 to $750. Remarks: Farrier for 37 years, blacksmith for 37 years, knifemaker for 25 years. Mark: KB inside horseshoe and anvil.

BAILEY, I.R.,
Lamorna Cottage, Common End, Colkirk, ENGLAND NR21 7JD, Phone: 01-328-856-183, admin@grommitbaileyknives.com; Web: www.grommitbaileyknives.com
Specialties: Hunters, utilities, Bowies, camp knives, fighters. Mainly influenced by Moran, Loveless and Lile. Technical: Primarily stock removal using flat ground 1095, 1075, and 80CrV2. Occasionally forges including own basic Damascus. Uses both native and exotic hardwoods, stag, Leather, Micarta and other synthetic handle materials, with brass or 301 stainless fittings. Does some filework and leather tooling. Does own heat treating. Remarks: Part-time maker since 2005. All knives and sheaths are sole authorship. Mark: Last name stamped.

BAILEY, JOSEPH D.,
3213 Jonesboro Dr, Nashville, TN 37214, Phone: 615-889-3172, jbknfemkr@aol.com
Specialties: Working and using straight knives; collector pieces. Patterns: Bowies, hunters, tactical, folders. Technical: 440C, ATS-34, Damascus and wire Damascus. Offers scrimshaw. Prices: $85 to $1200. Remarks: Part-time maker; first knife sold in 1988. Mark: Joseph D Bailey Nashville Tennessee.

BAKER, HERB,
14104 NC 87 N, Eden, NC 27288, Phone: 336-627-0338

BAKER, RAY,
PO Box 303, Sapulpa, OK 74067, Phone: 918-224-8013
Specialties: High-tech working straight knives. Patterns: Hunters, fighters, Bowies, skinners and boots of his design and to customer specs. Technical: Grinds 440C, 1095 spring steel or customer request; heat-treats. Custom-made scabbards for any knife. Prices: $125 to $500; some to $1000. Remarks: Full-time maker; first knife sold in 1981. Mark: First initial, last name.

BAKER, TONY,
707 Lake Highlands Dr, Allen, TX 75002, Phone: 214-543-1001, tonybakerknives@yahoo.com
Specialties: Hunting knives, integral made Technical: 154cm, S30V, and S90V Prices: Starting at $500. Prices: $200-$1200 Remarks: First knife made in 2001.

BAKER, WILD BILL,
Box 361, Boiceville, NY 12412, Phone: 914-657-8646
Specialties: Primitive knives, buckskinners. Patterns: Skinners, camp knives and Bowies. Technical: Works with L6, files and rasps. Prices: $100 to $350. Remarks: Part-time maker; first knife sold in 1989. Mark: Wild Bill Baker, Oak Leaf Forge, or both.

BALBACH, MARKUS,
Heinrich Worner Str.1-3, WeilmŸnster, GERMANY 35789, Phone: +49 (0) 6475-8911, Fax: 912986, Web: www.schmiede-balbach.de
Specialties: High-art knives and working/using straight knives and folders of his design and to customer specs. Patterns: Hunters and daggers. Technical: Stainless steel, one of Germany's greatest Smithies. Supplier for the forges of Solingen. Remarks: Full-time maker; first knife sold in 1984. Doing business as Schmiedewerkstatte M. Balbach. Mark: Initials stamped inside the handle.

BALL, BUTCH,
2161 Reedsville Rd., Floyd, VA 24091, Phone: 540-392-3485, ballknives@yahoo.com
Specialties: Fancy and Tactical Folders and Automatics. Patterns: Fixed and folders. Technical: Use various Damascus and ATS34, 154cm. Prices: $300 - $1500. Remarks: Part-time maker. Sold first knife in 1990. Mark: Ball or BCK with crossed knives.

BALL, KEN,
127 Sundown Manor, Mooresville, IN 46158, Phone: 317-834-4803
Specialties: Classic working/using straight knives of his design and to customer specs. Patterns: Hunters and utility/camp knives. Technical: Flat-grinds ATS-34. Offers filework. Prices: $150 to $400. Remarks: Part-time maker; first knife sold in 1994. Doing business as Ball Custom Knives. Mark: Last name.

BALLESTRA, SANTINO,
via D. Tempesta 11/17, Ventimiglia, ITALY 18039, Phone: 0184-215228, ladasin@libero.it
Specialties: Using and collecting straight knives. Patterns: Hunting, fighting, skinners, Bowies, medieval daggers and knives. Technical: Forges ATS-34, D2, O2, 1060 and his own Damascus. Uses ivory and silver. Prices: $500 to $2000; some higher. Remarks: Full-time maker; first knife sold in 1979. Mark: First initial, last name.

BALLEW, DALE,
PO Box 1277, Bowling Green, VA 22427, Phone: 804-633-5701
Specialties: Miniatures only to customer specs. Patterns: Bowies, daggers and fighters. Technical: Files 440C stainless; uses ivory, abalone, exotic woods and some precious stones. Prices: $100 to $800. Remarks: Part-time maker; first knife sold in 1988. Mark: Initials and last name.

BANAITIS, ROMAS,
84 Winthrop St., Medway, MA 02053, Phone: 774-248-5851, rbanaitis@verizon.net
Specialties: Designing art and fantasy knives. Patterns: Folders, daggers and fixed blades. Technical: Hand-carved blades, handles and fittings in stainless steel, sterling silver and titanium. Prices: Moderate to upscale. Remarks: First knife sold in 1996. Mark: Romas Banaitis.

BANKS, DAVID L.,
99 Blackfoot Ave, Riverton, WY 82501, Phone: 307-856-3154/Cell: 307-851-5599
Specialties: Heavy-duty working straight knives. Patterns: Hunters, Bowies and camp knives. Technical: Forges Damascus 1084-15N20, L6-W1 pure nickel, 5160, 52100 and his own Damascus; differential heat treat and tempers. Handles made of horn, antlers and exotic wood. Hand-stitched harness leather sheaths. Prices: $300 to $2000. Remarks: Part-time maker. Mark: Banks Blackfoot forged Dave Banks and initials connected.

BAREFOOT, JOE W.,
1654 Honey Hill, Wilmington, NC 28442, Phone: 910-641-1143
Specialties: Working straight knives of his design. Patterns: Hunters, fighters and boots; tantos and survival knives. Technical: Grinds D2, 440C and ATS-34. Mirror finishes. Uses ivory and stag on customer request only. Prices: $50 to

$160; some to $500. Remarks: Part-time maker; first knife sold in 1980. Mark: Bare footprint.

BARKER, JOHN,
5725 Boulder Bluff Dr., Cumming, GA 30040, Phone: 678-357-8586, barkerknives@bellsouth.net Web: www.barkerknives.com
Specialties: Tactical fixed blades and folders. Technical: Stock removal method and CPM and Carpenter powdered technology steels. Prices: $150 and up. Remarks: First knife made 2006. Mark: Snarling dog with "Barker" over the top of its head and "Knives" below.

BARKER, REGGIE,
603 S Park Dr, Springhill, LA 71075, Phone: 318-539-2958, wrbarker@cmaaccess.com; Web: www.reggiebarkerknives.com
Specialties: Camp knives and hatchets. Patterns: Bowie, skinning, hunting, camping, fighters, kitchen or customer design. Technical: Forges carbon steel and own pattern welded steels. Prices: $225 to $2000. Remarks: Full-time maker. Winner of 1999 and 2000 Spring Hammering Cutting contest. Winner of Best Value of Show 2001; Arkansas Knife Show and Journeyman Smith. Border Guard Forge. Mark: Barker JS.

BARKER, ROBERT G.,
2311 Branch Rd, Bishop, GA 30621, Phone: 706-769-7827
Specialties: Traditional working/using straight knives of his design. Patterns: Bowies, hunters and utility knives, ABS Journeyman Smith. Technical: Hand forged carbon and Damascus. Forges to shape high-carbon 5160, cable and chain. Differentially heat-treats. Prices: $200 to $500; some to $1000. Remarks: Spare-time maker; first knife sold in 1987. Mark: BARKER/J.S.

BARKER, STUART,
14 Belvoir Close, Oadby, Leicester, ENGLAND LE2 4SG, Phone: +44 7887 585411, sc_barker@hotmail.com Web: www.barkerknives.co.uk
Specialties: Fixed blade working knives of his design. Patterns: Kitchen, hunter, utility/camp knives. Technical: Grinds O1, Rw134 & Damasteel, hand rubbed or shot blast finishes. Prices: $150 - $1,000. Remarks: Part-time maker; first knife sold 2006. Mark: Last initial or last name.

BARKES, TERRY,
14844 N. Bluff Rd., Edinburgh, IN 46124, Phone: 812-526-6390, knifenpocket@sbcglobal.net; Web:http:// my.hsonline.net/wizard/TerryBarkesKnives.htm
Specialties: Traditional working straight knives of his designs. Patterns: Drop point hunters, boot knives, skinning, fighter, utility, all purpose, camp, and grill knives. Technical: Grinds 1095 - 1084 - 52100 - 01, Hollow grinds and flat grinds. Hand rubbed finish from 400 to 2000 grit or High polish buff. Hard edge and soft back, heat treat by maker. Likes File work, natural handle material, bone, stag, water buffalo horn, wildbeast bone, ironwood. Prices: $200 and up Remarks: Full-time maker, first knifge sold in 2005. Doing business as Barkes Knife Shop. Marks: Barkes - USA, Barkes Double Arrow - USA

BARLOW, JANA POIRIER,
3820 Borland Cir, Anchorage, AK 99517, Phone: 907-243-4581

BARNES, AUBREY G.,
11341 Rock Hill Rd, Hagerstown, MD 21740, Phone: 301-223-4587, a.barnes@myactv.net
Specialties: Classic Moran style reproductions and using knives of his own design. Patterns: Bowies, hunters, fighters, daggers and camping knives. Technical: Forges 5160, 1085, L6 and Damascus, Silver wire inlays. Prices: $500 to $5000. Remarks: Full-time maker; first knife sold in 1992. Doing business as Falling Waters Forge. Mark: First and middle initials, last name, M.S.

BARNES, GARY L.,
Box 138, New Windsor, MD 21776-0138, Phone: 410-635-6243, Fax: 410-635-6243, mail@glbarnes.com; Web: www.glbarnes.com or www.barnespneumatic.com
Specialties: Ornate button lock Damascus folders. Patterns: Barnes original. Technical: Forges own Damascus. Prices: Average $2500. Remarks: ABS Master Smith since 1983. Mark: Hand engraved logo of letter B pierced by dagger.

BARNES, GREGORY,
266 W Calaveras St, Altadena, CA 91001, Phone: 626-398-0053, snake@annex.com

BARNES, JACK,
PO Box 1315, Whitefish, MT 59937-1315, Phone: 406-862-6078

BARNES, MARLEN R.,
904 Crestview Dr S, Atlanta, TX 75551-1854, Phone: 903-796-3668, MRBlives@worldnet.att.net
Specialties: Hammer forges random and mosaic Damascus. Patterns: Hatchets, straight and folding knives. Technical: Hammer forges carbon steel using 5160, 1084 and 52100 with 15N20 and 203E nickel. Prices: $150 and up. Remarks: Part-time maker; first knife sold 1999. Mark: Script M.R.B., other side J.S.

BARNES, WENDELL,
PO Box 272, Clinton, MT 59825, Phone: 406-825-0908
Specialties: Working straight knives. Patterns: Hunters, folders, neck knives. Technical: Grinds 440C, ATS-34, D2 and Damascus. Prices: Start at $75. Remarks: Spare-time maker; first knife sold in 1996. Mark: First initial, split heart, last name.

BARNES JR., CECIL C.,
141 Barnes Dr, Center Ridge, AR 72027, Phone: 501-893-2267

BARNETT, BRUCE,
PO Box 447, Mundaring, WA, AUSTRALIA 6073, Phone: 61-4-19243855, bruce@barnettcustomknives.com; web: www.barnettcustomknives.com
Specialties: Most types of fixed blades, folders, carving sets. Patterns: Hunters, Bowies, Camp Knives, Fighters, Lockback and Slipjoint Folders. Prices: $200 up
Remarks: Part time maker. Member Australian Knifemakers Guild and ABS journeyman smith. Mark: Barnett + J.S.

BARNETT, VAN,
BARNETT INT'L INC, 1135 Terminal Way Ste #209, Reno, NV 89502, Phone: 304-727-5512; 775-513-6969; 775-686-9084, ImATimeMachine@gmail.com & illusionknives@gmail.com; Web: www.VanBarnett.com
Specialties: Collector grade one-of-a-kind / embellished high art daggers and art folders. Patterns: Art daggers and folders. Technical: Forges and grinds own Damascus. Prices: Upscale. Remarks: Designs and makes one-of-a-kind highly embellished art knives using high karat gold, diamonds and other gemstones, pearls, stone and fossil ivories, carved steel guards and blades, all knives are carved and or engraved, does own engraving, carving and other embellishments, sole authorship; full-time maker since 1981. Does one high art collaboration a year with Dellana. Member of ABS. Member Art Knife Invitational Group (AKI) Mark: VBARNETT

BARR, JUDSON C.,
1905 Pickwick Circle, Irving, TX 75060, Phone: 214-724-0564, judsonbarrknives@yahoo.com
Specialties: Bowies. Patterns: Sheffield and Early American. Technical: Forged carbon steel and Damascus. Also stock removal. Remarks: Journeyman member of ABS. Mark: Barr.

BARRETT, RICK L. (TOSHI HISA),
18943 CR 18, Goshen, IN 46528, Phone: 574-533-4297, barrettrick@hotmail.com
Specialties: Japanese-style blades from sushi knives to katana and fantasy pieces. Patterns: Swords, axes, spears/lances, hunter and utility knives. Technical: Forges and grinds Damascus and carbon steels, occasionally uses stainless. Prices: $250 to $4000+. Remarks: Full-time bladesmith, jeweler. Mark: Japanese mei on Japanese pieces and stylized initials.

BARRON, BRIAN,
123 12th Ave, San Mateo, CA 94402, Phone: 650-341-2683
Specialties: Traditional straight knives. Patterns: Daggers, hunters and swords. Technical: Grinds 440C, ATS-34 and 1095. Sculpts bolsters using an S-curve. Prices: $130 to $270; some to $1500. Remarks: Part-time maker; first knife sold in 1993. Mark: Diamond Drag "Barron."

BARRY, SCOTT,
Box 354, Laramie, WY 82073, Phone: 307-721-8038, scottyb@uwyo.edu
Specialties: Currently producing mostly folders, also make fixed blade hunters & fillet knives. Technical: Steels used are 440/C, ATS/34, 154/CM, S30V, Damasteel & Mike Norris stainless Damascus. Prices: Range from $300 $1000. Remarks: Part-time maker. First knife sold in 1972. Mark: DSBarry, etched on blade.

BARRY III, JAMES J.,
115 Flagler Promenade No., West Palm Beach, FL 33405, Phone: 561-832-4197
Specialties: High-art working straight knives of his design also high art tomahawks. Patterns: Hunters, daggers and fishing knives. Technical: Grinds 440C only. Prefers exotic materials for handles. Most knives embellished with filework, carving and scrimshaw. Many pieces designed to stand unassisted. Prices: $500 to $10,000. Remarks: Part-time maker; first knife sold in 1975. Guild member (Knifemakers) since 1991. Mark: Branded initials as a J and B together.

BARTH, J.D.,
101 4th St, PO Box 186, Alberton, MT 59820, Phone: 406-722-4557, mtdeerhunter@blackfoot.net; Web: www.jdbarthcustomknives.com
Specialties: Working and fancy straight knives of his design. LinerLock® folders, stainless and Damascus, fully file worked, nitre bluing. Technical: Grinds ATS-34, 440-C, stainless and carbon Damascus. Uses variety of natural handle materials and Micarta. Likes dovetailed bolsters. Filework on most knives, full and tapered tangs. Makes custom fit sheaths for each knife. Mark: Name over maker, city and state.

BARTLOW, JOHN,
14 Red Fox Dr., Sheridan, WY 82801, Phone: 307-673-4941, 2jbartlow@gmail.com
Specialties: Skinner/caper sets, classic working patterns, and known for bird-and-trout classics. Technical: ATS-34, CPM-154, damascus available on all LinerLocks. Prices: $400 to $2,500. Remarks: Full-time maker, Guild member from 1988. Mark: Bartlow Sheridan, Wyo.

BASKETT, BARBARA,
427 Sutzer Ck Rd, Eastview, KY 42732, Phone: 270-862-5019, baskettknives@windstream.net
Specialties: Hunters and LinerLocks. Technical: 440-C, CPM 154, S30V. Prices: $250 and up. Mark: B. Baskett.

BASKETT, LEE GENE,
427 Sutzer Ck. Rd., Eastview, KY 42732, Phone: 270-862-5019, Fax: Cell: 270-766-8724, baskettknives@hotmail.com Web: www.baskettknives.com
Specialties: Fancy working knives and fancy art pieces, often set up in fancy desk stands.
Patterns: Fighters, Bowies, and Survial Knives; lockback folders and liner locks along with traditional styles. Cutting competition knives.
Technical: Grinds O1, 440-c, S30V, power CPM154, CPM 4, D2, buys Damascus. Filework provided on most knives.
Prices: $250 and up.
Remarks: Part-time maker, first knife sold in 1980.
Mark: Baskett

BASSETT, DAVID J.,
P.O. Box 69-102, Glendene, Auckland, NEW ZEALAND 0645, Phone: 64 9 818 9033, Fax: 64 9 818 9013, david@customknifemaking.co.nz; Web:www.customknifemaking.co.nz
Specialties: Working/using knives. Patterns: Hunters, fighters, boot, skinners, tanto. Technical: Grinds 440C, 12C27, D2 and some Damascus via stock removal method. Prices: $150 to $500. Remarks: Part-time maker, first knife sold in 2006. Also carries range of natural and synthetic handle material, pin stock etc. for sale. Mark: Name over country in semi-circular design.

BATLEY, MARK S.,
PO Box 217, Wake, VA 23176, Phone: 804 776-7794

BATSON, JAMES,
176 Brentwood Lane, Madison, AL 35758, Phone: 256-971-6860
Specialties: Forged Damascus blades and fittings in collectible period pieces. Patterns: Integral art knives, Bowies, folders, American-styled blades and miniatures. Technical: Forges carbon steel and his Damascus. Prices: $150 to $1800; some to $4500. Remarks: Semi retired full-time maker; first knife sold in 1978. Mark: Name, bladesmith with horse's head.

BATSON, RICHARD G.,
6591 Waterford Rd, Rixeyville, VA 22737, Phone: 540-937-2318, mbatson6591@comcast.net
Specialties: Military, utility and fighting knives in working and presentation grade. Patterns: Daggers, combat and utility knives. Technical: Grinds O1, 1095 and 440C. Etches and scrimshaws; offers polished, Parkerized finishes. Prices: $400 to $1,750. Remarks: Very limited production to active-dute military and vets only. First knife sold in 1958. Mark: Bat in circle, hand-signed and serial numbered.

BATTS, KEITH,
500 Manning Rd, Hooks, TX 75561, Phone: 903-277-8466, kbatts@cableone.net
Specialties: Working straight knives of his design or to customer specs. Patterns: Bowies, hunters, skinners, camp knives and others. Technical: Forges 5160 and his Damascus; offers filework. Prices: $245 to $895. Remarks: Part-time maker; first knife sold in 1988. Mark: Last name.

BAUCHOP, ROBERT,
PO Box 330, Munster, KN, SOUTH AFRICA 4278, Phone: +27 39 3192449
Specialties: Fantasy knives; working and using knives of his design and to customer specs. Patterns: Hunters, swords, utility/camp knives, diver's knives and large swords. Technical: Grinds Sandvick 12C27, D2, 440C. Uses South African hardwoods red ivory, wild olive, African blackwood, etc. on handles. Prices: $200 to $800; some to $2000. Remarks: Full-time maker; first knife sold in 1986. Doing business as Bauchop Custom Knives and Swords. Mark: Viking helmet with Bauchop (bow and chopper) crest.

BAXTER, DALE,
291 County Rd 547, Trinity, AL 35673, Phone: 256-355-3626, dale@baxterknives.com
Specialties: Bowies, fighters, and hunters. Patterns: No patterns: all unique true customs. Technical: Hand forge and hand finish. Steels: 1095 and L6 for carbon blades, 1095/L6 for Damascus. Remarks: Full-time bladesmith and sold first knife in 1998. Mark: Dale Baxter (script) and J.S. on reverse.

BEAM, JOHN R.,
1310 Foothills Rd, Kalispell, MT 59901, Phone: 406-755-2593
Specialties: Classic, high-art and working straight knives of his design. Patterns: Bowies and hunters. Technical: Grinds 440C, Damascus and scrap. Prices: $175 to $600; some to $3000. Remarks: Part-time maker; first knife sold in 1950. Doing business as Beam's Knives. Mark: Beam's Knives.

BEASLEY, GENEO,
PO Box 339, Wadsworth, NV 89442, Phone: 775-575-2584

BEATTY, GORDON H.,
121 Petty Rd, Seneca, SC 29672, Phone: 864-882-6278
Specialties: Working straight knives, some fancy. Patterns: Traditional patterns, mini-skinners and letter openers. Technical: Grinds 440C, D2 and ATS-34; makes knives one-at-a-time. Prices: $75 to $450. Remarks: Part-time maker; first knife sold in 1982. Mark: Name.

BEATY, ROBERT B.,
CUTLER, 1995 Big Flat Rd, Missoula, MT 59804, Phone: 406-549-1818
Specialties: Plain and fancy working knives and collector pieces; will accept custom orders. Patterns: Hunters, Bowies, utility, kitchen and camp knives; locking folders. Technical: Grinds D-2, ATS-34, Dendritie D-2, makes all tool steel Damascus, forges 1095, 5160, 52100. Prices: $150 to $600, some to $1100. Remarks: Full-time maker; first knife sold 1995. Mark: Stainless: First name, middle initial, last name, city and state. Carbon: Last name stamped on Ricasso.

BEAUCHAMP, GAETAN,
125 de la Rivire, Stoneham, QC, CANADA G3C 0P6, Phone: 418-848-1914, Fax: 418-848-6859, knives@gbeauchamp.ca; Web: www.gbeauchamp.ca
Specialties: Working knives and folders of his design and to customer specs. Patterns: Hunters, fighters, fantasy knives. Technical: Grinds ATS-34, 440C, Damascus. Scrimshaws on ivory; specializes in buffalo horn and black backgrounds. Offers a variety of handle materials. Prices: Start at $250. Remarks: Full-time maker; first knife sold in 1992. Mark: Signature etched on blade.

BECKER, FRANZ,
AM Kreuzberg 2, Marktl, GERMANY 84533, Phone: 08678-8020
Specialties: Stainless steel knives in working sizes. Patterns: Semi- and full-integral knives; interframe folders. Technical: Grinds stainless steels; likes natural handle materials. Prices: $200 to $2000. Mark: Name, country.

BEERS, RAY,
2501 Lakefront Dr, Lake Wales, FL 33898, Phone: 443-841-4143, rbknives@copper.net

BEETS, MARTY,
390 N 5th Ave, Williams Lake, BC, CANADA V2G 2G4, Phone: 250-392-7199
Specialties: Working and collectable straight knives of his own design. Patterns: Hunter, skinners, Bowies and utility knives. Technical: Grinds various steels-does all his own work including heat treating. Uses a variety of handle material specializing in exotic hardwoods, antler and horn. Price: $125 to $400. Remarks: Wife, Sandy does handmade/hand stitched sheaths. First knife sold in 1988. Business name Beets Handmade Knives.

BEGG, TODD M.,
1341 N. McDowell Blvd., Ste. D, Petaluma, CA 94954, Phone: 707-242-1790, info@beggknives.com; Web: http://beggknives.net
Specialties: High-grade tactical folders and fixed blades. Patterns: Folders, integrals, fighters. Technical: Specializes in flipper folders using "IK135" bearing system. Price: $400 - $15,000. Remarks: Uses modern designs and materials.

BEHNKE, WILLIAM,
8478 Dell Rd, Kingsley, MI 49649, Phone: 231-263-7447, bill@billbehnkeknives.com Web: www.billbehnkeknives.com
Specialties: Hunters, belt knives, folders, hatchets, straight razors, high-end letter openers and tomahawks. Patterns: Traditional styling in moderate-sized straight and folding knives. Technical: Forges own damascus, prefers W-2. Prices: $150 to $2,000. Remarks: Part-time maker. Mark: Bill Behnke Knives.

BELL, DON,
Box 98, Lincoln, MT 59639, Phone: 406-362-3208, dlb@lintcel.net
Patterns: Folders, hunters and custom orders. Technical: Carbon steel 52100, 5160, 1095, 1084. Making own Damascus. Flat grinds. Natural handle material including fossil. ivory, pearl, & ironwork. Remarks: Full-time maker. First knife sold in 1999. Mark: Last name.

BELL, DONALD,
2 Division St, Bedford, NS, CANADA B4A 1Y8, Phone: 902-835-2623, donbell@accesswave.ca; Web: www.bellknives.com
Specialties: Fancy knives: carved and pierced folders of his own design. Patterns: Locking folders, pendant knives, jewelry knives. Technical: Grinds Damascus, pierces and carves blades. Prices: $500 to $2000, some to $3000. Remarks: Spare-time maker; first knife sold in 1993. Mark: Bell symbol with first initial inside.

BELL, GABRIEL,
88321 North Bank Lane, Coquille, OR 97423, Phone: 541-396-3605, gabriel@dragonflyforge.com; Web: www.dragonflyforge.com & tomboyama.com
Specialties: Full line of combat quality Japanese swords. Patterns: Traditional tanto to katana. Technical: Handmade steel and welded cable. Prices: Swords from bare blades to complete high art $1500 to $28,000. Remarks: Studied with father Michael Bell. Instruction in sword crafts. Working in partnership with Michael Bell. Mark: Dragonfly in shield or kunitoshi.

BELL, MICHAEL,
88321 N Bank Lane, Coquille, OR 97423, Phone: 541-396-3605, michael@dragonflyforge.com; Web: www.Dragonflyforge.com & tomboyama.com
Specialties: Full line of combat quality Japanese swords. Patterns: Traditional tanto to katana. Technical: Handmade steel and welded cable. Prices: Swords from bare blades to complete high art $1500 to $28,000. Remarks: Studied with Japanese master Nakajima Muneyoshi. Instruction in sword crafts. Working in partnership with son, Gabriel. Mark: Dragonfly in shield or tombo kunimitsu.

BELL, TONY,
PO Box 24, Woodland, AL 36280, Phone: 256-449-2655, tbell905@aol.com
Specialties: Hand forged period knives and tomahawks. Art knives and knives made for everyday use.Technical:Makes own Damascus. Forges 1095, 5160,1080,L6 steels. Does own heat treating. Prices:$75-$1200. Remarks:Full time maker. Mark:Bell symbol with initial T in the middle.

BENDIK, JOHN,
7076 Fitch Rd, Olmsted Falls, OH 44138

BENJAMIN JR., GEORGE,
3001 Foxy Ln, Kissimmee, FL 34746, Phone: 407-846-7259
Specialties: Fighters in various styles to include Persian, Moro and military. Patterns: Daggers, skinners and one-of-a-kind grinds. Technical: Forges O1, D2, A2, 5160 and Damascus. Favors Pakkawood, Micarta, and mirror or Parkerized finishes. Makes unique para-military leather sheaths. Prices: $150 to $600; some to $1200. Remarks: Doing business as The Leather Box. Mark: Southern Pride Knives.

BENNETT, BRETT C,
5105 Retreat Rd. NE, Kensington, OH 44427, Phone: 307-220-3919, brett@bennettknives.com; Web: www.bennettknives.com
Specialties: Hand-rubbed finish on all blades. Patterns: Most fixed blade patterns. Technical: ATS-34, D-2, 1084/15N20 Damascus, 1084 forged. Prices: $100 and up. Mark: "B.C. Bennett" in script or "Bennett" stamped in script.

BENNETT, GLEN C,
5821 S Stewart Blvd, Tucson, AZ 85706

BENNETT, PETER,
PO Box 143, Engadine, NSW, AUSTRALIA 2233, Phone: 02-520-4975 (home), Fax: 02-528-8219 (work)
Specialties: Fancy and embellished working and using straight knives to customer specs and in standard patterns. Patterns: Fighters, hunters, bird/trout and fillet knives. Technical: Grinds 440C, ATS-34 and Damascus. Uses rare Australian desert timbers for handles. Prices: $90 to $500; some to $1500. Remarks: Full-time maker; first knife sold in 1985. Mark: First and middle initials, last name; country.

BENNICA, CHARLES,
11 Chemin du Salet, Moules et Baucels, FRANCE 34190, Phone: +33 4 67 73 42 40, cbennica@bennica-knives.com; Web: www.bennica-knives.com
Specialties: Fixed blades and folding knives; the latter with slick closing mechanisms with push buttons to unlock blades. Unique handle shapes, signature to the maker. Technical: 416 stainless steel frames for folders and ATS-34 blades. Also specializes in Damascus.

BENSINGER, J. W.,
583 Jug Brook Rd., Marshfield, VT 05658, Phone: 802-917-1789, jwbensinger@gmail.com Web: www.vermontbladesmith.com
Specialties: Working hunters, bowies for work and defense, and Finnish patterns. Occasional folders. Technical: High performance handforged knives in 5160, 52100, 1080, and in-house damascus. Prices: Range from $130 for simple bushcraft knives to $500 for larger knives. Damascus prices on request. Remarks: First knife made in 1980 or so. Full-time maker. Customer designs welcome. Mark: "JWB" and year in cursive.

BENSON, DON,
2505 Jackson St #112, Escalon, CA 95320, Phone: 209-838-7921
Specialties: Working straight knives of his design. Patterns: Axes, Bowies, tantos and hunters. Technical: Grinds 440C. Prices: $100 to $150; some to $400. Remarks: Spare-time maker; first knife sold in 1980. Mark: Name.

BENTLEY, C L,
2405 Hilltop Dr, Albany, GA 31707, Phone: 912-432-6656

BER, DAVE,
656 Miller Rd, San Juan Island, WA 98250, Phone: 206-378-7230
Specialties: Working straight and folding knives for the sportsman; welcomes customer designs. Patterns: Hunters, skinners, Bowies, kitchen and fishing knives. Technical: Forges and grinds saw blade steel, wire Damascus, O1, L6, 5160 and 440C. Prices: $100 to $300; some to $500. Remarks: Full-time maker; first knife sold in 1985. Mark: Last name.

BERG, LEE,
PO Box 267, Ketchum, OK 74349, kilatstrike@wavelinx.net
Specialties: One-of-a-kind and investment-quality straight knives of his own design, incorporating traditional, period, Near East and Asian influence. Patterns: Daggers, fighters, hunters, bowies, short swords, full size and miniature. Technical: Stock removal with file, damascus, meteorite, O1, D2 and ATS-34. Prices: $200 and up. Remarks: Part-time maker; first knife sold in 1972. Mark: Full name.

BERG, LOTHAR,
37 Hillcrest Ln, Kitchener ON, CANADA NZK 1S9, Phone: 519-745-3260; 519-745-3260

BERGER, MAX A.,
5716 John Richard Ct, Carmichael, CA 95608, Phone: 916-972-9229, bergerknives@aol.com
Specialties: Fantasy and working/using straight knives of his design. Patterns: Fighters, hunters and utility/camp knives. Technical: Grinds ATS-34 and 440C. Offers fileworks and combinations of mirror polish and satin finish blades. Prices: $200 to $600; some to $2500. Remarks: Part-time maker; first knife sold in 1992. Mark: Last name.

BERGH, ROGER,
Dalkarlsa 291, Bygdea, SWEDEN 91598, Phone: 469-343-0061, knivroger@hotmail.com; Web: www.rogerbergh.com
Specialties: Collectible all-purpose straight-blade knives. Damascus steel blades, carving and artistic design knives are heavily influenced by nature and have an organic hand crafted feel.

BERGLIN, BRUCE,
17441 Lake Terrace Place, Mount Vernon, WA 98274, Phone: 360-422-8603, bruce@berglins.com
Specialties: Working fixed blades and folders of his own design. Patterns: Hunters, boots, bowies, utility, liner locks and slip joints some with vintage finish. Technical: Forges carbon steel, grinds carbon steel. Prefers natural handle material. Prices: Start at $300. Remarks: Part-time maker since 1998. Mark: (2 marks) 1. Last name; or 2. First initial, second initial & last name, surrounded with an oval.

BERTOLAMI, JUAN CARLOS,
Av San Juan 575, Neuquen, ARGENTINA 8300, fliabertolami@infovia.com.ar
Specialties: Hunting and country labor knives. All of them unique high quality

pieces and supplies collectors too. Technical: Austrian stainless steel and elephant, hippopotamus and orca ivory, as well as ebony and other fine woods for the handles.

BERTUZZI, ETTORE,
Via Partigiani 3, Seriate, Bergamo, ITALY 24068, Phone: 035-294262, Fax: 035-294262
Specialties: Classic straight knives and folders of his design, to customer specs and in standard patterns. Patterns: Bowies, hunters and locking folders. Technical: Grinds ATS-34, D3, D2 and various Damascus. Prices: $300 to $500. Remarks: Part-time maker; first knife sold in 1993. Mark: Name etched on ricasso.

BESEDICK, FRANK E,
1257 Country Club Road, Monongahela, PA 15063-1057, Phone: 724-292-8016, bxtr.bez3@verizon.net
Specialties: Traditional working and using straight knives of his design. Patterns: Hunters, utility/camp knives and miniatures; buckskinner blades and tomahawks. Technical: Forges and grinds 5160, O1 and Damascus. Offers filework and scrimshaw. Prices: $75 to $300; some to $750. Remarks: Part-time maker; first knife sold in 1990. Mark: Name or initials.

BESHARA, BRENT (BESH),
PO BOX 557, Holyrood, NL, CANADA A0A 2R0, Phone: 705-428-3152, BESH@beshknives.com Web: www.beshknives.com
Specialties: Fixed blade tools and knives. Patterns: BESH Wedge tools and knives. Technical: Custom design work, grinds 0-1, D-2, 440C, 154cm. Offers kydex sheathing Prices: Start at $250. Remarks: Inventor of BESH Wedge geometry, custom maker and designer since 2000. Retired (24yrs) Special Forces, Special Operations Navy bomb disposal diver. Lifelong martial artist. Mark: "BESH" stamped.

BEST, RON,
1489 Adams Lane, Stokes, NC 27884, Phone: 252-714-1264, ronbestknives@msn.com; Web: www.ronbestknives.com
Specialties: Folders and automatics. Patterns: Bowies, hunters, fighters, fantasy, daggers & swords. Technical: Grinds 440C, D-2 and ATS-34. Prices: $600 to $8000.

BETANCOURT, ANTONIO L.,
5718 Beefwood Ct., St. Louis, MO 63129, Phone: 314-306-1869, bet2001@charter.net
Specialties: One-of-a-kind fixed blades and art knives. Patterns: Hunters and Bowies with embellished handles. Technical: Uses cast sterling silver and lapidary with fine gemstones, fossil ivory, and scrimshaw. Grinds Damascus and 440C. Prices: $100 to $800. Remarks: Part-time maker, first knife sold in 1974. Mark: Initials in cursive.

BEUKES, TINUS,
83 Henry St, Risiville, Vereeniging, GT, SOUTH AFRICA 1939, Phone: 27 16 423 2053
Specialties: Working straight knives. Patterns: Hunters, skinners and kitchen knives. Technical: Grinds D2, 440C and chain, cable and stainless Damascus. Prices: $80 to $180. Remarks: Part-time maker; first knife sold in 1993. Mark: Full name, city, logo.

BEVERLY II, LARRY H,
PO Box 741, Spotsylvania, VA 22553, Phone: 540-846-5426, beverlyknives@aol.com
Specialties: Working straight knives, slip-joints and liner locks. Welcomes customer designs. Patterns: Bowies, hunters, guard less fighters and miniatures. Technical: Grinds 440C, A2 and O1. Prices: $125 to $1000. Remarks: Part-time maker; first knife sold in 1986. Mark: Initials or last name in script.

BEZUIDENHOUT, BUZZ,
PO BOX 28284, Malvern, KZN, SOUTH AFRICA 4055, Phone: 031-4632827, Fax: 031-4632827, buzzbee@mweb.co.za
Specialties: Working and Fancy Folders, my or customer design.Patterns: Boots, hunters, kitchen knives and utility/camp knives. Technical: Use 12-C-27 + stainless damascus, some carbon damascus. Uses local hardwoods, horn: kudu, impala, buffalo, giraffe bone and ivory for handles.
Prices: $250 to upscale. Remarks: Part-time maker; first knife sold in 1985. Member S.A. Knife Makers GuildMark: First name with a bee emblem.

BIGGERS, GARY,
5954 Chestnut Pl., Camarillo, CA 93012-4332, Phone: 805-484-0375
Specialties: Fixed blade knives of his design. Patterns: Hunters, boots/fighters, Bowies and utility knives. Technical: Grinds ATS-34, O1 and commercial Damascus. Prices: $150 to $550. Remarks: Part-time maker; first knife sold in 1996. Doing business as Ventura Knives. Mark: First and last name, city and state.

BILLGREN, PER,
Stallgatan 9, Soderfors, SWEDEN 81576, Phone: +46 293 30600, Fax: +46 293 30124, mail@damasteel.se Web:www.damasteel.se
Specialties: Damasteel, stainless Damascus steels. Patterns: Bluetongue, Heimskringla, Muhammad's ladder, Rose, Twist, Odin's eye, Vinland, Hakkapelliitta. Technical: Modern Damascus steel made by patented powder metallurgy method. Prices: $80 to $180. Remarks: Damasteel is available through distributors around the globe.

BINGENHEIMER, BRUCE,
553 Tiffany Dr., Spring Creek, NV 89815, Phone: 775-934-6295, mbing@citlink.net
Specialties: Forging fixed blade hunters, bowies, fighters. Technical: Forges own Damascus. Steel choices 5160, 1084. Damascus steels 15N20, 1080. Prices: $300 and up. Remarks: ABS Journeyman Smith 2010. Member of Montana Knife Makers Association and Oregon Knife Collector's Association. Mark: Bingenheimer (arched over) M B.

BIRDWELL, IRA LEE,
PO Box 1448, Congress, AZ 85332, Phone: 928-925-3258, heli.ira@gmail.com
Specialties: Special orders. Mark: Engraved signature.

BISH, HAL,
9347 Sweetbriar Trace, Jonesboro, GA 30236, Phone: 770-477-2422, hal-bish@hp.com

BISHER, WILLIAM (BILL),
1015 Beck Road, Denton, NC 27239, Phone: 336-859-4686, blackturtleforge@wildblue.net;Web: www.blackturtleforge.com
Specialties: Period pieces, also contemporary belt knives, friction folders. Patterns: Own design, hunters, camp/utility, Bowies, belt axes, neck knives, carving sets. Technical: Forges straight high carbon steels, and own Damascus, grinds ATS34 and 154CM. Uses natural handle materials (wood, bone, stag horn), micarta and stabilized wood. Prices: Starting at $75 - $2500. Remarks: Past president of North Carolina Custom Knifemakers Guild, member ABS, Full-time maker as of 2007, first knife made 1989, all work in house, blades and sheaths Mark: Last name under crown and turtle

BIZZELL, ROBERT,
145 Missoula Ave, Butte, MT 59701, Phone: 406-782-4403, patternweld@yahoo.com
Specialties: Damascus Bowies. Patterns: Composite, mosaic and traditional. Technical: Fixed blades & LinerLock® folders. Prices: Fixed blades start at $275. Folders start at $500. Remarks: Currently not taking orders. Mark: Hand signed.

BLACK, EARL,
3466 South, 700 East, Salt Lake City, UT 84106, Phone: 801-466-8395
Specialties: High-art straight knives and folders; period pieces. Patterns: Boots, Bowies and daggers; lockers and gents. Technical: Grinds 440C and 154CM. Buys some Damascus. Scrimshaws and engraves. Prices: $200 to $1800; some to $2500 and higher. Remarks: Full-time maker; first knife sold in 1980. Mark: Name, city, state.

BLACK, SCOTT,
27100 Leetown Rd, Picayune, MS 39466, Phone: 601-799-5939, copperheadforge@telepak.net
Specialties: Friction folders; fighters. Patterns: Bowies, fighters, hunters, smoke hawks, friction folders, daggers. Technical: All forged, all work done by him, own hand-stitched leather work; own heat-treating. Prices: $100 to $2200. Remarks: ABS Journeyman Smith. Cabel / Damascus/ High Carbone. Mark: Hot Mark - Copperhead Snake.

BLACK, TOM,
921 Grecian NW, Albuquerque, NM 87107, Phone: 505-344-2549, blackknives@comcast.net
Specialties: Working knives to fancy straight knives of his design. Patterns: Drop-point skinners, folders, using knives, Bowies and daggers. Technical: Grinds 440C, 154CM, ATS-34, A2, D2, CPM-154 and damascus. Offers engraving and scrimshaw. Prices: $250 and up; some over $8500. Remarks: Full-time maker; first knife sold in 1970. Mark: Name, city.

BLACKWELL, ZANE,
PO BOX 234, Eden, TX 76837, Phone: 325-869-8821, blackwellknives@hotmail.com; Web: www.blackwellknives.com
Specialties: Hunters and slip-joint folders. Patterns: Drop-point and clip-point hunters, and classic slip-joint patterns like single-blade trappers. Technical: Stainless steel blades and natural handle materials. Prices: Hunters start at $275, single-blade folders at $300. Remarks: Six-month back log. Mark: Zane Blackwell Eden Texas.

BLACKWOOD, NEIL,
7032 Willow Run, Lakeland, FL 33813, Phone: 863-812-5588, nblackwood4@gmail.com; Web: www.blackwoodcustomknives.blogspot.com
Specialties: Fixed blades and tactical folders. Technical: Blade steels D2 Talonite, Stellite, CPM S30V and RWL 34. Handle materials: G-10 carbon fiber and Micarta in the synthetics: giraffe bone and exotic woods on the natural side. Prices: $1000 to $1500. Remarks: Makes everything from the frames to the stop pins, pivot pins: everything but the stainless screws; one factory/custom collaboration (the Hybrid Hunter) with Outdoor Edge is in place and negotiations are under way for one with Benchmade. Collaborations with Boker. Mark: Blackwood

BLANCHARD, G R (GARY),
PO BOX 292, Dandridge, TN 37725, Phone: 865-397-9515, blanchardcustomknives@yahoo.com; Web: www.blanchardcustomknives.com
Specialties: Fancy folders with patented button blade release and high-art straight knives of his design. Patterns: Boots, daggers and locking folders. Technical: Grinds 440C and ATS-34 and Damascus. Engraves his knives. Prices: $1000 to $15,000 or more. Remarks: Full-time maker; first knife sold in 1989. Mark: First and middle initials, last name or last name only.

BLAUM, ROY,
319 N Columbia St, Covington, LA 70433, Phone: 985-893-1060
Specialties: Working straight knives and folders of his design; lightweight easy-open folders. Patterns: Hunters, boots, fishing and woodcarving/whittling knives. Technical: Grinds A2, D2, O1, 154CM and ATS-34. Offers leatherwork. Prices: $40 to $800; some higher. Remarks: Full-time maker; first knife sold in 1976. Mark: Engraved signature or etched logo.

BLOODWORTH CUSTOM KNIVES,
3502 W. Angelica Dr., Meridian, ID 83646, Phone: 208-888-7778
Patterns: Working straight knives, hunters, skinners, bowies, utility knives of his designs or customer specs. Scagel knives. Period knives and traditional frontier knives and sheaths. Technical: Grinds D2, ATS34, 154CM, 5160, 01, Damascus, Heat treats, natural and composite handle materials. Prices: $185.00 to $1,500. Remarks: Roger Smith knife maker. Full-time maker; first knife sold in 1978 Mark: Sword over BLOODWORTH.

BLOOMER, ALAN T,
PO Box 154, 116 E 6th St, Maquon, IL 61458, Phone: 309-875-3583 Cell: 309-371-8520, alant.bloomer@winco.net
Specialties: Folders & straight knives & custom pen maker. Patterns: All kinds. Technical: Does own heat treating. Prices: $400 to $1000. Remarks: Part-time maker. No orders. Mark: Stamp Bloomer.

BLUM, KENNETH,
1729 Burleson, Brenham, TX 77833, Phone: 979-836-9577
Specialties: Traditional working straight knives of his design. Patterns: Camp knives, hunters and Bowies. Technical: Forges 5160; grinds 440C and D2. Uses exotic woods and Micarta for handles. Prices: $150 to $300. Remarks: Part-time maker; first knife sold in 1978. Mark: Last name on ricasso.

BLYSTONE, RONALD L,
231 Bailey Road, Creekside, PA 15732, Phone: 724-397-2671, taxibly@hotmail.com
Specialties: Traditional forged working knives. Patterns: Hunting utility and skinners of his own design. Technical: Forges his own pattern welded Damascus using carbon steel. Prices: Starting at $150. Remarks: Spare-time maker. Mark: Initials - upsidedown R against the B, inside a circle, over the word FORGE

BOARDMAN, GUY,
39 Mountain Ridge R, New Germany, KZN, SOUTH AFRICA 3619, Phone: 031-726-921
Specialties: American and South African-styles. Patterns: Bowies, American and South African hunters, plus more. Technical: Grinds Bohler steels, some ATS-34. Prices: $100 to $600. Remarks: Part-time maker; first knife sold in 1986. Mark: Name, city, country.

BOCHMAN, BRUCE,
183 Howard Place, Grants Pass, OR 97526, Phone: 541-471-1985, 183bab@gmail.com
Specialties: Hunting, fishing, bird and tactical knives. Patterns: Hunters, fishing and bird knives. Technical: ATS34, 154CM, mirror or satin finish. Damascus. Prices: $250 to $350; some to $750. Remarks: Part-time maker; first knife sold in 1977. Mark: Custom Knives by B. Bochman

BODEN, HARRY,
Via Gellia Mill, Bonsall Matlock, Derbyshire, ENGLAND DE4 2AJ, Phone: 0629-825176
Specialties: Traditional working straight knives and folders of his design. Patterns: Hunters, locking folders and utility/camp knives. Technical: Grinds Sandvik 12C27, D2 and O1. Prices: £70 to £150; some to £300. Remarks: Full-time maker; first knife sold in 1986. Mark: Full name.

BODOLAY, ANTAL,
Rua Wilson Soares Fernandes #31, Planalto, Belo Horizonte, MG, BRAZIL MG-31730-700, Phone: 031-494-1885
Specialties: Working folders and fixed blades of his design or to customer specs; some art daggers and period pieces. Patterns: Daggers, hunters, locking folders, utility knives and Khukris. Technical: Grinds D6, high-carbon steels and 420 stainless. Forges files on request. Prices: $30 to $350. Remarks: Full-time maker; first knife sold in 1965. Mark: Last name in script.

BOEHLKE, GUENTER,
Parkstrasse 2, GERMANY 56412, Phone: 2602-5440, Boehlke-Messer@t-online.de; Web: www.boehlke-messer.de
Specialties: Classic working/using straight knives of his design. Patterns: Hunters, utility/camp knives and ancient remakes. Technical: Grinds Damascus, CPM-T-440V and 440C. Inlays gemstones and ivory. Prices: $220 to $700; some to $2000. Remarks: Spare-time maker; first knife sold in 1985. Mark: Name, address and bow and arrow.

BOGUSZEWSKI, PHIL,
PO Box 99329, Lakewood, WA 98499, Phone: 253-581-7096, knives01@aol.com
Specialties: Working folders—some fancy—mostly of his design. Patterns: Folders, slip-joints and lockers; also makes anodized titanium frame folders. Technical: Grinds BG42 and Damascus; offers filework. Prices: $550 to $3000. Remarks: Full-time maker; first knife sold in 1979. Mark: Name, city and state.

BOHRMANN, BRUCE,
61 Portland St, Yarmouth, ME 04096, Phone: 207-846-3385, bbohr@maine.rr.com; Web: Bohrmannknives.com
Specialties: Fixed-blade sporting, camp and hunting knives. Technical: Stock-removal maker using 13C26 Sandvik and 154CM stainless steels hardened to 58-60 Rockwell. Prices: $325-$395. Also, special "Heritage" production

using historic certified woods (from Washington's, Jefferson's, Madison's and Henry's Plantations; 45,000-50,000-year-old Kauri wood from New Zealand - $1,250. Remarks: Full-time maker; first knife made in 1955. Always developing new models and concepts, such as steak knives, fixed blades and miniatures with special pocket sheaths. All knives serial #'d and can be personalized by etching initials into blades. Mark: The letter "B" connected to and lying beneath deer antlers.

BOJTOS, ARPAD,
Dobsinskeho 10, 98403 Lucenec, SLOVAKIA, Phone: 00421-47 4333512; Cell: 00421-91 5875066, bojtos@stonline.sk; Web: www.arpadbojtos.sk
Specialties: Art knives, including over 100 folders. Patterns: Daggers, fighters and hunters. Technical: Grinds ATS-34 and stainless damascus. Carves on steel, handle materials and sheaths. Prices: $5000 to $10,000; some over. Remarks: Full-time maker; first knife sold in 1990. Mark: AB.

BOLDUC, GARY,
1419 Tanglewood Dr., Corona, CA 92882, Phone: 951-739-0137, gary@stillwaterwoods.com; Web: www.stillwaterwoods.com
Specialties: Fish fillet knives (larger sizes), medium 8" to large 10"-plus. Replica making of primitive Native Alaskan hunting and cutting tools, kitchen cutlery. Patterns: Hunters, skinners, fillet, boning, spear points and kitchen cutlery. Technical: High-quality stainless steel, mainly CTS-XHP and CPM154 for improved edge design. Prices: $200-$400 and up. Remarks: Full-time maker; first knife sold in 2007. Mark: First initial, last name with USA under.

BOLEWARE, DAVID,
PO Box 96, Carson, MS 39427, Phone: 601-943-5372
Specialties: Traditional and working/using straight knives of his design, to customer specs and in standard patterns. Patterns: Bowies, hunters and utility/camp knives. Technical: Grinds ATS-34, 440C and Damascus. Prices: $85 to $350; some to $600. Remarks: Part-time maker; first knife sold in 1989. Mark: First and last name, city, state.

BOLEY, JAMIE,
PO Box 477, Parker, SD 57053, Phone: 605-297-0014, jamie@polarbearforge.com
Specialties: Working knives and historical influenced reproductions. Patterns: Hunters, skinners, scramasaxes, and others.Technical: Forges 5160, O1, L6, 52100, W1, W2 makes own Damascus. Prices: Starts at $125. Remarks: Part-time maker. Mark: Polar bear paw print with name on the left side and Polar Bear Forge on the right.

BONASSI, FRANCO,
Via Nicoletta 4, Pordenone, ITALY 33170, Phone: 0434-550821, frank.bonassi@alice.it
Specialties: Fancy and working one-of-a-kind folder knives of his design. Patterns: Folders, linerlocks and back locks. Technical: Grinds CPM, ATS-34, 154CM and commercial Damascus. Uses only titanium foreguards and pommels. Prices: Start at $350. Remarks: Spare-time maker; first knife sold in 1988. Has made cutlery for several celebrities; Gen. Schwarzkopf, Fuzzy Zoeller, etc. Mark: FRANK.

BOOCO, GORDON,
175 Ash St, PO Box 174, Hayden, CO 81639, Phone: 970-276-3195
Specialties: Fancy working straight knives of his design and to customer specs. Patterns: Hunters and Bowies. Technical: Grinds 440C, D2 and A2. Heat-treats. Prices: $150 to $350; some $600 and higher. Remarks: Part-time maker; first knife sold in 1984. Mark: Last name with push dagger artwork.

BOOS, RALPH,
6018-37A Avenue NW, Edmonton, AB, CANADA T6L 1H4, Phone: 780-463-7094
Specialties: Classic, fancy and fantasy miniature knives and swords of his design and to customer specs. Patterns: Bowies, daggers and swords. Technical: Hand files O1, stainless and Damascus. Engraves and carves. Does heat bluing and acid etching. Prices: $125 to $350; some to $1000. Remarks: Part-time maker; first knife sold in 1982. Mark: First initials back to back.

BOOTH, PHILIP W,
301 S Jeffery Ave, Ithaca, MI 48847, Phone: 989-875-2844, Web: wwwphilipbooth.com
Specialties: Folding knives of his design using various mechanisms. Patterns: "Minnow" folding knives, a series of small folding knives started in 1996 and changing yearly. One of a kind hot-rod car themed folding knives. Technical: Grinds ATS-34, 1095 and commercial Damascus. Offers gun blue finishes and file work. Prices: $200 and up. Remarks: Part-time maker, first knife sold in 1991. Mark: Last name or name with city and map logo.

BORGER, WOLF,
Benzstrasse 8, Graben-Neudorf, GERMANY 76676, Phone: 07255-72303, Fax: 07255-72304, wolf@messerschmied.de; Web: www.messerschmied.de
Specialties: High-tech working and using straight knives and folders, many with corkscrews or other tools, of his design. Patterns: Hunters, Bowies and folders with various locking systems. Technical: Grinds 440C, ATS-34 and CPM. Uses stainless Damascus. Prices: $250 to $900; some to $1500. Remarks: Full-time maker; first knife sold in 1975. Mark: Howling wolf and name; first name on Damascus blades.

BOSE, REESE,
8810 N. County Rd. 375 E, Shelburn, IN 47879, Phone: 812-397-5114
Specialties: Traditional working and using knives in standard patterns and multi-blade folders. Patterns: Multi-blade slip-joints. Technical: ATS-34, D2, 154CM and CPM 440V. Prices: $600 to $3,000. Remarks: Full-time maker; first knife sold in 1992. Photos by Jack Busfield. Mark: R. Bose.

BOSE, TONY,
7252 N. County Rd, 300 E., Shelburn, IN 47879-9778, Phone: 812-397-5114
Specialties: Traditional working and using knives; multi-blade folders. Patterns: Multi-blade slip-joints. Technical: Grinds commercial Damascus, ATS-34 and D2. Prices: $400 to $1200. Remarks: Full-time maker; first knife sold in 1972. Mark: First initial, last name, city, state.

BOSSAERTS, CARL,
Rua Albert Einstein 906, Ribeirao Preto, SP, BRAZIL 14051-110, Phone: 016 633 7063
Specialties: Working and using straight knives of his design, to customer specs and in standard patterns. Patterns: Hunters, fighters and utility/camp knives. Technical: Grinds ATS-34, 440V and 440C; does filework. Prices: 60 to $400. Remarks: Part-time maker; first knife sold in 1992. Mark: Initials joined together.

BOST, ROGER E,
30511 Cartier Dr, Palos Verdes, CA 90275-5629, Phone: 310-541-6833, rogerbost@cox.net
Specialties: Hunters, fighters, boot, utility. Patterns: Loveless-style. Technical: ATS-34, BG-42, 440C, 59-61RC, stock removal and forge. Prices: $300 and up. Remarks: First knife sold in 1990. Cal. Knifemakers Assn., ABS. Mark: Diamond with initials inside and Palos Verdes California around outside.

BOSWORTH, DEAN,
329 Mahogany Dr, Key Largo, FL 33037, Phone: 305-451-1564, DLBOZ@bellsouth.net
Specialties: Free hand hollow ground working knives with hand rubbed satin finish, filework and inlays. Patterns: Bird and Trout, hunters, skinners, fillet, Bowies, miniatures. Technical: Using 440C, ATS-34, D2, Meier Damascus, custom wet formed sheaths. Prices: $250 and up. Remarks: Part-time maker; first knife made in 1985. Member Florida Knifemakers Assoc. Mark: BOZ stamped in block letters.

BOURBEAU, JEAN YVES,
15 Rue Remillard, Notre Dame, Ile Perrot, QC, CANADA J7V 8M9, Phone: 514-453-1069
Specialties: Fancy/embellished and fantasy folders of his design. Patterns: Bowies, fighters and locking folders. Technical: Grinds 440C, ATS-34 and Damascus. Carves precious wood for handles. Prices: $150 to $1000. Remarks: Part-time maker; first knife sold in 1994. Mark: Interlaced initials.

BOWLES, CHRIS,
PO Box 985, Reform, AL 35481, Phone: 205-375-6162
Specialties: Working/using straight knives, and period pieces. Patterns: Utility, tactical, hunting, neck knives, machetes, and swords. Grinds: 0-1, 154 cm, BG-42, 440V. Prices: $50 to $400 some higher. Remarks: Full-time maker. Mark: Bowles stamped or Bowles etched in script.

BOYD, FRANCIS,
1811 Prince St, Berkeley, CA 94703, Phone: 510-841-7210
Specialties: Folders and kitchen knives, Japanese swords. Patterns: Push-button sturdy locking folders; San Francisco-style chef's knives. Technical: Forges and grinds; mostly uses high-carbon steels. Prices: Moderate to heavy. Remarks: Designer. Mark: Name.

BOYE, DAVID,
PO Box 1238, Dolan Springs, AZ 86441, Phone: 800-853-1617, Fax: 928-767-4273, boye@cltlink.net; Web: www.boyeknives.com
Specialties: Folders and Boye Basics. Forerunner in the use of dendritic steel and dendritic cobalt for blades. Patterns: Lockback folders and fixed blade sheath knives in cobalt. Technical: Casts blades in cobalt. Prices: From $129 to $360. Remarks: Part-time maker; author of Step-by-Step Knifemaking. Mark: Name.

BOYES, TOM,
2505 Wallace Lake Rd., West Bend, WI 53090, Phone: 262-391-2172
Specialties: Hunters, skinners and fillets. Technical: Grinds ATS-34, 440C, O1 tool steel and Damascus. Prices: $60 to $1000. Remarks: First knife sold in 1998. Doing business as R. Boyes Knives.

BOYSEN, RAYMOND A,
125 E St Patrick, Rapid Ciy, SD 57701, Phone: 605-341-7752
Specialties: Hunters and Bowies. Technical: High performance blades forged from 52100 and 5160. Prices: $200 and up. Remarks: American Bladesmith Society Journeyman Smith. Part-time bladesmith. Mark: BOYSEN.

BRACH, PAUL,
4870 Widgeon Way, Cumming, GA 30028, Phone: 770-595-8952, Web: www.brachknives.com
Specialties: Standard and one-of-a-kind straight knives and locking folders. Nickel silver sheath fittings and gemstone settings used on high-end pieces. Patterns: Hunters, bowies, daggers, antique bowies and titanium-frame folders. Technical: Grinds CPM-154 and forges high-carbon steel. Usually flat or full convex grinds. Prices: $150 to $1,000+. Remarks: Part-time maker; first knife sold in 1984. Mark: Etched "Paul Brach maker Cumming, GA" or "Brach" stamped.

BRACKETT, JAMIN,
PO Box 387, Fallston, NC 28042, Phone: 704-718-3304, jaminbrackett@bellsouth.net; Web: brackettknives.com
Specialties: Hunting, camp, fishing, tactical, and general outdoor use. Handmade of my own design or to customer specs. Patterns: Drop point, tanto, fillet, and small EDC the "Tadpole", as well as large camp and tactical knives. Technical: Stock removal method, ATS-34 steel cryogenically treated to HRC

BRADBURN—BROOKER

59-61. Mirror polish and bead blasted finishes. Handle materials include exotic woods, stag, buffalo horn, colored laminates, Micarta, and G-10. Come hand stitched 8-9 OZ leather sheaths treated in beeswax saddle oil mixture. Tactical models include reinforced tactical nylon sheaths Mollie system compatible. Prices: Standard models $150-$325. Personalized engraving available, for gifts and special occasions. Remarks: Part-time maker. First knife made in 2009. Member of NC Custom Knifemakers Guild.Mark: "Brackett", in bold. Each knife and sheath numbered.

BRADBURN, GARY,
BRADBURN CUSTOM CUTLERY, 1714 Park Place, Wichita, KS 67203, Phone: 316-640-5684, gary@bradburnknives.com; Web:www.bradburnknives.com
Specialties: Specialize in clay-tempered Japanese-style knives and swords. Patterns: Also Bowies and fighters. Technical: Forge and/or grind carbon steel only. Prices: $150 to $1200. Mark: Initials GB stylized to look like Japanese character.

BRADFORD, GARRICK,
582 Guelph St, Kitchener, ON, CANADA N2H-5Y4, Phone: 519-576-9863

BRADLEY, DENNIS,
178 Bradley Acres Rd, Blairsville, GA 30512, Phone: 706-745-4364, bzbtaz@ brmemc.net; Web: www.dennisbradleyknives.com
Specialties: Working straight knives and folders, some high-art. Patterns: Hunters, boots and daggers; slip-joints and two-blades. Technical: Grinds ATS-34, D2, 440C and commercial Damascus. Prices: $100 to $500; some to $2000. Remarks: Part-time maker; first knife sold in 1973. Mark: BRADLEY KNIVES in double heart logo.

BRADLEY, GAYLE
1383 Old Garner Rd., Weatherford, TX 76088-8720, Phone: 817-504-2262, Bradleysblades@aol.com; Web: www.bradleysblades.com
Specialties: High-end folders with wedge locks of maker's own design or lock backs, and work/utility knives. Uses high-end materials, including lapidary work and black-lip-pearl handle inlays. Technical: Grinds blades from bar stock, performs own heat treating. Remarks: Full-time maker; first knife made in 1988.

BRADLEY, JOHN,
PO Box 33, Pomona Park, FL 32181, Phone: 386-649-4739, johnbradleyknives@ yahoo.com
Specialties: Fixed-blade using and art knives; primitive folders. Patterns: Skinners, Bowies, camp knives and primitive knives. Technical: Forged and ground 52100, 1095, O1 and Damascus. Prices: $250 to $2000. Remarks: Full-time maker; first knife sold in 1988. Mark: Last name.

BRANDSEY, EDWARD P,
4441 Hawkridge Ct, Janesville, WI 53546, Phone: 608-868-9010, ebrandsey@ centurytel.net
Patterns: Large bowies, hunters, neck knives and buckskinner-styles. Native American influence on some. An occasional tanto, art piece. Does own scrimshaw. See Egnath's second book. Now making locking liner folders. Technical: ATS-34, CPM154, 440-C, 0-1 and some damascus. Paul Bos heat treating past 20 years. Prices: $350 to $800; some to $4,000. Remarks: Full-time maker; first knife sold in 1973. Mark: Initials connected - registered Wisc. Trademark since March 1983.

BRANDT, MARTIN W,
833 Kelly Blvd, Springfield, OR 97477, Phone: 541-747-5422, oubob747@aol.com

BRANTON, ROBERT,
PO BOX 807, Awendaw, SC 29429, Phone: 843-928-3624, www.brantonknives.com
Specialties: Working straight knives of his design or to customer specs; throwing knives. Patterns: Hunters, fighters and some miniatures. Technical: Grinds ATS-34, A2 and 440C; forges 5160, O1. Offers hollow- or convex-grinds. Prices: $25 to $400. Remarks: Part-time maker; first knife sold in 1985. Doing business as Pro-Flyte, Inc. Mark: Last name; or first and last name, city, state.

BRASCHLER, CRAIG W.,
HC2 Box 498, Zalma, MO 63787, Phone: 573-495-2203
Specialties: Art knives, Bowies, utility hunters, slip joints, miniatures, engraving. Technical: Flat grinds. Does own selective heat treating. Does own engraving. Prices: Starting at $200. Remarks: Full-time maker since 2003. Mark: Braschler over Martin Oval stamped.

BRATCHER, BRETT,
11816 County Rd 302, Plantersville, TX 77363, Phone: 936-894-3788, Fax: (936) 894-3790, brett_bratcher@msn.com
Specialties: Hunting and skinning knives. Patterns: Clip and drop point. Hand forged. Technical: Material 5160, D2, 1095 and Damascus. Price: $200 to $500. Mark: Bratcher.

BRAY JR., W LOWELL,
6931 Manor Beach Rd, New Port Richey, FL 34652, Phone: 727-846-0830, brayknives@aol.com Web: www.brayknives.com
Specialties: Traditional working and using straight knives and collector pieces. Patterns: One of a kind pieces, hunters, fighters and utility knives. Technical: Grinds 440C and ATS-34; forges 52100 and Damascus. Prices: $125 to $800. Remarks: Spare-time maker; first knife sold in 1992. Mark: Lowell Bray Knives in shield or Bray Primitive in shield.

BREED, KIM,
733 Jace Dr, Clarksville, TN 37040, Phone: 931-980-4956, sfbreed@yahoo.com
Specialties: High end through working folders and straight knives. Patterns: Hunters, fighters, daggers, Bowies. His design or customers. Likes one-of-a-kind designs. Technical: Makes own Mosiac and regular Damascus, but will use stainless steels. Offers filework and sculpted material. Prices: $150 to $2000. Remarks: Full-time maker. First knife sold in 1990. Mark: Last name.

BREND, WALTER,
4094 Columbia Hwy., Ridge Springs, SC 29129, Phone: 256-736-3520, walterbrend@hotmail.com Web: www.brendknives.com
Specialties: Tactical-style knives, fighters, automatics. Technical: Grinds D-Z and 440C blade steels, 154CM steel. Prices: Micarta handles, titanium handles.

BRENNAN, JUDSON,
PO Box 1165, Delta Junction, AK 99737, Phone: 907-895-5153, Fax: 907-895-5404
Specialties: Period pieces. Patterns: All kinds of Bowies, rifle knives, daggers. Technical: Forges miscellaneous steels. Prices: Upscale, good value. Remarks: Muzzle-loading gunsmith; first knife sold in 1978. Mark: Name.

BRESHEARS, CLINT,
1261 Keats, Manhattan Beach, CA 90266, Phone: 310-372-0739, Fax: 310-372-0739, breshears1@verizon.net; Web: www.clintknives.com
Specialties: Working straight knives and folders. Patterns: Hunters, Bowies and survival knives. Folders are mostly hunters. Technical: Grinds 440C, 154CM and ATS-34; prefers mirror finishes. Prices: $125 to $750; some to $1800. Remarks: Part-time maker; first knife sold in 1978. Mark: First name.

BREUER, LONNIE,
PO Box 877384, Wasilla, AK 99687-7384
Specialties: Fancy working straight knives. Patterns: Hunters, camp knives and axes, folders and Bowies. Technical: Grinds 440C, AEB-L and D2; likes wire inlay, scrimshaw, decorative filing. Prices: $60 to $150; some to $300. Remarks: Part-time maker; first knife sold in 1977. Mark: Signature.

BREWER, CRAIG,
425 White Cedar, Killeen, TX 76542, Phone: 254-634-6934, craig6@ embargmail.com
Specialties: Folders; slip joints, some lock backs and an occasional liner lock. Patterns: I like the old traditional patterns. Technical: Grinds CPM steels most being CPM-154, 1095 for carbon and some Damascus. Prices: $450 and up. Remarks: Full-time maker, first knife sold in 2005.Mark: BREWER.

BRITTON, TIM,
PO Box 71, Bethania, NC 27010, Phone: 336-922-9582, timbritton@yahoo.com; Web: www.timbritton.com
Specialties: Small and simple working knives, sgian dubhs, slip joint folders and special tactical designs. Technical: Forges and grinds stainless steel. Prices: $165 to ???. Remarks: Veteran knifemaker. Mark: Etched signature.

BROADWELL, DAVID,
PO Box 4314, Wichita Falls, TX 76308, Phone: 940-782-4442, david@ broadwellstudios.com; Web: www.broadwellstudios.com
Specialties: Sculpted high-art straight and folding knives. Patterns: Daggers, sub-hilted fighters, folders, sculpted art knives and some Bowies. Technical: Grinds mostly Damascus; carves; prefers natural handle materials, including stone. Some embellishment. Prices: $500 to $4000; some higher. Remarks: Full-time maker since 1989; first knife sold in 1981. Mark: Stylized emblem bisecting "B"/with last name below.

BROCK, KENNETH L,
PO Box 375, 207 N Skinner Rd, Allenspark, CO 80510, Phone: 303-747-2547, brockknives@nedernet.net
Specialties: Custom designs, full-tang working knives and button lock folders of his design. Patterns: Hunters, miniatures and minis. Technical: Flat-grinds D2 and 440C; makes own sheaths; heat-treats. Prices: $75 to $800. Remarks: Full-time maker; first knife sold in 1978. Mark: Last name, city, state and serial number.

BRODZIAK, DAVID,
27 Stewart St, PO Box 1130, Albany, WA, AUSTRALIA 6331, Phone: 61 8 9841 3314, Fax: 61898115065, brodziakomninet.net.au; Web: www.brodziakcustomknives.com

BROMLEY, PETER,
BROMLEY KNIVES, 1408 S Bettman, Spokane, WA 99212, Phone: 509-534-4235, Fax: 509-536-2666
Specialties: Period Bowies, folder, hunting knives; all sizes and shapes. Patterns: Bowies, boot knives, hunters, utility, folder, working knives. Technical: High-carbon steel (1084, 1095 and 5160). Stock removal and forge. Prices: $85 to $750. Remarks: Almost full-time, first knife sold in 1987. A.B.S. Journeyman Smith. Mark: Bromley, Spokane, WA.

BROOKER, DENNIS,
55858 260th Ave., Chariton, IA 50049, Phone: 641-862-3263, dbrooker@ dbrooker.com Web: www.dbrooker.com
Specialties: Fancy straight knives and folders of his design. Obsidian and glass knives. Patterns: Hunters, folders and boots. Technical: Forges and grinds. Full-time engraver and designer; instruction available. Prices: Moderate to upscale. Remarks: Part-time maker. Takes no orders; sells only completed work. Mark: Name.

BROOKS, BUZZ,
2345 Yosemite Dr, Los Angles, CA 90041, Phone: 323-256-2892

BROOKS, MICHAEL,
2811 64th St, Lubbock, TX 79413, Phone: 806-438-3862, chiang@clearwire.net
Specialties: Working straight knives of his design or to customer specs. Patterns: Martial art, Bowies, hunters, and fighters. Technical: Grinds 440C, D2 and ATS-34; offers wide variety of handle materials. Prices: $75 & up. Remarks: Part-time maker; first knife sold in 1985. Mark: Initials.

BROOKS, STEVE R,
1610 Dunn Ave, Walkerville, MT 59701, Phone: 406-782-5114, Fax: 406-782-5114, steve@brooksmoulds.com; Web: brooksmoulds.com
Specialties: Working straight knives and folders; period pieces. Patterns: Hunters, Bowies and camp knives; folding lockers; axes, tomahawks and buckskinner knives; swords and stilettos. Technical: Damascus and mosaic Damascus. Some knives come embellished. Prices: $400 to $2000. Remarks: Full-time maker; first knife sold in 1982. Mark: Lazy initials.

BROOME, THOMAS A,
1212 E. Aliak Ave, Kenai, AK 99611-8205, Phone: 907-283-9128, tomlei@ptialaska.ent; Web: www.alaskanknives.com
Specialties: Working hunters and folders Patterns: Traditional and custom orders. Technical: Grinds ATS-34, BG-42, CPM-S30V. Prices: $175 to $350. Remarks: Full-time maker; first knife sold in 1979. Doing business as Thom's Custom Knives, Alaskan Man O; Steel Knives. Mark: Full name, city, state.

BROTHERS, DENNIS L.,
2007 Kent Rd., Oneonta, AL 35121, Phone: 205-466-3276, blademan@brothersblades.com Web: www.brothersblades.com
Specialties: Fixed blade hunting/working knives of maker's deigns. Works with customer designed specifications. Patterns: Hunters, camp knives, kitchen/utility, bird, and trout. Standard patterns and customer designed. Technical: Stock removal. Works with stainless and tool steels. SS cryo-treatment. Hollow and flat grinds. Prices: $200 - $400. Remarks: Sole authorship knives and customer leather sheaths. Part-time maker. Find on facebook "Brothers Blades by D.L. Brothers" Mark: "D.L. Brothers, 4B, Oneonta, AL" on obverse side of blade.

BROTHERS, ROBERT L,
989 Philpott Rd, Colville, WA 99114, Phone: 509-684-8922
Specialties: Traditional working and using straight knives and folders of his design and to customer specs. Patterns: Bowies, fighters and hunters. Technical: Grinds D2; forges Damascus. Makes own Damascus from saw steel wire rope and chain; part-time goldsmith and stone-setter. Prices: $100 to $400; some higher. Remarks: Part-time maker; first knife sold in 1986. Mark: Initials and year made.

BROUS, JASON,
5940 Matthews St., Goleta, CA 93110, Phone: 805-717-7192, contact@brousblades.com Web: www.brousblades.com
Patterns: Mostly fixed blades. Technical: Stock removal method using D2, CPM 154, 440c, ATS-34 or 1095 steels. Prices: $100 - $400. Remarks: Started May 2010.

BROUWER, JERRY,
Vennewaard 151, 1824 KD, Alkmaar, Netherlands, Phone: 00-31-618-774146, brouwern1@hotmail.nl; Web: www.brouwerknives.com
Specialties: Tactical fixed blades with epoxy-soaked Japanese wrapped handles, tactical and outdoor knives with Micarta or G-10 handles, tactical frame-lock folders. Fine, embellished knives for the demanding VIP. Patterns: Fixed-blade tantos, drop points, either V-ground or chisel ground, hunting knives, outdoor knives, folders, desk knives, pocket tools. Technical: Stock removal, only premium powder metallurgy steels and fine stainless damascus. Prices: $100 to $1,000. Remarks: Part-time maker; first knife sold in 2010. Mark: Laser etched "Brouwer" with a jack-o-lantern logo.

BROWER, MAX,
2016 Story St, Boone, IA 50036, Phone: 515-432-2938, mbrower@mchsi.com
Specialties: Hunters. Working/using straight knives. Patterns: Bowies, hunters and boots. Technical: Grinds 440C and ATS-34. Prices: $280 and up. Remarks: Spare-time maker; first knife sold in 1981. Mark: Last name.

BROWN, DENNIS G,
1633 N 197th Pl, Shoreline, WA 98133, Phone: 206-542-3997, denjilbro@msn.com

BROWN, DOUGLAS,
1500 Lincolnshire Way, Fort Worth, TX 76134, www.debrownphotography.com

BROWN, HAROLD E,
3654 NW Hwy 72, Arcadia, FL 34266, Phone: 863-494-7514, brknives@strato.net
Specialties: Fancy and exotic working knives. Patterns: Folders, slip-lock, locking several kinds. Technical: Grinds D2 and ATS-34. Embellishment available. Prices: $175 to $1000. Remarks: Part-time maker; first knife sold in 1976. Mark: Name and city with logo.

BROWN, JIM,
1097 Fernleigh Cove, Little Rock, AR 72210

BROWN, ROB E,
PO Box 15107, Emerald Hill, Port Elizabeth, EC, SOUTH AFRICA 6011, Phone: 27-41-3661086, Fax: 27-41-4511731, rbknives@global.co.za
Specialties: Contemporary-designed straight knives and period pieces. Patterns: Utility knives, hunters, boots, fighters and daggers. Technical: Grinds 440C, D2, ATS-34 and commercial Damascus. Knives mostly mirror finished;

African handle materials. Prices: $100 to $1500. Remarks: Full-time maker; first knife sold in 1985. Mark: Name and country.

BROWNE, RICK,
980 West 13th St, Upland, CA 91786, Phone: 909-985-1728
Specialties: Sheffield pattern pocket knives. Patterns: Hunters, fighters and daggers. No heavy-duty knives. Technical: Grinds ATS-34. Prices: Start at $450. Remarks: Part-time maker; first knife sold in 1975. Mark: R.E. Browne, Upland, CA.

BROWNING, STEVEN W,
3400 Harrison Rd, Benton, AR 72015, Phone: 501-316-2450

BRUCE, RICHARD L.,
13174 Surcease Mine Road, Yankee Hill, CA 95965, Phone: 530-532-0880, richardkarenbruce@yahoo.com
Specialties: Working straight knives. Prefers natural handle material; stag bone and woods. Admires the classic straight knife look. Patterns: Hunters, Fighters, Fishing Knives. Technical: Uses 01, 1095, L6, W2 steel. Stock removal method, flat grind, heat treats and tempers own knives. Builds own sheaths; simple but sturdy. Prices: $150-$400. Remarks: Sold first knife in 2006; part-time maker. Mark: RL Bruce.

BRUCE, RICHARD L.,
13174 Surcease Mine Road, Yankee Hill, CA 95965, Phone: 530-532-0880, Richardkarenbruce@yahoo.com
RL Bruce Custom Knives Mark: R.L. Bruce, Maker, Yankee Hill, Cal.

BRUNCKHORST, LYLE,
COUNTRY VILLAGE, 23706 7th Ave SE Ste B, Bothell, WA 98021, Phone: 425-402-3484, bronks@bronksknifeworks.com; Web: www.bronksknifeworks.com
Specialties: Forges own Damascus with 1084 and 15N20, forges 5160, 52100. Grinds CPM 154 CM, ATS-34, S30V. Hosts Biannual Northwest School of Knifemaking and Northwest Hammer In. Offers online and in-house sharpening services and knife sharpeners. Maker of the Double L Hoofknife. Traditional working and using knives, the new patent pending Xross-Bar Lock folders, tomahawks and irridescent RR spike knives. Patterns: Damascus Bowies, hunters, locking folders and featuring the ultra strong locking tactical folding knives. Prices: $185 to $1500; some to $3750. Remarks: Full-time maker; first knife made in 1976. Mark: Bucking horse or bronk.

BRUNER JR., FRED BRUNER BLADES,
E10910 W Hilldale Dr, Fall Creek, WI 54742, Phone: 715-877-2496, brunerblades@msn.com
Specialties: Pipe tomahawks, swords, makes his own. Patterns: Drop point hunters. Prices: $65 to $1500. Remarks: Voting member of the Knifemakers Guild. Mark: Fred Bruner.

BUCHANAN, THAD,
THAD BUCHANAN CUSTOM KNIVES, 915 NW Perennial Way, Prineville, OR 97754, Phone: 541-416-2556, knives@crestviewcable.com; Web: www.buchananblades.com
Specialties: Fixed blades. Patterns: Various hunters, trout, bird, utility, boots & fighters, including most Loveless patterns. Technical: Stock removal, high polish, variety handle materials. Prices: $450 to $2000. Remarks: 2005 and 2008 Blade Magazine handmade award for hunter/utility. 2006 Blade West best fixed blade award; 2008 Blade West best hunter/utility. 2010 and 2011 Best Fixed Blade at Plaza Cutlery Show. Mark: Thad Buchanan - maker

BUCHANAN, ZAC,
168 Chapel Dr., Eugene, OR 97404, Phone: 541-815-6706, zacbuchananknives@gmail.com; Web: www.zacbuchananknives.com
Specialties: R.W. Loveless-style fixed blades. Technical: Stock-removal knifemaker using CPM-154 blade steel, 416 stainless steel fittings and pre-ban elephant ivory, mammoth ivory, buffalo horn, stag and Micarta handles. Prices: $500 to $2,000. Remarks: Full-time maker; first knife sold in 2009. Mark: Zac Buchanan Eugene, Oregon.

BUCHARSKY, EMIL,
37 26321 SH627 Spruce Grove, Alberta, Canada T7Y 1C7, ebuch@telus.net; Web: www.ebuchknives.com
Specialties: Fancy working utility hunters and art folders, usually carved with overlays or inlays of damascus, hidden frames and screws. Patterns: Folders, hunters, bowies of maker's own design. Technical: Forges own damascus using 1095, 1084, 15N20 and nickel, stock-removal steels from Crucible, CPM alloys and UHB Elmax, natural handle materials of pearl, ancient ivory, bone, stabilized woods and others such as carbon fiber, titanium, stainless steel, mokume gane and gemstones. Prices: $400 to $1,000; art knives $1,500 and up. Remarks: Full-time maker; first knife made in 1989. Mark: Name, city and province in oval on fixed blades. Hand-engraved first name, initial and last name with year, in lower case, on folders.

BUCHNER, BILL,
PO Box 73, Idleyld Park, OR 97447, Phone: 541-498-2247, blazinhammer@earthlink.net; Web: www.home.earthlin.net/~blazinghammer
Specialties: Working straight knives, kitchen knives and high-art knives of his design. Technical: Uses W1, L6 and his own Damascus. Invented "spectrum metal" for letter openers, folder handles and jewelry. Likes sculpturing and carving in Damascus. Prices: $40 to $3000; some higher. Remarks: Full-time maker; first knife sold in 1978. Mark: Signature.

BUCKBEE, DONALD M,
243 South Jackson Trail, Grayling, MI 49738, Phone: 517-348-1386
Specialties: Working straight knives, some fancy, in standard patterns;

concentrating on kitchen knives. Patterns: Kitchen knives, hunters, Bowies. Technical: Grinds D2, 440C, ATS-34. Makes ultra-lights in hunter patterns. Prices: $100 to $250; some to $350. Remarks: Part-time maker; first knife sold in 1984. Mark: Antlered bee—a buck bee.

BUCKNER, JIMMIE H,
PO Box 162, Putney, GA 31782, Phone: 229-436-4182
Specialties: Camp knives, Bowies (one-of-a-kind), liner-lock folders, tomahawks, camp axes, neck knives for law enforcement and hide-out knives for body guards and professional people. Patterns: Hunters, camp knives, Bowies. Technical: Forges 1084, 5160 and Damascus (own), own heat treats. Prices: $195 to $795 and up. Remarks: Full-time maker; first knife sold in 1980, ABS Master Smith. Mark: Name over spade.

BUDELL, MICHAEL,
3733 Wieghat Ln., Brenham, TX 77833, Phone: 979-836-3148, mbbudell@att.net
Specialties: Slip Joint Folders. Technical: Grinds 01, 440C. File work springs, blades and liners. Natural material scales giraffe, mastadon ivory, elephant ivory, and jigged bone. Prices: $175 - $350. Remarks: Part-time maker; first knife sold 2006. Mark: XA

BUEBENDORF, ROBERT E,
108 Lazybrooke Rd, Monroe, CT 06468, Phone: 203-452-1769
Specialties: Traditional and fancy straight knives of his design. Patterns: Hand-makes and embellishes belt buckle knives. Technical: Forges and grinds 440C, O1, W2, 1095, his own Damascus and 154CM. Prices: $200 to $500. Remarks: Full-time maker; first knife sold in 1978. Mark: First and middle initials, last name and MAKER.

BULLARD, BENONI,
4416 Jackson 4, Bradford, AR 72020, Phone: 501-344-2672, benandbren@earthlink.net
Specialties: Bowies and hunters. Patterns: Camp knives, bowies, hunters, slip joints, folders, lock blades, miniatures, Hawks Tech. Technical: Makes own Damascus. Forges 5160, 1085, 15 N 20. Favorite is 5160. Prices: $150 - $1500. Remarks: Part-time maker. Sold first knife in 2006. Mark: Benoni with a star over the letter i.

BULLARD, RANDALL,
7 Mesa Dr., Canyon, TX 79015, Phone: 806-655-0590
Specialties: Working/using straight knives and folders of his design or to customer specs. Patterns: Hunters, locking folders and slip-joint folders. Technical: Grinds O1, ATS-34 and 440C. Does file work. Prices: $125 to $300; some to $500. Remarks: Part-time maker; first knife sold in 1993. Doing business as Bullard Custom Knives. Mark: First and middle initials, last name, maker, city and state.

BULLARD, TOM,
117 MC 8068, Flippin, AR 72634, Phone: 870-656-3428, tbullard8@live.com
Specialties: Traditional folders and hunters. Patterns: Bowies, hunters, single and 2-blade trappers, lockback folders. Technical: Grinds 440C, A2, D2, ATS-34 and O1. Prices: $175 and up. Remarks: Offers filework and engraving by Norvell Foster and Terry Thies. Does not make screw-together knives. Mark: T Bullard.

BUMP, BRUCE D.,
1103 Rex Ln, Walla Walla, WA 99362, Phone: 509 522-2219, brucebump1@gmail.com; Web: www.brucebumpknives.com
Specialties: "One-of-a-kind" folders to cut and shoots. Patterns: Damascus patterns including feather patterns. Technical: Dual threat weapons of his own design. Prices: Call for prices. Remarks: Full-time maker ABS mastersmith 2003. Mark: Bruce D. Bump "Custom", Bruce D. Bump "MS".

BURDEN, JAMES,
405 Kelly St, Burkburnett, TX 76354

BURGER, FRED,
Box 436, Munster, KZN, SOUTH AFRICA 4278, Phone: 27 39 3192316, info@swordcane.com; Web: www.swordcane.com
Specialties: Sword canes, folders, and fixed blades. Patterns: 440C and carbon steel blades. Technical: Double hollow ground and Poniard-style blades. Prices: $300 to $3000. Remarks: Full-time maker with son, Barry, since 1987. Member South African Guild. Mark: Last name in oval pierced by a dagger.

BURGER, PON,
12 Glenwood Ave, Woodlands, Bulawayo, ZIMBABWE 75514
Specialties: Collector's items. Patterns: Fighters, locking folders of traditional styles, buckles. Technical: Scrimshaws 440C blade. Uses polished buffalo horn with brass fittings. Cased in buffalo hide book. Prices: $450 to $1100. Remarks: Full-time maker; first knife sold in 1973. Doing business as Burger Products. Mark: Spirit of Africa.

BURGER, TIAAN,
69 Annie Botha Ave, Riviera,, Pretoria, GT, SOUTH AFRICA, tiaan_burger@hotmail.com
Specialties: Sliplock and multi-blade folder. Technical: High carbon or stainless with African handle materials Remarks: Occasional fixed blade knives.

BURKE, BILL,
20 Adams Ranch Rd., Boise, ID 83716, Phone: 208-336-3792, billburke@bladegallery.com
Specialties: Hand-forged working knives. Patterns: Fowler pronghorn, clip point and drop point hunters. Technical: Forges 52100 and 5160. Makes own Damascus from 15N20 and 1084. Prices: $450 and up. Remarks: Dedicated to fixed-blade high-performance knives. ABS Journeyman. Also makes "Ed Fowler" miniatures. Mark: Initials connected.

BURKE, DAN,
29 Circular Rd., Springdale, NL, CANADA A0J 1T0, Phone: 708-867-2026, dansknives@eastlink.ca
Specialties: Slip joint folders. Patterns: Traditional folders. Technical: Grinds D2 and BG-42. Prefers natural handle materials; heat-treats. Prices: $440 to $1900. Remarks: Full-time maker; first knife sold in 1976. Mark: First initial and last name.

BURNLEY, LUCAS,
1005 La Font Rd. SW, Albuquerque, NM 87105, Phone: 505-265-4297, burnleyknives@comcast.net
Specialties: Contemporary tactical fixed blade, and folder designs, some art knives. Patterns: Hybrids, neo Japanese, defensive, utility and field knives. Technical: Grinds CPM154, A2, D2, BG42, Stainless Damascus as well as titanium and aerospace composites. Prices: Most models $150 - $1000. Some specialty pieces higher. Remarks: Full-time maker, first knife sold in 2003. Mark: Last name, Burnley Knives, or Burnley Design.

BURRIS, PATRICK R,
11078 Crystal Lynn Ct, Jacksonville, FL 32226, Phone: 904-757-3938, burrispr@gmail.com
Specialties: Traditional straight knives and locking-liner folders. Patterns: Hunters, bowies, locking-liner folders. Technical: Flat grinds high-grade stainless and damascus. Remarks: Offers filework, embellishment, exotic materials and damascus Mark: Last name in script.

BURROWS, CHUCK,
WILD ROSE TRADING CO, 289 La Posta Canyon Rd, Durango, CO 81303, Phone: 970-259-8396, chuck@wrtcleather.com; Web: www.wrtcleather.com
Specialties: Presentation knives, hawks, and sheaths based on the styles of the American frontier incorporating carving, beadwork, rawhide, braintan, and other period correct materials. Also makes other period style knives such as Scottish Dirks and Moorish jambiyahs. Patterns: Bowies, Dags, tomahawks, war clubs, and all other 18th and 19th century frontier style edged weapons and tools. Technical: Carbon steel only: 5160, 1080/1084, 1095, O1, Damascus-Our Frontier Shear Steel, plus other styles available on request. Forged knives, hawks, etc. are made in collaborations with bladesmiths. Gib Guignard (under the name of Cactus Rose) and Mark Williams (under the name UB Forged). Blades are usually forge finished and all are given an aged period look. Prices: $500 plus. Remarks: Full-time maker, first knife sold in 1973. 40+ years experience working leather. Mark: A lazy eight or lazy eight with a capital T at the center. On leather either the lazy eight with T or a WRTC makers stamp.

BURROWS, STEPHEN R,
1020 Osage St, Humboldt, KS 66748, Phone: 816-921-1573
Specialties: Fantasy straight knives of his design, to customer specs and in standard patterns; period pieces. Patterns: Fantasy, bird and trout knives, daggers, fighters and hunters. Technical: Forges 5160 and 1095 high-carbon steel, O1 and his Damascus. Offers lost wax casting in bronze or silver of cross guards and pommels. Prices: $65 to $600; some to $2000. Remarks: Full-time maker; first knife sold in 1983. Doing business as Gypsy Silk. Mark: Etched name.

BUSCH, STEVE,
1989 Old Town Loop, Oakland, OR 97462, Phone: 541-459-2833, steve@buschcustomknives.com; Web: wwwbuschcustomknives.blademakers.com
Specialties: D/A automatic right and left handed, folders, fixed blade working mainly in Damascus file work, functional art knives, nitrate bluing, heat bluing most all scale materials. Prices: $150 to $2000. Remarks: Trained under Vallotton family 3 1/2 years on own since 2002. Mark: Signature and date of completion on all knives.

BUSFIELD, JOHN,
153 Devonshire Circle, Roanoke Rapids, NC 27870, Phone: 252-537-3949, Fax: 252-537-8704, busfield@charter.net; Web: www.busfieldknives.com
Specialties: Investor-grade folders; high-grade working straight knives. Patterns: Original price-style and trailing-point interframe and sculpted-frame folders, drop-point hunters and semi-skinners. Technical: Grinds 154CM and ATS-34. Offers interframes, gold frames and inlays; uses jade, agate and lapis. Prices: $275 to $2000. Remarks: Full-time maker; first knife sold in 1979. Mark: Last name and address.

BUSSE, JERRY,
11651 Co Rd 12, Wauseon, OH 43567, Phone: 419-923-6471
Specialties: Working straight knives. Patterns: Heavy combat knives and camp knives. Technical: Grinds D2, A2, INFI. Prices: $1100 to $3500. Remarks: Full-time maker; first knife sold in 1983. Mark: Last name in logo.

BUTLER, BART,
822 Seventh St, Ramona, CA 92065, Phone: 760-789-6431

BUTLER, JOHN,
777 Tyre Rd, Havana, FL 32333, Phone: 850-539-5742
Specialties: Hunters, Bowies, period. Technical: Damascus, 52100, 5160, L6 steels. Prices: $80 and up. Remarks: Making knives since 1986. Journeyman (ABS). Mark: JB.

BUTLER, JOHN R,
20162 6th Ave N E, Shoreline, WA 98155, Phone: 206-362-3847, rjjjrb@sprynet.com

BUXTON, BILL,
155 Oak Bend Rd, Kaiser, MO 65047, Phone: 573-348-3577, camper@yhti.net; Web: www.billbuxtonknives.com
Specialties: Forged fancy and working straight knives and folders. Mostly one-of-a-kind pieces. Patterns: Fighters, daggers, Bowies, hunters, linerlock folders, axes and tomahawks. Technical: Forges 52100, 0-1, 1080. Makes own Damascus (mosaic and random patterns) from 1080, 1095, 15n20, and powdered metals 1084 and 4800a. Offers sterling silver inlay, n/s pin patterning and pewter pouring on axe and hawk handles. Prices: $300 to $2,500. Remarks: Full-time maker, sold first knife in 1998. Mark: First initial and last name.

BUZEK, STANLEY,
PO Box 731, Waller, TX 77484, Phone: 936-372-1933, stan@sbuzekknives.com; Web: www.sbuzekknives.com
Specialties: Traditional slip-joint pocketknives, LinerLocks and frame-lock folders, and fixed-blade hunters and skinners. Technical: Grinds, heat treats and Rockwell tests CPM-154, and some traditional folders in O1 tool steel. Hand-rubbed finishes. Dyed jigged bone, mammoth ivory and fine stabilized woods. Prices: $250 and up. Remarks: Serious part-time maker; first knife sold in 2006. Mark: S. Buzek on riccasso.

BYBEE, BARRY J,
795 Lock Rd. E, Cadiz, KY 42211-8615
Specialties: Working straight knives of his design. Patterns: Hunters, fighters, boot knives, tantos and Bowies. Technical: Grinds ATS-34, 440C. Likes stag and Micarta for handle materials. Prices: $125 to $200; some to $1000. Remarks: Part-time maker; first knife sold in 1968. Mark: Arrowhead logo with name, city and state.

BYRD, WESLEY L,
189 Countryside Dr, Evensville, TN 37332, Phone: 423-775-3826, w.l.byrd@worldnet.att.net
Specialties: Hunters, fighters, Bowies, dirks, sgian dubh, utility, and camp knives. Patterns: Wire rope, random patterns. Twists, W's, Ladder, Kite Tail. Technical: Uses 52100, 1084, 5160, L6, and 15n20. Prices: Starting at $180. Remarks: Prefer to work with customer for their design preferences. ABS Journeyman Smith. Mark: BYRD, WB <X.

C

CABRERA, SERGIO B,
24500 Broad Ave, Wilmington, CA 90744

CAFFREY, EDWARD J,
2608 Central Ave West, Great Falls, MT 59404, Phone: 406-727-9102, caffreyknives@gmail.com; Web: www.caffreyknives.net
Specialties: One-of-a-kind using and collector quality pieces. Will accept some customer designs. Patterns: Bowies, folders, hunters, fighters, camp/utility, tomahawks and hatchets. Technical: Forges all types of Damascus, specializing in Mosaic Damascus, 52100, 5160, 1080/1084 and most other commonly used forged steels. Prices: Starting at $185; typical hunters start at $400; collector pieces can range into the thousands. Remarks: Offers one-on-one basic and advanced bladesmithing classes. ABS Mastersmith. Full-time maker. Mark: Stamped last name and MS on straight knives. Etched last name with MS on folders.

CALDWELL, BILL,
255 Rebecca, West Monroe, LA 71292, Phone: 318-323-3025
Specialties: Straight knives and folders with machined bolsters and liners. Patterns: Fighters, Bowies, survival knives, tomahawks, razors and push knives. Technical: Owns and operates a very large, well-equipped blacksmith and bladesmith shop with six large forges and eight power hammers. Prices: $400 to $3500; some to $10,000. Remarks: Full-time maker and self-styled blacksmith; first knife sold in 1962. Mark: Wild Bill and Sons.

CALLAHAN, F TERRY,
PO Box 880, Boerne, TX 78006, Phone: 830-981-8274, Fax: 830-981-8279, ftclaw@gvtc.com
Specialties: Custom hand-forged edged knives, collectible and functional. Patterns: Bowies, folders, daggers, hunters & camp knives . Technical: Forges 5160, 1095 and his own Damascus. Offers filework and handmade sheaths. Prices: $125 to $2000. Remarks: First knife sold in 1990. ABS/Journeyman Bladesmith. Mark: Initials inside a keystone symbol.

CALVERT JR., ROBERT W (BOB),
911 Julia, Rayville, LA 71269, Phone: 318-348-4490, rcalvert1@gmail.com
Specialties: Using and hunting knives; your design or his. Since 1990. Patterns: Forges own Damascus; all patterns. Technical: 5160, D2, 52100, 1084. Prefers natural handle material. Prices: $250 and up. Remarks: TOMB Member, ABS. Journeyman Smith. ABS Board of directors Mark: Calvert (Block) J S.

CAMBRON, HENRY,
169 Severn Way, Dallas, GA 30132-0317, Phone: 770-598-5721, worldclassknives@bellsouth.net; Web: www.worldclassknives.com
Specialties: Everyday carry, working and small neck knives. Patterns: Hunters, bowies, camp, utility and combat. Technical: Forge, stock removal, filework. Differential quench. Tuff-etched finish. Hand-sewn and Kydex sheaths. Prices: $65 to $650. Remarks: Full-time maker. Mark: First and last name over USA on blades. HC on sheaths.

CAMERER, CRAIG,
3766 Rockbridge Rd, Chesterfield, IL 62630, Phone: 618-753-2147, craig@camererknives.com; Web: www.camererknives.com
Specialties: Everyday carry knives, hunters and Bowies. Patterns: D-guard, historical recreations and fighters. Technical: Most of his knives are forged to shape. Prices: $100 and up. Remarks: Member of the ABS and PKA. Journeymen Smith ABS.

CAMERON, RON G,
PO Box 183, Logandale, NV 89021, Phone: 702-398-3356, rntcameron@mvdsl.com
Specialties: Fancy and embellished working/using straight knives and folders of his design. Patterns: Bowies, hunters and utility/camp knives. Technical: Grinds ATS-34, AEB-L and Devin Thomas Damascus or own Damascus from 1084 and 15N20. Does filework, fancy pins, mokume fittings. Uses exotic hardwoods, stag and Micarta for handles. Pearl & mammoth ivory. Prices: $175 to $850 some to $1000. Remarks: Part-time maker; first knife sold in 1994. Doing business as Cameron Handmade Knives. Mark: Last name, town, state or last name.

CAMPBELL, DICK,
196 Graham Rd, Colville, WA 99114, Phone: 509-684-6080, dicksknives@aol.com
Specialties: Working straight knives, folders & period pieces. Patterns: Hunters, fighters, boots: 19th century Bowies, Japanese swords and daggers. Technical: Grinds 440C, 154CM. Prices: $200 to $2500. Remarks: Full-time maker. First knife sold in 1975. Mark: Name.

CAMPBELL, DOUG,
46 W Boulder Rd., McLeod, MT 59052, Phone: 406-222-8153, dkcampbl@yahoo.com
Specialties: Sole authorship of most any fixed blade knife. Patterns: Capers, hunters, camp knives, bowies, fighters. Technical: Forged from 1084, 5160, 52100, and self forged pattern-welded Damascus. Prices: $150-$750. Remarks: Part-time knifesmith. Built first knife in 1987, tried to make every knife since better than the one before. ABS JourneymanSmith . Mark: Grizzly track surrounded by a C.

CAMPOS, IVAN,
R.XI de Agosto 107, Tatui, SP, BRAZIL 18270-000, Phone: 00-55-15-2518092, Fax: 00-55-15-2594368, ivan@ivancampos.com; Web: www.ivancompos.com
Specialties: Brazilian handmade and antique knives.

CANDRELLA, JOE,
1219 Barness Dr, Warminster, PA 18974, Phone: 215-675-0143
Specialties: Working straight knives, some fancy. Patterns: Daggers, boots, Bowies. Technical: Grinds 440C and 154CM. Prices: $100 to $200; some to $1000. Remarks: Part-time maker; first knife sold in 1985. Does business as Franjo. Mark: FRANJO with knife as J.

CANNADY, DANIEL L,
Box 301, 358 Parkwood Terrace, Allendale, SC 29810, Phone: 803-584-2813, Fax: 803-584-2813
Specialties: Working straight knives and folders in standard patterns. Patterns: Drop-point hunters, Bowies, skinners, fishing knives with concave grind, steak knives and kitchen cutlery. Technical: Grinds D2, 440C and ATS-34. Prices: $65 to $325; some to $1000. Remarks: Full-time maker; first knife sold in 1980. Mark: Last name above Allendale, S.C.

CANTER, RONALD E,
96 Bon Air Circle, Jackson, TN 38305, Phone: 731-668-1780, canterr@charter.net
Specialties: Traditional working knives to customer specs. Patterns: Beavertail skinners, Bowies, hand axes and folding lockers. Technical: Grinds 440C, Micarta & deer antler. Prices: $75 and up. Remarks: Spare-time maker; first knife sold in 1973. Mark: Three last initials intertwined.

CANTRELL, KITTY D,
19720 Hwy 78, Ramona, CA 92076, Phone: 760-788-8304

CAPDEPON, RANDY,
553 Joli Rd, Carencro, LA 70520, Phone: 318-896-4113, Fax: 318-896-8753
Specialties: Straight knives and folders of his design. Patterns: Hunters and locking folders. Technical: Grinds ATS-34, 440C and D2. Prices: $200 to $600. Remarks: Part-time maker; first knife made in 1992. Doing business as Capdepon Knives. Mark: Last name.

CAPDEPON, ROBERT,
829 Vatican Rd, Carencro, LA 70520, Phone: 337-896-8753, Fax: 318-896-8753
Specialties: Traditional straight knives and folders of his design. Patterns: Boots, hunters and locking folders. Technical: Grinds ATS-34, 440C and D2. Hand-rubbed finish on blades. Likes natural horn materials for handles, including ivory. Offers engraving. Prices: $250 to $750. Remarks: Full-time maker; first knife made in 1992. Mark: Last name.

CAREY, PETER,
P.O. Box 4712, Lago Vista, TX 78645, Phone: 512-358-4839, Web: www.careyblade.com
Specialties: Tactical folders, Every Day Carry to presentation grade. Working straight knives, hunters, and tactical. Patterns: High-tech patterns of his own design, Linerlocks, Framelocks, Flippers. Technical: Hollow grinds CPM154, 535VN, stainless Damascus, Stellite. Uses titanium, carbon fiber, G10, and select natural handle materials. Prices: Starting at $450. Remarks: Full-time maker, first knife sold in 2002. Mark: Last name in diamond.

custom knifemakers

CARLISLE—CHAMBERLAIN

CARLISLE, JEFF,
PO Box 282 12753 Hwy 200, Simms, MT 59477, Phone: 406-264-5693
CARPENTER, RONALD W,
Rt. 4 Box 323, Jasper, TX 75951, Phone: 409-384-4087
CARR, JOSEPH E.,
W183 N8974 Maryhill Drive, Menomonee Falls, WI 53051, Phone: 920-625-3607, carsmith1@SBCGlobal.net; Web: Hembrook3607@charter.net
Specialties: JC knives. Patterns: Hunters, Bowies, fighting knives, every day carries. Technical: Grinds ATS-34 and Damascus. Prices: $200 to $750. Remarks: Full-time maker for 2 years, being taught by Ron Hembrook.
CARR, TIM,
3660 Pillon Rd, Muskegon, MI 49445, Phone: 231-766-3582, tim@blackbearforgemi.com Web:www.blackbearforgemi.com
Specialties: Hunters, camp knives. Patterns: His or yours. Technical: Hand forges 5160, 52100 and Damascus. Prices: $125 to $700. Remarks: Part-time maker. Mark: The letter combined from maker's initials TRC.
CARRILLO, DWAINE,
C/O AIRKAT KNIVES, 1021 SW 15th St, Moore, OK 73160, Phone: 405-503-5879, Web: www.airkatknives.com
CARROLL, CHAD,
12182 McClelland, Grant, MI 49327, Phone: 231-834-9183, CHAD724@msn.com
Specialties: Hunters, Bowies, swords, tomahawks. Patterns: Fixed blades, folders. Prices: $100 to $2000. Remarks: ABS Journeyman May 2002. Mark: A backwards C next to a forward C, maker's initials.
CARSON, HAROLD J "KIT",
1076 Brizendine Lane, Vine Grove, KY 40175, Phone: 270 877-6300, Fax: 270 877 6338, KCKnives@bbtel.com; Web: www.kitcarsonknives.com/album
Specialties: Military fixed blades and folders; art pieces. Patterns: Fighters, D handles, daggers, combat folders and Crosslock-styles, tactical folders, tactical fixed blades. Technical: Grinds Stellite 6K, Talonite, CPM steels, Damascus. Prices: $400 to $750; some to $5000. Remarks: Full-time maker; first knife sold in 1973. BLADE Magazine Hall-Of-Fame Induction 2012. Mark: Name stamped or engraved.
CARTER, FRED,
5219 Deer Creek Rd, Wichita Falls, TX 76302, Phone: 904-723-4020
Specialties: High-art investor-class straight knives; some working hunters and fighters. Patterns: Classic daggers, Bowies; interframe, stainless and blued steel folders with gold inlay. Technical: Grinds a variety of steels. Uses no glue or solder. Engraves and inlays. Prices: Generally upscale. Remarks: Full-time maker. Mark: Signature in oval logo.
CARTER, MIKE,
2522 Frankfort Ave, Louisville, KY 40206, Phone: 502-387-4844, mike@cartercrafts.com Web: www.cartercrafts.com
Remarks: Voting Member Knifemakers Guild.
CARTER, MURRAY M,
22097 NW West Union Rd, Hillsboro, OR 97124, Phone: 503-447-1029, murray@cartercutlery.com; Web: www.cartercutlery.com
Specialties: Traditional Japanese cutlery, utilizing San soh ko (three layer) or Kata-ha (two layer) blade construction. Laminated neck knives, traditional Japanese etc. Patterns: Works from over 200 standard Japanese and North American designs. Technical: Hot forges and cold forges Hitachi white steel #1, Hitachi blue super steel exclusively. Prices: $800 to $10,000. Remarks: Owns and operates North America's most exclusive traditional Japanese bladesmithing school; web site available at which viewers can subscribe to 10 free knife sharpening and maintenance reports. Mark: Name in cursive, often appearing with Japanese characters. Other: Very interestng and informative monthly newsletter.
CARTER, SHAYNE,
5302 Rosewood Cir., Payson, UT 84651, Phone: 801-913-0181, shaynemcarter@hotmail.com
Specialties: Fixed blades. Patterns: Hunters, bowies and fighters. Technical: Flat grinds, hand finishes, forges blade steel, including own damascus, some 1084, 52100 and 5160. Remarks: Part-time maker; first damascus made in 1984.
CASEY, KEVIN,
10583 N. 42nd St., Hickory Corners, MI 49060, Phone: 269-719-7412, kevincasey@tds.net; Web: www.kevincaseycustomknives.com
Specialties: Fixed blades and folders. Patterns: Liner lock folders and feather Damascus pattern, mammoth ivory. Technical: Forges Damascus and carbon steels. Prices: Starting at $500 - $2500. Remarks: Member ABS, Knifemakers Guild, Custom Knifemakers Collectors Association.
CASHEN, KEVIN R,
5615 Tyler St, Hubbardston, MI 48845, Phone: 989-981-6780, kevin@cashenblades.com; Web: www.cashenblades.com
Specialties: Working straight knives, high art pattern welded swords, traditional renaissance and ethnic pieces. Patterns: Hunters, Bowies, utility knives, swords, daggers. Technical: Forges 1095, 1084 and his own O1/L6 Damascus. Prices: $100 to $4000+. Remarks: Full-time maker; first knife sold in 1985. Doing business as Matherton Forge. Mark: Black letter Old English initials and Master Smith stamp.

CASTEEL, DIANNA,
PO Box 63, Monteagle, TN 37356, Phone: 931-212-4341, ddcasteel@charter.net; Web: www.casteelcustomknives.com
Specialties: Small, delicate daggers and miniatures; most knives one-of-a-kind. Patterns: Daggers, boot knives, fighters and miniatures. Technical: Grinds 440C. Offers stainless Damascus. Prices: Start at $350; miniatures start at $250. Remarks: Full-time maker. Mark: Di in script.
CASTEEL, DOUGLAS,
PO Box 63, Monteagle, TN 37356, Phone: 931-212-4341, Fax: 931-723-1856, ddcasteel@charter.net; Web: www.casteelcustomknives.com
Specialties: One-of-a-kind collector-class period pieces. Patterns: Daggers, Bowies, swords and folders. Technical: Grinds 440C. Offers gold and silver castings. Offers stainless Damascus Prices: Upscale. Remarks: Full-time maker; first knife sold in 1982. Mark: Last name.
CASTELLUCIO, RICH,
220 Stairs Rd, Amsterdam, NY 12010, Phone: 518-843-5540, rcastellucio@nycap.rr.com
Patterns: Bowies, push daggers, and fantasy knives. Technical: Uses ATS-34, 440C, 154CM. I use stabilized wood, bone for the handles. Guards are made of copper, brass, stainless, nickle, and mokume.
CASTON, DARRIEL,
125 Ashcat Way, Folsom, CA 95630, Phone: 916-539-0744, darrielc@gmail.com
CASWELL, JOE,
173 S Ventu Park Rd, Newbury, CA 91320, Phone: 805-499-0707, Web:www.caswellknives.com
Specialties:Historic pattern welded knives and swords, hand forged. Also high precision folding and fixed blade "gentleman" and "tactical" knives of his design, period firearms. Inventor of the "In-Line" retractable pocket clip for folding knives. Patterns:Hunters, tactical/utility, fighters, bowies, daggers, pattern welded medieval swords, precision folders. Technical:Forges own Damascus especially historic forms. Sometimes uses modern stainless steels and Damascus of other makers. Makes some pieces entirely by hand, others using the latest CNC techniques and by hand. Makes sheaths too. Prices:$100-$5,500. Remarks:Full time makers since 1995. Making mostly historic recreations for exclusive clientele. Recently moving into folding knives and 'modern' designs. Mark:CASWELL or CASWELL USA Accompanied by a mounted knight logo.
CATOE, DAVID R,
4024 Heutte Dr, Norfolk, VA 23518, Phone: 757-480-3191
Technical: Does own forging, Damascus and heat treatments. Price: $200 to $500; some higher. Remarks: Part-time maker; trained by Dan Maragni 1985-1988; first knife sold 1989. Mark: Leaf of a camellia.
CAWTHORNE, CHRISTOPHER A,
PO Box 604, Wrangell, AK 99929, Phone: 661-902-3724, chriscawthorne@hotmail.com
Specialties: High-carbon steel, cable wire rope, silver wire inlay. Patterns: Forge welded Damascus and wire rope, random pattern. Technical: Hand forged, 50 lb. little giant power hammer, W-2, 0-1, L6, 1095. Prices: $650 to $2500. Remarks: School ABS 1985 w/Bill Moran, hand forged, heat treat. Mark: Cawthorne, forged in stamp.
CECCHINI, GUSTAVO T.,
R. XV Novembro 2841, Sao Jose Rio Preto, SPAIN 15015110, Phone: 55 1732224267, tomaki@terra.com.be Web: www.gtcknives.com
Specialties: Tactical and HiTech folders. Technical: Stock removal. Stainless steel fixed blades. S30V, S35Vn, S90V, CowryX, Damasteel, Chad Nichols SS damascus, RWL 34, CPM 154 CM, BG 42. Prices: $500 - $1500. Remarks: Full-time since 2004. Mark: Tang Stamp "GTC"
CEPRANO, PETER J.,
213 Townsend Brooke Rd., Auburn, ME 04210, Phone: 207-786-5322, bpknives@gmail.com
Specialties: Traditional working/using straight knives; tactical/defense straight knives. Own designs or to a customer's specs. Patterns: Hunters, skinners, utility, Bowies, fighters, camp and survival, neck knives. Technical: Forges 1095, 5160, W2, 52100 and old files; grinds CPM154cm, ATS-34, 440C, D2, CPMs30v, Damascus from other makes and other tool steels. Hand-sewn and tooled leather and Kydex sheaths. Prices: Starting at $125. Remarks: Full-time maker, first knife sold in 2001. Doing business as Big Pete Knives. Mark: Bold BPK over small BigPeteKnivesUSA.
CHAFFEE, JEFF L,
14314 N. Washington St, PO Box 1, Morris, IN 47033, Phone: 812-212-6188
Specialties: Fancy working and utility folders and straight knives. Patterns: Fighters, dagger, hunter and locking folders. Technical: Grinds commercial Damascus, 440C, ATS-34, D2 and O1. Prefers natural handle materials. Prices: $350 to $2000. Remarks: Part-time maker; first knife sold in 1988. Mark: Last name.
CHAMBERLAIN, CHARLES R,
PO Box 156, Barren Springs, VA 24313-0156, Phone: 703-381-5137
CHAMBERLAIN, JON A,
15 S. Lombard, E. Wenatchee, WA 98802, Phone: 509-884-6591
Specialties: Working and kitchen knives to customer specs; exotics on special order. Patterns: Over 100 patterns in stock. Technical: Prefers ATS-34, D2, L6 and Damascus. Prices: Start at $50. Remarks: First knife sold in 1986. Doing business as Johnny Custom Knifemakers. Mark: Name in oval with city and state enclosing.

CHAMBERLIN, JOHN A,
11535 Our Rd., Anchorage, AK 99516, Phone: 907-346-1524, Fax: 907-562-4583
Specialties: Art and working knives. Patterns: Daggers and hunters; some folders;. Technical: Grinds ATS-34, 440C, A2, D2 and Damascus. Uses Alaskan handle materials such as oosic, jade, whale jawbone, fossil ivory. Prices: Start at $200. Remarks: Favorite knives to make are double-edged. Does own heat treating and cryogenic deep freeze. Full-time maker; first knife sold in 1984. Mark: Name over English shield and dagger.

CHAMBERS, RONNY,
1900 W. Mississippi St., Beebe, AR 72012, Phone: 501-288-1476, chambersronny@yahoo.com; Web: www.chamberscustomknives.net

CHAMBLIN, JOEL,
960 New Hebron Church Rd, Concord, GA 30206, Phone: 678-588-6769, chamblinknives@yahoo.com Web: chamblinknives.com
Specialties: Fancy and working folders. Patterns: Fancy locking folders, traditional, multi-blades and utility. Technical: Uses ATS-34, CPM 154, and commercial Damascus. Offers filework. Prices: Start at $400. Remarks: Full-time maker; first knife sold in 1989. Mark: Last name.

CHAMPION, ROBERT,
7001 Red Rock Rd., Amarillo, TX 79118, Phone: 806-622-3970
Specialties: Traditional working straight knives. Patterns: Hunters, skinners, camp knives, Bowies, daggers. Technical: Grinds 440C and D2. Prices: $100 to $600. Remarks: Part-time maker; first knife sold in 1979. Stream-line hunters. Mark: Last name with dagger logo, city and state.

CHAPO, WILLIAM G,
45 Wildridge Rd, Wilton, CT 06897, Phone: 203-544-9424
Specialties: Classic straight knives and folders of his design and to customer specs; period pieces. Patterns: Boots, Bowies and locking folders. Technical: Forges stainless Damascus. Offers filework. Prices: $750 and up. Remarks: Full-time maker; first knife sold in 1989. Mark: First and middle initials, last name, city, state.

CHARD, GORDON R,
104 S. Holiday Lane, Iola, KS 66749, Phone: 620-365-2311, Fax: 620-365-2311, gchard@cox.net
Specialties: High tech folding knives in one-of-a-kind styles. Patterns: Liner locking folders of own design. Also fixed blade Art Knives. Technical: Clean work with attention to fit and finish. Blade steel mostly ATS-34 and 154CM, some CPM440V Vaso Wear and Damascus. Prices: $150 to $2500. Remarks: First knife sold in 1983. Mark: Name, city and state surrounded by wheat on each side.

CHASE, ALEX,
208 E. Pennsylvania Ave., DeLand, FL 32724, Phone: 386-734-9918, chase8578@bellsouth.net
Specialties: Historical steels, classic and traditional straight knives of his design and to customer specs. Patterns: Art, fighters, hunters and Japanese style. Technical: Forges O1-L6 Damascus, meteoric Damascus, 52100, 5160; uses fossil walrus and mastodon ivory etc. Prices: $150 to $1000; some to $3500. Remarks: Full-time maker; Guild member since 1996. Doing business as Confederate Forge. Mark: Stylized initials-A.C.

CHASE, JOHN E,
217 Walnut, Aledo, TX 76008, Phone: 817-441-8331, jchaseknives@sbcglobal.net
Specialties: Straight working knives in standard patterns or to customer specs. Patterns: Hunters, fighters, daggers and Bowies. Technical: Grinds D2, O1, 440C; offers mostly satin finishes. Prices: Start at $325. Remarks: Part-time maker; first knife sold in 1974. Mark: Last name in logo.

CHAUVIN, JOHN,
200 Anna St, Scott, LA 70583, Phone: 337-237-6138, Fax: 337-230-7980
Specialties: Traditional working and using straight knives of his design, to customer specs and in standard patterns. Patterns: Bowies, fighters, and hunters. Technical: Grinds ATS-34, 440C and O1 high-carbon. Paul Bos heat treating. Uses ivory, stag, oosic and stabilized Louisiana swamp maple for handle materials. Makes sheaths using alligator and ostrich. Prices: $200 and up. Bowies start at $500. Remarks: Part-time maker; first knife sold in 1995. Mark: Full name, city, state.

CHAUZY, ALAIN,
1 Rue de Paris, Seur-en-Auxios, FRANCE 21140, Phone: 03-80-97-03-30, Fax: 03-80-97-34-14
Specialties: Fixed blades, folders, hunters, Bowies-scagel-style. Technical: Forged blades only. Steels used XC65, 07C, and own Damascus. Prices: Contact maker for quote. Remarks: Part-time maker. Mark: Number 2 crossed by an arrow and name.

CHAVEZ, RAMON,
314 N. 5th St., Belen, NM 87002, Phone: 505-453-6008, ramonchavesknives@gmail.com; Web: www.handmadeblades.com
Specialties: Fixed blades and traditional everyday working knives, some custom. Patterns: Hunters, skinners, bushcraft, tactical, neck knives and utility. Technical: Grind/stock removal of CPM-D2 and D2. Handles are mostly canvas and linen phenolic resin, will use some stabilized woods. Thermal molding plastic for sheaths. Prices: Start at $175. Remarks: Part-time maker; first knife made in 1993, first knife sold in 2010. Mark: CHAVES USA with skeleton key.

CHEATHAM, BILL,
PO Box 636, Laveen, AZ 85339, Phone: 602-237-2786, blademan76@aol.com
Specialties: Working straight knives and folders. Patterns: Hunters, fighters, boots and axes; locking folders. Technical: Grinds 440C. Prices: $150 to $350; exceptional knives to $600. Remarks: Full-time maker; first knife sold in 1976. Mark: Name, city, state.

CHERRY, FRANK J,
3412 Tiley N.E., Albuquerque, NM 87110, Phone: 505-883-8643

CHEW, LARRY,
3025 De leon Dr., Weatherford, TX 76087, Phone: 817-573-8035, chewman@swbell.net; Web: www.voodooinside.com
Specialties: High-tech folding knives. Patterns: Double action automatic and manual folding patterns of his design. Technical: CAD designed folders utilizing roller bearing pivot design known as "VooDoo." Double action automatic folders with a variety of obvious and disguised release mechanisms, some with lock-outs. Prices: Manual folders start at $475, double action autos start at $750. Remarks: Made and sold first knife in 1988, first folder in 1989. Full-time maker since 1997. Mark: Name and location etched in blade, Damascus autos marked on spring inside frame. Earliest knives stamped LC.

CHILDERS, DAVID,
4106 Mossy Oaks, W. Spring, TX 77389, Phone: 281-353-4113, Web: www.davidchildersknives.com

CHINNOCK, DANIEL T.,
380 River Ridge Dr., Union, MO 63084, Phone: 314-276-6936, Web: www.DanChinnock.com; email: Sueanddanc@cs.com
Specialties: One of a kind folders in Damascus and Mammoth Ivory. Performs intricate pearl inlays into snake wood and giraffe bone. Makes matchimg ivory pistol grips for colt 1911's and Colt SAA. Patterns: New folder designs each year, thin ground and delicate gentleman's folders, large "hunting" folders in stainless Damascus and CPM154. Several standard models carried by Internet dealers. Prices: $500-$1500 Remarks: Full-time maker in 2005 and a voting member of the Knifemakers Guild. Performs intricate file work on all areas of knife. Mark: Signature on inside of backbar, starting in 2009 blades are stamped with a large "C" and "Dan" buried inside the "C".

CHOATE, MILTON,
1665 W. County 17-1/2, Somerton, AZ 85350, Phone: 928-627-7251, mccustom@juno.com
Specialties: Classic working and using straight knives of his design, to customer specs and in standard patterns. Patterns: Bowies, hunters and utility/camp knives. Technical: Grinds 440C; grinds and forges 1095 and 5160. Does filework on top and guards on request. Prices: $200 to $800. Remarks: Full-time maker, first knife made in 1990. All knives come with handmade sheaths by Judy Choate. Mark: Knives marked "Choate."

CHOMILIER, ALAIN AND JORIS,
20 rue des Hauts de Chanturgue, Clermont-Ferrand, FRANCE 63100, Phone: + 33 4 73 25 64 47, jo_chomilier@yahoo.fr
Specialties: One-of-a-kind knives; exclusive designs; art knives in carved patinated bronze, mainly folders, some straight knives and art daggers. Patterns: Liner-lock, side-lock, button-lock, lockback folders. Technical: Grind carbon and stainless damascus; also carve and patinate bronze. Prices: $400 to $3000, some to $4000. Remarks: Spare-time makers; first knife sold in 1995; Use fossil stone and ivory, mother-of-pearl, (fossil) coral, meteorite, bronze, gemstones, high karat gold. Mark: A. J. Chomilier in italics.

CHRISTENSEN, JON P,
516 Blue Grouse, Stevensville, MT 59870, Phone: 406-697-8377, jpcknives@gmail.com; Web: www.jonchristensenknives.com
Specialties: Hunting/utility knives, folders, art knives. Patterns: Mosaic damascusTechnical: Sole authorship, forges 01, 1084, 52100, 5160, Damascus from 1084/15N20. Prices: $220 and up. Remarks: ABS Mastersmith, first knife sold in 1999. Mark: First and middle initial surrounded by last initial.

CHURCHMAN, T W (TIM),
475 Saddle Horn Drive, Bandera, TX 78003, Phone: 210-240-0317, tim.churchman@nustarenergy.com
Specialties: Fancy and traditional straight knives. Bird/trout knives of his design and to customer specs. Patterns: Bird/trout knives, Bowies, daggers, fighters, boot knives, some miniatures. Technical: Grinds 440C, D2 and 154CM. Offers stainless fittings, fancy filework, exotic and stabilized woods, elk and other antler, and hand sewed lined sheaths. Also flower pins as a style. Prices: $350 to $450; some to $2,250. Remarks: Part-time maker; first knife made in 1981 after reading "KNIVES '81." Doing business as "Custom Knives Churchman Made." Mark: "Churchman" over Texas outline, "Bandera" under.

CLAIBORNE, JEFF,
1470 Roberts Rd, Franklin, IN 46131, Phone: 317-736-7443, jeff@claiborneknives.com; Web: www.claiborneknives.com
Specialties: Multi blade slip joint folders. All one-of-a-kind by hand, no jigs or fixtures, swords, straight knives, period pieces, camp knives, hunters, fighters, ethnic swords all periods. Handle: uses stag, pearl, oosic, bone ivory, mastodon-mammoth, elephant or exotic woods. Technical: Forges high-carbon steel, makes Damascus, forges cable grinds, O1, 1095, 5160, 52100, L6. Prices: $250 and up. Remarks: Part-time maker; first knife sold in 1989. Mark: Stylized initials in an oval.

CLAIBORNE, RON,
2918 Ellistown Rd, Knox, TN 37924, Phone: 615-524-2054, Bowie@icy.net
Specialties: Multi-blade slip joints, swords, straight knives. Patterns: Hunters, daggers, folders. Technical: Forges Damascus: mosaic, powder mosaic. Prefers bone and natural handle materials; some exotic woods. Prices: $125 to

CLARK—CONNOR

$2500. Remarks: Part-time maker; first knife sold in 1979. Doing business as Thunder Mountain Forge Claiborne Knives. Mark: Claiborne.

CLARK, D E (LUCKY),
413 Lyman Lane, Johnstown, PA 15909-1409
Specialties: Working straight knives and folders to customer specs. Patterns: Customer designs. Technical: Grinds D2, 440C, 154CM. Prices: $100 to $200; some higher. Remarks: Part-time maker; first knife sold in 1975. Mark: Name on one side; "Lucky" on other.

CLARK, HOWARD F,
115 35th Pl, Runnells, IA 50237, Phone: 515-966-2126, howard@mvforge.com; Web: mvforge.com
Specialties: Currently Japanese-style swords. Patterns: Katana. Technical: Forges L6 and 1086. Prices: $1200 to 5000. Remarks: Full-time maker; first knife sold in 1979. Doing business as Morgan Valley Forge. Prior Mark: Block letters and serial number on folders; anvil/initials logo on straight knives. Current Mark: Two character kanji "Big Ear."

CLARK, NATE,
604 Baird Dr, Yoncalla, OR 97499, nateclarkknives@hotmail.com; Web: www.nateclarkknives.com
Specialties: Automatics (push button and hidden release) ATS-34 mirror polish or satin finish, Damascus, pearl, ivory, abalone, woods, bone, Micarta, G-10, filework and carving and sheath knives. Prices: $100 to $2500. Remarks: Full-time knifemaker since 1996. Mark: Nate Clark on spring, spacer or blade.

CLARK, R W,
R.W. CLARK CUSTOM KNIVES, 17602 W. Eugene Terrace, Surprise, AZ 85388-5047, Phone: 909-279-3494, info@rwclarkknives.com
Specialties: Military field knives and Asian hybrids. Hand carved leather sheaths. Patterns: Fixed blade hunters, field utility and military. Also presentation and collector grade knives. Technical: First maker to use liquid metals LM1 material in knives. Other materials include S30V, O1, stainless and carbon Damascus. Prices: $75 to $2000. Average price $300. Remarks: Started knifemaking in 1990, full-time in 2000. Mark: R.W. Clark, Custom, Corona, CA in standard football shape. Also uses three Japanese characters, spelling Clark, on Asian Hybrids.

CLAY, WAYNE,
Box 125B, Pelham, TN 37366, Phone: 931-467-3472, Fax: 931-467-3076
Specialties: Working straight knives and folders in standard patterns. Patterns: Hunters and kitchen knives; gents and hunter patterns. Technical: Grinds ATS-34. Prices: $125 to $500; some to $1000. Remarks: Full-time maker; first knife sold in 1978. Mark: Name.

CLINCO, MARCUS,
821 Appelby Street, Venice, CA 90291, Phone: 818-610-9640, marcus@clincoknives.com; Web: www.clincoknives.com
Specialties: I make mostly fixed blade knives with an emphasis on everyday working and tactical models. Most of my knives are stock removal with the exception of my integral models including a one piece tactical model named the viper. Technical: Most working knife models in ATS 34. Integrals in O-1, D-2 and 440 C. Damascus in 1080 and 15 N 20. Large camp and Bowie models in 5160 and D-2. Handle materials used include micarta, stabilized wood, G-10 and occasionally stag and ivory. Prices: $200 - $600.

COATS, KEN,
317 5th Ave, Stevens Point, WI 54481, Phone: 715-544-0115, kandk_c@charter.net
Specialties: Does own jigged bone scales Patterns: Traditional slip joints - shadow patterns Technical: ATS-34 Blades and springs. Milled frames. Grinds ATS-34, 440C. Stainless blades and backsprings. Does all own heat treating and freeze cycle. Blades are drawn to 60RC. Nickel silver or brass bolsters on folders are soldered, neutralized and pinned. Handles are jigged bone, hardwoods antler, and Micarta. Cuts and jigs own bone, usually shades of brown or green. Prices: $300 and up

COCKERHAM, LLOYD,
1717 Carolyn Ave, Denham Springs, IA 70726, Phone: 225-665-1565

COFFEE, JIM,
2785 Rush Rd., Norton, OH 44203, Phone: 330-631-3355, jcoffee735@aol.com; Web: jcoffeecustomknives.com
Specialties: Stock Removal, hunters, skinners, fighters. Technical: Bowie handle material - stabilized wood, micarta, mammoth ivory, stag. Full tang and hidden tang. Steels - 0-1, d-2, 5160, damascus Prices: $150 to $500 and up. Remarks: Part-time maker since 2008.Mark: full name in a football etch.

COFFEY, BILL,
68 Joshua Ave, Clovis, CA 93611, Phone: 559-299-4259
Specialties: Working and fancy straight knives and folders of his design. Patterns: Hunters, fighters, utility, LinerLock® folders and fantasy knives. Technical: Grinds 440C, ATS-34, A-Z and commercial Damascus. Prices: $250 to $1000; some to $2500. Remarks: Full-time maker. First knife sold in 1993. Mark: First and last name, city, state.

COFFMAN, DANNY,
541 Angel Dr S, Jacksonville, AL 36265-5787, Phone: 256-435-1619
Specialties: Straight knives and folders of his design. Now making liner locks for $650 to $1200 with natural handles and contrasting Damascus blades and bolsters. Patterns: Hunters, locking and slip-joint folders. Technical: Grinds Damascus, 440C and D2. Offers filework and engraving. Prices: $100 to $400;

some to $800. Remarks: Spare-time maker; first knife sold in 1992. Doing business as Customs by Coffman. Mark: Last name stamped or engraved.

COHEA, JOHN M,
114 Rogers Dr., Nettleton, MS 38855, Phone: 662-322-5916, jhncohea@hotmail.com Web: http://jmcknives.blademakers.com
Specialties: Frontier style knives, hawks, and leather. Patterns: Bowies, hunters, patch/neck knives, tomahawks, and friction folders. Technical: Makes both forged and stock removal knives using high carbon steels and damascus. Uses natural handle materials that include antler, bone, ivory, horn, and figured hardwoods. Also makes rawhide covered sheaths that include fringe, tacks, antique trade beads, and other period correct materials. Prices: $100 - $1500, some higher. Remarks: Part-time maker, first knife sold in 1999. Mark: COHEA stamped on riccasso.

COHEN, N J (NORM),
2408 Sugarcone Rd, Baltimore, MD 21209, Phone: 410-484-3841, inquiry@njknives.com; Web:www.njcknives.com
Specialties: Working class knives. Patterns: Hunters, skinners, bird knives, push daggers, boots, kitchen and practical customer designs. Technical: Stock removal 440C, ATS-34. Uses Micarta, Corian. Some woods and stabilized woods in handles. Prices: $50 to $250. Remarks: Part-time maker; first knife sold in 1982. Mark: NJC engraved.

COLE, JAMES M,
505 Stonewood Blvd, Bartonville, TX 76226, Phone: 817-430-0302, dogcole@swbell.net

COLE, WELBORN I,
365 Crystal Ct, Athens, GA 30606, Phone: 404-261-3977
Specialties: Traditional straight knives of his design. Patterns: Hunters. Technical: Grinds 440C, ATS-34 and D2. Good wood scales. Prices: NA. Remarks: Full-time maker; first knife sold in 1983. Mark: Script initials.

COLEMAN, JOHN A,
7325 Bonita Way, Citrus Heights, CA 95610-3003, Phone: 916-335-1568, slimsknifes@yahoo.com
Specialties: Minis, hunters, bowies of his design or yours. Patterns: Plain to fancy file back working knives. Technical: Grinds 440C, ATS-34, 145CM, D2, 1095, 5160, 01. Some hand-forged blades. Exotic woods bone, antler and some ivory. Prices: $100 to $500. Remarks: Does some carving in handles. Part-time maker. First knife sold in 1989. OKCA 2010 Award winner for best mini of show. Mark: Cowboy setting on log whittling Slim's Custom Knives above cowboy and name and state under cowboy.

COLLINS, LYNN M,
138 Berkley Dr, Elyria, OH 44035, Phone: 440-366-7101
Specialties: Working straight knives. Patterns: Field knives, boots and fighters. Technical: Grinds D2, 154CM and 440C. Prices: Start at $200. Remarks: Spare-time maker; first knife sold in 1980. Mark: Initials, asterisks.

COLTER, WADE,
PO Box 2340, Colstrip, MT 59323, Phone: 406-748-4573; Shop: 406-748-2010; Fax: Cell: 406-740-1554
Specialties: Fancy and embellished straight knives, folders and swords of his design; historical and period pieces. Patterns: Bowies, swords and folders. Technical: Hand forges 52100 ball bearing steel and L6, 1090, cable and chain Damascus from 5N20 and 1084. Carves and makes sheaths. Prices: $250 to $3500. Remarks: SemiRetired; first knife sold in 1990. Doing business as "Colter's Hell" Forge. Mark: Initials on left side ricasso.

CONKLIN, GEORGE L,
Box 902, Ft. Benton, MT 59442, Phone: 406-622-3268, Fax: 406-622-3410, 7bbgrus@3rivers.net
Specialties: Designer and manufacturer of the "Brisket Breaker." Patterns: Hunters, utility/camp knives and hatchets. Technical: Grinds 440C, ATS-34, D2, 1095, 154CM and 5160. Offers some forging and heat-treats for others. Offers some jewelling. Prices: $65 to $200; some to $1000. Remarks: Full-time maker. Doing business as Rocky Mountain Knives. Mark: Last name in script.

CONLEY, BOB,
1013 Creasy Rd, Jonesboro, TN 37659, Phone: 423-753-3302
Specialties: Working straight knives and folders. Patterns: Lockers, two-blades, gents, hunters, traditional-styles, straight hunters. Technical: Grinds 440C, 154CM and ATS-34. Engraves. Prices: $250 to $450; some to $600. Remarks: Full-time maker; first knife sold in 1979. Mark: Full name, city, state.

CONN JR., C T,
206 Highland Ave, Attalla, AL 35954, Phone: 205-538-7688
Specialties: Working folders, some fancy. Patterns: Full range of folding knives. Technical: Grinds O2, 440C and 154CM. Prices: $125 to $300; some to $600. Remarks: Part-time maker; first knife sold in 1982. Mark: Name.

CONNOLLY, JAMES,
2486 Oro-Quincy Hwy, Oroville, CA 95966, Phone: 530-534-5363, rjconnolly@sbcglobal.net
Specialties: Classic working and using knives of his design. Patterns: Boots, Bowies, daggers and swords. Technical: Grinds ATS-34, BG42, A2, O1. Prices: $100 to $500; some to $1500. Remarks: Part-time maker; first knife sold in 1980. Doing business as Gold Rush Designs. Mark: First initial, last name, Handmade.

CONNOR, JOHN W,
PO Box 12981, Odessa, TX 79768-2981, Phone: 915-362-6901

CONNOR, MICHAEL,
Box 502, Winters, TX 79567, Phone: 915-754-5602
Specialties: Straight knives, period pieces, some folders. Patterns: Hunters to

camp knives to traditional locking folders to Bowies. Technical: Forges 5160, O1, 1084 steels and his own Damascus. Prices: Moderate to upscale. Remarks: Spare-time maker; first knife sold in 1974. ABS Master Smith 1983. Mark: Last name, M.S.

CONTI, JEFFREY D,
21104 75th St E, Bonney Lake, WA 98390, Phone: 253-447-4660, Fax: 253-512-8629
Specialties: Working straight knives. Patterns: Fighters and survival knives; hunters, camp knives and fishing knives. Technical: Grinds D2, 154CM and O1. Engraves. Prices: Start at $80. Remarks: Part-time maker; first knife sold in 1980. Does own heat treating. Mark: Initials, year, steel type, name and number of knife.

CONWAY, JOHN,
13301 100th Place NE, Kirkland, WA 98034, Phone: 425-823-2821, jcknives@Frontier.com
Specialties: Folders; working and Damascus. Straight knives, camp, utility and fighting knives. Patterns: LinerLock® folders of own design. Hidden tang straight knives of own design. Technical: Flat grinds forged carbon steels and own Damascus steel, including mosaic. Prices: $300 to $850. Remarks: Part-time maker since 1999. Mark: Oval with stylized initials J C inset.

COOGAN, ROBERT,
1560 Craft Center Dr, Smithville, TN 37166, Phone: 615-597-6801, http://iweb.tntech.edu/rcoogan/
Specialties: One-of-a-kind knives. Patterns: Unique items like ulu-style Appalachian herb knives. Technical: Forges; his Damascus is made from nickel steel and W1. Prices: Start at $100. Remarks: Part-time maker; first knife sold in 1979. Mark: Initials or last name in script.

COOK, JAMES R,
455 Anderson Rd, Nashville, AR 71852, Phone: 870 845 5173, jr@jrcookknives.com; Web: www.jrcookknives.com
Specialties: Working straight knives and folders of his design or to customer specs. Patterns: Bowies, hunters and camp knives. Technical: Forges 1084 and high-carbon Damascus. Prices: $500 to $10000. Remarks: Full-time maker; first knife sold in 1986. Mark: First and middle initials, last name.

COOK, LOUISE,
475 Robinson Ln, Ozark, IL 62972, Phone: 618-777-2932
Specialties: Working and using straight knives of her design and to customer specs; period pieces. Patterns: Bowies, hunters and utility/camp knives. Technical: Forges 5160. Filework; pin work; silver wire inlay. Prices: Start at $50/inch. Remarks: Part-time maker; first knife sold in 1990. Doing business as Panther Creek Forge. Mark: First name and Journeyman stamp on one side; panther head on the other.

COOK, MIKE,
475 Robinson Ln, Ozark, IL 62972, Phone: 618-777-2932
Specialties: Traditional working and using straight knives of his design and to customer specs. Patterns: Bowies, hunters and utility/camp knives. Technical: Forges 5160. Filework; pin work. Prices: Start at $50/inch. Remarks: Spare-time maker; first knife sold in 1991. Mark: First initial, last name and Journeyman stamp on one side; panther head on the other.

COOK, MIKE A,
10927 Shilton Rd, Portland, MI 48875, Phone: 517-242-1352, macook@hughes.net Web: www.artofishi.com
Specialties: Fancy/embellished and period pieces of his design. Patterns: Daggers, fighters and hunters. Technical: Stone bladed knives in agate, obsidian and jasper. Scrimshaws; opal inlays. Prices: $60 to $300; some to $800. Remarks: Part-time maker; first knife sold in 1988. Doing business as Art of Ishi. Mark: Initials and year.

COOMBS JR., LAMONT,
546 State Rt 46, Bucksport, ME 04416, Phone: 207-469-3057, Fax: 207-469-3057, theknifemaker@hotmail.com; Web: www.knivesby.com/coomb-knives.html
Specialties: Classic fancy and embellished straight knives; traditional working and using straight knives. Knives of his design and to customer specs. Patterns: Hunters, folders and utility/camp knives. Technical: Hollow- and flat-grinds ATS-34, 440C, A2, D2 and O1; grinds Damascus from other makers. Prices: $100 to $500; some to $3500. Remarks: Full-time maker; first knife sold in 1988. Mark: Last name on banner, handmade underneath.

COON, RAYMOND C,
21135 S.E. Tillstrom Rd, Damascus, OR 97089, Phone: 503-658-2252, Raymond@damascusknife.com; Web: Damascusknife.com
Specialties: Working straight knives in standard patterns. Patterns: Hunters, Bowies, daggers, boots and axes. Technical: Forges high-carbon steel and Damascus or 97089. Prices: Start at $235. Remarks: Full-time maker; does own leatherwork, makes own Damascus, daggers; first knife sold in 1995. Mark: First initial, last name.

COOPER, PAUL,
9 Woods St., Woburn, MA 01801, Phone: 781-938-0519, byksm@yahoo.com
Specialties: Forged, embellished, hand finished fixed-blade knives. Patterns: One of a kind designs, often inspired by traditional and historic pieces. Technical: Works in tool steel, damascus and natural materials. Prices: $500 - $2000. Remarks: Part-time maker, formally apprenticed under J.D. Smith. Sold first piece in 2006. Mark: Letter C inside bleeding heart.

COPELAND, THOM,
171 Country Line Rd S, Nashville, AR 71852, tcope@cswnet.com
Specialties: Hand forged fixed blades; hunters, Bowies and camp knives. Remarks: Member of ABS and AKA (Arkansas Knifemakers Association). Mark: Copeland.

COPPINS, DANIEL,
7303 Sherrard Rd, Cambridge, OH 43725, Phone: 740-439-4199
Specialties: Grinds 440 C, D-2. Antler handles. Patterns: Drop point hunters, fighters, Bowies, bird and trout daggers. Prices: $40 to $800. Remarks: Sold first knife in 2002. Mark: DC.

CORBY, HAROLD,
218 Brandonwood Dr, Johnson City, TN 37604, Phone: 423-926-9781
Specialties: Large fighters and Bowies; self-protection knives; art knives. Along with art knives and combat knives, Corby now has a all new automatic MO.PB1, also side lock MO LL-1 with titanium liners G-10 handles. Patterns: Sub-hilt fighters and hunters. Technical: Grinds 154CM, ATS-34 and 440C. Prices: $200 to $6000. Remarks: Full-time maker; first knife sold in 1969. Doing business as Knives by Corby. Mark: Last name.

CORDOVA, JOSEPH G,
1450 Lillie Dr, Bosque Farms, NM 87068, Phone: 505-869-3912, kcordova@rt66.com
Specialties: One-of-a-kind designs, some to customer specs. Patterns: Fighter called the 'Gladiator', hunters, boots and cutlery. Technical: Forges 1095, 5160; grinds ATS-34, 440C and 154CM. Prices: Moderate to upscale. Remarks: Full-time maker; first knife sold in 1953. Past chairman of American Bladesmith Society. Mark: Cordova made.

CORKUM, STEVE,
34 Basehoar School Rd, Littlestown, PA 17340, Phone: 717-359-9563, sco7129849@aol.com; Web: www.hawkknives.com

CORNWELL, JEFFREY,
Treasure Art Blades, PO Box 244014, Anchorage, AK 99524, Phone: 907-887-1661, cornwellsjej@alaska.net
Specialties: Organic, sculptural shapes of original design from damascus steel and mokume gane. Technical: Blade creations from Robert Eggerling damascus and Mike Sakmar mokume. Remarks: Free-time maker. Mark: Stylized J inside a circle.

COSTA, SCOTT,
409 Coventry Rd, Spicewood, TX 78669, Phone: 830-693-3431
Specialties: Working straight knives. Patterns: Hunters, skinners, axes, trophy sets, custom boxed steak sets, carving sets and bar sets. Technical: Grinds D2, ATS-34, 440 and Damascus. Heat-treats. Prices: $225 to $2000. Remarks: Full-time maker; first knife sold in 1985. Mark: Initials connected.

COTTRILL, JAMES I,
1776 Ransburg Ave, Columbus, OH 43223, Phone: 614-274-0020
Specialties: Working straight knives of his design. Patterns: Caters to the boating and hunting crowd; cutlery. Technical: Grinds O1, D2 and 440C. Likes filework. Prices: $95 to $250; some to $500. Remarks: Full-time maker; first knife sold in 1977. Mark: Name, city, state, in oval logo.

COUSINO, GEORGE,
7818 Norfolk, Onsted, MI 49265, Phone: 517-467-4911, cousinoknives@yahoo.com; Web: www.cousinoknives.com
Specialties: Hunters, Bowies using knives. Patterns: Hunters, Bowies, buckskinners, folders and daggers. Technical: Grinds 440C. Prices: $95 to $300. Remarks: Part-time maker; first knife sold in 1981. Mark: Last name.

COVER, JEFF,
11355AllenRd,Potosi,MO63664,Phone:573-749-0008,jeffcovercustomknives@hotmail.com
Specialties: Folders and straight knives. Patterns: Technical: Various knife steels and handle materials. Prices: $70 to $500.Mark: Jeff Cover J.C. Custom Knives.

COVER, RAYMOND A,
16235 State Hwy. U, Mineral Point, MO 63660, Phone: 573-749-3783
Specialties: High-tech working straight knives and folders in working patterns. Patterns: Slip joints, lockbacks, multi-blade folders. Technical: Various knife steels and handle materials. Prices: Swords from bare blades to complete high art $200 to $600. Mark: "R Cover"

COWLES, DON,
1026 Lawndale Dr, Royal Oak, MI 48067, Phone: 248-541-4619, don@cowlesknives.com; Web: www.cowlesknives.com
Specialties: Straight, non-folding pocket knives of his design. Patterns: Gentlemen's pocket knives. Technical: Grinds CPM154, S30V, Damascus, Talonite. Engraves; pearl inlays in some handles. Prices: Start at $300. Remarks: Full-time maker; first knife sold in 1994. Mark: Full name with oak leaf.

COX, COLIN J,
107 N. Oxford Dr, Raymore, MO 64083, Phone: 816-352-2122, Colin4knives@aol.com; Web: www.colincoxknives.com
Specialties: Working straight knives and folders of his design; period pieces. Patterns: Hunters, fighters and survival knives. Folders, two-blades, gents and hunters. Technical: Grinds D2, 440C, 154CM and ATS-34. Prices: $125 to $750; some to $4000. Remarks: Full-time maker; first knife sold in 1981. Mark: Full name, city and state.

COX, LARRY,
701 W. 13th St, Murfreesboro, AR 71958, Phone: 870-258-2429, Fax: Cell: 870-557-8062
Patterns: Hunters, camp knives, Bowies, and skinners. Technical: Forges carbon steel 1084, 1080, 15N29, 5160 and Damascus. Forges own pattern

welded Damascus as well as doing own heat treat. Prices: $150 and up. Remarks: Sole ownership; knives and sheaths. Part-time maker; first knife sold in 2007. Member ABS and Arkansas Knifemakers Association. Mark: COX.

COX, SAM,
1756 Love Springs Rd, Gaffney, SC 29341, Phone: 864-489-1892
Remarks: Started making knives in 1981 for another maker. 1st knife sold under own name in 1983. Full-time maker 1985-2009. Retired in 2010. Now part time. Mark: Different logo each year.

COYE, BILL,
PO Box 470684, Tulsa, OK 74147, Phone: 918-232-5721, info@coyeknives.com; Web: www.coyeknives.com
Specialties: Tactical and utility knives. Patterns: Fighters and utility. Technical: Grinds CPM154CM, 154CM, CTS-XHP and Elmax stainless steels. Prices: $210 to $320. Remarks: Part-time maker. First knife sold in 2009. Mark: COYE.

CRADDOCK, MIKE,
300 Blythe Dr., Thomasville, NC 27360, Phone: 336-382-8461, ncbladesmith@gmail.com
Specialties: Fighters, bowies. Patterns: Hunters and working knives. Technical: Forges and grinds high-carbon steel, and does own damascus. Prices: $350 to $1,500. Mark: CRADDOCK.

CRAIG, ROGER L,
2617 SW Seabrook Ave, Topeka, KS 66614, Phone: 785-249-4109
Specialties: Working and camp knives, some fantasy; all his design. Patterns: Fighters, hunter. Technical: Grinds 1095 and 5160. Most knives have file work. Prices: $50 to $250. Remarks: Part-time maker; first knife sold in 1991. Doing business as Craig Knives. Mark: Last name-Craig.

CRAIN, JACK W,
PO Box 212, Granbury, TX 76048, jack@jackcrainknives.com Web: www.jackcrainknives.com
Specialties: Fantasy and period knives; combat and survival knives. Patterns: One-of-a-kind art or fantasy daggers, swords and Bowies; survival knives. Technical: Forges Damascus; grinds stainless steel. Carves. Prices: $350 to $2500; some to $20,000. Remarks: Full-time maker; first knife sold in 1969. Designer and maker of the knives seen in the films Dracula 2000, Executive Decision, Demolition Man, Predator I and II, Commando, Die Hard I and II, Road House, Ford Fairlane and Action Jackson, and television shows War of the Worlds, Air Wolf, Kung Fu: The Legend Cont. and Tales of the Crypt. Mark: Stylized crane.

CRAMER, BRENT,
PO BOX 99, Wheatland, IN 47597, Phone: 812-881-9961, Bdcramer@juno.com Web: BDCramerKnives.com
Specialties: Traditional and custom working and using knives. Patterns: Traditional single blade slip-joint folders and standard fixed blades. Technical: Stock removal only. Pivot bushing construction on folders. Steel: D-2, 154 CM, ATS-34, CPM-D2, CPM-154CM, 0-1, 52100, A-2. All steels heat treated in shop with LN Cryo. Handle Material: Stag, Bone, Wood, Ivory, and Micarta. Prices: $150 - $550. Remarks: Part-time maker. First fixed blade sold in 2003. First folder sold in 2007. Mark: BDC and B.D.Cramer.

CRAWFORD, PAT AND WES,
205 N. Center, West Memphis, AR 72301, Phone: 870-732-2452, patcrawford1@earthlink.com; Web: www.crawfordknives.com
Specialties: Stainless steel Damascus. High-tech working self-defense and combat types and folders. Patterns: Tactical-more fancy knives now. Technical: Grinds S30V. Prices: $400 to $2000. Remarks: Full-time maker; first knife sold in 1973. Mark: Last name.

CRAWLEY, BRUCE R,
16 Binbrook Dr, Croydon, VIC, AUSTRALIA 3136
Specialties: Folders. Patterns: Hunters, lockback folders and Bowies. Technical: Grinds 440C, ATS-34 and commercial Damascus. Offers filework and mirror polish. Prices: $160 to $3500. Remarks: Part-time maker; first knife sold in 1990. Mark: Initials.

CRENSHAW, AL,
Rt 1 Box 717, Eufaula, OK 74432, Phone: 918-452-2128
Specialties: Folders of his design and in standard patterns. Patterns: Hunters, locking folders, slip-joint folders, multi blade folders. Technical: Grinds 440C, D2 and ATS-34. Does filework on back springs and blades; offers scrimshaw on some handles. Prices: $150 to $300; some higher. Remarks: Full-time maker; first knife sold in 1981. Doing business as A. Crenshaw Knives. Mark: First initial, last name, Lake Eufaula, state stamped; first initial last name in rainbow; Lake Eufaula across bottom with Okla. in middle.

CREWS, RANDY,
627 Cricket Trail Rd., Patriot, OH 45658, Phone: 740-379-2329, randy.crews@sbcglobal.net
Specialties: Fixed blades, bowies and hunters. Technical: 440C, Alabama Damascus, 1095 with file work. Stock removal method. Prices: Start at $150. Remarks: Collected knives for 30 years. Part-time maker; first knife made in 2002. Mark: Crews Patriot OH.

CRIST, ZOE,
HC 82 205, Marlinton, WV 24954, Phone: 304-799-6902, zoe@zoecristknives.com Web: www.zoecristknives.com
Specialties: Mosaic and classic pattern Damascus. Custom Damascus and traditional Damascus working and art knives. Also makes Mokume. Works to customer specs. Patterns: All Damascus hunters, bowies, fighters, neck,

boot, and high-end art knives. Technical: Makes all his own Damascus Steel from 1095, L6, 15n20. Forges all knives, heat treats, filework, differential heat treating. Prices: $150 - $2500. Remarks: Full-time maker, has been making knives since 1988, went full-time 2009. Also makes own leather sheaths. Mark: Small "z" with long tail on left side of blade at ricaso.

CROCKFORD, JACK,
1859 Harts Mill Rd, Chamblee, GA 30341, Phone: 770-457-4680
Specialties: Lockback folders. Patterns: Hunters, fishing and camp knives, traditional folders. Technical: Grinds A2, D2, ATS-34 and 440C. Engraves and scrimshaws. Prices: Start at $175. Remarks: Part-time maker; first knife sold in 1975. Mark: Name.

CROSS, KEVIN,
PO Box 38, Higganum, CT 06441, Phone: 860-345-3949, kevincross@comcast.net; Web: www.kdcknives.com
Specialties: Working/using and presentation grade fixed-blade knives and custom kitchen knives. Patterns: Hunters, skinners, fighters. Bowies, camp knives. Technical: Stock removal maker. Uses O1, 1095, 154 CPM as well as Damascus from Eggerling, Ealy, Donnelly, Nichols, Thomas and others. Most handles are natural materials such as burled and spalted woods, stag and ancient ivory. Prices: $200 - $1,200. Remarks: Part-time maker. First knife sold around 1997. Mark: Name, city and state.

CROSS, ROBERT,
RMB 200B, Manilla Rd, Tamworth, NSW, AUSTRALIA 2340, Phone: 067-618385

CROTTS, DAN,
PO Box 68, Elm Springs, AR 72728, Phone: 479-248-7116, dancrottsknives@yahoo.com Web: www.facebook.com/dancrottsknives
Specialties: User grade, hunting, tactical and folders. Technical: High-end tool steel. Prices: $2200. Remarks: Specializes in making performance blades. Mark: Crotts.

CROWDER, GARY L,
HC61 Box 364, Sallisaw, OK 74955, Phone: 918-775-9009, gcrowder99@yahoo.com
Specialties: Folders, multi-blades. Patterns: Traditional with a few sheath knives. Technical: Flat grinds ATS-34, D2 and others, as well as Damascus via stock-removal. Prices: $150 to $600. Remarks: Retired, part-time maker. First knife sold in 1994. Mark: small acid-etched "Crowder" on blade.

CROWDER, ROBERT,
Box 1374, Thompson Falls, MT 59873, Phone: 406-827-4754
Specialties: Traditional working knives to customer specs. Patterns: Hunters, Bowies, fighters and fillets. Technical: Grinds ATS-34, 154CM, 440C, Vascowear and commercial Damascus. Prices: $225 to $500; some to $2500. Remarks: Full-time maker; first knife sold in 1985. Mark: R Crowder signature & Montana.

CROWELL, JAMES L,
PO Box 822, 676 Newnata Cutoff, Mtn. View, AR 72560, Phone: 870-746-4215, crowellknives@yahoo.com; Web: www.crowellknives.com
Specialties: Bowie knives; fighters and working knives. Patterns: Hunters, fighters, Bowies, daggers and folders. Period pieces: War hammers, Japanese and European. Technical: Forges 10 series carbon steels as well as O1, L6 and his own Damascus. Prices: $425 to $4500; some to $7500. Remarks: Full-time maker; first knife sold in 1980. Earned ABS Master Bladesmith in 1986. 2011 Marked 25 years as an ABS Mastersmith. Mark: A shooting star.

CROWL, PETER,
5786 County Road 10, Waterloo, IN 46793, Phone: 260-488-2532, pete@petecrowlknives.com; Web: www.petecrowlknives.com
Specialties: Bowie, hunters. Technical: Forges 5160, 1080, W2, 52100. Prices: $200 and up. Remarks: ABS Journeyman smith. Mark: Last name in script.

CROWNER, JEFF,
1565 Samuel Drive, Cottage Grove, OR 97424, Phone: 541-201-3182, Fax: 541-579-3762
Specialties: Custom knife maker. I make some of the following: wilderness survival blades, martial art weapons, hunting blades. Technical: I differentially heat treat every knife. I use various steels like 5160, L-6, Cable Damascus, 52100, 6150, and some stainless types. I use the following for handle materials: TeroTuf by Columbia Industrial products and exotic hardwoods and horn. I make my own custom sheaths as well with either kydex or leather.

CROWTHERS, MARK F,
PO Box 4641, Rolling Bay, WA 98061-0641, Phone: 206-842-7501

CUCCHIARA, MATT,
387 W. Hagler, Fresno, CA 93711, Phone: 559-917-2328, matt@cucchiaraknives.com Web: www.cucchiaraknives.com
Specialties: I make large and small, plain or hand carved Ti handled Tactical framelock folders. All decoration and carving work done by maker. Also known for my hand carved Ti pocket clips. Prices: Start at around $400 and go as high as $1500 or so.

CULVER, STEVE,
5682 94th St, Meriden, KS 66512, Phone: 785-484-0146, Web: www.culverart.com
Specialties: Edged tools and weapons, collectible and functional. Patterns: Bowies, daggers, swords, hunters, folders and edged tools. Technical: Forges carbon steels and his own pattern welded steels. Prices: $500 to $5,000. Remarks: Full-time maker; first knife sold in 1989. Mark: Last name, M. S.

CUMMING, BOB,
CUMMING KNIVES, 35 Manana Dr, Cedar Crest, NM 87008, Phone: 505-286-0509, cumming@comcast.net; Web: www.cummingknives.com
Specialties: One-of-a-kind exhibition grade custom Bowie knives, exhibition grade and working hunters, bird & trout knives, salt and fresh water fillet knives. Low country oyster knives, custom tanto's plains Indian style sheaths & custom leather, all types of exotic handle materials, scrimshaw and engraving. Added folders in 2006. Custom oyster knives. Prices: $95 to $3500 and up. Remarks: Mentored by the late Jim Nolen, sold first knife in 1978 in Denmark. Retired U.S. Foreign Service Officer. Member NCCKG. Mark: Stylized CUMMING.

CURTISS, DAVID,
Curtiss Knives, PO Box 902, Granger, IN 46530, Phone: 574-651-2158, david@curtissknives.com; Web: www.curtissknives.com
Specialties: Specialize in custom tactical-style folders and flipper folders, with some of the best sellers being in the Nano and Cruze series. The Nano is now being produced by Boker Knives. Many new knife designs coming soon.

CURTISS, STEVE L,
PO Box 448, Eureka, MT 59914, Phone: 406-889-5510, Fax: 406-889-5510, slc@bladerigger.com; Web: http://www.bladerigger.com
Specialties: True custom and semi-custom production (SCP), specialized concealment blades; advanced sheaths and tailored body harnessing systems. Patterns: Tactical/personal defense fighters, swords, utility and custom patterns. Technical: Grinds A2 and Talonite®; heat-treats. Sheaths: Kydex or Kydex-lined leather laminated or Kydex-lined with Rigger Coat™. Exotic materials available. Prices: $50 to $10,000. Remarks: Full-time maker. Doing business as Blade Rigger L.L.C. Martial artist and unique defense industry tools and equipment. Mark: For true custom: Initials and for SCP: Blade Rigger.

D

DAILEY, G E,
577 Lincoln St, Seekonk, MA 02771, Phone: 508-336-5088, gedailey@msn.com; Web: www.gedailey.com
Specialties: One-of-a-kind exotic designed edged weapons. Patterns: Folders, daggers and swords. Technical: Reforges and grinds Damascus; prefers hollow-grinding. Engraves, carves, offers filework and sets stones and uses exotic gems and gold. Prices: Start at $1100. Remarks: Full-time maker. First knife sold in 1982. Mark: Last name or stylized initialed logo.

DAKE, C M,
19759 Chef Menteur Hwy, New Orleans, LA 70129-9602, Phone: 504-254-0357, Fax: 504-254-9501
Specialties: Fancy working folders. Patterns: Front-lock lockbacks, button-lock folders. Technical: Grinds ATS-34 and Damascus. Prices: $500 to $2500; some higher. Remarks: Full-time maker; first knife sold in 1988. Doing business as Bayou Custom Cutlery. Mark: Last name.

DAKE, MARY H,
Rt 5 Box 287A, New Orleans, LA 70129, Phone: 504-254-0357

DALLYN, KELLY,
124 Deerbrook Place S.E., Calgary, AB, CANADA T2J 6J5, Phone: 403-475-3056, info@dallyn-knives.com Web: dallyn-knives.com
Specialties: Kitchen, utility, and hunting knives

DAMASTEEL STAINLESS DAMASCUS,
3052 Isim Rd., Norman, OK 73026, Phone: 888-804-0683; 405-321-3614, damascus@newmex.com; Web: www.ssdamacus.com
Patterns: Rose, Odin's eye, 5, 20, 30 twists Hakkapelitta, TNT, and infinity, Big Rose, Mumin.

DAMLOVAC, SAVA,
10292 Bradbury Dr, Indianapolis, IN 46231, Phone: 317-839-4952
Specialties: Period pieces, fantasy, Viking, Moran type all Damascus daggers. Patterns: Bowies, fighters, daggers, Persian-style knives. Technical: Uses own Damascus, some stainless, mostly hand forges. Prices: $150 to $2500; some higher. Remarks: Full-time maker; first knife sold in 1993. Specialty, Bill Moran all Damascus dagger sets, in Moran-style wood case. Mark: "Sava" stamped in Damascus or etched in stainless.

D'ANDREA, JOHN,
8517 N Linwood Loop, Citrus Springs, FL 34433-5045, Phone: 352-489-2803, shootist1@tampabay.rr.com
Specialties: Fancy working straight knives and folders with filework and distinctive leatherwork. Patterns: Hunters, fighters, daggers, folders and an occasional sword. Technical: Grinds ATS-34, 154CM, 440C and D2. Prices: $220 to $1000. Remarks: Part-time maker; first knife sold in 1986. Mark: First name, last initial imposed on samurai sword.

D'ANGELO, LAURENCE,
14703 NE 17th Ave, Vancouver, WA 98686, Phone: 360-573-0546
Specialties: Straight knives of his design. Patterns: Bowies, hunters and locking folders. Technical: Grinds D2, ATS-34 and 440C. Hand makes all sheaths. Prices: $100 to $200. Remarks: Full-time maker; first knife sold in 1987. Mark: Football logo—first and middle initials, last name, city, state, Maker.

DANIEL, TRAVIS E,
PO Box 1223, Thomaston, GA 30286, Phone: 252-362-1229, tedsknives@mail.com
Specialties: Traditional working straight knives of his design or to customer specs. Patterns: Hunters, fighters and utility/camp knives. Technical: Grinds ATS-34, 440-C, 154CM, forges his own Damascus. Stock removal. Prices: $90 to $1200. Remarks: Full-time maker; first knife sold in 1976. Mark: TED.

DANIELS, ALEX,
1416 County Rd 415, Town Creek, AL 35672, Phone: 256-685-0943, akdknives@gmail.com; Web: http://alexdanielscustomknives.com
Specialties: Working and using straight knives and folders; period pieces, reproduction Bowies. Patterns: Mostly reproduction Bowies but offers full line of knives. Technical: BG-42, 440C, 1095, 52100 forged blades. Prices: $350 to $5500. Remarks: Full-time maker; first knife sold in 1963. Mark: First and middle initials, last name, city and state.

DANNEMANN, RANDY,
RIM RANCH, 27752 P25 Rd, Hotchkiss, CO 81419, randann14@gmail.com
Specialties: Hunting knives. Patterns: Utility hunters, trout. Technical: 440C and D2. Price: $95 to $450. Remarks: First knife sold 1974. Mark: R. Dannemann Colorado or stamped Dannemann.

DARBY, DAVID T,
30652 S 533 Rd, Cookson, OK 74427, Phone: 918-457-4868, knfmkr@fullnet.net
Specialties: Forged blades only, all styles. Prices: $350 and up. Remarks: ABS Journeyman Smith. Mark: Stylized quillion dagger incorporates last name (Darby).

DARBY, JED,
7878 E Co Rd 50 N, Greensburg, IN 47240, Phone: 812-663-2696
Specialties: Traditional working/using straight knives of his design and to customer specs. Patterns: Bowies, hunters and utility/camp knives. Technical: Grinds 440C, ATS-34 and Damascus. Prices: $70 to $550; some to $1000. Remarks: Full-time maker; first knife sold in 1992. Doing business as Darby Knives. Mark: Last name and year.

DARBY, RICK,
71 Nestingrock Ln, Levittown, PA 19054
Specialties: Working straight knives. Patterns: Boots, fighters and hunters with mirror finish. Technical: Grinds 440C and CPM440V. Prices: $125 to $300. Remarks: Part-time maker; first knife sold in 1974. Mark: First and middle initials, last name.

DARCEY, CHESTER L,
1608 Dominik Dr, College Station, TX 77840, Phone: 979-696-1656, DarceyKnives@yahoo.com
Specialties: Lockback, LinerLock® and scale release folders. Patterns: Bowies, hunters and utilities. Technical: Stock removal on carbon and stainless steels, forge own Damascus. Prices: $200 to $1000. Remarks: Part-time maker, first knife sold in 1999. Mark: Last name in script.

DARK, ROBERT,
2218 Huntington Court, Oxford, AL 36203, Phone: 256-831-4645, dark@darkknives.com; Web: www.darkknives.com
Specialties: Fixed blade working knives of maker's designs. Works with customer designed specifications. Patterns: Hunters, Bowies, camp knives, kitchen/utility, bird and trout. Standard patterns and customer designed. Technical: Forged and stock removal. Works with high carbon, stainless and Damascus steels. Hollow and flat grinds. Prices: $175 to $750. Remarks: Sole authorship knives and custom leather sheaths. Full-time maker. Mark: "R Dark" on left side of blade.

DARPINIAN, DAVE,
PO Box 2643, Olathe, KS 66063, Phone: 913-244-7114, darpo1956@yahoo.com Web: www.kansasknives.org
Specialties: Hunters, fighters, utilities, lock back folders. Patterns: Full range of straight knives including art daggers. Technical: Art grinds, Damascus, 1095, Clay temper hammon, Stock removal and forging. Prices: $300 to $1000. Remarks: First knife sold in 1986, part-time maker. Mark: Last name.

DAUGHTERY, TONY,
18661 Daughtery Ln., Loxley, AL 36551, Phone: 251-964-5670 or 251-213-0461

DAVIDSON, EDMUND,
3345 Virginia Ave, Goshen, VA 24439, Phone: 540-997-5651, Web: www.edmunddavidson.com
Specialties: High class art integrals. Patterns: Many hunters and art models. Technical: CPM 154-CM. Prices: $100 to infinity. Remarks: Full-time maker; first knife sold in 1986. Mark: Name in deer head or custom logos.

DAVIDSON, LARRY,
14249 River Rd., New Braunfels, TX 78132, Phone: 830-214-5144, lazza@davidsonknives.com; Web: www.davidsonknives.com

DAVIS, BARRY L,
4262 US 20, Castleton, NY 12033, Phone: 518-477-5036, daviscustomknives@yahoo.com
Specialties: Collector grade Damascus folders. Traditional designs with focus on turn-of-the-century techniques employed. Sole authorship. Forges own Damascus, does all carving, filework, gold work and piquet. Uses only natural handle material. Enjoys doing multi-blade as well as single blade folders and daggers. Prices: Prices range from $2000 to $7000. Remarks: First knife sold in 1980.

DAVIS, CHARLIE,
ANZA KNIVES, PO Box 457, Lakeside, CA 92040-9998, Phone: 619-561-9445, Fax: 619-390-6283, sales@anzaknives.com; Web: www.anzaknives.com
Specialties: Fancy and embellished working straight knives of his design. Patterns: Hunters, camp and utility knives. Technical: Grinds high-carbon files. Prices: $20 to $185, custom depends. Remarks: Full-time maker; first knife sold in 1980. Now offers custom. Mark: ANZA U.S.A.

DAVIS, DON,
8415 Coyote Run, Loveland, CO 80537-9665, Phone: 970-669-9016, Fax: 970-669-8072
Specialties: Working straight knives in standard patterns or to customer specs. Patterns: Hunters, utility knives, skinners and survival knives. Technical: Grinds 440C, ATS-34. Prices: $75 to $250. Remarks: Full-time maker; first knife sold in 1985. Mark: Signature, city and state.

DAVIS, JESSE W,
7398A Hwy 3, Sarah, MS 38665, Phone: 662-613-1644, jandddvais1@earthlink.net
Specialties: Working straight knives and boots in standard patterns and to customer specs. Patterns: Boot knives, daggers, fighters, subhilts & Bowies. Technical: Grinds A2, D2, 440C and commercial Damascus. Prices: $125 to $1000. Remarks: Full-time maker; first knife sold in 1977. Former member Knifemakers Guild (in good standing). Mark: Name or initials.

DAVIS, JOEL,
74538 165th, Albert Lea, MN 56007, Phone: 507-377-0808, joelknives@yahoo.com
Specialties: Complete sole authorship presentation grade highly complex pattern-welded mosaic Damascus blade and bolster stock. Patterns: To date Joel has executed over 900 different mosaic Damascus patterns in the past four years. Anything conceived by maker's imagination. Technical: Uses various heat colorable "high vibrancy" steels, nickel 200 and some powdered metal for bolster stock only. Uses 1095, 1075 and 15N20. High carbon steels for cutting edge blade stock only. Prices: 15 to $50 per square inch and up depending on complexity of pattern. Remarks: Full-time mosaic Damascus metal smith focusing strictly on never-before-seen mosaic patterns. Most of maker's work is used for art knives ranging between $1500 to $4500.

DAVIS, JOHN,
235 Lampe Rd, Selah, WA 98942, Phone: 509-697-3845, 509-945-4570, jdwelds@charter.net
Specialties: Damascus and mosaic Damascus, working folders, art knives and art folders. Technical: Some ATS-34 and stainless Damascus. Embellishes with fancy stabilized wood, mammoth and walrus ivory. Prices: Start at $150. Remarks: Part-time maker; first knife sold in 1996. Mark: Name city and state on Damascus stamp initials; name inside back RFR.

DAVIS, STEVE,
3370 Chatsworth Way, Powder Springs, GA 30127, Phone: 770-427-5740, bsdavis@bellsouth.net
Specialties: Gents and ladies folders. Patterns: Straight knives, slip-joint folders, locking-liner folders. Technical: Grinds ATS-34 forges own Damascus. Offers filework; prefers hand-rubbed finishes and natural handle materials. Uses pearl, ivory, stag and exotic woods. Prices: $250 to $800; some to $1500. Remarks: Full-time maker; first knife sold in 1988. Doing business as Custom Knives by Steve Davis. Mark: Name engraved on blade.

DAVIS, TERRY,
Box 111, Sumpter, OR 97877, Phone: 541-894-2307
Specialties: Traditional and contemporary folders. Patterns: Multi-blade folders, whittlers and interframe multiblades; sunfish patterns. Technical: Flat-grinds ATS-34. Prices: $400 to $1000; some higher. Remarks: Full-time maker; first knife sold in 1985. Mark: Name in logo.

DAVIS, VERNON M,
2020 Behrens Circle, Waco, TX 76705, Phone: 254-799-7671
Specialties: Presentation-grade straight knives. Patterns: Bowies, daggers, boots, fighters, hunters and utility knives. Technical: Hollow-grinds 440C, ATS-34 and D2. Grinds an aesthetic grind line near choil. Prices: $125 to $550; some to $5000. Remarks: Part-time maker; first knife sold in 1980. Mark: Last name and city inside outline of state.

DAVIS, W C,
1955 S 1251 Rd, El Dorado Springs, MO 64744, Phone: 417-876-1259
Specialties: Fancy working straight knives and folders. Patterns: Folding lockers and slip-joints; straight hunters, fighters and Bowies. Technical: Grinds A2, ATS-34, 154, CPM T490V and CPM 530V. Prices: $100 to $300; some to $1000. Remarks: Full-time maker; first knife sold in 1972. Mark: Name.

DAVIS JR., JIM,
5129 Ridge St, Zephyrhills, FL 33541, Phone: 813-779-9213 813-469-4241 Cell, jimdavisknives@aol.com
Specialties: Presentation-grade fixed blade knives w/composite hidden tang handles. Employs a variety of ancient and contemporary ivories. Patterns: One-of-a-kind gents, personal, and executive knives and hunters w/unique cam-lock pouch sheaths and display stands. Technical: Flat grinds ATS-34 and stainless Damascus w/most work by hand w/assorted files. Prices: $300 and up. Remarks: Full-time maker, first knives sold in 2000. Mark: Signature w/printed name over "HANDCRAFTED."

DAVISON, TODD A.,
415 So. Reed, Lyons, KS 67554, Phone: 620-894-0402, todd@tadscustomknives.com; Web: www.tadscustomknives.com
Specialties: Making working/using and collector folders of his design. All knives are truly made one of a kind. Each knife has a serial number inside the liner. Patterns: Single and double blade traditional slip-joint pocket knives. Technical: Free hand hollow ground blades, hand finished. Using only the very best materials possible. Holding the highest standards to fit & finish and detail. Does his own heat treating. ATS34 and D2 steel. Prices: $450 to $900, some

higher. Remarks: Full time maker, first knife sold in 1981. Mark: T.A. DAVISON stamped.

DAWKINS, DUDLEY L,
221 NW Broadmoor Ave., Topeka, KS 66606-1254, Phone: 785-817-9343, dawkind@reagan.com or dawkind@sbcglobal.net
Specialties: Stylized old or "Dawkins Forged" with anvil in center. New tang stamps. Patterns: Straight knives. Technical: Mostly carbon steel; some Damascus-all knives forged. Prices: Knives: $275 and up; Sheaths: $95 and up. Remarks: All knives supplied with wood-lined sheaths. ABS Member, sole authorship. Mark: Stylized "DLD or Dawkins Forged with anvil in center.

DAWSON, BARRY,
7760 E Hwy 69, Prescott Valley, AZ 86314, Phone: 928-255-9830, dawsonknives@yahoo.com; Web: www.dawsonknives.com
Specialties: Samurai swords, combat knives, collector daggers, tactical, folding and hunting knives. Patterns: Offers over 60 different models. Technical: Grinds 440C, ATS-34, own heat-treatment. Prices: $75 to $1500; some to $5000. Remarks: Full-time maker; first knife sold in 1975. Mark: Last name, USA in print or last name in script.

DAWSON, LYNN,
7760 E Hwy 69 #C-5 157, Prescott Valley, AZ 86314, Phone: 928-713-2812, lynnknives@yahoo.com; Web: www.lynnknives.com
Specialties: Swords, hunters, utility, and art pieces. Patterns: Over 25 patterns to choose from. Technical: Grinds 440C, ATS-34, own heat treating. Prices: $80 to $1000. Remarks: Custom work and her own designs. Mark: The name "Lynn" in print or script.

DE MARIA JR., ANGELO,
12 Boronda Rd, Carmel Valley, CA 93924, Phone: 831-659-3381, Fax: 831-659-1315, angelodemaria1@mac.com
Specialties: Damascus, fixed and folders, sheaths. Patterns: Mosaic and random. Technical: Forging 5160, 1084 and 15N20. Prices: $200+. Remarks: Part-time maker. Mark: Angelo de Maria Carmel Valley, CA etch or AdM stamp.

DE MESA, JOHN,
1565 W. Main St., STE. 208 #229, Lewisville, TX 75057, Phone: 972-310-3877, TogiArts@me.com; Web: http://togiarts.com/ and http://togiarts.com/CSC/index.html
Specialties: Japanese sword polishing. Technical: Traditional sword polishing of Japanese swords made by sword makers in Japan and U.S. Prices: Starting at $75 per inch. Remarks: Custom Swords Collaborations IN collaboration with Jose De Braga, we can mount Japanese style sword with custom carved handles, sword fittings and scabbards to customer specs.

DE WET, KOBUS,
2601 River Road, Yakima, WA 98902, Phone: 509-728-3736, kobus@moderndamascus.com, Web: www.moderndamascus.com
Specialties: Working and art knives Patterns: Every knife is unique. Fixed blades and folders. Hunting, Bowie, Tactical and Utility knives. Technical: I enjoy forging my own damascus steel, mainly from 15N20 and 1084. I also use stock removal and stainless steels. Prices: Starting at $200 Remarks: Part time maker, started in 2007 Mark: Circled "K" / Modern Damascus - Kobus de Wet

DEAN, HARVEY J,
3266 CR 232, Rockdale, TX 76567, Phone: 512-446-3111, Fax: 512-446-5060, dean@tex1.net; Web: www.harveydean.com
Specialties: Collectible, functional knives. Patterns: Bowies, hunters, folders, daggers, swords, battle axes, camp and combat knives. Technical: Forges 1095, O1 and his Damascus. Prices: $350 to $10,000. Remarks: Full-time maker; first knife sold in 1981. Mark: Last name and MS.

DEBAUD, JAKE,
2403 Springvale Lane, Dallas, TX 75234, Phone: 214-916-1891, jake.debaud@gmail.com Web: www.debaudknives.com
Specialties: Custom damascus art knives, hunting knives and tactical knives. Technical: A2, D2, 01, 1095 and some stainless if requested ATS-34 or 154CM and S30V. Remarks: Full-time maker. Have been making knives for three years.

DEBRAGA, JOSE C.,
1341 9e Rue, Trois Rivieres, QC, CANADA G8Y 2Z2, Phone: 418-948-5864, josecdebraga@cgocable.ca; Web: www.togiarts.com/CSC/Home.html
Specialties: Art knives, fantasy pieces and working knives of his design or to customer specs. Patterns: Knives with sculptured or carved handles, from miniatures to full-size working knives. Technical: Grinds and hand-files 440C and ATS-34. A variety of steels and handle materials available. Offers lost wax casting. Prices: Start at $300. Remarks: Full-time maker; wax modeler, sculptor and knifemaker; first knife sold in 1984. Mark: Initials in stylized script and serial number.

DEBRAGA, JOVAN,
141 Notre Dame des Victoir, Quebec, CANADA G2G 1J3, Phone: 418-997-0819/418-877-1915, jovancdebraga@msn.com
Specialties: Art knives, fantasy pieces and working knives of his design or to customer specs. Patterns: Knives with sculptured or carved handles, from miniatures to full-sized working knives. Technical: Grinds and hand-files 440C, and ATS-34. A variety of steels and handle materials available. Prices: Start at $300. Remarks: Full time maker. Sculptor and knifemaker. First knife sold in 2003. Mark: Initials in stylized script and serial number.

DEL RASO, PETER,
28 Mayfield Dr, Mt. Waverly, VIC, AUSTRALIA 3149, Phone: 613 98060644, delraso@optusnet.com.au
Specialties: Fixed blades, some folders, art knives. Patterns: Daggers, Bowies, tactical, boot, personal and working knives. Technical: Grinds ATS-34,

commercial Damascus and any other type of steel on request. Prices: $100 to $1500. Remarks: Part-time maker, first show in 1993. Mark: Maker's surname stamped.

DELAROSA, JIM,
2116 N Pontiac Dr, Janesville, WI 53545, Phone: 262-422-8604, D-knife@hotmail.com
Specialties: Working straight knives and folders of his design or customer specs. Patterns: Hunters, skinners, fillets, utility and locking folders. Technical: Grinds ATS-34, 440-C, D2, O1 and commercial Damascus. Prices: $100 to $500; some higher. Remarks: Part-time maker. Mark: First and last name.

DELL, WOLFGANG,
Am Alten Berg 9, Owen-Teck, GERMANY D-73277, Phone: 49-7021-81802, wolfgang@dell-knives.de; Web: www.dell-knives.de
Specialties: Fancy high-art straight of his design and to customer specs. Patterns: Fighters, hunters, Bowies and utility/camp knives. Technical: Grinds ATS-34, RWL-34, Elmax, Damascus (Fritz Schneider). Offers high gloss finish and engraving. Prices: $500 to $1000; some to $1600. Remarks: Full-time maker; first knife sold in 1992. Mark: Hopi hand of peace.

DELLANA,
STARLANI INT'L INC, 1135 Terminal Way Ste #209, Reno, NV 89502, Phone: 304-727-5512; 702-569-7827, 1dellana@gmail.com; Web: www.dellana.cc
Specialties: Collector grade fancy/embellished high art folders and art daggers. Patterns: Locking folders and art daggers. Technical: Forges her own Damascus and W-2. Engraves, does stone setting, filework, carving and gold/platinum fabrication. Prefers exotic, high karat gold, platinum, silver, gemstone and mother-of-pearl handle materials. Price: Upscale. Remarks: Sole authorship, full-time maker, first knife sold in 1994. Also does one high art collaboration a year with Van Barnett. Member: Art Knife Invitational and ABS. Mark: First name.

DELONG, DICK,
PO Box 1024, Centerville, TX 75833-1024, Phone: 903-536-1454
Specialties: Fancy working knives and fantasy pieces. Patterns: Hunters and small skinners. Technical: Grinds and files O1, D2, 440C and Damascus. Offers cocobolo and Osage orange for handles. Prices: Start at $50. Remarks: Part-time maker. Member of Art Knife Invitational. Voting member of Knifemakers Guild. Member of ABS. Mark: Last name; some unmarked.

DEMENT, LARRY,
PO Box 1807, Prince Fredrick, MD 20678, Phone: 410-586-9011
Specialties: Fixed blades. Technical: Forged and stock removal. Prices: $75 to $200. Remarks: Affordable, good feelin', quality knives. Part-time maker.

DEMPSEY, GORDON S,
PO Box 7497, N. Kenai, AK 99635, Phone: 907-394-0894, dempseygordon@aol.com
Specialties: Working straight knives. Patterns: Small hunters. Technical: Pattern-welded damascus and carbon steel. Prices: On request. Remarks: Part-time maker; first knife sold in 1974. Mark: Name.

DENNEHY, JOHN D,
2959 Zachary Drive, Loveland, CO 80537, Phone: 970-218-7128, www.thewildirishrose.com
Specialties: Working straight knives, throwers, and leatherworker's knives. Technical: 440C, & O1, heat treats own blades, part-time maker, first knife sold in 1989. Patterns: Small hunting to presentation Bowies, leatherworks round and head knives. Prices: $200 and up. Remarks: Custom sheath maker, sheath making seminars at the Blade Show.

DENNING, GENO,
CAVEMAN ENGINEERING, 135 Allenvalley Rd, Gaston, SC 29053, Phone: 803-794-6067, cden101656@aol.com; Web: www.cavemanengineering.com
Specialties: Mirror finish. Patterns: Hunters, fighters, folders. Technical: ATS-34, 440V, S-30-V D2. Prices: $100 and up. Remarks: Full-time maker since 1996. Sole income since 1999. Instructor at Montgomery Community College (Grinding Blades). A director of SCAK: South Carolina Association of Knifemakers. Mark: Troy NC.

DERESPINA, RICHARD,
, derespinaknives@yahoo.com Web: www.derespinaknives.com
Specialties: Custom fixed blades and folders, Kris and Karambit. Technical: I use the stock removal method. Steels I use are S30V, 154CM, D2, 440C, BG42. Handles made of G10 particularly Micarta, etc. Prices: $150 to $550 depending on model. Remarks: Full-time maker. Mark: My etched logos are two, my last name and Brooklyn NY mark as well as the Star/Yin Yang logo. The star being both representative of various angles of attack common in combat as well as being three triangles, each points to levels of metaphysical understanding. The Yin and Yang have my company initials on each side D & K. Yin and Yang shows the ever present physics of life.

DERINGER, CHRISTOPH,
625 Chemin Lower, Cookshire, QC, CANADA J0B 1M0, Phone: 819-345-4260, cdsab@sympatico.ca
Specialties: Traditional working/using straight knives and folders of his design and to customer specs. Patterns: Boots, hunters, folders, art knives, kitchen knives and utility/camp knives. Technical: Forges 5160, O1 and Damascus. Offers a variety of filework. Prices: Start at $250. Remarks: Full-time maker; first knife sold in 1989. Mark: Last name stamped/engraved.

DERR, HERBERT,
413 Woodland Dr, St. Albans, WV 25177, Phone: 304-727-3866
Specialties: Damascus one-of-a-kind knives, carbon steels also. Patterns: Birdseye, ladder back, mosaics. Technical: All styles functional as well as artistically pleasing. Prices: $90 to $175 carbon, Damascus $250 to $800. Remarks: All Damascus made by maker. Mark: H.K. Derr.

DESAULNIERS, ALAIN,
100 Pope Street, Cookshire, QC, CANADA J0B 1M0, pinklaperez@sympatico.ca Web: www.desoknives.com
Specialties: Mostly Loveless style knives. Patterns: Double grind fighters, hunters, daggers, etc. Technical: Stock removal, ATS-34, CPM. High-polished blades, tapered tangs, high-quality handles. Remarks: Full-time. Collaboration with John Young. Prices: $425 and up. Mark: Name and city in logo.

DESROSIERS, ADAM,
PO Box 1954, Petersburg, AK 99833, Phone: 907-518-4570, adam@alaskablades.com Web: www.alaskablades.com
Specialties: High performance, forged, carbon steel and damascus camp choppers, and hunting knives. Hidden tang, full tang, and full integral construction. High performance heat treating. Knife designs inspired by life in Alaskan bush. Technical: Hand forges tool steels and damascus. Sole authorship. Full range of handle materials, micarta to Ivory. Preferred steels: W-2, O-1, L-6, 15n20, 1095. Prices: $200 - $3000. Remarks: ABS member. Has trained with Masters around the world. Mark: DrsRosiers over Alaska, underlined with a rose.

DESROSIERS, HALEY,
PO Box 1954, Petersburg, AK 99833, Phone: 907-518-1416, haley@alaskablades.com Web: www.alaskablades.com
Specialties: Hunting knives, integrals and a few choppers, high performance. Technical: Hand forged blades designed for hard use, exotic wood, antler and ivory handles. Prices: $300 - $1500. Remarks: Forged first knife in 2001. Part-time bladesmith all year except for commercial fishing season. Mark: Capital HD.

DETMER, PHILLIP,
14140 Bluff Rd, Breese, IL 62230, Phone: 618-526-4834, jpdetmer@att.net
Specialties: Working knives. Patterns: Bowies, daggers and hunters. Technical: Grinds ATS-34 and D2. Prices: $60 to $400. Remarks: Part-time maker; first knife sold in 1977. Mark: Last name with dagger.

DEUBEL, CHESTER J.,
6211 N. Van Ark Rd., Tucson, AZ 85743, Phone: 520-444-5246, cjdeubel@yahoo.com; Web: www.cjdeubel.com
Specialties: Fancy working straight knives and folders of his or customer design, with intricate file work. Patterns: Fighters, Bowies, daggers, hunters, camp knives, and cowboy. Technical: Flat guard, hollow grind, antiqued, all types Damascus, 154cpm Stainsteel, high carbon steel, 440c Stainsteel. Prices: From $250 to $3500. Remarks: Started making part-time in 1980; went to full-time in 2000. Don Patch is my engraver. Mark: C.J. Deubel.

DEVERAUX, BUTCH,
PO Box 1356, Riverton, WY 82501, Phone: 307-851-0601, bdeveraux@wyoming.com; Web: www.deverauxknives.com
Specialties: Working straight knives. Patterns: Hunters, fighters and camp knives. Technical: Forged 52100 blade steel, brass guards, sheep-horn handles, as well as stag, cocobolo, she-oak and ironwood. Prices: $400 to $3,000.

DI MARZO, RICHARD,
1417 10th St S, Birmingham, AL 35205, Phone: 205-252-3331
Specialties: Handle artist. Scrimshaw carvings.

DIAZ, JOSE,
409 W. 12th Ave, Ellensburg, WA 98926, jose@diaztools.com Web: www.diaztools.com
Specialties: Affordable custom user-grade utility and camp knives. Also makes competition cutting knives. Patterns: Mas. Technical: Blade materials range from high carbon steels and Damascus to high performance tool and stainless steels. Uses both forge and stock removal methods in shaping the steel. Handle materials include Tero Tuf, Black Butyl Burl, Micarta, natural woods and G10. Prices: $65-$700. Remarks: Part-time knife maker; made first knife in 2008. Mark: Reclining tree frog with a smile, and "Diaz Tools."

DICK, DAN,
P.O. Box 2303, Hutchinson, KS 67504-2303, Phone: 620-669-6805, Dan@DanDickKnives.com; Web: www.dandickknives.com
Specialties: Traditional working/using fixed bladed knives of maker's design. Patterns: Hunters, skinners and utility knives. Technical: Stock removal maker using D2. Prefers such materials as exotic and fancy burl woods. Makes his own sheaths, all leather with tooling. Prices: $125 and up. Remarks: Part-time maker since 2006. Marks: Name in outline border of Kansas.

DICKERSON, GAVIN,
PO Box 7672, Petit, GT, SOUTH AFRICA 1512, Phone: +27 011-965-0988, Fax: +27 011-965-0988
Specialties: Straight knives of his design or to customer specs. Patterns: Hunters, skinners, fighters and Bowies. Technical: Hollow-grinds D2, 440C, ATS-34, 12C27 and Damascus upon request. Prefers natural handle materials; offers synthetic handle materials. Prices: $190 to $2500. Remarks: Part-time maker; first knife sold in 1982. Mark: Name in full.

DICKISON, SCOTT S,
179 Taylor Rd, Portsmouth, RI 02871, Phone: 401-847-7398, squared22@cox.net; Web: http://sqauredknives.com
Specialties: Straight knives, locking folders and slip joints of his design. Patterns: Sgain dubh, bird and trout knives. Technical: Forges and grinds commercial

Damascus, D2, O1 and sandvik stainless. Prices: $400 to $1000; some higher. Remarks: Part-time maker; first knife sold in 1989. Mark: Stylized initials.

DIETZ, ANTHONY P,
10519 Nevada Ave., Melrose Park, IL 60164, Phone: 847-845-9598, sukemitsu@sbcglobal.net Web: www.namahagesword.com or www.sukemitsu.com
Specialties: Japanese-style swords. Patterns: Katana, Wakizashi, Otanto, Kozuka. Technical: Tradition and some modern steels. All clay tempered and traditionally hand polished using Japanese wet stones. Remarks: Part-time maker. Prices: Varied, available on request. Mark: Blade tang signed in "SUKEMITSU."

DIETZ, HOWARD,
421 Range Rd, New Braunfels, TX 78132, Phone: 830-885-4662
Specialties: Lock-back folders, working straight knives. Patterns: Folding hunters, high-grade pocket knives. ATS-34, 440C, CPM 440V, D2 and stainless Damascus. Prices: $300 to $1000. Remarks: Full-time gun and knifemaker; first knife sold in 1995. Mark: Name, city, and state.

DIETZEL, BILL,
PO Box 1613, Middleburg, FL 32068, Phone: 904-282-1091
Specialties: Forged straight knives and folders. Patterns: His interpretations. Technical: Forges his Damascus and other steels. Prices: Middle ranges. Remarks: Likes natural materials; uses titanium in folder liners. Master Smith (1997). Mark: Name.

DIGANGI, JOSEPH M,
Box 950, Santa Cruz, NM 87567, Phone: 505-753-6414, Fax: 505-753-8144, Web: www.digangidesigns.com
Specialties: Kitchen and table cutlery. Patterns: French chef's knives, carving sets, steak knife sets, some camp knives and hunters. Holds patents and trademarks for "System II" kitchen cutlery set. Technical: Grinds ATS-34. Prices: $150 to $595; some to $1200. Remarks: Full-time maker; first knife sold in 1983. Mark: DiGangi Designs.

DILL, DAVE,
7404 NW 30th St, Bethany, OK 73008, Phone: 405-789-0750
Specialties: Folders of his design. Patterns: Various patterns. Technical: Hand-grinds 440C, ATS-34. Offers engraving and filework on all folders. Prices: Starting at $450. Remarks: Full-time maker; first knife sold in 1987. Mark: First initial, last name.

DILL, ROBERT,
1812 Van Buren, Loveland, CO 80538, Phone: 970-667-5144, Fax: 970-667-5144, dillcustomknives@msn.com
Specialties: Fancy and working knives of his design. Patterns: Hunters, Bowies and fighters. Technical: Grinds 440C and D2. Prices: $100 to $800. Remarks: Full-time maker; first knife sold in 1984. Mark: Logo stamped into blade.

DILLUVIO, FRANK J,
311 Whitetail Dr., Prudenville, MI 48651, Phone: 989-202-4051, fjdknives@hotmail.com; Web: www.fdilluviocustomknives.com
Specialties: Folders, fixed blades. Patterns: Many. Technical: Grinds 440-c, D-2. Precision fits. Prices: $225 and up. Remarks: Full-time maker; first knife sold in 1984. Mark: Name and state.

DINTRUFF, CHUCK,
1708 E. Martin Luther King Blvd., Seffner, FL 33584, Phone: 813-381-6916, DINTRUFFKNIVES@aol.com; Web: dintruffknives.com and spinwellfab.com

DION, GREG,
3032 S Jackson St, Oxnard, CA 93033, Phone: 519-981-1033
Specialties: Working straight knives, some fancy. Welcomes special orders. Patterns: Hunters, fighters, camp knives, Bowies and tantos. Technical: Grinds ATS-34, 154CM and 440C. Prices: $85 to $300; some to $600. Remarks: Part-time maker; first knife sold in 1985. Mark: Name.

DIOTTE, JEFF,
DIOTTE KNIVES, 159 Laurier Dr, LaSalle, ON, CANADA N9J 1L4, Phone: 519-978-2764

DIPPOLD, AL,
90 Damascus Ln, Perryville, MO 63775, Phone: 573-547-1119, adippold@midwest.net
Specialties: Fancy one-of-a-kind locking folders. Patterns: Locking folders. Technical: Forges and grinds mosaic and pattern welded Damascus. Offers filework on all folders. Prices: $500 to $3500; some higher. Remarks: Full-time maker; first knife sold in 1980. Mark: Last name in logo inside of liner.

DISKIN, MATT,
PO Box 653, Freeland, WA 98249, Phone: 360-730-0451, info@volcanknives.com; Web: www.volcanknives.com
Specialties: Damascus autos. Patterns: Dirks and daggers. Technical: Forges mosaic Damascus using 15N20, 1084, 02, 06, L6; pure nickel. Prices: Start at $500. Remarks; Full-time maker. Mark: Last name.

DIXON JR., IRA E,
PO Box 2581, Ventura, CA 93002-2581, irasknives@yahoo.com
Specialties: Straight knives of his design. Patterns: All patterns include art knives. Technical: Grinds CPM materials, Damascus and some tool steels. Prices: $275 to $2000. Remarks: Full-time maker; first knife sold in 1993. Mark: First name, Handmade.

DOBRATZ, ERIC,
25371 Hillary Lane, Laguna Hills, CA 92653, Phone: 949-233-5170, knifesmith@gmail.com
Specialties: Differentially quenched blades with Hamon of his design or with customer input. Patterns: Hunting, camp, kitchen, fighters, bowies, traditional tanto, and unique fixed blade designs. Technical: Hand-forged high carbon and damascus. Prefers natural material for handles; rare/exotic woods and stag, but also uses micarta and homemade synthetic materials. Prices: $150 - $1500. Remarks: Part-time maker; first knife made in 1995. Mark: Stylized Scarab beetle.

DODD, ROBERT F,
4340 E Canyon Dr, Camp Verde, AZ 86322, Phone: 928-567-3333, rfdknives@commspeed.net; Web: www.rfdoddknives.com
Specialties: Folders, fixed blade hunter/skinners, Bowies, daggers. Patterns: Drop point. Technical: ATS-34 and Damascus. Prices: $250 and up. Remarks: Hand tooled leather sheaths. Mark: R. F. Dodd, Camp Verde AZ.

DOGGETT, BOB,
1310 Vinetree Rd, Brandon, FL 33510, Phone: 813-205-5503, dogman@tampabay.rr.com; Web: www.doggettcustomknives.com
Specialties: Clean, functional working knives. Patterns: Classic-styled hunter, fighter and utility fixed blades; liner locking folders. Technical: Uses stainless steel and commercial Damascus, 416 stainless for bolsters and hardware, hand-rubbed satin finish, top quality handle materials and titanium liners on folders. Prices: Start at $175. Remarks: Part-time maker. Mark: Last name.

DOIRON, DONALD,
6 Chemin Petit Lac des Ced, Messines, QC, CANADA J0X-2J0, Phone: 819-465-2489

DOMINY, CHUCK,
PO Box 593, Colleyville, TX 76034, Phone: 817-498-4527
Specialties: Titanium LinerLock® folders. Patterns: Hunters, utility/camp knives and LinerLock® folders. Technical: Grinds 440C and ATS-34. Prices: $250 to $3000. Remarks: Full-time maker; first knife sold in 1976. Mark: Last name.

DOOLITTLE, MIKE,
13 Denise Ct, Novato, CA 94947, Phone: 415-897-3246
Specialties: Working straight knives in standard patterns. Patterns: Hunters and fishing knives. Technical: Grinds 440C, 154CM and ATS-34. Prices: $125 to $200; some to $750. Remarks: Part-time maker; first knife sold in 1981. Mark: Name, city and state.

DORNELES, LUCIANO OLIVEIRA,
Rua 15 De Novembro 2222, Nova Petropolis, RS, BRAZIL 95150-000, Phone: 011-55-54-303-303-90, tchebufalo@hotmail.com
Specialties: Traditional "true" Brazilian-style working knives and to customer specs. Patterns: Brazilian hunters, utility and camp knives, Bowies, Dirk. A master at the making of the true "Faca Campeira Gaucha," the true camp knife of the famous Brazilian Gauchos. A Dorneles knife is 100 percent hand-forged with sledge hammers only. Can make spectacular Damascus hunters/daggers. Technical: Forges only 52100 and his own Damascus, can put silver wire inlay on customer design handles on special orders; uses only natural handle materials. Prices: $250 to $1000. Mark: Symbol with L. Dorneles.

DOTSON, TRACY,
1280 Hwy C-4A, Baker, FL 32531, Phone: 850-537-2407
Specialties: Folding fighters and small folders. Patterns: LinerLock® and lockback folders. Technical: Hollow-grinds ATS-34 and commercial Damascus. Prices: Start at $250. Remarks: Part-time maker; first knife sold in 1995. Mark: Last name.

DOUCETTE, R,
CUSTOM KNIVES, 112 Memorial Dr, Brantford, ON, CANADA N3R 5S3, Phone: 519-756-9040, randy@randydoucetteknives.com; Web: www.randydoucetteknives.com
Specialties: Filework, tactical designs, multiple grinds. Patterns: Tactical folders, fancy folders, daggers, tantos, karambits. Technical: All knives are handmade. The only outsourcing is heat treatment. Prices: $500 to $2,500. Remarks: Full-time knifemaker; 2-year waiting list. Mark: R. Doucette

DOURSIN, GERARD,
Chemin des Croutoules, Pernes les Fontaines, FRANCE 84210
Specialties: Period pieces. Patterns: Liner locks and daggers. Technical: Forges mosaic Damascus. Prices: $600 to $4000. Remarks: First knife sold in 1983. Mark: First initial, last name and I stop the lion.

DOUSSOT, LAURENT,
1008 Montarville, St. Bruno, QC, CANADA J3V 3T1, Phone: 450-441-3298, doussot@skalja.com; Web: www.skalja.com, www.doussot-knives.com
Specialties: Fancy and embellished folders and fantasy knives. Patterns: Fighters and locking folders. Technical: Grinds ATS-34 and commercial Damascus. Scale carvings on all knives; most bolsters are carved titanium. Prices: $350 to $3000. Remarks: Part-time maker; first knife was sold in 1992. Mark: Stylized initials inside circle.

DOWNIE, JAMES T,
1295 - 906 Sandy Lane, Sarnia, Ontario, CANADA N7V 4K5, Phone: 519-491-8234, Web: www.ckg.org (click on members page)
Specialties: Serviceable straight knives and folders; period pieces. Patterns: Hunters, Bowies, camp knives, fillet and miniatures. Technical: Grinds D2, 440C and ATS-34, Damasteel, stainless steel Damascus. Prices: $150 and up. Remarks: Full-time maker, first knife sold in 1978. Mark: Signature of first and middle initials, last name.

DOWNING, LARRY,
12268 State Route 181 N, Bremen, KY 42325, Phone: 270-525-3523, larrydowning@bellsouth.net; Web: www.downingknives.com
Specialties: Working straight knives and folders. Patterns: From mini-knives to daggers, folding lockers to interframes. Technical: Forges and grinds 154CM, ATS-34 and his own Damascus. Prices: $195 to $950; some higher. Remarks: Part-time maker; first knife sold in 1979. Mark: Name in arrowhead.

DOWNING, TOM,
2675 12th St, Cuyahoga Falls, OH 44223, Phone: 330-923-7464
Specialties: Working straight knives; period pieces. Patterns: Hunters, fighters and tantos. Technical: Grinds 440C, ATs-34 and CPM-T-440V. Prefers natural handle materials. Prices: $150 to $900, some to $1500. Remarks: Part-time maker; first knife sold in 1979. Mark: First and middle initials, last name.

DOWNS, JAMES F,
2247 Summit View Rd, Powell, OH 43065, Phone: 614-766-5350, jfdowns1@yahoo.com
Specialties: Working straight knives of his design or to customer specs. Patterns: Folders, Bowies, boot, hunters, utility. Technical: Grinds 440C and other steels. Prefers mastodon ivory, all pearls, stabilized wood and elephant ivory. Prices: $75 to $1200. Remarks: Full-time maker; first knife sold in 1980. Mark: Last name.

DOX, JAN,
Zwanebloemlaan 27, Schoten, BELGIUM B 2900, Phone: 32 3 658 77 43, jan.dox@scarlet.be; Web: doxblades.weebly.com
Specialties: Working/using knives, from kitchen to battlefield. Patterns: Own designs, some based on traditional ethnic patterns (Scots, Celtic, Scandinavian and Japanese) or to customer specs. Technical: Grinds D2/A2 and stainless, forges carbon steels, convex edges. Handles: Wrapped in modern or traditional patterns, resin impregnated if desired. Natural or synthetic materials, some carved. Prices: $50 and up. Remarks: Spare-time maker, first knife sold 2001. Mark: Name or stylized initials.

DOZIER, BOB,
PO Box 1941, Springdale, AR 72765, Phone: 888-823-0023/479-756-0023, Fax: 479-756-9139, info@dozierknives.com; Web www.dozierknives.com
Specialties: Using knives (fixed blades and folders). Patterns: Some fine collector-grade knives. Technical: Uses D2. Prefers Micarta handle material. Prices: Using knives: $195 to $700. Remarks: Full-time maker; first knife sold in 1965. No longer doing semi-handmade line. Mark: State, made, last name in a circle (for fixed blades); Last name with arrow through 'D' and year over name (for folders).

DRAPER, AUDRA,
#10 Creek Dr, Riverton, WY 82501, Phone: 307-856-6807 or 307-851-0426 cell, adraper@wyoming.com; Web: www.draperknives.com
Specialties: One-of-a-kind straight and folding knives. Also pendants, earring and bracelets of Damascus. Patterns: Design custom knives, using, Bowies, and minis. Technical: Forge Damascus; heat-treats all knives. Prices: Vary depending on item. Remarks: Full-time maker; master bladesmith in the ABS. Member of the PKA; first knife sold in 1995. Mark: Audra.

DRAPER, MIKE,
#10 Creek Dr, Riverton, WY 82501, Phone: 307-856-6807, adraper@wyoming.com
Specialties: Mainly folding knives in tactical fashion, occasonal fixed blade. Patterns: Hunters, Bowies and camp knives, tactical survival. Technical: Grinds S30V stainless steel. Prices: Starting at $250+. Remarks: Full-time maker; first knife sold in 1996. Mark: Initials M.J.D. or name, city and state.

DREW, GERALD,
213 Hawk Ridge Dr, Mill Spring, NC 28756, Phone: 828-713-4762
Specialties: Blade ATS-34 blades. Straight knives. Patterns: Hunters, camp knives, some Bowies and tactical. Technical: ATS-34 preferred. Price: $65 to $400. Mark: GL DREW.

DRISCOLL, MARK,
4115 Avoyer Pl, La Mesa, CA 91941, Phone: 619-670-0695, markdriscoll91941@yahoo.com
Specialties: High-art, period pieces and working/using knives of his design or to customer specs; some fancy. Patterns: Swords, Bowies, fighters, daggers, hunters and primitive (mountain man-styles). Technical: Forges 52100, 5160, O1, L6, 1095, 15n20, W-2 steel and makes his own Damascus and mokume; also does multiple quench heat treating. Uses exotic hardwoods, ivory and horn, offers fancy file work, carving, scrimshaws. Prices: $150 to $550; some to $1500. Remarks: Part-time maker; first knife sold in 1986. Doing business as Mountain Man Knives. Mark: Double "M."

DROST, JASON D,
Rt 2 Box 49, French Creek, WV 26218, Phone: 304-472-7901
Specialties: Working/using straight knives of his design. Patterns: Hunters and utility/camp knives. Technical: Grinds 154CM and D2. Prices: $125 to $5000. Remarks: Spare-time maker; first knife sold in 1995. Mark: First and middle initials, last name, maker, city and state.

DROST, MICHAEL B,
Rt 2 Box 49, French Creek, WV 26218, Phone: 304-472-7901
Specialties: Working/using straight knives and folders of all designs. Patterns: Hunters, locking folders and utility/camp knives. Technical: Grinds ATS-34, D2 and CPM-T-440V. Offers dove-tailed bolsters and spacers, filework and scrimshaw. Prices: $125 to $400; some to $740. Remarks: Full-time maker; first knife sold in 1990. Doing business as Drost Custom Knives. Mark: Name, city and state.

DRUMM, ARMIN,
Lichtensteinstrasse 33, Dornstadt, GERMANY 89160, Phone: 49-163-632-2842, armin@drumm-knives.de; Web: www.drumm-knives.de
Specialties: One-of-a-kind forged and Damascus fixed blade knives and folders. Patterns: Classic Bowie knives, daggers, fighters, hunters, folders, swords. Technical: Forges own Damascus and carbon steels, filework, carved handles. Prices: $250 to $800, some higher. Remarks: First knife sold in 2001, member of the German Knifemakers Guild. Mark: First initial, last name.

DUCKER, BRIAN,
Lamorna Cottage, Common End, Colkirk, England NR21 7JD, Phone: 01-328-856-183, admin@grommitbaileyknives.com; Web: www.grommitbaileyknives.com
Specialties: Hunters, utility pieces, bowies, camp knives, fighters and folders. Technical: Stock removal and forged 1095, 1075 and 80CrV2. Forging own damascus, using exotic and native hardwoods, stag, leather, Micarta and other synthetic materials, with brass and 301 stainless steel fittings. Own leatherwork and heat treating. Remarks: Part-time maker since 2009, full time Dec. 2013. All knives and sheaths are sole authorship. Mark: GROMMIT UK MAKER & BAILEY GROMMIT MAKERS.

DUFF, BILL,
2801 Ash St, Poteau, OK 74953, Phone: 918-647-4458
Specialties: Straight knives and folders, some fancy. Patterns: Hunters, folders and miniatures. Technical: Grinds 440-C and commercial Damascus. Prices: $250 and up. Remarks: First knife sold in 1976. Mark: Bill Duff.

DUFOUR, ARTHUR J,
8120 De Armoun Rd, Anchorage, AK 99516, Phone: 907-345-1701
Specialties: Working straight knives from standard patterns. Patterns: Hunters, Bowies, camp and fishing knives—ground thin and pointed. Technical: Grinds 440C, ATS-34, AEB-L. Tempers 57-58R; hollow-grinds. Prices: $135; some to $250. Remarks: Part-time maker; first knife sold in 1970. Mark: Prospector logo.

DUGDALE, DANIEL J.,
11 Eleanor Road, Walpole, MA 02081, Phone: 508-668-3528, dlpdugdale@comcast.net
Specialties: Button-lock and straight knives of his design. Patterns: Utilities, hunters, skinners, and tactical. Technical: Falt grinds D-2 and 440C, aluminum handles with anodized finishes. Prices: $150 to $500. Remarks: Part-time maker since 1977. Mark: Deer track with last name, town and state.

DUNCAN, RON,
1462 County Road 1635, Cairo, MO 65239, Phone: 660-263-8949, www.duncanmadeknives.com
Remarks: Duncan Made Knives

DUNKERLEY, RICK,
PO Box 601, Lincoln, MT 59639, Phone: 406-210-4101, dunkerleyknives@gmail.com Web: www.dunkerleyknives.com
Specialties: Mosaic Damascus folders and carbon steel utility knives. Patterns: One-of-a-kind folders, standard hunters and utility designs. Technical: Forges 52100, Damascus and mosaic Damascus. Prefers natural handle materials. Prices: $200 and up. Remarks: Full-time maker; first knife sold in 1984. ABS Master Smith. Doing business as Dunkerley Custom Knives. Dunkerley handmade knives, sole authorship. Mark: Dunkerley, MS.

DUNLAP, JIM,
800 E. Badger Lee Rd., Sallisaw, OK 74955, Phone: 918-774-2700, dunlapknives@gmail.com
Specialties: Traditional slip-joint folders. Patterns: Single- and multi-blade traditional slip joints. Technical: Grinds ATS-34, CPM-154 and damascus. Prices: $250 and up. Remarks: Part-time maker; first knife sold in 2009. Mark: Dunlap.

DUNN, CHARLES K,
17740 GA Hwy 116, Shiloh, GA 31826, Phone: 706-846-2666
Specialties: Fancy and working straight knives and folders of his design and to customer specs. Patterns: Bowies, hunters and locking folders. Technical: Grinds 440C and ATS-34. Engraves; filework offered. Prices: $75 to $300. Remarks: Part-time maker; first knife sold in 1988. Mark: First initial, last name, city, state.

DUNN, STEVE,
376 Biggerstaff Rd, Smiths Grove, KY 42171, Phone: 270-563-9830, dunndeal@verizon.net; Web: www.stevedunnknives.com
Specialties: Working and using straight knives of his design; period pieces. Also offer engraving & gold inlays. Patterns: Hunters, skinners, Bowies, fighters, camp knives, folders, swords and battle axes. Technical: Forges own Damascus, 1075, 15N20, 52100, 1084, L6. Prices: Moderate to upscale. Remarks: Full-time maker; first knife sold in 1990. Mark: Last name and MS.

DURAN, JERRY T,
PO Box 9753, Albuquerque, NM 87119, Phone: 505-873-4676, jtdknives@hotmail.com; Web: http://www.google.com/profiles/jtdknivesLLC
Specialties: Tactical folders, Bowies, fighters, liner locks, autopsy and hunters. Patterns: Folders, Bowies, hunters and tactical knives. Technical: Forges own Damascus and forges carbon steel. Prices: Moderate to upscale. Remarks: Full-time maker; first knife sold in 1978. Mark: Initials in elk rack logo.

DURHAM, KENNETH,
BUZZARD ROOST FORGE, 10495 White Pike, Cherokee, AL 35616, Phone: 256-359-4287, www.home.hiwaay.net/~jamesd/
Specialties: Bowies, dirks, hunters. Patterns: Traditional patterns. Technical: Forges 1095, 5160, 52100 and makes own Damascus. Prices: $85 to $1600.

Remarks: Began making knives about 1995. Received Journeyman stamp 1999. Got Master Smith stamp in 2004. Mark: Bull's head with Ken Durham above and Cherokee AL below.

DURIO, FRED,
144 Gulino St, Opelousas, LA 70570, Phone: 337-948-4831/cell 337-351-2652, fdurio@yahoo.com
Specialties: Folders. Patterns: Liner locks; plain and fancy. Technical: Makes own Damascus. Prices: Moderate to upscale. Remarks: Full-time maker. Mark: Last name-Durio.

DUVALL, FRED,
10715 Hwy 190, Benton, AR 72015, Phone: 501-778-9360
Specialties: Working straight knives and folders. Patterns: Locking folders, slip joints, hunters, fighters and Bowies. Technical: Grinds D2 and CPM440V; forges 5160. Prices: $100 to $400; some to $800. Remarks: Part-time maker; first knife sold in 1973. Mark: Last name.

DWYER, DUANE,
120 N. Pacific St., L7, San Marcos, CA 92069, Phone: 760-471-8275, striderknives@aol.com Web: www.striderknives.com
Specialties: Primarily tactical. Patterns: Fixed and folders. Technical: Primarily stock removal specializing in highly technical materials. Prices: $100 and up, based on the obvious variables. Remarks: Full-time maker since 1996. ·

DYER, DAVID,
4531 Hunters Glen, Granbury, TX 76048, Phone: 817-573-1198
Specialties: Working skinners and early period knives. Patterns: Customer designs, his own patterns. Technical: Coal forged blades; 5160 and 52100 steels. Grinds D2, 1095, L6. Prices: $150 for neck knives and small (3" to 3-1/2"). To $600 for large blades and specialty blades. Mark: Last name DYER electro etched.

DYESS, EDDIE,
1005 Hamilton, Roswell, NM 88201, Phone: 505-623-5599, eddyess@msn.com
Specialties: Working and using straight knives in standard patterns. Patterns: Hunters and fighters. Technical: Grinds 440C, 154CM and D2 on request. Prices: $150 to $300, some higher. Remarks: Spare-time maker; first knife sold in 1980. Mark: Last name.

E

EAKER, ALLEN L,
416 Clinton Ave Dept KI, Paris, IL 61944, Phone: 217-466-5160
Specialties: Traditional straight knives and folders of his design. Patterns: Hunters, locking folders and slip-joint folders. Technical: Grinds 440C; inlays. Prices: $200 to $500. Remarks: Spare-time maker; first knife sold in 1994. Mark: Initials in tankard logo stamped on tang, serial number and surname on back.

EALY, DELBERT,
PO Box 121, Indian River, MI 49749, Phone: 231-238-4705

EATON, FRANK L JR,
5365 W. Meyer Rd., Farmington, MO 63640, Phone: 703-314-8708, eatontactical@me.com; Web: www.frankeatonknives.com
Specialties: Full tang/hidden tang fixed working and art knives of his own design. Patterns: Hunters, skinners, fighters, Bowies, tacticals and daggers. Technical: Stock removal maker, prefer using natural materials. Prices: $175 to $400. Remarks: Part-time maker - Active Duty Airborn Ranger-Making 4 years. Mark: Name over 75th Ranger Regimental Crest.

EATON, RICK,
313 Dailey Rd, Broadview, MT 59015, Phone: 406-667-2405, rick@eatonknives.com; Web: www.eatonknives.com
Specialties: Interframe folders and one-hand-opening side locks. Patterns: Bowies, daggers, fighters and folders. Technical: Grinds 154CM, ATS-34, 440C and other maker's Damascus. Makes own mosaic Damascus. Offers high-quality hand engraving, Bulino and gold inlay. Prices: Upscale. Remarks: Full-time maker; first knife sold in 1982. Mark: Full name or full name and address.

EBISU, HIDESAKU,
3-39-7 Koi Osako, Nishi Ku, Hiroshima, JAPAN 733 0816

ECHOLS, RODGER,
2853 Highway 371 W, Nashville, AR 71852-7577, Phone: 870-845-9173 or 870-845-0400, blademanechols@aol.com; Web: www.echolsknives.com
Specialties: Liner locks, auto-scale release, lock backs. Patterns: His or yours. Technical: Autos. Prices: $500 to $1700. Remarks: Likes to use pearl, ivory and Damascus the most. Made first knife in 1984. Part-time maker; tool and die maker by trade. Mark: Name.

EDDY, HUGH E,
211 E Oak St, Caldwell, ID 83605, Phone: 208-459-0536

EDGE, TOMMY,
1244 County Road 157, Cash, AR 72421, Phone: 501-477-5210, tedge@tex.net
Specialties: Fancy/embellished working knives of his design. Patterns: Bowies, hunters and utility/camping knives. Technical: Grinds 440C, ATS-34 and D2. Makes own cable Damascus; offers filework. Prices: $70 to $250; some to $1500. Remarks: Part-time maker; first knife sold in 1973. Mark: Stamped first initial, last name and stenciled name, city and state in oval shape.

EDMONDS, WARRICK,
, Adelaide Hills, SOUTH AUSTRALIA, Phone: 61-8-83900339, warrick@rifflebirdknives.com Web: www.rifflebirdknives.com
Specialties: Fixed blade knives with select and highly figured exotic or unique Australian wood handles. Themed collectors knives to individually designed working knives from Damascus, RWL34, 440C or high carbon steels. Patterns: Hunters, utilities and workshop knives, cooks knives with a Deco to Modern flavour. Hand sewn individual leather sheaths. Technical: Stock removal using only steel from well known and reliable sources. Prices: $250Aust to $1000Aust. Remarks: Part-time maker since 2004. Mark: Name stamped into sheath.

EDWARDS, MITCH,
303 New Salem Rd, Glasgow, KY 42141, Phone: 270-404-0758/270-404-0758, medwards@glasgow-ky.com; Web: www.traditionalknives.com
Specialties: Period pieces. Patterns: Neck knives, camp, rifleman and Bowie knives. Technical: All hand forged, forges own Damascus O1, 1084, 1095, L6, 15N20. Prices: $200 to $1000. Remarks: Journeyman Smith. Mark: Broken heart.

EHRENBERGER, DANIEL ROBERT,
1213 S Washington St, Mexico, MO 65265, Phone: 573-633-2010
Specialties: Affordable working/using straight knives of his design and to custom specs. Patterns: 10" western Bowie, fighters, hunting and skinning knives. Technical: Forges 1085, 1095, his own Damascus and cable Damascus. Prices: $80 to $500. Remarks: Full-time maker, first knife sold 1994. Mark: Ehrenberger JS.

EIRICH, WILLIAM,
61535 S. Hwy 97, Ste. 9-163, Bend, OR 97702, Phone: 541-280-8373, tapejet@live.com
Specialties: Hunting, folders, other. Technical: Stock removal. 154CM, 1050, M390, 5160, 01, 52100, ATS-34, and D2 steel. Prices: $200 and up. Remarks: First knife made 2004. Mark: Circle with an "E" in the center and a wing to the right of the circle with the name "Eirich" below framed by dots.

EKLUND, MAIHKEL,
Fone Stam V9, Farila, SWEDEN 82041, info@art-knives.com; Web: www.art-knives.com
Specialties: Collector-grade working straight knives. Patterns: Hunters, Bowies and fighters. Technical: Grinds ATS-34, Uddeholm and Dama steel. Engraves and scrimshaws. Prices: $200 to $2000. Remarks: Full-time maker; first knife sold in 1983. Mark: Initials or name.

ELDRIDGE, ALLAN,
7731 Four Winds Dr, Ft. Worth, TX 76133, Phone: 817-370-7778; Cell: 817-296-3528
Specialties: Fancy classic straight knives in standard patterns. Patterns: Hunters, Bowies, fighters, folders and miniatures. Technical: Grinds O1 and Damascus. Engraves silver-wire inlays, pearl inlays, scrimshaws and offers filework. Prices: $50 to $500; some to $1200. Remarks: Spare-time maker; first knife sold in 1965. Mark: Initials.

ELISHEWITZ, ALLEN,
3960 Lariat Ridge, New Braunfels, TX 78132, Phone: 830-899-5356, allen@elishewitzknives.com; Web: elishewitzknives.com
Specialties: Collectible high-tech working straight knives and folders of his design. Patterns: Working, utility and tactical knives. Technical: Designs and uses innovative locking mechanisms. All designs drafted and field-tested. Prices: $600 to $1000. Remarks: Full-time maker; first knife sold in 1989. Mark: Gold medallion inlaid in blade.

ELLEFSON, JOEL,
PO Box 1016, 310 S 1st St, Manhattan, MT 59741, Phone: 406-284-3111
Specialties: Working straight knives, fancy daggers and one-of-a-kinds. Patterns: Hunters, daggers and some folders. Technical: Grinds A2, 440C and ATS-34. Makes own mokume in bronze, brass, silver and shibuishi; makes brass/steel blades. Prices: $100 to $500; some to $2000. Remarks: Part-time maker; first knife sold in 1978. Mark: Stylized last initial.

ELLERBE, W B,
3871 Osceola Rd, Geneva, FL 32732, Phone: 407-349-5818
Specialties: Period and primitive knives and sheaths. Patterns: Bowies to patch knives, some tomahawks. Technical: Grinds Sheffield O1 and files. Prices: Start at $35. Remarks: Full-time maker; first knife sold in 1971. Doing business as Cypress Bend Custom Knives. Mark: Last name or initials.

ELLIOTT, JERRY,
4507 Kanawha Ave, Charleston, WV 25304, Phone: 304-925-5045, elliottknives@verizon.net
Specialties: Classic and traditional straight knives and folders of his design and to customer specs. Patterns: Hunters, locking folders and Bowies. Technical: Grinds ATS-34, 154CM, O1, D2 and T-440-V. All guards silver-soldered; bolsters are pinned on straight knives, spot-welded on folders. Prices: $80 to $265; some to $1000. Remarks: Full-time maker; first knife sold in 1972. Mark: First and middle initials, last name, knife maker, city, state.

ELLIS, WILLIAM DEAN,
2767 Edgar Ave, Sanger, CA 93657, Phone: 559-314-4459, urleebird@comcast.net; Web: www.billysblades.com
Specialties: Classic and fancy knives of his design. Patterns: Boots, fighters and utility knives. Technical: Grinds ATS-34, D2 and Damascus. Offers tapered tangs and six patterns of filework; tooled multi-colored sheaths. Prices: $250 to $1500Remarks: Part-time maker; first knife sold in 1991. Doing business as Billy's Blades. Also make shave-ready straight razors for actual use. Mark: "B" in a five-point star next to "Billy," city and state within a rounded-corner rectangle.

ELLIS, WILLY B,
1025 Hamilton Ave., Tarpon Springs, FL 34689, Phone: 727-942-6420, Web: www.willyb.com
Specialties: One-of-a-kind high art and fantasy knives of his design. Occasional customs full size and miniatures. Patterns: Bowies, fighters, hunters and others. Technical: Grinds 440C, ATS-34, 1095, carbon Damascus, ivory bone, stone and metal carving. Prices: $175 to $15,000. Remarks: Full-time maker, first knife made in 1973. Member Knifemakers Guild and FEGA. Jewel setting inlays. Mark: Willy B. or WB'S C etched or carved.

ELROD, ROGER R,
58 Dale Ave, Enterprise, AL 36330, Phone: 334-347-1863

EMBRETSEN, KAJ,
FALUVAGEN 67, Edsbyn, SWEDEN 82830, Phone: 46-271-21057, Fax: 46-271-22961, kay.embretsen@telia.com Web:www.embretsenknives.com
Specialties: Damascus folding knives. Patterns: Uses mammoth ivory and some pearl. Technical: Uses own Damascus steel. Remarks: Full time since 1983. Prices: $2500 to $8000. Mark: Name inside the folder.

EMERSON, ERNEST R,
1234 W. 254th, Harbor City, CA 90710, Phone: 310-539-5633, info@emersonknives.com; Web: www.emersonknives.com
Specialties: High-tech folders and combat fighters. Patterns: Fighters, LinerLock® combat folders and SPECWAR combat knives. Technical: Grinds 154CM and Damascus. Makes folders with titanium fittings, liners and locks. Chisel grind specialist. Prices: $550 to $850; some to $10,000. Remarks: Full-time maker; first knife sold in 1983. Mark: Last name and Specwar knives.

EMMERLING, JOHN,
1368 Pacific Way, Gearheart, OR 97138, Phone: 800-738-5434, ironwerks@linet.com

ENCE, JIM,
145 S 200 East, Richfield, UT 84701, Phone: 435-896-6206
Specialties: High-art period pieces (spec in California knives) art knives. Patterns: Art, boot knives, fighters, Bowies and occasional folders. Technical: Grinds 440C for polish and beauty boys; makes own Damascus. Prices: Upscale. Remarks: Full-time maker; first knife sold in 1977. Does own engraving, gold work and stone work. Guild member since 1977. Founding member of the AKI. Mark: Ence, usually engraved.

ENGLAND, VIRGIL,
1340 Birchwood St, Anchorage, AK 99508, Phone: 907-274-9494, WEB:www.virgilengland.com
Specialties: Edged weapons and equipage, one-of-a-kind only. Patterns: Axes, swords, lances and body armor. Technical: Forges and grinds as pieces dictate. Offers stainless and Damascus. Prices: Upscale. Remarks: A veteran knifemaker. No commissions. Mark: Stylized initials.

ENGLE, WILLIAM,
16608 Oak Ridge Rd, Boonville, MO 65233, Phone: 816-882-6277
Specialties: Traditional working and using straight knives of his design. Patterns: Hunters, Bowies and fighters. Technical: Grinds 440C, ATS-34 and 154 CM. Prices: $250 to $500; some higher. Remarks: Part-time maker; first knife sold in 1982. All knives come with certificate of authenticity. Mark: Last name in block lettering.

ENGLISH, JIM,
14586 Olive Vista Dr, Jamul, CA 91935, Phone: 619-669-0833
Specialties: Traditional working straight knives to customer specs. Patterns: Hunters, bowies, fighters, tantos, daggers, boot and utility/camp knives. Technical: Grinds 440C, ATS-34, commercial Damascus and customer choice. Prices: $130 to $350. Remarks: Part-time maker; first knife sold in 1985. In addition to custom line, also does business as Mountain Home Knives. Mark: Double "A," Double "J" logo.

ENNIS, RAY,
1220S 775E, Ogden, UT 84404, Phone: 800-410-7603, Fax: 501-621-2683, nifmakr@hotmail.com; Web:www.ennis-entrekusa.com

ENOS III, THOMAS M,
12302 State Rd 535, Orlando, FL 32836, Phone: 407-239-6205, tmenos3@att.net
Specialties: Heavy-duty working straight knives; unusual designs. Patterns: Swords, machetes, daggers, skinners, filleting, period pieces. Technical: Grinds 440C. Prices: $75 to $1500. Remarks: Full-time maker; first knife sold in 1972. No longer accepting custom requests. Will be making his own designs. Send SASE for listing of items for sale. Mark: Name in knife logo and year, type of steel and serial number.

ENTIN, ROBERT,
127 Pembroke St 1, Boston, MA 02118

EPTING, RICHARD,
4021 Cody Dr, College Station, TX 77845, Phone: 979-690-6496, rgeknives@hotmail.com; Web: www.eptingknives.com
Specialties: Folders and working straight knives. Patterns: Hunters, Bowies, and locking folders. Technical: Forges high-carbon steel and his own Damascus. Prices: $200 to $800; some to $1800. Remarks: Part-time maker, first knife sold 1996. Mark: Name in arch logo.

ERICKSON, DANIEL,
Ring Of Fire Forge, 20011 Welch Rd., Snohomish, WA 98296, Phone: 206-355-1793, Web: www.ringoffireforge.com
Specialties: Likes to fuse traditional and functional with creative concepts. Patterns: Hunters, fighters, bowies, folders, slip joints, art knives, the Phalanx. Technical: Forges own pattern-welded damascus blades (1080/15N20), 5160,

CruForgeV, 52100 and W2. Uses figured burls, stabilized woods, fossil ivories and natural and unique materials for handles. Custom stands and sheaths. Prices: $250 to $1,500. Remarks: Sole authorship, designer and inventor. Started making in 2003; first knife sold in 2004. ABS journeyman smith. Mark: "Ring of Fire" with Erickson moving through it.

ERICKSON, L.M.,
1379 Black Mountain Cir, Ogden, UT 84404, Phone: 801-737-1930
Specialties: Straight knives; period pieces. Patterns: Bowies, fighters, boots and hunters. Technical: Grinds 440C, 154CM and commercial Damascus. Prices: $200 to $900; some to $5000. Remarks: Part-time maker; first knife sold in 1981. Mark: Name, city, state.

ERICKSON, WALTER E.,
22280 Shelton Tr, Atlanta, MI 49709, Phone: 989-785-5262, wberic@racc2000.com
Specialties: Unusual survival knives and high-tech working knives. Patterns: Butterflies, hunters, tantos. Technical: Grinds ATS-34 or customer choice. Prices: $150 to $500; some to $1500. Remarks: Full-time maker; first knife sold in 1981. Mark: Using pantograph with assorted fonts (no longer stamping).

ERIKSEN, JAMES THORLIEF,
dba VIKING KNIVES, 3830 Dividend Dr, Garland, TX 75042, Phone: 972-494-3667, Fax: 972-235-4932, VikingKnives@aol.com
Specialties: Heavy-duty working and using straight knives and folders utilizing traditional, Viking original and customer specification patterns. Some high-tech and fancy/embellished knives available. Patterns: Bowies, hunters, skinners, boot and belt knives, utility/camp knives, fighters, daggers, locking folders, slip-joint folders and kitchen knives. Technical: Hollow-grinds 440C, D2, ASP-23, ATS-34, 154CM, Vascowear. Prices: $150 to $300; some to $600. Remarks: Full-time maker; first knife sold in 1985. Doing business as Viking Knives. For a color catalog showing 50 different models, mail $5 to above address. Mark: VIKING or VIKING USA for export.

ERNEST, PHIL (PJ),
PO Box 5240, Whittier, CA 90607-5240, Phone: 562-556-2324, hugger883562@yahoo.com; Web:www.ernestcustomknives.com
Specialties: Fixed blades. Patterns: Wide range. Many original as well as hunters, camp, fighters, daggers, bowies and tactical. Specialzin in Wharncliff's of all sizes. Technical: Grinds commercial Damascus, Mosaic Damascus. ATS-34, and 440C. Full Tangs with bolsters. Handle material includes all types of exotic hardwood, abalone, peal mammoth tooth, mammoth ivory, Damascus steel and Mosaic Damascus. Remarks: Full time maker. First knife sold in 1999. Prices: $200 to $1800. Some to $2500. Mark: Owl logo with PJ Ernest Whittier CA or PJ Ernest

ESPOSITO, EMMANUEL,
Via Reano 70, Buttigliera Alta TO, ITALY 10090, Phone: 39-011932-16-21, www.emmanuelmaker.it
Specialties: Folding knife with his patent system lock mechanism with mosaic inlay.

ESSEGIAN, RICHARD,
7387 E Tulare St, Fresno, CA 93727, Phone: 309-255-5950
Specialties: Fancy working knives of his design; art knives. Patterns: Bowies and some small hunters. Technical: Grinds A2, D2, 440C and 154CM. Engraves and inlays. Prices: Start at $600. Remarks: Part-time maker; first knife sold in 1986. Mark: Last name, city and state.

ESTABROOK, ROBBIE,
1014 Madge Ct., Conway, SC 29526, Phone: 803-917-3786, robbieestabrook@gmail.com

ETZLER, JOHN,
11200 N Island, Grafton, OH 44044, Phone: 440-748-2460, jetzler@bright.net; Web: members.tripod.com/~etzlerknives/
Specialties: High-art and fantasy straight knives and folders of his design and to customer specs. Patterns: Folders, daggers, fighters, utility knives. Technical: Forges and grinds nickel Damascus and tool steel; grinds stainless steels. Prefers exotic, natural materials. Prices: $250 to $1200; some to $6500. Remarks: Full-time maker; first knife sold in 1992. Mark: Name or initials.

EVANS, BRUCE A,
409 CR 1371, Booneville, MS 38829, Phone: 662-720-0193, beknives@avsia.com; Web: www.bruceevans.homestead.com/open.html
Specialties: Forges blades. Patterns: Hunters, Bowies, or will work with customer. Technical: 5160, cable Damascus, pattern welded Damascus. Prices: $200 and up. Mark: Bruce A. Evans Same with JS on reverse of blade.

EVANS, CARLTON,
PO Box 46, Gainesville, TX 76241, Phone: 817-886-9231, carlton@carltonevans.com; Web: www.carltonevans.com
Specialties: High end folders and fixed blades. Technical: Uses the stock removal methods. The materials used are of the highest quality. Remarks: Full-time knifemaker, voting member of Knifemakers Guild, member of the Texas Knifemakers and Collectors Association.

EVANS, PHIL,
594 SE 40th, Columbus, KS 66725, Phone: 620-249-0639, phil@glenviewforge.com Web: www.glenviewforge.com
Specialties: Working knives, hunters, skinners, also enjoys making Bowies and fighters, high carbon or Damascus. Technical: Forges own blades and makes own Damascus. Uses all kinds of ancient Ivory and bone. Stabilizes own native hardwoods. Prices: $150 - $1,500. Remarks: Part-time maker. Made first knife

in 1995. Mark: EVANS.

EVANS, RONALD B,
209 Hoffer St, Middleton, PA 17057-2723, Phone: 717-944-5464

EVANS, VINCENT K AND GRACE,
HC 1 Box 5275, Keaau, HI 96749-9517, Phone: 808-966-8978, evansvk@gmail.com Web: www.picturetrail.com/vevans
Specialties: Period pieces; swords. Patterns: Scottish, Viking, central Asian. Technical: Forges 5160 and his own Damascus. Prices: $700 to $4000; some to $8000. Remarks: Full-time maker; first knife sold in 1983. Mark: Last initial with fish logo.

EWING, JOHN H,
3276 Dutch Valley Rd, Clinton, TN 37716, Phone: 865-457-5757, johnja@comcast.net
Specialties: Working straight knives, hunters, camp knives. Patterns: Hunters. Technical: Grinds 440-D2. Forges 5160, 1095 prefers forging. Prices: $150 and up. Remarks: Part-time maker; first knife sold in 1985. Mark: First initial, last name, some embellishing done on knives.

F

FAIRLY, DANIEL,
2209 Bear Creek Canyon Rd, Bayfield, CO 81122, danielfairlyknives@gmail.com; Web: www.danielfairlyknives.com
Specialties: One of a kind handmade knives made for hard use. Patterns: Heavy duty choppers, every day carry and neck knives, Japanese influenced designs, ultra light titanium utilities. Technical: Grinds mostly tool steel and carbidized titanium in .050" to .360" thick material. Uses heavy duty handle materials and flared test tube fasteners or epoxy soaked wrapped handles. Most grinds are chisel; flat convex and hollow grinds used. Prices: $75 to $700. Remarks: Full-time maker since first knife sold in Feb. 2011. Mark: Fairly written in all capitals with larger F.

FANT JR., GEORGE,
1983 CR 3214, Atlanta, TX 75551-6515, Phone: (903) 846-2938

FARID, MEHR R,
8 Sidney Close, Tunbridge Wells, Kent, ENGLAND TN2 5QQ, Phone: 011-44-1892 520345, farid@faridknives.com; Web: www.faridknives.com
Specialties: Hollow handle survival knives. High tech folders. Patterns: Flat grind blades & chisel ground LinerLock® folders. Technical: Grinds 440C, CPMT-440V, CPM-420V, CPM-15V, CPM5125V, and T-1 high speed steel. Prices: $550 to $5000. Remarks: Full-time maker; first knife sold in 1991. Mark: First name stamped.

FARR, DAN,
285 Glen Ellyn Way, Rochester, NY 14618, Phone: 585-721-1388
Specialties: Hunting, camping, fighting and utility. Patterns: Fixed blades. Technical: Forged or stock removal. Prices: $150 to $750.

FASSIO, MELVIN G,
420 Tyler Way, Lolo, MT 59847, Phone: 406-544-1391
Specialties: Working folders to customer specs. Patterns: Locking folders, hunters and traditional-style knives. Technical: Grinds 440C. Prices: $125 to $350. Remarks: Part-time maker; first knife sold in 1975. Mark: Name and city, dove logo.

FAUCHEAUX, HOWARD J,
PO Box 206, Loreauville, LA 70552, Phone: 318-229-6467
Specialties: Working straight knives and folders; period pieces. Also a hatchet with capping knife in the handle. Patterns: Traditional locking knives, hunters, fighters and Bowies. Technical: Forges W2, 1095 and his own Damascus; stock removal D2. Prices: Start at $200. Remarks: Full-time maker; first knife sold in 1969. Mark: Last name.

FAUST, DICK,
624 Kings Hwy N, Rochester, NY 14617, Phone: 585-544-1948, dickfaustknives@mac.com
Specialties: High-performance working straight knives. Patterns: Hunters and utility/camp knives. Technical: Hollow grinds 154CM full tang. Exotic woods, stag and Micarta handles. Provides a custom leather sheath with each knife. Prices: From $200 to $600, some higher. Remarks: Full-time maker. Mark: Signature.

FAUST, JOACHIM,
Kirchgasse 10, Goldkronach, GERMANY 95497

FELIX, ALEXANDER,
PO Box 4036, Torrance, CA 90510, Phone: 310-320-1836, sgiandubh@dslextreme.com
Specialties: Straight working knives, fancy ethnic designs. Patterns: Hunters, Bowies, daggers, period pieces. Technical: Forges carbon steel and Damascus; forged stainless and titanium jewelry, gold and silver casting. Prices: $110 and up. Remarks: Jeweler, ABS Journeyman Smith. Mark: Last name.

FERGUSON, JIM,
32131 Via Bande, Temecula, CA 92592, Phone: 951-302-0267, Web: www.twistednickel.com www.howtomakeaknife.net
Specialties: Nickel Damascus, Bowies, daggers, push blades. Also makes swords, battle axes and utilities. Patterns: All styles. Technical: Sells in U.S. and Canada. Prices: $350 to $600, some to $1000. Mark: Jim Ferguson/USA. Also make swords, battle axes and utilities.

FERGUSON, JIM,
3543 Shadyhill Dr, San Angelo, TX 76904, Phone: 325-655-1061
Specialties: Straight working knives and folders. Patterns: Working belt knives, hunters, Bowies and some folders. Technical: Grinds ATS-34 and Vascowear. Flat-grinds hunting knives. Prices: $200 to $600; some to $1000. Remarks: Full-time maker; first knife sold in 1987. Mark: First and middle initials, last name.

FERGUSON, LEE,
1993 Madison 7580, Hindsville, AR 72738, Phone: 479-443-0084, info@fergusonknives.com; Web: www.fergusonknives.com
Specialties: Straight working knives and folders, some fancy. Patterns: Hunters, daggers, swords, locking folders and slip-joints. Technical: Grinds D2, 440C and ATS-34; heat-treats. Prices: $50 to $600; some to $4000. Remarks: Full-time maker; first knife sold in 1977. Mark: Full name.

FERGUSON, LINDA,
1993 Madison 7580, Hindsville, AR 72738, Phone: 479-443-0084, info@fergusonknives.com; Web: www.fergusonknives.com
Specialties: Mini knives. Patterns: Daggers & hunters. Technical: Hollow ground, stainless steel or Damascus. Prices: $65 to $250. Remarks: 2004 member Knifemakers Guild, Miniature Knifemakers Society. Mark: LF inside a Roman numeral 2.

FERRARA, THOMAS,
122 Madison Dr, Naples, FL 33942, Phone: 813-597-3363, Fax: 813-597-3363
Specialties: High-art, traditional and working straight knives and folders of all designs. Patterns: Boots, Bowies, daggers, fighters and hunters. Technical: Grinds 440C, D2 and ATS-34; heat-treats. Prices: $100 to $700; some to $1300. Remarks: Part-time maker; first knife sold in 1983. Mark: Last name.

FERRIER, GREGORY K,
3119 Simpson Dr, Rapid City, SD 57702, Phone: 605-342-9280

FERRY, TOM,
16005 SE 322nd St, Auburn, WA 98092, Phone: 253-939-4468, tomferryknives@Q.com; Web: tomferryknives.com
Specialties: Presentation grade knives. Patterns: Folders and fixed blades. Technical: Specialize in Damascus and engraving. Prices: $500 and up. Remarks: DBA: Soos Creek Ironworks. ABS Master Smith. Mark: Combined T and F in a circle and/or last name.

FILIPPOU, IOANNIS-MINAS,
23 Vryouron Str, Nea Smyrni 17122, Athens, GREECE 17122, Phone: (1) 935-2093, knifemaker_gr@yahoo.gr

FINCH, RICKY D,
1179 Hwy 844, West Liberty, KY 41472, Phone: 606-743-7151, finchknives@mrtc.com; Web: www.finchknives.com
Specialties: Traditional working/using straight knives of his design or to customer spec. Patterns: Hunters, skinners and utility/camp knives. LinerLock® of his design. Technical: Grinds 440C, ATS-34 and CPM154, hand rubbed stain finish, use Micarta, stabilized wood, natural and exotic. Prices: $85 to $225. Remarks: Part-time maker, first knife made 1994. Doing business as Finch Knives. Mark: Last name inside outline of state of Kentucky.

FIORINI, BILL,
703 W. North St., Grayville, IL 62844, Phone: 618-375-7191, smallflowerlonchura@yahoo.com
Specialties: Fancy working knives. Patterns: Hunters, boots, Japanese-style knives and kitchen/utility knives and folders. Technical: Forges own Damascus, mosaic and mokune-gane. Prices: Full range. Remarks: Full-time metal smith researching pattern materials. Mark: Orchid crest with name KOKA in Japanese.

FISHER, JAY,
1405 Edwards, Clovis, NM 88101, jayfisher@jayfisher.com Web: www.JayFisher.com
Specialties: High-art, working and collector's knives of his design and client's designs. Military working and commemoratives. Gemstone handles, Locking combat sheaths. Patterns: Hunters, daggers, folding knives, museum pieces and high-art sculptures. Technical: 440C, ATS-34, CPMS30V, D2, O1, CPM154CM, CPMS35VN. Prolific maker of stone-handled knives and swords. Prices: $850 to $150,000. Remarks: Full-time maker; first knife sold in 1980. High resolution etching, computer and manual engraving. Mark: Signature "JaFisher"

FISHER, JOSH,
JN Fisher Knives, 8419 CR 3615, Murchison, TX 75778, Phone: 903-203-2130, fisherknives@aol.com; Web: www.jnfisherknives.com
Specialties: Frame-handle fighters. Technical: Forge 5160 and 1084 blade steels. Prices: $125 to $1,000. Remarks: Part-time maker; first knife made in 2007. ABS journeyman smith. Mark: Josh Fisher etched. "JS" also etched on the reverse.

FISHER, LANCE,
9 Woodlawn Ave., Pompton Lakes, NJ 07442, Phone: 973-248-8447, lance.fisher@sandvik.com
Specialties: Wedding cake knives and servers, forks, etc. Including velvet lined wood display cases. Patterns: Drop points, upswept skinners, Bowies, daggers, fantasy, medieval, San Francisco style, chef or kitchen cutlery. Technical: Stock removal method only. Steels include but are not limited to CPM 154, D2, CPM S35VN, CPM S90V and Sandvik 13C26. Handle materials include stag, sheep horn, exotic woods, micarta, and G10 as well as reconstituted stone. Prices: $350 - $2000. Remarks: Part-time maker, will become full-time on retirement. Made and sold first knife in 1981 and has never looked back. Mark: Tang stamp.

FISK, JERRY,
10095 Hwy 278 W, Nashville, AR 71852, Phone: 870-845-4456, jerry@jerryfisk.com; Web: www.jerryfisk.com or Facebook: Jerry Fisk, MS Custom Knives
Specialties: Edged weapons, collectible and functional. Patterns: Bowies, daggers, swords, hunters, camp knives and others. Technical: Forges carbon steels and his own pattern welded steels. Prices: $1100 to $20,000. Remarks: National living treasure. Mark: Name, MS.

FISTER, JIM,
PO Box 307, Simpsonville, KY 40067
Specialties: One-of-a-kind collectibles and period pieces. Patterns: Bowies, camp knives, hunters, buckskinners, and daggers. Technical: Forges, 1085, 5160, 52100, his own Damascus, pattern and turkish. Prices: $150 to $2500. Remarks: Part-time maker; first knife sold in 1982. Mark: Name and MS.

FITCH, JOHN S,
45 Halbrook Rd, Clinton, AR 72031-8910, Phone: 501-893-2020

FITZGERALD, DENNIS M,
4219 Alverado Dr, Fort Wayne, IN 46816-2847, Phone: 219-447-1081
Specialties: One-of-a-kind collectibles and period pieces. Patterns: Skinners, fighters, camp and utility knives; period pieces. Technical: Forges 1085, 1095, L6, 5160, 52100, his own pattern and Turkish Damascus. Prices: $100 to $500. Remarks: Part-time maker; first knife sold in 1985. Doing business as The Ringing Circle. Mark: Name and circle logo.

FLINT, ROBERT,
2902 Aspen, Anchorage, AK 99517, Phone: 907-243-6706
Specialties: Working straight knives and folders. Patterns: Utility, hunters, fighters and gents. Technical: Grinds ATS-34, BG-42, D2 and Damascus. Prices: $150 and up. Remarks: Part-time maker, first knife sold in 1998. Mark: Last name; stylized initials.

FLOURNOY, JOE,
5750 Lisbon Rd, El Dorado, AR 71730, Phone: 870-863-7208, flournoy@ipa.net
Specialties: Working straight knives and folders. Patterns: Hunters, Bowies, camp knives, folders and daggers. Technical: Forges only high-carbon steel, steel cable and his own Damascus. Prices: $350 Plus. Remarks: First knife sold in 1977. Mark: Last name and MS in script.

FLYNT, ROBERT G,
15173 Christy Lane, Gulfport, MS 39503, Phone: 228-832-3378 or cell: 228-265-0410, robertflynt@cableone.net; Web: www.flyntstoneknifeworks.com
Specialties: All types of fixed blades: drop point, clip point, trailing point, bull-nose hunters, tactical, fighters and bowies. LinerLock, slip-joint and lockback folders. Technical: Using 154CM, CPM-154, ATS-34, 440C, CPM-3V and 52100 steels. Most blades made by stock removal, hollow and flat grind methods. Forges some cable damascus and uses numerous types of damascus purchased in billets from various makers. All filework and bluing done by the maker. Various wood handles, bone and horn materials, including some with wire inlay and other embellishments. Most knives sold with custom-fit leather sheaths, most include exotic skin inlay when appropriate. Prices: $150 and up, depending on embellishments on blade and sheath. Remarks: Full-time maker; first knife made in 1966. Knifemakers' Guild member. Mark: Last name in cursive letters or a knife striking a flint stone.

FOGARIZZU, BOITEDDU,
via Crispi 6, Pattada, ITALY 07016
Specialties: Traditional Italian straight knives and folders. Patterns: Collectible folders. Technical: forges and grinds 12C27, ATS-34 and his Damascus. Prices: $200 to $3000. Remarks: Full-time maker; first knife sold in 1958. Mark: Full name and registered logo.

FOGG, DON,
98 Lake St., Auburn, ME 04210, Phone: 205-483-0822, dfogg@dfoggknives.com; Web: www.dfoggknives.com
Specialties: Swords, daggers, Bowies and hunting knives. Patterns: Collectible folders. Technical: Hand-forged high-carbon and Damascus steel. Prices: $200 to $5000. Remarks: Full-time maker; first knife sold in 1976. Mark: 24K gold cherry blossom.

FONTENOT, GERALD J,
901 Maple Ave, Mamou, LA 70554, Phone: 318-468-3180

FORREST, BRIAN,
FORREST KNIVES, PO Box 611, Descanso, CA 91916, Phone: 619-445-6343, forrestforge@gmail.com; Web: www.forrestforge.biz
Specialties: Forged tomahawks, working knives, big Bowies. Patterns: Traditional and extra large Bowies. Technical: Hollow grinds: 440C, 1095, S160 Damascus. Prices"$125 and up. Remarks: Member of California Knifemakers Association. Full-time maker. First knife sold in 1971. Mark: Forrest USA/Tomahawks marked FF (Forrest Forge).

FORTHOFER, PETE,
5535 Hwy 93S, Whitefish, MT 59937, Phone: 406-862-2674
Specialties: Interframes with checkered wood inlays; working straight knives. Patterns: Interframe folders and traditional-style knives; hunters, fighters and Bowies. Technical: Grinds D2, 440C, 154CM and ATS-34. Prices: $350 to $2500; some to $1500. Remarks: Part-time maker; full-time gunsmith. First knife sold in 1979. Mark: Name and logo.

FOSTER, AL,
118 Woodway Dr, Magnolia, TX 77355, Phone: 936-372-9297
Specialties: Straight knives and folders. Patterns: Hunting, fishing, folders and Bowies. Technical: Grinds 440-C, ATS-34 and D2. Prices: $100 to $1000. Remarks: Full-time maker; first knife sold in 1981. Mark: Scorpion logo and name.

FOSTER, BURT,
23697 Archery Range Rd, Bristol, VA 24202, Phone: 276-669-0121, burt@burtfoster.com; Web:www.burtfoster.com
Specialties: Working straight knives, laminated blades, and some art knives of his design. Patterns: Bowies, hunters, daggers. Technical: Forges 52100, W-2 and makes own Damascus. Does own heat treating. Remarks: ABS MasterSmith. Full-time maker, believes in sole authorship. Mark: Signed "BF" initials.

FOSTER, NORVELL C,
7945 Youngsford Rd, Marion, TX 78124-1713, Phone: 830-914-2078
Specialties: Engraving; ivory handle carving. Patterns: American-large and small scroll-oak leaf and acorns. Prices: $25 to $400. Remarks: Have been engraving since 1957. Mark: N.C. Foster - Marion - Tex and current year.

FOSTER, RONNIE E,
95 Riverview Rd., Morrilton, AR 72110, Phone: 501-354-5389
Specialties: Working, using knives, some period pieces, work with customer specs. Patterns: Hunters, fighters, Bowies, liner-lock folders, camp knives. Technical: Forge-5160, 1084, O1, 15N20-makes own Damascus. Prices: $200 (start). Remarks: Part-time maker. First knife sold 1994. Mark: Ronnie Foster MS.

FOSTER, TIMOTHY L,
723 Sweet Gum Acres Rd, El Dorado, AR 71730, Phone: 870-863-6188

FOWLER, CHARLES R,
226 National Forest Rd 48, Ft McCoy, FL 32134-9624, Phone: 904-467-3215

FOWLER, ED A.,
Willow Bow Ranch, PO Box 1519, Riverton, WY 82501, Phone: 307-856-9815
Specialties: High-performance working and using straight knives. Patterns: Hunter, camp, bird, and trout knives and Bowies. New model, the gentleman's Pronghorn. Technical: Low temperature forged 52100 from virgin 5-1/2 round bars, multiple quench heat treating, engraves all knives, all handles domestic sheep horn processed and aged at least 5 years. Makes heavy duty hand-stitched waxed harness leather pouch type sheathes. Prices: $800 to $7000. Remarks: Full-time maker. First knife sold in 1962. Mark: Initials connected.

FOWLER, JERRY,
610 FM 1660 N, Hutto, TX 78634, Phone: 512-846-2860, fowler@inetport.com
Specialties: Using straight knives of his design. Patterns: A variety of hunting and camp knives, combat knives. Custom designs considered. Technical: Forges 5160, his own Damascus and cable Damascus. Makes sheaths. Prefers natural handle materials. Prices: Start at $150. Remarks: Part-time maker; first knife sold in 1986. Doing business as Fowler Forge Knife Works. Mark: First initial, last name, date and J.S.

FRALEY, D B,
1355 Fairbanks Ct, Dixon, CA 95620, Phone: 707-678-0393, dbtfnives@sbcglobal.net; Web:www.dbfraleyknives.com
Specialties Usable gentleman's fixed blades and folders. Patterns: Foure folders in four different sizes in liner lock and frame lock. Technical: Grinds CPMS30V, 154, 6K stellite. Prices: $250 and up. Remarks: Part time maker. First knife sold in 1990. Mark: First and middle initials, last name over a buffalo.

FRAMSKI, WALTER P,
24 Rek Ln, Prospect, CT 06712, Phone: 203-758-5634

FRANCE, DAN,
Box 218, Cawood, KY 40815, Phone: 606-573-6104
Specialties: Traditional working and using straight knives of his design. Patterns: Hunters, Bowies and utility/camp knives. Technical: Forges and grinds O1, 5160 and L6. Prices: $35 to $125; some to $350. Remarks: Spare-time maker; first knife sold in 1985. Mark: First name.

FRANCIS, JOHN D,
FRANCIS KNIVES, 18 Miami St., Ft. Loramie, OH 45845, Phone: 937-295-3941, jdfrancis72@gmail.com
Specialties: Utility and hunting-style fixed bladed knives of 440 C and ATS-34 steel; Micarta, exotic woods, and other types of handle materials. Prices: $90 to $150 range. Remarks: Exceptional quality and value at factory prices. Mark: Francis-Ft. Loramie, OH stamped on tang.

FRANK, HEINRICH H,
1147 SW Bryson St, Dallas, OR 97338, Phone: 503-831-1489, Fax: 503-831-1489
Specialties: High-art investor-class folders, handmade and engraved. Patterns: Folding daggers, hunter-size folders and gents. Technical: Grinds 07 and O1. Prices: $4800 to $16,000. Remarks: Full-time maker; first knife sold in 1965. Doing business as H.H. Frank Knives. Mark: Name, address and date.

FRANKLIN, MIKE,
9878 Big Run Rd, Aberdeen, OH 45101, Phone: 937-549-2598, Web: www.mikefranklinknives.com, hawgcustomknives.com
Specialties: High-tech tactical folders. Patterns: Tactical folders. Technical: Grinds CPM-T-440V, 440-C, ATS-34; titanium liners and bolsters; carbon fiber scales. Uses radical grinds and severe serrations. Prices: $100 to $1000. Remarks: Full-time maker; first knife sold in 1969. All knives made one at a time, 100% by the maker. Mark: Stylized boar with HAWG.

FRAPS, JOHN R,
3810 Wyandotte Tr, Indianapolis, IN 46240-3422, Phone: 317-849-9419, jfraps@att.net; Web: www.frapsknives.com
Specialties: Working and collector grade LinerLock® and slip joint folders. Patterns: One-of-a kind linerlocks and traditional slip joints. Technical: Flat and hollow grinds ATS-34, Damascus, Talonite, CPM S30V, 154Cm, Stellite 6K;

custom knifemakers

hand rubbed or mirror finish. Prices: $200 to $1500, some higher. Remarks: Voting member of the Knifemaker's Guild; Full-time maker; first knife sold in 1997. Mark: Cougar Creek Knives and/or name.

FRAZIER, JIM,
6315 Wagener Rd., Wagener, SC 29164, Phone: 803-564-6467, jbfrazierknives@gmail.com; Web: www.jbfrazierknives.com
Specialties: Hunters, semi skinners, oyster roast knives, bird and trout, folders, many patterns of own design with George Herron/Geno Denning influence. Technical: Stock removal maker using CPM-154, ATS-34, CPM-S30V and D2. Hollow grind, mainly mirror finish, some satin finish. Prefer to use natural handle material such as stag, horn, mammoth ivory, highly figured woods, some Micarta, others on request. Makes own leather sheaths on 1958 straight needle stitcher. Prices: $125 to $600. Remarks: Part-time maker since 1989. Mark: JB Frazier in arch with Knives under it. Stamp on sheath is outline of state of SC, JB Frazier Knives Wagener SC inside outline.

FRED, REED WYLE,
3149 X S, Sacramento, CA 95817, Phone: 916-739-0237
Specialties: Working using straight knives of his design. Patterns: Hunting and camp knives. Technical: Forges any 10 series, old files and carbon steels. Offers initialing upon request; prefers natural handle materials. Prices: $30 to $300. Remarks: Part-time maker; first knife sold in 1994. Doing business as R.W. Fred Knifemaker. Mark: Engraved first and last initials.

FREDEEN, GRAHAM,
5121 Finadene Ct., Colorado Springs, CO 80916, Phone: 719-331-5665, fredeenblades@hotmail.com Web: www.fredeenblades.com
Specialties: Working class knives to high-end custom knives. Traditional pattern welding and mosaic Damascus blades. Patterns: All types: Bowies, fighters, hunters, skinners, bird and trout, camp knives, utility knives, daggers, etc. Occasionally swords, both European and Asian. Technical: Differential heat treatment and Hamon. Damascus steel rings and jewelry. Hand forged blades and Damascus steel. High carbon blade steels: 1050, 1075/1080, 1084, 1095, 5160, 52100, W1, W2, O1, 15n20 Prices: $100 - $2,000. Remarks: Sole authorship. Part-time maker. First blade produced in 2005. Member of American Bladesmith Society and Professional Knifemaker's Association Mark: "Fredeen" etched on the ricasso or on/along the spine of the blade.

FREDERICK, AARON,
459 Brooks Ln, West Liberty, KY 41472-8961, Phone: 606-7432015, aaronf@mrtc.com; Web: www.frederickknives.com
Specialties: Makes most types of knives, but as for now specializes in the Damascus folder. Does all own Damascus and forging of the steel. Also prefers natural handle material such as ivory and pearl. Prefers 14k gold screws in most of the knives he do. Also offer several types of file work on blades, spacers, and liners. Has just recently started doing carving and can do a limited amount of engraving.

FREEMAN, MATT,
5767 N. Channing Way, Fresno, CA 93711, Phone: 559-375-4408, kathur420@yahoo.com; Web: www.youtube.com/FTWCM
Specialties: Fixed blades and butterfly knives. Technical: Using mostly 1084, 154CM, D2 and file steel, works in any requested materials via stock removal. Also does knife modifications and leather/Kydex work. Three months or less waiting list. Prices: $75+. Mark: "FTW," "FTWCM" or "FTW 3-13."

FREER, RALPH,
114 12th St, Seal Beach, CA 90740, Phone: 562-493-4925, Fax: same, ralphfreer@adelphia.net
Specialties: Exotic folders, liner locks, folding daggers, fixed blades. Patters: All original. Technical: Lots of Damascus, ivory, pearl, jeweled, thumb studs, carving ATS-34, 420V, 530V. Prices: $400 to $2500 and up. Mark: Freer in German-style text, also Freer shield.

FREY JR., W FREDERICK,
305 Walnut St, Milton, PA 17847, Phone: 570-742-9576, wffrey@ptd.net
Specialties: Working straight knives and folders, some fancy. Patterns: Wide range miniatures, boot knives and lock back folders. Technical: Grinds A2, O1 and D2; vaseo wear, cru-wear and CPM S90V. Prices: $100 to $250; some to $1200. Remarks: Spare-time maker; first knife sold in 1983. All knives include quality hand stitched leather sheaths. Mark: Last name in script.

FRIEDLY, DENNIS E,
12 Cottontail Lane E, Cody, WY 82414, Phone: 307-527-6811, friedlyknives@hotmail.com Web: www.friedlyknives.com
Specialties: Fancy working straight knives and daggers, lock back folders and liner locks. Also embellished bowies. Patterns: Hunters, fighters, short swords, minis and miniatures; new line of full-tang hunters/boots. Technical: Grinds 440C, commercial Damascus, mosaic Damascus and ATS-34 blades; prefers hidden tangs and full tangs. Both flat and hollow grinds. Prices: $350 to $2500. Some to $10,000. Remarks: Full-time maker; first knife sold in 1972. Mark: D.E. Friedly-Cody, WY. Friedly Knives

FRIGAULT, RICK,
1189 Royal Pines Rd, Golden Lake, ON, CANADA K0J 1X0, Phone: 613-401-2869, Web: www.rfrigaultknives.ca
Specialties: Fixed blades. Patterns: Hunting, tactical and large Bowies. Technical: Grinds ATS-34, 440-C, D-2, CPMS30V, CPMS60V, CPMS90V, BG42 and Damascus. Use G-10, Micarta, ivory, antler, ironwood and other stabilized woods for carbon fiber handle material. Makes leather sheaths by hand. Tactical blades include a Concealex sheath made by "On Scene

Tactical." Remarks: Sold first knife in 1997. Member of Canadian Knifemakers Guild. Mark: RFRIGAULT.

FRITZ, ERIK L,
837 River St Box 1203, Forsyth, MT 59327, Phone: 406-351-1101, tacmedic45@yahoo.com
Specialties: Forges carbon steel 1084, 5160, 52100 and Damascus. Patterns: Hunters, camp knives, bowies and folders as well as forged tactical. Technical: Forges own Mosaic and pattern welded Damascus as well as doing own heat treat. Prices: A$200 and up. Remarks: Sole authorship knives and sheaths. Part time maker first knife sold in 2004. ABS member. Mark: E. Fritz in arc on left side ricasso.

FRITZ, JESSE,
900 S. 13th St, Slaton, TX 79364, Phone: 806-828-5083
Specialties: Working and using straight knives in standard patterns. Patterns: Hunters, utility/camp knives and skinners with gut hook, Bowie knives, kitchen carving sets by request. Technical: Grinds 440C, O1 and 1095. Uses 1095 steel. Fline-napped steel design, blued blades, filework and machine jewelling. Inlays handles with turquoise, coral and mother-of-pearl. Makes sheaths. Prices: $85 to $275; some to $500. Mark: Last name only (FRITZ).

FRIZZELL, TED,
14056 Low Gap Rd, West Fork, AR 72774, Phone: 501-839-2516, mmhwaxes@aol.com Web: www.mineralmountain.com
Specialties: Swords, axes and self-defense weapons. Patterns: Small skeleton knives to large swords. Technical: Grinds 5160 almost exclusively—1/4" to 1/2"— bars some O1 and A2 on request. All knives come with Kydex sheaths. Prices: $45 to $1200. Remarks: Full-time maker; first knife sold in 1984. Doing business as Mineral Mountain Hatchet Works. Wholesale orders welcome. Mark: A circle with line in the middle; MM and HW within the circle.

FRIZZI, LEONARDO,
Via Kyoto 31, Firenze, ITALY 50126, Phone: 335-344750, postmaster@frizzi-knives.com; Web: www.frizzi-knives.com
Specialties: Fancy handmade one-of-a kind folders of his own design, some fixed blade and dagger. Patterns: Folders liner loch and back locks. Technical: Grinds rwl 34, cpm 154, cpm s30v, stainless damascus and the best craft damascus, own heat treating. I usually prefer satin finish the flat of the blade and mirror polish the hollow grind; special 18k gold, filework. Prices: $600 to $4,000. Remarks: Part-time maker, first knife sold in 2003. Mark: Full name, city, country, or initial, last name and city, or initial in square logo.

FRONEFIELD, DANIEL,
20270 Warriors Path, Peyton, CO 80831, Phone: 719-749-0226, dfronfld@hiwaay.com
Specialties: Fixed and folding knives featuring meteorites and other exotic materials. Patterns: San-mai Damascus, custom Damascus. Prices: $500 to $3000.

FROST, DEWAYNE,
1016 Van Buren Rd, Barnesville, GA 30204, Phone: 770-358-1426, lbrtyhill@aol.com
Specialties: Working straight knives and period knives. Patterns: Hunters, Bowies and utility knives. Technical: Forges own Damascus, cable, etc. as well as stock removal. Prices: $150 to $500. Remarks: Part-time maker ABS Journeyman Smith. Mark: Liberty Hill Forge Dewayne Frost w/liberty bell.

FRUHMANN, LUDWIG,
Stegerwaldstr 8, Burghausen, GERMANY 84489
Specialties: High-tech and working straight knives of his design. Patterns: Hunters, fighters and boots. Technical: Grinds ATS-34, CPM-T-440V and Schneider Damascus. Prefers natural handle materials. Prices: $200 to $1500. Remarks: Spare-time maker; first knife sold in 1990. Mark: First initial and last name.

FRY, JASON,
1701 North Willis, Abilene, TX 79603, Phone: 325-669-4805, frycustomknives@gmail.com; Web: www.frycustomknives.com
Specialties: Prefer drop points, both with or without bolsters. Prefer native Texas woods and often do contrasting wood bolsters. Also does own leather work. Patterns: Primarily EDC and hunting/skinning knives under 8 inches. Also slipjoint folders, primarily single blade trappers and jacks. Technical: 1080 carbon steel, D2 tool steel, and 154CM stainless. Make knives by stock removal and does own heat treating in a digitally controlled kiln. Prices: $150 to $400. Remarks: Part-time maker since July 2008. Mark: FRY placed on blade underneath jumping largemouth bass to reflect other interests.

FUEGEN, LARRY,
617 N Coulter Circle, Prescott, AZ 86303, Phone: 928-776-8777, fuegen@cableone.net; Web: www.larryfuegen.com
Specialties: High-art folders and classic and working straight knives. Patterns: Forged scroll folders, lockback folders and classic straight knives. Technical: Forges 5160, 1095 and his own Damascus. Works in exotic leather; offers elaborate filework and carving; likes natural handle materials, now offers own engraving. Prices: $600 to $12,000. Remarks: Full-time maker; first knife sold in 1975. Sole authorship on all knives. ABS Mastersmith. Mark: Initials connected.

FUJIKAWA, SHUN,
Sawa 1157, Kaizuka, Osaka, JAPAN 597 0062, Phone: 81-724-23-4032, Fax: 81-726-23-9229
Specialties: Folders of his design and to customer specs. Patterns: Locking folders. Technical: Grinds his own steel. Prices: $450 to $2500; some to $3000. Remarks: Part-time maker.

FUJISAKA, STANLEY,
45-004 Holowai St, Kaneohe, HI 96744, Phone: 808-247-0017, s.fuj@earthlink.net
Specialties: Fancy working straight knives and folders. Patterns: Hunters, boots, personal knives, daggers, collectible art knives. Technical: Grinds 440C, 154CM and ATS-34; clean lines, inlays. Prices: $400 to $2000; some to $6000. Remarks: Full-time maker; first knife sold in 1984. Mark: Name, city, state.

FUKUTA, TAK,
38-Umeagae-cho, Seki-City, Gifu, JAPAN, Phone: 0575-22-0264
Specialties: Bench-made fancy straight knives and folders. Patterns: Sheffield-type folders, Bowies and fighters. Technical: Grinds commercial Damascus. Prices: Start at $300. Remarks: Full-time maker. Mark: Name in knife logo.

FULLER, BRUCE A,
3366 Ranch Rd. 32, Blanco, TX 78606, Phone: 832-262-0529, fullcoforg@aol.com
Specialties: One-of-a-kind working/using straight knives and folders of his designs. Patterns: Bowies, hunters, folders, and utility/camp knives. Technical: Forges high-carbon steel and his own Damascus. Prefers El Solo Mesquite and natural materials. Offers filework. Prices: $200 to $500; some to $1800. Remarks: Spare-time maker; first knife sold in 1991. Doing business as Fullco Forge. Mark: Fullco, M.S.

FULLER, JACK A,
7103 Stretch Ct, New Market, MD 21774, Phone: 301-798-0119
Specialties: Straight working knives of his design and to customer specs. Patterns: Fighters, camp knives, hunters, tomahawks and art knives. Technical: Forges 5160, O1, W2 and his own Damascus. Does silver wire inlay and own leather work, wood lined sheaths for big camp knives. Prices: $400 and up. Remarks: Part-time maker. Master Smith in ABS; first knife sold in 1979. Mark: Fuller's Forge, MS.

FULTON, MICKEY,
406 S Shasta St, Willows, CA 95988, Phone: 530-934-5780
Specialties: Working straight knives and folders of his design. Patterns: Hunters, Bowies, lockback folders and steak knife sets. Technical: Hand-filed, sanded, buffed ATS-34, 440C and A2. Prices: $65 to $600; some to $1200. Remarks: Full-time maker; first knife sold in 1979. Mark: Signature.

G

GADBERRY, EMMET,
82 Purple Plum Dr, Hattieville, AR 72063, Phone: 501-354-4842

GADDY, GARY LEE,
205 Ridgewood Lane, Washington, NC 27889, Phone: 252-946-4359
Specialties: Working/using straight knives of his design; period pieces. Patterns: Bowies, hunters, utility/camp knives, oyster knives. Technical: Grinds ATS-34, O1; forges 1095. Prices: $175+ Remarks: Spare-time maker; first knife sold in 1991. No longer accepts orders. Mark: Quarter moon stamp.

GAETA, ANGELO,
R. Saldanha Marinho 1295, Centro Jau, SP, BRAZIL 17201-310, Phone: 0146-224543, Fax: 0146-224543
Specialties: Straight using knives to customer specs. Patterns: Hunters, fighting, daggers, belt push dagger. Technical: Grinds D6, ATS-34 and 440C stainless. Titanium nitride golden finish upon request. Prices: $60 to $300. Remarks: Full-time maker; first knife sold in 1992. Mark: First initial, last name.

GAETA, ROBERTO,
Rua Mandissununga 41, Sao Paulo, BRAZIL 05619-010, Phone: 11-37684626, karlaseno@uol.com.br
Specialties: Wide range of using knives. Patterns: Brazilian and North American hunting and fighting knives. Technical: Grinds stainless steel; likes natural handle materials. Prices: $500 to $800. Remarks: Full-time maker; first knife sold in 1979. Mark: BOB'G.

GAINES, BUDDY,
GAINES KNIVES, 155 Red Hill Rd., Commerce, GA 30530, Web: www.gainesknives.com
Specialties: Collectible and working folders and straight knives. Patterns: Folders, hunters, Bowies, tactical knives. Technical: Forges own Damascus, grinds ATS-34, D2, commercial Damascus. Prefers mother-of-pearl and stag. Prices: Start at $200. Remarks: Part-time maker, sold first knife in 1985. Mark: Last name.

GAINEY, HAL,
904 Bucklevel Rd, Greenwood, SC 29649, Phone: 864-223-0225, Web: www.scak.org
Specialties: Traditional working and using straight knives and folders. Patterns: Hunters, slip-joint folders and utility/camp knives. Technical: Hollow-grinds ATS-34 and D2; makes sheaths. Prices: $95 to $145; some to $500. Remarks: Full-time maker; first knife sold in 1975. Mark: Eagle head and last name.

GALLAGHER, BARRY,
135 Park St, Lewistown, MT 59457, Phone: 406-538-7056, Web: www.gallagherknives.com
Specialties: One-of-a-kind Damascus folders. Patterns: Folders, utility to high art, some straight knives, hunter, Bowies, and art pieces. Technical: Forges own mosaic Damascus and carbon steel, some stainless. Prices: $400 to $5000+. Remarks: Full-time maker; first knife sold in 1993. Doing business as Gallagher Custom Knives. Mark: Last name.

GAMBLE, FRANK,
4676 Commercial St SE #26, Salem, OR 97302, Phone: 503-581-7993, gamble6831@comcast.net
Specialties: Fantasy and high-art straight knives and folders of his design.

Patterns: Daggers, fighters, hunters and special locking folders. Technical: Grinds 440C and ATS-34; forges Damascus. Inlays; offers jewelling. Prices: $150 to $10,000. Remarks: Full-time maker; first knife sold in 1976. Mark: First initial, last name.

GAMBLE, ROGER,
18515 N.W. 28th Pl., Newberry, FL 32669, ROGERLGAMBLE@COX.NET
Specialties: Traditional working/using straight knives and folders of his design. Patterns: Liner locks and hunters. Technical: Grinds ATS-34 and Damascus. Prices: $150 to $2000. Remarks: Part-time maker; first knife sold in 1982. Doing business as Gamble Knives. Mark: First name in a fan of cards over last name.

GANN, TOMMY,
2876 State Hwy. 198, Canton, TX 75103, Phone: 903-848-9375
Specialties: Art and working straight knives of my design or customer preferences/design. Patterns: Bowie, fighters, hunters, daggers. Technical: Forges Damascus 52100 and grinds ATS-34 and D2. Prices: $200 to $2500. Remarks: Full-time knifemaker, first knife sold in 2002. ABS journey bladesmith. Mark: TGANN.

GANSHORN, CAL,
123 Rogers Rd., Regina, SK, CANADA S4S 6T7, Phone: 306-584-0524
Specialties: Working and fancy fixed blade knives. Patterns: Bowies, hunters, daggers, and filleting. Technical: Makes own forged Damascus billets, ATS, salt heat treating, and custom forges and burners. Prices: $250 to $1500. Remarks: Part-time maker. Mark: Last name etched in ricasso area.

GARAU, MARCELLO,
Via Alagon 42, Oristano, ITALY 09170, Phone: 00393479073454, marcellogarau@libero.it Web: www.knifecreator.com
Specialties: Mostly lock back folders with interframe. Technical: Forges own damascus for both blades and frames. Prices: 200 - 1800 Euro. Remarks: Full-time maker; first knife made in 1995. Attends Milano Knife Show and ECCKSHOW yearly. Mark: M.Garau inside handle.

GARCIA, MARIO EIRAS,
R. Edmundo Scanapieco 300, Caxingui, SP, BRAZIL 05516-070, Fax: 011-37214528
Specialties: Fantasy knives of his design; one-of-a-kind only. Patterns: Fighters, daggers, boots and two-bladed knives. Technical: Forges car leaf springs. Uses only natural handle material. Prices: $100 to $200. Remarks: Part-time maker; first knife sold in 1976. Mark: Two "B"s, one opposite the other.

GARDNER, ROBERT,
13462 78th Pl. N, West Palm Beach, FL 33412
Specialties: Straight blades, forged and clay hardened or differentialy heat treated. Kydex and leather sheath maker. Patterns: Working/using knives, some to customer specs, and high-end knives, daggers, bowies, ethnic knives, and Steelhead and Lil' Chub woodland survival/bushcraft knife set with an elaborate, versatile sheath system. Affordable hard-use production line of everyday carry belt knives, and less-expensive forged knives, neck knives and "wrench" knives. Technical: Grinds, forges and heat treats high-carbon 1084, 1095, 1075, W1, W2, 5160 and 52100 steels, some natural handle materials and Micarta for full-tang knives. Prices: $60 and up; sheaths $30 and up. Remarks: Full-time maker since 2010; first knife sold in 1986. Mark: Initials in angular script, stamped, engraved or etched.

GARNER, GEORGE,
7527 Calhoun Dr. NE, Albuquerque, NM 87109, Phone: 505-797-9317, razorbackblades@msn.com Web: www.razorbackblades.com
Specialties: High art locking liner folders and Daggers of his own design. Working and high art straight knives. Patterns: Bowies, daggers, fighters and locking liner folders. Technical: Grinds 440C, CPM-154, ATS34 and others. Damascus, Mosaic Damascus and Mokume. Makes own custom leather sheaths. Prices: $150 - $2,500. Remarks: Part-time maker since 1993. Full-time maker as of 2011. Company name is Razorback Blades. Mark: GEORGE GARNER.

GARNER, LARRY W,
13069 FM 14, Tyler, TX 75706, Phone: 903-597-6045, lwgarner@classicnet.net
Specialties: Fixed blade hunters and Bowies. Patterns: His designs or yours. Technical: Hand forges 5160. Prices: $200 to $500. Remarks: Apprentice bladesmith. Mark: Last name.

GARVOCK, MARK W,
RR 1, Balderson, ON, CANADA K1G 1A0, Phone: 613-833-2545, Fax: 613-833-2208, garvock@travel-net.com
Specialties: Hunters, Bowies, Japanese, daggers and swords. Patterns: Cable Damascus, random pattern welded or to suit. Technical: Forged blades; hi-carbon. Prices: $250 to $900. Remarks: CKG member and ABS member. Shipping and taxes extra. Mark: Big G with M in middle.

GATLIN, STEVE,
103 Marian Ct., Leesburg, GA 31763, Phone: 229-328-5074 or cell 229-435-2651, stevegatlinknives@hotmail.com; Web: www.stevegatlinknives.com
Specialties: Loveless-style knives, double-ground fighters and traditional hunters. Some tactical models of maker's design. Fixed blades only. Technical: Grinds CPM-154, ATS-34 and 154CM. Prices: $450 to $1,500 on base models. Remarks: Full-time maker six months a year, voting member of Knifemakers' Guild since 2009; first knife sold in 2008. Mark: Typical football shape with name on top and city below.

GAUDETTE, LINDEN L,
5 Hitchcock Rd, Wilbraham, MA 01095, Phone: 413-596-4896
Specialties: Traditional working knives in standard patterns. Patterns: Broad-bladed hunters, Bowies and camp knives; wood carver knives; locking folders. Technical: Grinds ATS-34, 440C and 154CM. Prices: $150 to $400; some higher. Remarks: Full-time maker; first knife sold in 1975. Mark: Last name in Gothic logo; used to be initials in circle.

GEDRAITIS, CHARLES J,
GEDRAITIS HAND CRAFTED KNIVES, 444 Shrewsbury St, Holden, MA 01520, Phone: 508-963-1861, gedraitisknives@yahoo.com; Web: www.gedraitisknives.com
Specialties: One-of-a-kind folders & automatics of his own design. Patterns: One-of-a-kind. Technical: Forges to shape mostly stock removal. Prices: $300 to $2500. Remarks: Full-time maker. Mark: 3 scallop shells with an initial inside each one: CJG.

GEORGE, HARRY,
3137 Old Camp Long Rd, Aiken, SC 29805, Phone: 803-649-1963, hdkk-george@scescape.net
Specialties: Working straight knives of his design or to customer specs. Patterns: Hunters, skinners and utility knives. Technical: Grinds ATS-34. Prefers natural handle materials, hollow-grinds and mirror finishes. Prices: Start at $70. Remarks: Part-time maker; first knife sold in 1985. Trained under George Herron. Member SCAK. Member Knifemakers Guild. Mark: Name, city, state.

GEORGE, LES,
6521 Fenwick Dr., Corpus Christi, TX 78414, Phone: 361-288-9777, les@georgeknives.com; Web: www.georgeknives.com
Specialties: Tactical frame locks and fixed blades. Patterns: Folders, balisongs, and fixed blades. Technical: CPM154, S30V, Chad Nichols Damascus. Prices: $200 to $800. Remarks: Full-time maker, first knife sold in 1992. Doing business as www.georgeknives.com. Mark: Last name over logo.

GEORGE, TOM,
550 Aldbury Dr, Henderson, NV 89014, tagmaker@aol.com
Specialties: Working straight knives, display knives, custom meat cleavers, and folders of his design. Patterns: Hunters, Bowies, daggers, buckskinners, swords and folders. Technical: Uses D2, 440C, ATS-34 and 154CM. Prices: $500 to $13,500. Remarks: Custom orders not accepted "at this time". Full-time maker. First knife 1982; first 350 knives were numbered; after that no numbers. Almost all his knives today are Bowies and swords. Creator and maker of the "Past Glories" series of knives. Mark: Tom George maker.

GEPNER, DON,
2615 E Tecumseh, Norman, OK 73071, Phone: 405-364-2750
Specialties: Traditional working and using straight knives of his design. Patterns: Bowies and daggers. Technical: Forges his Damascus, 1095 and 5160. Prices: $100 to $400; some to $1000. Remarks: Spare-time maker; first knife sold in 1991. Has been forging since 1954; first edged weapon made at 9 years old. Mark: Last initial.

GERNER, THOMAS,
PO Box 301, Walpole, WA, AUSTRALIA 6398, gerner@bordernet.com.au; Web: www.deepriverforge.com
Specialties: Forged working knives; plain steel and pattern welded. Patterns: Tries most patterns heard or read about. Technical: 5160, L6, O1, 52100 steels; Australian hardwood handles. Prices: $220 and up. Remarks: Achieved ABS Master Smith rating in 2001. Mark: Like a standing arrow and a leaning cross, T.G. in the Runic (Viking) alphabet.

GHIO, PAOLO,
4330 Costa Mesa, Pensacola, FL 32504-7849, Phone: 850-393-0135, paologhio@hotmail.com
Specialties: Folders, fillet knives and skinners. Patterns: Maker's own design, or will work from a customer's pattern. Technical: Stock removal, all work in house, including heat treat. Prices: $200 to $500. Mark: PKG.

GIAGU, SALVATORE AND DEROMA MARIA ROSARIA,
Via V Emanuele 64, Pattada (SS), ITALY 07016, Phone: 079-755918, Fax: 079-755918, coltelligiagupattada@tiscali.it Web: www.culterpattada.it
Specialties: Using and collecting traditional and new folders from Sardegna. Patterns: Folding, hunting, utility, skinners and kitchen knives. Technical: Forges ATS-34, 440, D2 and Damascus. Prices: $200 to $2000; some higher. Mark: First initial, last name and name of town and muflon's head.

GIBERT, PEDRO,
Los Alamos 410, San Martin de los Andes, Neuquen, ARGENTINA 8370, Phone: 054-2972-410868, rosademayo@infovia.com.ar
Specialties: Hand forges: Stock removal and integral. High quality artistic knives of his design and to customer specifications. Patterns: Country (Argentine gaucho-style), knives, folders, Bowies, daggers, hunters. Others upon request. Technical: Blade: Bohler k110 Austrian steel (high resistance to waste). Handles: (Natural materials) ivory elephant, killer whale, hippo, walrus tooth, deer antler, goat, ram, buffalo horn, bone, rhea, sheep, cow, exotic woods (South America native woods) hand carved and engraved guards and blades. Stainless steel guards, finely polished: semi-matte or shiny finish. Sheaths: Raw or tanned leather, hand-stitched; rawhide or cotton yarn embroidered. Box: One wood piece, hand carved. Wooden hinges and locks. Prices: $600 and up. Remarks: Full-time maker. Made first knife in 1987. Mark: Only a rose logo. Buyers initials upon request.

GIBO, GEORGE,
PO Box 4304, Hilo, HI 96720, Phone: 808-987-7002, geogibo@hilo808.net
Specialties: Straight knives and folders. Patterns: Hunters, bird and trout, utility, gentlemen and tactical folders. Technical: Grinds ATS-34, BG-42, Talonite, Stainless Steel Damascus. Prices: $250 to $1000. Remarks: Spare-time maker; first knife sold in 1995. Mark: Name, city and state around Hawaiian "Shaka" sign.

GILBERT, CHANTAL,
291 Rue Christophe-Colomb est #105, Quebec City, QC, CANADA G1K 3T1, Phone: 418-525-6961, Fax: 418-525-4666, gilbertc@medion.qc.ca; Web:www.chantalgilbert.com
Specialties: Straight art knives that may resemble creatures, often with wings, shells and antennae, always with a beak of some sort, fixed blades in a feminine style. Technical: ATS-34 and Damascus. Handle materials usually silver that she forms to shape via special molds and a press; ebony and fossil ivory. Prices: Range from $500 to $4000. Remarks: Often embellishes her art knives with rubies, meteorite, 18k gold and similar elements.

GILBREATH, RANDALL,
55 Crauswell Rd, Dora, AL 35062, Phone: 205-648-3902
Specialties: Damascus folders and fighters. Patterns: Folders and fixed blades. Technical: Forges Damascus and high-carbon; stock removal stainless steel. Prices: $300 to $1500. Remarks: Full-time maker; first knife sold in 1979. Mark: Name in ribbon.

GILJEVIC, BRANKO,
35 Hayley Crescent, Queanbeyan 2620, New South Wales, AUSTRALIA 0262977613
Specialties: Classic working straight knives and folders of his design. Patterns: Hunters, Bowies, skinners and locking folders. Technical: Grinds 440C. Offers acid etching, scrimshaw and leather carving. Prices: $150 to $1500. Remarks: Part-time maker; first knife sold in 1987. Doing business as Sambar Custom Knives. Mark: Company name in logo.

GINGRICH, JUSTIN,
3908 Barclay Way, Wade, NC 28395, Phone: 507-230-0398, justin@gingrichtactical.com Web: www.gingrichtactical.com
Specialties: Anything from bushcraft to tactical, heavy on the tactical. Patterns: Fixed blades and folders. Technical: Uses all types of steel and handle material, method is stock-removal. Prices: $30 - $1000. Remarks: Full-time maker. Mark: Tang stamp is the old Ranger Knives logo.

GIRTNER, JOE,
409 Catalpa Ave, Brea, CA 92821, Phone: 714-529-2388, conceptsinknives@aol.com
Specialties: Art knives and miniatures. Patterns: Mainly Damascus (some carved). Technical: Many techniques and materials combined. Wood carving knives and tools, hunters, custom orders. Prices: $55 to $3000. Mark: Name.

GITTINGER, RAYMOND,
6940 S Rt 100, Tiffin, OH 44883, Phone: 419-397-2517

GLOVER, RON,
100 West Church St., Mason, OH 45040, Phone: 513-404-7107, r.glover@zoomtown.com
Specialties: High-tech working straight knives and folders. Patterns: Hunters to Bowies; some interchangeable blade models; unique locking mechanisms. Technical: Grinds 440C, 154CM; buys Damascus. Prices: $70 to $500; some to $800. Remarks: Part-time maker; first knife sold in 1981. Mark: Name in script.

GLOVER, WARREN D,
dba BUBBA KNIVES, PO Box 475, Cleveland, GA 30528, Phone: 706-865-3998, Fax: 706-348-7176, warren@bubbaknives.net; Web: www.bubbaknives.net
Specialties: Traditional and custom working and using straight knives of his design and to customer request. Patterns: Hunters, skinners, bird and fish, utility and kitchen knives. Technical: Grinds 440, ATS-34 and stainless steel Damascus. Prices: $75 to $400 and up. Remarks: Full-time maker; sold first knife in 1995. Mark: Bubba, year, name, state.

GODDARD, WAYNE,
473 Durham Ave, Eugene, OR 97404, Phone: 541-689-8098, wgoddard44@comcast.net
Specialties: Working/using straight knives and folders. Patterns: Hunters and folders. Technical: Works exclusively with wire Damascus and his own-pattern welded material. Prices: $250 to $4000. Remarks: Full-time maker; first knife sold in 1963. Mark: Blocked initials on forged blades; regular capital initials on stock removal.

GODLESKY, BRUCE F.,
1002 School Rd., Apollo, PA 15613, Phone: 724-840-5786, brucegodlesky@yahoo.com; Web: www.birdforge.com
Specialties: Working/using straight knives and tomahawks, mostly forged. Patterns: Hunters, birds and trout, fighters and tomahawks. Technical: Most forged, some stock removal. Carbon steel only. 5160, O-1, W2, 10xx series. Makes own Damascus and welded cable. Prices: Starting at $75. Mark: BIRDOG FORGE.

GOERS, BRUCE,
3423 Royal Ct S, Lakeland, FL 33813, Phone: 941-646-0984
Specialties: Fancy working and using straight knives of his design and to customer specs. Patterns: Hunters, fighters, Bowies and fantasy knives. Technical: Grinds ATS-34, some Damascus. Prices: $195 to $600; some to $1300. Remarks: Part-time maker; first knife sold in 1990. Doing business as Vulture Cutlery. Mark: Buzzard with initials.

GOLDBERG, DAVID,
321 Morris Rd, Ft Washington, PA 19034, Phone: 215-654-7117, david@goldmountainforge.com; Web: www.goldmountainforge.com
Specialties: Japanese-style designs, will work with special themes in Japanese genre. Patterns: Kozuka, Tanto, Wakazashi, Katana, Tachi, Sword canes, Yari and Naginata. Technical: Forges his own Damascus and makes his own handmade tamehagane steel from straw ash, iron, carbon and clay. Uses traditional materials, carves fittings handles and cases. Hardens all blades in traditional Japanese clay differential technique. Remarks: Full-time maker; first knife sold in 1987. Japanese swordsmanship teacher (jaido) and Japanese self-defense teach (aikido). Mark: Name (kinzan) in Japanese Kanji on Tang under handle.

GOLDEN, RANDY,
6492 Eastwood Glen Dr, Montgomery, AL 36117, Phone: 334-271-6429, rgolden1@mindspring.com
Specialties: Collectable quality hand rubbed finish, hunter, camp, Bowie straight knives, custom leather sheaths with exotic skin inlays and tooling. Technical: Stock removal ATS-34, CPM154, S30V and BG-42. Natural handle materials primarily stag and ivory. Prices: $500 to $1500. Remarks: Full-time maker, member Knifemakers Guild, first knife sold in 2000. Mark: R. R. Golden Montgomery, AL.

GONZALEZ, LEONARDO WILLIAMS,
Ituzaingo 473, Maldonado, URUGUAY 20000, Phone: 598 4222 1617, Fax: 598 4222 1617, willyknives@hotmail.com
Specialties: Classic high-art and fantasy straight knives; traditional working and using knives of his design, in standard patterns or to customer specs. Patterns: Hunters, Bowies, daggers, fighters, boots, swords and utility/camp knives. Technical: Forges and grinds high-carbon and stainless Bohler steels. Prices: $100 to $2500. Remarks: Full-time maker; first knife sold in 1985. Mark: Willy, whale, R.O.U.

GOO, TAI,
5920 W Windy Lou Ln, Tucson, AZ 85742, Phone: 520-744-9777, taigoo@msn.com; Web: www.taigoo.com
Specialties: High art, neo-tribal, bush and fantasy. Technical: Hand forges, does own heat treating, makes own Damascus. Prices: $150 to $500 some to $10,000. Remarks: Full-time maker; first knife sold in 1978. Mark: Chiseled signature.

GOOD, D.R.,
D.R. Good Custom Knives and Weaponry, 6125 W. 100 S., Tipton, IN 46072, Phone: 765-963-6971, drntammigood@bluemarble.net
Specialties: Working knives, own design, Scagel style, "critter" knives, carved handles. Patterns: Bowies, large and small, neck knives and miniatures. Offers carved handles, snake heads, eagles, wolves, bear, skulls. Technical: Damascus, some stelite, 6K, pearl, ivory, moose. Prices: $150 - $1500. Remarks: Full-time maker. First knife was Bowie made from a 2-1/2 truck bumper in military. Mark: D.R. Good in oval and for minis, DR with a buffalo skull.

GOODE, BEAR,
PO Box 6474, Navajo Dam, NM 87419, Phone: 505-632-8184
Specialties: Working/using straight knives of his design and in standard patterns. Patterns: Bowies, hunters and utility/camp knives. Technical: Grinds 440C, ATS-34, 154-CM; forges and grinds 1095, 5160 and other steels on request; uses Damascus. Prices: $60 to $225; some to $500 and up. Remarks: Part-time maker; first knife sold in 1993. Doing business as Bear Knives. Mark: First and last name with a three-toed paw print.

GOODE, BRIAN,
203 Gordon Ave, Shelby, NC 28152, Phone: 704-434-6496, web:www.bgoodeknives.com
Specialties: Flat ground working knives with etched/antique or brushed finish. Patterns: Field, camp, hunters, skinners, survival, kitchen, maker's design or yours. Currently full tang only with supplied leather sheath. Technical: 0-1, D2 and other ground flat stock. Stock removal and differential heat treat preferred. Etched antique/etched satin working finish preferred. Micarta and hardwoods for strength. Prices: $150 to $700. Remarks: Part-time maker and full-time knife lover. First knife sold in 2004. Mark: B. Goode with NC separated by a feather.

GOODPASTURE, TOM,
13432 Farrington Road, Ashland, VA 23005, Phone: 804-752-8363, rtg007@aol.com; web: goodpastureknives.com
Specialties: Working/using straight knives of his own design, or customer specs. File knives and primative reproductions. Patterns: Hunters, bowies, small double-edge daggers, kitchen, custom miniatures and camp/utility. Technical: Stock removal, D-2, 0-1, 12C27, 420 HC, 52100. Forged blades of W-2, 1084, and 1095. Flat grinds only. Prices: $60 - $300. Remarks: Part-time maker, first knife sold at Blade Show 2005. Lifetime guarantee and sharpening. Mark: Early mark were initials RTG, current mark: Goodpasture.

GORDON, LARRY B,
23555 Newell Cir W, Farmington Hills, MI 48336, Phone: 248-477-5483, lbgordon1@aol.com
Specialties: Folders, small fixed blades. New design rotating scale release automatic. Patterns: Rotating handle locker. Ambidextrous fire (R&L) Prices: $450 minimum. Remarks: High line materials preferred. Mark: Gordon.

GORENFLO, JAMES T (JT),
9145 Sullivan Rd, Baton Rouge, LA 70818, Phone: 225-261-5868
Specialties: Traditional working and using straight knives of his design. Patterns: Bowies, hunters and utility/camp knives. Technical: Forges 5160, 1095, 52100 and his own Damascus. Prices: Start at $200. Remarks: Part-time maker; first knife sold in 1992. Mark: Last name or initials, J.S. on reverse.

GOSSMAN, SCOTT,
PO Box 41, Whiteford, MD 21160, Phone: 443-617-2444, scogos@peoplepc.com; Web:www.gossmanknives.com
Specialties: Heavy duty knives for big game hunting and survival. Patterns: Modified clip point/spear point blades, bowies, hunters, and bushcraft. Technical: Grinds D-2, A2, O1, CPM154, CPM535VN and 57 convex grinds and edges. Price: $65 to $500. Remarks: Full time maker does business as Gossman Knives. Mark: Gossman and steel type.

GOTTAGE, DANTE,
43227 Brooks Dr, Clinton Twp., MI 48038-5323, Phone: 810-286-7275
Specialties: Working knives of his design or to customer specs. Patterns: Large and small skinners, fighters, Bowies and fillet knives. Technical: Grinds O1, 440C and 154CM and ATS-34. Prices: $150 to $600. Remarks: Part-time maker; first knife sold in 1975. Mark: Full name in script letters.

GOTTAGE, JUDY,
43227 Brooks Dr, Clinton Twp., MI 48038-5323, Phone: 586-286-7275, jgottage@remaxmetropolitan.com
Specialties: Custom folders of her design or to customer specs. Patterns: Interframes or integral. Technical: Stock removal. Prices: $300 to $3000. Remarks: Full-time maker; first knife sold in 1980. Mark: Full name, maker in script.

GOTTSCHALK, GREGORY J,
12 First St. (Ft. Pitt), Carnegie, PA 15106, Phone: 412-279-6692
Specialties: Fancy working straight knives and folders to customer specs. Patterns: Hunters to tantos, locking folders to minis. Technical: Grinds 440C, 154CM, ATS-34. Now making own Damascus. Most knives have mirror finishes. Prices: Start at $150. Remarks: Part-time maker; first knife sold in 1977. Mark: Full name in crescent.

GOUKER, GARY B,
PO Box 955, Sitka, AK 99835, Phone: 907-747-3476
Specialties: Hunting knives for hard use. Patterns: Skinners, semi-skinners, and such. Technical: Likes natural materials, inlays, stainless steel. Prices: Moderate. Remarks: New Alaskan maker. Mark: Name.

GRAHAM, GORDON,
3145 CR 4008, New Boston, TX 75570, Phone: 903-293-2610, Web: www.grahamknives.com
Prices: $325 to $850. Mark: Graham.

GRANGER, PAUL J,
704 13th Ct. SW, Largo, FL 33770-4471, Phone: 727-953-3249, grangerknives@live.com Web: http://palehorsefighters.blogspot.com
Specialties: Working straight knives of his own design and a few folders. Patterns: 2.75" to 4" work knives, tactical knives and Bowies from 5"-9." Grinds CPM154-CM, ATS-34 and forges 52100 and 1084. Offers filework. Prices: $95 to $500. Remarks: Part-time maker since 1997. Sold first knife in 1997. Doing business as Granger Knives and Pale Horse Fighters. Member of ABS and Florida Knifemakers Association. Mark: "Granger" or "Palehorse Fighters."

GRAVELINE, PASCAL AND ISABELLE,
38 Rue de Kerbrezillic, Moelan-sur-Mer, FRANCE 29350, Phone: 33 2 98 39 73 33, atelier.graveline@wanadoo.fr; Web: www.graveline-coeuteliers.com
Specialties: French replicas from the 17th, 18th and 19th centuries. Patterns: Traditional folders and multi-blade pocket knives; traveling knives, fruit knives and fork sets; puzzle knives and friend's knives; rivet less knives. Technical: Grind 12C27, ATS-34, Damascus and carbon steel. Prices: $500 to $5000. Remarks: Full-time makers; first knife sold in 1992. Mark: Last name over head of ram.

GRAVES, DAN,
4887 Dixie Garden Loop, Shreveport, LA 71105, Phone: 318-865-8166, Web: wwwtheknifemaker.com
Specialties: Traditional forged blades and Damascus. Patterns: Bowies (D guard also), fighters, hunters, large and small daggers. Remarks: Full-time maker. Mark: Initials with circle around them.

GRAY, BOB,
8206 N Lucia Court, Spokane, WA 99208, Phone: 509-468-3924
Specialties: Straight working knives of his own design or to customer specs. Patterns: Hunter, fillet and carving knives. Technical: Forges 5160, L6 and some 52100; grinds 440C. Prices: $100 to $600. Remarks: Part-time knifemaker; first knife sold in 1991. Doing business as Hi-Land Knives. Mark: HI-L.

GRAY, DANIEL,
GRAY KNIVES, 686 Main Rd., Brownville, ME 04414, Phone: 207-965-2191, mail@grayknives.com; Web: www.grayknives.com
Specialties: Straight knives, fantasy, folders, automatics and traditional of his own design. Patterns: Automatics, fighters, hunters. Technical: Grinds O1, 154CM and D2. Prices: From $155 to $750. Remarks: Full-time maker; first knife sold in 1974. Mark: Gray Knives.

GREBE, GORDON S,
PO Box 296, Anchor Point, AK 99556-0296, Phone: 907-235-8242
Specialties: Working straight knives and folders, some fancy. Patterns: Tantos, Bowies, boot fighter sets, locking folders. Technical: Grinds stainless steels; likes 1/4" inch stock and glass-bead finishes. Prices: $75 to $250; some to $2000. Remarks: Full-time maker; first knife sold in 1968. Mark: Initials in lightning logo.

GRECO, JOHN,
100 Mattie Jones Rd, Greensburg, KY 42743, Phone: 270-932-3335, johngreco@grecoknives.com; Web: www.grecoknives.com
Specialties: Folders. Patterns: Tactical, fighters, camp knives, short swords. Technical: Stock removal carbon steel. Prices: Affordable. Remarks: Full-time maker since 1979. First knife sold in 1979. Mark: GRECO

GREEN, BILL,
6621 Eastview Dr, Sachse, TX 75048, Phone: 972-463-3147
Specialties: High-art and working straight knives and folders of his design and to customer specs. Patterns: Bowies, hunters, kitchen knives and locking folders. Technical: Grinds ATS-34, D2 and 440V. Hand-tooled custom sheaths. Prices: $70 to $350; some to $750. Remarks: Part-time maker; first knife sold in 1990. Mark: Last name.

GREEN, WILLIAM (BILL),
46 Warren Rd, View Bank, VIC, AUSTRALIA 3084, Fax: 03-9459-1529
Specialties: Traditional high-tech straight knives and folders. Patterns: Japanese-influenced designs, hunters, Bowies, folders and miniatures. Technical: Forges O1, D2 and his own Damascus. Offers lost wax castings for bolsters and pommels. Likes natural handle materials, gems, silver and gold. Prices: $400 to $750; some to $1200. Remarks: Full-time maker. Mark: Initials.

GREENAWAY, DON,
3325 Dinsmore Tr, Fayetteville, AR 72704, Phone: 501-521-0323
Specialties: Liner locks and bowies. Prices: $150 to $1500. Remarks: 20 years experience.Mark:Greenaway over Fayetteville, Ark.

GREENE, CHRIS,
707 Cherry Lane, Shelby, NC 28150, Phone: 704-434-5620

GREENE, DAVID,
570 Malcom Rd, Covington, GA 30209, Phone: 770-784-0657
Specialties: Straight working using knives. Patterns: Hunters. Technical: Forges mosaic and twist Damascus. Prefers stag and desert ironwood for handle material.

GREENE, STEVE,
DUNN KNIVES INC, PO Box 307 1449 Nocatee St., Intercession City, FL 33848, Phone: 800-245-6483, s.greene@earthlink.net; Web: www.dunnknives.com
Specialties: Skinning & fillet knives. Patterns: Skinners, drop points, clip points and fillets. Technical: CPM-S30V powdered metal steel manufactured by Niagara Specialty Metals. Prices: $100 to $350. Mark: Dunn by Greene and year. Remarks: Full-time knifemaker. First knife sold in 1972. Each knife is handcrafted and includes holster-grade leather sheath.

GREENFIELD, G O,
2605 15th St #310, Everett, WA 98201, Phone: 425-244-2902, garyg1946@yahoo.com
Specialties: High-tech and working straight knives and folders of his design. Patterns: Boots, daggers, hunters and one-of-a-kinds. Technical: Grinds ATS-34, D2, 440C and T-440V. Makes sheaths for each knife. Prices: $100 to $800; some to $10,000. Remarks: Part-time maker; first knife sold in 1978. Mark: Springfield®, serial number.

GREGORY, MATTHEW M.,
74 Tarn Tr., Glenwood, NY 14069, Phone: 716-863-1215, mgregoryknives@yahoo.com; Web: www.mgregoryknives.com
Patterns: Wide variation of styles, as I make what I like to make. Bowies, fighters, Neo-American/Japanese-inspired blades, occasionally kitchen knives. Technical: Forging and stock removal, using forging steels such as 1084, 1095, W2 and CruForgeV, as well as high-alloy steels like CPM-3V and CPM-S110V. Hamon (blade temper line) development and polishing. Prices: $350 and up. Remarks: Part-time maker since 2005. Mark: M. Gregory.

GREGORY, MICHAEL,
211 Calhoun Rd, Belton, SC 29627, Phone: 864-338-8898, gregom.123@charter.net
Specialties: Interframe folding knives, working hunters and period pieces. Hand rubbed finish. Patterns: Hunters, bowies, daggers, and folding knives. Technical: Grinds ATS-34 and other makers damascus. Prices: $150 and up. Remarks: Full-time maker; first knife sold in 1980. Mark: Name, city in logo.

GREINER, RICHARD,
1073 E County Rd 32, Green Springs, OH 44836, Phone: 419-483-4613, rgreiner7295@yahoo.com
Specialties: High-carbon steels, edge hardened. Patterns: Most. Technical: Hand forged. Prices: $125 and up. Remarks: Have made knives for 30 years. Mark: Maple leaf.

GREISS, JOCKL,
Herrenwald 15, Schenkenzell, GERMANY 77773, Phone: +49 7836 95 71 69 or +49 7836 95 55 76, www.jocklgreiss@yahoo.com
Specialties: Classic and working straight knives of his design. Patterns: Bowies, daggers and hunters. Technical: Uses only Jerry Rados Damascus. All knives are one-of-a-kind made by hand; no machines are used. Prices: $700 to $2000; some to $3000. Remarks: Full-time maker; first knife sold in 1984. Mark: An "X" with a long vertical line through it.

GREY, PIET,
PO Box 363, Naboomspruit, LP, SOUTH AFRICA 0560, Phone: 014-743-3613
Specialties: Fancy working and using straight knives of his design. Patterns: Fighters, hunters and utility/camp knives. Technical: Grinds ATS-34 and AEB-L; forges and grinds Damascus. Solder less fitting of guards. Engraves and scrimshaws. Prices: $125 to $750; some to $1500. Remarks: Part-time

maker; first knife sold in 1970. Mark: Last name.

GRIFFIN, RENDON AND MARK,
9706 Cedardale, Houston, TX 77055, Phone: 713-468-0436
Specialties: Working folders and automatics of their designs. Patterns: Standard lockers and slip-joints. Technical: Most blade steels; stock removal. Prices: Start at $350. Remarks: Rendon's first knife sold in 1966; Mark's in 1974. Mark: Last name logo.

GRIFFIN JR., HOWARD A,
14299 SW 31st Ct, Davie, FL 33330, Phone: 954-474-5406, mgriffin18@aol.com
Specialties: Working straight knives and folders. Patterns: Hunters, Bowies, locking folders with his own push-button lock design. Technical: Grinds 440C. Prices: $100 to $200; some to $500. Remarks: Part-time maker; first knife sold in 1983. Mark: Initials.

GRIMES, MARK,
PO BOX 1293, Bedford, TX 76095, Phone: 817-416-7507
Specialties: Qs. Patterns: Hunters, fighters, bowies. Technical: Custom hand forged 1084 steel blades full and hidden tang, heat treating, sheathes. Prices: $150-$400. Remarks: Part-time maker, first knife sold in 2009. Mark: Last name.

GRIZZARD, JIM,
3626 Gunnels Ln., Oxford, AL 36203, Phone: 256-403-1232, grizzardforgiven@aol.com
Specialties: Hand carved art knives inspired by sole authorship. Patterns: Fixedblades, folders, and swords. Technical: Carving handles, artgrinding, forged and stock removal. Prices: Vary. Remarks: Uses knives mostly as a ministry to bless others. Mark: FOR HIS GLORY CUSTOM KNIVES OR j grizzard in a grizzly bear.

GROSPITCH, ERNIE,
18440 Amityville Dr, Orlando, FL 32820, Phone: 407-568-5438, shrpknife@aol.com; Web: www.erniesknives.com
Specialties: Bowies, hunting, fishing, kitchen, lockback folders, leather craft. Patterns: His design or customer. Technical: Stock removal using most available steels. Prices: $140 and up. Remarks: Full-time maker, sold first knife in 1990. Mark: Etched name/maker city and state.

GROSS, W W,
109 Dylan Scott Dr, Archdale, NC 27263-3858
Specialties: Working knives. Patterns: Hunters, boots, fighters. Technical: Grinds. Prices: Moderate. Remarks: Full-time maker. Mark: Name.

GROSSMAN, STEWART,
24 Water St #419, Clinton, MA 01510, Phone: 508-365-2291; 800-mysword
Specialties: Miniatures and full-size knives and swords. Patterns: One-of-a-kind miniatures—jewelry, replicas—and wire-wrapped figures. Full-size art, fantasy and combat knives, daggers and modular systems. Technical: Forges and grinds most metals and Damascus. Uses gems, crystals, electronics and motorized mechanisms. Prices: $20 to $300; some to $4500 and higher. Remarks: Full-time maker; first knife sold in 1985. Mark: G1.

GRUSSENMEYER, PAUL G,
310 Kresson Rd, Cherry Hill, NJ 08034, Phone: 856-428-1088, pgrussentne@comcast.net; Web: www.pgcarvings.com
Specialties: Assembling fancy and fantasy straight knives with his own carved handles. Patterns: Bowies, daggers, folders, swords, hunters and miniatures. Technical: Uses forged steel and Damascus, stock removal and knapped obsidian blades. Prices: $250 to $4000. Remarks: Spare-time maker; first knife sold in 1991. Mark: First and last initial hooked together on handle.

GUARNERA, ANTHONY R,
42034 Quail Creek Dr, Quartzhill, CA 93536, Phone: 661-722-4032
Patterns: Hunters, camp, Bowies, kitchen, fighter knives. Technical: Forged and stock removal. Prices: $100 and up.

GUINN, TERRY,
13026 Hwy 6 South, Eastland, TX 76448, Phone: 254-629-8603, Web: www.terryguinn.com
Specialties: Working fixed blades and balisongs. Patterns: Almost all types of folding and fixed blades, from patterns and "one of a kind". Technical: Stock removal all types of blade steel with preference for air hardening steel. Does own heat treating, all knives Rockwell tested in shop. Prices: $200 to $2,000. Remarks: Part time maker since 1982, sold first knife 1990. Mark: Full name with cross in the middle.

GUNTER, BRAD,
13 Imnaha Rd., Tijeras, NM 87059, Phone: 505-281-8080

GUNTHER, EDDIE,
11 Nedlands Pl Burswood, Auckland, NEW ZEALAND 2013, Phone: 006492722373, eddit.gunther49@gmail.com
Specialties: Drop point hunters, boot, Bowies. All mirror finished. Technical: Grinds D2, 440C, 12c27. Prices: $250 to $800. Remarks: Part-time maker, first knife sold in 1986. Mark: Name, city, country.

H

HAAS, RANDY,
HHH Knives, 6518 Chard St., Marlette, MI 48453, Phone: 989-635-7059, Web: www.hhhcustomknives.com
Specialties: Handmade custom kitchen and culinary knives, hunters, fighters, folders and art knives. Technical: Damascus maker and sales. Remarks: Full-time maker for 10 years. Mark: Three H's with a knife behind the HHH.

HACKNEY, DANA A.,
33 Washington St., Monument, CO 80132, Phone: 719-481-3940; Cell: 719-651-5634, shacknee@peoplepc.com and dshackney@Q.com; Web: www.hackneycustomknives.com
Specialties: Hunters, bowies, and everyday carry knives, and some kitchen cutlery. Technical: ABS journeyman smith who forges 1080 series, 5160, 0-1, W-2, and his own damascus. Uses CPM154 mostly for stainless knives. Prices: $100 and up. Remarks: Sole ownership knives and sheaths. Full-time maker as of July 2012. Sold first knife in 2005. ABS, MKA, and PKA member. Mark: Last name, HACKNEY on left-side ricasso.

HAGEN, DOC,
PO Box 58, 41780 Kansas Point Ln, Pelican Rapids, MN 56572, Phone: 218-863-8503, dochagen@gmail.com; Web: www.dochagencustomknives.com
Specialties: Folders. Autos:bolster release-dual action. Slipjoint foldersPatterns: Defense-related straight knives; wide variety of folders. Technical: Dual action release, bolster release autos. Prices: $300 to $800; some to $3000. Remarks: Full-time maker; first knife sold in 1975. Makes his own Damascus. Mark: DOC HAGEN in shield, knife, banner logo; or DOC.

HAGGERTY, GEORGE S,
PO Box 88, Jacksonville, VT 05342, Phone: 802-368-7437, swewater@sover.net
Specialties: Working straight knives and folders. Patterns: Hunters, claws, camp and fishing knives, locking folders and backpackers. Technical: Forges and grinds W2, 440C and 154CM. Prices: $85 to $300. Remarks: Part-time maker; first knife sold in 1981. Mark: Initials or last name.

HAGUE, GEOFF,
Unit 5, Project Workshops, Lains Farm, Quarley, Hampshire, UNITED KINGDOM SP11 8PX, Phone: (+44) 01672-870212, Fax: (+44) 01672 870212, geoff@hagueknives.com; Web: www.hagueknives.com
Specialties: Quality folding knives. Patterns: Back lock, locking liner, slip joint, and friction folders. Technical: RWL34, D2, titanium, and some gold decoraqtion. Mainly natural handle materials. Prices: $900 to $2,000. Remarks: Full-time maker. Mark: Last name.

HAINES, JEFF,
Haines Custom Knives, 901 A E. Third St., Wauzeka, WI 53826, Phone: 608-875-5325, jeffhaines@centurytel.net; Web: www.hainescustomknives.com
Patterns: Hunters, skinners, camp knives, customer designs welcome. Technical: Forges 1095, 5160, and Damascus, grinds A2. Prices: $75 and up. Remarks: Part-time maker since 1995. Mark: Last name.

HALE, LLOYD,
3492 Kerr Hill Rd., Lynnville, TN 38472, Phone: 931-424-5846, lloydahale@gmail.com
Specialties: Museum-grade, one-of-a-kind daggers, folders and sub-hilt fighting knives. Remarks: Full-time maker for 44+ years. Spent 20+ years creating a one-of-a-kind knife collection for Owsley Brown Frazier of Louisville, KY. I don't accept orders anymore.

HALFRICH, JERRY,
340 Briarwood, San Marcos, TX 78666, Phone: 512-353-2582, Fax: 512-392-3659, jerryhalfrich@grandecom.net; Web: www.halfrichknives.com
Specialties: Working knives and specialty utility knives for the professional and serious hunter. Uses proven designs in both straight and folding knives. Plays close attention to fit and finish. Art knives on special request. Patterns: Hunters, skinners, lock back liner lock. Technical: Grinds both flat and hollow D2, damasteel, BG42 makes high precision folders. Prices: $300 to $600, sometimes $1000. Remarks: Full-time maker since 2000. DBA Halfrich Custom Knives. Mark: Halfrich, San Marcos, TX in a football shape.

HALL, JEFF,
179 Niblick Rd, # 180, Paso Robles, CA 93446, Phone: 562-594-4740, info@nemesis-knives.com; Web: www.nemisis-knives.com
Specialties: Collectible and working folders and fixed blades of his design. Technical: Grinds CPM-S35VN, CPM-154, and various makers' damascus. Patterns: Fighters, gentleman's, hunters and utility knives. Prices: $100 and up. Remarks: Full-time maker. First knife sold 1998. Mark: Last name.

HALL, KEN,
606 Stevenson Cove Rd., Waynesville, NC 28785, Phone: 828-627-2135, khall@hallenergyconsulting.com; Web: http://www.hallenergyconsulting.com/KHKindex.html
Specialties: Standard and one-of-a-kind fixed-blade knives with leather sheaths. Patterns: Hunters, bowies, fighters, chef's knives and tantos. Technical: Forges high-carbon steel, flat grinds. Prices: $150 to $700+. Remarks: Part-time maker; first knives sold in 2010. Mark: Etched "Ken Hall" or "KHall JS."

HALLIGAN, ED,
3434 Sun Lit Grove, San Antonio, TX 78247, Phone: 210-912-8167, beano101010@yahoo.com
Specialties: Working straight knives and folders, some fancy. Patterns: Liner locks, hunters, skinners, boots, fighters and swords. Technical: Grinds ATS-34; forges 5160; makes cable and pattern Damascus. Prices: $160 to $2500. Remarks: Full-time maker; first knife sold in 1985. Doing business as Halligan Knives. Mark: Last name, city, state and USA.

HAMLET JR., JOHNNY,
300 Billington, Clute, TX 77531, Phone: 979-265-6929, nifeman@swbell.net; Web: www.hamlets-handmade-knives.com
Specialties: Working straight knives and folders. Patterns: Hunters, fighters, fillet and kitchen knives, locking folders. Likes upswept knives and trailing-points. Technical: Grinds 440C, D2, ATS-34. Makes sheaths. Prices: $125 and up. Remarks: Full-time maker; sold first knife in 1988. Mark: Hamlet's Handmade in script.

HAMMOND, HANK,
189 Springlake Dr, Leesburg, GA 31763, Phone: 229-434-1295, godogs57@bellsouth.net
Specialties: Traditional hunting and utility knives of his design. Will also design and produce knives to customer's specifications. Patterns: Straight or sheath knives, hunters skinners as well as Bowies and fighters. Technical: Grinds (hollow and flat grinds) CPM 154CM, ATS-34. Also uses Damascus and forges 52100. Offers filework on blades. Handle materials include all exotic woods, red stag, sambar stag, deer, elk, oosic, bone, fossil ivory, Micarta, etc. All knives come with sheath handmade for that individual knife. Prices: $100 up to $500. Remarks: Part-time maker. Sold first knife in 1981. Doing business as Double H Knives. Mark: "HH" inside 8 point deer rack.

HAMMOND, JIM,
PO Box 486, Arab, AL 35016, Phone: 256-586-4151, jim@jimhammondknives.com; Web: www.jimhammondknives.com
Specialties: High-tech fighters and folders. Patterns: Proven-design fighters. Technical: Grinds 440C, 440V, S30V and other specialty steels. Prices: $385 to $1200; some to $9200. Remarks: Full-time maker; first knife sold in 1977. Designer for Columbia River Knife and Tool. Mark: Full name, city, state in shield logo.

HAMMOND, RAY,
633 Devon Brooke Dr., Woodstock, GA 30188, Phone: 678-300-2883, rayhammond01@yahoo.com; Web: www.biggamehuntingblades.com
Specialties: hunters, capers, camp knives and bowies. Technical: Stock removal and forged blades. Prices: $300 and up. Remarks: Part-time maker; first knife built in 2008. Mark: Capital letters RH surrounded by a broken circle, pierced by a knife silhouette, atop the circle is my name, and below the circle the words "custom knives." Will soon alter this to be simply my last name.

HANCOCK, TIM,
10805 N. 83rd St, Scottsdale, AZ 85260, Phone: 480-998-8849
Specialties: High-art and working straight knives and folders of his design and to customer preferences. Patterns: Bowies, fighters, daggers, tantos, swords, folders. Technical: Forges Damascus and 52100; grinds ATS-34. Makes Damascus. Silver-wire inlays; offers carved fittings and file work. Prices: $500 to $10,000. Remarks: Full-time maker; first knife sold in 1988. Master Smith ABS. Mark: Last name or heart.

HAND, BILL,
PO Box 717, 1103 W. 7th St., Spearman, TX 79081, Phone: 806-659-2967, Fax: 806-659-5139, klinker43@yahoo.com
Specialties: Traditional working and using straight knives and folders of his design or to customer specs. Patterns: Hunters, Bowies, folders and fighters. Technical: Forges 5160, 52100 and Damascus. Prices: Start at $150. Remarks: Part-time maker; Journeyman Smith. Current delivery time 12 to 16 months. Mark: Stylized initials.

HANSEN, LONNIE,
PO Box 4956, Spanaway, WA 98387, Phone: 253-847-4632, lonniehansen@msn.com; Web: lchansen.com
Specialties: Working straight knives of his design. Patterns: Tomahawks, tantos, hunters, fillet. Technical: Forges 1086, 52100, grinds 440V, BG-42. Prices: Starting at $300. Remarks: Part-time maker since 1989. Mark: First initial and last name. Also first and last initial.

HANSEN, ROBERT W,
35701 University Ave NE, Cambridge, MN 55008, Phone: 763-689-3242
Specialties: Working straight knives, folders and integrals. Patterns: From hunters to minis, camp knives to miniatures; folding lockers and slip-joints in original styles. Technical: Grinds O1, 440C and 154CM; likes filework. Prices: $100 to $450; some to $600. Remarks: Part-time maker; first knife sold in 1983. Mark: Fish w/h inside surrounded by Bob Hansen maker.

HANSON III, DON L.,
PO Box 13, Success, MO 65570-0013, Phone: 573-674-3045, Web: www.sunfishforge.com; Web: www.donhansonknives.com
Specialties: One-of-a-kind damascus folders, slip joints and forged fixed blades. Patterns: Small, fancy pocket knives, large folding fighters and Bowies. Technical: Forges own pattern welded Damascus, file work and carving also carbon steel blades with hamons. Prices: $800 and up. Remarks: Full-time maker, first knife sold in 1984. ABS mastersmith. Mark: Sunfish.

HARA, KOJI,
292-2 Osugi, Seki-City, Gifu, JAPAN 501-3922, Phone: 0575-24-7569, Fax: 0575-24-7569, info@knifehousehara.com; Web: www.knifehousehara.com
Specialties: High-tech and working straight knives of his design; some folders. Patterns: Hunters, locking folders and utility/camp knives. Technical: Grinds Cowry X, Cowry Y and ATS-34. Prefers high mirror polish; pearl handle inlay. Prices: $400 to $2500. Remarks: Full-time maker; first knife sold in 1980. Doing business as Knife House "Hara." Mark: First initial, last name in fish.

HARDING, CHAD,
12365 Richland Ln, Solsberry, IN 47459, hardingknives@yahoo.com; Web: http://hardingknives.weeby.com
Specialties: Hunters and camp knives, occasional fighters or bowies. No folders. Technical: Hand forge 90% of work. Prefer 10XX steels and tool steels. Makes own damascus and cable and chainsaw chain damascus. 100% sole authorship on knives and sheaths. Mostly natural handle material, prefer wood

and stag. Prices: $150 to $1,000. Remarks: Part-time maker, member of ABS. First knife sold in 2005. Mark: Last name.

HARDY, DOUGLAS E,
114 Cypress Rd, Franklin, GA 30217, Phone: 706-675-6305

HARDY, SCOTT,
639 Myrtle Ave, Placerville, CA 95667, Phone: 530-622-5780, Web: www.innercite.com/~shardy
Specialties: Traditional working and using straight knives of his design. Patterns: Most anything with an edge. Technical: Forges carbon steels. Japanese stone polish. Offers mirror finish; differentially tempers. Prices: $100 to $1000. Remarks: Part-time maker; first knife sold in 1982. Mark: First initial, last name and Handmade with bird logo.

HARKINS, J A,
PO Box 218, Conner, MT 59827, Phone: 406-821-1060, kutter@customknives.net; Web: customknives.net
Specialties: OTFs. Patterns: OTFs, Automatics, Folders. Technical: Grinds ATS-34. Engraves; offers gem work. Prices: $1500 and up. Remarks: Celebrating 20th year as full-time maker . Mark: First and middle initials, last name.

HARLEY, LARRY W,
348 Deerfield Dr, Bristol, TN 37620, Phone: 423-878-5368 (shop); cell: 423-530-1133, Web: www.lonesomepineknives.com
Specialties: One-of-a-kind Persian in one-of-a-kind Damascus. Working knives, period pieces. Technical: Forges and grinds ATS-34, 440c, L6, 15, 20, 1084, and 52100. Patterns: Full range of straight knives, tomahawks, razors, buck skinners and hog spears. Prices: $200 and up. Mark: Pine tree.

HARLEY, RICHARD,
348 Deerfield Dr, Bristol, TN 37620, Phone: 423-878-5368; cell: 423-408-5720
Specialties: Hunting knives, Bowies, friction folders, one-of-a-kind. Technical: Forges 1084, S160, 52100, Lg. Prices: $150 to $1000. Mark: Pine tree with name.

HARM, PAUL W,
818 Young Rd, Attica, MI 48412, Phone: 810-724-5582, harm@blclinks.net
Specialties: Early American working knives. Patterns: Hunters, skinners, patch knives, fighters, folders. Technical: Forges and grinds 1084, O1, 52100 and own Damascus. Prices: $75 to $1000. Remarks: First knife sold in 1990. Mark: Connected initials.

HARNER III, "BUTCH" LLOYD R.,
745 Kindig Rd., Littlestown, PA 17340, butch@harnerknives.com; Web: www.harnerknives.com
Specialties: Kitchen knives and straight razors. Technical: CPM-3V, CPM-154 and various Carpenter powdered steel alloys. Remarks: Full-time maker since 2007. Mark: L.R. Harner (2005-Sept. 2012) and Harner III (after Oct. 2012)

HARRINGTON, ROGER,
P.O. Box 157, Battle, East Sussex, ENGLAND TN 33 3 DD, Phone: 0854-838-7062, info@bisonbushcraft.co.uk; Web: www.bisonbushcraft.co.uk
Specialties: Working straight knives to his or customer's designs, flat saber Scandinavia-style grinds on full tang knives, also hollow and convex grinds. Technical: Grinds O1, D2, Damascus. Prices: $200 to $800. Remarks: First knife made by hand in 1997 whilst traveling around the world. Mark: Bison with bison written under.

HARRIS, CASS,
19855 Fraiser Hill Ln, Bluemont, VA 20135, Phone: 540-554-8774, Web: www.tdogforge.com
Prices: $160 to $500.

HARRIS, JAY,
991 Johnson St, Redwood City, CA 94061, Phone: 415-366-6077
Specialties: Traditional high-tech straight knives and folders of his design. Patterns: Daggers, fighters and locking folders. Technical: Uses 440C, ATS-34 and CPM. Prices: $250 to $850. Remarks: Spare-time maker; first knife sold in 1980.

HARRIS, JEFFERY A,
214 Glen Cove Dr, Chesterfield, MO 63017, Phone: 314-469-6317, Fax: 314-469-6374, jeffro135@aol.com
Remarks: Purveyor and collector of handmade knives.

HARRIS, JOHN,
14131 Calle Vista, Riverside, CA 92508, Phone: 951-653-2755, johnharrisknives@yahoo.com
Specialties: Hunters, daggers, Bowies, bird and trout, period pieces, Damascus and carbon steel knives, forged and stock removal. Prices: $200 to $1000.

HARRIS, RALPH DEWEY,
2607 Bell Shoals Rd, Brandon, FL 33511, Phone: 813-681-5293, Fax: 813-654-8175
Specialties: Collector quality interframe folders. Patterns: High tech locking folders of his own design with various mechanisms. Technical: Grinds 440C, ATS-34 and commercial Damascus. Offers various frame materials including 416ss, and titanium; file worked frames and his own engraving. Prices: $400 to $3000. Remarks: Full-time maker; first knife sold in 1978. Mark: Last name, or name and city.

HARRISON, BRIAN,
BFH KNIVES, 2359 E Swede Rd, Cedarville, MI 49719, Phone: 906-430-0720, bfh_knives@yahoo.com
Specialties: High grade fixed blade knives. Patterns: Many sizes & variety of patterns from small pocket carries to large combat and camp knives. Mirror and bead blast finishes. All handles of high grade materials from ivory to highly figured stabilized woods to stag, deer & moose horn and Micarta. Hand sewn fancy sheaths for pocket or belt. Technical: Flat & hollow grinds usually ATS-34 but some O1, L6 and stellite 6K. Prices: $150 to $1200. Remarks: Full-time maker, sole authorship. Made first knife in 1980, sold first knife in 1999. Received much knowledge from the following makers: George Young, Eric Erickson, Webster Wood, Ed Kalfayan who are all generous men. Mark: Engraved blade outline w/BFH Knives over the top edge, signature across middle & Cedarville, MI underneath.

HARRISON, JIM (SEAMUS),
721 Fairington View Dr, St. Louis, MO 63129, Phone: 314-894-2525, jrh@seamusknives.com; Web: www.seamusknives.com
Specialties: "Crossover" folders, liner-locks and frame-locks. Patterns: Uber, Author, Skyyy Folders, Grant Survivor, Fixed blade. Technical: Use CPM S30V and 154, Stellite 6k and S.S. Damascus by Norris, Thomas and Damasteel. Prices: Folders $375 to $1,000. Remarks: Full-time maker since 2008, Maker since 1999. Mark: Seamus

HARSEY, WILLIAM H.,
82710 N. Howe Ln, Creswell, OR 97426, Phone: 519-895-4941, harseyjr@cs.com
Specialties: High-tech kitchen and outdoor knives. Patterns: Folding hunters, trout and bird folders; straight hunters, camp knives and axes. Technical: Grinds; etches. Prices: $125 to $300; some to $1500. Folders start at $350. Remarks: Full-time maker; first knife sold in 1979. Mark: Full name, state, U.S.A.

HART, BILL,
647 Cedar Dr, Pasadena, MD 21122, Phone: 410-255-4981
Specialties: Fur-trade era working straight knives and folders. Patterns: Springback folders, skinners, Bowies and patch knives. Technical: Forges and stock removes 1095 and 5160 wire Damascus. Prices: $100 to $600. Remarks: Part-time maker; first knife sold in 1986. Mark: Name.

HARTMAN, ARLAN (LANNY),
6102 S Hamlin Cir, Baldwin, MI 49304, Phone: 231-745-4029
Specialties: Working straight knives and folders. Patterns: Drop-point hunters, coil spring lockers, slip-joints. Technical: Flat-grinds D2, 440C and ATS-34. Prices: $300 to $2000. Remarks: Part-time maker; first knife sold in 1982. Mark: Last name.

HARTMAN, TIM,
3812 Pedroncelli Rd NW, Albuquerque, NM 87107, Phone: 505-385-6924, tbonz1@comcast.net
Specialties: Exotic wood scales, sambar stag, filework, hunters. Patterns: Fixed blade hunters, skinners, utility and hiking. Technical: 154CM, Ats-34 and D2. Mirror finish and contoured scales. Prices: Start at $200-$450. Remarks: Started making knives in 2004. Mark: 3 lines Ti Hartman, Maker, Albuquerque NM

HARVEY, HEATHER,
HEAVIN FORGE, PO Box 768, Belfast, MP, SOUTH AFRICA 1100, Phone: 27-13-253-0914, heather@heavinforge.co.za; Web: www.heavinforge.co.za
Specialties: Integral hand forged knives, traditional African weapons, primitive folders and by-gone forged-styles. Patterns: All forged knives, war axes, spears, arrows, forks, spoons, and swords. Technical: Own carbon Damascus and mokume. Also forges stainless, brass, copper and titanium. Traditional forging and heat-treatment methods used. Prices: $300 to $5000, average $1000. Remarks: Full-time maker and knifemaking instructor. Master bladesmith with ABS. First Damascus sold in 1995, first knife sold in 1998. Often collaborate with husband, Kevin (ABS MS) using the logo "Heavin." Mark: First name and sur name, oval shape with "M S" in middle.

HARVEY, KEVIN,
HEAVIN FORGE, PO Box 768, Belfast, LP, SOUTH AFRICA 1100, Phone: 27-13-253-0914, info@heavinforge.co.za Web: www.heavinforge.co.za
Specialties: Large knives of presentation quality and creative art knives. Patterns: Fixed blades of Bowie, dagger and fighter-styles, occasionally folders and swords. Technical: Stock removal of stainless and forging of carbon steel and own Damascus. Indigenous African handle materials preferred. Own engraving Often collaborate with wife, Heather (ABS MS) under the logo "Heavin." Prices: $500 to $5000 average $1500. Remarks: Full-time maker and knifemaking instructor. Master bladesmith with ABS. First knife sold in 1984. Mark: First name and surname, oval with "M S" in the middle.

HARVEY, MAX,
14 Bass Rd, Bull Creek, Pert , WA, AUSTRALIA 6155, Phone: 09-332-7585
Specialties: Daggers, Bowies, fighters and fantasy knives. Patterns: Hunters, Bowies, tantos and skinners. Technical: Hollow-and flat-grinds 440C, ATS-34, 154CM and Damascus. Offers gem work. Prices: $250 to $4000. Remarks: Part-time maker; first knife sold in 1981. Mark: First and middle initials, last name.

HARVEY, MEL,
P.O. Box 176, Nenana, AK 99760, Phone: 907-832-5660, tinker1@nenana.net
Specialties: Fixed blade knives for hunting and fishing. Patterns: Hunters, skinners. Technical: Stock removal on ATS-34, 440C, 01, 1095; Damascus blades using 1095 and 15N20. Prices: Starting at $350. Remarks: ABS member, attended Bill Moran School; 50+ knives sold since 2007. Mark: Mel Harvey over serial number over Nenana, AK.

HASLINGER, THOMAS,
164 Fairview Dr SE, Calgary, AB, CANADA T2H 1B3, Phone: 403-253-9628, Web: www.haslinger-knives.com; www.haslinger-culinary.com
Specialties: One-of-a-kind using, working and art knives HCK signature

sweeping grind lines. Maker of New Generation and Evolution Chef series. Differential heat treated stainless steel. Patterns: Likes to work with customers on design. Technical: Grinds various specialty alloys, including Damascus, High end satin finish. Prefers natural handle materials e.g. ancient ivory stag, pearl, abalone, stone and exotic woods. Does inlay work with stone, some sterling silver, niobium and gold wire work. Custom sheaths using matching woods or hand stitched with unique leather. Offers engraving. Prices: $300 and up. Remarks: Full-time maker; first knife sold in 1994. Doing business as Haslinger Custom Knives. Mark: Two marks used, high end work uses stylized initials, other uses elk antler with Thomas Haslinger, Canada, handcrafted above.

HAWES, CHUCK,
HAWES FORGE, PO Box 176, Weldon, IL 61882, Phone: 217-736-2479
Specialties: 95 percent of all work in own Damascus. Patterns: Slip-joints liner locks, hunters, Bowie's, swords, anything in between. Technical: Forges everything, uses all high-carbon steels, no stainless. Prices: $150 to $4000. Remarks: Like to do custom orders, his style or yours. Sells Damascus. Full-time maker since 1995. Mark: Small football shape. Chuck Hawes maker Weldon, IL.

HAWK, GRANT AND GAVIN,
Box 401, Idaho City, ID 83631, Phone: 208-392-4911, Web: www.9-hawkknives.com
Specialties: Large folders with unique locking systems D.O.G. lock, toad lock. Technical: Grinds ATS-34, titanium folder parts. Prices: $450 and up. Remarks: Full-time maker. Mark: First initials and last names.

HAWKINS, BUDDY,
PO Box 5969, Texarkana, TX 75505-5969, Phone: 903-838-7917, buddyhawkins@cableone.net

HAWKINS, RADE,
110 Buckeye Rd, Fayetteville, GA 30214, Phone: 770-964-1177, radeh@bellsouth.net; Web: wwwhawkinscustomknives.com
Specialties: All styles. Patterns: All styles. Technical: Grinds and forges. Makes own Damascus Prices: Start at $190. Remarks: Full-time maker; first knife sold in 1972. Member knifemakers guild, ABS Journeyman Smith. Mark: Rade Hawkins Custom Knives.

HAWKINS JR., CHARLES R.,
2764 Eunice, San Angelo, TX 76901, Phone: 325-947-7875, chawk12354@aol.com; Web: www.hawkcustomknives.com
Specialties: Custom knives, fixed blades, railroad spike knives and rasp file knives. Technical: Stock removal and some forging, using 1095 and 440C steel. Prices: $135 and up. Remarks: Part-time maker; first knife sold in 2008. Mark: Full name, city and state.

HAYES, SCOTTY,
Texarkana College, 2500 N Robinson Rd., Tesarkana, TX 75501, Phone: 903-838-4541, ext. 3236, Fax: 903-832-5030, shayes@texakanacollege.edu; Web: www.americanbladesmith.com/2005ABSo/o20schedule.htm
Specialties: ABS School of Bladesmithing.

HAYES, WALLY,
9960, 9th Concession, RR#1, Essex, ON, CANADA N8M-2X5, Phone: 519-776-1284, Web: www.hayesknives.com
Specialties: Classic and fancy straight knives and folders. Patterns: Daggers, Bowies, fighters, tantos. Technical: Forges own Damascus and O1; engraves. Prices: $150 to $14,000. Mark: Last name, M.S. and serial number.

HAYNES, JERRY,
260 Forest Meadow Dr, Gunter, TX 75058, Phone: 903-433-1424, jhaynes@arrow-head.com; Web: http://www.arrow-head.com
Specialties: Working straight knives and folders of his design, also historical blades. Patterns: Hunters, skinners, carving knives, fighters, renaissance daggers, locking folders and kitchen knives. Technical: Grinds ATS-34, CPM, Stellite 6K, D2 and acquired Damascus. Prefers exotic handle materials. Has B.A. in design. Studied with R. Buckminster Fuller. Prices: $200 to $1200. Remarks: Part-time maker. First knife sold in 1953. Mark: Arrowhead and last name.

HAYS, MARK,
HAYS HANDMADE KNIVES, 1008 Kavanagh Dr., Austin, TX 78748, Phone: 512-292-4410, markhays@austin.rr.com
Specialties: Working straight knives and folders. Patterns inspired by Randall and Stone. Patterns: Bowies, hunters and slip-joint folders. Technical: 440C stock removal. Repairs and restores Stone knives. Prices: Start at $200. Remarks: Part-time maker, brochure available, with Stone knives 1974-1983, 1990-1991. Mark: First initial, last name, state and serial number.

HEADRICK, GARY,
122 Wilson Blvd, Juan Les Pins, FRANCE 06160, Phone: 033 610282885, headrick-gary@wanadoo.fr; Web: couteaux-scrimshaw.com
Specialties: Hi-tech folders with natural furnishings. Back lock & back spring. Patterns: Damascus and mokumes. Technical: Self made Damascus all steel (no nickel). All chassis titanium. Prices: $500 to $2000. Remarks: Full-time maker for last 7 years. German Guild-French Federation. 10 years active. Mark: HEADRICK on ricosso is new marking.

HEANEY, JOHN D,
9 Lefe Court, Haines City, FL 33844, Phone: 863-422-5823, jdh199@msn.com; Web: www.heaneyknives.com
Specialties: Forged 5160, O1 and Damascus. Prefers using natural handle material such as bone, stag and oosic. Plans on using some of the various ivories on future knives. Prices: $250 and up.Remarks: ABS member. Received journeyman smith stamp in June. Mark: Heaney JS.

HEASMAN, H G,
28 St Mary's Rd, Llandudno, N. Wales, UNITED KINGDOM LL302UB, Phone: (UK)0492-876351
Specialties: Miniatures only. Patterns: Bowies, daggers and swords. Technical: Files from stock high-carbon and stainless steel. Prices: $400 to $600. Remarks: Part-time maker; first knife sold in 1975. Doing business as Reduced Reality. Mark: NA.

HEATH, WILLIAM,
PO Box 131, Bondville, IL 61815, Phone: 217-863-2576
Specialties: Classic and working straight knives, folders. Patterns: Hunters and Bowies LinerLock® folders. Technical: Grinds ATS-34, 440C, 154CM, Damascus, handle materials Micarta, woods to exotic materials snake skins cobra, rattle snake, African flower snake. Does own heat treating. Prices: $75 to $300 some $1000. Remarks: Full-time maker. First knife sold in 1979. Mark: W. D. HEATH.

HEBEISEN, JEFF,
310 19th Ave N, Hopkins, MN 55343, Phone: 952-935-4506, jhebeisen@peoplepc.com
Specialties: One of a kind fixed blade of any size up to 16". Patterns: Miniature, Hunters, Skinners, Daggers, Bowies, Fighters and Neck knives. Technical: Stock removal using CPM-154, D2, 440C. Handle mterial varies depending on intended use, mostly natural materials such as bone, horn, antler, and wood. Filework on many. Heavy duty sheaths made to fit. Prices: From $100 to $750. Remarks: Full-time maker. First knife sold in 2007. Mark: Started new mark in 2012: J. Hebeisen, Hopkins, MN. Older mark: arched name over buffalo skull.

HEDGES, DEE,
192 Carradine Rd., Bedfordale, WA, AUSTRALIA 6112, dark_woods_forge@yahoo.com.au; Web: www.darkwoodsforge.com
Patterns: Makes any and all patterns and style of blades from working blades to swords to Japanese inspired. Favors exotic and artistic variations and unique one-off pieces. Technical: Forges all blades from a range of steels, favoring 1084, W2, 52100, 5160 and Damascus steels she makes from a 1084/15n20 mix. Prices: Start at $200. Remarks: Full-time bladesmith and jeweller. Started making blades professionally in 1999, earning my Journeyman Smith rating in 2010. Mark: "Dark Woods" atop an ivy leaf, with "Forge" underneath.

HEDLUND, ANDERS,
Samstad 400, Brastad, SWEDEN 45491, Phone: 46-523-139 48, anderskniv@passagen.se; Web: http://hem.passagen.se/anderskniv
Specialties: Fancy high-end collectible folders, high-end collectible Nordic hunters with leather carvings on the sheath. Carvings combine traditional designs with own designs. Patterns: Own designs. Technical: Grinds most steels, but prefers mosaic Damascus and RWL-34. Prefers mother-of-pearl, mammoth, and mosaic steel for folders. Prefers desert ironwood, mammoth, stabilized arctic birch, willow burl, and Damascus steel or RWL-34 for stick tang knives. Prices: Starting at $750 for stick tang knives and staring at $1500 for folders. Remarks: Part-time maker, first knife sold in 1988. Nordic champion (five countries) several times and Swedish champion 20 times in different classes. Mark: Stylized initials or last name.

HEDRICK, DON,
131 Beechwood Hills, Newport News, VA 23608, Phone: 757-877-8100, donaldhedrick@cox.net
Specialties: Working straight knives; period pieces and fantasy knives. Patterns: Hunters, boots, Bowies and miniatures. Technical: Grinds 440C and commercial Damascus. Also makes micro-mini Randall replicas. Prices: $150 to $550; some to $1200. Remarks: Part-time maker; first knife sold in 1982. Mark: First initial, last name in oval logo.

HEFLIN, CHRISTOPHER M,
6013 Jocely Hollow Rd, Nashville, TN 37205, Phone: 615-352-3909, blix@bellsouth.net

HEGWALD, J L,
1106 Charles, Humboldt, KS 66748, Phone: 316-473-3523
Specialties: Working straight knives, some fancy. Patterns: Makes Bowies, miniatures. Technical: Forges or grinds O1, L6, 440C; mixes materials in handles. Prices: $35 to $200; some higher. Remarks: Part-time maker; first knife sold in 1983. Mark: First and middle initials.

HEHN, RICHARD KARL,
Lehnmuehler Str 1, Dorrebach, GERMANY 55444, Phone: 06724 3152
Specialties: High-tech, full integral working knives. Patterns: Hunters, fighters and daggers. Technical: Grinds CPM T-440V, CPM T-420V, forges his own stainless Damascus. Prices: $1000 to $10,000. Remarks: Full-time maker; first knife sold in 1963. Mark: Runic last initial in logo.

HEIMDALE, J E,
7749 E 28 CT, Tulsa, OK 74129, Phone: 918-640-0784, heimdale@sbcglobal.net
Specialties: Art knives Patterns: Bowies, daggers Technical: Makes allcomponents and handles - exotic woods and sheaths. Uses Damascus blades by other Blademakers, notably R.W. Wilson. Prices: $300 and up. Remarks: Part-time maker. First knife sold in 1999. Marks: JEHCO

HEINZ, JOHN,
611 Cafferty Rd, Upper Black Eddy, PA 18972, Phone: 610-847-8535, Web: www.herugrim.com
Specialties: Historical pieces / copies. Technical: Makes his own steel. Prices: $150 to $800. Mark: "H."

HEITLER, HENRY,
8106 N Albany, Tampa, FL 33604, Phone: 813-933-1645
Specialties: Traditional working and using straight knives of his design and to customer specs. Patterns: Fighters, hunters, utility/camp knives and fillet knives. Technical: Flat-grinds ATS-34; offers tapered tangs. Prices: $135 to $450; some to $600. Remarks: Part-time maker; first knife sold in 1990. Mark: First initial, last name, city, state circling double H's.

HELSCHER, JOHN W,
2645 Highway 1, Washington, IA 52353, Phone: 319-653-7310

HELTON, ROY,
HELTON KNIVES, 2941 Comstock St., San Diego, CA 92111, Phone: 858-277-5024

HEMPERLEY, GLEN,
13322 Country Run Rd, Willis, TX 77318, Phone: 936-228-5048, hemperley.com
Specialties: Specializes in hunting knives, does fixed and folding knives.

HENDRICKS, SAMUEL J,
2162 Van Buren Rd, Maurertown, VA 22644, Phone: 703-436-3305
Specialties: Integral hunters and skinners of thin design. Patterns: Boots, hunters and locking folders. Technical: Grinds ATS-34, 440C and D2. Integral liners and bolsters of N-S and 7075 T6 aircraft aluminum. Does leatherwork. Prices: $50 to $250; some to $500. Remarks: Full-time maker; first knife sold in 1992. Mark: First and middle initials, last name, city and state in football-style logo.

HENDRICKSON, E JAY,
4204 Ballenger Creek Pike, Frederick, MD 21703, Phone: 301-663-6923, Fax: 301-663-6923, ejayhendrickson@comcast.net
Specialties: Specializes in silver wire inlay. Patterns: Bowies, Kukri's, camp, hunters, and fighters. Technical: Forges 06, 1084, 5160, 52100, D2, L6 and W2; makes Damascus. Moran-styles on order. Prices: $400 to $8,000. Remarks: Full-time maker; first knife made in 1972; first knife sold in 1974. Mark: Last name, M.S.

HENDRICKSON, SHAWN,
2327 Kaetzel Rd, Knoxville, MD 21758, Phone: 301-432-4306
Specialties: Hunting knives. Patterns: Clip points, drop points and trailing point hunters. Technical: Forges 5160, 1084 and L6. Prices: $175 to $400.

HENDRIX, JERRY,
HENDRIX CUSTOM KNIVES, 175 Skyland Dr. Ext., Clinton, SC 29325, Phone: 864-833-2659, jhendrix@backroads.net
Specialties: Traditional working straight knives of all designs. Patterns: Hunters, utility, boot, bird and fishing. Technical: Grinds ATS-34 and 440C. Prices: $85 to $275. Remarks: Full-time maker. Hand stitched, waxed leather sheaths. Mark: Full name in shape of knife.

HENDRIX, WAYNE,
9636 Burton's Ferry Hwy, Allendale, SC 29810, Phone: 803-584-3825, Fax: 803-584-3825, whendrixknives@gmail.com Web: www.hendrixknives.com
Specialties: Working/using knives of his design. Patterns: Hunters and fillet knives. Technical: Grinds ATS-34, D2 and 440C. Prices: $100 and up. Remarks: Full-time maker; first knife sold in 1985. Mark: Last name.

HENNINGSSON, MICHAEL,
Tralasvagen 1, Vastra Frolunda (Gothenburg), SWEDEN, Phone: 46 31-471073; Cell: 46702555745, michael.henningsson@gmail.com; Web: henningssonknives.wordpress.com
Specialties: Handmade folding knives, mostly tactical liner locks and frame locks. Patterns: Own design in both engravings and knife models. Technical: All kinds of stee; such as Damascus, but prefer clean RWL-43. Tweaking a lot with hand engraving and therefore likes clean steel mostly. Work a lot with inlays of various materials. Prices: Starting at $1200 and up, depending on decoration and engravings. Remarks: Part-time maker, first knife sold in 2010. Mark: Hand engraved name or a Viking sail with initials in runes

HENRIKSEN, HANS J,
Birkegaardsvej 24, Helsinge, DENMARK 3200, Fax: 45 4879 4899
Specialties: Zirconia ceramic blades. Patterns: Customer designs. Technical: Slip-cast zirconia-water mix in plaster mould; offers hidden or full tang. Prices: White blades start at $10cm; colored +50 percent. Remarks: Part-time maker; first ceramic blade sold in 1989. Mark: Initial logo.

HENSLEY, WAYNE,
PO Box 904, Conyers, GA 30012, Phone: 770-483-8938
Specialties: Period pieces and fancy working knives. Patterns: Boots to Bowies, locking folders to miniatures. Large variety of straight knives. Technical: Grinds ATS-34, 440C, D2 and commercial Damascus. Prices: $85 and up. Remarks: Full-time maker; first knife sold in 1974. Mark: Last name.

HERB, MARTIN,
2500 Starwood Dr, Richmond, VA 23229

HERBST, GAWIE,
PO Box 59158, Karenpark, Akasia, GT, SOUTH AFRICA 0118, Phone: +27 72 060 3687, Fax: +27 12 549 1876, gawie@herbst.co.za Web: www.herbst.co.za
Specialties: Hunters, Utility knives, Art knives and Liner lock folders.

HERBST, PETER,
Komotauer Strasse 26, Lauf a.d. Pegn., GERMANY 91207, Phone: 09123-13315, Fax: 09123-13379
Specialties: Working/using knives and folders of his design. Patterns: Hunters, fighters and daggers; interframe and integral. Technical: Grinds CPM-T-440V,

UHB-Elmax, ATS-34 and stainless Damascus. Prices: $300 to $3000; some to $8000. Remarks: Full-time maker; first knife sold in 1981. Mark: First initial, last name.

HERBST, THINUS,
PO Box 59158, Karenpark, Akasia, GT, SOUTH AFRICA 0118, Phone: +27 82 254 8016, thinus@herbst.co.za; Web: www.herbst.co.za
Specialties: Plain and fancy working straight knives of own design and liner lock folders. Patterns: Hunters, utility knives, art knives, and liner lock folders. Technical: Prefer exotic materials for handles. Most knives embellished with file work, carving and scrimshaw. Prices: $200 to $2000. Remarks: Full-time maker, member of the Knifemakers Guild of South Africa.

HERMAN, TIM,
517 E. 126 Terrace, Olathe, KS 66061-2731, Phone: 913-839-1924, HermanKnives@comcast.net
Specialties: Investment-grade folders of his design; interframes and bolster frames. Patterns: Interframes and new designs in carved stainless. Technical: Grinds ATS-34 and damasteel Damascus. Engraves and gold inlays with pearl, jade, lapis and Australian opal. Prices: $1500 to $20,000 and up. Remarks: Full-time maker; first knife sold in 1978. Inventor of full-color bulino engraving since 1993. Mark: Etched signature.

HERNDON, WM R "BILL",
32520 Michigan St, Acton, CA 93510, Phone: 661-269-5860, bherndons1@roadrunner.com
Specialties: Straight knives, plain and fancy. Technical: Carbon steel (white and blued), Damascus, stainless steels. Prices: Start at $175. Remarks: Full-time maker; first knife sold in 1976. American Bladesmith Society journeyman smith. Mark: Signature and/or helm logo.

HERRING, MORRIS,
Box 85 721 W Line St, Dyer, AR 72935, Phone: 501-997-8861, morrish@ipa.com

HETHCOAT, DON,
Box 1764, Clovis, NM 88101, Phone: 575-762-5721, dhethcoat@plateautel.net; Web: www.donhethcoat.com
Specialties: Liner locks, lock backs and multi-blade folder patterns. Patterns: Hunters, Bowies. Technical: Grinds stainless; forges Damascus. Prices: Moderate to upscale. Remarks: Full-time maker; first knife sold in 1969. Mark: Last name on all.

HIBBEN, DARYL,
PO Box 172, LaGrange, KY 40031-0172, Phone: 502-222-0983, dhibben1@bellsouth.net
Specialties: Working straight knives, some fancy to customer specs. Patterns: Hunters, fighters, Bowies, short sword, art and fantasy. Technical: Grinds 440C, ATS-34, 154CM, Damascus; prefers hollow-grinds. Prices: $275 and up. Remarks: Full-time maker; first knife sold in 1979. Mark: Etched full name in script.

HIBBEN, GIL,
PO Box 13, LaGrange, KY 40031, Phone: 502-222-1397, Fax: 502-222-2676, gil@hibbenknives.com Web: www.hibbenknives.com
Specialties: Working knives and fantasy pieces to customer specs. Patterns: Full range of straight knives, including swords, axes and miniatures; some locking folders. Technical: Grinds ATS-34, 440C and D2. Prices: $300 to $2000; some to $10,000. Remarks: Full-time maker; first knife sold in 1957. Maker and designer of Rambo III knife; made swords for movie Marked for Death and throwing knife for movie Under Seige; made belt buckle knife and knives for movie Perfect Weapon; made knives featured in movie Star Trek the Next Generation , Star Trek Nemesis. 1990 inductee Cutlery Hall of Fame; designer for United Cutlery. Official klingon armourer for Star Trek. Knives also for movies of the Expendables and the Expendables sequel. Over 37 movies and TV productions. President of the Knifemakers Guild. Celebrating 55 years since first knife sold. Mark: Hibben Knives. City and state, or signature.

HIBBEN, JOLEEN,
PO Box 172, LaGrange, KY 40031, Phone: 502-222-0983, dhibben1@bellsouth.net
Specialties: Miniature straight knives of her design; period pieces. Patterns: Hunters, axes and fantasy knives. Technical: Grinds Damascus, 1095 tool steel and stainless 440C or ATS-34. Uses wood, ivory, bone, feathers and claws on/for handles. Prices: $60 to $600. Remarks: Spare-time maker; first knife sold in 1991. Design knives, make & tool leather sheathes. Produced first inlaid handle in 2005, used by Daryl on a dagger. Mark: Initials or first name.

HIBBEN, WESTLEY G,
14101 Sunview Dr, Anchorage, AK 99515
Specialties: Working straight knives of his design or to customer specs. Patterns: Hunters, fighters, daggers, combat knives and some fantasy pieces. Technical: Grinds 440C mostly. Filework available. Prices: $200 to $400; some to $3000. Remarks: Part-time maker; first knife sold in 1988. Mark: Signature.

HICKS, GARY,
341 CR 275, Tuscola, TX 79562, Phone: 325-554-9762

HIELSCHER, GUY,
PO Box 992, 6550 Otoe Rd., Alliance, NE 69301, Phone: 308-762-4318, g-hielsc@bbcwb.net Web: www.ghknives.com
Specialties: Working Damascus fixed blade knives. Patterns: Hunters, fighters, capers, skinners, bowie, drop point. Technical: Forges own Damascus using 1018 and 0-1 tool steels. Prices: $285 and up. Remarks: Member of PKA. Part-time maker; sold first knife in 1988. Mark: Arrowhead with GH inside.

HIGH, TOM,
5474 S 1128 Rd, Alamosa, CO 81101, Phone: 719-589-2108, www.rockymountainscrimshaw.com
Specialties: Hunters, some fancy. Patterns: Drop-points in several shapes; some semi-skinners. Knives designed by and for top outfitters and guides. Technical: Grinds ATS-34; likes hollow-grinds, mirror finishes; prefers scrimable handles. Prices: $300 to $8000.. Remarks: Full-time maker; first knife sold in 1965. Limited edition wildlife series knives. Mark: Initials connected; arrow through last name.

HILL, HOWARD E,
41785 Mission Lane, Polson, MT 59860, Phone: 406-883-3405, Fax: 406-883-3486, knifeman@bigsky.net
Specialties: Autos, complete new design, legal in Montana (with permit). Patterns: Bowies, daggers, skinners and lockback folders. Technical: Grinds 440C; uses micro and satin finish. Prices: $150 to $1000. Remarks: Full-time maker; first knife sold in 1981. Mark: Persuader.

HILL, RICK,
20 Nassau, Maryville, IL 62062-5618, Phone: 618-288-4370
Specialties: Working knives and period pieces to customer specs. Patterns: Hunters, locking folders, fighters and daggers. Technical: Grinds D2, 440C and 154CM; forges his own Damascus. Prices: $75 to $500; some to $3000. Remarks: Part-time maker; first knife sold in 1983. Mark: Full name in hill shape logo.

HILL, STEVE E,
217 Twin Lake Tr., Spring Branch, TX 78070, Phone: 830-624-6258 (cell) or 830-885-6108 (home), kingpirateboy2@juno.com or kingpirateboy2@gvtc.com; Web: www.stevehillknives.com
Specialties: Fancy manual and automatic LinerLock® folders, small fixed blades and classic Bowie knives. Patterns: Classic to cool folding and fixed blade designs. Technical: Grinds Damascus and occasional 440C, D2. Prefers natural handle materials; offers elaborate filework, carving, and inlays. Prices: $400 to $6000, some higher. Remarks: Full-time maker; first knife sold in 1978. Google search: Steve Hill custom knives. Mark: First initial, last name and handmade. (4400, D2). Damascus folders: mark inside handle.

HILLMAN, CHARLES,
225 Waldoboro Rd, Friendship, ME 04547, Phone: 207-832-4634
Specialties: Working knives of his own or custom design. Heavy Scagel influence. Patterns: Hunters, fishing, camp and general utility. Occasional folders. Technical: Grinds D2 and 440C. File work, blade and handle carving, engraving. Natural handle materials-antler, bone, leather, wood, horn. Sheaths made to order. Prices: $60 to $500. Remarks: Part-time maker; first knife sold 1986. Mark: Last name in oak leaf.

HINDERER, RICK,
5373 Columbus Rd., Shreve, OH 44676, Phone: 330-263-0962, Fax: 330-263-0962, rhind64@earthlink.net; Web: www.rickhindererknives.com
Specialties: Working tactical knives, and some one-of-a kind. Patterns: Makes his own. Technical: Grinds Duratech 20 CV and CPM S30V. Prices: $150 to $4000. Remarks: Full-time maker doing business as Rick Hinderer Knives, first knife sold in 1988. Mark: R. Hinderer.

HINDMARCH, GARTH,
PO Box 135, Carlyle, SK, CANADA S0C 0R0, Phone: 306-453-2568
Specialties: Working and fancy straight knives, Bowies. Patterns: Hunters, skinners, Bowies. Technical: Grind 440C, ATS-34, some Damascus. Prices: $175 - $700. Remarks: Part-time maker; first knife sold 1994. All knives satin finish. Does file work, offers engraving, stabilized wood, Giraffe bone, some Micarta. Mark: First initial last name, city, province.

HINK III, LES,
1599 Aptos Lane, Stockton, CA 95206, Phone: 209-547-1292
Specialties: Working straight knives and traditional folders in standard patterns or to customer specs. Patterns: Hunting and utility/camp knives; others on request. Technical: Grinds carbon and stainless steels. Prices: $80 to $200; some higher. Remarks: Part-time maker; first knife sold in 1980. Mark: Last name, or last name 3.

HINMAN, THEODORE,
186 Petty Plain Road, Greenfield, MA 01301, Phone: 413-773-0448, armenemargosian@verizon.net
Specialties: Tomahawks and axes. Offers classes in bladesmithing and toolmaking.

HINSON AND SON, R,
2419 Edgewood Rd, Columbus, GA 31906, Phone: 706-327-6801
Specialties: Working straight knives and folders. Patterns: Locking folders, liner locks, combat knives and swords. Technical: Grinds 440C and commercial Damascus. Prices: $200 to $450; some to $1500. Remarks: Part-time maker; first knife sold in 1983. Son Bob is co-worker. Mark: HINSON, city and state.

HINTZ, GERALD M,
5402 Sahara Ct, Helena, MT 59602, Phone: 406-458-5412
Specialties: Fancy, high-art, working/using knives of his design. Patterns: Bowies, hunters, daggers, fish fillet and utility/camp knives. Technical: Forges ATS-34, 440C and D2. Animal art in horn handles or in the blade. Prices: $75 to $400; some to $1000. Remarks: Part-time maker; first knife sold in 1980. Doing business as Big Joe's Custom Knives. Will take custom orders. Mark: F.S. or W.S. with first and middle initials and last name.

HIRAYAMA, HARUMI,
4-5-13 Kitamachi, Warabi City, Saitama, JAPAN 335-0001, Phone: 048-443-2248, Fax: 048-443-2248, swanbird3@gmail.com; Web: www.ne.jp/asahi/harumi/knives
Specialties: High-tech working knives of her design. Patterns: Locking folders, interframes, straight gents and slip-joints. Technical: Grinds 440C or equivalent; uses natural handle materials and gold. Prices: Start at $2500. Remarks: Part-time maker; first knife sold in 1985. Mark: First initial, last name.

HIROTO, FUJIHARA,
2-34-7 Koioosako, Nishi-ku, Hiroshima, JAPAN, Phone: 082-271-8389, fjhr8363@crest.ocn.ne.jp

HITCHMOUGH, HOWARD,
95 Old Street Rd, Peterborough, NH 03458-1637, Phone: 603-924-9646, Fax: 603-924-9595, hhrlm@comcast.net; Web: www.hitchmoughknives.com
Specialties: High class folding knives. Patterns: Lockback folders, liner locks, pocket knives. Technical: Uses ATS-34, stainless Damascus, titanium, gold and gemstones. Prefers hand-rubbed finishes and natural handle materials. Prices: $2500 - $7500. Remarks: Full-time maker; first knife sold in 1967. Mark: Last name.

HOBART, GENE,
100 Shedd Rd, Windsor, NY 13865, Phone: 607-655-1345

HOCKENSMITH, DAN,
104 North Country Rd 23, Berthoud, CO 80513, Phone: 970-231-6506, blademan@skybeam.com; Web: www.dhockensmithknives.com
Specialties: Traditional working and using straight knives of his design. Patterns: Hunters, Bowies, folders and utility/camp knives. Technical: Uses his Damascus, 5160, carbon steel, 52100 steel and 1084 steel. Hand forged. Prices: $250 to $1500. Remarks: Part-time maker; first knife sold in 1987. Mark: Last name or stylized "D" with H inside.

HODGE III, JOHN,
422 S 15th St, Palatka, FL 32177, Phone: 904-328-3897
Specialties: Fancy straight knives and folders. Patterns: Various. Technical: Pattern-welded Damascus—"Southern-style." Prices: To $1000. Remarks: Part-time maker; first knife sold in 1981. Mark: JH3 logo.

HOEL, STEVE,
PO Box 283, Pine, AZ 85544, Phone: 602-476-4278
Specialties: Investor-class folders, straight knives and period pieces of his design. Patterns: Folding interframes lockers and slip-joints; straight Bowies, boots and daggers. Technical: Grinds 154CM, ATS-34 and commercial Damascus. Prices: $600 to $1200; some to $7500. Remarks: Full-time maker. Mark: Initial logo with name and address.

HOFER, LOUIS,
BOX 125, Rose Prairie, BC, CANADA V0C 2H0, Phone: 250-827-3999, ldhofer@xplornet.com
Specialties: Damascus knives, working knives, fixed blade bowies, daggers. Patterns: Hunting, skinning, custom. Technical: Wild damascus, random damascus. Prices: $450 and up. Remarks: Part-time maker since 1995. Mark: Logo of initials.

HOFFMAN, JAY,
Hoffman Haus + Heraldic Device, 911 W Superior St., Munising, MI 49862, Phone: 906-387-3440, hoffmanhaus1@yahoo.com; Web: www.hoffmanhausknives.com
Technical: Scrimshaw, metal carving, own casting of hilts and pommels, etc. Most if not all leather work for sheaths. Remarks: Has been making knives for 50 + years. Professionally since 1991. Mark: Early knives marked "Hoffman Haus" and year. Now marks "Hoffman Haus Knives" on the blades. Starting in 2010 uses heraldic device. Will build to your specs. Lag time 1-2 months.

HOFFMAN, KEVIN L,
28 Hopeland Dr, Savannah, GA 31419, Phone: 912-920-3579, Fax: 912-920-3579, kevh052475@aol.com; Web: www.KLHoffman.com
Specialties: Distinctive folders and fixed blades. Patterns: Titanium frame lock folders. Technical: Sculpted guards and fittings cast in sterling silver and 14k gold. Grinds ATS-34, CPM S30V Damascus. Makes kydex sheaths for his fixed blade working knives. Prices: $400 and up. Remarks: Full-time maker since 1981. Mark: KLH.

HOGAN, THOMAS R,
2802 S. Heritage Ave, Boise, ID 83709, Phone: 208-362-7848

HOGSTROM, ANDERS T,
Halmstadsvagen 36, Johanneshov, SWEDEN 12153, Phone: 46 702 674 574, andershogstrom@hotmail.com or info@andershogstrom.com; Web: www.andershogstrom.com
Specialties: Short and long daggers, fighters and swords For select pieces makes wooden display stands. Patterns: Daggers, fighters, short knives and swords and an occasional sword. Technical: Grinds 1050 High Carbon, Damascus and stainless, forges own Damasus on occasion, fossil ivories. Does clay tempering and uses exotic hardwoods. Prices: Start at $850. Marks: Last name in maker's own signature.

HOKE, THOMAS M,
3103 Smith Ln, LaGrange, KY 40031, Phone: 502-222-0350
Specialties: Working/using knives, straight knives. Own designs and customer specs. Patterns: Daggers, Bowies, hunters, fighters, short swords. Technical: Grind 440C, Damascus and ATS-34. Filework on all knives. Tooling on sheaths (custom fit on all knives). Any handle material, mostly exotic. Prices: $100 to

$700; some to $1500. Remarks: Full-time maker, first knife sold in 1986. Mark: Dragon on banner which says T.M. Hoke.

HOLBROOK, H L,
PO Box 483, Sandy Hook, KY 41171, Phone: Home: 606-738-9922 Cell: 606-794-1497, hhknives@mrtc.com
Specialties: Traditional working using straight knives of his design, to customer specs and in standard patterns. Stabilized wood. Patterns: Hunters, mild tacticals and neck knives with kydex sheaths. Technical: Grinds CPM154CM, 154CM. Blades have hand-rubbed satin finish. Uses exotic woods, stag and Micarta. Hand-sewn sheath with each straight knife. Prices: $125 - $400. Remarks: Part-time maker; first knife sold in 1983. Doing business as Holbrook Knives. Mark: Name, city, state.

HOLDER, D'ALTON,
18910 McNeil Rd., Wickenburg, AZ 85390, Phone: 928-684-2025, Fax: 623-878-3964, dholderknives@cox.net; Web: d'holder.com
Specialties: Deluxe working knives and high-art hunters. Patterns: Drop-point hunters, fighters, Bowies. Technical: Grinds ATS-34; uses amber and other materials in combination on stick tangs. Prices: $400 to $1000; some to $2000. Remarks: Full-time maker; first knife sold in 1966. Mark: D'HOLDER, city and state.

HOLLOWAY, PAUL,
714 Burksdale Rd, Norfolk, VA 23518, Phone: 757-547-6025, houdini969@yahoo.com
Specialties: Working straight knives and folders to customer specs. Patterns: Lockers and slip-joints; fighters and boots; fishing and push knives, from swords to miniatures. Technical: Grinds A2, D2, 154CM, 440C and ATS-34. Prices: $210 to $1,200; some to $1,500 or higher. Remarks: Part-time maker; semi-retired; first knife sold in 1981. Mark: Name and city in logo.

HOOK, BOB,
3247 Wyatt Rd, North Pole, AK 99705, Phone: 907-488-8886, grayling@alaska.net; Web: www.alaskaknifeandforge.com
Specialties: Forged carbon steel. Damascus blades. Patterns: Pronghorns, bowies, drop point hunters and knives for the kitchen. Technical: 5160, 52100, carbon steel and 1084 and 15N20 pattern welded steel blades are hand forged. Heat treated and ground by maker. Handles are natural materials from Alaska. I favor sole authorship of each piece. Prices: $300-$1000. Remarks: Journeyman smith with ABS. I have attended the Bill Moran School of Bladesmithing. Knife maker since 2000. Mark: Hook.

HORN, DES,
PO Box 322, Onrusrivier, WC, SOUTH AFRICA 7201, Phone: 27283161795, Fax: +27866280824, deshorn@usa.net
Specialties: Folding knives. Patterns: Ball release side lock mechanism and interframe automatics. Technical: Prefers working in totally stainless materials. Prices: $800 to $7500. Remarks: Full-time maker. Enjoys working in gold, titanium, meteorite, pearl and mammoth. Mark: Des Horn.

HORN, JESS,
2526 Lansdown Rd, Eugene, OR 97404, Phone: 541-463-1510, jandahorn@earthlink.net
Specialties: Investor-class working folders; period pieces; collectibles. Patterns: High-tech design and finish in folders; liner locks, traditional slip-joints and featherweight models. Technical: Grinds ATS-34, 154CM. Prices: Start at $1000. Remarks: Full-time maker; first knife sold in 1968. Mark: Full name or last name.

HORNE, GRACE,
The Old Public Convenience, 469 Fulwood Road, Sheffield, UNITED KINGDOM S10 3QA, gracehorne@hotmail.co.uk Web: www.gracehorn.co.uk
Specialties: Knives of own design, mainly slip-joint folders. Technical: Grinds RWL34, Damasteel and own Damascus for blades. Scale materials vary from traditional (coral, wood, precious metals, etc) to unusual (wool, fabric, felt, etc). Prices: $500 - $1500Remarks: Part-time maker. Mark: 'gH' and 'Sheffield'.

HORRIGAN, JOHN,
433 C.R. 200 D, Burnet, TX 78611, Phone: 512-756-7545, jhorrigan@yahoo.com Web: www.eliteknives.com
Specialties: High-end custom knives. Prices: $200 - $6500. Remarks: Part-time maker. Obtained Mastersmith stamp 2005. First knife made in 1982. Mark: Horrigan M.S.

HORTON, SCOT,
PO Box 451, Buhl, ID 83316, Phone: 208-543-4222
Specialties: Traditional working stiff knives and folders. Patterns: Hunters, skinners, utility, hatchets and show knives. Technical: Grinds ATS-34 and D-2 tool steel. Prices: $400 to $2500. Remarks: First knife sold in 1990. Mark: Full name in arch underlined with arrow, city, state.

HOSSOM, JERRY,
3585 Schilling Ridge, Duluth, GA 30096, Phone: 770-449-7809, jerry@hossom.com; Web: www.hossom.com
Specialties: Working straight knives of his own design. Patterns: Fighters, combat knives, modern Bowies and daggers, modern swords, concealment knives for military and LE uses. Technical: Grinds 154CM, S30V, CPM-3V, CPM-154 and stainless Damascus. Uses natural and synthetic handle materials. Prices: $350-1500, some higher. Remarks: Full-time maker since 1997. First knife sold in 1983. Mark: First initial and last name, includes city and state since 2002.

HOSTETLER, LARRY,
10626 Pine Needle Dr., Fort Pierce, FL 34945, Phone: 772-465-8352, hossknives@bellsouth.net Web: www.hoss-knives.com
Specialties: EDC working knives and custom collector knives. Utilizing own designs and customer designed creations. Maker uses a wide variety of exotic materials. Patterns: Bowies, hunters and folders. Technical: Stock removal, grinds ATS-34, carbon and stainless Damascus, embellishes most pieces with file work. Prices: $200 - $1500. Some custom orders higher. Remarks: Motto: "EDC doesn't have to be ugly." First knife made in 2001, part-time maker, voting member in the Knife Maker's Guild. Doing business as "Hoss Knives." Mark: "Hoss" etched into blade with a turn of the century fused bomb in place of the "O" in Hoss.

HOUSE, CAMERON,
2001 Delaney Rd Se, Salem, OR 97306, Phone: 503-585-3286, chouse357@aol.com
Specialties: Working straight knives. Patterns: Hunters, Bowies, fighters. Technical: Grinds ATS-34, 530V, 154CM. Remarks: Part-time maker, first knife sold in 1993. Prices: $150 and up. Mark: HOUSE.

HOUSE, GARY,
2851 Pierce Rd, Ephrata, WA 98823, Phone: 509-754-3272, spindry101@aol.com
Specialties: Bowies, hunters, daggers and some swords. Patterns: Unlimited, SW Indian designs, geometric patterns, bowies, hunters and daggers. Technical: Mosaic damascus bar stock, forged blades, using 1084, 15N20 and some nickel. Forged company logos and customer designs in mosaic damascus. Prices: $500 & up. Remarks: Some of the finest and most unique patterns available. ABS master smith. Marks: Initials GTH, G hanging T, H.

HOWARD, DURVYN M,
4220 McLain St S, Hokes Bluff, AL 35903, Phone: 256-492-5720, Fax: Cell: 256-504-1853
Specialties: Collectible upscale folders; one-of-a-kind, gentlemen's folders. Multiple patents. Patterns: Conceptual designs; each unique and different. Technical: Uses natural and exotic materials and precious metals. Prices: $5000 to $25,000. Remarks: Full-time maker; by commission or available work. Mark: Howard; or Howard in Garamond Narrow "etched."

HOWE, TORI,
30020 N Stampede Rd, Athol, ID 83801, Phone: 208-449-1509, wapiti@knifescales.com; Web:www.knifescales.com
Specialties Custom knives, knife scales & Damascus blades. Remarks: Carry James Luman polymer clay knife scales.

HOWELL, JASON G,
1112 Sycamore, Lake Jackson, TX 77566, Phone: 979-297-9454, tinyknives@yahoo.com; Web:www.howellbladesmith.com
Specialties: Fixed blades and LinerLock® folders. Makes own Damascus. Patterns: Clip and drop point. Prices: $150 to $750. Remarks: Likes making Mosaic Damascus out of the ordinary stuff. Member of TX Knifemakers and Collectors Association; apprentice in ABS; working towards Journeyman Stamp. Mark: Name, city, state.

HOWELL, KEITH A.,
67 Hidden Oaks Dr., Oxford, AL 36203, Phone: 256-283-3269, keith@howellcutlery.com; Web: www.howellcutlery.com
Specialties: Working straight knives and folders of his design or to customer specs. Patterns: Hunters, utility pieces, neck knives, everyday carry knives and friction folders. Technical: Grinds damascus, 1095 and 154CM. Prices: $100 to $250. Remarks: Part-time maker; first knife sold in 2007. Mark: Last name.

HOWELL, LEN,
550 Lee Rd 169, Opelika, AL 36804, Phone: 334-749-1942
Specialties: Traditional and working knives of his design and to customer specs. Patterns: Buckskinner, hunters and utility/camp knives. Technical: Forges cable Damascus, 1085 and 5160; makes own Damascus. Mark: Engraved last name.

HOWELL, TED,
1294 Wilson Rd, Wetumpka, AL 36092, Phone: 205-569-2281, Fax: 205-569-1764
Specialties: Working/using straight knives and folders of his design; period pieces. Patterns: Bowies, fighters, hunters. Technical: Forges 5160, 1085 and cable. Offers light engraving and scrimshaw; filework. Prices: $75 to $250; some to $450. Remarks: Part-time maker; first knife sold in 1991. Doing business as Howell Co. Mark: Last name, Slapout AL.

HOWSER, JOHN C,
54 Bell Ln, Frankfort, KY 40601, Phone: 502-875-3678, howsercustomknives@fewpb.net
Specialties: Slip joint folders (old patterns-multi blades). Patterns: Traditional slip joint folders, lockbacks, hunters and fillet knives. Technical: Steel S30V, CPM154, ATS-34 and D2. Prices: $200 to $600 some to $800. Remarks: Full-time maker; first knife sold in 1974. Mark: Signature or stamp.

HOY, KEN,
54744 Pinchot Dr, North Fork, CA 93643, Phone: 209-877-7805

HRISOULAS, JIM,
SALAMANDER ARMOURY, 284-C Lake Mead Pkwy #157, Henderson, NV 89105, Phone: 702-566-8551, www.atar.com
Specialties: Working straight knives; period pieces. Patterns: Swords, daggers and sgian dubhs. Technical: Double-edged differential heat treating. Prices: $85 to $175; some to $600 and higher. Remarks: Full-time maker; first knife sold in 1973. Author of The Complete Bladesmith, The Pattern Welded Blade

and The Master Bladesmith. Doing business as Salamander Armory. Mark: 8R logo and sword and salamander.

HUCKABEE, DALE,
254 Hwy 260, Maylene, AL 35114, Phone: 205-664-2544, huckabeeknives@hotmail.com; Web: http://dalehuckabeeknives.weebly.com
Specialties: Fixed blade hunter and Bowies of his design. Technical: Steel used: 5160, 1084, and Damascus. Prices: $225 and up, depending on materials used. Remarks: Hand forged. Journeyman Smith. Part-time maker. Mark: Stamped Huckabee J.S.

HUCKS, JERRY,
KNIVES BY HUCKS, 1807 Perch Road, Moncks Corner, SC 29461, Phone: 843-761-6481, Fax: Cell: 843-708-1649
Specialties: Drop points, bowies and oyster knives. Patterns: To customer specs or maker's own design. Technical: CPM-154, ATS-34, 5160, 15N20, D2 and 1095 mostly for damascus billets. Prices: $200 and up. Remarks: Full-time maker, retired as a machinist in 1990. Makes sheaths sewn by hand with some carving. Will custom make to order or by sketch. Mark: Robin Hood hat with Moncks Corner under.

HUDSON, ANTHONY B,
PO Box 368, Amanda, OH 43102, Phone: 740-969-4200, abhudsonknives@yahoo.com; Web: abhudsonknives.com
Specialties: Hunting knives, fighters, survival, period pieces (U.S.) Remarks: ABS Journeyman Smith. Mark: A.B. HUDSON (except for period pieces).

HUDSON, C ROBBIN,
497 Groton Hollow Rd, Rummney, NH 03266, Phone: 603-786-9944, bladesmith8@gmail.com
Specialties: High-art working knives. Patterns: Hunters, Bowies, fighters and kitchen knives. Technical: Forges W2, nickel steel, pure nickel steel, composite and mosaic Damascus; makes knives one-at-a-time. Prices: 500 to $1200; some to $5000. Remarks: Full-time maker; first knife sold in 1970. Mark: Last name and MS.

HUDSON, ROB,
340 Roush Rd, Northumberland, PA 17857, Phone: 570-473-9588, robscustknives@aol.com Web:www.robscustomknives.com
Specialties: Presentation hunters and Bowies. Technical: Hollow grinds CPM-154 stainless and stainless Damascus. Prices: $400 to $2000. Remarks: Full-time maker. Does business as Rob's Custom Knives. Mark: Capital R, Capital H in script.

HUDSON, ROBERT,
3802 Black Cricket Ct, Humble, TX 77396, Phone: 713-454-7207
Specialties: Working straight knives of his design. Patterns: Bowies, hunters, skinners, fighters and utility knives. Technical: Grinds D2, 440C, 154CM and commercial Damascus. Prices: $85 to $350; some to $1500. Remarks: Part-time maker; first knife sold in 1980. Mark: Full name, handmade, city and state.

HUGHES, DAN,
301 Grandview Bluff Rd, Spencer, TN 38585, Phone: 931-946-3044
Specialties: Working straight knives to customer specs. Patterns: Hunters, fighters, fillet knives. Technical: Grinds 440C and ATS-34. Prices: $55 to $175; some to $300. Remarks: Part-time maker; first knife sold in 1984. Mark: Initials.

HUGHES, DARYLE,
10979 Leonard, Nunica, MI 49448, Phone: 616-837-6623, hughes.builders@verizon.net
Specialties: Working knives. Patterns: Buckskinners, hunters, camp knives, kitchen and fishing knives. Technical: Forges and grinds 52100 and Damascus. Prices: $125 to $1000. Remarks: Part-time maker; first knife sold in 1979. Mark: Name and city in logo.

HUGHES, ED,
280 1/2 Holly Lane, Grand Junction, CO 81503, Phone: 970-243-8547, edhughes26@msn.com
Specialties: Working and art folders. Patterns: Buys Damascus. Technical: Grinds stainless steels. Engraves. Prices: $300 and up. Remarks: Full-time maker; first knife sold in 1978. Mark: Name or initials.

HUGHES, LAWRENCE,
207 W Crestway, Plainview, TX 79072, Phone: 806-293-5406
Specialties: Working and display knives. Patterns: Bowies, daggers, hunters, buckskinners. Technical: Grinds D2, 440C and 154CM. Prices: $125 to $300; some to $2000. Remarks: Full-time maker; first knife sold in 1979. Mark: Name with buffalo skull in center.

HUGHES, TONY,
Tony Hughes Forged Blades, 7536 Trail North Dr., Littleton, CO 80125, Phone: 303-941-1092, tonhug@msn.com
Specialties: Fixed blades, bowies/fighters and hunters of maker's own damascus steel. Technical: Forges damascus and mosaic-damascus blades. Fittings are 416 stainless steel, 1095-and-nickel damascus, 1080-and-15N20 damascus or silicon bronze. Prefers ivory, desert ironwood, blackwood, ebony and other burls. Prices: $450 and up. Remarks: Full-time ABS journeyman smith forging knives for 20 years. Mark: Tony Hughes and JS on the other side.

HULETT, STEVE,
115 Yellowstone Ave, West Yellowstone, MT 59758-0131, Phone: 406-646-4116, Web: www.seldomseenknives.com
Specialties: Classic, working/using knives, straight knives, folders. Your design, custom specs. Patterns: Utility/camp knives, hunters, and LinerLock folders, lock back pocket knives. Technical: Grinds 440C stainless steel, O1 Carbon, 1095. Shop is retail and knife shop; people watch their knives being made. We do everything in house: "all but smelt the ore, or tan the hide." Prices:

Strarting $250 to $7000. Remarks: Full-time maker; first knife sold in 1994. Mark: Seldom seen knives/West Yellowstone Montana.

HULSEY, HOYT,
379 Shiloh, Attalla, AL 35954, Phone: 256-538-6765
Specialties: Traditional working straight knives and folders of his design. Patterns: Hunters and utility/camp knives. Technical: Grinds 440C, ATS-34, O1 and A2. Prices: $75 to $250. Remarks: Part-time maker; first knife sold in 1989. Mark: Hoyt Hulsey Attalla AL.

HUME, DON,
2731 Tramway Circle NE, Albuquerque, NM 87122, Phone: 505-796-9451

HUMENICK, ROY,
PO Box 55, Rescue, CA 95672, rhknives@gmail.com; Web: www.humenick.com
Specialties: Traditional multiblades and tactical slipjoints. Patterns: Original folder and fixed blade designs, also traditional patterns. Technical: Grinds premium steels and Damascus. Prices: $350 and up; some to $1500. Remarks: First knife sold in 1984. Mark: Last name in ARC.

HUMPHREY, LON,
83 Wilwood Ave., Newark, OH 43055, Phone: 740-644-1137, ironcrossforge@hotmail.com
Specialties: Hunters, tacticals, and bowie knives. Prices: I make knives that start in the $150 range and go up to $1000 for a large bowie. Remarks: Has been blacksmithing since age 13 and progressed to the forged blade.

HUMPHREYS, JOEL,
90 Boots Rd, Lake Placid, FL 33852, Phone: 863-773-0439
Specialties: Traditional working/using straight knives and folders of his design and in standard patterns. Patterns: Hunters, folders and utility/camp knives. Technical: Grinds ATS-34, D2, 440C. All knives have tapered tangs, mitered bolster/handle joints, handles of horn or bone fitted sheaths. Prices: $135 to $225; some to $350. Remarks: Part-time maker; first knife sold in 1990. Doing business as Sovereign Knives. Mark: First name or "H" pierced by arrow.

HUNT, MAURICE,
10510NCR650E, Brownsburg, IN 46112, Phone: 317-892-2982, mdhuntknives@juno.com
Patterns: Bowies, hunters, fighters. Prices: $200 to $800. Remarks: Part-time maker. Journeyman Smith.

HUNTER, HYRUM,
285 N 300 W, PO Box 179, Aurora, UT 84620, Phone: 435-529-7244
Specialties: Working straight knives of his design or to customer specs. Patterns: Drop and clip, fighters dagger, some folders. Technical: Forged from two-piece Damascus. Prices: Prices are adjusted according to size, complexity and material used. Remarks: Will consider any design you have. Part-time maker; first knife sold in 1990. Mark: Initials encircled with first initial and last name and city, then state. Some patterns are numbered.

HUNTER, RICHARD D,
7230 NW 200th Ter, Alachua, FL 32615, Phone: 386-462-3150
Specialties: Traditional working/using knives of his design or customer suggestions; filework. Patterns: Folders of various types, Bowies, hunters, daggers. Technical: Traditional blacksmith; hand forges high-carbon steel (5160, 1084, 52100) and makes own Damascus; grinds 440C and ATS-34. Prices: $200 and up. Remarks: Part-time maker; first knife sold in 1992. Mark: Last name in capital letters.

HURST, COLE,
1583 Tedford, E. Wenatchee, WA 98802, Phone: 509-884-9206
Specialties: Fantasy, high-art and traditional straight knives. Patterns: Bowies, daggers and hunters. Technical: Blades are made of stone; handles are made of stone, wood or ivory and embellished with fancy woods, ivory or antlers. Prices: $100 to $300; some to $2000. Remarks: Spare-time maker; first knife sold in 1985. Mark: Name and year.

HURST, JEFF,
PO Box 247, Rutledge, TN 37861, Phone: 865-828-5729, jhurst@esper.com
Specialties: Working straight knives and folders of his design. Patterns: Tomahawks, hunters, boots, folders and fighters. Technical: Forges W2, O1 and his own Damascus. Makes mokume. Prices: $250 to $600. Remarks: Full-time maker; first knife sold in 1984. Doing business as Buzzard's Knob Forge. Mark: Last name; partnered knives are marked with Newman L. Smith, handle artisan, and SH in script.

HUSIAK, MYRON,
PO Box 238, Altona, VIC, AUSTRALIA 3018, Phone: 03-315-6752
Specialties: Straight knives and folders of his design or to customer specs. Patterns: Hunters, fighters, lock-back folders, skinners and boots. Technical: Forges and grinds his own Damascus, 440C and ATS-34. Prices: $200 to $900. Remarks: Part-time maker; first knife sold in 1974. Mark: First initial, last name in logo and serial number.

HUTCHESON, JOHN,
SURSUM KNIFE WORKS, 1237 Brown's Ferry Rd., Chattanooga, TN 37419, Phone: 423-667-6193, sursum5071@aol.com; Web: www.sursumknife.com
Specialties: Straight working knives, hunters. Patterns: Customer designs, hunting, speciality working knives. Technical: Grinds D2, S7, O1 and 5160, ATS-34 on request. Prices: $100 to $300, some to $600. Remarks: First knife sold 1985, also produces a mid-tech line. Doing business as Sursum Knife Works. Mark: Family crest boar's head over 3 arrows.

custom knifemakers

HUTCHINSON, ALAN,
315 Scenic Hill Road, Conway, AR 72034, Phone: 501-470-9653, mama_wolfie@yahoo.com
　Specialties: Bowie knives, fighters and working/hunter knives. Technical: Forges 10 series carbon steels as well as 5160 and 01. Prices: Range from $150 and up. Remarks: Prefers natural handle materials, full-time maker, first forged blade in 1970. Mark: Last name.

HYTOVICK, JOE "HY",
14872 SW 111th St, Dunnellon, FL 34432, Phone: 800-749-5339, Fax: 352-489-3732, hyclassknives@aol.com
　Specialties: Straight, folder and miniature. Technical: Blades from Wootz, Damascus and Alloy steel. Prices: To $5000. Mark: HY.

I

IKOMA, FLAVIO,
R Manoel Rainho Teixeira 108, Presidente Prudente, SP, BRAZIL 19031-220, Phone: 0182-22-0115, fikoma@itelesonica.com.br
　Specialties: Tactical fixed blade knives, LinerLock® folders and balisongs. Patterns: Utility and defense tactical knives built with hi-tech materials. Technical: Grinds S30V and Damasteel. Prices: $500 to $1000. Mark: Ikoma hand made beside Samurai.

IMBODEN II, HOWARD L.,
620 Deauville Dr, Dayton, OH 45429, Phone: 513-439-1536
　Specialties: One-of-a-kind hunting, flint, steel and art knives. Technical: Forges and grinds stainless, high-carbon and Damascus. Uses obsidian, cast sterling silver, 14K and 18K gold guards. Carves ivory animals and more. Prices: $65 to $25,000. Remarks: Full-time maker; first knife sold in 1986. Doing business as Hill Originals. Mark: First and last initials, II.

IMEL, BILLY MACE,
1616 Bundy Ave, New Castle, IN 47362, Phone: 765-529-1651
　Specialties: High-art working knives, period pieces and personal cutlery. Patterns: Daggers, fighters, hunters; locking folders and slip-joints with interframes. Technical: Grinds D2, 440C and 154CM. Prices: $300 to $2000; some to $6000. Remarks: Part-time maker; first knife sold in 1973. Mark: Name in monogram.

IRIE, MICHAEL L,
MIKE IRIE HANDCRAFT, 1606 Auburn Dr., Colorado Springs, CO 80909, Phone: 719-572-5330, mikeirie@aol.com
　Specialties: Working fixed blade knives and handcrafted blades for the do-it-yourselfer. Patterns: Twenty standard designs along with custom. Technical: Blades are ATS-34, BG-43, 440C with some outside Damascus. Prices: Fixed blades $95 and up, blade work $45 and up. Remarks: Formerly dba Wood, Irie and Co. with Barry Wood. Full-time maker since 1991. Mark: Name.

ISAO, OHBUCHI,
702-1 Nouso, Yame-City, Fukuoka, JAPAN, Phone: 0943-23-4439, www.5d.biglobe.ne.jp/~ohisao/

ISHIHARA, HANK,
86-18 Motomachi, Sakura City, Chiba, JAPAN, Phone: 043-485-3208, Fax: 043-485-3208
　Specialties: Fantasy working straight knives and folders of his design. Patterns: Boots, Bowies, daggers, fighters, hunters, fishing, locking folders and utility camp knives. Technical: Grinds ATS-34, 440C, D2, 440V, CV-134, COS25 and Damascus. Engraves. Prices: $250 to $1000; some to $10,000. Remarks: Full-time maker; first knife sold in 1987. Mark: HANK.

J

JACKS, JIM,
344 S. Hollenbeck Ave, Covina, CA 91723-2513, Phone: 626-331-5665
　Specialties: Working straight knives in standard patterns. Patterns: Bowies, hunters, fighters, fishing and camp knives, miniatures. Technical: Grinds Stellite 6K, 440C and ATS-34. Prices: Start at $100. Remarks: Spare-time maker; first knife sold in 1980. Mark: Initials in diamond logo.

JACKSON, CHARLTON R,
6811 Leyland Dr, San Antonio, TX 78239, Phone: 210-601-5112

JACKSON, DAVID,
214 Oleander Ave, Lemoore, CA 93245, Phone: 559-925-8547, jnbcrea@lemoorenet.com
　Specialties: Forged steel. Patterns: Hunters, camp knives, Bowies. Prices: $150 and up. Mark: G.D. Jackson - Maker - Lemoore CA.

JACQUES, ALEX,
10 Exchange St., Apt 1, East Greenwich, RI 02818, Phone: 617-771-4441, customrazors@gmail.com Web: www.customrazors.com
　Specialties: One-of-a-kind, heirloom quality straight razors … functional art. Technical: Damascus, 01, CPM154, and various other high-carbon and stainless steels. Prices: $450 and up. Remarks: First knife sold in 2008. Mark: Jack-O-Lantern logo with "A. Jacques" underneath.

JAKSIK JR., MICHAEL,
427 Marschall Creek Rd, Fredericksburg, TX 78624, Phone: 830-997-1119
　Mark: MJ or M. Jaksik.

JANSEN VAN VUUREN, LUDWIG,
311 Brighton Rd., Waldronville 9018, Dunedin, New Zealand, Phone: 64-3-7421012, ludwig@nzhandmadeknives.co.nz; Web: www.nzhandmadeknives.co.nz
　Specialties: Fixed-blade knives of his design or custom specifications. Patterns: Hunting, fishing, bird-and-trout and chef's knives. Technical: Stock-removal maker, Sandvik 12C27, D2, O1, Damasteel, damascus and other blade steels on request. Handle material includes Micarta, antler and a wide selection of woods. Prices: Starting at $200 and up. Remarks: Part-time maker since 2008. Mark: L J van Vuuren.

JARVIS, PAUL M,
30 Chalk St, Cambridge, MA 02139, Phone: 617-547-4355 or 617-661-3015
　Specialties: High-art knives and period pieces of his design. Patterns: Japanese and Mid-Eastern knives. Technical: Grinds Myer Damascus, ATS-34, D2 and O1. Specializes in height-relief Japanese-style carving. Works with silver, gold and gems. Prices: $200 to $17,000. Remarks: Part-time maker; first knife sold in 1978.

JEAN, GERRY,
25B Cliffside Dr, Manchester, CT 06040, Phone: 860-649-6449
　Specialties: Historic replicas. Patterns: Survival and camp knives. Technical: Grinds A2, 440C and 154CM. Handle slabs applied in unique tongue-and-groove method. Prices: $125 to $250; some to $1000. Remarks: Spare-time maker; first knife sold in 1973. Mark: Initials and serial number.

JEFFRIES, ROBERT W,
Route 2 Box 227, Red House, WV 25168, Phone: 304-586-9780, wvknifeman@hotmail.com; Web: www.jeffriesknileswv.tripod.com
　Specialties: Hunters, Bowies, daggers, lockback folders and LinerLock push buttons. Patterns: Skinning types, drop points, typical working hunters, folders one-of-a-kind. Technical: Grinds all types of steel. Makes his own Damascus. Prices: $125 to $600. Private collector pieces to $3000. Remarks: Starting engraving. Custom folders of his design. Part-time maker since 1988. Mark: Name etched or on plate pinned to blade.

JENKINS, MITCH,
194 East 500 South, Manti, Utah 84642, Phone: 435-813-2532, mitch.jenkins@gmail.com Web: MitchJenkinsKnives.com
　Specialties: Hunters, working knives. Patterns: Johnson and Loveless Style. Drop points, skinners and semi-skinners, Capers and utilities. Technical: 154CM and ATS-34. Experimenting with S30V and love working with Damascus on occasion. Prices: $150 and up. Remarks: Slowly transitioning to full-time maker; first knife made in 2008. Mark: Jenkins Manti, Utah and M. Jenkins, Utah.

JENSEN, JOHN LEWIS,
JENSEN KNIVES, 437 S. Orange Grove Blvd. #3, Pasadena, CA 91105, Phone: 323-559-7454, Fax: 626-449-1148, john@jensenknives.com; Web: www.jensenknives.com
　Specialties: Designer and fabricator of modern, original one-of-a-kind, hand crafted, custom ornamental edged weaponry. Combines skill, precision, distinction and the finest materials, geared toward the discriminating art collector. Patterns: Folding knives and fixed blades, daggers, fighters and swords. Technical: High embellishment, BFA 96 Rhode Island School of Design: jewelry and metalsmithing. Grinds 440C, ATS-34, Damascus. Works with custom made Damascus to his specs. Uses gold, silver, gemstones, pearl, titanium, fossil mastodon and walrus ivories. Carving, file work, soldering, deep etches Damascus, engraving, layers, bevels, blood grooves. Also forges his own Damascus. Prices: Start at $10,000. Remarks: Available on a first come basis and via commission based on his designs. Knifemakers Guild voting member and ABS apprenticesmith and member of the Society of North American Goldsmiths. Mark: Maltese cross/butterfly shield.

JERNIGAN, STEVE,
3082 Tunnel Rd., Milton, FL 32571, Phone: 850-994-0802, Fax: 850-994-0802, jerniganknives@mchsi.com
　Specialties: Investor-class folders and various theme pieces. Patterns: Array of models and sizes in side plate locking interframes and conventional liner construction. Technical: Grinds ATS-34, CPM-T-440V and Damascus. Inlays mokume (and minerals) in blades and sculpts marble cases. Prices: $650 to $1800; some to $6000. Remarks: Full-time maker, first knife sold in 1982. Mark: Last name.

JOBIN, JACQUES,
46 St Dominique, Levis, QC, CANADA G6V 2M7, Phone: 418-833-0283, Fax: 418-833-8378
　Specialties: Fancy and working straight knives and folders; miniatures. Patterns: Minis, fantasy knives, fighters and some hunters. Technical: ATS-34, some Damascus and titanium. Likes native snake wood. Heat-treats. Prices: Start at $250. Remarks: Full-time maker; first knife sold in 1986. Mark: Signature on blade.

JOEHNK, BERND,
Posadowskystrasse 22, Kiel, GERMANY 24148, Phone: 0431-7297705, Fax: 0431-7297705
　Specialties: One-of-a-kind fancy/embellished and traditional straight knives of his design and from customer drawing. Patterns: Daggers, fighters, hunters and letter openers. Technical: Grinds and file 440C, ATS-34, powder metal orgical, commercial Damascus and various stainless and corrosion-resistant steels. Prices: Upscale. Remarks: Likes filework. Leather sheaths. Offers engraving. Part-time maker; first knife sold in 1990. Doing business as metal design kiel. All knives made by hand. Mark: From 2005 full name and city, with certificate.

JOHANNING CUSTOM KNIVES, TOM,
1735 Apex Rd, Sarasota, FL 34240 9386, Phone: 941-371-2104, Fax: 941-378-9427, Web: www.survivalknives.com
  Specialties: Survival knives. Prices: $375 to $775.

JOHANSSON, ANDERS,
Konstvartarevagen 9, Grangesberg, SWEDEN 77240, Phone: 46 240 23204, Fax: +46 21 358778, www.scrimart.u.se
  Specialties: Scandinavian traditional and modern straight knives. Patterns: Hunters, fighters and fantasy knives. Technical: Grinds stainless steel and makes own Damascus. Prefers water buffalo and mammoth for handle material. Prices: Start at $100. Remarks: Spare-time maker; first knife sold in 1994. Works together with scrimshander Viveca Sahlin. Mark: Stylized initials.

JOHNS, ROB,
1423 S. Second, Enid, OK 73701, Phone: 405-242-2707
  Specialties: Classic and fantasy straight knives of his design or to customer specs; fighters for use at Medieval fairs. Patterns: Bowies, daggers and swords. Technical: Forges and grinds 440C, D2 and 5160. Handles of nylon, walnut or wire-wrap. Prices: $150 to $350; some to $2500. Remarks: Full-time maker; first knife sold in 1980. Mark: Medieval Customs, initials.

JOHNSON, C E GENE,
1240 Coan Street, Chesterton, IN 46304, Phone: 219-787-8324, ddjlady55@aol.com
  Specialties: Lock-back folders and springers of his design or to customer specs. Patterns: Hunters, Bowies, survival lock-back folders. Technical: Grinds D2, 440C, A18, O1, Damascus; likes filework. Prices: $100 to $2000. Remarks: Full-time maker; first knife sold in 1975. Mark: Gene.

JOHNSON, DAVID A,
1791 Defeated Creek Rd, Pleasant Shade, TN 37145, Phone: 615-774-3596, artsmith@mwsi.net

JOHNSON, GORDON A.,
981 New Hope Rd, Choudrant, LA 71227, Phone: 318-768-2613
  Specialties:Using straight knives and folders of my design, or customers. Offering filework and hand stitched sheaths. Patterns: Hunters, bowies, folders and miniatures. Technical: Forges 5160, 1084, 52100 and my own Damascus. Some stock removal on working knives and miniatures. Prices: Mid range. Remarks: First knife sold in 1990. ABS apprentice smith. Mark: Interlocking initials G.J. or G. A. J.

JOHNSON, JERRY,
PO Box 491, Spring City, Utah 84662, Phone: 435-851-3604 or 435-462-3688, Web: sanpetesilver.com
  Specialties: Hunter, fighters, camp. Patterns: Multiple. Prices: $225 - $3000. Mark: Jerry E. Johnson Spring City, UT in several fonts.

JOHNSON, JERRY L,
29847 260th St, Worthington, MN 56187, Phone: 507-376-9253; Cell: 507-370-3523, Web: jljknives.com
  Specialties:Straight knives, hunters, bowies, and fighting knives. Patterns: Drop points, trailing points, bowies, and some favorite Loveless patterns. Technical: Grinds ATS 34, 440C, S30V, forges own damascus, mirror finish, satin finish, file work and engraving done by self. Prices: $250 to $1500. Remarks: Part-time maker since 1991, member of knifemakers guild since 2009. Mark: Name over a sheep head or elk head with custom knives under the head.

JOHNSON, JOHN R,
5535 Bob Smith Ave, Plant City, FL 33565, Phone: 813-986-4478, rottyjohn@msn.com
  Specialties: Hand forged and stock removal. Technical: High tech. Folders. Mark: J.R. Johnson Plant City, FL.

JOHNSON, JOHN R,
PO Box 246, New Buffalo, PA 17069, Phone: 717-834-6265, jrj@jrjknives.com; Web: www.jrjknives.com
  Specialties: Working hunting and tactical fixed blade sheath knives. Patterns: Hunters, tacticals, Bowies, daggers, neck knives and primitives. Technical: Flat, convex and hollow grinds. ATS-34, CPM154CM, L6, O1, D2, 5160, 1095 and Damascus. Prices: $60 to $700. Remarks: Full-time maker, first knife sold in 1996. Doing business as JRJ Knives. Custom sheath made by maker for every knife, Mark: Initials connected.

JOHNSON, MIKE,
38200 Main Rd, Orient, NY 11957, Phone: 631-323-3509, mjohnsoncustomknives@hotmail.com
  Specialties: Large Bowie knives and cutters, fighters and working knives to customer specs. Technical: Forges 5160, O1. Prices: $325 to $1200. Remarks: Full-time bladesmith. Mark: Johnson.

JOHNSON, R B,
Box 11, Clearwater, MN 55320, Phone: 320-558-6128, Fax: 320-558-6128, rb@rbjohnsonknives.com; Web: rbjohnsonknives.com
  Specialties: Liner locks with titanium, mosaic Damascus. Patterns: LinerLock® folders, skeleton hunters, frontier Bowies. Technical: Damascus, mosaic Damascus, A-2, O1, 1095. Prices: $200 and up. Remarks: Full-time maker since 1973. Not accepting orders. Mark: R B Johnson (signature).

JOHNSON, RANDY,
2575 E Canal Dr, Turlock, CA 95380, Phone: 209-632-5401
  Specialties: Folders. Patterns: Locking folders. Technical: Grinds Damascus. Prices: $200 to $400. Remarks: Spare-time maker; first knife sold in 1989. Doing business as Puedo Knifeworks. Mark: PUEDO.

JOHNSON, RICHARD,
W165 N10196 Wagon Trail, Germantown, WI 53022, Phone: 262-251-5772, rlj@execpc.com; Web: http://www.execpc.com/~rlj/index.html
  Specialties: Custom knives and knife repair.

JOHNSON, RUFFIN,
215 LaFonda Dr, Houston, TX 77060, Phone: 281-448-4407
  Specialties: Working straight knives and folders. Patterns: Hunters, fighters and locking folders. Technical: Grinds 440C and 154CM; hidden tangs and fancy handles. Prices: $450 to $650; some to $1350. Remarks: Full-time maker; first knife sold in 1972. Mark: Wolf head logo and signature.

JOHNSON, RYAN M,
3103 Excelsior Ave., Signal Mountain, TN 37377, Phone: 866-779-6922, rmjtactical@gmail.com Web: www.rmjforge.com www.rmjtactical.com
  Specialties: Historical and Tactical Tomahawks. Some period knives and folders. Technical: Forges a variety of steels including own Damascus. Prices: $500 - $1200 Remarks: Full-time maker began forging in 1986. Mark: Sledge-hammer with halo.

JOHNSON, STEVEN R,
202 E 200 N, PO Box 5, Manti, UT 84642, Phone: 435-835-7941, srj@mail.manti.com; Web: www.srjknives.com
  Specialties: Investor-class working knives. Patterns: Hunters, fighters, boots. Technical: Grinds CPM 154-CM, CTS 40-CP and CTS-XHP. Prices: $1,500 to $20,000. Remarks: Full-time maker; first knife sold in 1972. Also see SR Johnson forum on www.knifenetwork.com. Mark: Registered trademark, including name, city, state, and optional signature mark.

JOHNSON, TOMMY,
144 Poole Rd., Troy, NC 27371, Phone: 910-975-1817, tommy@tjohnsonknives.com Web: www.tjohnsonknives.com
  Specialties: Straight knives for hunting, fishing, utility, and linerlock and slip joint folders since 1982.

JOHNSON, WM. C. "BILL",
225 Fairfield Pike, Enon, OH 45323, Phone: 937-864-7802, wjohnson64@woh.RR.com
  Patterns: From hunters to art knives as well as custom canes, some with blades. Technical: Stock removal method utilizing 440C, ATS34, 154CPM, and custom Damascus. Prices: $175 to over $2500, depending on design, materials, and embellishments. Remarks: Full-time maker. First knife made in 1978. Member of the Knifemakers Guild since 1982. Mark: Crescent shaped WM. C. "BILL" JOHNSON, ENON OHIO. Also uses an engraved or electro signature on some art knives and on Damascus blades.

JOHNSTON, DR. ROBT,
PO Box 9887 1 Lomb Mem Dr, Rochester, NY 14623

JOKERST, CHARLES,
9312 Spaulding, Omaha, NE 68134, Phone: 402-571-2536
  Specialties: Working knives in standard patterns. Patterns: Hunters, fighters and pocketknives. Technical: Grinds 440C, ATS-34. Prices: $90 to $170. Remarks: Spare-time maker; first knife sold in 1984. Mark: Early work marked RCJ; current work marked with last name and city.

JONES, BARRY M AND PHILLIP G,
221 North Ave, Danville, VA 24540, Phone: 804-793-5282
  Specialties: Working and using straight knives and folders of their design and to customer specs; combat and self-defense knives. Patterns: Bowies, fighters, daggers, swords, hunters and LinerLock® folders. Technical: Grinds 440C, ATS-34 and D2; flat-grinds only. All blades hand polished. Prices: $100 to $1000, some higher. Remarks: Part-time makers; first knife sold in 1989. Mark: Jones Knives, city, state.

JONES, CURTIS J,
210 Springfield Ave, Washington, PA 15301-5244, Phone: 724-225-8829
  Specialties: Big Bowies, daggers, his own style of hunters. Patterns: Bowies, daggers, hunters, swords, boots and miniatures. Technical: Grinds 440C, ATS-34 and D2. Fitted guards only; does not solder. Heat-treats. Custom sheaths: hand-tooled and stitched. Prices: $125 to $1500; some to $3000. Remarks: Full-time maker; first knife sold in 1975. Mail orders accepted. Mark: Stylized initials on either side of three triangles interconnected.

JONES, ENOCH,
7278 Moss Ln, Warrenton, VA 20187, Phone: 540-341-0292
  Specialties: Fancy working straight knives. Patterns: Hunters, fighters, boots and Bowies. Technical: Forges and grinds O1, W2, 440C and Damascus. Prices: $100 to $350; some to $1000. Remarks: Part-time maker; first knife sold in 1982. Mark: First name.

JONES, FRANKLIN (FRANK) W,
6030 Old Dominion Rd, Columbus, GA 31909, Phone: 706-563-6051, frankscuba@bellsouth.net
  Specialties: Traditional/working/tactical/period straight knives of his or your design. Patterns: Hunters, skinners, utility/camp, Bowies, fighters, kitchen, neck knives, Harley chains. Technical: Forges using 5160, O1, 52100, 1084 1095 and Damascus. Also stock removal of stainless steel. Prices: $150 to $1000. Remarks: Full-time, American Bladesmith Society Journeyman Smith. Mark: F.W. Jones, Columbus, GA.

JONES, JACK P.,
17670 Hwy. 2 East, Ripley, MS 38663, Phone: 662-837-3882, jacjones@ripleycable.net
  Specialties: Working knives in classic design. Patterns: Hunters, fighters, and

JONES—KELLY

Bowies. Technical: Grinds D2, A2, CPM-154, CTS-XHP and ATS-34. Prices: $200 and up. Remarks: Full-time maker since retirement in 2005, first knife sold in 1976. Mark: J.P. Jones, Ripley, MS.

JONES, JOHN A,
779 SW 131 Hwy, Holden, MO 64040, Phone: 816-682-0238
Specialties: Working, using knives. Hunters, skinners and fighters. Technical: Grinds D2, O1, 440C, 1095. Prefers forging; creates own Damascus. File working on most blades. Prices: $50 to $500. Remarks: Part-time maker; first knife sold in 1996. Doing business as Old John Knives. Mark: OLD JOHN and serial number.

JONES, ROGER MUDBONE,
GREENMAN WORKSHOP, 320 Prussia Rd, Waverly, OH 45690, Phone: 740-739-4562, greenmanworkshop@yahoo.com
Specialties: Working in cutlery to suit working woodsman and fine collector. Patterns: Bowies, hunters, folders, hatchets in both period and modern style, scale miniatures a specialty. Technical: All cutlery hand forged to shape with traditional methods; multiple quench and draws, limited Damascus production hand carves wildlife and historic themes in stag/antler/ivory, full line of functional and high art leather. All work sole authorship. Prices: $50 to $5000 Remarks: Full-time maker/first knife sold in 1979. Mark: Stamped R. Jones hand made or hand engraved sig. W/Bowie knife mark.

JORGENSEN, CARSON,
1805 W Hwy 116, Mt Pleasant, UT 84647, tcjorgensenknife@gmail.com; Web: tcjknives.com
Specialties: Stock removal, Loveless Johnson and young styles. Prices: Most $100 to $800.

K

K B S, KNIVES,
RSD 181, North Castlemaine, VIC, AUSTRALIA 3450, Phone: 0011 61 3 54 705864, Fax: 0011 61 3 54 706233
Specialties: Bowies, daggers and miniatures. Patterns: Art daggers, traditional Bowies, fancy folders and miniatures. Technical: Hollow or flat grind, most steels. Prices: $200 to $600+. Remarks: Full-time maker; first knife sold in 1983. Mark: Initials and address in Southern Cross motif.

KACZOR, TOM,
375 Wharncliffe Rd N, Upper London, ON, CANADA N6G 1E4, Phone: 519-645-7640

KAGAWA, KOICHI,
1556 Horiyamashita, Hatano-Shi, Kanagawa, JAPAN
Specialties: Fancy high-tech straight knives and folders to customer specs. Patterns: Hunters, locking folders and slip-joints. Technical: Uses 440C and ATS-34. Prices: $500 to $2000; some to $20,000. Remarks: Part-time maker; first knife sold in 1986. Mark: First initial, last name-YOKOHAMA.

KAIN, CHARLES,
KAIN DESIGNS, 1736 E. Maynard Dr., Indianapolis, IN 46227, Phone: 317-781-9549, Fax: 317-781-8521, charles@kaincustomknives.com; Web: www.kaincustomknives.com
Specialties: Unique Damascus art folders. Patterns: Any. Technical: Specialized & patented mechanisms. Remarks: Unique knife & knife mechanism design. Mark: Kain and Signet stamp for unique pieces.

KAJIN, AL,
PO Box 1047, 342 South 6th Ave, Forsyth, MT 59327, Phone: 406-346-2442, kajinknives@cablemt.net
Specialties: Utility/working knives, hunters, kitchen cutlery. Produces own Damascus steel from 15N20 and 1084 and cable. Forges 52100, 5160, 1084, 15N20 and O1. Stock removal ATS-34, D2, O1, and L6. Patterns: All types, especially like to work with customer on their designs. Technical: Maker since 1989. ABS member since 1995. Does own differential heat treating, cryogenic soaking when appropriate. Does all leather work. Prices: Stock removal starts at $250. Forged blades and Damascus starts at $300. Kitchen cutlery starts at $100. Remarks: Likes to use exotic woods. Mark: Interlocked AK on forged blades, etched stylized Kajin in outline of Montana on stock removal knives.

KANKI, IWAO,
691-2 Tenjincho, Ono-City, Hyogo, JAPAN 675-1316, Phone: 07948-3-2555, Web: www.chiyozurusadahide.jp
Specialties: Plane, knife. Prices: Not determined yet. Remarks:Masters of traditional crafts designated by the Minister of International Trade and Industry (Japan). Mark: Chiyozuru Sadahide.

KANSEI, MATSUNO,
109-8 Uenomachi, Nishikaiden, Gifu, JAPAN 501-1168, Phone: 81-58-234-8643
Specialties: Folders of original design. Patterns: LinerLock® folder. Technical: Grinds VG-10, Damascus. Prices: $350 to $2000. Remarks: Full-time maker. First knife sold in 1993. Mark: Name.

KANTER, MICHAEL,
ADAM MICHAEL KNIVES, 14550 West Honey Ln., New Berlin, WI 53151, Phone: 262-860-1136, mike@adammichaelknives.com; Web: www.adammichaelknives.com
Specialties: Fixed blades and folders. Patterns: Drop point hunters, Bowies and fighters. Technical: Jerry Rados Damascus, BG42, CPM, S60V and S30V. Prices: $375 and up. Remarks: Ivory, mammoth ivory, stabilized woods, and pearl handles. Mark: Engraved Adam Michael.

KARP, BOB,
PO Box 47304, Phoenix, AZ 85068, Phone: 602 870-1234
602 870-1234, Fax: 602-331-0283
Remarks: Bob Karp "Master of the Blade."

KATO, SHINICHI,
Rainbow Amalke 402, Moriyama-ku Nagoya, Aichi, JAPAN 463-0002, Phone: 81-52-736-6032, skato-402@u0l.gate01.com
Specialties: Flat grind and hand finish. Patterns: Bowie, fighter. Hunting and folding knives. Technical: Hand forged,flat grind. Prices: $100 to $2000. Remarks: Part-time maker. Mark: Name.

KATSUMARO, SHISHIDO,
2-6-11 Kamiseno, Aki-ku, Hiroshima, JAPAN, Phone: 090-3634-9054, Fax: 082-227-4438, shishido@d8.dion.ne.jp

KAUFFMAN, DAVE,
4 Clark Creek Loop, Montana City, MT 59634, Phone: 406-442-9328
Specialties: Field grade and exhibition grade hunting knives and ultra light folders. Patterns: Fighters, Bowies and drop-point hunters. Technical: S30V and SS Damascus. Prices: $155 to $1200. Remarks: Full-time maker; first knife sold in 1989. On the cover of Knives '94. Mark: First and last name, city and state.

KAY, J WALLACE,
332 Slab Bridge Rd, Liberty, SC 29657

KAZSUK, DAVID,
PO Box 39, Perris, CA 92572-0039, Phone: 909-780-2288, ddkaz@hotmail.com
Specialties: Hand forged. Prices: $150+. Mark: Last name.

KEARNEY, JAROD,
1505 Parkersburg Turnpike, Swoope, VA 24479, jarodkearney@gmail.com Web: www.jarodkearney.com
Patterns: Bowies, skinners, hunters, Japanese blades, Sgian Dubhs

KEESLAR, JOSEPH F,
391 Radio Rd, Almo, KY 42020, Phone: 270-753-7919, Fax: 270-753-7919, sjkees@apex.net
Specialties: Classic and contemporary Bowies, combat, hunters, daggers and folders. Patterns: Decorative filework, engraving and custom leather sheaths available. Technical: Forges 5160, 52100 and his own Damascus steel. Prices: $300 to $3000. Remarks: Full-time maker; first knife sold in 1976. ABS Master Smith, and 50 years as a bladesmith (1962-2012). Mark: First and middle initials, last name in hammer, knife and anvil logo, M.S.

KEESLAR, STEVEN C,
115 Lane 216 Hamilton Lake, Hamilton, IN 46742, Phone: 260-488-3161, sskeeslar@hotmail.com
Specialties: Traditional working/using straight knives of his design and to customer specs. Patterns: Bowies, hunters, utility/camp knives. Technical: Forges 5160, files 52100 Damascus. Prices: $100 to $600; some to $1500. Remarks: Part-time maker; first knife sold in 1976. ABS member. Mark: Fox head in flames over Steven C. Keeslar.

KEETON, WILLIAM L,
6095 Rehobeth Rd SE, Laconia, IN 47135-9550, Phone: 812-969-2836, wlkeeton@hughes.net; Web: www.keetoncustomknives.com
Specialties: Plain and fancy working knives. Patterns: Hunters and fighters; locking folders and slip-joints. Names patterns after Kentucky Derby winners. Technical: Grinds any of the popular alloy steels. Prices: $185 to $8000. Remarks: Full-time maker; first knife sold in 1971. Mark: Logo of key.

KEHIAYAN, ALFREDO,
Cuzco 1455 Ing., Maschwitz, Buenos Aires, ARGENTINA B1623GXU, Phone: 540-348-4442212, Fax: 54-077-75-4493-5359, alfredo@kehiayan.com.ar; Web: www.kehiayan.com.ar
Specialties: Functional straight knives. Patterns: Utility knives, skinners, hunters and boots. Technical: Forges and grinds SAE 52.100, SAE 6180, SAE 9260, SAE 5160, 440C and ATS-34, titanium with nitride. All blades mirror-polished; makes leather sheath and wood cases. Prices: From $350 up. Remarks: Full-time maker; first knife sold in 1983. Some knives are satin finish (utility knives). Mark: Name.

KEISUKE, GOTOH,
105 Cosumo-City Otozu 202, Oita-city, Oita, JAPAN, Phone: 097-523-0750, k-u-an@ki.rim.or.jp

KELLER, BILL,
12211 Las Nubes, San Antonio, TX 78233, Phone: 210-653-6609
Specialties: Primarily folders, some fixed blades. Patterns: Autos, liner locks and hunters. Technical: Grinds stainless and Damascus. Prices: $400 to $1000, some to $4000. Remarks: Part-time maker, first knife sold 1995. Mark: Last name inside outline of Alamo.

KELLEY, GARY,
17485 SW Pheasant Lane, Aloha, OR 97006, Phone: 503-649-7867, garykelley@thebladmaker.com; Web: wwwthebladmaker.com
Specialties: Primitive knives and blades. Patterns: Fur trade era rifleman's knives, tomahawks, and hunting knives. Technical: Hand-forges and precision investment casts. Prices: $35 to $125. Remarks: Family business. Doing business as The Blademaker. Mark: Fir tree logo.

KELLY, DAVE,
865 S. Shenandoah St., Los Angeles, CA 90035, Phone: 310-657-7121, dakcon@sbcglobal.net
Specialties: Collector and user one-of-a-kind (his design) fixed blades, liner lock folders, and leather sheaths. Patterns: Utility and hunting fixed blade knives with

hand-sewn leather sheaths, Gentleman liner lock folders. Technical: Grinds carbon steels, hollow, convex, and flat. Offers clay differentially hardened blades, etched and polished. Uses Sambar stag, mammoth ivory, and high-grade burl woods. Hand-sewn leather sheaths for fixed blades and leather pouch sheaths for folders. Prices: $250 to $750, some higher. Remarks: Full-time maker, first knife made in 2003. Mark: First initial, last name with large K.

KELLY, STEVEN,
11407 Spotted Fawn Ln., Bigfork, MT 59911, Phone: 406-837-1489, www. skknives.com
Technical: Damascus from 1084 or 1080 and 15n20. 52100.

KELSEY, NATE,
5901 Arctic Blvd., Unit M, Anchorage, AK 99518, Phone: 907-360-4469, edgealaska@mac.com; Web: www.edgealaska.com
Specialties: Forges high-performance 52100, stock removal on 154CM for Extreme Duty Worldwide. Patterns: Hunters, fighters and bowies. Prices: Material dependent, $175 to $3,000. Remarks: Maker since 1990, member ABS. Mark: EDGE ALASKA.

KELSO, JIM,
577 Collar Hill Rd, Worcester, VT 05682, Phone: 802-229-4254, Fax: 802-229-0595, kelsomaker@gmail.com; Web:www.jimkelso.com
Specialties: Fancy high-art straight knives and folders that mix Eastern and Western influences. Only uses own designs. Patterns: Daggers, swords and locking folders. Technical: Works with top bladesmiths. Prices: $6,000 to $30,000 . Remarks: Full-time maker; first knife sold in 1980. Mark: Stylized initials.

KEMP, LAWRENCE,
8503 Water Tower Rd, Ooltewah, TN 37363, Phone: 423-344-2357, larry@kempknives.com Web: www.kempknives.com
Specialties: Bowies, hunters and working knives. Patterns: Bowies, camp knives, hunters and skinners. Technical: Forges carbon steel, and his own Damascus. Prices: $250 to $1500. Remarks: Part-time maker, first knife sold in 1991. ABS Journeyman Smith since 2006. Mark: L.A. Kemp.

KENNEDY JR., BILL,
PO Box 850431, Yukon, OK 73085, Phone: 405-354-9150
Specialties: Working straight knives and folders. Patterns: Hunters, minis, fishing, and pocket knives. Technical: Grinds D2, 440C, ATS-34, BG42. Prices: $110 and up. Remarks: Part-time maker; first knife sold in 1980. Mark: Last name and year made.

KERANEN, PAUL,
4122 S. E. Shiloh Ct., Tacumseh, KS 66542, Phone: 785-220-2141, pk6269@yahoo.com
Specialties:Specializes in Japanese style knives and swords. Most clay tempered with hamon. Patterns: Does bowies, fighters and hunters. Technical: Forges and grinds carbons steel only. Make my own Damascus. Prices: $75 to $800. Mark: Keranen arched over anvil.

KERN, R W,
20824 Texas Trail W, San Antonio, TX 78257-1602, Phone: 210-698-2549, rkern@ev1.net
Specialties: Damascus, straight and folders. Patterns: Hunters, Bowies and folders. Technical: Grinds ATS-34, 440C and BG42. Forges own Damascus. Prices: $200 and up. Remarks: First knives 1980; retired; work as time permits. Member ABS, Texas Knifemaker and Collectors Association. Mark: Outline of Alamo with kern over outline.

KEYES, DAN,
6688 King St, Chino, CA 91710, Phone: 909-628-8329

KEYES, GEOFF P.,
13027 Odell Rd NE, Duvall, WA 98019, Phone: 425-844-0758, 5ef@polarisfarm.com/ Web: www5elementsforge.com
Specialties: Working grade fixed blades, 19th century style gents knives. Patterns: Fixed blades, your design or mine. Technical: Hnad-forged 5160, 1084, and own Damascus. Prices: $200 and up. Remarks: Geoff Keyes DBA 5 Elements Forge, ABS Journeyman Smith. Mark: Early mark KEYES etched in script. New mark as of 2009: pressed GPKeyes.

KHALSA, JOT SINGH,
368 Village St, Millis, MA 02054, Phone: 508-376-8162, Fax: 508-532-0517, jotkhalsa@comcast.net; Web: www.khalsakirpans.com, www.lifeknives.com, and www.thekhalsaraj.com
Specialties: Liner locks, one-of-a-kind daggers, swords, and kirpans (Sikh daggers) all original designs. Technical: Forges own Damascus, uses others high quality Damascus including stainless, and grinds stainless steels. Uses natural handle materials frequently unusual minerals. Pieces are frequently engraved and more recently carved. Prices: Start at $700.

KHARLAMOV, YURI,
Oboronnay 46, Tula, RUSSIA 300007
Specialties: Classic, fancy and traditional knives of his design. Patterns: Daggers and hunters. Technical: Forges only Damascus with nickel. Uses natural handle materials; engraves on metal; carves on nut-tree; silver and pearl inlays. Prices: $600 to $2380; some to $4000. Remarks: Full-time maker; first knife sold in 1988. Mark: Initials.

KI, SHIVA,
5222 Ritterman Ave, Baton Rouge, LA 70805, Phone: 225-356-7274, shivakicustomknives@netzero.net; Web: www.shivakicustomknives.com
Specialties: Working straight knives and folders. Patterns: Emphasis on personal defense knives, martial arts weapons. Technical: Forges and grinds; makes own Damascus; prefers natural handle materials. Prices: $550 to $10,000.Remarks:

Full-time maker; first knife sold in 1981. Mark: Name with logo.

KIEFER, TONY,
112 Chateaugay Dr, Pataskala, OH 43062, Phone: 740-927-6910
Specialties: Traditional working and using straight knives in standard patterns. Patterns: Bowies, fighters and hunters. Technical: Grinds 440C and D2; forges D2. Flat-grinds Bowies; hollow-grinds drop-point and trailing-point hunters. Prices: $110 to $300; some to $200. Remarks: Spare-time maker; first knife sold in 1988. Mark: Last name.

KILBY, KEITH,
1902 29th St, Cody, WY 82414, Phone: 307-587-2732
Specialties: Works with all designs. Patterns: Mostly Bowies, camp knives and hunters of his design. Technical: Forges 52100, 5160, 1095, Damascus and mosaic Damascus. Prices: $250 to $3500. Remarks: Part-time maker; first knife sold in 1974. Doing business as Foxwood Forge. Mark: Name.

KILEY, MIKE AND JANDY,
ROCKING K KNIVES, 1325 Florida, Chino Valley, AZ 86323, Phone: 928-910-2647
Specialties: Period knives for cowboy action shooters and mountain men. Patterns: Bowies, drop-point hunters, skinners, sheepsfoot blades and spear points. Technical: Steels are 1095, O-1, Damascus and others upon request. Handles include all types of wood, with cocobolo, ironwood, rosewood, maple and bacote being favorites as well as buffalo horn, stag, elk antler, mammoth ivory, giraffe boon, sheep horn and camel bone. Prices: $100 to $500 depending on style and materials. Hand-tooled leather sheaths by Jan and Mike. Mark: Stylized K on one side; Kiley on the other.

KILPATRICK, CHRISTIAN A,
6925 Mitchell Ct, Citrus Hieghts, CA 95610, Phone: 916-729-0733, crimsonkil@gmail.com; Web:www.crimsonknives.com
Specialties: All forged weapons (no firearms) from ancient to modern. All blades produced are first and foremost useable tools, and secondly but no less importantly, artistic expressions. Patterns: Hunters, bowies, daggers, swords, axes, spears, boot knives, bird knives, ethnic blades and historical reproductions. Customer designs welcome. Technical: Forges and grinds, makes own Damascus. Does file work. Prices: $125 to $3200. Remarks: 26 year part time maker. First knife sold in 2002.

KIMBERLEY, RICHARD L.,
86-B Arroyo Hondo Rd, Santa Fe, NM 87508, Phone: 505-820-2727
Specialties: Fixed-blade and period knives. Technical: O1, 52100, 9260 steels. Remarks: Member ABS. Marketed under "Kimberleys of Santa Fe." Mark: "By D. KIMBERLEY SANTA FE NM."

KIMSEY, KEVIN,
198 Cass White Rd. NW, Cartersville, GA 30121, Phone: 770-387-0779 and 770-655-8879
Specialties: Tactical fixed blades and folders. Patterns: Fighters, folders, hunters and utility knives. Technical: Grinds 440C, ATS-34 and D2 carbon. Prices: $100 to $400; some to $600. Remarks: Three-time Blade magazine award winner, knifemaker since 1983. Mark: Rafter and stylized KK.

KING, BILL,
14830 Shaw Rd, Tampa, FL 33625, Phone: 813-961-3455, billkingknives@yahoo.com
Specialties: Folders, lockbacks, liner locks, automatics and stud openers. Patterns: Wide varieties; folders. Technical: ATS-34 and some Damascus; single and double grinds. Offers filework and jewel embellishment; nickel-silver Damascus and mokume bolsters. Prices: $150 to $475; some to $850. Remarks: Full-time maker; first knife sold in 1976. All titanium fitting on liner-locks; screw or rivet construction on lock-backs. Mark: Last name in crown.

KING, FRED,
430 Grassdale Rd, Cartersville, GA 30120, Phone: 770-382-8478, Web: http://www.fking83264@aol.com
Specialties: Fancy and embellished working straight knives and folders. Patterns: Hunters, Bowies and fighters. Technical: Grinds ATS-34 and D2: forges 5160 and Damascus. Offers filework. Prices: $100 to $3500. Remarks: Spare-time maker; first knife sold in 1984. Mark: Kings Edge.

KING JR., HARVEY G,
32170 Hwy K4, Alta Vista, KS 66834, Phone: 785-499-5207, Web: www.harveykingknives.com
Specialties: Traditional working and using straight knives of his design and to customer specs. Patterns: Hunters, Bowies and fillet knives. Technical: Grinds O1, A2 and D2. Prefers natural handle materials; offers leatherwork. Prices: Start at $125. Remarks: Full-time maker; first knife sold in 1988. Mark: Name, city, state, and serial number.

KINKER, MIKE,
8755 E County Rd 50 N, Greensburg, IN 47240, Phone: 812-663-5277, kinkercustomknives@gmail.com
Specialties: Working/using knives, straight knives. Starting to make folders. Your design. Patterns: Boots, daggers, hunters, skinners, hatchets. Technical: Grind 440C and ATS-34, others if required. Damascus, dovetail bolsters, jeweled blade. Prices: $125 to 375; some to $1000. Remarks: Part-time maker; first knife sold in 1991. Doing business as Kinker Custom Knives. Mark: Kinker

KINNIKIN, TODD,
EUREKA FORGE, 7 Capper Dr., Pacific, MO 63069-3603, Phone: 314-938-6248
Specialties: Mosaic Damascus. Patterns: Hunters, bowies, folders and automatics. Technical: Forges own mosaic Damascus with tool steel Damascus edge. Prefers natural, fossil and artifact handle materials. Prices: $1200 to $2400.

custom knifemakers

KIOUS—KRAFT

Remarks: Full-time maker; first knife sold in 1994. Mark: Initials connected.

KIOUS, JOE,
1015 Ridge Pointe Rd, Kerrville, TX 78028, Phone: 830-367-2277, kious@hctc.net
Specialties: Investment-quality interframe and bolstered folders. Patterns: Folder specialist, all types. Technical: Both stainless and non-stainless Damascus. Also uses CPM 154CM, M4, and CPM D2. Prices: $1300 to $5000; some to $10,000. Remarks: Full-time maker; first knife sold in 1969. Mark: Last name, city and state or last name only.

KIRK, RAY,
PO Box 1445, Tahlequah, OK 74465, Phone: 918-207-8076, ray@rakerknives.com; Web: www.rakerknives.com
Specialties: Folders, skinners fighters, and Bowies. Patterns: Neck knives and small hunters and skinners. Full and hidden-tang integrals from 52100 round bar. Technical: Forges all knives from 52100 and own damascus. Prices: $65 to $3000. Remarks: Started forging in 1989; makes own Damascus. Mark: Stamped "Raker" on blade.

KIRKES, BILL,
235 Oaklawn Cir., Little Rock, AR 72206, Phone: 501-551-0135, bill@kirkesknives.com; Web: www.kirkesknives.com
Specialties: Handforged fixed blades. Technical: High-carbon 5160 and 1084 blade steels. Will build to customer's specs, prefers to use natural handle material. Remarks: ABS Journeyman smith. Mark: Kirkes.

KITSMILLER, JERRY,
67277 Las Vegas Dr, Montrose, CO 81401, Phone: 970-249-4290
Specialties: Working straight knives in standard patterns. Patterns: Hunters, boots. Technical: Grinds ATS-34 and 440C only. Prices: $75 to $200; some to $300. Remarks: Spare-time maker; first knife sold in 1984. Mark: JandS Knives.

KLAASEE, TINUS,
PO Box 10221, George, WC, SOUTH AFRICA 6530
Specialties: Hunters, skinners and utility knives. Patterns: Uses own designs and client specs. Technical: N690 stainless steel 440C Damascus. Prices: $700 and up. Remarks: Use only indigenous materials. Hardwood, horns and ivory. Makes his own sheaths and boxes. Mark: Initials and sur name over warthog.

KLEIN, KEVIN,
129 Cedar St., Apt. 2, Boston, MA 02119, Phone: 609-937-8949, kevin.a.klein779@gmail.com
Specialties: Forged damascus blades using 15N20 and 1084. Remarks: Full-time maker; first knife made in 2012. Apprentice to J.D. Smith starting in 2012. Mark: KAK? or ?, depending on piece.

KNAPP, MARK,
Mark Knapp Custom Knives, 1971 Fox Ave, Fairbanks, AK 99701, Phone: 907-452-7477, info@markknappcustomknives.com; Web: www.markknappcustomknives.com
Specialties: Mosaic handles of exotic natural materials from Alaska and around the world. Folders, fixed blades, full and hidden tangs. Patterns: Folders, hunters, skinners, and camp knives. Technical: Forges own Damascus, uses both forging and stock removal with ATS-34, 154CM, stainless Damascus, carbon steel and carbon Damascus. Prices: $800-$3000. Remarks: Full time maker, sold first knife in 2000. Mark: Mark Knapp Custom Knives Fairbanks, AK.

KNAPTON, CHRIS C.,
76 Summerland Dr., Henderson, Aukland, NEW ZEALAND, Phone: 098-353-598, knappo@xtra.co.nz
Specialties: Working and fancy straight knives of his own design. Patterns: Utility, hunters, skinners, Persian, all full tang. Technical: Predominate knife steel 12C27, also in use CPM154. High class natural and synthetic handle materials used. All blades made via the stock removal method and flat ground. Prices: $180 - $450; some higher. Remarks: Part-time maker. Mark: Stylized letter K and country name.

KNICKMEYER, HANK,
6300 Crosscreek, Cedar Hill, MO 63016, Phone: 636-285-3210
Specialties: Complex mosaic Damascus constructions. Patterns: Fixed blades, swords, folders and automatics. Technical: Mosaic Damascus with all tool steel Damascus edges. Prices: $500 to $2000; some $3000 and higher. Remarks: Part-time maker; first knife sold in 1989. Doing business as Dutch Creek Forge and Foundry. Mark: Initials connected.

KNICKMEYER, KURT,
6344 Crosscreek, Cedar Hill, MO 63016, Phone: 314-274-0481

KNIGHT, JASON,
110 Paradise Pond Ln, Harleyville, SC 29448, Phone: 843-452-1163, jasonknightknives.com
Specialties: Bowies. Patterns: Bowies and anything from history or his own design. Technical: 1084, 5160, O1, 52102, Damascus/forged blades. Prices: $200 and up. Remarks: Bladesmith. Mark: KNIGHT.

KNIPSCHIELD, TERRY,
808 12th Ave NE, Rochester, MN 55906, Phone: 507-288-7829, terry@knipknives.com; Web: www.knipknives.com
Specialties: Folders and fixed blades and leatherworking knives. Patterns: Variations of traditional patterns and his own new designs. Technical: Stock removal. Grinds CPM-154CM, ATS-34, stainless Damascus, 01. Prices: $60 to $1200 and higher for upscale folders. Mark: Etchd logo on blade, KNIP with shield image.

KNOTT, STEVE,
KNOTT KNIVES, 203 Wild Rose, Guyton, GA 31312, Phone: 912-536-7651, knottknives@yahoo.com; FaceBook: Knott Knives/Steve Knott
Technical: Uses ATS-34/440C and some commercial Damascus, single and double grinds with mirror or satin finishes. Patterns: Hunters, boot knives, bowies, and tantos, slip joint, LinerLock and lock-back folders. Uses a wide variety of handle materials to include ironwood, coca-bola and colored stabilized wood, also horn, bone and ivory upon customer request. Remarks: First knife sold in 1991. Part-time maker.

KNOWLES, SHAWN,
750 Townsbury Rd, Great Meadows, NJ 07838, Phone: 973-670-3307, skcustomknives@gmail.com Web: shawnknowlescustomknives.com

KNUTH, JOSEPH E,
3307 Lookout Dr, Rockford, IL 61109, Phone: 815-874-9597
Specialties: High-art working straight knives of his design or to customer specs. Patterns: Daggers, fighters and swords. Technical: Grinds 440C, ATS-34 and D2. Prices: $150 to $1500; some to $15,000. Remarks: Full-time maker; first knife sold in 1989. Mark: Initials on bolster face.

KOHLS, JERRY,
N4725 Oak Rd, Princeton, WI 54968, Phone: 920-295-3648
Specialties: Working knives and period pieces. Patterns: Hunters-boots and Bowies, your designs or his. Technical: Grinds, ATS-34 440c 154CM and 1095 and commercial Damascus. Remarks: Part-time maker. Mark: Last name.

KOJETIN, W,
20 Bapaume Rd Delville, Germiston, GT, SOUTH AFRICA 1401, Phone: 27118733305/mobile 27836256208
Specialties: High-art and working straight knives of all designs. Patterns: Daggers, hunters and his own Man hunter Bowie. Technical: Grinds D2 and ATS-34; forges and grinds 440B/C. Offers "wrap-around" pava and abalone handles, scrolled wood or ivory, stacked filework and setting of faceted semi-precious stones. Prices: $185 to $600; some to $11,000. Remarks: Spare-time maker; first knife sold in 1962. Mark: Billy K.

KOLITZ, ROBERT,
W9342 Canary Rd, Beaver Dam, WI 53916, Phone: 920-887-1287
Specialties: Working straight knives to customer specs. Patterns: Bowies, hunters, bird and trout knives, boots. Technical: Grinds O1, 440C; commercial Damascus. Prices: $50 to $100; some to $500. Remarks: Spare-time maker; first knife sold in 1979. Mark: Last initial.

KOMMER, RUSS,
4609 35th Ave N, Fargo, ND 58102, Phone: 701-281-1826, russkommer@yahoo.com Web: www.russkommerknives.com
Specialties: Working straight knives with the outdoorsman in mind. Patterns: Hunters, semi-skinners, fighters, folders and utility knives, art knives. Technical: Hollow-grinds ATS-34, 440C and 440V. Prices: $125 to $850; some to $3000. Remarks: Full-time maker; first knife sold in 1995. Mark: Bear paw—full name, city and state or full name and state.

KOPP, TODD M,
PO Box 3474, Apache Jct., AZ 85217, Phone: 480-983-6143, tmkopp@msn.com
Specialties: Classic and traditional straight knives. Fluted handled daggers. Patterns: Bowies, boots, daggers, fighters, hunters, swords and folders. Technical: Grinds 5160, 440C, ATS-34. All Damascus steels, or customers choice. Some engraving and filework. Prices: $200 to $1200; some to $4000. Remarks: Part-time maker; first knife sold in 1989. Mark: Last name in Old English, some others name, city and state.

KOSTER, STEVEN C,
16261 Gentry Ln, Huntington Beach, CA 92647, Phone: 714-907-7250, kosterknives@verizon.net Web: www.kosterhandforgedknives.com
Specialties: Walking sticks, hand axes, tomahawks, Damascus.Patterns: Ladder, twists, round horn. Technical: Use 5160, 52100, 1084, 1095 steels. Ladder, twists, Prices: $200 to $1000. Remarks: Wood and leather sheaths with silver furniture. ABS Journeyman 2003. California knifemakers member. Mark: Koster squeezed between lines.

KOVACIK, ROBERT,
Erenburgova 23, 98401 Lucenec, SLOVAKIA, Phone: Mobil:00421907644800, kovacikart@gmail.com Web: www.robertkovacik.com
Specialties: Engraved hunting knives, guns engraved; Knifemakers. Technical: Fixed blades, folder knives, miniatures. Prices: $350 to $10,000 U.S. Mark: R.

KOVAR, EUGENE,
2626 W 98th St., Evergreen Park, IL 60642, Phone: 708-636-3724/708-790-4115, baldemaster333@aol.com
Specialties: One-of-a-kind miniature knives only. Patterns: Fancy to fantasy miniature knives; knife pendants and tie tacks. Technical: Files and grinds nails, nickel-silver and sterling silver. Prices: $5 to $35; some to $100. Mark: GK.

KOYAMA, CAPTAIN BUNSHICHI,
3-23 Shirako-cho, Nakamura-ku, Nagoya, Aichi, JAPAN City 453-0817, Phone: 052-461-7070, Fax: 052-461-7070
Specialties: Innovative folding knife. Patterns: General purpose one hand. Technical: Grinds ATS-34 and Damascus. Prices: $400 to $900; some to $1500. Remarks: Part-time maker; first knife sold in 1994. Mark: Captain B. Koyama and the shoulder straps of CAPTAIN.

KRAFT, STEVE,
408 NE 11th St, Abilene, KS 67410, Phone: 785-263-1411
Specialties: Folders, lockbacks, scale release auto, push button auto. Patterns: Hunters, boot knives and fighters. Technical: Grinds ATS-34, Damascus; uses titanium, pearl, ivory etc. Prices: $500 to $2500. Remarks: Part-time maker; first

knife sold in 1984. Mark: Kraft.

KRAPP, DENNY,
1826 Windsor Oak Dr, Apopka, FL 32703, Phone: 407-880-7115
Specialties: Fantasy and working straight knives of his design. Patterns: Hunters, fighters and utility/camp knives. Technical: Grinds ATS-34 and 440C. Prices: $85 to $300; some to $800. Remarks: Spare-time maker; first knife sold in 1988. Mark: Last name.

KRAUSE, JIM,
3272 Hwy H, Farmington, MO 63640, Phone: 573-756-7388, james_krause@sbcglobal.net
Specialties: Folders, fixed blades, neck knives. Patterns: Stock removal. Technical: K390, CPM-S35VN, CPM-S30V, most CPM steel, 1095, stainless and high-carbon damascus from the best makers. Remarks: Full-time maker; first knife made in 2000. Mark: Krause Handmade with Christian fish.

KRAUSE, ROY W,
22412 Corteville, St. Clair Shores, MI 48081, Phone: 810-296-3995, Fax: 810-296-2663
Specialties: Military and law enforcement/Japanese-style knives and swords. Patterns: Combat and back-up, Bowies, fighters, boot knives, daggers, tantos, wakazashis and katanas. Technical: Grinds ATS-34, A2, D2, 1045, O1 and commercial Damascus; differentially hardened Japanese-style blades. Prices: Moderate to upscale. Remarks: Full-time maker. Mark: Last name on traditional knives; initials in Japanese characters on Japanese-style knives.

KREGER, THOMAS,
1996 Dry Branch Rd., Lugoff, SC 29078, Phone: 803-438-4221, tdkreger@bellsouth.net
Specialties: South Carolina/George Herron style working/using knives. Customer designs considered. Patterns: Hunters, skinners, fillet, liner lock folders, kitchen, and camp knives. Technical: Hollow and flat grinds of ATS-34, CPM154CM, and 5160. Prices: $100 and up. Remarks: Full-time maker. President of the South Carolina Association of Knifemakers 2002-06. Mark: TDKreger.

KREH, LEFTY,
210 Wichersham Way, "Cockeysville", MD 21030

KREIBICH, DONALD L.,
1638 Commonwealth Circle, Reno, NV 89503, Phone: 775-746-0533, dmkreno@sbcglobal.net
Specialties: Working straight knives in standard patterns. Patterns: Bowies, boots and daggers; camp and fishing knives. Technical: Grinds 440C, 154CM and ATS-34; likes integrals. Prices: $100 to $200; some to $500. Remarks: Part-time maker; first knife sold in 1980. Mark: First and middle initials, last name.

KRESSLER, D F,
Mittelweg 31 i, D-28832 Achim, GERMANY 28832, Phone: +49 (0) 42 02/76-5742, Fax: +49 (0) 42 02/7657 41, info@kresslerknives.com; Web: www.kresslerknives.com
Specialties: High-tech integral and interframe knives. Patterns: Hunters, fighters, daggers. Technical: Grinds new state-of-the-art steels; prefers natural handle materials. Prices: Upscale. Mark: Name in logo.

KUBASEK, JOHN A,
74 Northhampton St, Easthampton, MA 01027, Phone: 413-527-7917, jaknife01@yahoo.com
Specialties: Left- and right-handed LinerLock® folders of his design or to customer specs. Also new knives made with Ripcord patent. Patterns: Fighters, tantos, drop points, survival knives, neck knives and belt buckle knives. Technical: Grinds 154CM, S30 and Damascus. Prices: $395 to $1500. Remarks: Part-time maker; first knife sold in 1985. Mark: Name and address etched.

KUKULKA, WOLFGANG,
Golf Tower 2, Apt. 107, Greens, PO BOX 126229, Dubai, UNITED ARAB EMIRATES, Phone: 00971-50-2201047, wolfgang.kukulka@hotmail.com
Specialties: Fully handmade from various steels: Damascus Steel, Japanese Steel, 1.2842, 1.2379, K110, K360, M390 microclean Patterns: Handles made from stabilized wood, different hard woods, horn and various materials Technical: Hardness of blades: 58-67 HRC.

L

LADD, JIM S,
1120 Helen, Deer Park, TX 77536, Phone: 713-479-7286
Specialties: Working knives and period pieces. Patterns: Hunters, boots and Bowies plus other straight knives. Technical: Grinds D2, 440C and 154CM. Prices: $125 to $225; some to $550. Remarks: Part-time maker; first knife sold in 1965. Mark: First and middle initials, last name.

LADD, JIMMIE LEE,
1120 Helen, Deer Park, TX 77536, Phone: 713-479-7186
Specialties: Working straight knives. Patterns: Hunters, skinners and utility knives. Technical: Grinds 440C and D2. Prices: $75 to $225. Remarks: First knife sold in 1979. Mark: First and middle initials, last name.

LAINSON, TONY,
114 Park Ave, Council Bluffs, IA 51503, Phone: 712-322-5222
Specialties: Working straight knives, liner locking folders. Technical: Grinds 154CM, ATS-34, 440C buys Damascus. Handle materials include Micarta, carbon fiber G-10 ivory pearl and bone. Prices: $95 to $600. Remarks: Part-time maker; first knife sold in 1987. Mark: Name and state.

LAIRSON SR., JERRY,
HC 68 Box 970, Ringold, OK 74754, Phone: 580-876-3426, bladesmt@brightok.net; Web: www.lairson-custom-knives.net
Specialties: Damascus collector grade knives & high performance field grade hunters & cutting competition knives. Patterns: Damascus, random, raindrop, ladder, twist and others. Technical: All knives hammer forged. Mar TemperingPrices: Field grade knives $300. Collector grade $400 & up. Mark: Lairson. Remarks: Makes any style knife but prefer fighters and hunters. ABS Mastersmith, AKA member, KGA member. Cutting competition competitor.

LAKE, RON,
3360 Bendix Ave, Eugene, OR 97401, Phone: 541-484-2683
Specialties: High-tech working knives; inventor of the modern interframe folder. Patterns: Hunters, boots, etc.; locking folders. Technical: Grinds 154CM and ATS-34. Patented interframe with special lock release tab. Prices: $2200 to $3000; some higher. Remarks: Full-time maker; first knife sold in 1966. Mark: Last name.

LALA, PAULO RICARDO P AND LALA, ROBERTO P.,
R Daniel Martins 636, Presidente Prudente, SP, BRAZIL 19031-260, Phone: 0182-210125, korthknives@terra.com.br; Web: www.ikbsknifetech.com
Specialties: Straight knives and folders of all designs to customer specs. Patterns: Bowies, daggers fighters, hunters and utility knives. Technical: Grinds and forges D6, 440C, high-carbon steels and Damascus. Prices: $60 to $400; some higher. Remarks: Full-time makers; first knife sold in 1991. All stainless steel blades are ultra sub-zero quenched. Mark: Sword carved on top of anvil under KORTH.

LAMB, CURTIS J,
3336 Louisiana Ter, Ottawa, KS 66067-8996, Phone: 785-242-6657

LAMBERT, JARRELL D,
2321 FM 2982, Granado, TX 77962, Phone: 512-771-3744
Specialties: Traditional working and using straight knives of his design and to customer specs. Patterns: Bowies, hunters, tantos and utility/camp knives. Technical: Grinds ATS-34; forges W2 and his own Damascus. Makes own sheaths. Prices: $80 to $600; some to $1000. Remarks: Part-time maker; first knife sold in 1982. Mark: Etched first and middle initials, last name; or stamped last name.

LAMBERT, KIRBY,
2131 Edgar St, Regina, SK, CANADA S4N 3K8, kirby@lambertknives.com; Web: www.lambertknives.com
Specialties: Tactical/utility folders. Tactical/utility Japanese style fixed blades. Prices: $200 to $1500 U.S. Remarks: Full-time maker since 2002. Mark: Black widow spider and last name Lambert.

LAMEY, ROBERT M,
15800 Lamey Dr, Biloxi, MS 39532, Phone: 228-396-9066, Fax: 228-396-9022, rmlamey@ametro.net; Web: www.lameyknives.com
Specialties: Bowies, fighters, hard use knives. Patterns: Bowies, fighters, hunters and camp knives. Technical: Forged and stock removal. Prices: $125 to $350. Remarks: Lifetime reconditioning; will build to customer designs, specializing in hard use, affordable knives. Mark: LAMEY.

LAMPSON, FRANK G,
1407 Bannon Cir., Chino Valley, AZ 86323, Phone: 916-549-3241, fglampson@yahoo.com
Specialties: Working folders; one-of-a-kinds. Patterns: Folders, hunters, utility knives, fillet knives and Bowies. Technical: Grinds ATS-34, 440C and 154CM. Prices: $100 to $750; some to $3500. Remarks: Full-time maker; first knife sold in 1971. Mark: Name in fish logo.

LANCASTER, C G,
No 2 Schoonwinkel St, Parys, Free State, SOUTH AFRICA, Phone: 0568112090
Specialties: High-tech working and using knives of his design and to customer specs. Patterns: Hunters, locking folders and utility/camp knives. Technical: Grinds Sandvik 12C27, 440C and D2. Offers anodized titanium bolsters. Prices: $450 to $750; some to $1500. Remarks: Part-time maker; first knife sold in 1990. Mark: Etched logo.

LANCE, BILL,
PO Box 4427, Eagle River, AK 99577, Phone: 907-694-1487
Specialties: Ulu sets and working straight knives; limited issue sets. Patterns: Several ulu patterns, drop-point skinners. Technical: Uses ATS-34 and AEBL; ivory, horn and high-class wood handles. Prices: $145 to $500; art sets to $7,500. Remarks: First knife sold in 1981. Mark: Last name over a lance.

LANCE, LUCAS,
3600 N. Charley, Wasilla, AK 99654, Phone: 907-357-0349, lucas@lanceknives.com; Web: www.lanceknives.com
Specialties: Working with materials native to Alaska such as fossilized ivory, bone, musk ox bone, sheep horn, moose antler, all combined with exotic materials from around the world. Patterns: Fully functional knives of my own design. Technical: Mainly stock removal, flat grinds in ATS-34, 440C, 5160 and various makes of American-made damascus. Prices: $165 to $850. Remarks: Second-generation knifemaker who grew up and trained in father, Bill Lance's, shop. First knife designed and made in 1994. Mark: Last name over a lance.

LANDERS, JOHN,
758 Welcome Rd, Newnan, GA 30263, Phone: 404-253-5719
Specialties: High-art working straight knives and folders of his design. Patterns: Hunters, fighters and slip-joint folders. Technical: Grinds 440C, ATS-34, 154CM and commercial Damascus. Prices: $85 to $250; some to $500.

LANG—LEE

LANG, DAVID,
Remarks: Part-time maker; first knife sold in 1989. Mark: Last name.

LANG, DAVID,
6153 Cumulus Circle, Kearns, UT 84118, Phone: 801-809-1241, dknifeguy@msn.com
Specialties: Hunters, Fighters, Push Daggers, Upscale Art Knives, Folders. Technical: Flat grind, hollow grind, hand carving, casting. Remarks: Will work from my designs or to your specifications. I have been making knives 10 years and have gleaned help from Jerry Johnson, Steven Rapp, Earl Black, Steven Johnson, and many others. Prices: $225 - $3000. Mark: Dland over UTAH.

LANGLEY, GENE H,
1022 N. Price Rd, Florence, SC 29506, Phone: 843-669-3150
Specialties: Working knives in standard patterns. Patterns: Hunters, boots, fighters, locking folders and slip-joints. Technical: Grinds 440C, 154CM and ATS-34. Prices: $125 to $450; some to $1000. Remarks: Part-time maker; first knife sold in 1979. Mark: Name.

LANGLEY, MICK,
1015 Centre Crescent, Qualicum Beach, BC, CANADA V9K 2G6, Phone: 250-752-4261
Specialties: Period pieces and working knives. Patterns: Bowies, push daggers, fighters, boots. Some folding lockers. Technical: Forges 5160, 1084, W2 and his own Damascus. Prices: $250 to $2500; some to $4500. Remarks: Full-time maker, first knife sold in 1977. Mark: Langley with M.S. (for ABS Master Smith)

LANKTON, SCOTT,
8065 Jackson Rd. R-11, Ann Arbor, MI 48103, Phone: 313-426-3735
Specialties: Pattern welded swords, krisses and Viking period pieces. Patterns: One-of-a-kind. Technical: Forges W2, L6 nickel and other steels. Prices: $600 to $12,000. Remarks: Part-time bladesmith, full-time smith; first knife sold in 1976. Mark: Last name logo.

LAOISLAV, SANTA-LASKY,
Hrochot 264, 97637 Hrochot, SLOVAKIA, Phone: +421-905-544-280, santa.ladislav@pobox.sk; Web: www.lasky.sk
Specialties: Damascus hunters, daggers and swords. Patterns: Carious Damascus patterns. Prices: $300 to $6000 U.S. Mark: L or Lasky.

LAPEN, CHARLES,
Box 529, W. Brookfield, MA 01585
Specialties: Chef's knives for the culinary artist. Patterns: Camp knives, Japanese-style swords and wood working tools, hunters. Technical: Forges 1075, car spring and his own Damascus. Favors narrow and Japanese tangs. Prices: $200 to $400; some to $2000. Remarks: Part-time maker; first knife sold in 1972. Mark: Last name.

LAPLANTE, BRETT,
4545 CR412, McKinney, TX 75071, Phone: 972-838-9191, blap007@aol.com
Specialties: Working straight knives and folders to customer specs. Patterns: Survival knives, Bowies, skinners, hunters. Technical: Grinds D2 and 440C. Heat-treats. Prices: $200 to $800. Remarks: Part-time maker; first knife sold in 1987. Mark: Last name in Canadian maple leaf logo.

LARAMIE, MARK,
301 McCain St., Raeford, NC 28376, Phone: 978-502-2726, mark@malknives.com; Web: www.malknives.com
Specialties: Traditional fancy & art knives. Patterns: Slips, back-lock L/L, automatics, single and multi blades. Technical: Free hand ground blades of D2, 440, and Damascus. Mark: M.A.L. Knives w/fish logo.

LARGIN, KEN,
KELGIN Knifemakers Co-Op, 104 Knife Works Ln, Sevierville, TN 37876, Phone: 765-969-5012, kelginfinecutlery@gmail.com; Web: wwwkelgin.com
Specialties: Retired from general knifemaking. Only take limited orders in meteorite damascus or solid meteorite blades. Patterns: Any. Technical: Stock removal or forged. Prices: $500 & up. Remarks: Runs the Kelgin Knife Makers Co-op at Smoky Mtn. Knife Works. Mark: K.C. Largin (Kelgin mark retired in 2004).

LARK, DAVID,
6641 Schneider Rd., Kingsley, MI 49649, Phone: 231-342-1076, dblark58@yahoo.com
Specialties: Traditional straight knives, art knives, folders. Patterns: All types. Technical: Grinds all types of knife making steel and makes damascus. Prices: $600 and up. Remarks: Full-time maker, custom riflemaker, and engraver. Mark: Lark in script and DBL on engraving.

LARSON, RICHARD,
549 E Hawkeye Ave, Turlock, CA 95380, Phone: 209-668-1615, lebatardknives@aol.com
Specialties: Sound working knives, lightweight folders, practical tactical knives. Patterns: Hunters, trout and bird knives, fish fillet knives, Bowies, tactical sheath knives, one- and two-blade folders. Technical: Grinds ATS-34, A2, D2, CPM 3V and commercial. Damascus; forges and grinds 52100, O1 and 1095. Machines folder frames from aircraft aluminum. Prices: $40 to $650. Remarks: Full-time maker. First knife made in 1974. Offers knife repair, restoration and sharpening. All knives are serial numbered and registered in the name of original purchaser. Mark: Stamped last name or etched logo of last name, city, and state.

LARY, ED,
1016 19th St., Mosinee, WI 54455, laryblades@hotmail.com
Specialties: Upscale hunters and art knives with display presentations. Patterns: Hunters, period pieces. Technical: Grinds all steels, heat treats, fancy file work and engraving. Prices: Upscale. Remarks: Full-time maker since 1974. Mark: Hand engraved "Ed Lary" in script.

LAURENT, KERMIT,
1812 Acadia Dr, LaPlace, LA 70068, Phone: 504-652-5629
Specialties: Traditional and working straight knives and folders of his design. Patterns: Bowies, hunters, utilities and folders. Technical: Forges own Damascus, plus uses most tool steels and stainless. Specializes in altering cable patterns. Uses stabilized handle materials, especially select exotic woods. Prices: $100 to $2500; some to $50,000. Remarks: Full-time maker; first knife sold in 1982. Doing business as Kermit's Knife Works. Favorite material is meteorite Damascus. Mark: First name.

LAWRENCE, ALTON,
201 W Stillwell, De Queen, AR 71832, Phone: 870-642-7643, Fax: 870-642-4023, uncle21@riversidemachine.net; Web: riversidemachine.net
Specialties: Classic straight knives and folders to customer specs. Patterns: Bowies, hunters, folders and utility/camp knives. Technical: Forges 5160, 1095, 1084, Damascus and railroad spikes. Prices: Start at $100. Remarks: Part-time maker; first knife sold in 1988. Mark: Last name inside fish symbol.

LAY, L J,
602 Mimosa Dr, Burkburnett, TX 76354, Phone: 940-569-1329
Specialties: Working straight knives in standard patterns; some period pieces. Patterns: Drop-point hunters, Bowies and fighters. Technical: Grinds ATS-34 to mirror finish; likes Micarta handles. Prices: Moderate. Remarks: Full-time maker; first knife sold in 1985. Mark: Name or name with ram head and city or stamp L J Lay.

LAY, R J (BOB),
Box 1225, Logan Lake, BC, CANADA V0K 1W0, Phone: 250-523-9923, Fax: SAME, rjlay@telus.net
Specialties: Traditional-styled, fancy straight knifes of his design. Specializing in hunters. Patterns: Bowies, fighters and hunters. Technical: Grinds 440C, ATS-34, S30V, CPM-154CM. Uses exotic handle and spacer material. File cut, prefers narrow tang. Sheaths available. Price: $200 to $500, some to $5000. Remarks: Full-time maker, first knife sold in 1976. Doing business as Lay's Custom Knives. Mark: Signature acid etched.

LEAVITT JR., EARL F,
Pleasant Cove Rd Box 306, E. Boothbay, ME 04544, Phone: 207-633-3210
Specialties: 1500-1870 working straight knives and fighters; pole arms. Patterns: Historically significant knives, classic/modern custom designs. Technical: Flat-grinds O1; heat-treats. Filework available. Prices: $90 to $350; some to $1000. Remarks: Full-time maker; first knife sold in 1981. Doing business as Old Colony Manufactory. Mark: Initials in oval.

LEBATARD, PAUL M,
14700 Old River Rd, Vancleave, MS 39565, Phone: 228-826-4137, Fax: Cell phone: 228-238-7461, lebatardknives@aol.com
Specialties: Sound working hunting and fillet knives, folding knives, practical tactical knives. Patterns: Hunters, trout and bird knives, fish fillet knives, kitchen knives, Bowies, tactical sheath knives, one- and two-blade folders. Technical: Grinds ATS-34, D-2, CPM 3-V, CPM-154CM, and commercial Damascus; forges and grinds 1095, 01, and 52100. Prices: $75 to $650; some to $1200. Remarks: Full-time maker, first knife made in 1974. Charter member Gulf Coast Custom Knifemakers; Voting member Knifemaker's Guild. Mark: Stamped last name, or etched logo of last name, city, and state. Other: All knives are serial numbered and registered in the name of the original purchaser.

LEBER, HEINZ,
Box 446, Hudson's Hope, BC, CANADA V0C 1V0, Phone: 250-783-5304
Specialties: Working straight knives of his design. Patterns: 20 models, from capers to Bowies. Technical: Hollow-grinds D2 and M2 steel; mirror-finishes and full tang only. Likes moose, elk, stone sheep for handles. Prices: $175 to $1000. Remarks: Full-time maker; first knife sold in 1975. Mark: Initials connected.

LEBLANC, GARY E,
7342 145th Ave, Royalton, MN 56373, Phone: 320-232-0245, butternutcove@hotmail.com
Specialties: Hunting and fishing, some kitchen knives and the Air Assualt tactical knife. Does own leather and Kydex work. Patterns: Stock removal. Technical: Mostly ATS34 for spec knives--orders, whatever the customer desires. Prices: Full range: $85 for parring knife, up $4000 plus fro collector grade hunter and fillet set. Remarks: First knife in 1998. Mark: Circular with star in center and LEBLANC on upper curve and KNIFEWORKS on lower curve.

LECK, DAL,
Box 1054, Hayden, CO 81639, Phone: 970-276-3663
Specialties: Classic, traditional and working knives of his design and in standard patterns; period pieces. Patterns: Boots, daggers, fighters, hunters and push daggers. Technical: Forges O1 and 5160; makes his own Damascus. Prices: $175 to $700; some to $1500. Remarks: Part-time maker; first knife sold in 1990. Doing business as The Moonlight Smithy. Mark: Stamped: hammer and anvil with initials.

LEE, RANDY,
PO Box 1873, St. Johns, AZ 85936, Phone: 928-337-2594, Fax: 928-337-5002, randylee.knives@yahoo.com; Web.www.randyleeknives.com
Specialties: Traditional working and using straight knives of his design. Patterns: Bowies, fighters, hunters, daggers. Technical: Grinds ATS-34, 440C Damascus, and 154CPM. Offers sheaths. Prices: $325 to $2500. Remarks: Full-time maker; first knife sold in 1979. Mark: Full name, city, state.

LELAND, STEVE,
2300 Sir Francis Drake Blvd, Fairfax, CA 94930-1118, Phone: 415-457-0318, Fax: 415-457-0995, Web: www.stephenleland@comcast.net
Specialties: Traditional and working straight knives and folders of his design. Patterns: Hunters, fighters, Bowies, chefs. Technical: Grinds O1, ATS-34 and 440C. Does own heat treat. Makes nickel silver sheaths. Prices: $150 to $750; some to $1500. Remarks: Part-time maker; first knife sold in 1987. Doing business as Leland Handmade Knives. Mark: Last name.

LEMAIRE, RYAN M.,
14045 Leon Rd., Abbeville, LA 70510, Phone: 337-893-1937, ryanlemaire@yahoo.com
Specialties: All styles. Enjoys early American and frontier styles. Also, office desk sets for hunters and fishermen. Patterns: Hunters, camp knives, miniatures and period styles. Technical: Stock removal, carbon steel, stainless steel and damascus. Some forging of guards. Leather and wooden sheaths. Prices: Vary. Remarks: Member of American Bladesmith Society and Louisiana Craft Guild. Mark: First name, city and state in oval.

LEMCKE, JIM L,
10649 Haddington Ste 180, Houston, TX 77043, Phone: 888-461-8632, Fax: 713-461-8221, jimll@hal-pc.org; Web: www.texasknife.com
Specialties: Large supply of custom ground and factory finished blades; knife kits; leather sheaths; in-house heat treating and cryogenic tempering; exotic handle material (wood, ivory, oosik, horn, stabilized woods); machines and supplies for knifemaking; polishing and finishing supplies; heat treat ovens; etching equipment; bar, sheet and rod material (brass, stainless steel, nickel silver); titanium sheet material. Catalog. $4.

LEMOINE, DAVID C,
1037 S College St, Mountain Home, AR 72653, Phone: 870-656-4730, dlemoine@davidlemoineknives.com; Web: davidlemoineknives.com
Specialties: Superior edge geometry on high performance custom classic and tactical straight blades and liner lock folders. Patterns: Hunters, skinners, bird and trout, fillet, camp, tactical, and military knives. Some miniatures. Technical: Flat and hollow grinds, CPMS90V, CPMS35V, CPMS30V, D2, A2, O1, 440C, ATS34, 154cm, Damasteel, Chad Nichols, Devin Thomas, and Robert Eggerling Damascus. Hidden and full tapered tangs, ultra-smooth folding mechanisms. File work, will use most all handle materials, does own professional in-house heat treatment and Rockwell testing. Hot blueing. Prices: $250 and up. Remarks: Part-time maker, giving and selling knives since 1986. Each patron receives a NIV Sportsman's Field Bible. Mark: Name, city and state in full oval with cross in the center. Reverse image on other side. The cross never changes.

LENNON, DALE,
459 County Rd 1554, Alba, TX 75410, Phone: 903-765-2392, devildaddy1@netzero.net
Specialties: Working / using knives. Patterns: Hunters, fighters and Bowies. Technical: Grinds high carbon steels, ATS-34, forges some. Prices: Starts at $120. Remarks: Part-time maker, first knife sold in 2000. Mark: Last name.

LEONARD, RANDY JOE,
188 Newton Rd, Sarepta, LA 71071, Phone: 318-994-2712

LEONE, NICK,
9 Georgetown Dr, Pontoon Beach, IL 62040, Phone: 618-792-0734, nickleone@sbcglobal.net
Specialties: 18th century period straight knives. Patterns: Fighters, daggers, bowies. Besides period pieces makes modern designs. Technical: Forges 5160, W2, O1, 1098, 52100 and his own Damascus. Prices: $100 to $1000; some to $3500. Remarks: Full-time maker; first knife sold in 1987. Doing business as Anvil Head Forge. Mark: AHF, Leone, NL

LERCH, MATTHEW,
N88 W23462 North Lisbon Rd, Sussex, WI 53089, Phone: 262-246-6362, Web: www.lerchcustomknives.com
Specialties: Folders and folders with special mechanisms. Patterns: Interframe and integral folders; lock backs, assisted openers, side locks, button locks and liner locks. Technical: Grinds ATS-34, 1095, 440 and Damascus. Offers filework and embellished bolsters. Prices: $900 and up. Remarks: First knife made in 1986. Mark: Last name.

LESSWING, KEVIN,
29A East 34th St, Bayonne, NJ 07002, Phone: 551-221-1841, klesswing@excite.com
Specialties: Traditonal working and using straight knives of his design or to customer specs. A few folders. Makes own leather sheaths. Patterns: Hunters, daggers, bowies, bird and trout. Technical: Forges high carbon and tool steels, makes own Damascus, grinds CPM154CM, Damasteel, and other stainless steels. Does own heat treating. Remarks: Voting member of Knifemakers Guild, part-time maker. Mark: KL on early knives, LESSWING on Current knives.

LEU, POHAN,
PO BOX 15423, Rio Rancho, NM 87174, Phone: 949-300-6412, pohanleu@hotmail.com Web: www.leucustom.com
Specialties: Japanese influenced fixed blades made to your custom specifications. Knives and swords. A2 tool steel, Stock Removal. Prices: $180 and up. Remarks: Full-time; first knife sold in 2003. Mark: LEU or PL.

LEVENGOOD, BILL,
15011 Otto Rd, Tampa, FL 33624, Phone: 813-961-5688, bill.levengood@verison.net; Web: www.levengoodknives.com
Specialties: Working straight knives and folders. Patterns: Hunters, Bowies, folders and collector pieces. Technical: Grinds ATS-34, S-30V, CPM-154 and Damascus. Prices: $175 to $1500. Remarks: Full time maker; first knife sold in

1983. Mark: Last name, city, state.

LEVIN, JACK,
201 Brighton 1st Road, Suite 3R, Brooklyn, NY 11235, Phone: 718-415-7911, jacklevin1@yahoo.com
Specialties: Folders with mechanisms.

LEVINE, BOB,
101 Westwood Dr, Tullahoma, TN 37388, Phone: 931-454-9943, levineknives@msn.com
Specialties: Working left- and right-handed LinerLock® folders. Patterns: Hunters and folders. Technical: Grinds ATS-34, 440C, D2, O1 and some Damascus; hollow and some flat grinds. Uses fossil ivory, Micarta and exotic woods. Provides custom leather sheath with each fixed knife. Prices: Starting at $275. Remarks: Full-time maker; first knife sold in 1984. Voting member Knifemakers Guild, German Messermaher Guild. Mark: Name and logo.

LEWIS, BILL,
PO Box 63, Riverside, IA 52327, Phone: 319-629-5574, wildbill37@geticonnect.com
Specialties: Folders of all kinds including those made from one-piece of white tail antler with or without the crown. Patterns: Hunters, folding hunters, fillet, Bowies, push daggers, etc. Prices: $20 to $200. Remarks: Full-time maker; first knife sold in 1978. Mark: W.E.L.

LEWIS, MIKE,
21 Pleasant Hill Dr, DeBary, FL 32713, Phone: 386-753-0936, dragonsteel@prodigy.net
Specialties: Traditional straight knives. Patterns: Swords and daggers. Technical: Grinds 440C, ATS-34 and 5160. Frequently uses cast bronze and cast nickel guards and pommels. Prices: $100 to $750. Remarks: Part-time maker; first knife sold in 1988. Mark: Dragon Steel and serial number.

LEWIS, TOM R,
1613 Standpipe Rd, Carlsbad, NM 88220, Phone: 575-885-3616, lewisknives@carlsbadnm.com; Web: www.cavemen.net/lewisknives/
Specialties: Traditional working straight knives. Patterns: Outdoor knives, hunting knives and Bowies. Technical: Grinds ATS-34 forges 5168 and O1. Makes wire, pattern welded and chainsaw Damascus. Prices: $140 to $1500. Remarks: Part-time maker; first knife sold in 1980. Doing business as TR Lewis Handmade Knives. Mark: Lewis family crest.

LICATA, STEVEN,
LICATA CUSTOM KNIVES, 146 Wilson St. 1st Floor, Boonton, NJ 07005, Phone: 973-588-4909, kniveslicata@aol.com; Web: www.licataknives.com
Specialties: Fantasy swords and knives. One-of-a-kind sculptures in steel. Prices: $200 to $25,000.

LIEBENBERG, ANDRE,
8 Hilma Rd, Bordeaux, Randburg, GT, SOUTH AFRICA 2196, Phone: 011-787-2303
Specialties: High-art straight knives of his design. Patterns: Daggers, fighters and swords. Technical: Grinds 440C and 12C27. Prices: $250 to $500; some $4000 and higher. Giraffe bone handles with semi-precious stones. Remarks: Spare-time maker; first knife sold in 1990. Mark: Initials.

LIEGEY, KENNETH R,
288 Carney Dr, Millwood, WV 25262, Phone: 304-273-9545
Specialties: Traditional working/using straight knives of his design and to customer specs. Patterns: Hunters, utility/camp knives, miniatures. Technical: Grinds 440C. Prices: $75 to $150; some to $300. Remarks: Spare-time maker; first knife sold in 1977. Mark: First and middle initials, last name.

LIGHTFOOT, GREG,
RR #2, Kitscoty, AB, CANADA T0B 2P0, Phone: 780-846-2812; 780-800-1061, Pitbull@lightfootknives.com; Web: www.lightfootknives.com
Specialties: Stainless steel and Damascus. Patterns: Boots, fighters and locking folders. Technical: Grinds BG-42, 440C, D2, CPM steels, Stellite 6K. Offers engraving. Prices: $500 to $2000. Remarks: Full-time maker; first knife sold in 1988. Doing business as Lightfoot Knives. Mark: Shark with Lightfoot Knives below.

LIN, MARCUS,
4616 Rollando Dr., Unit G, Rolling Hills Estates, CA 90274, Phone: 808-636-0977, marcuslin7@gmail.com; Web: www.linknives.com
Specialties: Working knives. Patterns: Original patterns from the Loveless Shop designed by R.W. Loveless, and maker's own patterns. Technical: Main blade material is ATS34/154CM. Experience with many other alloys, Stellite 6K, Damasteel, and tool steels. Prices: $150 to $1650. Remarks: Part-time maker since 2004. Mentored by: R.W. Loveless and Jim Merritt. Sole authorship work, except for heat treat which is done by Paul Bos Heat Treating. Mark: Two used: "Marcus Lin, maker, Loveless Design" and "LIN, CALIFORNIA" (with Chinese characters on left side for "Forest.")

LINKLATER, STEVE,
8 Cossar Dr, Aurora, ON, CANADA L4G 3N8, Phone: 905-727-8929, knifman@sympatico.ca
Specialties: Traditional working/using straight knives and folders of his design. Patterns: Fighters, hunters and locking folders. Technical: Grinds ATS-34, 440V and D2. Prices: $125 to $350; some $600. Remarks: Part-time maker; first knife sold in 1987. Doing business as Links Knives. Mark: LINKS.

LISCH, DAVID K,
9239 8th Ave. SW, Seattle, WA 98106, Phone: 206-919-5431, Web: www.davidlisch.com
Specialties: One-of-a-kind collectibles, straight knives of own design and to customer specs. Patterns: Hunters, skinners, Bowies, and fighters. Technical: Forges all his own Damascus under 360-pound air hammer. Forges and

custom knifemakers

chisels wrought iron, pure iron, and bronze butt caps. Prices: Starting at $800. Remarks: Full-time blacksmith, part-time bladesmith. Mark: D. Lisch J.S.

LISTER JR., WELDON E,
116 Juniper Ln, Boerne, TX 78006, Phone: 210-269-0102, wlister@grtc.com; Web: www.weldonlister.com

Specialties: One-of-a-kind fancy and embellished folders. Patterns: Locking and slip-joint folders. Technical: Commercial Damascus and O1. All knives embellished. Engraves, inlays, carves and scrimshaws. Prices: Upscale. Remarks: Spare-time maker; first knife sold in 1991. Mark: Last name.

LITTLE, GARY M,
94716 Conklin Meadows Ln, PO Box 156, Broadbent, OR 97414, Phone: 503-572-2656

Specialties: Fancy working knives. Patterns: Hunters, tantos, Bowies, axes and buckskinners; locking folders and interframes. Technical: Forges and grinds O1, L6m, 1095, and 15N20; makes his own Damascus; bronze fittings. Prices: $120 to $1500. Remarks: Full-time maker; first knife sold in 1979. Doing business as Conklin Meadows Forge. Mark: Name, city and state.

LITTLE, LARRY,
1A Cranberry Ln, Spencer, MA 01562, Phone: 508-885-2301, littcran@aol.com

Specialties: Working straight knives of his design or to customer specs. Likes Scagel-style. Patterns: Hunters, fighters, Bowies, folders. Technical: Grinds and forges L6, O1, 5160, 1095, 1080. Prefers natural handle material especially antler. Uses nickel silver. Makes own heavy duty leather sheath. Prices: Start at $125. Remarks: Part-time maker. First knife sold in 1985. Offers knife repairs. Mark: Little on one side, LL brand on the other.

LIVESAY, NEWT,
3306 S. Dogwood St, Siloam Springs, AR 72761, Phone: 479-549-3356, Fax: 479-549-3357, newt@newtlivesay.com; Web:www.newtlivesay.com

Specialties: Combat utility knives, hunting knives, titanium knives, swords, axes, KYDWX sheaths for knives and pistols, custom orders.

LIVINGSTON, ROBERT C,
PO Box 6, Murphy, NC 28906, Phone: 704-837-4155

Specialties: Art letter openers to working straight knives. Patterns: Minis to machetes. Technical: Forges and grinds most steels. Prices: Start at $20. Remarks: Full-time maker; first knife sold in 1988. Doing business as Mystik Knifeworks. Mark: MYSTIK.

LOCKETT, LOWELL C.,
344 Spring Hill Dr., Canton, GA 30115, Phone: 678-880-9789, lcl1932@gmail.com or spur1932@windstream.net

Technical: Forges 5160, 1095 and other blade steels, and uses desert ironwood, ivory and other handle materials. Prices: $150 to $1,500.

LOCKETT, STERLING,
527 E Amherst Dr, Burbank, CA 91504, Phone: 818-846-5799

Specialties: Working straight knives and folders to customer specs. Patterns: Hunters and fighters. Technical: Grinds. Prices: Moderate. Remarks: Spare-time maker. Mark: Name, city with hearts.

LOERCHNER, WOLFGANG,
WOLFE FINE KNIVES, PO Box 255, Bayfield, ON, CANADA N0M 1G0, Phone: 519-565-2196

Specialties: Traditional straight knives, mostly ornate. Patterns: Small swords, daggers and stilettos; locking folders and miniatures. Technical: Grinds D2, 440C and 154CM; all knives hand-filed and flat-ground. Prices: Vary. Remarks: Part-time maker; first knife sold in 1983. Doing business as Wolfe Fine Knives. Mark: WOLFE.

LONEWOLF, J AGUIRRE,
481 Hwy 105, Demorest, GA 30535, Phone: 706-754-4660, Fax: 706-754-8470, lonewolfandsons@windstream.net, Web: www.knivesbylonewolf.com www.eagleswinggallery.com

Specialties: High-art working and using straight knives of his design. Patterns: Bowies, hunters, utility/camp knives and fine steel blades. Technical: Forges Damascus and high-carbon steel. Most knives have hand-carved moose antler handles. Prices: $55 to $500; some to $2000. Remarks: Full-time maker; first knife sold in 1980. Doing business as Lonewolf and Sons LLC. Mark: Stamp.

LONG, GLENN A,
10090 SW 186th Ave, Dunnellon, FL 34432, Phone: 352-489-4272, galong99@att.net

Specialties: Classic working and using straight knives of his design and to customer specs. Patterns: Hunters, Bowies, utility. Technical: Grinds 440C D2 and 440V. Prices: $85 to $300; some to $800. Remarks: Part-time maker; first knife sold in 1990. Mark: Last name inside diamond.

LONGWORTH, DAVE,
1200 Red Oak Ridge, Felicity, OH 45120, Phone: 513-876-2372

Specialties: High-tech working knives. Patterns: Locking folders, hunters, fighters and elaborate daggers. Technical: Grinds O1, ATS-34, 440C; buys Damascus. Prices: $125 to $600; some higher. Remarks: Part-time maker; first knife sold in 1980. Mark: Last name.

LOOS, HENRY C,
210 Ingraham, New Hyde Park, NY 11040, Phone: 516-354-1943, hcloos@optonline.net

Specialties: Miniature fancy knives and period pieces of his design. Patterns: Bowies, daggers and swords. Technical: Grinds O1 and 440C. Uses sterling, 18K, rubies and emeralds. All knives come with handmade hardwood cases. Prices: $90 to $195; some to $250. Remarks: Spare-time maker; first knife sold

in 1990. Mark: Script last initial.

LORO, GENE,
2457 State Route 93 NE, Crooksville, OH 43731, Phone: 740-982-4521, Fax: 740-982-1249, geney@aol.com

Specialties: Hand forged knives. Patterns: Damascus, Random, Ladder, Twist, etc. Technical: ABS Journeyman Smith. Prices: $200 and up. Remarks: Loro and hand forged by Gene Loro. Mark: Loro. Retired engineer.

LOTT, SHERRY,
1100 Legion Park Rd, Greensburg, KY 42743, Phone: 270-932-2212, info@greenriverleather.com

Specialties: One-of-a-kind, usually carved handles. Patterns: Art. Technical: Carbon steel, stock removal. Prices: Moderate. Mark: Sherry Lott. Remarks: First knife sold in 1994.

LOUKIDES, DAVID E,
76 Crescent Circle, Cheshire, CT 06410, Phone: 203-271-3023, Loussharp1@sbcglobal.net; Web: www.prayerknives.com

Specialties: Hand forged working blades and collectible pieces. Patterns: Chef knives, bowies, and hunting knives. . Technical: Uses 1084, 1095, 5160, W2, and O1.Prices: Normally $200 to $1,000. Remarks: part-time maker, Journeyman Bladesmith, Full-time Journeyman Toolmaker. Mark: LOUKIDES, or previously on older knives, initial DEL

LOVE, ED,
19443 Mill Oak, San Antonio, TX 78258, Phone: 210-497-1021, Fax: 210-497-1021, annaedlove@sbcglobal.net

Specialties: Hunting, working knives and some art pieces. Technical: Grinds ATS-34, and 440C. Prices: $150 and up. Remarks: Part-time maker. First knife sold in 1980. Mark: Name in a weeping heart.

LOVESTRAND, SCHUYLER,
1136 19th St SW, Vero Beach, FL 32962, Phone: 772-778-0282, Fax: 772-466-1126, lovestranded@aol.com

Specialties: Fancy working straight knives of his design and to customer specs; unusual fossil ivories. Patterns: Hunters, fighters, Bowies and fishing knives. Technical: Grinds stainless steel. Prices: $550 to $2,500. Remarks: Part-time maker; first knife sold in 1982. Mark: Name in logo.

LOVETT, MICHAEL,
PO Box 121, Mound, TX 76558, Phone: 254-865-9956, michaellovett@embarqmail.com

Specialties: The Loveless Connection Knives as per R.W. Loveless-Jim Merritt. Patterns: All Loveless Patterns and Original Lovett Patterns. Technical: Complicated double grinds and premium fit and finish. Prices: $1000 and up. Remarks: High degree of fit and finish - Authorized collection by R. W. Loveless Mark: Loveless Authorized football or double nude.

LOZIER, DON,
5394 SE 168th Ave, Ocklawaha, FL 32179, Phone: 352-625-3576

Specialties: Fancy and working straight knives of his design and in standard patterns. Patterns: Daggers, fighters, boot knives, and hunters. Technical: Grinds ATS-34, 440C and Damascus. Most pieces are highly embellished by notable artisans. Taking limited number of orders per annum. Prices: Start at $250; most are $1250 to $3000; some to $12,000. Remarks: Full-time maker. Mark: Name.

LUCHAK, BOB,
15705 Woodforest Blvd, Channelview, TX 77530, Phone: 281-452-1779

Specialties: Presentation knives; start of The Survivor series. Patterns: Skinners, Bowies, camp axes, steak knife sets and fillet knives. Technical: Grinds 440C. Offers electronic etching; filework. Prices: $50 to $1500. Remarks: Full-time maker; first knife sold in 1983. Doing business as Teddybear Knives. Mark: Full name, city and state with Teddybear logo.

LUCHINI, BOB,
1220 Dana Ave, Palo Alto, CA 94301, Phone: 650-321-8095, rwluchin@bechtel.com

LUCIE, JAMES R,
4191 E. Fruitport Rd., Fruitport, MI 49415, Phone: 231-865-6390, scagel@netonecom.net

Specialties: Hand-forges William Scagel-style knives. Patterns: Authentic scagel-style knives and miniatures. Technical: Forges 5160, 52100 and 1084 and forges his own pattern welded Damascus steel. Prices: Start at $750. Remarks: Full-time maker; first knife sold in 1975. Believes in sole authorship of his work. ABS Journeyman Smith. Mark: Scagel Kris with maker's name and address.

LUCKETT, BILL,
108 Amantes Ln, Weatherford, TX 76088, Phone: 817-320-1568, luckettknives@gmail.com Web: www.billluckettcustomknives.com

Specialties: Uniquely patterned robust straight knives. Patterns: Fighters, Bowies, hunters. Technical: 154CM stainless.Prices: $550 to $1500. Remarks: Part-time maker; first knife sold in 1975. Knifemakers Guild Member. Mark: Last name over Bowie logo.

LUDWIG, RICHARD O,
57-63 65 St, Maspeth, NY 11378, Phone: 718-497-5969

Specialties: Traditional working/using knives. Patterns: Boots, hunters and utility/camp knives folders. Technical: Grinds 440C, ATS-34 and BG42. File work on guards and handles; silver spacers. Offers scrimshaw. Prices: $325 to $400; some to $2000. Remarks: Full-time maker. Mark: Stamped first initial, last name, state.

LUI, RONALD M,
4042 Harding Ave, Honolulu, HI 96816, Phone: 808-734-7746

Specialties: Working straight knives and folders in standard patterns. Patterns:

Hunters, boots and liner locks. Technical: Grinds 440C and ATS-34. Prices: $100 to $700. Remarks: Spare-time maker; first knife sold in 1988. Mark: Initials connected.

LUMAN, JAMES R,
Clear Creek Trail, Anaconda, MT 59711, Phone: 406-560-1461
Specialties: San Mai and composite end patterns. Patterns: Pool and eye Spirograph southwest composite patterns. Technical: All patterns with blued steel; all made by him. Prices: $200 to $800. Mark: Stock blade removal. Pattern welded steel. Bottom ricasso JRL.

LUNDSTROM, JAN-AKE,
Mastmostigen 8, Dals-Langed, SWEDEN 66010, Phone: 0531-40270
Specialties: Viking swords, axes and knives in cooperation with handle makers. Patterns: All traditional-styles, especially swords and inlaid blades. Technical: Forges his own Damascus and laminated steel. Prices: $200 to $1000. Remarks: Full-time maker; first knife sold in 1985; collaborates with museums. Mark: Runic.

LUNDSTROM, TORBJORN (TOBBE),
Norrskenet 4, Are, SWEDEN 83013, 9lundstrm@telia.com Web: http://tobbeiare.se/site/
Specialties: Hunters and collectible knives. Patterns: Nordic-style hunters and art knives with unique materials such as mammoth and fossil walrus ivory. Technical: Uses forged blades by other makers, particularly Mattias Styrefors who mostly uses 15N20 and 20C steels and is a mosaic blacksmith. Remarks: First knife made in 1986.

LUNN, GAIL,
434 CR 1422, Mountain Home, AR 72653, Phone: 870-424-2662, gail@lunnknives.com; Web: www.lunnknives.com
Specialties: Fancy folders and double action autos, some straight blades. Patterns: One-of-a-kind, all types. Technical: Stock removal, hand made. Prices: $300 and up. Remarks: Fancy file work, exotic materials, inlays, stone etc. Mark: Name in script.

LUNN, LARRY A,
434 CR 1422, Mountain Home, AR 72653, Phone: 870-424-2662, larry@lunnknives.com; Web: www.lunnknives.com
Specialties: Fancy folders and double action autos; some straight blades. Patterns: All types; his own designs. Technical: Stock removal; commercial Damascus. Prices: $125 and up. Remarks: File work inlays and exotic materials. Mark: Name in script.

LUPOLE, JAMIE G,
KUMA KNIVES, 285 Main St., Kirkwood, NY 13795, Phone: 607-775-9368, jlupole@stny.rr.com
Specialties: Working and collector grade fixed blades, ethnic-styled blades. Patterns: Fighters, Bowies, tacticals, hunters, camp, utility, personal carry knives, some swords. Technical: Forges and grinds 10XX series and other high-carbon steels, grinds ATS-34 and 440C, will use just about every handle material available. Prices: $80 to $500 and up. Remarks: Part-time maker since 1999. Marks: "KUMA" hot stamped, name, city and state-etched, or "Daiguma saku" in kanji.

LUTZ, GREG,
127 Crescent Rd, Greenwood, SC 29646, Phone: 864-229-7340
Specialties: Working and using knives and period pieces of his design and to customer specs. Patterns: Fighters, hunters and swords. Technical: Forges 1095 and O1; grinds ATS-34. Differentially heat-treats forged blades; uses cryogenic treatment on ATS-34. Prices: $50 to $350; some to $1200. Remarks: Part-time maker; first knife sold in 1986. Doing business as Scorpion Forge. Mark: First initial, last name.

LYLE III, ERNEST L,
LYLE KNIVES, PO Box 1755, Chiefland, FL 32644, Phone: 352-490-6693, ernestlyle@msn.com
Specialties: Fancy period pieces; one-of-a-kind and limited editions. Patterns: Arabian/Persian influenced fighters, military knives, Bowies and Roman short swords; several styles of hunters. Technical: Grinds 440C, D2 and 154 CM. Engraves. Prices: $200 - $7500. Remarks: Full-time maker; first knife sold in 1972. Mark: Lyle Knives over Chiefland, Fla.

LYNCH, TAD,
140 Timberline Dr., Beebe, AR 72012, Phone: 501-626-1647, lynchknives@yahoo.com Web: lynchknives.com
Specialties: Forged fixed blades. Patterns: Bowies, choppers, fighters, hunters. Technical: Hand-forged W-2, 1084, 1095 clay quenched 52100, 5160. Prices: Starting at $250. Remarks: Part-time maker, also offers custom leather work via wife Amy Lynch. Mark: T.D. Lynch over anvil.

LYNN, ARTHUR,
29 Camino San Cristobal, Galisteo, NM 87540, Phone: 505-466-3541, lynnknives@aol.com
Specialties: Handforged Damascus knives. Patterns: Folders, hunters, Bowies, fighters, kitchen. Technical: Forges own Damascus. Prices: Moderate.

LYTTLE, BRIAN,
Box 5697, High River, AB, CANADA T1V 1M7, Phone: 403-558-3638, brian@lyttleknives.com; Web: www.lyttleknives.com
Specialties: Fancy working straight knives and folders; art knives. Patterns: Bowies, daggers, dirks, sgian dubhs, folders, dress knives, tantos, short swords. Technical: Forges Damascus steel; engraving; scrimshaw; heat-treating; classes. Prices: $450 to $15,000. Remarks: Full-time maker; first knife

M

MACCAUGHTRY, SCOTT F.,
Fullerton Forge, 1824 Sorrel St, Camarillo, CA 93010, Phone: 805-750-2137, smack308@hotmail.com
Specialties: Fixed blades and folders. Technical: Forges 5160, 52100, W2 and his own damascus using 1084 and 15N20 steels. Prices: $275 and up. Remarks: ABS journeyman smith. Mark: S. MacCaughtry in script, and J.S. on the back side.

MACDONALD, DAVID,
2824 Hwy 47, Los Lunas, NM 87031, Phone: 505-866-5866

MACDONALD, JOHN,
310 Rte 27, Apt 18, Raymond, NH 03077, Phone: 603-244-2988
Specialties: Working/using straight knives of his design and to customer specs. Patterns: Japanese cutlery, Bowies, hunters and working knives. Technical: Grinds O1, L6 and ATS-34. Swords have matching handles and scabbards with Japanese flair. Prices: $70 to $250; some to $500. Remarks: Part-time maker; first knife sold in 1988. Custom knife cases made from pine and exotic hardwoods for table display or wall hanging. Doing business as Mac the Knife. Mark: Initials.

MACKIE, JOHN,
13653 Lanning, Whittier, CA 90605, Phone: 562-945-6104
Specialties: Forged. Patterns: Bowie and camp knives. Technical: Attended ABS Bladesmith School. Prices: $75 to $500. Mark: JSM in a triangle.

MACKRILL, STEPHEN,
PO Box 1580, Pinegowrie, Johannesburg, GT, SOUTH AFRICA 2123, Phone: 27-11-474-7139, Fax: 27-11-474-7139, info@mackrill.co.za; Web: www.mackrill.net
Specialties: Art fancy, historical, collectors and corporate gifts cutlery. Patterns: Fighters, hunters, camp, custom lock back and LinerLock® folders. Technical: N690, 12C27, ATS-34, silver and gold inlay on handles; wooden and silver sheaths. Prices: $330 and upwards. Remarks: First knife sold in 1978. Mark: Mackrill fish with country of origin.

MADRULLI, MME JOELLE,
Residence Ste Catherine B1, Salon De Provence, FRANCE 13330

MAE, TAKAO,
1-119 1-4 Uenohigashi, Toyonaka, Osaka, JAPAN 560-0013, Phone: 81-6-6852-2758, Fax: 81-6-6481-1649, takamae@nifty.com
Remarks: Distinction stylish in art-forged blades, with lacquered ergonomic handles.

MAESTRI, PETER A,
S11251 Fairview Rd, Spring Green, WI 53588, Phone: 608-546-4481
Specialties: Working straight knives in standard patterns. Patterns: Camp and fishing knives, utility green-river-styled. Technical: Grinds 440C, 154CM and 440A. Prices: $15 to $45; some to $150. Remarks: Full-time maker; first knife sold in 1981. Provides professional cutler service to professional cutters. Mark: CARISOLO, MAESTRI BROS., or signature.

MAGEE, JIM,
741 S. Ohio St., Salina, KS 67401, Phone: 785-820-6928, jimmagee@cox.net
Specialties: Working and fancy folding knives. Patterns: Liner locking folders, favorite is his Persian. Technical: Grinds ATS-34, Devin Thomas & Eggerling Damascus, titanium. Liners Prefer mother-of-pearl handles. Prices: Start at $225 to $1200. Remarks: Part-time maker, first knife sold in 2001. Purveyor since 1982. Past president of the Professional Knifemakers Association Mark: Last name.

MAGRUDER, JASON,
460 Arnos Rd, Unit 66, Talent, OR 97540, Phone: 719-210-1579, belstain@hotmail.com; jason@magruderknives.com; web: MagruderKnives.com
Specialties: Unique and innovative designs combining the latest modern materials with traditional hand craftsmanship. Patterns: Fancy neck knives. Tactical gents folders. Working straight knives. Technical: Flats grinds CPM3v, CPM154, ATS34, 1080, and his own forged damascus. Hand carves carbon fiber, titanium, wood, ivory, and pearl handles. Filework and carving on blades. Prices: $150 and up. Remarks: Part-time maker; first knife sold in 2000. Mark: Last name.

MAHOMEDY, A R,
PO Box 76280, Marble Ray, KZN, SOUTH AFRICA 4035, Phone: +27 31 577 1451, arm-koknives@mweb.co.za; Web: www.arm-koknives.co.za
Specialties: Daggers and elegant folders of own design finished with finest exotic materials currently available. Technical: Via stock removal, grinds Damasteel, Damascus and the famous hardenable stainless steels. Prices: U.S. $650 and up. Remarks: Part-time maker. First knife sold in 1995. Voting member knifemakers guild of SA, FEGA member starting out Engraving. Mark: Initials A R M crowned with a "Minaret."

MAHOMEDY, HUMAYD A.R.,
PO BOX 76280, Marble Ray, KZN, SOUTH AFRICA 4035, Phone: +27 31 577 1451, arm-koknives@mweb.co.za
Specialties: Tactical folding and fixed blade knives. Patterns: Fighters, utilities, tacticals, folders and fixed blades, daggers, modern interpretation of Bowies. Technical: Stock-removal knives of Bohler N690, Bohler K110, Bohler K460, Sandvik 12C27, Sandvik RWL 34. Handle materials used are G10, Micarta, Cape Buffalo horn, Water Buffalo horn, Kudu horn, Gemsbok horn, Giraffe bone, Elephant ivory, Mammoth ivory, Arizona desert ironwood, stabilised and dyed burls. Prices: $250 - $1000. Remarks: First knife sold in 2002. Full-time

knifemaker since 2002. First person of color making knives full-time in South Africa. Doing business as HARM EDGED TOOLS. Mark: HARM and arrow over EDGED TOOLS.

MAIENKNECHT, STANLEY,
38648 S R 800, Sardis, OH 43946

MAINES, JAY,
SUNRISE RIVER CUSTOM KNIVES, 5584 266th St., Wyoming, MN 55092, Phone: 651-462-5301, jaymaines@fronternet.net; Web: http://www.sunrisecustomknives.com
Specialties: Heavy duty working, classic and traditional fixed blades. Some high-tech and fancy embellished knives available. Patterns: Hunters, skinners, fillet, bowies tantos, boot daggers etc. etc. Technical: Hollow ground, stock removal blades of 440C, ATS-34 and CPM S-90V. Prefers natural handle materials, exotic hard woods, and stag, rams and buffalo horns. Offers dovetailed bolsters in brass, stainless steel and nickel silver. Custom sheaths from matching wood or hand-stitched from heavy duty water buffalo hide. Prices: Moderate to up-scale. Remarks: Part-time maker; first knife sold in 1992. Doing business as Sunrise River Custom Knives. Offers fixed blade knives repair and handle conversions. Mark: Full name under a Rising Sun logo.

MAISEY, ALAN,
PO Box 197, Vincentia, NSW, AUSTRALIA 2540, Phone: 2-4443 7829, tosanaji@excite.com
Specialties: Daggers, especially krisses; period pieces. Technical: Offers knives and finished blades in Damascus and nickel Damascus. Prices: $75 to $2000; some higher. Remarks: Part-time maker; provides complete restoration service for krisses. Trained by a Japanese Kris smith. Mark: None, triangle in a box, or three peaks.

MAJORS, CHARLIE,
1911 King Richards Ct, Montgomery, TX 77316, Phone: 713-826-3135, charliemajors@sbcglobal.net
Specialties: Fixed-blade hunters and slip-joint and lock-back folders. Technical: Practices stock removal method, preferring CPM154 steel and natural handle materials such as ironwood, stag, and mammoth ivory. Also takes customer requests. Does own heat treating and cryogenic quenching. Remarks: First knife made in 1980.

MAKOTO, KUNITOMO,
3-3-18 Imazu-cho, Fukuyama-city, Hiroshima, JAPAN, Phone: 084-933-5874, kunitomo@po.iijnet.or.jp

MALABY, RAYMOND J,
835 Calhoun Ave, Juneau, AK 99801, Phone: 907-586-6981, Fax: 907-523-8031, malaby@gci.net
Specialties: Straight working knives. Patterns: Hunters, skiners, Bowies, and camp knives. Technical: Hand forged 1084, 5160, O1 and grinds ATS-34 stainless. Prices: $195 to $400. Remarks: First knife sold in 1994. Mark: First initial, last name, city, and state.

MALLOY, JOE,
1039 Schwabe St, Freeland, PA 18224, Phone: 570-436-6416, jdmalloy@msn.com
Specialties: Working straight knives and lock back folders—plain and fancy—of his design. Patterns: Hunters, utility, folders, tactical designs. Technical: 154CM, ATS-34, 440C, D2 and A2, damascus, other exotic steel on request. Prices: $100 to $1800. Remarks: Part-time maker; first knife sold in 1982. Mark: First and middle initials, last name, city and state.

MANARO, SAL,
10 Peri Ave., Holbrook, NY 11741, Phone: 631-737-1180, maker@manaroknives.com
Specialties: Tactical folders, bolstered titanium LinerLocks, handmade folders, and fixed blades with hand-checkered components. Technical: Compound grinds, hidden fasteners and welded components, with blade steels including CPM-154, damascus, Stellite, D2, S30V and O-1 by the stock-removal method of blade making. Prices: $500 and up. Remarks: Part-time maker, made first knife in 2001. Mark: Last name with arrowhead underline.

MANDT, JOE,
3735 Overlook Dr. NE, St. Petersburg, FL 33703, Phone: 813-244-3816, jmforge@mac.com
Specialties: Forged Bowies, camp knives, hunters, skinners, fighters, boot knives, military style field knives. Technical: Forges plain carbon steel and high carbon tool steels, including W2, 1084, 5160, O1, 9260, 15N20, cable Damascus, pattern welded Damascus, flat and convex grinds. Prefers natural handle materials, hand-rubbed finishes, and stainless low carbon steel, Damascus and wright iron fittings. Does own heat treat. Prices: $150 to $750. Remarks: Part-time maker, first knife sold in 206. Mark: "MANDT".

MANEKER, KENNETH,
RR 2, Galiano Island, BC, CANADA V0N 1P0, Phone: 604-539-2084
Specialties: Working straight knives; period pieces. Patterns: Camp knives and hunters; French chef knives. Technical: Grinds 440C, 154CM and Vascowear. Prices: $50 to $200; some to $300. Remarks: Part-time maker; first knife sold in 1981. Doing business as Water Mountain Knives. Mark: Japanese Kanji of initials, plus glyph.

MANKEL, KENNETH,
7836 Cannonsburg Rd, PO Box 35, Cannonsburg, MI 49317, Phone: 616-874-6955, Fax: 616-8744-4053

MANLEY, DAVID W,
3270 Six Mile Hwy, Central, SC 29630, Phone: 864-654-1125, dmanleyknives@wmconnect.com
Specialties: Working straight knives of his design or to custom specs. Patterns: Hunters, boot and fighters. Technical: Grinds 440C and ATS-34. Prices: $60 to $250. Remarks: Part-time maker; first knife sold in 1994. Mark: First initial, last name, year and serial number.

MANN, MICHAEL L,
IDAHO KNIFE WORKS, PO Box 144, Spirit Lake, ID 83869, Phone: 509 994-9394, Web: www.idahoknifeworks.com
Specialties: Good working blades-historical reproduction, modern or custom design. Patterns: Cowboy Bowies, Mountain Man period blades, old-style folders, designer and maker of "The Cliff Knife", hunter knives, hand ax and fish fillet. Technical: High-carbon steel blades-hand forged 5160. Stock removed 15N20 steel. Also Damascus. Prices: $130 to $670+. Remarks: Made first knife in 1965. Full-time making knives as Idaho Knife Works since 1986. Functional as well as collectible. Each knife truly unique! Mark: Four mountain peaks are his initials MM.

MANN, TIM,
BLADEWORKS, PO Box 1196, Honokaa, HI 96727, Phone: 808-775-0949, Fax: 808-775-0949, birdman@shaka.com
Specialties: Hand-forged knives and swords. Patterns: Bowies, tantos, pesh kabz, daggers. Technical: Use 5160, 1050, 1075, 1095 and ATS-34 steels, cable Damascus. Prices: $200 to $800. Remarks: Just learning to forge Damascus. Mark: None yet.

MARAGNI, DAN,
RD 1 Box 106, Georgetown, NY 13072, Phone: 315-662-7490
Specialties: Heavy-duty working knives, some investor class. Patterns: Hunters, fighters and camp knives, some Scottish types. Technical: Forges W2 and his own Damascus; toughness and edge-holding a high priority. Prices: $125 to $500; some to $1000. Remarks: Full-time maker; first knife sold in 1975. Mark: Celtic initials in circle.

MARCHAND, RICK,
Wildertools, 681 Middleton Lane, Wheatley, ON, CANADA N0P 2P0, Phone: 519-825-9726, rickmarchand@wildertools.com
Specialties: Specializing in multicultural, period stylized blades and accoutrements. Technical: Hand forged from 1070/84 and 5160 steel. Prices: $175 - $900. Remarks: 3 years full-time maker. ABS Apprentice Smith. Mark: Tang stamp: "MARCHAND" along with two Japanese-style characters resembling "W" and "M."

MARINGER, TOM,
2692 Powell St., Springdale, AR 72764, maringer@arkansas.net; Web: shirepost.com/cutlery
Specialties: Working straight and curved blades with stainless steel furniture and wire-wrapped handles. Patterns: Subhilts, daggers, boots, swords. Technical: Grinds D-2, A-2, ATS-34. May be safely disassembled by the owner via pommel screw or pegged construction. Prices: $2000 to $3000, some to $20,000. Remarks: Former full-time maker, now part-time. First knife sold in 1975. Mark: Full name, year, and serial number etched on tang under handle.

MARKLEY, KEN,
7651 Cabin Creek Lane, Sparta, IL 62286, Phone: 618-443-5284
Specialties: Traditional working and using knives of his design and to customer specs. Patterns: Fighters, hunters and utility/camp knives. Technical: Forges 5160, 1095 and L6; makes his own Damascus; does file work. Prices: $150 to $800; some to $2000. Remarks: Part-time maker; first knife sold in 1991. Doing business as Cabin Creek Forge. Mark: Last name, JS.

MARLOWE, CHARLES,
10822 Poppleton Ave, Omaha, NE 68144, Phone: 402-933-5065, cmarlowe1@cox.net; Web: www.marloweknives.com
Specialties: Folding knives and balisong. Patterns: Tactical pattern folders. Technical: Grind ATS-34, S30V, CPM154, 154CM, Damasteel, others on request. Forges/grinds 1095 on occasion. Prices: Start at $450. Remarks: First knife sold in 1993. Full-time since 1999. Mark: Turtle logo with Marlowe above, year below.

MARLOWE, DONALD,
2554 Oakland Rd, Dover, PA 17315, Phone: 717-764-6055
Specialties: Working straight knives in standard patterns. Patterns: Bowies, fighters, boots and utility knives. Technical: Grinds D2 and 440C. Integral design hunter models. Prices: $130 to $850. Remarks: Spare-time maker; first knife sold in 1977. Mark: Last name.

MARSH, JEREMY,
6169 3 Mile NE, Ada, MI 49301, Phone: 616-889-1945, steelbean@hotmail.com; Web: www.marshcustomknives.com
Specialties: Locking liner folders, dressed-up gents knives, tactical knives, and dress tacticals. Technical: CPM S30V stainless and Damascus blade steels using the stock-removal method of bladesmithing. Prices: $450 to $1500. Remarks: Self-taught, part-time knifemaker; first knife sold in 2004. Mark: Maker's last name and large, stylized M.

MARSHALL, STEPHEN R,
975 Harkreader Rd, Mt. Juliet, TN 37122

MARTIN, BRUCE E,
Rt. 6, Box 164-B, Prescott, AR 71857, Phone: 501-887-2023
Specialties: Fancy working straight knives of his design. Patterns: Bowies, camp

knives, skinners and fighters. Technical: Forges 5160, 1095 and his own Damascus. Uses natural handle materials; filework available. Prices: $75 to $350; some to $500. Remarks: Full-time maker; first knife sold in 1979. Mark: Name in arch.

MARTIN, GENE,
PO Box 396, Williams, OR 97544, Phone: 541-846-6755, bladesmith@customknife.com
Specialties: Straight knives and folders. Patterns: Fighters, hunters, skinners, boot knives, spring back and lock back folders. Technical: Grinds ATS-34, 440C, Damascus and 154CM. Prices: $150 to $2500. Remarks: Full-time maker; first knife sold in 1993. Doing business as Provision Forge. Mark: Name and/or crossed staff and sword.

MARTIN, HAL W,
781 Hwy 95, Morrilton, AR 72110, Phone: 501-354-1682, hal.martin@sbcglobal.net
Specialties: Hunters, Bowies and fighters. Prices: $250 and up. Mark: MARTIN.

MARTIN, HERB,
2500 Starwood Dr, Richmond, VA 23229, Phone: 804-747-1675, hamjlm@hotmail.com
Specialties: Working straight knives. Patterns: Skinners, hunters and utility. Technical: Hollow grinds ATS-34, and Micarta handles. Prices: $85 to $125. Remarks: Part-time Maker. First knife sold in 2001. Mark: HA MARTIN.

MARTIN, MICHAEL W,
Box 572, Jefferson St, Beckville, TX 75631, Phone: 903-678-2161
Specialties: Classic working/using straight knives of his design and in standard patterns. Patterns: Hunters. Technical: Grinds ATS-34, 440C, O1 and A2. Bead blasted, Parkerized, high polish and satin finishes. Sheaths are handmade. Also hand forges cable Damascus. Prices: $185 to $280 some higher. Remarks: Part-time maker; first knife sold in 1995. Doing business as Michael W. Martin Knives. Mark: Name and city, state in arch.

MARTIN, PETER,
28220 N. Lake Dr, Waterford, WI 53185, Phone: 262-706-3076, Web: www.petermartinknives.com
Specialties: Fancy, fantasy and working straight knives and folders of his design and in standard patterns. Patterns: Bowies, fighters, hunters, locking folders and liner locks. Technical: Forges own Mosaic Damascus, powdered steel and his own Damascus. Prefers natural handle material; offers file work and carved handles. Prices: Moderate. Remarks: Full-time maker; first knife sold in 1988. Doing business as Martin Custom Products. Mark: Martin Knives.

MARTIN, RANDALL J,
51 Bramblewood St, Bridgewater, MA 02324, Phone: 508-279-0682
Specialties: High tech folding and fixed blade tactical knives employing the latest blade steels and exotic materials. Employs a unique combination of 3d-CNC machining and hand work on both blades and handles. All knives are designed for hard use. Clean, radical grinds and ergonomic handles are hallmarks of RJ's work, as is his reputation for producing "Scary Sharp" knives. Technical: Grinds CPM30V, CPM 3V, CPM154CM, A2 and stainless Damascus. Other CPM alloys used on request. Performs all heat treating and cryogenic processing in-house. Remarks: Full-time maker since 2001 and materials engineer. Former helicopter designer. First knife sold in 1976.

MARTIN, TONY,
PO Box 10, Arcadia, MO 63621, Phone: 573-546-2254, arcadian@charter.net; Web: www.arcadianforge.com
Specialties: Specializes in historical designs, esp. puukko, skean dhu. Remarks: Premium quality blades, exotic wood handles, unmatched fit and finish. Mark: AF.

MARTIN, WALTER E,
570 Cedar Flat Rd, Williams, OR 97544, Phone: 541-846-6755

MARTIN, JOHN ALEXANDER,
821 N Grand Ave, Okmulgee, OK 74447, Phone: 918-758-1099, jam@jamblades.com; Web: www.jamblades.com
Specialties: Inlaid and engraved handles. Patterns: Bowies, fighters, hunters and traditional patterns. Swords, fixed blade knives, folders and axes. Technical: Forges 5160, 1084, 10XX, O1, L6 and his own Damascus. Prices: Start at $300. Remarks: Part-time maker. Mark: Two initials with last name and MS or 5 pointed star.

MARZITELLI, PETER,
19929 35A Ave, Langley, BC, CANADA V3A 2R1, Phone: 604-532-8899, marzitelli@shaw.ca
Specialties: Specializes in unique functional knife shapes and designs using natural and synthetic handle materials. Patterns: Mostly folders, some daggers and art knives. Technical: Grinds ATS-34, S/S Damascus and others. Prices: $220 to $1000 (average $375). Remarks: Full-time maker; first knife sold in 1984. Mark: Stylized logo reads "Marz."

MASON, BILL,
9306 S.E. Venns St., Hobe Sound, FL 33455, Phone: 772-545-3649
Specialties: Combat knives; some folders. Patterns: Fighters to match knife types in book Cold Steel. Technical: Grinds O1, 440C and ATS-34. Prices: $115 to $250; some to $350. Remarks: Spare-time maker; first knife sold in 1979. Mark: Initials connected.

MASSEY, AL,
Box 14 Site 15 RR#2, Mount Uniacke, NS, CANADA B0N 1Z0, Phone: 902-866-4754, armjan@eastlink.ca
Specialties: Working knives and period pieces. Patterns: Swords and daggers of Celtic to medieval design, Bowies. Technical: Forges 5160, 1084 and 1095. Makes own Damascus. Prices: $200 to $500, damascus $300-$1000. Remarks: Part-time maker, first blade sold in 1988. Mark: Initials and JS on Ricasso.

MASSEY, ROGER,
4928 Union Rd, Texarkana, AR 71854, Phone: 870-779-1018
Specialties: Traditional and working straight knives and folders of his design and to customer specs. Patterns: Bowies, hunters, daggers and utility knives. Technical: Forges 1084 and 52100, makes his own Damascus. Offers filework and silver wire inlay in handles. Prices: $200 to $1500; some to $2500. Remarks: Part-time maker; first knife sold in 1991. Mark: Last name, M.S.

MASSEY, RON,
61638 El Reposo St., Joshua Tree, CA 92252, Phone: 760-366-9239 after 5 p.m., Fax: 763-366-4620
Specialties: Classic, traditional, fancy/embellished, high art, period pieces, working/using knives, straight knives, folders, and automatics. Your design, customer specs, about 175 standard patterns. Patterns: Automatics, hunters and fighters. All folders are side-locking folders. Unless requested as lock books slip joint he specializes or custom designs. Technical: ATS-34, D-2 upon request. Engraving, filework, scrimshaw, most of the exotic handle materials. All aspects are performed by him: inlay work in pearls or stone, handmade Pem' work. Prices: $110 to $2500; some to $6000. Remarks: Part-time maker; first knife sold in 1976.

MATA, LEONARD,
3583 Arruza St, San Diego, CA 92154, Phone: 619-690-6935

MATHEWS, CHARLIE AND HARRY,
TWIN BLADES, 121 Mt Pisgah Church Rd., Statesboro, GA 30458, Phone: 912-865-9098, twinblades@bulloch.net; Web: www.twinxblades.com
Specialties: Working straight knives, carved stag handles. Patterns: Hunters, fighters, Bowies and period pieces. Technical: Grinds D2, CPMS30V, CPM3V, ATS-34 and commercial Damascus; handmade sheaths some with exotic leather, filework. Forges 1095, 1084, and 5160. Prices: Starting at $125. Remarks: Twin brothers making knives full-time under the label of Twin Blades. Charter members Georgia Custom Knifemakers Guild. Members of The Knifemakers Guild. Mark: Twin Blades over crossed knives, reverse side steel type.

MATSUNO, KANSEI,
109-8 Uenomachi, Nishikaiden, Gifu-City, JAPAN 501-1168, Phone: 81 58 234 8643

MATSUOKA, SCOT,
94-415 Ukalialii Place, Mililani, HI 96789, Phone: 808-625-6658, Fax: 808-625-6658, scottym@hawaii.rr.com; Web: www.matsuokaknives.com
Specialties: Folders, fixed blades with custom hand-stitched sheaths. Patterns: Gentleman's knives, hunters, tactical folders. Technical: CPM 154CM, 440C, 154, BG42, bolsters, file work, and engraving. Prices: Starting price $350. Remarks: Part-time maker, first knife sold in 2002. Mark: Logo, name and state.

MATSUSAKI, TAKESHI,
MATSUSAKI KNIVES, 151 Ono-Cho, Sasebo-shi, Nagasaki, JAPAN, Phone: 0956-47-2938, Fax: 0956-47-2938
Specialties: Working and collector grade front look and slip joint. Patterns: Sheffierd type folders. Technical: Grinds ATS-34 k-120. Price: $250 to $1000, some to $8000. Remarks: Part-time maker, first knife sold in 1990. Mark: Name and initials.

MAXEN, MICK,
2 Huggins Welham Green, Hatfield, Herts, UNITED KINGDOM AL97LR, Phone: 01707 261213, mmaxen@aol.com
Specialties: Damascus and Mosaic. Patterns: Medieval-style daggers and Bowies. Technical: Forges CS75 and 15N20 / nickel Damascus. Mark: Last name with axe above.

MAXFIELD, LYNN,
382 Colonial Ave, Layton, UT 84041, Phone: 801-544-4176, lcmaxfield@msn.com
Specialties: Sporting knives, some fancy. Patterns: Hunters, fishing, fillet, special purpose; some locking folders. Technical: Grinds 440-C, 154-CM, CPM154, D2, CPM S30V, and Damascus. Prices: $125 to $400; some to $900. Remarks: Part-time maker; first knife sold in 1979. Mark: Name, city and state.

MAXWELL, DON,
1484 Celeste Ave, Clovis, CA 93611, Phone: 559-299-2197, maxwellknives@aol.com; Web: maxwellknives.com
Specialties: Fancy folding knives and fixed blades of his design. Patterns: Hunters, fighters, utility/camp knives, LinerLock® folders, flippers and fantasy knives. Technical: Grinds 440C, ATS-34, D2, CPM 154, and commercial Damascus. Prices: $250 to $1000; some to $2500. Remarks: Full-time maker; first knife sold in 1987. Mark: Last name only or Maxwell MAX-TAC.

MAY, CHARLES,
10024 McDonald Rd., Aberdeen, MS 39730, Phone: 662-369-0404, charlesmayknives@yahoo.com; Web: charlesmayknives.blademakers.com
Specialties: Fixed-blade sheath knives. Patterns: Hunters and fillet knives. Technical: Scandinavian-ground D2 and S30V blades, black micarta and wood handles, nickel steel pins with maker's own pocket carry or belt-loop pouches. Prices: $215 to $495. Mark: "Charles May Knives" and a knife in a circle.

MAYNARD, LARRY JOE,
PO Box 493, Crab Orchard, WV 25827
Specialties: Fancy and fantasy straight knives. Patterns: Big knives; a Bowie with a full false edge; fighting knives. Technical: Grinds standard steels. Prices: $350 to $500; some to $1000. Remarks: Full-time maker; first knife sold in 1986. Mark: Middle and last initials.

MAYNARD, WILLIAM N.,
2677 John Smith Rd, Fayetteville, NC 28306, Phone: 910-425-1615
　　Specialties: Traditional and working straight knives of all designs. Patterns: Combat, Bowies, fighters, hunters and utility knives. Technical: Grinds 440C, ATS-34 and commercial Damascus. Offers fancy filework; handmade sheaths. Prices: $100 to $300; some to $750. Remarks: Full-time maker; first knife sold in 1988. Mark: Last name.

MAYO JR., HOMER,
18036 Three Rivers Rd., Biloxi, MS 39532, Phone: 228-326-8298
　　Specialties: Traditional working straight knives, folders and tactical. Patterns: Hunters, fighters, tactical, bird, Bowies, fish fillet knives and lightweight folders. Technical: Grinds 440C, ATS-34, D-2, Damascus, forges and grinds 52100 and custom makes sheaths. Prices: $100 to $1000. Remarks: Part-time maker Mark: All knives are serial number and registered in the name of the original purchaser, stamped last name or etched.

MAYO JR., TOM,
67 412 Alahaka St, Waialua, HI 96791, Phone: 808-637-6560, mayot001@hawaii.rr.com; Web: www.mayoknives.com
　　Specialties: Framelocks/tactical knives. Patterns: Combat knives, hunters, Bowies and folders. Technical: Titanium/stellite/S30V. Prices: $500 to $1000. Remarks: Full-time maker; first knife sold in 1982. Mark: Volcano logo with name and state.

MAYVILLE, OSCAR L,
2130 E. County Rd 910S, Marengo, IN 47140, Phone: 812-338-4159
　　Specialties: Working straight knives; period pieces. Patterns: Kitchen cutlery, Bowies, camp knives and hunters. Technical: Grinds A2, O1 and 440C. Prices: $50 to $350; some to $500. Remarks: Full-time maker; first knife sold in 1984. Mark: Initials over knife logo.

MCABEE, WILLIAM,
27275 Norton Grade, Colfax, CA 95713, Phone: 530-389-8163
　　Specialties: Working/using knives. Patterns: Fighters, Bowies, Hunters. Technical: Grinds ATS-34. Prices: $75 to $200; some to $350. Remarks: Part-time maker; first knife sold in 1990. Mark: Stylized WM stamped.

MCCALLEN JR., HOWARD H,
110 Anchor Dr, So Seaside Park, NJ 08752

MCCARLEY, JOHN,
4165 Harney Rd, Taneytown, MD 21787
　　Specialties: Working straight knives; period pieces. Patterns: Hunters, Bowies, camp knives, miniatures, throwing knives. Technical: Forges W2, O1 and his own Damascus. Prices: $150 to $300; some to $1000. Remarks: Part-time maker; first knife sold in 1977. Mark: Initials in script.

MCCARTY, HARRY,
1479 Indian Ridge Rd, Blaine, TN 37709, harry@indianridgeforge.com; Web: www.indianridgeforge.com
　　Specialties: Period pieces. Patterns: Trade knives, Bowies, 18th and 19th century folders and hunting swords. Technical: Forges and grinds high-carbon steel. Prices: $75 to $1300. Remarks: Full-time maker; first knife sold in 1977. Doing business as Indian Ridge Forge. Mark: Stylized initials inside a shamrock.

MCCLURE, JERRY,
3052 Isim Rd, Norman, OK 73026, Phone: 405-321-3614, jerry@jmcclureknives.net; Web: www.jmcclureknives.net
　　Specialties: Gentleman's folder, linerlock with my jeweled pivot system of eight rubies, forged one-of-a-kind Damascus Bowies, and a line of hunting/camp knives. Patterns: Folders, Bowie, and hunting/camp Technical Forges own Damascus, also uses Damasteel and does own heat treating. Prices $500 to $3,000 and up Remarks Full-time maker, made first knife in 1965. Mark J.MCCLURE

MCCLURE, MICHAEL,
803 17th Ave, Menlo Park, CA 94025, Phone: 650-323-2596, mikesknives@att.net; Web: www.customknivesbymike.com
　　Specialties: Working/using straight knives of his design and to customer specs. Patterns: Bowies, hunters, skinners, utility/camp, tantos, fillets and boot knives. Technical: Forges high-carbon and Damascus; also grinds stainless, all grades. Prices: Start at $200. Remarks: Part-time maker; first knife sold in 1991. ABS Journeyman Smith. Mark: Mike McClure.

MCCONNELL JR., LOYD A,
309 County Road 144-B, Marble Falls, TX 78654, Phone: 830-798-8087, ccknives@ccknives.com; Web: www.ccknives.com
　　Specialties: Working straight knives and folders, some fancy. Patterns: Hunters, boots, Bowies, locking folders and slip-joints. Technical: Grinds CPM Steels, ATS-34 and BG-42 and commercial Damascus. Prices: $450 to $10,000. Remarks: Full-time maker; first knife sold in 1975. Doing business as Cactus Custom Knives. Markets product knives under name: Lone Star Knives. Mark: Name, city and state in cactus logo.

MCCORNOCK, CRAIG,
MCC MTN OUTFITTERS, 4775 Rt. 212/PO 162, Willow, NY 12495, Phone: 845-679-9758, Mccmtn@aol.com; Web: www.mccmtn.com
　　Specialties: Carry, utility, hunters, defense type knives and functional swords. Patterns: Drop points, hawkbills, tantos, waklzashis, katanas Technical: Stock removal, forged and Damascus, (yes, he still flints knap). Prices: $200 to $2000. Mark: McM.

MCCOUN, MARK,
14212 Pine Dr, DeWitt, VA 23840, Phone: 804-469-7631, mccounandsons@live.com
　　Specialties: Working/using straight knives of his design and in standard patterns; custom miniatures. Patterns: Locking liners, integrals. Technical: Grinds Damascus, ATS-34 and 440C. Prices: $150 to $500. Remarks: Part-time maker; first knife sold in 1989. Mark: Name, city and state.

MCCRACKIN, KEVIN,
3720 Hess Rd, House Springs, MO 63051, Phone: 636-677-6066

MCCRACKIN AND SON, V J,
3720 Hess Rd, House Springs, MO 63051, Phone: 636-677-6066
　　Specialties: Working straight knives in standard patterns. Patterns: Hunters, Bowies and camp knives. Technical: Forges L6, 5160, his own Damascus, cable Damascus. Prices: $125 to $700; some to $1500. Remarks: Part-time maker; first knife sold in 1983. Son Kevin helps make the knives. Mark: Last name, M.S.

MCCULLOUGH, JERRY,
274 West Pettibone Rd, Georgiana, AL 36033, Phone: 334-382-7644, ke4er@alaweb.com
　　Specialties: Standard patterns or custom designs. Technical: Forge and grind scrap-tool and Damascus steels. Use natural handle materials and turquoise trim on some. Filework on others. Prices: $65 to $250 and up. Remarks: Part-time maker. Mark: Initials (JM) combined.

MCDONALD, RICH,
5010 Carmel Rd., Hillboro, OH 45133, Phone: 937-466-2071, rmclongknives@aol.com; Web: www.longknivesandleather.com
　　Specialties: Traditional working/using and art knives of his design. Patterns: Bowies, hunters, folders, primitives and tomahawks. Technical: Forges 5160, 1084, 1095, 52100 and his own Damascus. Fancy filework. Prices: $200 to $1500. Remarks: Full-time maker; first knife sold in 1994. Mark: First and last initials connected.

MCDONALD, ROBERT J,
14730 61 Court N, Loxahatchee, FL 33470, Phone: 561-790-1470
　　Specialties: Traditional working straight knives to customer specs. Patterns: Fighters, swords and folders. Technical: Grinds 440C, ATS-34 and forges own Damascus. Prices: $150 to $1000. Remarks: Part-time maker; first knife sold in 1988. Mark: Electro-etched name.

MCDONALD, W.J. "JERRY",
7173 Wickshire Cove E, Germantown, TN 38138, Phone: 901-756-9924, wjmcdonaldknives@msn.com; Web: www.mcdonaldknives.com
　　Specialties: Classic and working/using straight knives of his design and in standard patterns. Patterns: Bowies, hunters kitchen and traditional spring back pocket knives. Technical: Grinds ATS-34, 154CM, D2, 440V, BG42 and 440C. Prices: $125 to $1000. Remarks: Full-time maker; first knife sold in 1989. Mark: First and middle initials, last name, maker, city and state. Some of his knives are stamped McDonald in script.

MCFALL, KEN,
PO Box 458, Lakeside, AZ 85929, Phone: 928-537-2026, Fax: 928-537-8066, knives@citlink.net
　　Specialties: Fancy working straight knives and some folders. Patterns: Daggers, boots, tantos, Bowies; some miniatures. Technical: Grinds D2, ATS-34 and 440C. Forges his own Damascus. Prices: $200 to $1200. Remarks: Part-time maker; first knife sold in 1984. Mark: Name, city and state.

MCFARLIN, ERIC E,
PO Box 2188, Kodiak, AK 99615, Phone: 907-486-4799
　　Specialties: Working knives of his design. Patterns: Bowies, skinners, camp knives and hunters. Technical: Flat and convex grinds 440C, A2 and AEB-L. Prices: Start at $200. Remarks: Part-time maker; first knife sold in 1989. Mark: Name and city in rectangular logo.

MCFARLIN, J W,
3331 Pocohantas Dr, Lake Havasu City, AZ 86404, Phone: 928-453-7612, Fax: 928-453-7612, aztheedge@NPGcable.com
　　Technical: Flat grinds, D2, ATS-34, 440C, Thomas and Peterson Damascus. Remarks: From working knives to investment. Customer designs always welcome. 100 percent handmade. Made first knife in 1972. Prices: $150 to $3000. Mark: Hand written in the blade.

MCGHEE, E. SCOTT,
7136 Lisbon Rd., Clarkton, NC 28433, Phone: 910-448-2224, guineahogforge@gmail.com; Web: www.guineahogforge.com
　　Specialties: Hunting knives, kitchen blades, presentation blades, tactical knives and sword canes. Technical: Forge and stock removal, all flat-ground blades, including 1080-and-15N20 damascus, 1084, O1 and W2. Prices: $200 to $2,000. Remarks: Planning to be full time in 2014; first knife sold in 2009. Currently an ABS journeyman smith. Mark: E. Scott McGhee (large print) above Guinea Hog Forge (small print).

MCGILL, JOHN,
PO Box 302, Blairsville, GA 30512, Phone: 404-745-4686
　　Specialties: Working knives. Patterns: Traditional patterns; camp knives. Technical: Forges L6 and 9260; makes Damascus. Prices: $50 to $250; some to $500. Remarks: Full-time maker; first knife sold in 1982. Mark: XYLO.

MCGOWAN, FRANK E,
12629 Howard Lodge Rd., Sykesville, MD 21784, Phone: 443-745-2611, fmcgowan11@verizon.net
　　Specialties: Fancy working knives and folders to customer specs. Patterns: Survivor knives, fighters, fishing knives, folders and hunters. Technical: Grinds

and forges O1, 440C, 5160, ATS-34, 52100, or customer choice. Prices: $100 to $1000; some more. Remarks: Full-time maker; first knife sold in 1986. Mark: Last name.

MCGRATH, PATRICK T,
8343 Kenyon Ave, Westchester, CA 90045, Phone: 310-338-8764, hidinginLA@excite.com

MCGRODER, PATRICK J,
5725 Chapin Rd, Madison, OH 44057, Phone: 216-298-3405, Fax: 216-298-3405
Specialties: Traditional working/using knives of his design. Patterns: Bowies, hunters and utility/camp knives. Technical: Grinds ATS-34, D2 and customer requests. Does reverse etching; heat-treats; prefers natural handle materials; custom made sheath with each knife. Prices: $125 to $250. Remarks: Part-time maker. Mark: First and middle initials, last name, maker, city and state.

MCGUANE IV, THOMAS F,
410 South 3rd Ave, Bozeman, MT 59715, Phone: 406-586-0248, Web: http://www.thomasmcguane.com
Specialties: Multi metal inlaid knives of handmade steel. Patterns: Lock back and LinerLock® folders, fancy straight knives. Technical: 1084/1SN20 Damascus and Mosaic steel by maker. Prices: $1000 and up. Mark: Surname or name and city, state.

MCHENRY, WILLIAM JAMES,
Box 67, Wyoming, RI 02898, Phone: 401-539-8353
Specialties: Fancy high-tech folders of his design. Patterns: Locking folders with various mechanisms. Technical: One-of-a-kind only, no duplicates. Inventor of the Axis Lock. Most pieces disassemble and feature top-shelf materials including gold, silver and gems. Prices: Upscale. Remarks: Full-time maker; first knife sold in 1988. Former goldsmith. Mark: Last name or first and last initials.

MCINTYRE, SHAWN,
71 Leura Grove, Hawthornm, E VIC, AUSTRALIA 3123, Phone: 61 3 9813 2049/Cell 61 412 041 062, macpower@netspace.net.au; Web: www.mcintyreknives.com
Specialties: Damascus & CS fixed blades and art knives. Patterns: Bowies, hunters, fighters, kukris, integrals. Technical: Forges, makes own Damascus including pattern weld, mosaic, and composite multi-bars form O1 & 15N20 Also uses 1084, W2, and 52100. Prices: $275 to $2000. Remarks: Full-time maker since 1999. Mark: Mcintyre in script.

MCKEE, NEIL,
674 Porter Hill Rd., Stevensville, MT 59870, Phone: 406-777-3507, mckeenh@peoplepc.com
Specialties: Early American. Patterns: Nessmuk, DeWeese, French folders, art pieces. Technical: Engraver. Prices: $150 to $1000. Mark: Oval with initials.

MCKENZIE, DAVID BRIAN,
2311 B Ida Rd, Campbell River, BC, CANADA V9W-4V7

MCKIERNAN, STAN,
11751 300th St, Lamoni, IA 50140, Phone: 641-784-6873/641-781-0368, slmck@hotmailc.om
Specialties: Self-sheathed knives and miniatures. Patterns: Daggers, ethnic designs and individual styles. Technical: Grinds Damascus and 440C. Prices: $200 to $500, some to $1500. Mark: "River's Bend" inside two concentric circles.

MCLENDON, HUBERT W,
125 Thomas Rd, Waco, GA 30182, Phone: 770-574-9796
Specialties: Using knives; his design or customer's. Patterns: Bowies and hunters. Technical: Hand ground or forged ATS-34, 440C and D2. Prices: $100 to $300. Remarks: First knife sold in 1978. Mark: McLendon or Mc.

MCLUIN, TOM,
36 Fourth St, Dracut, MA 01826, Phone: 978-957-4899, tmcluin@comcast.net; Web: www.mcluinknives.com
Specialties: Working straight knives and folders of his design. Patterns: Boots, hunters and folders. Technical: Grinds ATS-34, 440C, O1 and Damascus; makes his own mokume. Prices: $100 to $400; some to $700. Remarks: Part-time maker; first knife sold in 1991. Mark: Last name.

MCLURKIN, ANDREW,
2112 Windy Woods Dr, Raleigh, NC 27607, Phone: 919-834-4693, mclurkincustomknives.com
Specialties: Collector grade folders, working folders, fixed blades, and miniatures. Knives made to order and to his design. Patterns: Locking liner and lock back folders, hunter, working and tactical designs. Technical: Using patterned Damascus, Mosaic Damascus, ATS-34, BG-42, and CPM steels. Prefers natural handle materials such as pearl, ancient ivory and stabilized wood. Also using synthetic materials such as carbon fiber, titanium, and G10. Prices: $250 and up. Mark: Last name. Mark is often on inside of folders.

MCNABB, TOMMY,
CAROLINA CUSTOM KNIVES, PO Box 327, Bethania, NC 27010, Phone: 336-924-6053, tommy@tmcnabb.com; Web: carolinaknives.com
Specialties: Classic and working knives of his own design or to customer's specs. Patterns: Traditional bowies. Tomahawks, hunters and customer designs. Technical: Forges his own Damascus steel, hand forges or grinds ATS-34 and other hi-tech steels. Prefers mirror finish or satin finish on working knives. Uses exotic or natural handle material and stabilized woods. Price: $300-$3500. Remarks: Full time maker. Made first knife in 1982. Mark" "Carolina Custom Knives" on stock removal blades "T. McNabb" on custom orders and Damascus knives.

MCNEES, JONATHAN,
15203 Starboard Pl, Northport, AL 35475, Phone: 205-391-8383, jmackusmc@yahoo.com; Web: www.mcneescustomknives.com
Specialties: Tactical, outdoors, utility. Technical: Stock removal method utilizing carbon and stainless steels to include 1095, cpm154, A2, cpms35v. Remarks: Part-time maker, first knife made in 2007. Mark: Jmcnees

MCRAE, J MICHAEL,
6100 Lake Rd, Mint Hill, NC 28227, Phone: 704-545-2929, scotia@carolina.rr.com; Web: www.scotiametalwork.com
Specialties: Scottish dirks, sgian dubhs, broadswords. Patterns: Traditional blade styles with traditional and slightly non-traditional handle treatments. Technical: Forges 5160 and his own Damascus. Prefers stag and exotic hardwoods for handles, many intricately carved. Prices: Starting at $125, some to $3500. Remarks: Journeyman Smith in ABS, member of ABANA. Full-time maker, first knife sold in 1982. Doing business as Scotia Metalwork. Mark: Last name underlined with a claymore.

MCWILLIAMS, SEAN,
PO Box 1685, Carbondale, CO 81623, Phone: 970-963-7489, ironventure@q.com; Web: www.seanmcwilliamsforge.com
Specialties: Tactical, survival and working knives in Kydex-and-nylon sheaths. Patterns: Fighters, bowies, hunters and sports knives, period pieces, swords, martial arts blades and some folders. Technical: Forges only, including ATS-34, BG-42, CPM-S30V, CPM-90V and his own damascus. Prices: $165 to $2,500. Remarks: Full-time maker; first knife sold in 1972. Mark: Stylized bear paw.

MEERDINK, KURT,
248 Yulan Barryville Rd., Barryville, NY 12719-5305, Phone: 845-557-0783
Specialties: Working straight knives. Patterns: Hunters, Bowies, tactical and neck knives. Technical: Grinds ATS-34, 440C, D2, Damascus. Prices: $95 to $1100. Remarks: Full-time maker, first knife sold in 1994. Mark: Meerdink Maker, Rio NY.

MEERS, ANDREW,
1100 S Normal Ave., Allyn Bldg MC 4301, Carbondale, IL 62901, Phone: 774-217-3574, namsuechool@gmail.com
Specialties: Pattern welded blades, in the New England style. Patterns: Can do open or closed welding and fancies middle eastern style blades. Technical: 1095, 1084, 15n20, 5160, w1, w2 steels Remarks: Part-time maker attending graduate school at SIUC; looking to become full-time in the future as well as earn ABS Journeyman status. Mark: Korean character for south.

MEIER, DARYL,
75 Forge Rd, Carbondale, IL 62901, Phone: 618-549-3234, Web: www.meiersteel.com
Specialties: One-of-a-kind knives and swords. Patterns: Collaborates on blades. Technical: Forges his own Damascus, W1 and A203E, 440C, 431, nickel 200 and clad steel. Prices: $250 to $450; some to $6000. Remarks: Full-time smith and researcher since 1974; first knife sold in 1974. Mark: Name or circle/arrow symbol or SHAWNEE.

MELIN, GORDON C,
14207 Coolbank Dr, La Mirada, CA 90638, Phone: 562-946-5753

MELOY, SEAN,
7148 Rosemary Lane, Lemon Grove, CA 91945-2105, Phone: 619-465-7173
Specialties: Traditional working straight knives of his design. Patterns: Bowies, fighters and utility/camp knives. Technical: Grinds 440C, ATS-34 and D2. Prices: $125 to $300. Remarks: Part-time maker; first knife sold in 1985. Mark: Broz Knives.

MENEFEE, RICKY BOB,
2440 County Road 1322, Blawchard, OK 73010, rmenefee@pldi.net
Specialties: Working straight knives and pocket knives. Patterns: Hunters, fighters, minis & Bowies. Technical: Grinds ATS-34, 440C, D2, BG42 and S30V. Price: $130 to $1000. Remarks: Part-time maker, first knife sold in 2001. Member of KGA of Oklahoma, also Knifemakers Guild. Mark: Menefee made or Menefee stamped in blade.

MENSCH, LARRY C,
Larry's Knife Shop, 578 Madison Ave, Milton, PA 17847, Phone: 570-742-9554
Specialties: Custom orders. Patterns: Bowies, daggers, hunters, tantos, short swords and miniatures. Technical: Grinds ATS-34, stainless steel Damascus; blade grinds hollow, flat and slack. Filework; bending guards and fluting handles with finger grooves. Prices: $200 and up. Remarks: Full-time maker; first knife sold in 1993. Doing business as Larry's Knife Shop. Mark: Connected capital "L" and small "m" in script.

MERCER, MIKE,
149 N. Waynesville Rd, Lebanon, OH 45036, Phone: 513-932-2837, mmercer08445@roadrunner.com
Specialties: Miniatures and autos. Patterns: All folder patterns. Technical: Diamonds and gold, one-of-a-kind, Damascus, O1, stainless steel blades. Prices: $500 to $5000. Remarks: Carved wax - lost wax casting. Mark: Stamp - Mercer.

MERCHANT, TED,
7 Old Garrett Ct, White Hall, MD 21161, Phone: 410-343-0380
Specialties: Traditional and classic working knives. Patterns: Bowies, hunters, camp knives, fighters, daggers and skinners. Technical: Forges W2 and 5160; makes own Damascus. Makes handles with wood, stag, horn, silver and gem stone inlay; fancy filework. Prices: $125 to $600; some to $1500. Remarks: Full-time maker; first knife sold in 1985. Mark: Last name.

MERZ III, ROBERT L,
1447 Winding Canyon, Katy, TX 77493, Phone: 281-391-2897, bobmerz@consolidated.net; Web: www.merzknives.com
   Specialties: Folders. Prices: $350 to $1,400. Remarks: Full time maker; first knife sold in 1974. Mark: MERZ.

MESHEJIAN, MARDI,
5 Bisbee Court 109 PMB 230, Santa Fe, NM 87508, Phone: 505-310-7441, toothandnail13@yahoo.com
   Specialties: One-of-a-kind fantasy and high art straight knives & folders. Patterns: Swords, daggers, folders and other weapons. Technical: Forged steel Damascus and titanium Damascus. Prices: $300 to $5000 some to $7000. Mark: Stamped stylized "M."

MESSER, DAVID T,
134 S Torrence St, Dayton, OH 45403-2044, Phone: 513-228-6561
   Specialties: Fantasy period pieces, straight and folding, of his design. Patterns: Bowies, daggers and swords. Technical: Grinds 440C, O1, 06 and commercial Damascus. Likes fancy guards and exotic handle materials. Prices: $100 to $225; some to $375. Remarks: Spare-time maker; first knife sold in 1991. Mark: Name stamp.

METHENY, H A "WHITEY",
7750 Waterford Dr, Spotsylvania, VA 22551, Phone: 540842-1440, Fax: 540-582-3095, hametheny@aol.com; Web: www.methenyknives.com
   Specialties: Working and using straight knives of his design and to customer specs. Patterns: Hunters and kitchen knives. Technical: Grinds 440C and ATS-34. Offers filework; tooled custom sheaths. Prices: $350 to $450. Remarks: Spare-time maker; first knife sold in 1990. Mark: Initials/full name football logo.

METSALA, ANTHONY,
30557 103rd St. NW, Princeton, MN 55371, Phone: 763-389-2628, acmetsala@izoom.net; Web: www.metsalacustomknives.com
   Specialties: Sole authorship one-off mosaic Damascus liner locking folders, sales of makers finished one-off mosaic Damascus blades. Patterns: Except for a couple EDC folding knives, maker does not use patterns. Technical: Forges own mosaic Damascus carbon blade and bolster material. All stainless steel blades are heat treated by Paul Bos. Prices: $250 to $1500. Remarks: Full-time knifemaker and Damascus steel maker, first knife sold in 2005. Mark: A.C. Metsala or Metsala.

METZ, GREG T,
c/o Yellow Pine Bar HC 83, BOX 8080, Cascade, ID 83611, Phone: 208-382-4336, metzenterprise@yahoo.com
   Specialties: Hunting and utility knives. Prices: $350 and up. Remarks: Natural handle materials; hand forged blades; 1084 and 1095. Mark: METZ (last name).

MEYER, CHRISTOPHER J,
737 Shenipsit Lake Rd, Tolland, CT 06084, Phone: 860-875-1826, shenipsitforge.cjm@gmail.com
   Specialties: Handforged tool steels. Technical: Forges tool steels, grinds stainless. Remarks: Spare-time maker; sold first knife in 2003. Mark: Name and/or "Shenipsit Forge."

MICHINAKA, TOSHIAKI,
I-679 Koyamacho-nishi, Tottori-shi, Tottori, JAPAN 680-0947, Phone: 0857-28-5911
   Specialties: Art miniature knives. Patterns: Bowies, hunters, fishing, camp knives & miniatures. Technical: Grinds ATS-34 and 440C. Prices: $300 to $900 some higher. Remarks: Part-time maker. First knife sold in 1982. Mark: First initial, last name.

MICKLEY, TRACY,
42112 Kerns Dr, North Mankato, MN 56003, Phone: 507-947-3760, tracy@mickleyknives.com; Web: www.mickleyknives.com
   Specialties: Working and collectable straight knives using mammoth ivory or burl woods, LinerLock® folders. Patterns: Custom and classic hunters, utility, fighters and Bowies. Technical: Grinding 154-CM, BG-42 forging O1 and 52100. Prices: Starting at $325 Remarks: Part-time since 1999. Mark: Last name.

MIDGLEY, BEN,
PO Box 577, Wister, OK 74966, Phone: 918-655-6701, mauricemidgley@windstream.net
   Specialties: Multi-blade folders, slip-joints, some lock-backs and hunters. File work, engraving and scrimshaw. Patterns: Reproduce old patterns, trappers, muskrats, stockman, whittlers, lockbacks an hunters. Technical: Grinds ATS-34, 440C, 12-C-27, CPM-154, some carbon steel, and commercial Damascus. Prices: $385 to $1875. Remarks: Full-time maker, first knife sold in 2002. Mark: Name, city, and state stamped on blade.

MIKOLAJCZYK, GLEN,
4650 W. 7 Mile Rd., Caledonia, WI 53108, Phone: 414-791-0424, Fax: 262-835-9697, glenmikol@aol.com Web: www.customtomahawk.com
   Specialties: Pipe hawks, fancy folders, bowies, long blades, hunting knives, all of his own design. Technical: Sole-author, forges own Damascus and powdered steel. Works with ivory, bone, tortoise, horn and antlers, tiger maple, pearl for handle materials. Designs and does intricate file work and custom sheaths. Enjoys exotic handle materials. Prices: Moderate. Remarks: Founded Weg Von Wennig Forge in 2003, first knife sold in 2004. Also, designs and builds mini-forges. Will build upon request. International sales accepted. Mark: Tomahawk and name.

MILES JR., C R "IRON DOCTOR",
1541 Porter Crossroad, Lugoff, SC 29078, Phone: 803-438-5816
   Specialties: Traditional working straight knives of his design or made to custom specs. Patterns: Hunters, fighters, utility camp knives and hatches. Technical: Grinds O1, D2, ATS-34, 440C, 1095, and 154 CPM. Forges 18th century style cutlery of high carbon steels. Also forges and grinds old files and farrier's rasps to make knives. Custom leather sheaths. Prices: $100 and up. Remarks: Part-time maker, first knife sold in 1997. Member of South Carolina Association of Knifemakers since 1997. Mark: Iron doctor plus name and serial number.

MILITANO, TOM,
CUSTOM KNIVES, 77 Jason Rd., Jacksonville, AL 36265-6655, Phone: 256-435-7132, jeffkin57@aol.com
   Specialties: Fixed blade, one-of-a-kind knives. Patterns: Bowies, fighters, hunters and tactical knives. Technical: Grinds 440C, CPM 154CM, A2, and Damascus. Hollow grinds, flat grinds, and decorative filework. Prices: $150 plus. Remarks: Part-time maker. Sold first knives in the mid to late 1980s. Memberships: Founding member of New England Custom Knife Association. Mark: Name engraved in ricasso area - type of steel on reverse side.

MILLARD, FRED G,
27627 Kopezyk Ln, Richland Center, WI 53581, Phone: 608-647-5376
   Specialties: Working/using straight knives of his design or to customer specs. Patterns: Bowies, hunters, utility/camp knives, kitchen/steak knives. Technical: Grinds ATS-34, O1, D2 and 440C. Makes sheaths. Prices: $110 to $300. Remarks: Full-time maker; first knife sold in 1993. Doing business as Millard Knives. Mark: Mallard duck in flight with serial number.

MILLER, DON,
21049 Uncompahgre Rd., Montrose, CO 81403, Phone: 800-318-8127, masterdon_1@yahoo.com; Web: www.masterdonknives.com, http://uncbb.com (pg. 3)

MILLER, HANFORD J,
Box 97, Cowdrey, CO 80434, Phone: 970-723-4708
   Specialties: Working knives in Moran styles, Bowie, period pieces, Cinquedea. Patterns: Daggers, Bowies, working knives. Technical: All work forged: W2, 1095, 5160 and Damascus. ABS methods; offers fine silver repousse, scabboard mountings and wire inlay, oak presentation cases. Prices: $400 to $1000; some to $3000 and up. Remarks: Full-time maker; first knife sold in 1968. Mark: Initials or name within Bowie logo.

MILLER, JAMES P,
9024 Goeller Rd, RR 2, Box 28, Fairbank, IA 50629, Phone: 319-635-2294, Web: www.damascusknives.biz
   Specialties: All tool steel Damascus; working knives and period pieces. Patterns: Hunters, Bowies, camp knives and daggers. Technical: Forges and grinds 1095, 52100, 440C and his own Damascus. Prices: $175 to $500; some to $1500. Remarks: Full-time maker; first knife sold in 1970. Mark: First and middle initials, last name with knife logo.

MILLER, M A,
11625 Community Center Dr, Unit #1531, Northglenn, CO 80233, Phone: 303-280-3816
   Specialties: Using knives for hunting. 3-1/2"-4" Loveless drop-point. Made to customer specs. Patterns: Skinners and camp knives. Technical: Grinds 440C, D2, O1 and ATS-34 Damascus miniatures. Prices: $225 to $350; miniatures $75 to $150. Remarks: Part-time maker; first knife sold in 1988. Mark: Last name stamped in block letters or first and middle initials, last name, maker, city and state with triangles on either side etched.

MILLER, MICHAEL,
3030 E Calle Cedral, Kingman, AZ 86401, Phone: 928-757-1359, mike@mmilleroriginals.com
   Specialties: Hunters, Bowies, and skinners with exotic burl wood, stag, ivory and gemstone handles. Patterns: High carbon steel knives. Technical: High carbon and nickel alloy Damascus and high carbon and meteorite Damascus. Also mosaic Damascus. Prices: $235 to $4500. Remarks: Full-time maker since 2002, first knife sold 2000; doing business as M Miller Originals. Mark: First initial and last name with 'handmade' underneath.

MILLER, MICHAEL E,
910146 S. 3500 Rd., Chandler, OK 74834, Phone: 918-377-2411, mimiller1@brightok.net
   Specialties: Traditional working/using knives of his design. Patterns: Bowies, hunters and kitchen knives. Technical: Grinds ATS-34, CPM 440V; forges Damascus and cable Damascus and 52100. Prefers scrimshaw, fancy pins, basket weave and embellished sheaths. Prices: $80 to $300; some to $500. Remarks: Part-time maker; first knife sold in 1984. Doing business as Miller Custom Knives. Member of KGA of Oklahoma and Salt Fork Blacksmith Association. Mark: First and middle initials, last name, maker.

MILLER, NATE,
Sportsman's Edge, 1075 Old Steese Hwy N, Fairbanks, AK 99712, Phone: 907-479-4774, sportsmansedge@gci.net Web: www.alaskasportsmansedge.com
   Specialties: Fixed blade knives for hunting, fishing, kitchen and collector pieces. Patterns: Hunters, skinners, utility, tactical, fishing, camp knives-your pattern or mine. Technical: Stock removal maker, ATS-34, 154CM, 440C, D2, 1095, other steels on request. Handle material includes micarta, horn, antler, fossilized ivory and bone, wide selection of woods. Prices: $225-$800. Remarks: Full time maker since 2002. Mark: Nate Miller, Fairbanks, AK.

MILLER, R D,
10526 Estate Lane, Dallas, TX 75238, Phone: 214-348-3496
   Specialties: One-of-a-kind collector-grade knives. Patterns: Boots, hunters,

Bowies, camp and utility knives, fishing and bird knives, miniatures. Technical: Grinds a variety of steels to include O1, D2, 440C, 154CM and 1095. Prices: $65 to $300; some to $900. Remarks: Full-time maker; first knife sold in 1984. Mark: R.D. Custom Knives with date or bow and arrow logo.

MILLER, RICK,
516 Kanaul Rd, Rockwood, PA 15557, Phone: 814-926-2059
Specialties: Working/using straight knives of his design and in standard patterns. Patterns: Bowies, daggers, hunters and friction folders. Technical: Grinds L6. Forges 5160, L6 and Damascus. Patterns for Damascus are random, twist, rose or ladder. Prices: $75 to $250; some to $400. Remarks: Part-time maker; first knife sold in 1982. Mark: Script stamp "R.D.M."

MILLER, RONALD T,
12922 127th Ave N, Largo, FL 34644, Phone: 813-595-0378 (after 5 p.m.)
Specialties: Working straight knives in standard patterns. Patterns: Combat knives, camp knives, kitchen cutlery, fillet knives, locking folders and butterflies. Technical: Grinds D2, 440C and ATS-34; offers brass inlays and scrimshaw. Prices: $45 to $325; some to $750. Remarks: Part-time maker; first knife sold in 1984. Mark: Name, city and state in palm tree logo.

MILLER, STEVE,
1376 Pine St., Clearwater, FL 33756, Phone: 727-461-4180, millknives@aol.com; Web: www.millerknives.com
Patterns: Bowies, hunters, skinners, folders. Technical: 440-C, ATS-34, Sandvic Stainless, CPM-S30-V, Damascus. Exotic hardwoods, bone, horn, antler, ivory, synthetics. All leather work and sheaths made by me and handstitched. Remarks: Have been making custom knives for sale since 1990. Part-time maker, hope to go full time in about five and a half years (after retirement from full-time job). Mark: Last name inside a pentagram.

MILLER, TERRY,
P.O. Box 262, Healy, AK 99743, Phone: 907-683-1239, terry@denalidomehome.com
Specialties: Alaskan ulas with wood or horn. Remarks: New to knifemaking (4 years).

MILLS, LOUIS G,
9450 Waters Rd, Ann Arbor, MI 48103, Phone: 734-668-1839
Specialties: High-art Japanese-style period pieces. Patterns: Traditional tantos, daggers and swords. Technical: Makes steel from iron; makes his own Damascus by traditional Japanese techniques. Prices: $900 to $2000; some to $8000. Remarks: Spare-time maker. Mark: Yasutomo in Japanese Kanji.

MILLS, MICHAEL,
151 Blackwell Rd, Colonial Beach, VA 22443-5054, Phone: 804-224-0265
Specialties: Working knives, hunters, skinners, utility and Bowies. Technical: Forge 5160 differential heat-treats. Prices: $300 and up. Remarks: Part-time maker, ABS Journeyman. Mark: Last name in script.

MINCHEW, RYAN,
2510 Mary Ellen, Pampa, TX 79065, Phone: 806-669-3983, ryan@minchewknives.com Web: www.minchewknives.com
Specialties: Hunters and folders. Patterns: Standard hunter, bird, and trout. Prices: $150 to $500. Mark: Minchew.

MINK, DAN,
PO Box 861, 196 Sage Circle, Crystal Beach, FL 34681, Phone: 727-786-5408, blademkr@gmail.com
Specialties: Traditional and working knives of his design. Patterns: Bowies, fighters, folders and hunters. Technical: Grinds ATS-34, 440C and D2. Blades and tanges embellished with fancy filework. Uses natural and rare handle materials. Prices: $125 to $450. Remarks: Part-time maker; first knife sold in 1985. Mark: Name and star encircled by custom made, city, state.

MINNICK, JIM & JOYCE,
144 North 7th St, Middletown, IN 47356, Phone: 765-354-4108, jmjknives@aol.com; Web: www.minnickknives.com
Specialties: Lever-lock folding art knives, liner-locks. Patterns: Stilettos, Persian and one-of-a-kind folders. Technical: Grinds and carves Damascus, stainless, and high-carbon. Prices: $950 to $7000. Remarks: Part-time maker; first knife sold in 1976. Husband and wife team. Mark: Minnick and JMJ.

MIRABILE, DAVID,
PO BOX 20417, Juneau, AK 99802, Phone: 907-321-1103, dmirabile02@gmail.com; Web: www.mirabileknives.com
Specialties: Elegant edged weapons and hard use Alaskan knives. Patterns: Fighters, personal carry knives, special studies of the Tlinget dagger. Technical: Uses W-2, 1080, 15n20, 1095, 5160, and his own Damascus, and stainless/high carbon San Mai.

MITCHELL, JAMES A,
PO Box 4646, Columbus, GA 31904, Phone: 404-322-8582
Specialties: Fancy working knives. Patterns: Hunters, fighters, Bowies and locking folders. Technical: Grinds D2, 440C and commercial Damascus. Prices: $100 to $400; some to $900. Remarks: Part-time maker; first knife sold in 1976. Sells knives in sets. Mark: Signature and city.

MITCHELL, MAX DEAN AND BEN,
3803 VFW Rd, Leesville, LA 71440, Phone: 318-239-6416
Specialties: Hatchet and knife sets with folder and belt and holster all match. Patterns: Hunters, 200 L6 steel. Technical: L6 steel; soft back, hand edge. Prices: $300 to $500. Remarks: Part-time makers; first knife sold in 1965. Custom orders only; no stock. Mark: First names.

MITCHELL, WM DEAN,
PO Box 2, Warren, TX 77664, Phone: 409-547-2213
Specialties: Functional and collectable cutlery. Patterns: Personal and

collector's designs. Technical:Forges own Damascus and carbon steels. Prices: Determined by the buyer. Remarks:Gentleman knifemaker. ABS Master Smith 1994.Mark: Full name with anvil and MS or WDM and MS.

MITSUYUKI, ROSS,
PO Box 29577, Honolulu, HI 96820, Phone: 808-671-3335, Fax: 808-671-3335, rossman@hawaiiantel.net; Web:www.picturetrail.com/homepage/mrbing
Specialties: Working straight knives and engraving titanium & 416 S.S. Patterns: Hunting, fighters, utility knives and boot knives. Technical: 440C, BG42, ATS-34, S30V, CPM154, and Damascus. Prices: $100 and up. Remarks: Spare-time maker, first knife sold in 1998. Mark: (Honu) Hawaiian sea turtle.

MIVILLE-DESCHENES, ALAIN,
1952 Charles A Parent, Quebec, CANADA G2B 4B2, Phone: 418-845-0950, Fax: 418-845-0950, amd@miville-deschenes.com; Web: www.miville-deschenes.com
Specialties: Working knives of his design or to customer specs and art knives. Patterns: Bowies, skinner, hunter, utility, camp knives, fighters, art knives. Technical: Grinds ATS-34, CPMS30V, 0-1, D2, and sometime forge carbon steel. Prices: $250 to $700; some higher. Remarks: Part-time maker; first knife sold in 2001. Mark: Logo (small hand) and initials (AMD).

MOELLER, HARALD,
#17-493 Pioneer Crescent, Parksville, BC, CANADA V9P 1V2, Phone: 250-248-0391, moeknif@shaw.ca; Web: www.collectiblecustomknives.com
Specialties: Collector grade San Fransisco Dagger; small fighters, Fantasy Axes, Bowies, Survival Knives. Special design award winning liner lock folders; Viper throwing knives. Technical: Steels - 440-C, ATS34, damascus, etc. Materials: mammoth, Abalone, MOP, Black Water Buffalo, 14K Gold, rubies, diamonds, etc. Prices: Throwing knives - $80 to $350; Fighters - $400 to $600; Axe - $3200; Folders - $600 to $3400; Dagger - Up to $9,000 Remarks: Now part time maker, first knife sold in 1979. member Southern California Blades; Member Oregon Knife Collectors Assoc.Mark: Moeller

MOEN, JERRY,
4478 Spring Valley Rd., Dallas, TX 75244, Phone: 972-839-1609, jmoen@moencustomknives.com Web: moencustomknives.com
Specialties: Hunting, pocket knives, fighters tactical, and exotic. Prices: $750 to $2500.

MOJZIS, JULIUS,
B S Timravy 6, 98511 Halic, SLOVAKIA, julius.mojzis@gmail.com; Web: www.juliusmojzis.com
Specialties: Art Knives. Prices: USD $2000. Mark: MOJZIS.

MONCUS, MICHAEL STEVEN,
1803 US 19 N, Smithville, GA 31787, Phone: 912-846-2408

MONTANO, GUS A,
11217 Westonhill Dr, San Diego, CA 92126-1447, Phone: 619-273-5357
Specialties: Traditional working/using straight knives of his design. Patterns: Boots, Bowies and fighters. Technical: Grinds 1095 and 5160; grinds and forges cable. Double or triple hardened and triple drawn; hand-rubbed finish. Prefers natural handle materials. Prices: $200 to $400; some to $600. Remarks: Spare-time maker; first knife sold in 1997. Mark: First initial and last name.

MONTEIRO, VICTOR,
31 Rue D'Opprebais, Maleves Ste Marie, BELGIUM 1360, Phone: 010 88 0441, victor.monteiro@skynet.be
Specialties: Working and fancy straight knives, folders and integrals of his design. Patterns: Fighters, hunters and kitchen knives. Technical: Grinds ATS-34, 440C, D2, Damasteel and other commercial Damascus, embellishment, filework and domed pins. Prices: $300 to $1000, some higher. Remarks: Part-time maker; first knife sold in 1989. Mark: Logo with initials connected.

MONTELL, TY,
PO BOX 1312, Thatcher, AZ 85552, Phone: 928-792-4509, Fax: Cell: 575-313-4373, montellfamily@aol.com
Specialties: Automatics, slip-joint folders, hunting and miniatures.Technical: Stock removal. Steel of choice is CPM-154, Devin Thomas Damascus. Prices: $250 and up. Remarks: First knife made in 1980. Mark: Tang stamp - Montell.

MOONEY, MIKE,
19432 E. Cloud Rd., Queen Creek, AZ 85142, Phone: 480-244-7768, mike@moonblades.com; Web: www.moonblades.com
Specialties: Hand-crafted high-performing straight knives of his or customer's design. Patterns: Bowies, fighters, hunting, camp and kitchen users or collectible. Technical: Flat-grind, hand-rubbed finish, S30V, CMP-154, Damascus, any steel. Prices: $300 to $3000. Remarks: Doing business as moonblades.com. Commissions are welcome. Mark: M. Mooney followed by crescent moon.

MOORE, DAVY,
Moyriesk, Quin, Co Clare, IRELAND, Phone: 353 (0)65 6825975, davy@mooreireland.com; Web: http://www.mooreireland.com
Specialties: Traditional and Celtic outdoor hunting and utility knives. Patterns: Traditional hunters and skinners, Celtic pattern hunting knives, Bushcrafting, fishing, utility/camp knives. Technical: Stock removal knives 01, D2, RWL 34, ATS 34, CPM 154, Damasteel (various).Prices: 250-1700 Euros.Remarks: Full-time maker, first knife sold in 2004. Mark: Three stars over rampant lion / MOORE over Ireland.

MOORE, JAMES B,
1707 N Gillis, Ft. Stockton, TX 79735, Phone: 915-336-2113
Specialties: Classic working straight knives and folders of his design. Patterns: Hunters, Bowies, daggers, fighters, boots, utility/camp knives, locking folders

and slip-joint folders. Technical: Grinds 440C, ATS-34, D2, L6, CPM and commercial Damascus. Prices: $85 to $700; exceptional knives to $1500. Remarks: Full-time maker; first knife sold in 1972. Mark: Name, city and state.

MOORE, JON P,
304 South N Rd, Aurora, NE 68818, Phone: 402-849-2616, Web: www.sharpdecisionknives.com
Specialties: Working and fancy straight knives using antler, exotic bone, wood and Micarta. Will use customers antlers on request. Patterns: Hunters, skinners, camp Bowies. Technical: Hand forged high carbon steel. Makes his own Damascus. Remarks: Full-time maker, sold first knife in 2003, member of ABS - apprentice. Does on location knife forging demonstrations. Mark: Signature.

MOORE, MARVE,
HC 89 Box 393, Willow, AK 99688, Phone: 907-232-0478, marvemoore@aol.com
Specialties: Fixed blades forged and stock removal. Patterns: Hunter, skinners, fighter, short swords. Technical: 100 percent of his work is done by hand. Prices: $100 to $500. Remarks: Also makes his own sheaths. Mark: -MM-.

MOORE, MICHAEL ROBERT,
70 Beauliew St, Lowell, MA 01850, Phone: 978-479-0589, Fax: 978-441-1819

MOORE, TED,
340 E Willow St, Elizabethtown, PA 17022, Phone: 717-367-3939, tedmoore@tedmooreknives.com; Web: www.tedmooreknives.com
Specialties: Damascus folders, cigar cutters, high art. Patterns: Slip joints, linerlock, cigar cutters. Technical: Grinds Damascus and stainless steels. Prices: $250 and up. Remarks: Part-time maker; first knife sold 1993. Mark: Moore U.S.A.

MORETT, DONALD,
116 Woodcrest Dr, Lancaster, PA 17602-1300, Phone: 717-746-4888

MORGAN, JEFF,
9200 Arnaz Way, Santee, CA 92071, Phone: 619-448-8430
Specialties: Early American style knives. Patterns: Hunters, bowies, etc. Technical: Carbon steel and carbon steel damascus. Prices: $60 to $400

MORGAN, TOM,
14689 Ellett Rd, Beloit, OH 44609, Phone: 330-537-2023
Specialties: Working straight knives and period pieces. Patterns: Hunters, boots and presentation tomahawks. Technical: Grinds O1, 440C and 154CM. Prices: Knives, $65 to $200; tomahawks, $100 to $325. Remarks: Full-time maker; first knife sold in 1977. Mark: Last name and type of steel used.

MORRIS, C H,
1590 Old Salem Rd, Frisco City, AL 36445, Phone: 334-575-7425
Specialties: LinerLock® folders. Patterns: Interframe liner locks. Technical: Grinds 440C and ATS-34. Prices: Start at $350. Remarks: Full-time maker; first knife sold in 1973. Doing business as Custom Knives. Mark: First and middle initials, last name.

MORRIS, ERIC,
306 Ewart Ave, Beckley, WV 25801, Phone: 304-255-3951

MORRIS, MICHAEL S.,
609 S. Main St., Yale, MI 48097, Phone: 810-887-7817, michaelmorrisknives@gmail.com
Specialties: Hunting and Tactical fixed blade knives of his design made from files. Technical: All knives hollow ground on 16" wheel. Hand stitches his own sheaths also. Prices: From $60 to $350 with most in the $90 to $125 range. Remarks: Machinist since 1980, made his first knife in 1984, sold his first knife in 2004. Now full-time maker. Mark: Last name with date of manufacture.

MOSES, STEVEN,
1610 W Hemlock Way, Santa Ana, CA 92704

MOSIER, DAVID,
1725 Millburn Ave., Independence, MO 64056, Phone: 816-796-3479, dmknives@aol.com Web: www.dmknives.com
Specialties: Tactical folders and fixed blades. Patterns: Fighters and concealment blades. Technical: Uses S35VN, CPM 154, S30V, 154CM, ATS-34, 440C, A2, D2, Stainless damascus, and Damasteel. Fixed blades come with Kydex sheaths made by maker. Prices: $150 to $1000. Remarks: Full-time maker, business name is DM Knives. Mark: David Mosier Knives encircling sun.

MOSIER, JOSHUA J,
SPRING CREEK KNIFE WORKS, PO Box 476/608 7th St, Deshler, NE 68340, Phone: 402-365-4386, joshmoiser50@gmail.com; Web:www.sc-kw.com
Specialties: Working straight and folding knives of his designs with customer specs. Patterns: Hunter/utility LinerLock® folders. Technical: Forges random pattern Damascus, 01, and 5160. Prices: $85 and up. Remarks: Part-time maker, sold first knife in 1986. Mark: SCKW.

MOULTON, DUSTY,
135 Hillview Lane, Loudon, TN 37774, Phone: 865-408-9779, Web: www.moultonknives.com
Specialties: Fancy and working straight knives. Patterns: Hunters, fighters, fantasy and miniatures. Technical: Grinds ATS-34 and Damascus. Prices: $300 to $2000. Remarks: Full-time maker; first knife sold in 1991. Now doing engraving on own knives as well as other makers. Mark: Last name.

MOYER, RUSS,
1266 RD 425 So, Havre, MT 59501, Phone: 406-395-4423
Specialties: Working knives to customer specs. Patterns: Hunters, Bowies and survival knives. Technical: Forges W2 & 5160. Prices: $150 to $350. Remarks: Part-time maker; first knife sold in 1976. Mark: Initials in logo.

MULKEY, GARY,
533 Breckenridge Rd, Branson, MO 65616, Phone: 417-335-0123, gary@mulkeyknives.com; Web: www.mulkeyknives.com
Specialties: Sole authorship damascus and high-carbon steel hunters, bowies and fighters. Patterns: Fixed blades (hunters, bowies, and fighters). Prices: $450 and up. Remarks: Full-time maker since 1997. Mark: MUL above skeleton key.

MULLER, JODY,
3359 S. 225th Rd., Goodson, MO 65663, Phone: 417-752-3260, mullerforge2@hotmail.com; Web: www.mullerforge.com
Specialties: Hand engraving, carving and inlays, fancy folders and oriental styles. Patterns: One-of-a-kind fixed blades and folders in all styles. Technical: Forges own Damascus and high carbon steel. Prices: $300 and up. Remarks: Full-time knifemaker, does hand engraving, carving and inlay. All work done by maker. Mark: Muller

MUNJAS, BOB,
600 Beebe Rd., Waterford, OH 45786, Phone: 740-336-5538, Web: hairofthebear.com
Specialties: Damascus and carbon steel sheath knives. Patterns: Hunters and neck knives. Technical: My own Damascus, 5160, 1095, 1984, L6, and W2. Forge and stock removal. Does own heat treating and makes own sheaths. Prices: $100 to $500. Remarks: Part-time maker. Mark: Moon Munjas.

MURSKI, RAY,
12129 Captiva Ct, Reston, VA 22091-1204, Phone: 703-264-1102, rmurski@gmail.com
Specialties: Fancy working/using folders of his design. Patterns: Hunters, slip-joint folders and utility/camp knives. Technical: Grinds CPM-3V Prices: $125 to $500. Remarks: Spare-time maker; first knife sold in 1996. Mark: Engraved name with serial number under name.

MUTZ, JEFF,
8210 Rancheria Dr. Unit 7, Rancho Cucamonga, CA 91730, Phone: 909-559-7129, jmutzknives@hotmail.com; Web: www.jmutzknives.com
Specialties: Traditional working/using fixed blade and slip-jointed knives of own design and customer specs. Patterns: Hunters, skinners, and folders. Technical: Forges and grinds all steels Offers scrimshaw. Prices: $225 to $800. Remarks: Full-time maker, first knife sold in 1998. Mark: First initial, last name over "maker."

MYERS, PAUL,
644 Maurice St, Wood River, IL 62095, Phone: 618-258-1707
Specialties: Fancy working straight knives and folders. Patterns: Full range of folders, straight hunters and Bowies; tie tacks; knife and fork sets. Technical: Grinds D2, 440C, ATS-34 and 154CM. Prices: $100 to $350; some to $3000. Remarks: Full-time maker; first knife sold in 1974. Mark: Initials with setting sun on front; name and number on back.

MYERS, STEVE,
1429 Carolina Ave., Springfield, IL 62702, Phone: 217-416-0800, myersknives@ymail.com
Specialties: Working straight knives and integrals. Patterns: Camp knives, hunters, skinners, Bowies, and boot knives.Technical: Forges own Damascus and high carbon steels. Prices: $250 to $1,000. Remarks: Full-time maker, first knife sold in 1985. Mark: Last name in logo.

N

NADEAU, BRIAN,
SHARPBYDESIGN LLC, 8 Sand Hill Rd., Stanhope, NJ 07874, Phone: 862-258-0792, nadeau@sharpbydesign.com; Web: www.sharpbydesign.com
Specialties: High-quality tactical fixed blades and folders, collector and working blades. All blades and sheaths of maker's own design. Designs, writes programs and machines all components on CNC equipment, nothing water jet; everything hand finished. Technical: Works with new CPM steels, but loves to get an order for a W2 blade with a nice hamon or temper line. Prices: $100 and up. Remarks: Part-time maker. Mark: Name in script, or initials "BN" skewed on top of one another.

NARASADA, MAMORU,
9115-8 Nakaminowa, Minowa-machi, Kamiina-gun, NAGANO, JAPAN 399-4601, Phone: 81-265-79-3960, Fax: 81-265-79-3960
Specialties: Utility working straight knife. Patterns: Hunting, fishing, and camping knife. Technical: Grind and forges / ATS34, VG10, 440C, CRM07. Prices: $150 to $500, some higher. Remarks: First knife sold in 2003. Mark: M.NARASADA with initial logo.

NATEN, GREG,
1804 Shamrock Way, Bakersfield, CA 93304-3921
Specialties: Fancy and working/using folders of his design. Patterns: Fighters, hunters and locking folders. Technical: Grinds 440C, ATS-34 and CPM440V. Heat-treats; prefers desert ironwood, stag and mother-of-pearl. Designs and sews leather sheaths for straight knives. Prices: $175 to $600; some to $950. Remarks: Spare-time maker; first knife sold in 1992. Mark: Last name above battle-ax, handmade.

NAUDE, LOUIS,
15 Auction St, Dalsig, Malmesbury, WC, SOUTH AFRICA 7560, Phone: +27-0-21-981-0079, info@louisnaude.co.za Web: www.louisnaude.co.za
Specialties: Folders, Hunters, Custom.. Patterns: See Website. Technical: Stock removal, African materials.Prices: See website. Remarks: Still the tool! Mark: Louis Naude Knives with family crest.

NEALY, BUD,
125 Raccoon Way, Stroudsburg, PA 18360, Phone: 570-402-1018, Fax: 570-402-1018, bnealy@ptd.net; Web: www.budnealyknifemaker.com
Specialties: Original design concealment knives with designer multi-concealment sheath system. Patterns: Fixed Blades and Folders Technical: Grinds CPM 154, XHP, and Damascus. Prices: $200 to $2500. Remarks: Full-time maker; first knife sold in 1980. Mark: Name, city, state or signature.

NEASE, WILLIAM,
2336 Front Rd., LaSalle, ON, CANADA Canada N9J 2C4, wnease@hotmail.com Web: www.unsubtleblades.com
Specialties: Hatchets, choppers, and Japanese-influenced designs. Technical: Stock removal. Works A-2, D-2, S-7, O-1, powder stainless alloys, composite laminate blades with steel edges. Prices: $125 to $2200. Remarks: Part-time maker since 1994. Mark: Initials W.M.N. engraved in cursive on exposed tangs or on the spine of blades.

NEDVED, DAN,
206 Park Dr, Kalispell, MT 59901, bushido2222@yahoo.com
Specialties: Slip joint folders, liner locks, straight knives. Patterns: Mostly traditional or modern blend with traditional lines. Technical: Grinds ATS-34, 440C, 1095 and uses other makers Damascus. Prices: $95 and up. Mostly in the $150 to $200 range. Remarks: Part-time maker, averages 2 a month. Mark: Dan Nedved or Nedved with serial # on opposite side.

NEELY, GREG,
5419 Pine St, Bellaire, TX 77401, Phone: 713-991-2677, gtneely64@comcast.net
Specialties: Traditional patterns and his own patterns for work and/or collecting. Patterns: Hunters, Bowies and utility/camp knives. Technical: Forges own Damascus, 1084, 5160 and some tool steels. Differentially tempers. Prices: $225 to $5000. Remarks: Part-time maker; first knife sold in 1987. Mark: Last name or interlocked initials, MS.

NEILSON, J,
291 Scouten Rd., Wyalusing, PA 18853, Phone: 570-746-4944, mountainhollow@epix.net; Web: www.mountainhollow.net
Specialties: Working and collectable fixed blade knives. Patterns: Hunter/fighters, Bowies, neck knives and daggers. Technical: 1084, 1095, 5160, W-2, 52100, maker's own Damascus. Prices: $175 to $2500. Remarks: ABS Master Smith, full-time maker, first knife sold in 2000, doing business as Neilson's Mountain Hollow. Each knife comes with a sheath. Mark: J. Neilson MS.

NELL, CHAD,
2491 S. 2110E Cir., St. George, UT 84790, Phone: 435-229-6442, chad@nellknives.com; Web: www.nellknives.com
Specialties: Fixed blade working knives. Patterns: hunters, fighters, daggers. Technical: Grinds CPM-154, ATS-34. Prices: Starting at $300. Remarks: Full-time maker since Sep 2011, First knife made in May 2010. Mark: Nell Knives, Nell Knives Kona, Hi, C. Nell Kona, Hawaii and C. Nell Utah, USA.

NELSON, KEN,
2712 17th St., Racine, WI 53405, Phone: 262-456-7519 or 262-664-5293, ken@ironwolfonline.com Web: www.ironwolfonline.com
Specialties: Working straight knives, period pieces. Patterns: Utility, hunters, dirks, daggers, throwers, hawks, axes, swords, pole arms and blade blanks as well. Technical: Forges 5160, 52100, W2, 10xx, L6, carbon steels and own Damascus. Does his own heat treating. Prices: $50 to $350, some to $3000. Remarks: Part-time maker. First knife sold in 1995. Doing business as Iron Wolf Forge. Mark: Stylized wolf paw print.

NETO JR.,, NELSON DE CARVALHO, HENRIQUE M.,
R. Joao Margarido No 20-V, Braganca Paulista, SP, BRAZIL 12900-000, Phone: 011-7843-6889, Fax: 011-7843-6889
Specialties: Straight knives and folders. Patterns: Bowies, katanas, jambyias and others. Technical: Forges high-carbon steels. Prices: $70 to $3000. Remarks: Full-time makers; first knife sold in 1990. Mark: HandN.

NEVLING, MARK,
BURR OAK KNIVES, PO Box 9, Hume, IL 61932, Phone: 217-887-2522, burroakknives@aol.com; Web: www.burroakknives.com
Specialties: Straight knives and folders of his own design. Patterns: Hunters, fighters, Bowies, folders, and small executive knives. Technical: Convex grinds, Forges, uses only high-carbon and Damascus. Prices: $200 to $2000. Remarks: Full-time maker, first knife sold 1988. Apprentice Damascus smith to George Werth and Doug Ponzio.

NEWBERRY, ALLEN,
PO BOX 301, Lowell, AR 72745, Phone: 479-530-6439, newberry@newberryknives.com Web: www.newberryknives.com
Specialties: Fixed blade knives both forged and stock removal. Patterns: Traditional patterns as well as newer designs inspired by historical and international blades. Technical: Uses 1095, W2, 5160, 154-CM, other steels by request. Prices: $150 to $450+. Remarks: Many of the knives feature hamons. Mark: Newberry with a capital N for forged pieces and newberry with a lower case n for stock removal pieces.

NEWCOMB, CORBIN,
628 Woodland Ave, Moberly, MO 65270, Phone: 660-263-4639
Specialties: Working straight knives and folders; period pieces. Patterns: Hunters, axes, Bowies, folders, buckskinned blades and boots. Technical: Hollow-grinds D2, 440C and 154CM; prefers natural handle materials. Makes own Damascus; offers cable Damascus. Prices: $100 to $500. Remarks: Full-time maker; first knife sold in 1982. Doing business as Corbin Knives. Mark: First name and serial number.

NEWHALL, TOM,
3602 E 42nd Stravenue, Tucson, AZ 85713, Phone: 520-721-0562, gggaz@aol.com

NEWTON, LARRY,
1758 Pronghorn Ct, Jacksonville, FL 32225, Phone: 904-537-2066, lnewton1@comcast.net; Web: larrynewtonknives.com
Specialties: Traditional and slender high-grade gentlemen's automatic folders, locking liner type tactical, and working straight knives. Patterns: Front release locking folders, interframes, hunters, and skinners. Technical: Grinds Damascus, ATS-34, 440C and D2. Prices: Folders start at $350, straights start at $150. Remarks: Retired teacher. Full-time maker. First knife sold in 1989. Won Best Folder for 2008 - Blade Magazine.Mark: Last name.

NEWTON, RON,
223 Ridge Ln, London, AR 72847, Phone: 479-293-3001, rnewton@centurylink.net; Web: www.ronnewtonknives.com
Specialties: All types of folders and fixed blades. Blackpowder gun knife combos. Patterns: Traditional slip joint, multi-blade patterns, antique bowie repros. Technical: Forges traditional and mosaic damascus. Performs engraving and gold inlay. Prices: $500 and up. Remarks: Creates hidden mechanisms in assisted opening folders. Mark: NEWTON M.S. in a western invitation font."

NICHOLS, CALVIN,
710 Colleton Rd., Raleigh, NC 27610, Phone: 919-523-4841, calvin.nichols@nicholsknives.com; Web: http://nicholsknives.com
Specialties: Flame-colored high carbon damascus. Patterns: Fixed blades or folders, bowies and daggers. Technical: Stock removal. Prices: Start at $200. Remarks: Full-time maker, 22 years experience, own heat treating, 2012 Best Custom and High Art winner, National and North Carolina Knifemakers Guild member. Mark: First, last name--city, state.

NICHOLS, CHAD,
1125 Cr 185, Blue Springs, MS 38828, Phone: 662-538-5966, chadn28@hotmail.com Web: chadnicholsdamascus.com
Specialties: Gents folders and everyday tactical/utility style knives and fixed hunters. Technical: Makes own stainless damascus, mosaic damascus, and high carbon damascus. Prices: $450 - $1000. Mark: Name and Blue Springs.

NICHOLSON, R. KENT,
PO Box 204, Phoenix, MD 21131, Phone: 410-323-6925
Specialties: Large using knives. Patterns: Bowies and camp knives in the Moran-style. Technical: Forges W2, 9260, 5160; makes Damascus. Prices: $150 to $995. Remarks: Part-time maker; first knife sold in 1984. Mark: Name.

NIELSON, JEFF V,
1060 S Jones Rd, Monroe, UT 84754, Phone: 435-527-4242, jvn1u205@hotmail.com
Specialties: Classic knives of his design and to customer specs. Patterns: Fighters, hunters; miniatures. Technical: Grinds 440C stainless and Damascus. Prices: $100 to $1200. Remarks: Part-time maker; first knife sold in 1991. Mark: Name, location.

NIEMUTH, TROY,
3143 North Ave, Sheboygan, WI 53083, Phone: 414-452-2927
Specialties: Period pieces and working/using straight knives of his design and to customer specs. Patterns: Hunters and utility/camp knives. Technical: Grinds 440C, 1095 and A2. Prices: $85 to $350; some to $500. Remarks: Full-time maker; first knife sold in 1995. Mark: Etched last name.

NILSSON, JONNY WALKER,
Tingstigen 11, Arvidsjaur, SWEDEN 93333, Phone: (46)960-13048, 0960.1304@telia.com; Web: www.jwnknives.com
Specialties: High-end collectible Nordic hunters, engraved reindeer antler. World class freehand engravings. Matching engraved sheaths in leather, bone and Arctic wood with inlays. Combines traditional techniques and design with his own innovations. Master Bladesmith who specializes in forging mosaic Damascus. Sells unique mosaic Damascus bar stock to other makers. Patterns: Own designs and traditional Sami designs. Technical: Mosaic Damascus of UHB 20 C 15N20 with pure nickel, hardness HRC 58-60. Prices: $1500 to $6000. Remarks: Full-time maker since 1988. Nordic Champion (5 countries) numerous times, 50 first prizes in Scandinavian shows. Yearly award in his name in Nordic Championship. Knives inspired by 10,000 year old indigenous Sami culture. Mark: JN on sheath, handle, custom wood box. JWN on blade.

NIRO, FRANK,
1948 Gloaming Dr, Kamloops, B.C., CANADA V1S1P8, Phone: 250-372-8332, niro@telus.net
Specialties: Liner locking folding knives in his designs in what might be called standard patterns. Technical: Enjoys grinding mosaic Damascus with pure nickel of the make up for blades that are often double ground; as well as meteorite for bolsters which are then etched and heat colored. Uses 416 stainless for spacers with inlays of natural materials, gem stones with also file work. Liners are made from titanium are most often fully file worked and anodized. Only uses natural materials particularly mammoth ivory for scales. Prices: $500 to $1500 Remarks: Full time maker. Has been selling knives for over thirty years. Mark: Last name on the inside of the spacer.

NISHIUCHI, MELVIN S,
6121 Forest Park Dr, Las Vegas, NV 89156, Phone: 702-501-3724, msnknives@yahoo.com
Specialties: Collectable quality using/working knives. Patterns: Locking liner folders, fighters, hunters and fancy personal knives. Technical: Grinds ATS-34

and Devin Thomas Damascus; prefers semi-precious stone and exotic natural handle materials. Prices: $375 to $2000. Remarks: Part-time maker; first knife sold in 1985. Mark: Circle with a line above it.

NOLEN, STEVE,
2069 Palomino Tr, Keller, TX 76248-3102, Phone: 903-786-2454, nolen_tx@netzero.net; Web: www.nolenknives.com
Specialties: Working knives; display pieces. Patterns: Wide variety of straight knives, butterflies and buckles. Technical: Grind D2, 440C and 154CM. Offer filework; make exotic handles. Prices: $150 to $800; some higher. Remarks: Full-time maker; Steve is third generation maker. Mark: NK in oval logo.

NOLTE, STEVE,
10801 Gram B Cir., Lowell, AR 72745, Phone: 479-629-1676, snolte@alertalarmsys.com; Web: www.snolteknives.com
Specialties: Fancy hunters and skinners, a few fighters, some collector-grade, high-art knives. One-of-a-kind mosaic handle creations including exotic stone work. Technical: Mostly high-carbon damascus, some stainless damascus with very few straight stainless blades. Hollow grinds. Prices: Start at $295. All prices include handmade sheaths, mostly exotic leathers. Mark: S.Nolte.

NORDELL, INGEMAR,
Skarp vagen 5, Fšrila, SWEDEN 82041, Phone: 0651-23347, ingi@ingemarnordell.se; Web: www.ingemarnordell.se
Specialties: Classic working and using straight knives. Patterns: Hunters, Bowies and fighters. Technical: Forges and grinds ATS-34, D2 and Sandvik. Prices: $300 to $3,000. Remarks: Part-time maker; first knife sold in 1985. Mark: Initials or name.

NOREN, DOUGLAS E,
14676 Boom Rd, Springlake, MI 49456, Phone: 616-842-4247, gnoren@icsdata.com
Specialties: Hand forged blades, custom built and made to order. Hand file work, carving and casting. Stag and stacked handles. Replicas of Scagel and Joseph Rogers. Hand tooled custom made sheaths. Technical: Master smith, 5160, 52100 and 1084 steel. Prices: Start at $250. Remarks: Sole authorship, works in all mediums, ABS Mastersmith, all knives come with a custom hand-tooled sheath. Also makes anvils. Enjoys the challenge and meeting people.

NORFLEET, ROSS W,
4110 N Courthouse Rd, Providence Forge, VA 23140-3420, Phone: 804-966-2596, rossknife@aol.com
Specialties: Classic, traditional and working/using knives of his design or in standard patterns. Patterns: Hunters and folders. Technical: Hollow-grinds 440C and ATS-34. Prices: $150 to $550. Remarks: Part-time maker; first knife sold in 1992. Mark: Last name.

NORTON, DON,
95N Wilkison Ave, Port Townsend, WA 98368-2534, Phone: 306-385-1978
Specialties: Fancy and plain straight knives. Patterns: Hunters, small Bowies, tantos, boot knives, fillets. Technical: Prefers 440C, Micarta, exotic woods and other natural handle materials. Hollow-grinds all knives except fillet knives. Prices: $185 to $2800; average is $200. Remarks: Full-time maker; first knife sold in 1980. Mark: Full name, Hsi Shuai, city, state.

NOWACKI, STEPHEN R.,
167 King Georges Ave, Regents Park, Southampton, Hampshire, ENGLAND SO154LD, Phone: 023 8032 5405, stephen.nowacki@hotmail.co.uk Web: www.whitetigerknives.com
Specialties: Hand-forged, bowies, daggers, tactical blades, hunters and mountain-man style folders. Technical: Flat grinds 0-1, 1084, 5160, and hand forged Damascus. Heat treats and uses natural handle materials. Prices: $200 - $1500. Remarks: Part-time maker. First knife sold in 2000. Doing business as White Tiger Knives. Mark: Stylized W T.

NOWLAND, RICK,
3677 E Bonnie Rd, Waltonville, IL 62894, Phone: 618-279-3170, ricknowland@frontiernet.net
Specialties: Slip joint folders in traditional patterns. Patterns: Trapper, whittler, sowbelly, toothpick and copperhead. Technical: Uses ATS-34, bolsters and liners have integral construction. Prices: $225 to $1000. Remarks: Part-time maker. Mark: Last name.

NUCKELS, STEPHEN J,
1105 Potomac Ave, Hagerstown, MD 21742, Phone: 301-739-1287, sgnucks@myactv.net
Specialties: Traditional using/working/everyday carry knives and small neck knives. Patterns: Hunters, bowies, Drop and trailing point knives, frontier styles. Technical: Hammer forges carbon steels, stock removal. Modest silver wire inlay and file work. Sheath work. Remarks: Spare-time maker forging under Potomac Forge, first knife made in 2008. Member W.F. Moran Jr. Foundation, American Bladesmith Society. Mark: Initials.

NUNN, GREGORY,
HC64 Box 2107, Castle Valley, UT 84532, Phone: 435-259-8607
Specialties: High-art working and using knives of his design; new edition knife with handle made from anatomized dinosaur bone, first ever made. Patterns: Flaked stone knives. Technical: Uses gem-quality agates, jaspers and obsidians for blades. Prices: $250 to $2300. Remarks: Full-time maker; first knife sold in 1989. Mark: Name, knife and edition numbers, year made.

O

OATES, LEE,
PO BOX 1391, La Porte, TX 77572, Phone: 281-471-6060, bearoates@att.net Web: www.bearclawknives.com
Specialties: Friction folders, period correct replicas, traditional, working and primitive knives of my design or to customer specs. Patterns: Bowies, teflon-coated fighters, daggers, hunters, fillet and kitchen cutlery. Technical: Heat treating services for other makers. Forges carbon, 440C, D2, and makes own Damascus, stock removal on SS and kitchen cutlery, Teflon coatings available on custom hunters/fighters, makes own sheaths. Remarks: Full-time maker and heat treater since 1996. First knive sold in 1988. Mark: Harmony (yin/yang) symbol with two bear tracks inside all forged blades; etched "Commanche Cutlery" on SS kitchen cutlery.

O'BRIEN, MIKE J.,
3807 War Bow, San Antonio, TX 78238, Phone: 210-256-0673, obrien8700@att.net
Specialties: Quality straight knives of his design. Patterns: Mostly daggers (safe queens), some hunters. Technical: Grinds 440c, ATS-34, and CPM-154. Emphasis on clean workmanship and solid design. Likes hand-rubbed blades and fittings, exotic woods. Prices: $300 to $700 and up. Remarks: Part-time maker, made first knife in 1988. Mark: O'BRIEN in semi-circle.

OCHS, CHARLES F,
124 Emerald Lane, Largo, FL 33771, Phone: 727-536-3827, Fax: 727-536-3827, charlesox@oxforge.com; Web: www.oxforge.com
Specialties: Working knives; period pieces. Patterns: Hunters, fighters, Bowies, buck skinners and folders. Technical: Forges 52100, 5160 and his own Damascus. Prices: $150 to $1800; some to $2500. Remarks: Full-time maker; first knife sold in 1978. Mark: OX Forge.

OCHS, ERIC,
PO BOX 1311, Sherwood, OR 97140, Phone: 503-925-9790, Fax: 503-925-9790, eric@ochs.com Web: www.ochssherworx.com
Specialties: Tactical folders and flippers, as well as fixed blades for tactical, hunting, camping and chopping uses. Patterns: Tactical liner- and frame-lock folders with texture in various synthetic and natural materials. Technical: Focus on powder metals, including CPM-S30V, Elmax, CPM-154, CPM-3V and CPM-S35VN, as well as damascus steels. Flat, hollow and compound convex grinds. Prices: $200 - $1,500. Remarks: Full-time maker; made first knife in 2008 and started selling knives in mid-2009. Mark: The words "Ochs Sherworx" separated by an eight point compass insignia.

ODGEN, RANDY W,
10822 Sage Orchard, Houston, TX 77089, Phone: 713-481-3601

ODOM JR., VICTOR L.,
PO Box 572, North, SC 29112, Phone: 803-247-2749, cell 803-608-0829, vlodom3@tds.net Web: www.knifemakercentral.com
Specialties: Forged knives and tomahawks; stock removal knives. Patterns: Hunters, Bowies, George Herron patterns, and folders. Technical: Use 1095, 5160, 52100 high carbon and alloy steels, ATS-34, and 154 CM. Prices: Straight knives $60 and up. Folders $250 and up. Remarks: Student of Mr. George Henron. SCAK.ORG. Secretary of the Couth Carolina Association of Knifemakers. Mark: Steel stamp "ODOM" and etched "Odom Forge North, SC" plus a serial number.

OGDEN, BILL,
OGDEN KNIVES, PO Box 52, Avis
AVIS, PA 17721, Phone: 570-974-9114
Specialties: One-of-a-kind, liner-lock folders, hunters, skinners, minis. Technical: Grinds ATS-34, 440-C, D2, 52100, Damascus, natural and unnatural handle materials, hand-stitched custom sheaths. Prices: $50 and up. Remarks: Part-time maker since 1992. Marks: Last name or "OK" stamp (Ogden Knives).

OGLETREE JR., BEN R,
2815 Israel Rd, Livingston, TX 77351, Phone: 409-327-8315
Specialties: Working/using straight knives of his design. Patterns: Hunters, kitchen and utility/camp knives. Technical: Grinds ATS-34, W1 and 1075; heat-treats. Prices: $200 to $400. Remarks: Part-time maker; first knife sold in 1955. Mark: Last name, city and state in oval with a tree on either side.

O'HARE, SEAN,
1831 Rte. 776, Grand Manan, NB, CANADA E5G 2H9, Phone: 506-662-8524, sean@ohareknives.com; Web: www.ohareknives.com
Specialties: Fixed blade hunters and folders. Patterns: Small to large hunters and daily carry folders. Technical: Stock removal, flat ground. Prices: $220 USD to $1200 USD. Remarks: Strives to balance aesthetics, functionality and durability. Mark: 1st line - "OHARE KNIVES", 2nd line - "CANADA."

OLIVE, MICHAEL E,
6388 Angora Mt Rd, Leslie, AR 72645, Phone: 870-363-4668
Specialties: Fixed blades. Patterns: Bowies, camp knives, fighters and hunters. Technical: Forged blades of 1084, W2, 5160, Damascus of 1084, and1572. Prices: $250 and up. Remarks: Received J.S. stamp in 2005. Mark: Olive.

OLIVER, TODD D,
719 Artesian Rd. #63, Cheyenne, WY 82007, Phone: 812-821-5928, tdblues7@aol.com
Specialties: Damascus hunters and daggers. High-carbon as well. Patterns: Ladder, twist random. Technical: Sole author of all his blades. Prices: $350 and up. Remarks: Learned bladesmithing from Jim Batson at the ABS school and Damascus from Billy Merritt in Indiana. Mark: T.D. Oliver Spencer IN. Two crossed swords and a battle ax.

OLSON, DARROLD E,
PO Box 1182, McMinnville, OR 97128, Phone: 541-285-1412
Specialties: Straight knives and folders of his design and to customer specs. Patterns: Hunters, liner locks and slip joints. Technical: Grinds ATS-34, 154CM and 440C. Uses anodized titanium; sheaths wet-molded. Prices: $125 to $550 and up. Remarks: Part-time maker; first knife sold in 1989. Mark: Name, type of steel and year.

OLSON, JOE,
210 W. Simson Ave, Geyser, MT 59447, Phone: 406-735-4404, joekeri@3rivers. net Web: www.olsonhandmade.com
Specialties: Theme based art knives specializing in mosaic Damascus autos, folders, and straight knives, all sole authorship. Patterns: Mas. Technical: Foix. Prices: $300 to $5000 with most in the $3500 range. Remarks: Full-time maker for 15 years. Mark: Folders marked OLSON relief carved into back bar. Carbon steel straight knives stamped OLSON, forged hunters also stamped JS on reverse side.

OLSON, ROD,
Box 5973, High River, AB, CANADA T1V 1P6, Phone: 403-652-0885, rod. olson@hotmail.com
Patterns: Button lock folders. Technical: Grinds RWL 34 blade steel, titanium frames. Prices: Mid range. Remarks: Part-time maker; first knife sold in 1979. Mark: Last name.

OLSZEWSKI, STEPHEN,
1820 Harkney Hill Rd, Coventry, RI 02816, Phone: 401-397-4774, blade5377@ yahoo.com; Web: www.olszewskiknives.com
Specialties: Lock back, liner locks, automatics (art knives). Patterns: One-of-a-kind art knives specializing in figurals. Technical: Damascus steel, titanium file worked liners, fossil ivory and pearl. Double actions. Prices: $400 to $20,000. Remarks: Will custom build to your specifications. Quality work with guarantee. Mark: SCO inside fish symbol. Also "Olszewski."

O'MACHEARLEY, MICHAEL,
129 Lawnview Dr., Wilmington, OH 45177, Phone: 937-728-2818, omachearleycustomknives@yahoo.com
Specialties: Forged and Stock removal; hunters, skinners, bowies, plain to fancy. Technical: ATS-34 and 5160, forges own Damascus. Prices: $180-$1000 and up. Remarks: Full-time maker, first knife made in 1999. Mark: Last name and shamrock.

O'MALLEY, DANIEL,
4338 Evanston Ave N, Seattle, WA 98103, Phone: 206-527-0315
Specialties: Custom chef's knives. Remarks: Making knives since 1997.

ONION, KENNETH J,
47-501 Hui Kelu St, Kaneohe, HI 96744, Phone: 808-239-1300, shopjunky@aol. com; Web: www.kenonionknives.com
Specialties: Folders featuring speed safe as well as other invention gadgets. Patterns: Hybrid, art, fighter, utility. Technical: S30V, CPM 154V, Cowry Y, SQ-2 and Damascus. Prices: $500 to $20,000. Remarks: Full-time maker; designer and inventor. First knife sold in 1991. Mark: Name and state.

O'QUINN, W. LEE,
2654 Watson St., Elgin, SC 29045, Phone: 803-438-8322, wleeoquinn@ bellsouth.net; Web: www.creativeknifeworks.com
Specialties: Hunters, utility, working, tactical and neck knives. Technical: Grinds ATS-34, CPM-154, 5160, D2, 1095 and damascus steels. Prices: Start at $100. Remarks: Member of South Carolina Association of Knifemakers. Mark: O'Quinn.

ORFORD, BEN,
Nethergreen Farm, Ridgeway Cross, Malvern, Worcestershire, ENGLAND WR13 5JS, Phone: 44 01886 880410, web: www.benorford.com
Specialties: Working knives for woodcraft and the outdoorsman, made to his own designs. Patterns: Mostly flat Scandinavian grinds, full and partial tang. Also makes specialist woodcraft tools and hook knives. Custom leather sheaths by Lois, his wife. Technical: Grinds and forges 01, EN9, EN43, EN45 plus recycled steels. Heat treats. Prices: $25 - $650. Remarks: Full-time maker; first knife made in 1997. Mark: Celtic knot with name underneath.

ORTEGA, BEN M,
165 Dug Rd, Wyoming, PA 18644, Phone: 717-696-3234

ORTON, RICH,
739 W. Palm Dr., Covina, CA 91722, Phone: 626-332-3441, rorton2@ca.rr.com
Specialties: Straight knives only. Patterns: Fighters, hunters, skinners. Technical: Grinds ATS-34. Heat treats by Paul Bos. Prices: $100 to $1000. Remarks: Full-time maker; first knife sold in 1992. Doing business as Orton Knife Works. Mark: Last name, city state (maker)

OSBORNE, DONALD H,
5840 N McCall, Clovis, CA 93611, Phone: 559-299-9483, Fax: 559-298-1751, oforge@sbcglobal.net
Specialties: Traditional working using straight knives and folder of his design. Patterns: Working straight knives, Bowies, hunters, camp knives and folders. Technical: Forges carbon steels and makes Damascus. Grinds ATS-34, 154CM, and 440C. Prices: $150 and up. Remarks: Part-time maker. Mark: Last name logo and J.S.

OSBORNE, WARREN,
#2-412 Alysa Ln, Waxahachie, TX 75167, Phone: 972-935-0899, Fax: 972-937-9004, ossie6@mac.com Web: www.osborneknives.com
Specialties: Investment grade collectible, interframes, one-of-a-kinds; unique locking mechanisms and cutting competition knives. Patterns: Folders; bolstered and interframes; conventional lockers, front lockers and back lockers; some slip-joints; some high-art pieces. Technical: Grinds CPM M4, BG42, CPM S30V, Damascus - some forged and stock removed cutting competition knives. Prices: $1200 to $3500; some to $5000. Interframes $1250 to $3000. Remarks: Full-time maker; first knife sold in 1980. Mark: Last name in boomerang logo.

OTT, FRED,
1257 Rancho Durango Rd, Durango, CO 81303, Phone: 970-375-9669, fredsknives@wildblue.net
Patterns: Bowies, hunters tantos and daggers. Technical: Forges 1086M, W2 and Damascus. Prices: $250 to $2,000. Remarks: Full-time maker. Mark: Last name.

OTT, TED,
154 Elgin Woods Ln., Elgin, TX 78621, Phone: 512-413-2243, tedottknives@aol.com
Specialties: Fixed blades, chef knives, butcher knives, bowies, fillet and hunting knives. Technical: Use mainly CPM powder steel, also ATS-34 and D-2. B>Prices: $250 - $1000, depending on embellishments, including scrimshaw and engraving. Remarks: Part-time maker; sold first knife in 1993. Won world cutting competition title in 2010 and 2012, along with the Bladesports championship. Mark: Ott Knives Elgin Texas.

OUYE, KEITH,
PO Box 25307, Honolulu, HI 96825, Phone: 808-395-7000, keith@keithouyeknives.com; Web: www.keithouyeknives.com
Specialties: Folders with 1/8 blades and titanium handles. Patterns: Tactical design with liner lock and flipper. Technical: Blades are stainless steel ATS 34, CPM154 and S30V. Titanium liners (.071) and scales 3/16 pivots and stop pin, titanium pocket clip. Heat treat by Paul Bos. Prices: $495 to $995, with engraved knives starting at $1,200. Remarks: Engraving done by C.J. Cal, Bruce Shaw, Lisa Tomlin and Tom Ferry. Retired, so basically a full time knifemaker. Sold first fixed blade in 2004 and first folder in 2005. Mark: Ouye/Hawaii with steel type on back side Other: Selected by Blade Magazine (March 2006 issue) as one of five makers to watch in 2006.

OVEREYNDER, T R,
1800 S. Davis Dr, Arlington, TX 76013, Phone: 817-277-4812, Fax: 817-277-4812, trovereynder@gmail.com or tom@overeynderknives.com; Web: www. overeynderknives.com
Specialties: Highly finished collector-grade knives. Multi-blades. Patterns: Fighters, Bowies, daggers, locking folders, 70 percent collector-grade multi blade slip joints, 25 percent interframe, 5 percent fixed blade Technical: Grinds CPM-D2, BG-42, S60V, S30V, CPM154, CPM M4, CTS-XHP, RWL-34 vendor supplied Damascus. Has been making titanium-frame folders since 1977. Prices: $750 to $2000, some to $7000. Remarks: Full-time maker; first knife made in 1977. Doing business as TRO Knives. Mark: T.R. OVEREYNDER KNIVES, city and state.

OWENS, DONALD,
2274 Lucille Ln, Melbourne, FL 32935, Phone: 321-254-9765

OWENS, JOHN,
14500 CR 270, Nathrop, CO 81236, Phone: 719-207-0067
Specialties: Hunters. Prices: $225 to $425 some to $700. Remarks: Spare-time maker. Mark: Last name.

OWNBY, JOHN C,
708 Morningside Tr., Murphy, TX 75094-4365, Phone: 972-442-7352, john@johnownby.com; Web: www.johnownby.com
Specialties: Hunters, utility/camp knives. Patterns: Hunters, locking folders and utility/camp knives. Technical: 440C, D2 and ATS-34. All blades are flat ground. Prefers natural materials for handles—exotic woods, horn and antler. Prices: $150 to $350; some to $500. Remarks: Part-time maker; first knife sold in 1993. Doing business as John C. Ownby Handmade Knives. Mark: Name, city, state.

OYSTER, LOWELL R,
543 Grant Rd, Corinth, ME 04427, Phone: 207-884-8663
Specialties: Traditional and original designed multi-blade slip-joint folders. Patterns: Hunters, minis, camp and fishing knives. Technical: Grinds O1; heat-treats. Prices: $55 to $450; some to $750. Remarks: Full-time maker; first knife sold in 1981. Mark: A scallop shell.

P

PACKARD, BOB,
PO Box 311, Elverta, CA 95626, Phone: 916-991-5218
Specialties: Traditional working/using straight knives of his design and to customer specs. Patterns: Hunters, fishing knives, utility/camp knives. Technical: Grinds ATS-34, 440C; Forges 52100, 5168 and cable Damascus. Prices: $75 to $225. Mark: Engraved name and year.

PACKARD, RONNIE,
301 White St., Bonham, TX 75418, Phone: 903-227-3131, packardknives@gmail.com; Web: www.packardknives.com
Specialties: Bowies, folders (lockback, slip joint, frame lock, Hobo knives) and hunters of all sizes. Technical: Grinds 440C, ATS-34, D2 and stainless damascus. Makes own sheaths, does heat treating and sub-zero quenching in shop. Prices: $160 to $2,000. Remarks: Part-time maker; first knife sold in 1975. Mark: Last name over year.

PADILLA, GARY,
PO Box 5706, Bellingham, WA 98227, Phone: 360-756-7573, gkpadilla@yahoo.com
Specialties: Unique knives of all designs and uses. Patterns: Hunters, kitchen knives, utility/camp knives and obsidian ceremonial knives. Technical: Grinds 440C, ATS-34, O1 and Damascus. Prices: Generally $100 to $200. Remarks:

PAGE—PATRICK

Part-time maker; first knife sold in 1977. Mark: Stylized name.

PAGE, LARRY,
1200 Mackey Scott Rd, Aiken, SC 29801-7620, Phone: 803-648-0001
Specialties: Working knives of his design. Patterns: Hunters, boots and fighters. Technical: Grinds ATS-34. Prices: Start at $85. Remarks: Part-time maker; first knife sold in 1983. Mark: Name, city and state in oval.

PAGE, REGINALD,
6587 Groveland Hill Rd, Groveland, NY 14462, Phone: 716-243-1643
Specialties: High-art straight knives and one-of-a-kind folders of his design. Patterns: Hunters, locking folders and slip-joint folders. Technical: Forges O1, 5160 and his own Damascus. Prefers natural materials but will work with Micarta. Remarks: Spare-time maker; first knife sold in 1985. Mark: First initial, last name.

PAINTER, TONY,
87 Fireweed Dr, Whitehorse, YT, CANADA Y1A 5T8, Phone: 867-633-3323, jimmies@klondiker.com; Web: www.tonypainterdesigns.com
Specialties: One-of-a-kind using knives, some fancy, fixed and folders. Patterns: No fixed patterns. Technical: Grinds ATS-34, D2, O1, S30V, Damascus satin finish. Prefers to use exotic woods and other natural materials. Micarta and G10 on working knives. Prices: Starting at $200. Remarks: Full-time knifemaker and carver. First knife sold in 1996. Mark: Two stamps used: initials TP in a circle and painter.

PALIKKO, J-T,
B30 B1 Suomenlinna, 00190 Helsinki, FINLAND, Phone: 358-400-699687, jt@kp-art.fi; Web: www.art-helsinki.com
Specialties: One-of-a-kind knives and swords. Patterns: Own puukko models, hunters, integral & semi-integral knives, swords & other historical weapons and friction folders. Technical: Forges 52100 & other carbon steels, Damasteel stainless damascus & RWL-34, makes own damascus steel, makes carvings on walrus ivory and antler. Prices: Starting at $250. Remarks: Full-time maker; first knife sold in 1989. Mark: JT

PALM, RIK,
10901 Scripps Ranch Blvd, San Diego, CA 92131, Phone: 858-530-0407, rikpalm@knifesmith.com; Web: www.knifesmith.com
Specialties: Sole authorship of one-of-a-kind unique art pieces, working/using knives and sheaths. Patterns: Carved nature themed knives, camp, hunters, friction folders, tomahawks, and small special pocket knives. Technical: Makes own Damascus, forges 5160H, 1084, 1095, W2, O1. Does his own heat treating including clay hardening. Prices: $80 and up. Remarks: American Bladesmith Society Journeyman Smith. First blade sold in 2000. Mark: Stamped, hand signed, etched last name signature.

PALMER, TAYLOR,
TAYLOR-MADE SCENIC KNIVES INC., Box 97, Blanding, UT 84511, Phone: 435-678-2523, taylormadewoodeu@citlink.net
Specialties: Bronze carvings inside of blade area. Prices: $250 and up. Mark: Taylor Palmer Utah.

PANAK, PAUL S,
6103 Leon Rd., Andover, OH 44003, Phone: 330-442-2724, burn@burnknives.com; Web: www.burnknives.com
Specialties: Italian-styled knives. DA OTF's, Italian style stilettos. Patterns: Vintage-styled Italians, fighting folders and high art gothic-styles all with various mechanisms. Technical: Grinds ATS-34, 154 CM, 440C and Damascus. Prices: $800 to $3000. Remarks: Full-time maker, first knife sold in 1998. Mark: "Burn."

PANCHENKO, SERGE,
5927 El Sol Way, Citrus Heights, CA 95621, Phone: 916-588-8821, serge@sergeknives.com Web: www.sergeknives.com
Specialties: Unique art knives using natural materials, copper and carbon steel for a rustic look. Patterns: Art knives, tactical folders, Japanese- and relic-style knives. Technical: Forges carbon steel, grinds carbon and stainless steels. Prices: $100 to $800. Remarks: Part-time maker, first knife sold in 2008. Mark: SERGE

PARDUE, JOE,
PO Box 569, Hillister, TX 77624, Phone: 409-429-7074, Fax: 409-429-5657, joepardue@hughes.net; Web: www.melpardueknives.com/Joepardueknives/index.htm

PARDUE, MELVIN M,
4461 Jerkins Rd., Repton, AL 36475, Phone: 251-248-2686, mpardue@frontiernet.net; Web: www.pardueknives.com
Specialties: Folders, collectable, combat, utility and tactical. Patterns: Lockback, liner lock, push button; all blade and handle patterns. Technical: Grinds 154CM, 440C, 12C27. Forges mokume and Damascus. Uses titanium. Prices: $400 to $1600. Remarks: Full-time maker, Guild member, ABS member, AFC member. First knife made in 1957; first knife sold professionally in 1974. Mark: Mel Pardue.

PARKER, CLIFF,
6350 Tulip Dr, Zephyrhills, FL 33544, Phone: 813-973-1682, cooldamascus@aol.com Web: cliffparkerknives.com
Specialties: Damascus gent knives. Patterns: Locking liners, some straight knives. Technical: Mostly use 1095, 1084, 15N20, 203E and powdered steel. Prices: $700 to $2100. Remarks: Making own Damascus and specializing in mosaics; first knife sold in 1996. Full-time beginning in 2000. Mark: CP.

PARKER, J E,
11 Domenica Cir, Clarion, PA 16214, Phone: 814-226-4837, jimparkerknives@hotmail.com Web:www.jimparkerknives.com
Specialties: Fancy/embellished, traditional and working straight knives of his design and to customer specs. Engraving and scrimshaw by the best in the business. Patterns: Bowies, hunters and LinerLock® folders. Technical: Grinds 440C, 440V, ATS-34 and nickel Damascus. Prefers mastodon, oosik, amber and malachite handle material. Prices: $75 to $5200. Remarks: Full-time maker; first knife sold in 1991. Doing business as Custom Knife. Mark: J E Parker and Clarion PA stamped or etched in blade.

PARKER, ROBERT NELSON,
1527 E Fourth St, Royal Oak, MI 48067, Phone: 248-545-8211, rnparkerknives@wowway.com; Web:classicknifedesign@wowway.com
Specialties: Traditional working and using straight knives of his design. Patterns: Chutes, subhilts, hunters, and fighters. Technical: Grinds ATS-34; GB-42, S-30V, BG-42, ATS, 34-D-Z, no forging, hollow and flat grinds, full and hidden tangs. Hand-stitched leather sheaths. Prices: $400 to $1400; some to $2000. Remarks: Full-time maker; first knife sold in 1986. I do forge sometimes. Mark: Full name.

PARKS, BLANE C,
15908 Crest Dr, Woodbridge, VA 22191, Phone: 703-221-4680
Specialties: Knives of his design. Patterns: Boots, Bowies, daggers, fighters, hunters, kitchen knives, locking and slip-joint folders, utility/camp knives, letter openers and friction folders. Technical: Grinds ATS-34, 440C, D2 and other carbon steels. Offers filework, silver wire inlay and wooden sheaths. Prices: Start at $250 to $650; some to $1000. Remarks: Part-time maker; first knife sold in 1993. Doing business as B.C. Parks Knives. Mark: First and middle initials, last name.

PARKS, JOHN,
3539 Galilee Church Rd, Jefferson, GA 30549, Phone: 706-367-4916
Specialties: Traditional working and using straight knives of his design. Patterns: Hunters, integral bolsters, and personal knives. Technical: Forges 1095 and 5168. Prices: $275 to $600; some to $800. Remarks: Part-time maker; first knife sold in 1989. Mark: Initials.

PARLER, THOMAS O,
11 Franklin St, Charleston, SC 29401, Phone: 803-723-9433

PARRISH, ROBERT,
271 Allman Hill Rd, Weaverville, NC 28787, Phone: 828-645-2864
Specialties: Heavy-duty working knives of his design or to customer specs. Patterns: Survival and duty knives; hunters and fighters. Technical: Grinds 440C, D2, O1 and commercial Damascus. Prices: $200 to $300; some to $6000. Remarks: Part-time maker; first knife sold in 1970. Mark: Initials connected, sometimes with city and state.

PARRISH III, GORDON A,
940 Lakloey Dr, North Pole, AK 99705, Phone: 907-488-0357, ga-parrish@gci.net
Specialties: Classic and high-art straight knives of his design and to customer specs; working and using knives. Patterns: Bowies and hunters. Technical: Grinds tool steel and ATS-34. Uses mostly Alaskan handle materials. Prices: Starting at $225. Remarks: Spare-time maker; first knife sold in 1980. Mark: Last name, FBKS. ALASKA

PARSONS, LARRY,
1038 W Kyle Way, Mustang, OK 73064, Phone: 405-376-9408, Fax: 405-376-9408, l.j.parsons@sbcglobal.net
Specialties: Variety of sheaths from plain leather, geometric stamped, also inlays of various types. Prices: Starting at $35 and up

PARSONS, PETE,
5905 High Country Dr., Helena, MT 59602, Phone: 406-202-0181, Parsons14@MT.net; Web: www.ParsonsMontanaKnives.com
Specialties: Forged utility blades in straight steel or Damascus (will grind stainless on customer request). Folding knives of my own design. Patterns: Hunters, fighters, Bowies, hikers, camp knives, everyday carry folders, tactical folders, gentleman's folders. Some customer designed pieces. Technical: Forges carbon steel, grinds carbon steel and some stainless. Forges own Damascus. Mark: Left side of blade PARSONS stamp or Parsons Helena, MT etch.

PARTRIDGE, JERRY D.,
P.O. Box 977, DeFuniak Springs, FL 32435, Phone: 850-520-4873, jerry@partridgeknives.com; Web: www.partridgeknives.com
Specialties: Fancy and working straight knives and straight razors of his designs. Patterns: Hunters, skinners, fighters, chef's knives, straight razors, neck knives, and miniatures. Technical: Grinds 440C, ATS-34, carbon Damascus, and stainless Damascus. Prices: $250 and up, depending on materials used. Remarks: Part-time maker, first knife sold in 2007. Mark: Partridge Knives logo on the blade; Partridge or Partridge Knives engraved in script.

PASSMORE, JIMMY D,
316 SE Elm, Hoxie, AR 72433, Phone: 870-886-1922

PATRICK, BOB,
12642 24A Ave, S. Surrey, BC, CANADA V4A 8H9, Phone: 604-538-6214, Fax: 604-888-2683, bob@knivesonnet.com; Web: www.knivesonnet.com
Specialties: Maker's designs only, No orders. Patterns: Bowies, hunters, daggers, throwing knives. Technical: D2, 5160, Damascus. Prices: Good value. Remarks: Full-time maker; first knife sold in 1987. Doing business as Crescent Knife Works. Mark: Logo with name and province or Crescent Knife Works.

PATRICK, CHUCK,
4650 Pine Log Rd., Brasstown, NC 28902, Phone: 828-837-7627, chuckandpeggypatrick@gmail.com Web: www.chuckandpeggypatrick.com
 Specialties: Period pieces. Patterns: Hunters, daggers, tomahawks, pre-Civil War folders. Technical: Forges hardware, his own cable and Damascus, available in fancy pattern and mosaic. Prices: $150 to $1000; some higher. Remarks: Full-time maker. Mark: Hand-engraved name or flying owl.

PATRICK, PEGGY,
4650 Pine Log Rd., Brasstown, NC 28902, Phone: 828-837-7627, chuckandpeggypatrick@gmail.com Web: www.chuckandpeggypatrick.com
 Specialties: Authentic period and Indian sheaths, braintan, rawhide, beads and quill work. Technical: Does own braintan, rawhide; uses only natural dyes for quills, old color beads.

PATRICK, WILLARD C,
PO Box 5716, Helena, MT 59604, Phone: 406-458-6552, wilamar@mt.net
 Specialties: Working straight knives and one-of-a-kind art knives of his design or to customer specs. Patterns: Hunters, Bowies, fish, patch and kitchen knives. Technical: Grinds ATS-34, 1095, O1, A2 and Damascus. Prices: $100 to $2000. Remarks: Full-time maker; first knife sold in 1989. Doing business as Wil-A-Mar Cutlery. Mark: Shield with last name and a dagger.

PATTAY, RUDY,
8739 N. Zurich Way, Citrus Springs, FL 34434, Phone: 516-318-4538, dolphin51@att.net; Web: www.pattayknives.com
 Specialties: Fancy and working straight knives of his design. Patterns: Bowies, hunters, utility/camp knives, drop point, skinners. Technical: Hollow-grinds ATS-34, 440C, O1. Offers commercial Damascus, stainless steel soldered guards; fabricates guard and butt cap on lathe and milling machine. Heat-treats. Prefers synthetic handle materials. Offers hand-sewn sheaths. Prices: $100 to $350; some to $500. Remarks: Full-time maker; first knife sold in 1990. Mark: First initial, last name in sorcerer logo.

PATTERSON, PAT,
Box 246, Barksdale, TX 78828, Phone: 830-234-3586, pat@pattersonknives.com
 Specialties: Traditional fixed blades and LinerLock folders. Patterns: Hunters and folders. Technical: Grinds 440C, ATS-34, D2, O1 and Damascus. Prices: $250 to $1000. Remarks: Full-time maker. First knife sold in 1991. Mark: Name and city.

PATTON, DICK AND ROB,
6803 View Ln, Nampa, ID 83687, Phone: 208-468-4123, grpatton@pattonknives.com; Web: www.pattonknives.com
 Specialties: Custom Damascus, hand forged, fighting knives, Bowie and tactical. Patterns: Mini Bowie, Merlin Fighter, Mandrita Fighting Bowie. Prices: $100 to $2000.

PATTON, PHILLIP,
PO BOX 113, Yoder, IN 46798, phillip@pattonblades.com Web: www.pattonblades.com
 Specialties: Tactical fixed blades, including fighting, camp, and general utility blades. Also makes Bowies and daggers. Known for leaf and recurve blade shapes. Technical: Forges carbon, stainless, and high alloy tool steels. Makes own damascus using 1084/15n20 or O1/L6. Makes own carbon/stainless laminated blades. For handle materials, prefers high end woods and sythetics. Uses 416 ss and bronze for fittings. Prices: $175 - $1000 for knives; $750 and up for swords. Remarks: Full-time maker since 2005. Two-year backlog. ABS member. Mark: "Phillip Patton" with Phillip above Patton.

PAULO, FERNANDES R,
Raposo Tavares No 213, Lencois Paulista, SP, BRAZIL 18680, Phone: 014-263-4281
 Specialties: An apprentice of Jose Alberto Paschoarelli, his designs are heavily based on the later designs. Technical: Grinds tool steels and stainless steels. Part-time knifemaker. Prices: Start from $100. Mark: P.R.F.

PAWLOWSKI, JOHN R,
111 Herman Melville Ave, Newport News, VA 23606, Phone: 757-870-4284, Fax: 757-223-5935, www.virginiacustomcutlery.com
 Specialties: Traditional working and using straight knives and folders. Patterns: Hunters, Bowies, fighters and camp knives. Technical: Stock removal, grinds 440C, ATS-34, 154CM and buys Damascus. Prices: $150 to $500; some higher. Remarks: Part-time maker, first knife sold in 1983, Knifemaker Guild Member. Mark: Name with attacking eagle.

PEAGLER, RUSS,
PO Box 1314, Moncks Corner, SC 29461, Phone: 803-761-1008
 Specialties: Traditional working straight knives of his design and to customer specs. Patterns: Hunters, fighters, boots. Technical: Hollow-grinds 440C, ATS-34 and O1; uses Damascus steel. Prefers bone handles. Prices: $85 to $300; some to $500. Remarks: Spare-time maker; first knife sold in 1983. Mark: Initials.

PEARCE, LOGAN,
1013 Dogtown Rd, De Queen, AR 71832, Phone: 580-212-0995, night_everclear@hotmail.com; Web: www.pearceknives.com
 Specialties: Edged weapons, art knives, stright working knives. Patterns: Bowie, hunters, tomahawks, fantasy, utility, daggers, and slip-joint. Technical: Fprges 1080, L6, 5160, 440C, steel cable, and his own Damascus. Prices: $35 to $500. Remarks: Full-time maker, first knife sold in 1992. Doing business as Pearce Knives Mark: Name

PEASE, W D,
657 Cassidy Pike, Ewing, KY 41039, Phone: 606-845-0387, Web: www.wdpeaseknives.com
 Specialties: Display-quality working folders. Patterns: Fighters, tantos and boots; locking folders and interframes. Technical: Grinds ATS-34 and

commercial Damascus; has own side-release lock system. Prices: $500 to $1000; some to $3000. Remarks: Full-time maker; first knife sold in 1970. Mark: First and middle initials, last name and state. W. D. Pease Kentucky.

PEELE, BRYAN,
219 Ferry St, PO Box 1363, Thompson Falls, MT 59873, Phone: 406-827-4633, banana_peele@yahoo.com
 Specialties: Fancy working and using knives of his design. Patterns: Hunters, Bowies and fighters. Technical: Grinds 440C, ATS-34, D2, O1 and commercial Damascus. Prices: $110 to $300; some $900. Remarks: Part-time maker; first knife sold in 1985. Mark: The Elk Rack, full name, city, state.

PELLEGRIN, MIKE,
MP3 Knives, 107 White St., Troy, IL 62294-1126, Phone: 618-667-6777, Web: MP3knives.com
 Specialties: Lockback folders with stone inlays, and one-of-a-kind art knives with stainless steel or damascus handles. Technical: Stock-removal method of blade making using 440C, Damasteel or high-carbon damascus blades. Prices: $800 and up. Remarks: Making knives since 2000. Mark: MP (combined) 3.

PENDLETON, LLOYD,
24581 Shake Ridge Rd, Volcano, CA 95689, Phone: 209-296-3353, Fax: 209-296-3353
 Specialties: Contemporary working knives in standard patterns. Patterns: Hunters, fighters and boots. Technical: Grinds and ATS-34; mirror finishes. Prices: $400 to $900 Remarks: Full-time maker; first knife sold in 1973. Mark: First initial, last name logo, city and state.

PENDRAY, ALFRED H,
13950 NE 20th St, Williston, FL 32696, Phone: 352-528-6124
 Specialties: Working straight knives and folders; period pieces. Patterns: Fighters and hunters, axes, camp knives and tomahawks. Technical: Forges Wootz steel; makes his own Damascus; makes traditional knives from old files and rasps. Prices: $125 to $1000; some to $3500. Remarks: Part-time maker; first knife sold in 1954. Mark: Last initial in horseshoe logo.

PENFOLD, MICK,
PENFOLD KNIVES, 5 Highview Close, Tremar, Cornwall, ENGLAND PL14 5SJ, Phone: 01579-345783, mickpenfold@btinternet.com
 Specialties: Hunters, fighters, Bowies. Technical: Grinds 440C, ATS-34, Damasteel, and Damascus. Prices: $200 to $1800. Remarks: Part-time maker. First knives sold in 1999. Mark: Last name.

PENNINGTON, C A,
163 Kainga Rd, Kainga Christchurch, NEW ZEALAND 8009, Phone: 03-3237292, capennington@xtra.co.nz
 Specialties: Classic working and collectors knives. Folders a specialty. Patterns: Classical styling for hunters and collectors. Technical: Forges his own all tool steel Damascus. Grinds D2 when requested. Prices: $240 to $2000. Remarks: Full-time maker; first knife sold in 1988. Color brochure $3. Mark: Name, country.

PEPIOT, STEPHAN,
73 Cornwall Blvd, Winnipeg, MB, CANADA R3J-1E9, Phone: 204-888-1499
 Specialties: Working straight knives in standard patterns. Patterns: Hunters and camp knives. Technical: Grinds 440C and industrial hack-saw blades. Prices: $75 to $125. Remarks: Spare-time maker; first knife sold in 1982. Not currently taking orders. Mark: PEP.

PERRY, CHRIS,
1654 W. Birch, Fresno, CA 93711, Phone: 559-246-7446, chris.perry4@comcast.net
 Specialties: Traditional working/using straight knives of his design. Patterns: Boots, hunters and utility/camp knives. Technical: Grinds ATS-34, Damascus, 416ss fittings, silver and gold fittings, hand-rubbed finishes. Prices: Starting at $250. Remarks: Part-time maker, first knife sold in 1995. Mark: Name above city and state.

PERRY, JIM,
Hope Star PO Box 648, Hope, AR 71801, jenn@comfabinc.com

PERRY, JOHN,
9 South Harrell Rd, Mayflower, AR 72106, Phone: 501-470-3043, jpknives@cyberback.com
 Specialties: Investment grade and working folders; Antique Bowies and slip joints. Patterns: Front and rear lock folders, liner locks, hunters and Bowies. Technical: Grinds CPM440V, D2 and making own Damascus. Offers filework. Prices: $375 to $1200; some to $3500. Remarks: Part-time maker; first knife sold in 1991. Doing business as Perry Custom Knives. Mark: Initials or last name in high relief set in a diamond shape.

PERRY, JOHNNY,
PO Box 35, Inman, SC 29349, Phone: 864-431-6390, perr3838@bellsouth.net
 Mark: High Ridge Forge.

PERSSON, CONNY,
PL 588, Loos, SWEDEN 82050, Phone: +46 657 10305, Fax: +46 657 413 435, connyknives@swipnet.se; Web: www.connyknives.com
 Specialties: Mosaic Damascus. Patterns: Mosaic Damascus. Technical: Straight knives and folders. Prices: $1000 and up. Mark: C. Persson.

PETEAN, FRANCISCO AND MAURICIO,
R. Dr. Carlos de Carvalho Rosa 52, Birigui, SP, BRAZIL 16200-000, Phone: 0186-424786
 Specialties: Classic knives to customer specs. Patterns: Bowies, boots, fighters, hunters and utility knives. Technical: Grinds D6, 440C and high-

carbon steels. Prefers natural handle material. Prices: $70 to $500. Remarks: Full-time maker; first knife sold in 1985. Mark: Last name, hand made.

PETERSEN, DAN L,
10610 SW 81st, Auburn, KS 66402, Phone: 785-256-2640, dan@petersenknives.com; Web: www.petersenknives.com
Specialties: Period pieces and forged integral hilts on hunters and fighters. Patterns: Texas-style Bowies, boots and hunters in high-carbon and Damascus steel. Technical: Precision heat treatments. Bainite blades with mantensite cores. Prices: $400 to $5000. Remarks: First knife sold in 1978. ABS Master Smith. Mark: Stylized initials.

PETERSON, CHRIS,
Box 143, 2175 W Rockyford, Salina, UT 84654, Phone: 435-529-7194
Specialties: Working straight knives of his design. Patterns: Large fighters, boots, hunters and some display pieces. Technical: Forges O1 and meteor. Makes and sells his own Damascus. Engraves, scrimshaws and inlays. Prices: $150 to $600; some to $1500. Remarks: Full-time maker; first knife sold in 1986. Mark: A drop in a circle with a line through it.

PETERSON, ELDON G,
368 Antelope Trl, Whitefish, MT 59937, Phone: 406-862-2204, draino@digisys.net; Web: http://www.kmg.org/egpeterson
Specialties: Fancy and working folders, any size. Patterns: Lockback interframes, integral bolster folders, liner locks, and two-blades. Technical: Grinds 440C and ATS-34. Offers gold inlay work, gem stone inlays and engraving. Prices: $285 to $5000. Remarks: Full-time maker; first knife sold in 1974. Mark: Name, city and state.

PETERSON, LLOYD (PETE) C,
64 Halbrook Rd, Clinton, AR 72031, Phone: 501-893-0000, wmblade@cyberback.com
Specialties: Miniatures and mosaic folders. Prices: $250 and up. Remarks: Lead time is 6-8 months. Mark: Pete.

PFANENSTIEL, DAN,
1824 Lafayette Ave, Modesto, CA 95355, Phone: 209-575-5937, dpfan@sbcglobal.net
Specialties: Japanese tanto, swords. One-of-a-kind knives. Technical: Forges simple carbon steels, some Damascus. Prices: $200 to $1000. Mark: Circle with wave inside.

PHILIPPE, D A,
PO Box 306, Cornish, NH 03746, Phone: 603-543-0662
Specialties: Traditional working straight knives. Patterns: Hunters, trout and bird, camp knives etc. Technical: Grinds ATS-34, 440C, A-2, Damascus, flat and hollow ground. Exotic woods and antler handles. Brass, nickel silver and stainless components. Prices: $125 to $800. Remarks: Full-time maker, first knife sold in 1984. Mark: First initial, last name.

PHILLIPS, ALISTAIR,
, Amaroo, ACT, AUSTRALIA 2914, alistair.phillips@knives.mutantdiscovery.com; Web: http://knives.mutantdiscovery.com
Specialties: Slipjoint folders, forged or stock removal fixed blades. Patterns: Single blade slipjoints, smaller neck knives, and hunters. Technical: Flat grnds O1, ATS-34, and forged 1055. Prices: $80 to $400. Remarks: Part-time maker, first knife made in 2005. Mark: Stamped signature.

PHILLIPS, DENNIS,
16411 West Bennet Rd, Independence, LA 70443, Phone: 985-878-8275
Specialties: Specializes in fixed blade military combat tacticals.

PHILLIPS, DONAVON,
905 Line Prairie Rd., Morton, MS 39117, Phone: 662-907-0322, bigdknives@gmail.com
Specialties: Flat ground, tapered tang working/using knives. Patterns: Hunters, Capers, Fillet, EDC, Field/Camp/Survival, Competition Cutters. Will work with customers on custom designs or changes to own designs. Technical: Stock removal maker using CPM-M4, CPM-154, and other air-hardening steels. Will use 5160 or 52100 on larger knives. G-10 or rubber standard, will use natural material if requested including armadillo. Kydex sheath is standard, outsourced leather available.†Heat treat is done by maker. Prices: $100 - $1000 Remarks: Part-time/hobbyist maker. First knife made in 2004; first sold 2007. Mark: Mark is etched, first and last name forming apex of triangle, city and state at the base, D in center.

PHILLIPS, SCOTT C,
671 California Rd, Gouverneur, NY 13642, Phone: 315-287-1280, Web: www.mangusknives.com
Specialties: Sheaths in leather. Fixed blade hunters, boot knives, Bowies, buck skinners (hand forged and stock removal). Technical: 440C, 5160, 1095 and 52100. Prices: Start at $125. Remarks: Part-time maker; first knife sold in 1993. Mark: Before "2000" as above after S Mangus.

PICKENS, SELBERT,
2295 Roxalana Rd, Dunbar, WV 25064, Phone: 304-744-4048
Specialties: Using knives. Patterns: Standard sporting knives. Technical: Stainless steels; stock removal method. Prices: Moderate. Remarks: Part-time maker. Mark: Name.

PICKETT, TERRELL,
66 Pickett Ln, Lumberton, MS 39455, Phone: 601-794-6125, pickettfence66@bellsouth.net
Specialties: Fix blades, camp knives, Bowies, hunters, & skinners. Forge and stock removal and some firework. Technical: 5160, 1095, 52100, 440C and ATS-

34. Prices: Range from $150 to $550. Mark: Logo on stock removal T.W. Pickett and on forged knives Terrell Pickett's Forge.

PIENAAR, CONRAD,
19A Milner Rd, Bloemfontein, Free State, SOUTH AFRICA 9300, Phone: 027 514364180, Fax: 027 514364180
Specialties: Fancy working and using straight knives and folders of his design, to customer specs and in standard patterns. Patterns: Hunters, locking folders, cleavers, kitchen and utility/camp knives. Technical: Grinds 12C27, D2 and ATS-34. Uses some Damascus. Embellishments; scrimshaws; inlays gold. Knives come with wooden box and custom-made leather sheath. Prices: $300 to $1000. Remarks: Part-time maker; first knife sold in 1981. Doing business as C.P. Knifemaker. Makes slip joint folders and liner locking folders. Mark: Initials and serial number.

PIERCE, HAROLD L,
106 Lyndon Lane, Louisville, KY 40222, Phone: 502-429-5136
Specialties: Working straight knives, some fancy. Patterns: Big fighters and Bowies. Technical: Grinds D2, 440C, 154CM; likes sub-hilts. Prices: $150 to $450; some to $1200. Remarks: Full-time maker; first knife sold in 1982. Mark: Last name with knife through the last initial.

PIERCE, RANDALL,
903 Wyndam, Arlington, TX 76017, Phone: 817-468-0138

PIERGALLINI, DANIEL E,
4011 N. Forbes Rd, Plant City, FL 33565, Phone: 813-754-3908, Fax: 813-754-3908, coolnifedad@wildblue.net
Specialties: Traditional and fancy straight knives and folders of his design or to customer's specs. Patterns: Hunters, fighters, skinners, working and camp knives. Technical: Grinds 440C, O1, D2, ATS-34, some Damascus; forges his own mokume. Uses natural handle material. Prices: $450 to $800; some to $1800. Remarks: Part-time maker; sold first knife in 1994. Mark: Last name, city, state or last name in script.

PIESNER, DEAN,
1786 Sawmill Rd, Conestogo, ON, CANADA N0B 1N0, Phone: 519-664-3648, dean47@rogers.com
Specialties: Classic and period pieces of his design and to customer specs. Patterns: Bowies, skinners, fighters and swords. Technical: Forges 5160, 52100, steel Damascus and nickel-steel Damascus. Makes own mokume gane with copper, brass and nickel silver. Silver wire inlays in wood. Prices: Start at $150. Remarks: Full-time maker; first knife sold in 1990. Mark: First initial, last name, JS.

PITMAN, DAVID,
PO Drawer 2566, Williston, ND 58802, Phone: 701-572-3325

PITT, DAVID F,
6812 Digger Pine Ln, Anderson, CA 96007, Phone: 530-357-2393, handcannons@tds.net or bearpawcustoms@dtds.net; Web: http://bearpawcustoms.blademakers.com
Specialties: Fixed blade, hunters and hatchets. Flat ground mirror finish. Patterns: Hatchets with gut hook, small gut hooks, guards, bolsters or guard less. Technical: Grinds A2, 440C, 154CM, ATS-34, D2. Prices: $150 to $1,000. Remarks: All work done in-house including heat treat. Mark: Bear paw with David F. Pitt Maker.

PLOPPERT, TOM,
1407 2nd Ave. SW, Cullman, AL 35055, Phone: 256-962-4251, tomploppert3@bellsouth.net
Specialties: Highly finished single- to multiple-blade slip-joint folders in standard and traditional patterns, some lockbacks. Technical: Hollow grinds CPM-154, 440V, damascus and other steels upon customer request. Uses elephant ivory, mammoth ivory, bone and pearl. Mark: Last name stamped on main blade.

PLUNKETT, RICHARD,
29 Kirk Rd, West Cornwall, CT 06796, Phone: 860-672-3419; Toll free: 888-KNIVES-8
Specialties: Traditional, fancy folders and straight knives of his design. Patterns: Slip-joint folders and small straight knives. Technical: Grinds O1 and stainless steel. Offers many different file patterns. Prices: $150 to $450. Remarks: Full-time maker; first knife sold in 1994. Mark: Signature and date under handle scales.

PODMAJERSKY, DIETRICH,
9219 15th Ave NE, Seatlle, WA 98115, Phone: 206-552-0763, podforge@gmail.com; Web: podforge.com
Specialties: Kitchen, utility and art knives, blending functionality with pleasing lines. Technical: Stainless and carbon steel, utilizing stock removal or forging where appropriate. All heat traeting is done in house, including cryogenic as needed. Prices: $150 and up.

POIRIER, RICK,
1149 Sheridan Rd., McKees Mills, New Brunswick E4V 2W7, Canada, Phone: 506-525-2818, ripknives@gmail.com
Specialties: Working straight knives of his design or to customer specs, hunters, fighters, bowies, utility, camp, tantos and short swords. Technical: Forges own damascus and cable damascus using 1084, 15N20, O1 and mild steel. Forges/grinds mostly O1 and W2. Varied handle materials inlcude G-10, Micarta, wood, bone, horn and Japanese cord wrap. Prices: $200 and up. Remarks: Full-time maker, apprenticed under ABS master smith Wally Hayes; first knife sold in 1998. Marks: R P (pre. 2007), RIP (2007 on), also etches gravestone RIP.

POLK, CLIFTON,
4625 Webber Creek Rd, Van Buren, AR 72956, Phone: 479-474-3828, cliffpolkknives1@aol.com; Web: www.polkknives.com
Specialties: Fancy working folders. Patterns: One blades spring backs in five sizes, LinerLock®, automatics, double blades spring back folder with standard drop & clip blade or bird knife with drop and vent hook or cowboy's knives with drop and hoof pick and straight knives. Technical: Uses D2 & ATS-34. Makes all own Damascus using 1084, 1095, O1, 15N20, 5160. Using all kinds of exotic woods. Stag, pearls, ivory, mastodon ivory and other bone and horns. Prices: $200 to $3000. Remarks: Retired fire fighter, made knives since 1974. Mark: Polk.

POLK, RUSTY,
5900 Wildwood Dr, Van Buren, AR 72956, Phone: 870-688-3009, polkknives@yahoo.com; Web: www.facebook.com/polkknives
Specialties: Skinners, hunters, Bowies, fighters and forging working knives fancy Damascus, daggers, boot knives, survival knives, and folders. Patterns: Drop point, and forge to shape. Technical: ATS-34, 440C, Damascus, D2, 51/60, 1084, 15N20, does all his forging. Prices: $200 to $2000. Mark: R. Polk.

POLLOCK, WALLACE J,
806 Russet Valley Dr., Cedar Park, TX 78613, Phone: 512-918-0528, jarlsdad@gmail.com; Web: www.pollackknives.com
Specialties: Using knives, skinner, hunter, fighting, camp knives. Patterns: Use his own patterns or yours. Traditional hunters, daggers, fighters, camp knives. Technical: Grinds ATS-34, D-2, BG-42, makes own Damascus, D-2, 0-1, ATS-34, prefer D-2, handles exotic wood, horn, bone, ivory. Remarks: Full-time maker, sold first knife 1973. Prices: $250 to $2500. Mark: Last name, maker, city/state.

POLZIEN, DON,
1912 Inler Suite-L, Lubbock, TX 79407, Phone: 806-791-0766, blindinglightknives.net
Specialties: Traditional Japanese-style blades; restores antique Japanese swords, scabbards and fittings. Patterns: Hunters, fighters, one-of-a-kind art knives. Technical: 1045-1050 carbon steels, 440C, D2, ATS-34, standard and cable Damascus. Prices: $150 to $2500. Remarks: Full-time maker. First knife sold in 1990. Mark: Oriental characters inside square border.

PONZIO, DOUG,
10219 W State Rd 81, Beloit, WI 53511, Phone: 608-313-3223, prfgdoug@hughes.net; Web: www.ponziodamascus.com
Specialties: Mosaic Damascus, stainless Damascus. Mark: P.F.

POOLE, MARVIN O,
PO Box 552, Commerce, GA 30529, Phone: 803-225-5970
Specialties: Traditional working/using straight knives and folders of his design and in standard patterns. Patterns: Bowies, fighters, hunters, locking folders, bird and trout knives. Technical: Grinds 440C, D2, ATS-34. Prices: $50 to $150; some to $750. Remarks: Part-time maker; first knife sold in 1980. Mark: First initial, last name, year, serial number.

POTIER, TIMOTHY F,
PO Box 711, Oberlin, LA 70655, Phone: 337-639-2229, tpotier@hotmail.com
Specialties: Classic working and using straight knives to customer specs; some collectible. Patterns: Hunters, Bowies, utility/camp knives and belt axes. Technical: Forges carbon steel and his own Damascus; offers filework. Prices: $300 to $1800; some to $4000. Remarks: Part-time maker; first knife sold in 1981. Mark: Last name, MS.

POTTER, BILLY,
6323 Hyland Dr., Dublin, OH 43017, Phone: 614-589-8324, potterknives@yahoo.com; Web: www.potterknives.com
Specialties: Working straight knives; his design or to customers patterns. Patterns: Bowie, fighters, utilities, skinners, hunters, folding lock blade, miniatures and tomahawks. Technical: Grinds and forges, carbon steel, L6, 0-1, 1095, 5160, 1084 and 52000. Grinds 440C stainless. Forges own Damascus. Handles: prefers exotic hardwood, curly and birdseye maples. Bone, ivory, antler, pearl and horn. Some scrimshaw. Prices: Start at $100 up to $800. Remarks: Part-time maker; first knife sold 1996. Mark: First and last name (maker).

POWELL, JAMES,
2500 North Robinson Rd, Texarkana, TX 75501

POWELL, ROBERT CLARK,
PO Box 321, 93 Gose Rd., Smarr, GA 31086, Phone: 478-994-5418
Specialties: Composite bar Damascus blades. Patterns: Art knives, hunters, combat, tomahawks. Patterns: Hand forges all blades. Prices: $300 and up. Remarks: ABS Journeyman Smith. Mark: Powell.

POWERS, WALTER R.,
PO BOX 82, Lolita, TX 77971, Phone: 361-874-4230, carlyn@laward.net Web: waltscustomknives.blademakers.com
Specialties: Skinners and hunters. Technical: Uses mainly CPMD2, CPM154 and CPMS35VN, but will occasionally use 3V. Stock removal. Prices: $140 - $200. Remarks: Part-time maker; first knife made in 2002. Mark: WP

PRATER, MIKE,
PRATER AND COMPANY, 81 Sanford Ln., Flintstone, GA 30725, cmprater@aol.com; Web: www.casecustomknives.com
Specialties: Customizing factory knives. Patterns: Buck knives, case knives, hen and rooster knives. Technical: Manufacture of mica pearl. Prices: Varied. Remarks: First knife sold in 1980. Mark: Mica pearl.

PRESSBURGER, RAMON,
59 Driftway Rd, Howell, NJ 07731, Phone: 732-363-0816
Specialties: BG-42. Only knifemaker in U.S.A. that has complete line of affordable hunting knives made from BG-42. Patterns: All types hunting styles.

Technical: Uses all steels; main steels are D-2 and BG-42. Prices: $75 to $500. Remarks: Full-time maker; has been making hunting knives for 30 years. Makes knives to your patterning. Mark: NA.

PRESTI, MATT,
5280 Middleburg Rd, Union Bridge, MD 21791, Phone: 410-775-1520; Cell: 240-357-3592
Specialties: Hunters and chef's knives, fighters, bowies, and period pieces. Technical: Forges 5160, 52100, 1095, 1080, W2, and O1 steels as well as his own Damascus. Does own heat treating and makes sheaths. Prefers natural handle materials, particularly antler and curly maple. Prices: $150 and up. Remarks: Part-time knifemaker who made his first knife in 2001. Mark: MCP.

PRICE, DARRELL MORRIS,
92 Union, Plymouth, Devon, ENGLAND PL1 3EZ, Phone: 0752 223546
Specialties: Traditional Japanese knives, Bowies and high-art knives. Technical: Nickel Damascus and mokume. Prices: $1000 to $4000. Remarks: Part-time maker; first knife sold in 1990. Mark: Initials and Japanese name—Kuni Shigae.

PRICE, TIMMY,
PO Box 906, Blairsville, GA 30514, Phone: 706-745-5111

PRIDGEN JR., LARRY,
PO BOX 707, Fitzgerald, GA 31750, Phone: 229-591-0013, pridgencustomknives@gmail.com Web: www.pridgencustomknives.com
Specialties: Bowie and Liner Lock Folders. Patterns: Bowie, fighter, skinner, trout, liner lock, and custom orders. Technical: I do stock removal and use carbon and stainless Damascus and stainless steel. Prices: $250 and up. Remarks: Each knife comes with a hand-crafted custom sheath and life-time guarantee. Mark: Distinctive logo that looks like a brand with LP and a circle around it.

PRIMOS, TERRY,
932 Francis Dr, Shreveport, LA 71118, Phone: 318-686-6625, tprimos@sport.rr.com or terry@primosknives.com; Web: www.primosknives.com
Specialties: Traditional forged straight knives. Patterns: Hunters, Bowies, camp knives, and fighters. Technical: Forges primarily 1084 and 5160; also forges Damascus. Prices: $250 to $600. Remarks: Full-time maker; first knife sold in 1993. Mark: Last name.

PRINSLOO, THEUNS,
PO Box 2263, Bethlehem, Free State, SOUTH AFRICA 9700, Phone: 27824663885, theunsmes@yahoo.com; Web: www.theunsprinsloo.co.za
Specialties: Handmade folders and fixed blades. Technical: Own Damascus and mokume. I try to avoid CNC work, laser cutting and machining as much as possible. Prices: $650 and up. Mark: Handwritten name with bushman rock art and mountain scene.

PRITCHARD, RON,
613 Crawford Ave, Dixon, IL 61021, Phone: 815-284-6005
Specialties: Plain and fancy working knives. Patterns: Variety of straight knives, locking folders, interframes and miniatures. Technical: Grinds 440C, 154CM and commercial Damascus. Prices: $100 to $200; some to $1500. Remarks: Part-time maker; first knife sold in 1979. Mark: Name and city.

PROVENZANO, JOSEPH D,
39043 Dutch Lane, Ponchatoula, LA 70454, Phone: 225-615-4846
Specialties: Working straight knives and folders in standard patterns. Patterns: Hunters, Bowies, folders, camp and fishing knives. Technical: Grinds ATS-34, 440C, 154CM, CPM 4400V, CPM420V and Damascus. Hollow-grinds hunters. Prices: $110 to $300; some to $1000. Remarks: Part-time maker; first knife sold in 1980. Mark: Joe-Pro.

PROVOST, J.C.,
1634 Lakeview Dr., Laurel, MS 39440, Phone: 601-498-1143, jcprovost2@gmail.com; Web: www.jcprovost.com
Specialties: Classic working straight knives and folders. Patterns: Hunters, skinners, bowies, daggers, fighters, fillet knives, chef's and steak knives, folders and customs. Technical: Grinds 440C, CPM-154 and commercial damascus. Prices: $175 and up. Remarks: Part-time maker; first knife made in 1979. Taught by R.W. Wilson. Mark: Name, city and state.

PRUYN, PETER,
Brothersville Custom Knives, 1328 NW "B" St., Grants Pass, OR 97526, Phone: 631-793-9052, Fax: 541-479-1889, brothersvilleknife@gmail.com Web: brothersvilleknife.com
Specialties: Fixed blade hunters, fighters, and chef knives. Technical: Damascus, hi-carbon and stainless steels. Prices: $200 - $1,000. Remarks: Full-time maker, first knife sold in 2009. Mark: Anvil with "Brothersville" crested above.

PULIS, VLADIMIR,
CSA 230-95, 96701 Kremnica, SLOVAKIA, Phone: 00421 903 340076, vpulis@gmail.com; Web: www.vpulis.host.sk
Specialties: Fancy and high-art straight knives of his design. Patterns: Daggers and hunters. Technical: Forges Damascus steel. All work done by hand. Prices: $250 to $3000; some to $10,000. Remarks: Full-time maker; first knife sold in 1990. Mark: Initials in sixtagon.

PURSLEY, AARON,
8885 Coal Mine Rd, Big Sandy, MT 59520, Phone: 406-378-3200
Specialties: Fancy working knives. Patterns: Locking folders, straight hunters and daggers, personal wedding knives and letter openers. Technical: Grinds

O1 and 440C; engraves. Prices: $900 to $2500. Remarks: Full-time maker; first knife sold in 1975. Mark: Initials connected with year.

PURVIS, BOB AND ELLEN,
2416 N Loretta Dr, Tucson, AZ 85716, Phone: 520-795-8290, repknives2@cox.net
Specialties: Hunter, skinners, Bowies, using knives, gentlemen folders and collectible knives. Technical: Grinds ATS-34, 440C, Damascus, Dama steel, heat-treats and cryogenically quenches. We do gold-plating, salt bluing, scrimshawing, filework and fashion handmade leather sheaths. Materials used for handles include exotic woods, mammoth ivory, mother-of-pearl, G-10 and Micarta. Prices: $165 to $800. Remarks: Knifemaker since retirement in 1984. Selling them since 1993. Mark: Script or print R.E. Purvis ~ Tucson, AZ or last name only.

PUTNAM, DONALD S,
590 Wolcott Hill Rd, Wethersfield, CT 06109, Phone: 860-563-9718, Fax: 860-563-9718, dpknives@cox.net
Specialties: Working knives for the hunter and fisherman. Patterns: His design or to customer specs. Technical: Uses stock removal method, O1, W2, D2, ATS-34, 154CM, 440C and CPM REX 20; stainless steel Damascus on request. Prices: $250 and up. Remarks: Full-time maker; first knife sold in 1985. Mark: Last name with a knife outline.

Q

QUAKENBUSH, THOMAS C,
2426 Butler Rd, Ft Wayne, IN 46808, Phone: 219-483-0749

QUARTON, BARR,
PO Box 4335, McCall, ID 83638, Phone: 208-634-3641
Specialties: Plain and fancy working knives; period pieces. Patterns: Hunters, tantos and swords. Technical: Forges and grinds 154CM, ATS-34 and his own Damascus. Prices: $180 to $450; some to $4500. Remarks: Part-time maker; first knife sold in 1978. Doing business as Barr Custom Knives. Mark: First name with bear logo.

QUATTLEBAUM, CRAIG,
912 Scooty Dr., Beebe, AR 72012-3454, mustang376@gci.net
Specialties: Traditional straight knives and one-of-a-kind knives of his design; period pieces. Patterns: Bowies and fighters. Technical: Forges 5168, 1095 and own Damascus. Prices: $300 to $2000. Remarks: Part-time maker; first knife sold in 1988. Mark: Stylized initials.

QUESENBERRY, MIKE,
110 Evergreen Cricle, Blairsden, CA 96103, Phone: 775-233-1527, quesenberry@psln.com; Web: www.quesenberryknives.com
Specialties: Hunters, daggers, Bowies, and integrals. Technical: Forges 52100, 1095, 1084, 5160. Makes own Damascus. Will use stainless on customer requests. Does own heat-treating and own leather work. Prices: Starting at $300. Remarks: Parttime maker. ABS member since 2006. Journeyman Bladesmith Mark: Last name.

R

RABUCK, JASON,
W3080 Hay Lake Road, Springbrook, WI 54875, Phone: 715-766-8220, sales@rabuckhandmadeknives.com; web: www.rabuckhandmadeknives.com
Patterns: Hunters, skinners, camp knives, fighters, survival/tactical, neck knives, kitchen knives. Include whitetail antler, maple, walnut, as well as stabilized woods and micarta. Technical: Flat grinds 1095, 5160, and 0-1 carbon steels. Blades are finished with a hand-rubbed satin blade finish. Hand stitched leather sheaths specifically fit to each knife. Boot clips, swivel sheaths, and leg ties include some of the available sheath options. Prices: $140 - $560. Remarks: Also knife restoration (handle replacement, etc.) Custom and replacement sheath work available for any knife. Mark: "RABUCK" over a horseshoe

RACHLIN, LESLIE S,
412 Rustic Ave., Elmira, NY 14905, Phone: 607-733-6889, lrachlin@stry.rr.com
Specialties: Classic and working kitchen knives, carving sets and outdoors knives. Technical: Grinds 440C or cryogenically heat-treated A2. Prices: $65 to $1,400. Remarks: Spare-time maker; first knife sold in 1989. Doing business as Tinkermade Knives. Mark: LSR

RADER, MICHAEL,
P.O. Box 393, Wilkeson, WA 98396, Phone: 253-255-7064, michael@raderblade.com; Web: www.raderblade.com
Specialties: Swords, kitchen knives, integrals. Patterns: Non traditional designs. Inspired by various cultures. Technical: Damascus is made with 1084 and 15N-20, forged blades in 52100, W2 and 1084. Prices: $350 - $5,000 Remarks: ABS Journeyman Smith Mark: ABS Mastersmith Mark "Rader" on one side, "M.S." on other

RADOS, JERRY F,
134 Willie Nell Rd., Columbia, KY 42728, Phone: 606-303-3334, jerry@radosknives.com Web: www.radosknives.com
Specialties: Deluxe period pieces. Patterns: Hunters, fighters, locking folders, daggers and camp knives. Technical: Forges and grinds his own Damascus which he sells commercially; makes pattern-welded Turkish Damascus. Prices: Start at $900. Remarks: Full-time maker; first knife sold in 1981. Mark: Last name.

RAFN, DAN C.,
Smedebakken 24, Hadsten, DENMARK 8370, contact@dcrknives.com Web: www.dcrknives.com
Specialties: One of a kind collector art knives of own design. Patterns: Mostly fantasy style fighters and daggers. But also swords, hunters, and folders.

Technical: Grinds RWL-34, sleipner steel, damasteel, and hand forges Damascus. Prices: Start at $500. Remarks: Part-time maker since 2003. Mark: Rafn. or DCR. or logo.

RAGSDALE, JAMES D,
160 Clear Creek Valley, Ellijay, GA 30536, Phone: 706-636-3180, jimmarrags@etcmail.com
Specialties: Fancy and embellished working knives of his design or to customer specs. Patterns: Hunters, folders and fighters. Technical: Grinds 440C, ATS-34 and A2. Uses some Damascus Prices: $150 and up. Remarks: Full-time maker; first knife sold in 1984. Mark: Fish symbol with name above, town below.

RAINVILLE, RICHARD,
126 Cockle Hill Rd, Salem, CT 06420, Phone: 860-859-2776, w1jo@snet.net
Specialties: Traditional working straight knives. Patterns: Outdoor knives, including fishing knives. Technical: L6, 400C, ATS-34. Prices: $100 to $800. Remarks: Full-time maker; first knife sold in 1982. Mark: Name, city, state in oval logo.

RALEY, R. WAYNE,
825 Poplar Acres Rd, Collierville, TN 38017, Phone: 901-853-2026

RALPH, DARREL,
BRIAR KNIVES, 12034 S. Profit Row, Founcy, TX 75126, Phone: 469-728-7242, dralph@earthlink.net; Web: www.darrelralph.com
Specialties: Tactical and tactical dress folders and fixed blades. Patterns: Daggers, fighters and swords. Technical: High tech. Forges his own damascus, nickel and high-carbon. Uses mokume and damascus, mosaics and special patterns. Engraves and heat treats. Prefers pearl, ivory and abalone handle material; uses stones and jewels. Prices: $600 to $30,000. Remarks: Full-time maker; first knife sold in 1987. Doing business as Briar Knives. Mark: DDR.

RAMONDETTI, SERGIO,
VIA MARCONI N 24, CHIUSA DI PESIO (CN), ITALY 12013, Phone: 0171 734490, Fax: 0171 734490, info@ramon-knives.com Web: www.ramon-knives.com
Specialties: Folders and straight knives of his design. Patterns: Utility, hunters and skinners. Technical: Grinds RWL-34 and Damascus. Prices: $500 to $2000. Remarks: Part-time maker; first knife sold in 1999. Mark: Logo (S.Ramon) with last name.

RAMSEY, RICHARD A,
8525 Trout Farm Rd, Neosho, MO 64850, Phone: 417-451-1493, rams@direcway.com; Web: www.ramseyknives.com
Specialties: Drop point hunters. Patterns: Various Damascus. Prices: $125 to $1500. Mark: RR double R also last name-RAMSEY.

RANDALL, PATRICK,
Patrick Knives, 160 Mesa Ave., Newbury Park, CA 91320, Phone: 818-292-3811, pat@patrickknives.com; Web: www.patrickknives.com
Specialties: Chef's and kitchen knives, bowies, hunters and utility folding knives. Technical: Preferred materials include 440C, 154CM, CPM-3V, 1084, 1095 and ATS-34. Handle materials include stabilized wood, Micarta, stag and jigged bone. Prices: $125 to $225. Remarks: Part-time maker since 2005.

RANDALL, STEVE,
3438 Oak Ridge Cir., Lincolnton, NC 28092, Phone: 704-732-2498, steve@ksrblades.com; Web: www.ksrblades.com
Specialties: Mostly working straight knives and one-of-a-kind pieces, some fancy fixed blades. Patterns: Bowies, hunters, choppers, camp and utility knives. Technical: Forged high-carbon-steel blades; 5160, 52100, W2, CruForgeV, high-carbon simple steels like 1075, 1084 and 1095. Prices: $275 and up. Remarks: Part-time maker, first knife sold in 2009. Earned journeyman smith rating in 2012. Doing business as Knives By Steve Randall or KSR Blades. Mark: KS Randall on left side, JS on right side.

RANDALL JR., JAMES W,
11606 Keith Hall Rd, Keithville, LA 71047, Phone: 318-925-6480, Fax: 318-925-1709, jw@jwrandall.com; Web: www.jwrandall.com
Specialties: Collectible and functional knives. Patterns: Bowies, hunters, daggers, swords, folders and combat knives. Technical: Forges 5160, 1084, O1 and his Damascus. Prices: $400 to $8000. Remarks: Part-time. First knife sold in 1998. Mark: JW Randall, MS.

RANDALL MADE KNIVES,
4857 South Orange Blossom Trail, Orlando, FL 32839, Phone: 407-855-8075, Fax: 407-855-9054, Web: http://www.randallknives.com
Specialties: Working straight knives. Patterns: Hunters, fighters and Bowies. Technical: Forges and grinds O1 and 440B. Prices: $170 to $550; some to $450. Remarks: Full-time maker; first knife sold in 1937. Mark: Randall made, city and state in scimitar logo.

RANDOW, RALPH,
7 E. Chateau Estates Dr., Greenbrier, AR 72058, Phone: 318-729-3368, randow@dishmail.net

RANKL, CHRISTIAN,
Possenhofenerstr 33, Munchen, GERMANY 81476, Phone: 0049 01 71 3 66 26 79, Fax: 0049 8975967265, Web: http://www.german-knife.com/german-knifemakers-guild.html
Specialties: Tail-lock knives. Patterns: Fighters, hunters and locking folders. Technical: Grinds ATS-34, D2, CPM1440V, RWL 34 also stainless Damascus. Prices: $450 to $950; some to $2000. Remarks: Part-time maker; first knife sold in 1989. Mark: Electrochemical etching on blade.

RAPP, STEVEN J,
8033 US Hwy 25-70, Marshall, NC 28753, Phone: 828-649-1092
Specialties: Gold quartz; mosaic handles. Patterns: Daggers, Bowies, fighters

and San Francisco knives. Technical: Hollow- and flat-grinds 440C and Damascus. Prices: Start at $500. Remarks: Full-time maker; first knife sold in 1981. Mark: Name and state.

RAPPAZZO, RICHARD,
142 Dunsbach Ferry Rd, Cohoes, NY 12047, Phone: 518-783-6843
Specialties: Damascus locking folders and straight knives. Patterns: Folders, dirks, fighters and tantos in original and traditional designs. Technical: Hand-forges all blades; specializes in Damascus; uses only natural handle materials. Prices: $400 to $1500. Remarks: Part-time maker; first knife sold in 1985. Mark: Name, date, serial number.

RARDON, A D,
1589 SE Price Dr, Polo, MO 64671, Phone: 660-354-2330
Specialties: Folders, miniatures. Patterns: Hunters, buck skinners, Bowies, miniatures and daggers. Technical: Grinds O1, D2, 440C and ATS-34. Prices: $150 to $2000; some higher. Remarks: Full-time maker; first knife sold in 1954. Mark: Fox logo.

RARDON, ARCHIE F,
1589 SE Price Dr, Polo, MO 64671, Phone: 660-354-2330
Specialties: Working knives. Patterns: Hunters, Bowies and miniatures. Technical: Grinds O1, D2, 440C, ATS-34, cable and Damascus. Prices: $50 to $500. Remarks: Part-time maker. Mark: Boar hog.

RASSENTI, PETER,
218 Tasse, St-Eustache, Quebec J7P 4C2, Canada, Phone: 450-598-6250, guireandgimble@hotmail.com
Specialties: Tactical mono-frame folding knives.

RAY, ALAN W,
1287 FM 1280 E, Lovelady, TX 75851, awray@rayzblades.com; Web: www.rayzblades.com
Specialties: Working straight knives of his design. Patterns: Hunters. Technical: Forges 01, L6 and 5160 for straight knives. Prices: $200 to $1000. Remarks: Full-time maker; first knife sold in 1979. Mark: Stylized initials.

REBELLO, INDIAN GEORGE,
358 Elm St, New Bedford, MA 02740-3837, Phone: 508-951-2719, indgeo@juno.com; Web: www.indiangeorgesknives.com
Specialties: One-of-a-kind fighters and Bowies. Patterns: To customer's specs, hunters and utilities. Technical: Forges his own Damascus, 5160, 52100, 1084, 1095, cable and O1. Grinds S30V, ATS-34, 154CM, 440C, D2 and A2. Prices: Starting at $250. Remarks: Full-time maker, first knife sold in 1991. Doing business as Indian George's Knives. Founding father and President of the Southern New England Knife-Makers Guild. Member of the N.C.C.A. and A.B.S. Mark: Indian George's Knives.

RED, VERNON,
2020 Benton Cove, Conway, AR 72034, Phone: 501-450-7284, knivesvr@conwaycorp.net
Specialties: Custom design straight knives or folders of own design or customer's. Patterns: Hunters, fighters, Bowies, folders. Technical: Hollow grind, flat grind, stock removal and forged blades. Uses 440C, D-2, ATS-34, 1084, 1095, and Damascus. Prices: $150 and up. Remarks: Made first knife in 1982, first folder in 1992. Member of (AKA) Arkansas Knives Association. Doing business as Custom Made Knives by Vernon Red. Mark: Last name.

REDD, BILL,
2647 West 133rd Circle, Broomfield, Colorado 80020, Phone: 303-469-9803, knifeinfo@reddknives.com and unlimited_design@msn.com; Web: www.reddknives.com
Prices: Contact maker. Remarks: Full-time custom maker, member of PKA and RMBC (Rocky Mountain Blade Collectors). Mark: Redd Knives, Bill Redd.

REDDIEX, BILL,
27 Galway Ave, Palmerston North, NEW ZEALAND, Phone: 06-357-0383, Fax: 06-358-2910
Specialties: Collector-grade working straight knives. Patterns: Traditional-style Bowies and drop-point hunters. Technical: Grinds 440C, D2 and O1; offers variety of grinds and finishes. Prices: $130 to $750. Remarks: Full-time maker; first knife sold in 1980. Mark: Last name around kiwi bird logo.

REED, JOHN M,
3937 Sunset Cove Dr., Port Orange, FL 32129, Phone: 386-310-4569
Specialties: Hunter, utility, some survival knives. Patterns: Trailing Point, and drop point sheath knives. Technical: ATS-34, Rockwell 60 exotic wood or natural material handles. Prices: $135 to $450. Depending on handle material. Remarks: Likes the stock removal method. "Old Fashioned trainling point blades." Handmade and sewn leather sheaths. Mark: "Reed" acid etched on left side of blade.

REEVE, CHRIS,
2949 Victory View Way, Boise, ID 83709-2946, Phone: 208-375-0367, Fax: 208-375-0368, crkinfo@chrisreeve.com; Web: www.chrisreeve.com
Specialties: Originator and designer of the One Piece range of fixed blade utility knives and of the Sebenza Integral Lock folding knives made by Chris Reeve Knives. Currently makes only one or two pieces per year himself. Patterns: Art folders and fixed blades; one-of-a-kind. Technical: Grinds specialty stainless steels, Damascus and other materials to his own design. Prices: $1000 and upwards. Remarks: Full-time in knife business; first knife sold in 1982. Mark: Signature and date.

REEVES, J.R.,
5181 South State Line, Texarkana, AR 71854, Phone: 870-773-5777, jos123@netscape.com
Specialties: Working straight knives of my design and customer design if a good flow. Patterns: Hunters, fighters, bowies, camp, bird, and trout knives. Technical: Forges and grinds 5160, 1084, 15n20, L6, 52100 and some damascus. Also some stock removal 440C, 01, D2, and 154 CM steels. I offer flat or hollow grinds. Natural handle material to include Sambar stag, desert Ironwood, sheep horn, other stabilized exotic woods and ivory. Custom filework offered. Prices: $200 - $1500. Remarks: Full-time maker, first knife sold in 1985. Mark: JR Reeves.

REGGIO JR., SIDNEY J,
PO Box 851, Sun, LA 70463, Phone: 504-886-5886
Specialties: Miniature classic and fancy straight knives of his design or in standard patterns. Patterns: Fighters, hunters and utility/camp knives. Technical: Grinds 440C, ATS-34 and commercial Damascus. Engraves; scrimshaws; offers filework. Hollow grinds most blades. Prefers natural handle material. Offers handmade sheaths. Prices: $85 to $250; some to $500. Remarks: Part-time maker; first knife sold in 1988. Doing business as Sterling Workshop. Mark: Initials.

REID, JIM,
6425 Cranbrook St. NE, Albuquerque, NM 87111, jhrabq7@Q.com
Specialties: Fixed-blade knives. Patterns: Hunting, neck, and cowboy bowies. Technical: A2, D2, and damascus, stock removal. Prices: $125 to $300. Mark: Jim Reid over New Mexico zia sign.

RENNER, TERRY,
TR Blades, Inc., 707 13th Ave. Cir. W, Palmetto, FL 34221, Phone: 941-729-3226; 941-545-6320, terrylmusic@gmail.com Web: www.trblades.com
Specialties: High art folders and straight-blades, specialty locking mechanisms. Designer of the Neckolas knife by CRKT. Deep-relief carving. Technical: Prefer CPM154, S30V, 1095 carbon, damascus by Rob Thomas, Delbert Ealey, Bertie Reitveld, Todd Fischer, Joel Davis. Does own heat treating. Remarks: Full-time maker of 2005. Formerly in bicylce manufacturing business, with patents for tooling and fixtures. President of the Florida Knifemaker's Association since 2009. Mark: TR* stylized

REPKE, MIKE,
4191 N. Euclid Ave., Bay City, MI 48706, Phone: 517-684-3111
Specialties: Traditional working and using straight knives of his design or to customer specs; classic knives; display knives. Patterns: Hunters, Bowies, skinners, fighters boots, axes and swords. Technical: Grind 440C. Offer variety of handle materials. Prices: $99 to $1500. Remarks: Full-time makers. Doing business as Black Forest Blades. Mark: Knife logo.

REVERDY, NICOLE AND PIERRE,
5 Rue de L'egalite', Romans, FRANCE 26100, Phone: 334 75 05 10 15, Web: http://www.reverdy.com
Specialties: Art knives; legend pieces. Pierre and Nicole, his wife, are creating knives of art with combination of enamel on pure silver (Nicole) and poetic Damascus (Pierre) such as the "La dague a la licorne." Patterns: Daggers, folding knives Damascus and enamel, Bowies, hunters and other large patterns. Technical: Forges his Damascus and "poetic Damascus"; where animals such as unicorns, stags, dragons or star crystals appear, works with his own EDM machine to create any kind of pattern inside the steel with his own touch. Prices: $2000 and up. Remarks: Full-time maker since 1989; first knife sold in 1986. Nicole (wife) collaborates with enamels. Mark: Reverdy.

REVISHVILI, ZAZA,
2102 Linden Ave, Madison, WI 53704, Phone: 608-243-7927
Specialties: Fancy/embellished and high-art straight knives and folders of his design. Patterns: Daggers, swords and locking folders. Technical: Uses Damascus; silver filigree, silver inlay in wood; enameling. Prices: $1000 to $9000; some to $15,000. Remarks: Full-time maker; first knife sold in 1987. Mark: Initials, city.

REXFORD, TODD,
518 Park Dr., Woodland Park, CO 80863, Phone: 719-650-6799, todd@rexfordknives.com; Web: www.rexfordknives.com
Specialties: Dress tactical and tactical folders and fixed blades. Technical: I work in stainless steels, stainless damascus, titanium, Stellite and other high performance alloys. All machining and part engineering is done in house.

REXROAT, KIRK,
527 Sweetwater Circle Box 224, Wright, WY 82732, Phone: 307-464-0166, rexknives@vcn.com; Web: www.rexroatknives.com
Specialties: Using and collectible straight knives and folders of his design or to customer specs. Patterns: Bowies, hunters, folders. Technical: Forges Damascus patterns, mosaic and 52100. Prices: $400 and up. Remarks: Part-time maker, Master Smith in the ABS; first knife sold in 1984. Doing business as Rexroat Knives. Mark: Last name.

REYNOLDS, DAVE,
1404 Indian Creek, Harrisville, WV 26362, Phone: 304-643-2889, wvreynolds@zoomintevnet.net
Specialties: Working straight knives of his design. Patterns: Bowies, kitchen and utility knives. Technical: Grinds and forges L6, 1095 and 440C. Heat-treats. Prices: $50 to $85; some to $175. Remarks: Full-time maker; first knife sold in 1980. Doing business as Terra-Gladius Knives. Mark: Mark on special orders only; serial number on all knives.

REYNOLDS, JOHN C,
#2 Andover HC77, Gillette, WY 82716, Phone: 307-682-6076
Specialties: Working knives, some fancy. Patterns: Hunters, Bowies, tomahawks and buck skinners; some folders. Technical: Grinds D2, ATS-34,

RHEA—ROBERTS

440C and forges own Damascus and knives. Scrimshaws. Prices: $200 to $3000. Remarks: Spare-time maker; first knife sold in 1969. Mark: On ground blades JC Reynolds Gillette, WY, on forged blades, initials make the mark-JCR.

RHEA, LIN,
413 Grant 291020, Prattsville, AR 72129, Phone: 870-699-5095, lwrhea2@windstream.net; Web: www.rheaknives.com
Specialties: Traditional and early American styled Bowies in high carbon steel or Damascus. Patterns: Bowies, hunters and fighters. Technical: Filework wire inlay. Sole authorship of construction, Damascus and embellishment. Prices: $280 to $1500. Remarks: Serious part-time maker and rated as a Master Smith in the ABS.

RHO, NESTOR LORENZO,
Prinera Junta 589, Junin, Buenos Aires, ARGENTINA CP 6000, Phone: +54-236-154670686, info@cuchillosrho.com.ar; Web: www.cuchillosrho.com.ar
Specialties: Classic and fancy straight knives of his design. Patterns: Bowies, fighters and hunters. Technical: Grinds 420C, 440C, 1084, 5160, 52100, L6 and W1. Offers semi-precious stones on handles, acid etching on blades and blade engraving. Prices: $90 to $500, some to $1500. Remarks: Full-time maker; first knife sold in 1975. Mark: Name.

RIBONI, CLAUDIO,
Via L Da Vinci, Truccazzano (MI), ITALY, Phone: 02 95309010, Web: www.riboni-knives.com

RICARDO ROMANO, BERNARDES,
Rua Coronel Rennò 1261, Itajuba MG, BRAZIL 37500, Phone: 0055-2135-622-5896
Specialties: Hunters, fighters, Bowies. Technical: Grinds blades of stainless and tools steels. Patterns: Hunters. Prices: $100 to $700. Mark: Romano.

RICHARD, RAYMOND,
31047 SE Jackson Rd., Gresham, OR 97080, Phone: 503-663-1219, rayskee13@hotmail.com; Web: www.hawknknives.com
Specialties: Hand-forged knives, tomahawks, axes, and spearheads, all one-of-a-kind. Prices: $200 and up, some to $3000. Remarks: Full-time maker since 1994. Mark: Name on spine of blades.

RICHARDS, CHUCK,
7243 Maple Tree Lane SE, Salem, OR 97317, Phone: 503-569-5549, woodchuckforge@gmail.com; Web: www.acrichardscustomknives.com
Specialties: Fixed blade Damascus. One-of-a-kind. Patterns: Hunters, fighters. Prices: $300 to $1,500+ Remarks: Likes to work with customers on a truly custom knife. Mark: A.C. Richards J.S. or ACR J.S.

RICHARDS, RALPH (BUD),
6413 Beech St, Bauxite, AR 72011, Phone: 501-602-5367, DoubleR042@aol.com; Web: www.ralphrichardscustomknives.com
Specialties: Forges 55160, 1084, and 15N20 for Damascus. S30V, 440C, and others. Wood, mammoth, giraffe and mother of pearl handles.

RICHARDSON JR., PERCY,
1400 SM Tucker Rd., Pollok, TX 75969, Phone: 936-288-1690, Percy@Richardsonhandmadeknives.com; Web: www.Richardsonhandmadeknives.com
Specialties: Working straight knives and folders. Patterns: Hunters, skinners, bowies, fighters and folders. Technical: Mostly grinds CPM-154. Prices: $175 - $750 some bowies to $1200. Remarks: Full-time maker, first knife sold in 1990. Doing business as Richardsons Handmade Knives. Mark: Texas star with last name across it.

RICHERSON, RON,
P.O. Box 51, Greenburg, KY 42743, Phone: 270-405-0491, Fax: 270-932-5601, RRicherson1@windstream.net
Specialties: Collectible and functional fixed blades, locking liners, and autos of his design. Technical: Grinds ATS-34, S30V, S60V, CPM-154, D2, 440, high carbon steel, and his and others' Damascus. Prefers natural materials for handles and does both stock removal and forged work, some with embellishments. Prices: $250 to $850, some higher. Remarks: Full-time maker. Member American Bladesmith Society. Made first knife in September 2006, sold first knife in December 2006. Mark: Name in oval with city and state. Also name in center of oval Green River Custom Knives.

RICKE, DAVE,
1209 Adams St, West Bend, WI 53090, Phone: 262-334-5739, R.L5710@sbcglobal.net
Specialties: Working knives; period pieces. Patterns: Hunters, boots, Bowies; locking folders and slip joints. Technical: Grinds ATS-34, A2, 440C and 154CM. Prices: $145 and up. Remarks: Full-time maker; first knife sold in 1976. Mark: Last name.

RICKS, KURT J.,
Darkhammer Forge, 29 N. Center, Trenton, UT 84338, Phone: 435-563-3471, kopsh@hotmail.com; http://darkhammerworks.tripod.com
Specialties: Fixed blade working knives of all designs and to customer specs. Patterns: Fighters, daggers, hunters, swords, axes, and spears. Technical: Uses a coal fired forge. Forges high carbon, tool and spring steels. Does own heat treat on forge. Prefers natural handle materials. Leather sheaths available. Prices: Start at $50 plus shipping. Remarks: A knife should be functional first and pretty second. Part-time maker; first knife sold in 1994. Mark: Initials.

RIDER, DAVID M,
PO Box 5946, Eugene, OR 97405-0911, Phone: 541-343-8747

RIDLEY, ROB,
RR1, Sundre, AB, CANADA T0M 1X0, Phone: 405-556-1113, rob@rangeroriginal.com; www.rangeroriginal.com, www.knifemaker.ca
Specialties: The knives I make are mainly fixed blades, though I'm exploring the complex world of folders. Technical: I favour high-end stainless alloys and exotic handle materials because a knife should provide both cutting ability and bragging rights. Remarks: I made my first knife in 1998 and still use that blade today. I've gone from full time, to part time, to hobby maker, but I still treasure time in the shop or spent with other enthusiasts. Operates Canadian Knifemakers Supply

RIEPE, RICHARD A,
17604 E 296 St, Harrisonville, MO 64701

RIETVELD, BERTIE,
PO Box 53, Magaliesburg, GT, SOUTH AFRICA 1791, Phone: 2783 232 8766, bertie@rietveldknives.com; Web: www.rietveldknives.com
Specialties: Art daggers, Bolster lock folders, Persian designs, embraces elegant designs. Patterns: Mostly one-of-a-kind. Technical: Sole authorship, work only in own Damascus, gold inlay, blued stainless fittings. Prices: $500 - $8,000 Remarks: First knife made in 1979. Annual shows attended: ECCKS, Blade Show, Milan Show, South African Guild Show. Marks: Logo is elephant in half circle with name, enclosed in Stanhope lens

RIGNEY JR., WILLIE,
191 Colson Dr, Bronston, KY 42518, Phone: 606-679-4227
Specialties: High-tech period pieces and fancy working knives. Patterns: Fighters, boots, daggers and push knives. Technical: Grinds 440C and 154CM; buys Damascus. Most knives are embellished. Prices: $150 to $1500; some to $10,000. Remarks: Full-time maker; first knife sold in 1978. Mark: First initial, last name.

RINKES, SIEGFRIED,
Am Sportpl 2, Markterlbach, GERMANY 91459

RIZZI, RUSSELL J,
37 March Rd, Ashfield, MA 01330, Phone: 413-625-2842
Specialties: Fancy working and using straight knives and folders of his design or to customer specs. Patterns: Hunters, locking folders and fighters. Technical: Grinds 440C, D2 and commercial Damascus. Prices: $150 to $750; some to $2500. Remarks: Part-time maker; first knife sold in 1990. Mark: Last name, Ashfield, MA.

ROBBINS, BILL,
2160 E. Fry Blvd., Ste. C5, Sierra Vista, AZ 85635-2794, billknifemaker@aol.com
Specialties: Plain and fancy working straight knives. Makes to his designs and most anything you can draw. Patterns: Hunting knives, utility knives, and Bowies. Technical: Grinds ATS-34, 440C, tool steel, high carbon, buys Damascus. Prices: $70 to $450. Remarks: Part-time maker, first knife sold in 2001. Mark: Last name or desert scene with name.

ROBBINS, HOWARD P,
1310 E. 310th Rd., Flemington, MO 65650, Phone: 417-282-5055, ARobb1407@aol.com
Specialties: High-tech working knives with clean designs, some fancy. Patterns: Folders, hunters and camp knives. Technical: Grinds 440C. Heat-treats; likes mirror finishes. Offers leatherwork. Prices: $100 to $500; some to $1000. Remarks: Full-time maker; first knife sold in 1982. Mark: Name, city and state.

ROBERTS, CHUCK,
PO Box 7174, Golden, CO 80403, Phone: 303-642-2388, chuck@crobertsart.com; Web: www.crobertsart.com
Specialties: Price daggers, large Bowies, hand-rubbed satin finish. Patterns: Bowies and California knives. Technical: Grinds 440C, 5160 and ATS-34. Handles made of stag, ivory or mother-of-pearl. Prices: $1250. Remarks: Full-time maker. Company name is C. Roberts - Art that emulates the past. Mark: Last initial or last name.

ROBERTS, GEORGE A,
PO Box 31228, 211 Main St., Whitehorse, YT, CANADA Y1A 5P7, Phone: 867-667-7099, Fax: 867-667-7099, gr1898@northwestel.net; Web: www.yuk-biz.com/bandit blades
Specialties: Mastadon ivory, fossil walrus ivory handled knives, scrimshawed or carved. Patterns: Side lockers, fancy bird and trout knives, hunters, fillet blades. Technical: Grinds stainless Damascus, all surgical steels. Prices: Up to $3500 U.S. Remarks: Full-time maker; first knives sold in 1986. Doing business as Bandit Blades. Most recent works have gold nuggets in fossilized Mastadon ivory. Something new using mosaic pins in mokume bolster and in mosaic Damascus, it creates a new look. Mark: Bandit Yukon with pick and shovel crossed.

ROBERTS, JACK,
10811 Sagebluff Dr, Houston, TX 77089, Phone: 281-481-1784, jroberts59@houston.rr.com
Specialties: Hunting knives and folders, offers scrimshaw by wife Barbara. Patterns: Drop point hunters and LinerLock® folders. Technical: Grinds 440-C, offers file work, texturing, natural handle materials and Micarta. Prices: $200 to $800 some higher. Remarks: Part-time maker, sold first knife in 1965. Mark: Name, city, state.

ROBERTS, MICHAEL,
601 Oakwood Dr, Clinton, MS 39056, Phone: 601-540-6222, Fax: 601-213-4891
Specialties: Working and using knives in standard patterns and to customer specs. Patterns: Hunters, Bowies, tomahawks and fighters. Technical: Forges 5160, O1, 1095 and his own Damascus. Uses only natural handle materials.

Prices: $145 to $500; some to $1100. Remarks: Part-time maker; first knife sold in 1988. Mark: Last name or first and last name in Celtic script.

ROBERTS, T. C. (TERRY),
1795 Berry Lane, Fayetteville, AR 72701, Phone: 479-442-4493, carolcroberts@cox.net
Specialties: Working straight knives and folders of the maker's original design. Patterns: Bowies, daggers, fighters, locking folders, slip joints to include multiblades and whittlers. Technical: Grinds all types of carbon and stainless steels and commercially available Damascus. Works in stone and casts in bronze and silver. Some inlays and engraving. Prices: $250 - $3500. Remarks: Full-time maker; sold first knife in 1983. Mark: Stamp is oval with initials inside.

ROBERTSON, LEO D,
3728 Pleasant Lake Dr, Indianapolis, IN 46227, Phone: 317-882-9899, ldr52@juno.com
Specialties: Hunting and folders. Patterns: Hunting, fillet, Bowie, utility, folders and tantos. Technical: Uses ATS-34, 154CM, 440C, 1095, D2 and Damascus steels. Prices: Fixed knives $75 to $350, folders $350 to $600. Remarks: Handles made with stag, wildwoods, laminates, mother-of-pearl. Made first knife in 1990. Member of American Bladesmith Society. Mark: Logo with full name in oval around logo.

ROBINSON, CALVIN,
5501 Twin Creek Circle, Pace, FL 32571, Phone: 850 572 1504, calvinshandmadeknives@yahoo.com; Web: www.CalvinRobinsonKnives.com
Specialties: Working knives of my own design. Patterns: Hunters, fishing, folding and kitchen and purse knives. Technical: Now using 14C28N stainless blade steel, as well as 12C27, 13C26 and D2. Prices: $180 to $2500. Remarks: Full-time maker. Probationary member and voting member of the Knifemaker's Guild. Mark: Calvin Robinson Pace, Florida.

ROBINSON, CHARLES (DICKIE),
PO Box 221, Vega, TX 79092, Phone: 806-676-6428, dickie@amaonline.com; Web: www.robinsonknives.com
Specialties: Classic and working/using knives. Does his own engraving. Patterns: Bowies, daggers, fighters, hunters and camp knives. Technical: Forges O1, 5160, 52100 and his own Damascus. Prices: $350 to $850; some to $5000. Remarks: Part-time maker; first knife sold in 1988. Doing business as Robinson Knives. ABS Master Smith. Mark: Robinson MS.

ROBINSON, CHUCK,
SEA ROBIN FORGE, 1423 Third Ave., Picayune, MS 39466, Phone: 601-798-0060, robi5515@bellsouth.net
Specialties: Deluxe period pieces and working / using knives of his design and to customer specs. Patterns: Bowies, fighters, hunters, utility knives and original designs. Technical: Forges own damascus, 52100, O1, W2, L6 and 1070 thru 1095. Prices: Start at $225. Remarks: First knife 1958. Mark: Fish logo, anchor and initials C.R.

ROBINSON III, REX R,
10531 Poe St, Leesburg, FL 34788, Phone: 352-787-4587
Specialties: One-of-a-kind high-art automatics of his design. Patterns: Automatics, liner locks and lock back folders. Technical: Uses tool steel and stainless Damascus and mokume; flat grinds. Hand carves folders. Prices: $1800 to $7500. Remarks: First knife sold in 1988. Mark: First name inside oval.

ROCHFORD, MICHAEL R,
PO Box 577, Dresser, WI 54009, Phone: 715-755-3520, mrrochford@centurytel.net
Specialties: Working straight knives and folders. Classic Bowies and Moran traditional. Patterns: Bowies, fighters, hunters: slip-joint, locking and liner locking folders. Technical: Grinds ATS-34, 440C, 154CM and D-2; forges W2, 5160, and his own Damascus. Offers metal and metal and leather sheaths. Filework and wire inlay. Prices: $150 to $1000; some to $2000. Remarks: Part-time maker; first knife sold in 1984. Mark: Name.

RODDY, ROY "TIM",
7640 Hub-Bedford Rd., Hubbard, OH 44425, Phone: 330-770-5921, pfr2rtr@hotmail.com
Specialties: Any type of knife a customer wants, large knives, small knives and anything in between. Patterns: Hunters, fighters, martial arts knives, hide-outs, neck knives, throwing darts and locking-liner folders. Leather or Kydex sheaths with exotic-skin inlays. Technical: 440C, D2, ATS-34 or damascus blade steels. Remarks: Started making knives 25 years ago. Mark: Railroad sign (circle with an X inside and an R on either side of the X).

RODEBAUGH, JAMES L,
4875 County Rd, Carpenter, WY 82054

RODEWALD, GARY,
447 Grouse Ct, Hamilton, MT 59840, Phone: 406-363-2192
Specialties: Bowies of his design as inspired from historical pieces. Patterns: Hunters, Bowies and camp/combat. Forges 5160 1084 and his own Damascus of 1084, 15N20, field grade hunters AT-34-440C, 440V, and BG42. Prices: $200 to $1500. Remarks: Sole author on knives, sheaths done by saddle maker. Mark: Rodewald.

RODKEY, DAN,
18336 Ozark Dr, Hudson, FL 34667, Phone: 727-863-8264
Specialties: Traditional straight knives of his design and in standard patterns. Patterns: Boots, fighters and hunters. Technical: Grinds 440C, D2 and ATS-34. Prices: Start at $200. Remarks: Full-time maker; first knife sold in 1985. Doing business as Rodkey Knives. Mark: Etched logo on blade.

ROE JR., FRED D,
4005 Granada Dr, Huntsville, AL 35802, Phone: 205-881-6847
Specialties: Highly finished working knives of his design; period pieces.

Patterns: Hunters, fighters and survival knives; locking folders; specialty designs like diver's knives. Technical: Grinds 154CM, ATS-34 and Damascus. Field-tests all blades. Prices: $125 to $250; some to $2000. Remarks: Part-time maker; first knife sold in 1980. Mark: Last name.

ROEDER, DAVID,
426 E. 9th Pl., Kennewick, WA 99336, d.roeder1980@yahoo.com
Specialties: Fixed blade field and exposition grade knives. Patterns: Favorite styles are Bowie and hunter. Technical: Forges primarily 5160 and 52100. Makes own Damascus. Prices: Start at $150. Remarks: Made first knife in September, 1996. Mark: Maker's mark is a D and R with the R resting at a 45-degree angle to the lower right of the D.

ROGERS, RAY,
PO Box 126, Wauconda, WA 98859, Phone: 509-486-8069, knives@rayrogers.com; Web: www.rayrogers.com
Specialties: LinerLock® folders. Asian and European professional chef's knives. Patterns: Rayzor folders, chef's knives and cleavers of his own and traditional designs, drop point hunters and fillet knives. Technical: Stock removal S30V, 440, 1095, O1 Damascus and other steels. Does all own heat treating, clay tempering, some forging G-10, Micarta, carbon fiber on folders, stabilized burl woods on fixed blades. Prices: $200 to $450. Remarks: Knives are made one-at-a-time to the customer's order. Happy to consider customizing knife designs to suit your preferences and sometimes create entirely new knives when necessary. As a full-time knifemaker is willing to spend as much time as it takes (usually through email) discussing the options and refining details of a knife's design to insure that you get the knife you really want.

ROGERS, RICHARD,
PO Box 769, Magdalena, NM 87825, Phone: 575-838-7237, r.s.rogers@hotmail.com
Specialties: Sheffield-style folders and multi-blade folders. Patterns: Folders: various traditional patterns. One-of-a-kind fixed blades: Bowies, daggers, hunters, utility knives. Technical: Mainly uses ATS-34 and prefer natural handle materials. Prices: $400 and up. Mark: Last name.

ROGHMANS, MARK,
607 Virginia Ave, LaGrange, GA 30240, Phone: 706-885-1273
Specialties: Classic and traditional knives of his design. Patterns: Bowies, daggers and fighters. Technical: Grinds ATS-34, D2 and 440C. Prices: $250 to $500. Remarks: Part-time maker; first knife sold in 1984. Doing business as LaGrange Knife. Mark: Last name and/or LaGrange Knife.

ROHN, FRED,
7675 W Happy Hill Rd, Coeur d'Alene, ID 83814, Phone: 208-667-0774
Specialties: Hunters, boot knives, custom patterns. Patterns: Drop points, double edge, etc. Technical: Grinds 440 or 154CM. Prices: $85 and up. Remarks: Part-time maker. Mark: Logo on blade; serial numbered.

ROLLERT, STEVE,
PO Box 65, Keenesburg, CO 80643-0065, Phone: 303-732-4858, steve@doveknives.com; Web: www.doveknives.com
Specialties: Highly finished working knives. Patterns: Variety of straight knives; locking folders and slip-joints. Technical: Forges and grinds W2, 1095, ATS-34 and his pattern-welded, cable Damascus and nickel Damascus. Prices: $300 to $1000; some to $3000. Remarks: Full-time maker; first knife sold in 1980. Doing business as Dove Knives. Mark: Last name in script.

ROMEIS, GORDON,
1521 Coconut Dr., Fort Myers, FL 33901, Phone: 239-940-5060, gordonromeis@gmail.com Web: Romeisknives.com
Specialties: Smaller using knives. Patterns: I have a number of standard designs that include both full tapered tangs and narrow tang knives. Custom designs are welcome. Many different types. No folders. Technical: Standard steel is 440C. Also uses Alabama Damascus steel. Prices: Start at $165. Remarks: I am a part-time maker however I do try to keep waiting times to a minimum. Mark: Either my name, city, and state or simply ROMEIS depending on the knife.

RONZIO, N. JACK,
PO Box 248, Fruita, CO 81521, Phone: 970-858-0921

ROOT, GARY,
644 East 14th St, Erie, PA 16503, Phone: 814-459-0196
Specialties: Damascus Bowies with hand carved eagles, hawks and snakes for handles. Few folders made. Patterns: Daggers, fighters, hunter/field knives. Technical: Using handforged Damascus from Ray Bybar Jr (M.S.) and Robert Eggerling. Grinds D2, 440C, 1095 and 5160. Some 5160 is hand forged. Prices: $80 to $300 some to $1000. Remarks: Full time maker, first knife sold in 1976. Mark: Name over Erie, PA.

ROSE, BOB,
PO BOX 126, Wagontown, PA 19376, Phone: 484-883-3925, medit8@meditationsociety.com Web: www.bobroseknives.com
Patterns: Bowies, fighters, drop point hunters, daggers, bird and trout, camp, and other fixed blade styles. Technical: Mostly using 1095 and damascus steel, desert ironwood and other top-of-the-line exotic woods as well as mammoth tooth. Prices: $49 - $300. Remarks: Been making and selling knives since 2004. "Knife Making is a meditation technique for me."

ROSE, DEREK W,
14 Willow Wood Rd, Gallipolis, OH 45631, Phone: 740-446-4627

ROSE II, DOUN T,
Ltc US Special Operations Command (ret), 1795/96 W Sharon Rd SW, Fife Lake, MI 49633, Phone: 231-645-1369, Web: www.rosecutlery.com
Specialties: Straight working, collector and presentation knives to a high level of fit and finish. Design in collaboration with customer. Patterns: Field knives, Scagel, Bowies, period pieces, axes and tomahawks, fishing and hunting spears and fine. Technical: Forged and billet ground, high carbon and stainless steel appropriate to end use. Sourced from: Crucible, Frye, Admiral and Starret. Some period pieces from recovered stock. Makes own damascus and mokume gane. Remarks: Full-time maker, ABS since 2000, William Scagel Memorial Scholarship 2002, Bill Moran School of Blade Smithing 2003, Apprentice under Master Blacksmith Dan Nickels at Black Rock Forge current. Mark: Last name ROSE in block letters with five petal "wild rose" in place of O. Doing business as Rose Cutlery.

ROSENBAUGH, RON,
2806 Stonegate Dr, Crystal Lake, IL 60012, Phone: 815-477-0027, ron@rosenbaughknives.com; Web: www.rosenbaughknives.com
Specialties: Fancy and plain working knives using own designs, collaborations, and traditional patterns. Patterns: Bird, trout, boots, hunters, fighters, some Bowies. Technical: Grinds high alloy stainless, tool steels, and Damascus; forges 1084,5160, 52100, carbon and spring steels. Prices: $150 to $1000. Remarks: Part-time maker, first knife sold in 2004. Mark: Last name, logo, city.

ROSENFELD, BOB,
955 Freeman Johnson Rd, Hoschton, GA 30548, Phone: 770-867-2647, www.1bladesmith@msn.com
Specialties: Fancy and embellished working/using straight knives of his design and in standard patterns. Patterns: Daggers, hunters and utility/camp knives. Technical: Forges 52100, A203E, 1095 and L6 Damascus. Offers engraving. Prices: $125 to $650; some to $1000. Remarks: Full-time maker; first knife sold in 1984. Also makes folders; ABS Journeyman. Mark: Last name or full name, Knifemaker.

ROSS, D L,
27 Kinsman St, Dunedin, NEW ZEALAND, Phone: 64 3 464 0239, Fax: 64 3 464 0239
Specialties: Working straight knives of his design. Patterns: Hunters, various others. Technical: Grinds 440C. Prices: $100 to $450; some to $700 NZ (not U.S. $). Remarks: Part-time maker; first knife sold in 1988. Mark: Dave Ross, Maker, city and country.

ROSS, STEPHEN,
534 Remington Dr, Evanston, WY 82930, Phone: 307-789-7104
Specialties: One-of-a-kind collector-grade classic and contemporary straight knives and folders of his design and to customer specs; some fantasy pieces. Patterns: Combat and survival knives, hunters, boots and folders. Technical: Grinds stainless and tool steels. Engraves, scrimshaws. Makes leather sheaths. Prices: $160 to $3000. Remarks: Part-time-time maker; first knife sold in 1971. Mark: Last name in modified Roman; sometimes in script.

ROSS, TIM,
3239 Oliver Rd, Thunder Bay, ON, CANADA P7G 1S9, Phone: 807-935-2667, Fax: 807-935-3179, rosscustomknives@gmail.com
Specialties: Fixed blades, natural handle material. Patterns: Hunting, fishing, Bowies, fighters. Technical: 440C, D2, 52100, Cable, 5160, 1084, L6, W2. Prices: $150 to $750 some higher. Remarks: Forges and stock removal. Mark: Ross Custom Knives.

ROSSDEUTSCHER, ROBERT N,
133 S Vail Ave, Arlington Heights, IL 60005, Phone: 847-577-0404, Web: www.rnrknives.com
Specialties: Frontier-style and historically inspired knives. Patterns: Trade knives, Bowies, camp knives and hunting knives, tomahawks and lances. Technical: Most knives are hand forged, a few are stock removal. Prices: $135 to $1500. Remarks: Journeyman Smith of the American Bladesmith Society. Mark: Back-to-back "R's", one upside down and backwards, one right side up and forward in an oval. Sometimes with name, town and state; depending on knife style.

ROTELLA, RICHARD A,
643 75th St, Niagara Falls, NY 14304
Specialties: Working knives of his design. Patterns: Various fishing, hunting and utility knives; folders. Technical: Grinds ATS-34. Prefers hand-rubbed finishes. Prices: $65 to $450; some to $900. Remarks: Spare-time maker; first knife sold in 1977. Not taking orders at this time; only sells locally. Mark: Name and city in stylized waterfall logo.

ROULIN, CHARLES,
113 B Rt. de Soral, Geneva, SWITZERLAND 1233, Phone: 022-757-4479, Fax: 079-218-9754, charles.roulin@bluewin.ch; Web: www.coutelier-roulin.com
Specialties: Fancy high-art straight knives and folders of his design. Patterns: Bowies, locking folders, slip-joint folders and miniatures. Technical: Grinds 440C, ATS-34 and D2. Engraves; carves nature scenes and detailed animals in steel, ivory, on handles and blades. Prices: $500 to $3000; some to Euro: 14,600. Remarks: Full-time maker; first knife sold in 1988. Mark: Symbol of fish with name or name engraved.

ROUSH, SCOTT,
Big Rock Forge, 31920 Maki Rd, Washburn, WI 54891, Phone: 715-373-2334, scott@bigrockforge.com; Web: bigrockforge.com
Specialties: Forged blades representing a diversity of styles from trasditional hunters, fighters, camp knives, and EDC's to artistic pieces of cultural and historical inspiration with an emphasis in unique materials. Technical: Forges Aldo 1084, W2, low MN 1075, stainless/high carbon san mai, wrought iron/high carbon san mai, damascus. Prices: $85 to $1000 Remarks: Full-time maker; first knife sold in 2010.Mark: Stamped initials (SAR) set in a diamond.

ROWE, FRED,
BETHEL RIDGE FORGE, 3199 Roberts Rd, Amesville, OH 45711, Phone: 866-325-2164, fred.rowe@bethelridgeforge.com; Web: www.bethelridgeforge.com
Specialties: Damascus and carbon steel sheath knives. Patterns: Bowies, hunters, fillet small kokris. Technical: His own Damascus, 52100, O1, L6, 1095 carbon steels, mosaics. Prices: $200 to $2000. Remarks: All blades are clay hardened. Mark: Bethel Ridge Forge.

ROYER, KYLE,
1962 State Route W, Mountain View, MO 65548, Phone: 417-934-6394, Fax: 417-247-5572, royerknifeworks@live.com Web: www.royerknifeworks.com
Specialties: I currently specialize in fixed blades. Technical: I forge many different patterns of damascus using mostly 1080 and 15n20. Remarks: I am a full-time maker and nineteen years old (12-05-90). I received my ABS Journeyman Smith Stamp at the 2009 Blade Show in Atlanta.

ROZAS, CLARK D,
1436 W "G" St, Wilmington, CA 90744, Phone: 310-518-0488
Specialties: Hand forged blades. Patterns: Pig stickers, toad stabbers, whackers, choppers. Technical: Damascus, 52100, 1095, 1084, 5160. Prices: $200 to $600. Remarks: A.B.S. member; part-time maker since 1995. Mark: Name over dagger.

RUA, GARY,
400 Snell St., Apt. 2, Fall River, MA 02721, Phone: 508-677-2664
Specialties: Working straight knives of his design. 1800 to 1900 century standard patterns. Patterns: Bowies, hunters, fighters, and patch knives. Technical: Forges and grinds. Damascus, 5160, 1095, old files. Uses only natural handle material. Prices: $350 - $2000. Remarks: Part-time maker. (Harvest Moon Forge) Mark: Last name.

RUANA KNIFE WORKS,
Box 520, Bonner, MT 59823, Phone: 406-258-5368, Fax: 406-258-2895, info@ruanaknives.com; Web: www.ruanaknives.com
Specialties: Working knives and period pieces. Patterns: Variety of straight knives. Technical: Forges 5160 chrome alloy for Bowies and 1095. Prices: $200 and up. Remarks: Full-time maker; first knife sold in 1938. Brand new non catalog knives available on ebay under seller name ruanaknives. For free catalog email regular mailing address to info@ruanaknives.com Mark: Name.

RUCKER, THOMAS,
194 Woodhaven Ct., Nacogdoches, TX 75965, Phone: 832-216-8122, admin@knivesbythomas.com Web: www.knivesbythomas.com
Specialties: Personal design and custom design. Hunting, tactical, folding knives, and cutlery. Technical: Design and grind ATS34, D2, O1, Damascus, and VG10. Prices: $150 - $5,000. Remarks: Full-time maker and custom scrimshaw and engraving done by wife, Debi Rucker. First knife done in 1969; first design sold in 1975 Mark: Etched logo and signature.

RUPERT, BOB,
301 Harshaville Rd, Clinton, PA 15026, Phone: 724-573-4569, rbrupert@aol.com
Specialties: Wrought period pieces with natural elements. Patterns: Elegant straight blades, friction folders. Technical: Forges colonial 7; 1095; 5160; diffuse mokume-gane and Damascus. Prices: $150 to $1500; some higher. Remarks: Part-time maker; first knife sold in 1980. Evening hours studio since 1980. Likes simplicity that disassembles. Mark: R etched in Old English.

RUPLE, WILLIAM H,
201 Brian Dr., Pleasanton, TX 78064, Phone: 830-569-0007, bknives@devtex.net
Specialties: Multi-blade folders, slip joints, some lock backs. Patterns: Like to reproduce old patterns. Offers filework and engraving. Technical: Grinds CPM-154 and other carbon and stainless steel and commercial Damascus. Prices: $950 to $2500. Remarks: Full-time maker; first knife sold in 1988. Mark: Ruple.

RUSS, RON,
5351 NE 160th Ave, Williston, FL 32696, Phone: 352-528-2603, RussRs@aol.com
Specialties: Damascus and mokume. Patterns: Ladder, rain drop and butterfly. Technical: Most knives, including Damascus, are forged from 52100-E. Prices: $65 to $2500. Mark: Russ.

RUSSELL, MICK,
4 Rossini Rd, Pari Park, Port Elizabeth, EC, SOUTH AFRICA 6070
Specialties: Art knives. Patterns: Working and collectible bird, trout and hunting knives, defense knives and folders. Technical: Grinds D2, 440C, ATS-34 and Damascus. Offers mirror or satin finishes. Prices: Start at $100. Remarks: Full-time maker; first knife sold in 1986. Mark: Stylized rhino incorporating initials.

RUSSELL, TOM,
6500 New Liberty Rd, Jacksonville, AL 36265, Phone: 205-492-7866
Specialties: Straight working knives of his design or to customer specs. Patterns: Hunters, folders, fighters, skinners, Bowies and utility knives. Technical: Grinds D2, 440C and ATS-34; offers filework. Prices: $75 to $225. Remarks: Part-time maker; first knife sold in 1987. Full-time tool and die maker. Mark: Last name with tulip stamp.

RUTH, MICHAEL G,
3101 New Boston Rd, Texarkana, TX 75501, Phone: 903-832-7166/cell:903-277-3663, Fax: 903-832-4710, mike@ruthknives.com; Web: www.ruthknives.com
Specialties: Hunters, bowies & fighters. Damascus & carbon steel. Prices: $375 & up. Mark: Last name.

RUTH, JR., Michael,
5716 Wilshire Dr., Texarkana, TX 75503, Phone: 903-293-2663, michael@ruthlesscustomknives.com; Web: www.ruthlesscustomknives.com
Specialties: Custom hand-forged blades, utilizing high carbon and Damascus steels. Patterns: Bowies, hunters and fighters ranging from field to presentation-grade pieces. Technical: Steels include 5160, 1084, 15n20, W-2, 1095, and O-1. Handle materials include a variety of premium hardwoods, stag, assorted ivories and micarta. Mark: 8-pointed star with capital "R" in center.

RUUSUVUORI, ANSSI,
Verkkotie 38, Piikkio, FINLAND 21500, Phone: 358-50-520 8057, anssi.ruusuvuori@akukon.fi; Web: www.mmkhorasani.com/razmafzar/smiths
Specialties: Traditional and modern puukko knives and hunters. Sole author except for Damascus steel. Technical: Forges mostly 1080 steel. Prices: $200 to $500; some to $1200. Remarks: Part-time maker. Mark: A inside a circle (stamped)

RYBAR JR., RAYMOND B,
2328 South Sunset Dr., Came Verde, AZ 86322, Phone: 928-567-6372, ray@rybarknives.com; Web: www.rybarknives.com
Specialties: Straight knives or folders with customers name, logo, etc. in mosaic pattern. Patterns: Common patterns plus mosaics of all types. Technical: Forges own Damascus. Primary forging of self smelted steel - smelting classes. Prices: $200 to $1200; Bible blades to $10,000. Remarks: Master Smith (A.B.S.) Primary focus toward Biblicaly themed blades Mark: Rybar or stone church forge or Rev. 1:3 or R.B.R. between diamonds.

RYBERG, GOTE,
Faltgatan 2, Norrahammar, SWEDEN 56200, Phone: 4636-61678

RYDBOM, JEFF,
PO Box 548, Annandale, MN 55302, Phone: 320-274-9639, jry1890@hotmail.com
Specialties: Ring knives. Patterns: Hunters, fighters, Bowie and camp knives. Technical: Straight grinds O1, A2, 1566 and 5150 steels. Prices: $150 to $1000. Remarks: No pinning of guards or pommels. All silver brazed. Mark: Capital "C" with J R inside.

RYUICHI, KUKI,
504-7 Tokorozawa-Shinmachi, Tokorozawa-city, Saitama, JAPAN, Phone: 042-943-3451

RZEWNICKI, GERALD,
8833 S Massbach Rd, Elizabeth, IL 61028-9714, Phone: 815-598-3239

S

SAINDON, R BILL,
233 Rand Pond Rd, Goshen, NH 03752, Phone: 603-863-1874, dayskiev71@aol.com
Specialties: Collector-quality folders of his design or to customer specs. Patterns: Latch release, LinerLock® and lockback folders. Technical: Offers limited amount of own Damascus; also uses Damas makers steel. Prefers natural handle material, gold and gems. Prices: $500 to $4000. Remarks: Full-time maker; first knife sold in 1981. Doing business as Daynia Forge. Mark: Sun logo or engraved surname.

SAKAKIBARA, MASAKI,
20-8 Sakuragaoka 2-Chome, Setagaya-ku, Tokyo, JAPAN 156-0054, Phone: 81-3-3420-0375

SAKMAR, MIKE,
903 S. Latson Rd. #257, Howell, MI 48843, Phone: 517-546-6388, Fax: 517-546-6399, sakmarent@yahoo.com; Web: www.sakmarenterprises.com
Specialties: Mokume in various patterns and alloy combinations. Patterns: Bowies, fighters, hunters and integrals. Technical: Grinds ATS-34, Damascus and high-carbon tool steels. Uses mostly natural handle materials—elephant ivory, walrus ivory, stag, wildwood, oosic, etc. Makes mokume for resale. Prices: $250 to $2500; some to $4000. Remarks: Part-time maker; first knife sold in 1990. Supplier of mokume. Mark: Last name.

SALLEY, JOHN D,
3965 Frederick-Ginghamsburg Rd., Tipp City, OH 45371, Phone: 937-698-4588, Fax: 937-698-4131
Specialties: Fancy working knives and art pieces. Patterns: Hunters, fighters, daggers and some swords. Technical: Grinds ATS-34, 12C27 and W2; buys Damascus. Prices: $85 to $1000; some to $6000. Remarks: Part-time maker; first knife sold in 1979. Mark: First initial, last name.

SAMPSON, LYNN,
381 Deakins Rd, Jonesborough, TN 37659, Phone: 423-348-8373
Specialties: Highly finished working knives, mostly folders. Patterns: Locking folders, slip-joints, interframes and two-blades. Technical: Grinds D2, 440C and ATS-34; offers extensive filework. Prices: Start at $300. Remarks: Full-time maker; first knife sold in 1982. Mark: Name and city in logo.

SANDBERG, RONALD B,
24784 Shadowwood Ln, Brownstown, MI 48134-9560, Phone: 734-671-6866, msc2009@comcast.net
Specialties: Good looking and functional hunting knives, filework, mixing of handle materials. Patterns: Hunters, skinners and Bowies. Prices: $120 and up. Remarks: Full lifetime workmanship guarantee. Mark: R.B. SANDBERG

SANDERS, BILL,
335 Bauer Ave, PO Box 957, Mancos, CO 81328, Phone: 970-533-7223, Fax: 970-533-7390, billsand@frontier.net; Web: www.billsandershandmadeknives.com
Specialties: Survival knives, working straight knives, some fancy and some fantasy, of his design. Patterns: Hunters, boots, utility knives, using belt knives. Technical: Grinds 440C, ATS-34 and commercial Damascus. Provides wide variety of handle materials. Prices: $170 to $800. Remarks: Full-time maker. Formerly of Timberline Knives. Mark: Name, city and state.

SANDERS, MICHAEL M,
PO Box 1106, Ponchatoula, LA 70454, Phone: 225-294-3601, sanders@bellsouth.net
Specialties: Working straight knives and folders, some deluxe. Patterns: Hunters, fighters, Bowies, daggers, large folders and deluxe Damascus miniatures. Technical: Grinds O1, D2, 440C, ATS-34 and Damascus. Prices: $75 to $650; some higher. Remarks: Full-time maker; first knife sold in 1967. Mark: Name and state.

SANDOW, BRENT EDWARD,
50 O'Halloran Road, Howick, Auckland, NEW ZEALAND 2014, Phone: 64 9 537 4166, knifebug@vodafone.co.nz; Web: www.brentsandowknives.com
Specialties: Tactical fixed blades, hunting, camp, Bowie. Technical: All blades made by stock removal method. Prices: From US $200 upward. Mark: Name etched or engraved.

SANDOW, NORMAN E,
63 B Moore St, Howick, Auckland, NEW ZEALAND, Phone: 095328912, sanknife@xtra.co.nz
Specialties: Quality LinerLock® folders. Working and fancy straight knives. Some one-of-a-kind. Embellishments available. Patterns: Most patterns, hunters, boot, bird and trout, etc., and to customer's specs. Technical: Predominate knife steel ATS-34. Also in use 12C27, D2 and Damascus. High class handle material used on both folders and straight knives. All blades made via the stock removal method. Prices: $350 to $4000. Remarks: Full-time maker. Mark: Norman E Sandow in semi-circular design.

SANDS, SCOTT,
2 Lindis Ln, New Brighton, Christchurch 9, NEW ZEALAND
Specialties: Classic working and fantasy swords. Patterns: Fantasy, medieval, celtic, viking, katana, some daggers. Technical: Forges own Damascus; 1080 and L6; 5160 and L6; O1 and L6. All hand-polished, does own heat-treating, forges non-Damascus on request. Prices: $1500 to $15,000+. Remarks: Full-time maker; first blade sold in 1996. Mark: Stylized Moon.

SANFORD, DICK,
9 Satsop Court, Montesano, WA 98563, Phone: 360-249-5776, richardsanfo364@centurytel.net
Remarks: Ten years experience hand forging knives

SANTIAGO, ABUD,
Av Gaona 3676 PB, Buenos Aires, ARGENTINA 1416, Phone: 5411 4612 8396, info@phi-sabud.com; Web: www.phi-sabud.com/blades.html

SANTINI, TOM,
101 Clayside Dr, Pikeville, NC 27863, Phone: 586-354-0245, tomsantiniknives@hotmail.com; Web: www.tomsantiniknives.com
Specialties: working/using straight knives, tactical, and some slipjoints Technical: Grinds ATS-34, S-90-V, D2, and damascus. I handstitch my leather sheaths. Prices: $150 - $500. Remarks: Full-time maker, first knife sold in 2004. Mark: Full name.

SARGANIS, PAUL,
2215 Upper Applegate Rd, Jacksonville, OR 97530, Phone: 541-899-2831, paulsarganis@hotmail.com; Web: www.sarganis.50megs.com
Specialties: Hunters, folders, Bowies. Technical: Forges 5160, 1084. Grinds ATS-34 and 440C. Prices: $120 to $500. Remarks: Spare-time maker, first knife sold in 1987. Mark: Last name.

SASS, GARY N,
2048 Buckeye Dr, Sharpsville, PA 16150, Phone: 724-866-6165, gnsass@yahoo.com
Specialties: Working straight knives of his design or to customer specifications. Patterns: Hunters, fighters, utility knives, push daggers. Technical: Grinds 440C, ATS-34 and Damascus. Uses exotic wood, buffalo horn, warthog tusk and semi-precious stones. Prices: $50 to $250, some higher. Remarks: Part-time maker. First knife sold in 2003. Mark: Initials G.S. formed into a diamond shape or last name.

SAVIANO, JAMES,
124 Wallis St., Douglas, MA 01516, Phone: 508-476-7644, jimsaviano@gmail.com
Specialties: Straight knives. Patterns: Hunters, bowies, fighters, daggers, short swords. Technical: Hand-forged high-carbon and my own damascus steel. Prices: Starting at $300. Remarks: ABS mastersmith, maker since 2000, sole authorship. Mark: Last name or stylized JPS initials.

SAWBY, SCOTT,
480 Snowberry Ln, Sandpoint, ID 83864, Phone: 208-263-4253, scotmar@dishmail.net; Web: www.sawbycustomknives.com
Specialties: Folders, working and fancy. Patterns: Locking folders, patent locking systems and interframes. Technical: Grinds D2, 440C, CPM154, ATS-34, S30V, and Damascus. Prices: $700 to $3000. Remarks: Full-time maker; first knife sold in 1974. Engraving by wife Marian. Mark: Last name, city and state.

custom knifemakers

SCARROW, WIL,
c/o LandW Mail Service, PO Box 1036, Gold Hill, OR 97525, Phone: 541-855-1236, willsknife@earthlink.net
Specialties: Carving knives, also working straight knives in standard patterns or to customer specs. Patterns: Carving, fishing, hunting, skinning, utility, swords and Bowies. Technical: Forges and grinds: A2, L6, W1, D2, 5160, 1095, 440C, AEB-L, ATS-34 and others on request. Offers some filework. Prices: $105 to $850; some higher. Prices include sheath (carver's $40 and up). Remarks: Spare-time maker; first knife sold in 1983. Two to eight month construction time on custom orders. Doing business as Scarrow's Custom Stuff and Gold Hill Knife works (in Oregon). Carving knives available at Raven Dog Enterprises. Contact at Ravedog@aol.com. Mark: SC with arrow and year made.

SCHALLER, ANTHONY BRETT,
5609 Flint Ct. NW, Albuquerque, NM 87120, Phone: 505-899-0155, brett@schallerknives.com; Web: www.schallerknives.com
Specialties: Straight knives and locking-liner folders of his design and in standard patterns. Patterns: Boots, fighters, utility knives and folders. Technical: Grinds CPM154, S30V, and stainless Damascus. Offers filework, hand-rubbed finishes and full and narrow tangs. Prefers exotic woods or Micarta for handle materials, G-10 and carbon fiber to handle materials. Prices: $100 to $350; some to $500. Remarks: Part-time maker; first knife sold in 1990. Mark: A.B. Schaller - Albuquerque NM - handmade.

SCHEID, MAGGIE,
124 Van Stallen St, Rochester, NY 14621-3557
Specialties: Simple working straight knives. Patterns: Kitchen and utility knives; some miniatures. Technical: Forges 5160 high-carbon steel. Prices: $100 to $200. Remarks: Part-time maker; first knife sold in 1986. Mark: Full name.

SCHEMPP, ED,
PO Box 1181, Ephrata, WA 98823, Phone: 509-754-2963, Fax: 509-754-3212, edschempp@yahoo.com
Specialties: Mosaic Damascus and unique folder designs. Patterns: Primarily folders. Technical: Grinds CPM440V; forges many patterns of mosaic using powdered steel. Prices: $100 to $400; some to $2000. Remarks: Part-time maker; first knife sold in 1991. Doing business as Ed Schempp Knives. Mark: Ed Schempp Knives over five heads of wheat, city and state.

SCHEMPP, MARTIN,
PO Box 1181, 5430 Baird Springs Rd NW, Ephrata, WA 98823, Phone: 509-754-2963, Fax: 509-754-3212
Specialties: Fantasy and traditional straight knives of his design, to customer specs and in standard patterns; Paleolithic-styles. Patterns: Fighters and Paleolithic designs. Technical: Uses opal, Mexican rainbow and obsidian. Offers scrimshaw. Prices: $15 to $100; some to $250. Remarks: Spare-time maker; first knife sold in 1995. Mark: Initials and date.

SCHEURER, ALFREDO E FAES,
Av Rincon de los Arcos 104, Col Bosque Res del Sur, Distrito Federal, MEXICO 16010, Phone: 5676 47 63
Specialties: Fancy and fantasy knives of his design. Patterns: Daggers. Technical: Grinds stainless steel; casts and grinds silver. Sets stones in silver. Prices: $2000 to $3000. Remarks: Spare-time maker; first knife sold in 1989. Mark: Symbol.

SCHIPPNICK, JIM,
PO Box 326, Sanborn, NY 14132, Phone: 716-731-3715, ragnar@ragweedforge.com; Web: www.ragweedforge.com
Specialties: Nordic, early American, rustic. Mark: Runic R. Remarks: Also imports Nordic knives from Norway, Sweden and Finland.

SCHLUETER, DAVID,
2136 Cedar Gate Rd., Madison Heights, VA 24572, Phone: 434-384-8642, drschlueter@hotmail.com
Specialties: Japanese-style swords. Patterns: Larger blades. O-tanto to Tachi, with focus on less common shapes. Technical: Forges and grinds carbon steels, heat-treats and polishes own blades, makes all fittings, does own mounting and finishing. Prices: Start at $3000. Remarks: Sells fully mounted pieces only, doing business as Odd Frog Forge. Mark: Full name and date.

SCHMITZ, RAYMOND E,
PO Box 1787, Valley Center, CA 92082, Phone: 760-749-4318

SCHNEIDER, CRAIG M,
5380 N Amity Rd, Claremont, IL 62421, Phone: 217-377-5715, raephtownslam@att.blackberry.net
Specialties: Straight knives of his own design. Patterns: Bowies, hunters, tactical, bird & trout. Technical: Forged high-carbon steel and Damascus. Flat grind and differential heat treatment use a wide selection of handle, guard and bolster material, also offers leather sheaths. Prices: $150 to $3000. Remarks: Part-time maker; first knife sold in 1985. Mark: Stylized initials.

SCHNEIDER, HERMAN J.,
14084 Apple Valley Rd, Apple Valley, CA 92307, Phone: 760-946-9096
Specialties: Presentation pieces, Fighters, Hunters. Prices: Starting at $900. Mark: H.J. Schneider-Maker or maker's last name.

SCHOEMAN, CORRIE,
Box 28596, Danhof, Free State, SOUTH AFRICA 9310, Phone: 027 51 4363528 Cell: 027 82-3750789, corries@intekom.co.za
Specialties: High-tech folders of his design or to customer's specs. Patterns: Linerlock folders and automatics. Technical: ATS-34, Damascus or stainless Damascus with titanium frames; prefers exotic materials for handles. Prices:

$650 to $2000. Remarks: Full-time maker; first knife sold in 1984. All folders come with filed liners and back and jeweled inserts. Mark: Logo in knife shape engraved on inside of back bar.

SCHOENFELD, MATTHEW A,
RR #1, Galiano Island, BC, CANADA V0N 1P0, Phone: 250-539-2806
Specialties: Working knives of his design. Patterns: Kitchen cutlery, camp knives, hunters. Technical: Grinds 440C. Prices: $85 to $500. Remarks: Part-time maker; first knife sold in 1978. Mark: Signature, Galiano Is. B.C., and date.

SCHOENINGH, MIKE,
49850 Miller Rd, North Powder, OR 97867, Phone: 541-856-3239

SCHOLL, TIM,
1389 Langdon Rd, Angier, NC 27501, Phone: 910-897-2051, tschollknives@live.com
Specialties: Fancy and working/using straight knives and folders of his design and to customer specs. Patterns: Bowies, hunters, tomahawks, daggers & fantasy knives. Technical: Forges high carbon and tool steel makes Damascus, grinds ATS-34 and D2 on request. Prices: $150 to $6000. Remarks: Part-time maker; first knife sold in 1990. Doing business as Tim Scholl Custom Knives. President North Carolina Custom Knifemakers Guild. Journeyman Smith American Bladesmith Society member Professional Knifemakers Association. Mark: S pierced by arrow.

SCHRADER, ROBERT,
55532 Gross De, Bend, OR 97707, Phone: 541-598-7301
Specialties: Hunting, utility, Bowie. Patterns: Fixed blade. Prices: $150 to $600.

SCHRAP, ROBERT G,
CUSTOM LEATHER KNIFE SHEATH CO., 7024 W Wells St, Wauwatosa, WI 53213-3717, Phone: 414-771-6472, Fax: 414-479-9765, knifesheaths@aol.com; Web: www.customsheaths.com
Specialties: Leatherwork. Prices: $35 to $100. Mark: Schrap in oval.

SCHROEN, KARL,
4042 Bones Rd, Sebastopol, CA 95472, Phone: 707-823-4057, Fax: 707-823-2914, Web: http://users.ap.net/~schroen
Specialties: Using knives made to fit. Patterns: Sgian dubhs, carving sets, wood-carving knives, fishing knives, kitchen knives and new cleaver design. Technical: Forges A2, ATS-34, D2 and L6 cruwear S30V S90V. Prices: $150 to $6000. Remarks: Full-time maker; first knife sold in 1968. Author of The Hand Forged Knife. Mark: Last name.

SCHUCHMANN, RICK,
3975 Hamblen Dr, Cincinnati, OH 45255, Phone: 513-553-4316
Specialties: Replicas of antique and out-of-production Scagels and Randalls, primarily miniatures. Patterns: All sheath knives, mostly miniatures, hunting and fighting knives, some daggers and hatchets. Technical: Stock removal, 440C and O1 steel. Most knives are flat ground, some convex. Prices: $175 to $600 and custom to $4000. Remarks: Part-time maker, sold first knife in 1997. Knives on display in the Randall Museum. Sheaths are made exclusively at Sullivan's Holster Shop, Tampa, FL Mark: SCAR.

SCHWARZER, LORA SUE,
119 Shoreside Trail, Crescent City, FL 32112, Phone: 386-698-2840, auntielora57@yahoo.com
Specialties: Scagel style knives. Patterns: Hunters and miniatures Technical: Forges 1084 and Damascus. Prices: Start at $400. Remarks: Part-time maker; first knife sold in 1997. Journeyman Bladesmith, American Bladesmith Society. Now working with Steve Schwarzer on some projects. Mark: Full name - JS on reverse side.

SCHWARZER, STEPHEN,
119 Shoreside Trail, Crescent City, FL 32112, Phone: 386-698-2840, Fax: 386-698-2840, schwarzeranvil@gmail.com; Web: www.steveschwarzer.com
Specialties: Mosaic Damascus and picture mosaic in folding knives. All Japanese blades are finished working with Wally Hostetter considered the top Japanese lacquer specialist in the U.S.A. Also produces a line of carbon steel skinning knives at $300. Patterns: Folders, axes and buckskinner knives. Technical: Specializes in picture mosaic Damascus and powder metal mosaic work. Sole authorship; all work including carving done in-house. Most knives have file work and carving. Hand carved steel and precious metal guards. Prices: $1500 to $5000, some higher; carbon steel and primitive knives much less. Remarks: Full-time maker; first knife sold in 1976, considered by many to be one of the top mosaic Damascus specialists in the world. Mosaic Master level work. I am now working with Lora Schwarzer on some projects. Mark: Schwarzer + anvil.

SCIMIO, BILL,
4554 Creek Side Ln., Spruce Creek, PA 16683, Phone: 814-632-3751, sprucecreekforge@gmail.com Web: www.sprucecreekforge.com
Specialties: Hand-forged primitive-style knives with curly maple, antler, bone and osage handles.

SCORDIA, PAOLO,
Via Terralba 144, Torrimpietra, Roma, ITALY 00050, Phone: 06-61697231, paolo.scordia@uni.net; Web: www.scordia-knives.com
Specialties: Working, fantasy knives, Italian traditional folders and fixed blades of own design. Patterns: Any. Technical: Forge mosaic Damascus, forge blades, welds own mokume and grinds ATS-34, etc. use hardwoods and Micarta for handles, brass and nickel-silver for fittings. Makes sheaths. Prices: $200 to $2000, some to $4000. Remarks: Part-time maker; first knife sold in 1988. Mark: Sun and moon logo and ititials.

SCROGGS, JAMES A,
108 Murray Hill Dr, Warrensburg, MO 64093, Phone: 660-747-2568, jscroggsknives@embarqmail.com
Specialties: Straight knives, prefers light weight. Patterns: Hunters, hideouts, and fighters. Technical: Grinds CPM-154 stainless plus experiments in steel. Prefers handles of walnut in English, bastonge, American black. Also uses myrtle, maple, Osage orange. Prices: $200 to $1000. Remarks: 1st knife sold in 1985. Full-time maker, no orders taken. Mark: SCROGGS in block or script.

SCULLEY, PETER E,
340 Sunset Dr, Rising Fawn, GA 30738, Phone: 706-398-0169

SEARS, MICK,
8146 Featherun Rd, Kershaw, SC 29067, Phone: 803-475-4937
Specialties: Scots and confederate reproductions; Bowies and fighters. Patterns: Bowies, fighters. Technical: Grinds 440C and 1095. Prices: $50 to $150; some to $300. Remarks: Full-time maker; first knife sold in 1975. Doing business as Mick's Custom Knives. Mark: First name.

SEATON, DAVID D,
1028 South Bishop Ave, #237, Rolla, MO 65401, Phone: 573-465-3193, aokcustomknives@gmail.com
Specialties: Gentleman's and Lady's folders. Patterns: Liner lock folders of own design and to customer specs, lockbacks, slipjoints, some stright knives, tactical folders, skinners, fighters, and utility knives. Technical: Grinds ATS 34, O1, 1095, 154CM, CPM154, commercial Damascus. Blades are mostly flat ground, some hollow ground. Does own heat treating, tempering, and Nitre Bluing. Prefers natural handle materials such as ivory, mother of pearl, bone, and exotic woods, some use of G10 and micarta on hard use knives. Use gem stones, gold, silver on upscale knives, offers some carving, filework, and engrving. Prices: $150 to $600 avg; some to $1500 and up depending on materials and embellishments. Remarks: First knife sold in 2002, part-time maker, doing business at AOK Custom Knives. Mark: full or last name engraved on blade.

SEIB, STEVE,
7914 Old State Road, Evansville, IN 47710, Phone: 812-867-2231, sseib@insightbb.com
Specialties: Working straight knives. Pattern: Skinners, hunters, bowies and camp knives. Technical: Forges high-carbon and makes own damascus. Remarks: Part-time maker. ABS member. Mark: Last name.

SELF, ERNIE,
950 O'Neill Ranch Rd, Dripping Springs, TX 78620-9760, Phone: 512-940-7134, ernieself@hillcountrytx.net
Specialties: Traditional and working straight knives and folders of his design and in standard patterns. Patterns: Hunters, locking folders and slip-joints. Technical: Grinds 440C, D2, 440V, ATS-34 and Damascus. Offers fancy filework. Prices: $250 to $1000; some to $2500. Remarks: Full-time maker; first knife sold in 1982. Also customizes Buck 110's and 112's folding hunters. Mark: In oval shape - Ernie Self Maker Dripping Springs TX.

SELLEVOLD, HARALD,
PO Box 4134, S Kleivesmau:2, Bergen, NORWAY N5835, Phone: 47 55-310682, haraldsellevold@c2i.net; Web:knivmakeren.com
Specialties: Norwegian-styles; collaborates with other Norse craftsmen. Patterns: Distinctive ferrules and other mild modifications of traditional patterns; Bowies and friction folders. Technical: Buys Damascus blades; blacksmiths his own blades. Semi-gemstones used in handles; gemstone inlay. Prices: $350 to $2000. Remarks: Full-time maker; first knife sold in 1980. Mark: Name and country in logo.

SELZAM, FRANK,
Martin Reinhard Str 23, Bad Koenigshofen, GERMANY 97631, Phone: 09761-5980, frankselzam.de
Specialties: Hunters, working knives to customers specs, hand tooled and stitched leather sheaths large stock of wood and German stag horn. Patterns: Mostly own design. Technical: Forged blades, own Damascus, also stock removal stainless. Prices: $250 to $1500. Remark: First knife sold in 1978. Mark: Last name stamped.

SENTZ, MARK C,
4084 Baptist Rd, Taneytown, MD 21787, Phone: 410-756-2018
Specialties: Fancy straight working knives of his design. Patterns: Hunters, fighters, folders and utility/camp knives. Technical: Forges 1085, 1095, 5160, 5155 and his Damascus. Most knives come with wood-lined leather sheath or wooden presentation sheath. Prices: Start at $275. Remarks: Full-time maker; first knife sold in 1989. Doing business as M. Charles Sentz Gunsmithing, Inc. Mark: Last name.

SERAFEN, STEVEN E,
24 Genesee St, New Berlin, NY 13411, Phone: 607-847-6903
Specialties: Traditional working/using straight knives of his design and to customer specs. Patterns: Bowies, fighters, hunters. Technical: Grinds ATS-34, 440C, high-carbon steel. Prices: $175 to $600; some to $1200. Remarks: Part-time maker; first knife sold in 1990. Mark: First and middle initial, last name in script.

SERVEN, JIM,
PO Box 1, Fostoria, MI 48435, Phone: 517-795-2255
Specialties: Highly finished unique folders. Patterns: Fancy working folders, axes, miniatures and razors; some straight knives. Technical: Grinds 440C; forges his own Damascus. Prices: $150 to $800; some to $1500. Remarks: Full-time maker; first knife sold in 1971. Mark: Name in map logo.

SEVEY CUSTOM KNIFE,
94595 Chandler Rd, Gold Beach, OR 97444, Phone: 541-247-2649, sevey@charter.net; Web: www.seveyknives.com
Specialties: Fixed blade hunters. Patterns: Drop point, trailing paint, clip paint, full tang, hidden tang. Technical: D-2, and ATS-34 blades, stock removal. Heat treatment by Paul Bos. Prices: $225 and up depending on overall length and grip material. Mark: Sevey Custom Knife.

SFREDDO, RODRIGO MENEZES,
cep g5 150-000, Rua 15 De Setembro 66, Nova Petropolis, RS, BRAZIL 95150-000, Phone: 011-55-54-303-303-90, www.brazilianbladesmiths.com.br; www.sbccutelaria.org.br
Specialties: Integrals, Bowies, hunters, dirks & swords. Patterns: Forges his own Damascus and 52100 steel. Technical: Specialized in integral knives and Damascus. Prices: From $350 and up. Most around $750 to $1000. Remarks: Considered by many to be the Brazil's best bladesmith. ABS SBC Member. Mark: S. Sfreddo on the left side of the blade.

SHADLEY, EUGENE W,
209 NW 17th Street, Grand Rapids, MN 55744, Phone: 218-999-7197 or 218-244-8628, Fax: call first, ShadleyKnives@hotmail.com
Specialties: Gold frames are available on some models. Patterns: Whittlers, stockman, sowbelly, congress, trapper, etc. Technical: Grinds ATS-34, 416 frames. Prices: Starts at $600, some models up to $15,000. Remarks: Full-time maker; first knife sold in 1985. Doing business as Shadley Knives. Mark: Last name.

SHADMOT, BOAZ,
MOSHAV PARAN D N, Arava, ISRAEL 86835, srb@arava.co.il

SHARP, DAVID,
17485 Adobe St., Hesperia, CA 92345, Phone: 520-370-1899, sharpwerks@gmail.com or david@sharpwerks.com; Web: www.sharpwerks.com
Specialties: Fixed blades. Patterns: Original and real Loveless pattern utilities, hunters and fighters. Technical: Stock removal, tool steel and stainless steel, hollow grind, machine finish, full polish, various handle materials. Prices: $300 to $1,500. Remarks: Part-time maker, first knife sold in 2011. Mark: "Sharpwerks" on original designs; "D. Sharp" on Loveless designs.

SHARRIGAN, MUDD,
111 Bradford Rd, Wiscasset, ME 04578-4457, Phone: 207-882-9820, Fax: 207-882-9835
Specialties: Custom designs; repair straight knives, custom leather sheaths. Patterns: Daggers, fighters, hunters, crooked knives and seamen working knives; traditional Scandinavian-styles. Technical: Forges 1095, 5160, and W2. Prices: $50 to $325; some to $1200. Remarks: Full-time maker; first knife sold in 1982. Mark: Swallow tail carving. Mudd engraved.

SHEEHY, THOMAS J,
4131 NE 24th Ave, Portland, OR 97211-6411, Phone: 503-493-2843
Specialties: Hunting knives and ulus. Patterns: Own or customer designs. Technical: 1095/O1 and ATS-34 steel. Prices: $35 to $200. Remarks: Do own heat treating; forged or ground blades. Mark: Name.

SHEELY, "BUTCH" FOREST,
15784 Custarrd, Grand Rapids, OH 43522, Phone: 419-308-3471, sheelyblades@gmail.com
Specialties: Traditional bowies and pipe tomahawks. Patterns: Bowies, hunters, integrals, dirks, axes and hawks. Technical: Forges 5160, 52100, 1084, 1095, and Damascus.Prices: $150 to $1500;Remarks: Full-time bladesmith part-time blacksmith; first knife sold in 1982. ABS Journeysmith, sole author of all knives and hawks including hand sewn leather sheaths, doing business as Beaver Creek Forge. Mark: First and last name above Bladesmith.

SHEETS, STEVEN WILLIAM,
6 Stonehouse Rd, Mendham, NJ 07945, Phone: 201-543-5882

SHIFFER, STEVE,
PO Box 582, Leakesville, MS 39451, Phone: 601-394-4425, aiifish2@yahoo.com; Web: wwwchoctawplantationforge.com
Specialties: Bowies, fighters, hard use knives. Patterns: Fighters, hunters, combat/utility knives. Walker pattern LinerLock® folders. Allen pattern scale and bolster release autos. Technical: Most work forged, stainless stock removal. Makes own Damascus. O1 and 5160 most used also 1084, 440c, 154cm, s30v. Prices: $125 to $1000. Remarks: First knife sold in 2000, all heat treatment done by maker. Doing business as Choctaw Plantation Forge. Mark: Hot mark sunrise over creek.

SHINOSKY, ANDY,
3117 Meanderwood Dr, Canfield, OH 44406, Phone: 330-702-0299, andrew@shinosky.com; Web: www.shinosky.com
Specialties: Collectable folders and interframes. Patterns: Drop point, spear point, trailing point, daggers. Technical: Grinds ATS-34 and Damascus. Prefers natural handle materials. Most knives are engraved by Andy himself. Prices: Start at $800. Remarks: Part-time maker/engraver. First knife sold in 1992. Mark: Name.

SHIPLEY, STEVEN A,
800 Campbell Rd Ste 137, Richardson, TX 75081, Phone: 972-644-7981, Fax: 972-644-7985, steve@shipleysphotography.com
Specialties: Hunters, skinners and traditional straight knives. Technical: Hand grinds ATS-34, 440C and Damascus steels. Each knife is custom sheathed by his son, Dan. Prices: $175 to $2000. Remarks: Part-time maker; like smooth lines and unusual handle materials. Mark: S A Shipley.

custom knifemakers

SHOEMAKER, CARROLL,
380 Yellowtown Rd, Northup, OH 45658, Phone: 740-446-6695
Specialties: Working/using straight knives of his design. Patterns: Hunters, utility/camp and early American backwoodsmen knives. Technical: Grinds ATS-34; forges old files, O1 and 1095. Uses some Damascus; offers scrimshaw and engraving. Prices: $100 to $175; some to $350. Remarks: Spare-time maker; first knife sold in 1977. Mark: Name and city or connected initials.

SHOEMAKER, SCOTT,
316 S Main St, Miamisburg, OH 45342, Phone: 513-859-1935
Specialties: Twisted, wire-wrapped handles on swords, fighters and fantasy blades; new line of seven models with quick-draw, multi-carry Kydex sheaths. Patterns: Bowies, boots and one-of-a-kinds in his design or to customer specs. Technical: Grinds A6 and ATS-34; buys Damascus. Hand satin finish is standard. Prices: $100 to $1500; swords to $8000. Remarks: Part-time maker; first knife sold in 1984. Mark: Angel wings with last initial, or last name.

SHOGER, MARK O,
14780 SW Osprey Dr Suite 345, Beaverton, OR 97007, Phone: 503-579-2495, mosdds@msn.com
Specialties: Working and using straight knives and folders of his design; fancy and embellished knives. Patterns: Hunters, Bowies, daggers and folders. Technical: Forges O1, W2, 1084, 5160, 52100 and 1084/15n20 pattern weld. Remarks: Spare-time maker. Mark: Last name or stamped last initial over anvil.

SHROPSHIRE, SHAWN,
PO Box 453, Piedmont, OK 73078, Phone: 405-833-5239, shawn@sdsknifeworks.com; Web: www.sdsknifeworks.com
Specialties: Working straight knives and frontier style period pieces. Patterns: Bowies, hunters, skinners, fighters, patch/neck knives.Technical: Grinds D2, 154CMandsomeDamascus,forges1084,5160.Prices: Startingat$125. Remarks: Part-time maker; first knife sold in 1997. Doing business as SDS Knifeworks. Mark: Etched "SDS Knifeworks - Oklahoma" in an oval or "SDS" tang stamp.

SHULL, JAMES,
5146 N US 231 W, Rensselaer, IN 47978, Phone: 219-866-0436, nbjs@netnitco.net Web: www.shullhandforgedknives.com
Specialties: Working knives of hunting, fillet, Bowie patterns. Technical: Forges or uses 1095, 5160, 52100 & O1. Prices: $100 to $300. Remarks: DBA Shull Handforged Knives. Mark: Last name in arc.

SIBERT, SHANE,
PO BOX 241, Gladstone, OR 97027, Phone: 503-650-2082, shane.sibert@comcast.net Web: www.sibertknives.com
Specialties: Innovative light weight hiking and backpacking knives for outdoorsman and adventurers, progressive fixed blade combat and fighting knives. One-of-a-kind knives of various configurations. Titanium frame lock folders. Patterns: Modern configurations of utility/camp knives, bowies, modified spear points, daggers, tantos, recurves, clip points and spine serrations. Technical: Stock removal. Specializes in CPM S30V, CPM S35VN, CPM D2, CPM 3V, stainless damascus. Micarta, G-10, stabilized wood and titanium. Prices. $200 - $1000, some pieces $1500 and up. Remarks: Full-time maker, first knife sold in 1994. Mark: Stamped "SIBERT" and occasionally uses electro-etch with oval around last name.

SIBRIAN, AARON,
4308 Dean Dr, Ventura, CA 93003, Phone: 805-642-6950
Specialties: Tough working knives of his design and in standard patterns. Patterns: Makes a "Viper utility"—a kukri derivative and a variety of straight using knives. Technical: Grinds 440C and ATS-34. Offers traditional Japanese blades; soft backs, hard edges, temper lines. Prices: $60 to $100; some to $250. Remarks: Spare-time maker; first knife sold in 1989. Mark: Initials in diagonal line.

SIMMONS, H R,
1100 Bay City Rd, Aurora, NC 27806, Phone: 252-916-2241
Specialties: Working/using straight knives of his design. Patterns: Fighters, hunters and utility/camp knives. Technical: Forges and grinds Damascus and L6; grinds ATS-34. Prices: $150 and up. Remarks: Part-time maker; first knife sold in 1987. Doing business as HRS Custom Knives, Royal Forge and Trading Company. Mark: HRS.

SIMONELLA, GIANLUIGI,
Via Battiferri 33, Maniago, ITALY 33085, Phone: 01139-427-730350
Specialties: Traditional and classic folding and working/using knives of his design and to customer specs. Patterns: Bowies, fighters, hunters, utility/camp knives. Technical: Forges ATS-34, D2, 440C. Prices: $250 to $400; some to $1000. Remarks: Full-time maker; first knife sold in 1988. Mark: Wilson.

SINCLAIR, J E,
520 Francis Rd, Pittsburgh, PA 15239, Phone: 412-793-5778
Specialties: Fancy hunters and fighters, liner locking folders. Patterns: Fighters, hunters and folders. Technical: Flat-grinds and hollow grind, prefers hand rubbed satin finish. Uses natural handle materials. Prices: $185 to $800. Remarks: Part-time maker; first knife sold in 1995. Mark: First and middle initials, last name and maker.

SINYARD, CLESTON S,
27522 Burkhardt Dr, Elberta, AL 36530, Phone: 334-987-1361, nimoforge1@gulftel.com; Web: www.knifemakersguild
Specialties:Workingstraightknivesandfoldersofhisdesign.Patterns:Hunters, buckskinners, Bowies, daggers, fighters and all-Damascus folders. Technical: Makes Damascus from 440C, stainless steel, D2 and regular high-carbon steel.

forges "forefinger pad" into hunters and skinners. Prices: In Damascus $450 to $1500; some $2500. Remarks: Full-time maker; first knife sold in 1980. Doing business as Nimo Forge. Mark: Last name, U.S.A. in anvil.

SISKA, JIM,
48 South Maple St, Westfield, MA 01085, Phone: 413-642-3059, siskaknives@comcast.net
Specialties: Traditional working straight knives, no folders. Patterns: Hunters, fighters, Bowies and one-of-a-kinds; folders. Technical: Grinds D2, A2, 54CM and ATS-34; buys Damascus. Likes exotic woods. Prices: $300 and up. Remarks: Part-time. Mark: Siska in Old English.

SJOSTRAND, KEVIN,
1541 S Cain St, Visalia, CA 93292, Phone: 559-625-5254
Specialties: Traditional and working/using straight knives and folders of his design or to customer specs. Patterns: Fixed blade hunters, Bowies, utility/camp knives. Technical: Grinds ATS-34, 440C and 1095. Prefers high polished blades and full tang. Natural and stabilized hardwoods, Micarta and stag handle material. Prices: $150 to $400. Remarks: Part-time maker; first knife sold in 1992. Doing business as Black Oak Blades. Mark: SJOSTRAND

SKIFF, STEVEN,
SKIFF MADE BLADES, PO Box 537, Broadalbin, NY 12025, Phone: 518-883-4875, skiffmadeblades @hotmail.com; Web: www.skiffmadeblades.com
Specialties: Custom using/collector grade straight blades and LinerLock® folders of maker's design or customer specifications. Patterns: Hunters, utility/camp knives, tactical/fancy art folders. Prices: Straight blades $225 and up. Folders $450 and up. Technical: Stock removal hollow ground ATS-34, 154 CM, S30V, and tool steel. Damascus-Devon Thomas, Robert Eggerling, Mike Norris and Delbert Ealy. Nickel silver and stainless in-house heat treating. Handle materials: man made and natural woods (stabilized). Horn shells sheaths for straight blades, sews own leather and uses sheaths by "Tree-Stump Leather." Remarks: First knife sold 1997. Started making folders in 2000. Mark: SKIFF on blade of straight blades and in inside of backspacer on folders.

SLEE, FRED,
9 John St, Morganville, NJ 07751, Phone: 732-591-9047
Specialties: Working straight knives, some fancy, to customer specs. Patterns: Hunters, fighters, fancy daggers and folders. Technical: Grinds D2, 440C and ATS-34. Prices: $285 to $1100. Remarks: Part-time maker; first knife sold in 1980. Mark: Letter "S" in Old English.

SLOAN, DAVID,
PO BOX 83, Diller, NE 68342, Phone: 402-793-5755, sigp22045@hotmail.com
Specialties: Hunters, choppers and fighters. Technical: Forged blades of W2, 1084 and Damascus. Prices: Start at $225. Remarks: Part-time maker, made first knife in 2002, received JS stamp 2010. Mark: Sloan JS.

SLOAN, SHANE,
4226 FM 61, Newcastle, TX 76372, Phone: 940-846-3290
Specialties: Collector-grade straight knives and folders. Patterns: Uses stainless Damascus, ATS-34 and 12C27. Bowies, lockers, slip-joints, fancy folders, fighters and period pieces. Technical: Grinds D2 and ATS-34. Uses hand-rubbed satin finish. Prefers rare natural handle materials. Prices: $250 to $6500. Remarks: Full-time maker; first knife sold in 1985. Mark: Name and city.

SLOBODIAN, SCOTT,
PO Box 1498, San Andreas, CA 95249, Phone: 209-286-1980, Fax: 209-286-1982, info@slobodianswords.com; Web: www.slobodianswords.com
Specialties: Japanese-style knives and swords, period pieces, fantasy pieces and miniatures. Patterns: Small kweikens, tantos, wakazashis, katanas, traditional samurai swords. Technical: Flat-grinds 1050, commercial Damascus. Prices: Prices start at $1500. Remarks: Full-time maker; first knife sold in 1987. Mark: Blade signed in Japanese characters and various scripts.

SMALE, CHARLES J,
509 Grove Ave, Waukegan, IL 60085, Phone: 847-244-8013

SMALL, ED,
Rt 1 Box 178-A, Keyser, WV 26726, Phone: 304-298-4254, coldanvil@gmail.com
Specialties: Working knives of his design; period pieces. Patterns: Hunters, daggers, buckskinners and camp knives; likes one-of-a-kinds, very primitive bowies. Technical: Forges and grinds W2, L6 and his own Damascus. Prices: $150 to $1500. Remarks: Full-time maker; first knife sold in 1978. Mark: Script initials connected.

SMART, STEVE,
907 Park Row Cir, McKinney, TX 75070-3847, Phone: 214-837-4216, Fax: 214-837-4111
Specialties: Working/using straight knives and folders of his design, to customer specs and in standard patterns. Patterns: Bowies, hunters, kitchen knives, locking folders, utility/camp, fishing and bird knives. Technical: Grinds ATS-34, D2, 440C and O1. Prefers mirror polish or satin finish; hollow-grinds all blades. All knives come with sheath. Offers some filework. Prices: $95 to $225; some to $500. Remarks: Spare-time maker; first knife sold in 1983. Mark: Name, Custom, city and state in oval.

SMIT, GLENN,
627 Cindy Ct, Aberdeen, MD 21001, Phone: 410-272-2959, wolfsknives@comcast.net; Web: www.facebook.com/Wolf'sKnives
Specialties: Working and using straight and folding knives of his design or to customer specs. Customizes and repairs all types of cutlery. Exclusive maker of Dave Murphy Style knives. Patterns: Hunters, Bowies, daggers, fighters, utility/camp, folders, kitchen knives and miniatures, Murphy combat, C.H.A.I.K., Little 88 and Tiny 90-styles. Technical: Grinds 440C, ATS-34, O1, A2 also grinds 6AL4V titanium allox for blades. Reforges commercial Damascus

and makes cast aluminum handles. Prices: Miniatures start at $50; full-size knives start at $100. Remarks: Spare-time maker; first knife sold in 1986. Doing business as Wolf's Knives. Mark: G.P. SMIT, with year on reverse side, Wolf's Knives-Murphy's way with date.

SMITH, J D,
69 Highland, Roxbury, MA 02119, Phone: 617-989-0723, jdsmith02119@yahoo.com
Specialties: Fighters, Bowies, Persian, locking folders and swords. Patterns: Bowies, fighters and locking folders. Technical: Forges and grinds D2, his Damascus, O1, 52100 etc. and wootz-pattern hammer steel. Prices: $500 to $2000; some to $5000. Remarks: Full-time maker; first knife sold in 1987. Doing business as Hammersmith. Mark: Last initial alone or in cartouche.

SMITH, J.B.,
21 Copeland Rd., Perkinston, MS 39573, Phone: 228-380-1851
Specialties: Traditional working knives for the hunter and fisherman. Patterns: Hunters, Bowies, and fishing knives; copies of 1800 period knives. Technical: Grinds ATS-34, 440C. Prices: $100 to $800. Remarks: Full-time maker, first knife sold in 1972. Mark: J.B. Smith MAKER PERKINSTON, MS.

SMITH, JERRY,
JW Smith & Sons Custom Knives, 111 S Penn Ave, Oberlin, KS 67749, Phone: 785-475-2695, jerry@jwsmithandsons.com Web: www.jwsmithandsons.com
Specialties: Fixed blade and folding knives. Technical: Steels used D2, A2, O1, 154 CM, 154 CPM. Stock removal, heat treat in house, all leather work in house. Prices: $240. Remarks: Full-time knifemaker. First knife made in 2004. Slogan: "Cut Like You Mean It"

SMITH, JOHN M,
3450 E Beguelin Rd, Centralia, IL 62801, Phone: 618-249-6444, jknife@frontiernet.net
Specialties: Folders. Patterns: Folders. Prices: $250 to $2500. Remarks: First knife sold in 1980. Not taking orders at this time on fixed blade knives. Part-time maker. Mark: Etched signature or logo.

SMITH, JOHN W,
1322 Cow Branch Rd, West Liberty, KY 41472, Phone: 606-743-3599, jwsknive@mrtc.com; Web: www.jwsmithknives.com
Specialties: Fancy and working locking folders of his design or to customer specs. Patterns: Interframes, traditional and daggers. Technical: Grinds 530V and his own Damascus. Offers gold inlay, engraving with gold inlay, hand-fitted mosaic pearl inlay and filework. Prefers hand-rubbed finish. Pearl and ivory available. Prices: Utility pieces $375 to $650. Art knives $1200 to $10,000. Remarks: Full-time maker. Mark: Initials engraved inside diamond.

SMITH, JOSH,
Box 753, Frenchtown, MT 59834, Phone: 406-626-5775, joshsmithknives@gmail.com; Web: www.joshsmithknives.com
Specialties: Mosaic, Damascus, LinerLock folders, automatics, Bowies, fighters, etc. Patterns: All kinds. Technical: Advanced Mosaic and Damascus. Prices: $450 and up. Remarks: A.B.S. Master Smith. Mark: Josh Smith with last two digits of the current year.

SMITH, LACY,
PO BOX 188, Jacksonville, AL 36265, Phone: 256-310-4619, sales@smith-knives.com; Web: www.smith-knives.com

SMITH, LENARD C,
PO Box D68, Valley Cottage, NY 10989, Phone: 914-268-7359

SMITH, MICHAEL J,
1418 Saddle Gold Ct, Brandon, FL 33511, Phone: 813-431-3790, smithknife@hotmail.com; Web: www.smithknives.com
Specialties: Fancy high art folders of his design. Patterns: Locking locks and automatics. Technical: Uses ATS-34, non-stainless and stainless Damascus; hand carves folders, prefers ivory and pearl. Hand-rubbed satin finish. Liners are 6AL4V titanium. Prices: $500 to $3000. Remarks: Full-time maker; first knife sold in 1989. Mark: Name, city, state.

SMITH, NEWMAN L.,
865 Glades Rd Shop #3, Gatlinburg, TN 37738, Phone: 423-436-3322, thesmithshop@aol.com; Web: www.thesmithsshop.com
Specialties: Collector-grade and working knives. Patterns: Hunters, slip-joint and lock-back folders, some miniatures. Technical: Grinds O1 and ATS-34; makes fancy sheaths. Prices: $165 to $750; some to $1000. Remarks: Full-time maker; first knife sold in 1984. Partners part-time to handle Damascus blades by Jeff Hurst; marks these with SH connected. Mark: First and middle initials, last name.

SMITH, RALPH L,
525 Groce Meadow Rd, Taylors, SC 29687, Phone: 864-444-0819, ralph_smith1@charter.net; Web: www.smithhandcraftedknives.com
Specialties: Working knives: straight and folding knives. Hunters, skinners, fighters, bird, boot, Bowie and kitchen knives. Technical: Concave Grind D2, ATS 34, 440C, steel hand finish or polished. Prices: $125 to $350 for standard models. Remarks: First knife sold in 1976. KMG member since 1981. SCAK founding member and past president. Mark: SMITH handcrafted knives in SC state outline.

SMITH, RAYMOND L,
217 Red Chalk Rd, Erin, NY 14838, Phone: 607-795-5257, Bladesmith@wildblue.net; Web: www.theanvilsedge.com
Specialties: Working/using straight knives and folders to customer specs and in standard patterns; period pieces. Patterns: Bowies, hunters, skip-joints. Technical: Forges 5160, 52100, 1018, 15N20, 1084, ATS 34. Damascus and wire cable Damascus. Filework. Prices: $125 to $1500; estimates for custom orders. Remarks: Full-time maker; first knife sold in 1991. ABS Master Smith. Doing

business as The Anvils Edge. Mark: Ellipse with RL Smith, Erin NY MS in center.

SMITH, RICK,
BEAR BONE KNIVES, 1843 W Evans Creek Rd., Rogue River, OR 97537, Phone: 541-582-4144, BearBoneSmith@msn.com; Web: www.bearbone.com
Specialties: Classic, historical style Bowie knives, hunting knives and various contemporary knife styles. Technical: Blades are either forged or made by stock removal method depending on steel used. Also forge weld wire Damascus. Does own heat treating and tempering using digital even heat kiln. Stainless blades are sent out for cryogenic "freeze treat." Preferred steels are O1, tool, 5160, 1095, 1084, ATS-34, 154CM, 440C and various high carbon Damascus. Prices: $350 to $1500. Custom leather sheaths available for knives. Remarks: Full-time maker since 1997. Serial numbers no longer put on knives. Official business name is "Bear Bone Knives." Mark: Early maker's mark was "Bear Bone" over capital letters "RS" with downward arrow between letters and "Hand Made" underneath letters. Mark on small knives is 3/8 circle containing "RS" with downward arrow between letters. Current mark since 2003 is "R Bear Bone Smith" arching over image of coffin Bowie knife with two shooting stars and "Rogue River, Oregon" underneath.

SMITH, SHAWN,
2644 Gibson Ave, Clouis, CA 93611, Phone: 559-323-6234, kslc@sbcglobal.net
Specialties: Working and fancy straight knives. Patterns: Hunting, trout, fighters, skinners. Technical: Hollow grinds ATS-34, 154CM, A-2. Prices: $150.00 and up. Remarks: Part time maker. Mark: Shawn Smith handmade.

SMITH JR., JAMES B "RED",
Rt 2 Box 1525, Morven, GA 31638, Phone: 912-775-2844
Specialties: Folders. Patterns: Rotating rear-lock folders. Technical: Grinds ATS-34, D2 and Vascomax 350. Prices: Start at $350. Remarks: Full-time maker; first knife sold in 1985. Mark: GA RED in cowboy hat.

SMOCK, TIMOTHY E,
1105 N Sherwood Dr, Marion, IN 46952, Phone: 765-664-0123

SNODY, MIKE,
346 S. Commercial, Ste. #6, Aransas Pass, TX 78336, Phone: 361-443-0161, info@snodyknives.com; Web: www.snodygallery.com
Specialties: High performance straight knives in traditional and Japanese-styles. Patterns: Skinners, hunters, tactical, Kwaiken and tantos. Technical: Grinds BG42, ATS-34, 440C and A2. Offers full or tapered tangs, upgraded handle materials such as fossil ivory, coral and exotic woods. Traditional diamond wrap over stingray on Japanese-style knives. Sheaths available in leather or Kydex. Prices: $100 to $1000. Remarks: Part-time maker; first knife sold in 1999. Mark: Name over knife maker.

SNOW, BILL,
4824 18th Ave, Columbus, GA 31904, Phone: 706-576-4390, tipikw@knology.net
Specialties: Traditional working/using straight knives and folders of his design and to customer specs. Offers engraving and scrimshaw. Patterns: Bowies, fighters, hunters and folders. Technical: Grinds ATS-34, 440V, 440C, 420V, CPM350, BG42, A2, D2, 5160, 52100 and O1; forges if needed. Cryogenically quenches all steels; inlaid handles; some integrals; leather or Kydex sheaths. Prices: $125 to $700; some to $3500. Remarks: Now also have 530V, 10V and 3V steels in use. Full-time maker; first knife sold in 1958. Doing business as Tipi Knife works. Mark: Old English scroll "S" inside a tipi.

SNYDER, MICHAEL TOM,
PO Box 522, Zionsville, IN 46077-0522, Phone: 317-873-6807, wildcatcreek@indy.pr.com

SOAPER, MAX H.,
2375 Zion Rd, Henderson, KY 42420, Phone: 270-827-8143
Specialties: Primitive Longhunter knives, scalpers, camp knives, cowboy Bowies, neck knives, working knives, period pieces from the 18th century. Technical: Forges 5160, 1084, 1095; all blades differentially heat treated. Prices: $80 to $800. Remarks: Part-time maker since 1989. Mark: Initials in script.

SOLOMON, MARVIN,
23750 Cold Springs Rd, Paron, AR 72122, Phone: 501-821-3170, mardot@swbell.net; Web: www.coldspringsforge.com
Specialties: Traditional working and using straight knives of his design and to customer specs, also lock back 7 LinerLock® folders. Patterns: Single blade folders. Technical: Forges 5160, 1095, O1 and random Damascus. Prices: $125 to $1000. Remarks: Part-time maker; first knife sold in 1990. Doing business as Cold Springs Forge. Mark: Last name.

SONNTAG, DOUGLAS W,
902 N 39th St, Nixa, MO 65714, Phone: 417-693-1640, Fax: 417-582-1392, dougsonntag@gmail.com
Specialties: Working knives; art knives. Patterns: Hunters, boots, straight working knives; Bowies, some folders, camp/axe sets. Technical: Grinds D2, ATS-34, forges own Damascus; does own heat treating. Prices: $225 and up. Remarks: Full-time maker; first knife sold in 1986. Mark: Etched name in arch.

SONNTAG, JACOB D,
14148 Trisha Drive St, Robert, MO 65584, Phone: 337-378-7090, Jake0372@live.com
Specialties: Working knives, some art knives. Patterns: Hunters, bowies, and tomahawks. Technical: Grinds D2, ATS34 and Damascus. Forges some Damascus and tomahawks; does own heat treating. Prices: $200 and up. Remarks: Part-time maker; first knife sold in 2010. Mark: Etched name or stamped

SONNTAG, KRISTOPHER D,
902 N 39th St, Nixa, MO 65714, Phone: 417-838-8327, kriss@buildit.us
Specialties: Working fixed blades, hunters, skinners, using knives. Patterns: Hunters, bowies, skinners. Technical: Grinds D2, ATS 34, Damascus. Makes some Damascus; does own heat treating. Prices: $200 and up.Remarks: Part-time maker; first knife sold in 2010. Mark: Etched name or stamped

SONTHEIMER, G DOUGLAS,
12604 Bridgeton Dr, Potomac, MD 20854, Phone: 301-948-5227
Specialties: Fixed blade knives. Patterns: Whitetail deer, backpackers, camp, claws, fillet, fighters. Technical: Hollow Grinds. Price: $500 and up. Remarks: Spare-time maker; first knife sold in 1976. Mark: LORD.

SOPPERA, ARTHUR,
Pilatusblick, Oberer Schmidberg, Ulisbach, SWITZERLAND 9631, Phone: 71-988 23 27, Fax: 71-988 47 57, doublelock@hotmail.com; Web: www.sopperaknifeart.ch
Specialties: High-art, high-tech knives of his design. Patterns: Locking folders, and fixed blade knives. Technical: Grinds ATS-34 and commercial Damascus. Folders have button lock of his own design; some are fancy folders in jeweler's fashion. Also makes jewelry with integrated small knives. Prices: $300 to $1500, some $2500 and higher. Remarks: Full-time maker; first knife sold in 1986. Mark: Stylized initials, name, country.

SORNBERGER, JIM,
25126 Overland Dr, Volcano, CA 95689, Phone: 209-295-7819
Specialties: Classic San Francisco-style knives. Collectible straight knives. Patterns: Forges 1095-1084/15W2. Makes own Damascus and powder metal. Fighters, daggers, Bowies; miniatures; hunters, custom canes, liner locks folders. Technical: Grinds 440C, 154CM and ATS-34; engraves, carves and embellishes. Prices: $500 to $20,000 in gold with gold quartz inlays. Remarks: Full-time maker; first knife sold in 1970. Mark: First initial, last name, city and state.

SOWELL, BILL,
100 Loraine Forest Ct, Macon, GA 31210, Phone: 478- 994-9863, billsowell@reynoldscable.net
Specialties: Antique reproduction Bowies, forging Bowies, hunters, fighters, and most others. Also folders. Technical: Makes own Damascus, using 1084/15N20, also making own designs in powder metals, forges 5160-1095-1084, and other carbon steels, grinds ATS-34. Prices: Starting at $150 and up. Remarks: Part-time maker. Sold first knife in 1998. Does own leather work. ABS Master Smith. Mark: Iron Horse Forge - Sowell - MS.

SPARKS, BERNARD,
PO Box 73, Dingle, ID 83233, Phone: 208-847-1883, dogknifeii@juno.com; Web: www.sparksknives.com
Specialties: Maker engraved, working and art knives. Straight knives and folders of his own design. Patterns: Locking inner-frame folders, hunters, fighters, one-of-a-kind art knives. Technical: Grinds 530V steel, 440-C, 154CM, ATS-34, D-2 and forges by special order; triple temper, cryogenic soak. Mirror or hand finish. New Liquid metal steel. Prices: $300 to $2000. Remarks: Full-time maker, first knife sold in 1967. Mark: Last name over state with a knife logo on each end of name. Prior 1980, stamp of last name.

SPICKLER, GREGORY NOBLE,
5614 Mose Cir, Sharpsburg, MD 21782, Phone: 301-432-2746

SPINALE, RICHARD,
4021 Canterbury Ct, Lorain, OH 44053, Phone: 440-282-1565
Specialties: High-art working knives of his design. Patterns: Hunters, fighters, daggers and locking folders. Technical: Grinds 440C, ATS-34 and 07; engraves. Offers gold bolsters and other deluxe treatments. Prices: $300 to $1000; some to $3000. Remarks: Spare-time maker; first knife sold in 1976. Mark: Name, address, year and model number.

SPIVEY, JEFFERSON,
9244 W Wilshire, Yukon, OK 73099, Phone: 405-371-9304, jspivey5@cox.net
Specialties: The Saber tooth: a combination hatchet, saw and knife. Patterns: Built for the wilderness, all are one-of-a-kind. Technical: Grinds chromemoly steel. The saw tooth spine curves with a double row of biangular teeth. Prices: Start at $275. Remarks: First knife sold in 1977. As of September 2006 Spivey knives has resumed production of the Sabertooth knife (one word trademark). Mark: Name and serial number.

SPRAGG, WAYNE E,
252 Oregon Ave, Lovell, WY 82431, Phone: 307-548-7212
Specialties: Working straight knives, some fancy. Patterns: Folders. Technical: Forges carbon steel and makes Damascus. Prices: $200 and up. Remarks: All stainless heat-treated by Paul Bos. Carbon steel in shop heat treat. Mark: Last name front side w/s initials on reverse side.

SPROKHOLT, ROB,
Burgerweg 5, Gatherwood, NETHERLANDS 1754 KB Burgerbrug, Phone: 0031 6 51230225, Fax: 0031 84 2238446, info@gatherwood.nl; Web: www.gatherwood.nl
Specialties: One-of-a-kind knives. Top materials collector grade, made to use. Patterns: Outdoor knives (hunting, sailing, hiking), Bowies, man's surviving companions MSC, big tantos, folding knives. Technical: Handles mostly stabilized or oiled wood, ivory, Micarta, carbon fibre, G10. Stiff knives are full tang. Characteristic one row of massive silver pins or tubes. Folding knives have a LinerLock® with titanium or Damascus powdersteel liner thumb can have any stone you like. Stock removal grinder: flat or convex. Steel 440-C, RWL-34, ATS-34, PM damascener steel. Prices: Start at 320 euro. Remarks: Writer of the first Dutch knifemaking book, supply shop for knife enthusiastic. First knife sold in 2000. Mark: Gatherwood in an eclipse etched blade or stamped in an intarsia of silver in the spine.

ST. CLAIR, THOMAS K,
12608 Fingerboard Rd, Monrovia, MD 21770, Phone: 301-482-0264

STAFFORD, RICHARD,
104 Marcia Ct, Warner Robins, GA 31088, Phone: 912-923-6372, Fax: Cell: 478-508-5821, rnrstafford@cox.net
Specialties: High-tech straight knives and some folders. Patterns: Hunters in several patterns, fighters, boots, camp knives, combat knives and period pieces. Technical: Grinds ATS-34 and 440C. Machine satin finish offered. Prices: Starting at $150. Remarks: Part-time maker; first knife sold in 1983. Mark: R. W. STAFFORD GEORGIA.

STAINTHORP, GUY,
4 Fisher St, Brindley Ford, Stroke-on-Trent, ENGLAND ST8 7QJ, Phone: 07946 469 888, guystainthorp@hotmail.com Web: http://stainthorpknives.co.uk/index.html
Specialties: Tactical and outdoors knives to his own design. Patterns: Hunting, survival and occasionally folding knives. Technical: Grinds RWL-34, O1, S30V, Damasteel. Micarta, G10 and stabilised wood/bone for handles. Prices: $200 - $1000. Remarks: Full-time knifemaker. Mark: Squared stylised GS over "Stainthorp".

STALCUP, EDDIE,
PO Box 2200, Gallup, NM 87305, Phone: 505-863-3107, sharon.stalcup@gmail.com
Specialties: Working and fancy hunters, bird and trout. Special custom orders. Patterns: Drop point hunters, locking liner and multi blade folders. Technical: ATS-34, 154 CM, 440C, CPM 154 and S30V. Prices: $150 to $1500. Remarks: Scrimshaw, exotic handle material, wet formed sheaths. Membership Arizona Knife Collectors Association. Southern California blades collectors & professional knife makers assoc. Mark: E.F. Stalcup, Gallup, NM.

STANCER, CHUCK,
62 Hidden Ranch Rd NW, Calgary, AB, CANADA T3A 5S5, Phone: 403-295-7370, stancerc@telusplanet.net
Specialties: Traditional and working straight knives. Patterns: Bowies, hunters and utility knives. Technical: Forges and grinds most steels. Prices: $175 and up. Remarks: Part-time maker. Mark: Last name.

STANFORD, PERRY,
405 N Walnut #9, Broken Arrow, OK 74012, Phone: 918-251-7983 or 866-305-5690, stanfordoutdoors@valornet.com; Web: www.stanfordoutdoors.homestead.com
Specialties: Drop point, hunting and skinning knives, handmade sheaths. Patterns: Stright, hunting, and skinners. Technical: Grinds 440C, ATS-34 and Damascus. Prices: $65 to $275. Remarks: Part-time maker, first knife sold in 2007. Knifemaker supplier, manufacturer of paper sharpening systems. Doing business as Stanford Outdoors. Mark: Company name and nickname.

STANLEY, JOHN,
604 Elm St, Crossett, AR 71635, Phone: 970-304-3005
Specialties: Hand forged fixed blades with engraving and carving. Patterns: Scottish dirks, skeans and fantasy blades. Technical: Forge high-carbon steel, own Damascus. Prices $70 to $500. Remarks: All work is sole authorship. Offers engraving and carving services on other knives and handles. Mark: Varies.

STAPEL, CHUCK,
Box 1617, Glendale, CA 91209, Phone: 213-66-KNIFE, Fax: 213-669-1577, www.stapelknives.com
Specialties: Working knives of his design. Patterns: Variety of straight knives, tantos, hunters, folders and utility knives. Technical: Grinds D2, 440C and AEB-L. Prices: $185 to $12,000. Remarks: Full-time maker; first knife sold in 1974. Mark: Last name or last name, U.S.A.

STAPLETON, WILLIAM E,
BUFFALO 'B' FORGE, 5425 Country Ln, Merritt Island, FL 32953
Specialties: Classic and traditional knives of his design and customer spec. Patterns: Hunters and using knives. Technical: Forges, O1 and L6 Damascus, cable Damascus and 5160; stock removal on request. Prices: $150 to $1000. Remarks: Part-time maker, first knife sold 1990. Doing business as Buffalo "B" Forge. Mark: Anvil with S initial in center of anvil.

STATES, JOSHUA C,
43905 N 16th St, New River, AZ 85087, Phone: 623-826-3809, Web: www.dosgatosforge.com
Specialties: Design and fabrication of forged working and art knives from O1 and my own damascus. Stock removal from 440C and CM154 upon request. Folders from 440C, CM154 and Damascus. Flat and Hollow grinds. Knives made to customer specs and/or design.Patterns: Bowies, hunters, daggers, chef knives, and exotic shapes. Technical: Damascus is 1095, 1084, O1 and 15N20. Carved or file-worked fittings from various metals including my own mokume gane and Damascus.Prices: $150 to $1500. Remarks: Part-time maker with waiting list. First knife sold in 2006. Mark: Initials JCS inside small oval, or Dos Gatos Forge. Unmarked knives come with certificate of authorship.

STECK, VAN R,
260 W Dogwood Ave, Orange City, FL 32763, Phone: 407-416-1723, van@thudknives.com
Specialties: Specializing in double-edged grinds. Free-hand grinds: folders, spears, bowies, swords and miniatures. Patterns: Tomahawks with a crane for the spike, tactical merged with nature.Technical: Hamon lines, folder lock of own design, the arm-lock! Prices: $50 - $1500. Remarks: Builds knives designed by Laci Szabo or builds to customer design. Studied with Reese

Weiland on folders and automatics. Mark: GEISHA holding a sword with initials and THUD KNIVES in a circle.

STEGALL, KEITH,
701 Outlet View Dr, Wasilla, AK 99654, Phone: 907-376-0703, kas5200@yahoo.com
Specialties: Traditional working straight knives. Patterns: Most patterns. Technical: Grinds 440C and 154CM. Prices: $100 to $300. Remarks: Spare-time maker; first knife sold in 1987. Mark: Name and state with anchor.

STEGNER, WILBUR G,
9242 173rd Ave SW, Rochester, WA 98579, Phone: 360-273-0937, wilbur@wgsk.net; Web: www.wgsk.net
Specialties: Working/using straight knives and folders of his design. Patterns: Hunters and locking folders. Technical: Makes his own Damascus steel. Prices: $100 to $1000; some to $5000. Remarks: Full-time maker; first knife sold in 1979. Google search key words-"STEGNER KNIVES." Best folder awards NWKC 2009, 2010 and 2011. Mark: First and middle initials, last name in bar over shield logo.

STEIER, DAVID,
7722 Zenith Way, Louisville, KY 40219, Phone: 502-969-8409, umag300@aol.com; Web: www.steierknives.com
Specialties: Folding LinerLocks, Bowies, slip joints, lockbacks, and straight hunters. Technical: Stock removal blades of 440C, ATS-34, and Damascus from outside sources like Robert Eggerling and Mike Norris. Prices: $150 for straight hunters to $1400 for fully decked-out folders. Remarks: First knife sold in 1979. Mark: Last name STEIER.

STEIGER, MONTE L,
Box 186, Genesee, ID 83832, Phone: 208-285-1769, montesharon@genesee-id.com
Specialties: Traditional working/using straight knives of all designs. Patterns: Hunters, utility/camp knives, fillet and chefs. Carving sets and steak knives. Technical: Grinds 1095, O1, 440C, ATS-34. Handles of stacked leather, natural wood, Micarta or pakkawood. Each knife comes with right- or left-handed sheath. Prices: $110 to $600. Remarks: Spare-time maker; first knife sold in 1988. Retired librarian Mark: First initial, last name, city and state.

STEIGERWALT, KEN,
507 Savagehill Rd, Orangeville, PA 17859, Phone: 570-683-5156, Web: www.steigerwaltknives.com
Specialties: Carving on bolsters and handle material. Patterns: Folders, button locks and rear locks. Technical: Grinds ATS-34, 440C and commercial Damascus. Experiments with unique filework. Prices: $500 to $5000. Remarks: Full-time maker; first knife sold in 1981. Mark: Kasteigerwalt

STEINAU, JURGEN,
Julius-Hart Strasse 44, Berlin, GERMANY 01162, Phone: 372-6452512, Fax: 372-645-2512
Specialties: Fantasy and high-art straight knives of his design. Patterns: Boots, daggers and switch-blade folders. Technical: Grinds 440B, 2379 and X90 Cr.Mo.V. 78. Prices: $1500 to $2500; some to $3500. Remarks: Full-time maker; first knife sold in 1984. Mark: Symbol, plus year, month day and serial number.

STEINBERG, AL,
5244 Duenas, Laguna Woods, CA 92653, Phone: 949-951-2889, lagknife@fea.net
Specialties: Fancy working straight knives to customer specs. Patterns: Hunters, Bowies, fishing, camp knives, push knives and high end kitchen knives. Technical: Grinds O1, 440C and 154CM. Prices: $60 to $2500. Remarks: Full-time maker; first knife sold in 1972. Mark: Signature, city and state.

STEINBRECHER, MARK W,
1122 92nd Place, Pleasant Prairie, WI 53158-4939
Specialties: Working and fancy folders. Patterns: Daggers, pocket knives, fighters and gents of his own design or to customer specs. Technical: Hollow grinds ATS-34, O1 other makers Damascus. Uses natural handle materials: stag, ivories, mother-of-pearl. File work and some inlays. Prices: $500 to $1200, some to $2500. Remarks: Part-time maker, first folder sold in 1989. Mark: Name etched or handwritten on ATS-34; stamped on Damascus.

STEINGASS, T.K.,
194 Mesquite Lane, Hedgesville, WV 25427, Phone: 304-268-1161, tksteingass@frontier.com; Web: http://steingassknives.com
Specialties: Loveless style hunters and fighters and sole authorship knives: Man Knife, Silent Hunter, and Silent Fighter. Harpoon Grind Camp Knife and Harpoon Grind Man Hunter. Technical: Stock removal, use CPM 154, S3V and occasionally 1095 or O1 for camp choppers. Prices: $200 to $500. Remarks: Part-time maker; first knife made in 2010. Mark: STEINGASS.

STEKETEE, CRAIG A,
871 NE US Hwy 60, Billings, MO 65610, Phone: 417-744-2770, stekknives04@yahoo.com
Specialties: Classic and working straight knives and swords of his design. Patterns: Bowies, hunters, and Japanese-style swords. Technical: Forges his own Damascus; bronze, silver and Damascus fittings, offers filework. Prefers exotic and natural handle materials. Prices: $200 to $4000. Remarks: Full-time maker. Mark: STEK.

STEPHAN, DANIEL,
2201 S Miller Rd, Valrico, FL 33594, Phone: 727-580-8617, knifemaker@verizon.net
Specialties: Art knives, one-of-a-kind.

STERLING, MURRAY,
693 Round Peak Church Rd, Mount Airy, NC 27030, Phone: 336-352-5110, Fax: Fax: 336-352-5105, sterck@surry.net; Web: www.sterlingcustomknives.com
Specialties: Single and dual blade folders. Interframes and integral dovetail frames. Technical: Grinds ATS-34 or Damascus by Mike Norris and/or Devin Thomas. Prices: $300 and up. Remarks: Full-time maker; first knife sold in 1991. Mark: Last name stamped.

STERLING, THOMAS J,
ART KNIVES BY, 120 N Pheasant Run, Coupeville, WA 98239, Phone: 360-678-9269, Fax: 360-678-9269, netsuke@comcast.net; Web: www.bladegallery.com Or www.sterlingsculptures.com
Specialties: Since 2003 Tom Sterling and Dr. J.P. Higgins have created a unique collaboration of one-of-a-kind, ultra-quality art knives with percussion or pressured flaked stone blades and creatively sculpted handles. Their knives are often highly influenced by the traditions of Japanese netsuke and unique fusions of cultures, reflecting stylistically integrated choices of exotic hardwoods, fossil ivories and semi-precious materials, contrasting inlays and polychromed and pyrographed details. Prices: $300 to $900. Remarks: Limited output ensures highest quality artwork and exceptional levels of craftsmanship. Mark: Signatures Sterling and Higgins.

STETTER, J. C.,
115 E College Blvd PMB 180, Roswell, NM 88201, Phone: 505-627-0978
Specialties: Fixed and folding. Patterns: Traditional and yours. Technical: Forged and ground of varied materials including his own pattern welded steel. Prices: Start at $250. Remarks: Full-time maker, first knife sold 1989. Mark: Currently "J.C. Stetter."

STEWART, EDWARD L,
4297 Audrain Rd 335, Mexico, MO 65265, Phone: 573-581-3883
Specialties: Fixed blades, working knives some art. Patterns: Hunters, Bowies, utility/camp knives. Technical: Forging 1095-W-2-I-6-52100 makes own Damascus. Prices: $85 to $500. Remarks: Part-time maker first knife sold in 1993. Mark: First and last initials-last name.

STEYN, PETER,
PO Box 76, Welkom, Freestate, SOUTH AFRICA 9460, Phone: 27 57 3522015, Fax: 27 57 3523566, Web: www.petersteynknives.com email: info@petersteynknives.com
Specialties: Fixed blade working knives of own design, tendency toward tactical creative & artistic styles all with hand stitched leather sheaths. Patterns: Hunters, skinners, fighters & wedge ground daggers. Technical: Grinds 12C27, D2, N690. Blades are bead-blasted in plain or camo patterns & own exclusive crator finish. Prefers synthetic handle materials also uses cocobolo & ironwood. Prices: $200-$600. Remarks: Full time maker, first knife sold 2005, member of South African Guild. Mark: Letter 'S' in shape of pyramid with full name above & 'Handcrafted' below.

STICE, DOUGLAS W,
PO Box 12815, Wichita, KS 67277, Phone: 316-295-6855, doug@sticecraft.com; Web: www.sticecraft.com
Specialties: Working fixed blade knives of own design. Patterns: Tacticals, hunters, skinners,utility, and camp knives. Technical: Grinds CPM154CM, 154CM, CPM3V, Damascus; uses 18" contact grinds where wheel for hollow grinds, also flat. Prices: $100 to $750. Remarks: Full-time maker; first professional knife made in 2009. All knives have serial numbers and include certificate of authenticity. Mark: Stylized "Stice" stamp.

STIDHAM, DANIEL,
3106 Mill Cr. Rd., Gallipolis, Ohio 45631, Phone: 740-446-1673, danstidham@yahoo.com
Specialties: Fixed blades, folders, Bowies and hunters. Technical: 440C, Alabama Damascus, 1095 with filework. Prices: Start at $150. Remarks: Has made fixed blades since 1961, folders since 1986. Also sells various knife brands. Mark: Stidham Knives Gallipolis, Ohio 45631.

STIMPS, JASON M,
374 S Shaffer St, Orange, CA 92866, Phone: 714-744-5866

STIPES, DWIGHT,
2651 SW Buena Vista Dr, Palm City, FL 34990, Phone: 772-597-0550, dwightstipes@adelphia.net
Specialties: Traditional and working straight knives in standard patterns. Patterns: Boots, Bowies, daggers, hunters and fighters. Technical: Grinds 440C, D2 and D3 tool steel. Handles of natural materials, animal, bone or horn. Prices: $75 to $150. Remarks: Full-time maker; first knife sold in 1972. Mark: Stipes.

STOKES, ED,
22614 Cardinal Dr, Hockley, TX 77447, Phone: 713-351-1319
Specialties: Working straight knives and folders of all designs. Patterns: Boots, Bowies, daggers, fighters, hunters and miniatures. Technical: Grinds ATS-34, 440C and D2. Offers decorative butt caps, tapered spacers on handles and finger grooves, nickel-silver inlays, handmade sheaths. Prices: $185 to $290; some to $350. Remarks: Full-time maker; first knife sold in 1973. Mark: First and last name, Custom Knives with Apache logo.

STONE, JERRY,
PO Box 1027, Lytle, TX 78052, Phone: 830-709-3042
Specialties: Traditional working and using folders of his design and to customer specs; fancy knives. Patterns: Fighters, hunters, locking folders and slip joints. Also make automatics. Technical: Grinds 440C and ATS-34. Offers filework. Prices: $175 to $1000. Remarks: Full-time maker; first knife sold in 1973. Mark: Name over Texas star/town and state underneath.

STORCH, ED,
RR 4, Mannville, AB, CANADA T0B 2W0, Phone: 780-763-2214, storchkn@agt.net; Web: www.storchknives.com
Specialties: Working knives, fancy fighting knives, kitchen cutlery and art knives. Knifemaking classes. Technical: Forges his own Damascus. Grinds ATS-34. Builds friction folders. Salt heat treating. Prices: $45 to $750 (U.S.). Remarks: Part-time maker; first knife sold in 1984. Hosts annual Northwest Canadian Knifemakers Symposium; 60 to 80 knifemakers and families. Mark: Last name.

STORMER, BOB,
34354 Hwy E, Dixon, MO 65459, Phone: 636-734-2693, bs34354@gmail.com
Specialties: Straight knives, using collector grade. Patterns: Bowies, skinners, hunters, camp knives. Technical: Forges 5160, 1095. Prices: $200 to $500. Remarks: Part-time maker, ABS Journeyman Smith 2001. Mark: Setting sun/fall trees/initials.

STOUT, CHARLES,
RT3 178 Stout Rd, Gillham, AR 71841, Phone: 870-386-5521

STOUT, JOHNNY,
1205 Forest Trail, New Braunfels, TX 78132, Phone: 830-606-4067, johnny@stoutknives.com; Web: www.stoutknives.com
Specialties: Folders, some fixed blades. Working knives, some fancy. Patterns: Hunters, tactical, Bowies, automatics, liner locks and slip-joints. Technical: Grinds stainless and carbon steels; forges own Damascus. Prices: $450 to $895; some to $3500. Remarks: Full-time maker; first knife sold in 1983. Hosts semi-annual Guadalupe Forge Hammer-in and Knifemakers Rendezvous. Mark: Name and city in logo with serial number.

STRAIGHT, KENNETH J,
11311 103 Lane N, Largo, FL 33773, Phone: 813-397-9817

STRANDE, POUL,
Soster Svenstrup Byvej 16, Viby Sj., Dastrup, DENMARK 4130, Phone: 46 19 43 05, Fax: 46 19 53 19, Web: www.poulstrande.com
Specialties: Classic fantasy working knives; Damasceret blade, Nikkel Damasceret blade, Lamineret: Lamineret blade with Nikkel. Patterns: Bowies, daggers, fighters, hunters and swords. Technical: Uses carbon steel and 15C20 steel. Prices: NA. Remarks: Full-time maker; first knife sold in 1985. Mark: First and last initials.

STRAUB, SALEM F.,
324 Cobey Creek Rd., Tonasket, WA 98855, Phone: 509-486-2627, vorpalforge@hotmail.com Web: www.prometheanknives.com
Specialties: Elegant working knives, fixed blade hunters, utility, skinning knives; liner locks. Makes own horsehide sheaths. Patterns: A wide range of syles, everything from the gentleman's pocket to the working kitchen, integrals, Bowies, folders, check out my website to see some of my work for ideas. Technical: Forges several carbon steels, 52100, W1, etc. Grinds stainless and makes/uses own Damascus, cable, san mai, stadard patterns. Likes clay quenching, hamons, hand rubbed finishes. Flat, hollow, or convex grinds. Prefers synthetic handle materials. Hidden and full tapered tangs. Prices: $150 - $600, some higher. Remarks: Full-time maker. Doing what it takes to make your knife ordering and buying experience positive and enjoyable; striving to exceed expectations. All knives backed by lifetime guarantee. Mark: "Straub" stamp or "Promethean Knives" etched. Some older pieces stamped "Vorpal" though no longer using this mark. Other: Feel free to call or e-mail anytime. I love to talk knives.

STRICKLAND, DALE,
1440 E Thompson View, Monroe, UT 84754, Phone: 435-896-8362
Specialties: Traditional and working straight knives and folders of his design and to customer specs. Patterns: Hunters, folders, miniatures and utility knives. Technical: Grinds Damascus and 440C. Prices: $120 to $350; some to $500. Remarks: Part-time maker; first knife sold in 1991. Mark: Oval stamp of name, Maker.

STRIDER, MICK,
STRIDER KNIVES, 120 N Pacific Unit L-7, San Marcos, CA 92069, Phone: 760-471-8275, Fax: 503-218-7069, striderguys@striderknives.com; Web: www.striderknives.com

STRONG, SCOTT,
1599 Beaver Valley Rd, Beavercreek, OH 45434, Phone: 937-426-9290
Specialties: Working knives, some deluxe. Patterns: Hunters, fighters, survival and military-style knives, art knives. Technical: Forges and grinds O1, A2, D2, 440C and ATS-34. Uses no solder; most knives disassemble. Prices: $75 to $450; some to $1500. Remarks: Spare-time maker; first knife sold in 1983. Mark: Strong Knives.

STROYAN, ERIC,
Box 218, Dalton, PA 18414, Phone: 717-563-2603
Specialties: Classic and working/using straight knives and folders of his design. Patterns: Hunters, locking folders, slip-joints. Technical: Forges Damascus; grinds ATS-34, D2. Prices: $200 to $600; some to $2000. Remarks: Part-time maker; first knife sold in 1968. Mark: Signature or initials stamp.

STUART, MASON,
24 Beech Street, Mansfield, MA 02048, Phone: 508-339-8236, smasonknives@verizon.net Web: smasonknives.com
Specialties: Straight knives of his design, standard patterns. Patterns: Bowies, hunters, fighters and neck knives. Technical: Forges and grinds. Damascus, 5160, 1095, 1084, old files. Uses only natural handle material. Prices: $350 -

2,000. Remarks: Part-time maker. Mark: First initial and last name.

STUART, STEVE,
Box 168, Gores Landing, ON, CANADA K0K 2E0, Phone: 905-440-6910, stevestuart@xplornet.com
Specialties: Straight knives. Patterns: Tantos, fighters, skinners, file and rasp knives. Technical: Uses 440C, CPM154, CPMS30V, Micarta and natural handle materials. Prices: $60 to $400. Remarks: Part-time maker. Mark: SS.

STYREFORS, MATTIAS,
Unbyn 23, Boden, SWEDEN 96193, infor@styrefors.com
Specialties: Damascus and mosaic Damascus. Fixed blade Nordic hunters, folders and swords. Technical: Forges, shapes and grinds Damascus and mosaic Damascus from mostly UHB 15N20 and 20C with contrasts in nickel and 15N20. Hardness HR 58. Prices: $800 to $3000. Remarks: Full-time maker since 1999. International reputation for high end Damascus blades. Uses stabilized Arctic birch and willow burl, horn, fossils, exotic materials, and scrimshaw by Viveca Sahlin for knife handles. Hand tools and hand stitches leather sheaths in cow raw hide. Works in well equipped former military forgery in northern Sweden. Mark: MS.

SUEDMEIER, HARLAN,
762 N 60th Rd, Nebraska City, NE 68410, Phone: 402-873-4372
Patterns: Straight knives. Technical: Forging hi carbon Damascus. Prices: Starting at $175. Mark: First initials & last name.

SUGIHARA, KEIDOH,
4-16-1 Kamori-Cho, Kishiwada City, Osaka, JAPAN F596-0042, Fax: 0724-44-2677
Specialties: High-tech working straight knives and folders of his design. Patterns: Bowies, hunters, fighters, fishing, boots, some pocket knives and liner-lock folders. Technical: Grinds ATS-34, COS-25, buys Damascus and high-carbon steels. Prices $60 to $4000. Remarks: Full-time maker, first knife sold in 1980. Mark: Initial logo with fish design.

SUGIYAMA, EDDY K,
2361 Nagayu, Naoirimachi Naoirigun, Oita, JAPAN, Phone: 0974-75-2050
Specialties: One-of-a-kind, exotic-style knives. Patterns: Working, utility and miniatures. Technical: CT rind, ATS-34 and D2. Prices: $400 to $1200. Remarks: Full-time maker. Mark: Name or cedar mark.

SUMMERS, ARTHUR L,
1310 Hess Rd, Concord, NC 28025, Phone: 704-787-9275 Cell: 704-305-0735, arthursummers88@hotmail.com
Specialties: Drop points, clip points, straight blades. Patterns: Hunters, Bowies and personal knives. Technical: Grinds 440C, ATS-34, D2 and Damascus. Prices: $250 to $1000. Remarks: Full-time maker; first knife sold in 1988. Mark: Serial number is the date.

SUMMERS, DAN,
2675 NY Rt. 11, Whitney Pt., NY 13862, Phone: 607-692-2391, dansumm11@msn.com
Specialties: Period knives and tomahawks. Technical: All hand forging. Prices: Most $100 to $400.

SUMMERS, DENNIS K,
827 E. Cecil St, Springfield, OH 45503, Phone: 513-324-0624
Specialties: Working/using knives. Patterns: Fighters and personal knives. Technical: Grinds 440C, A2 and D2. Makes drop and clip point. Prices: $75 to $200. Remarks: Part-time maker; first knife sold in 1995. Mark: First and middle initials, last name, serial number.

SUNDERLAND, RICHARD,
Av Infraganti 23, Col Lazaro Cardenas, Puerto Escondido, OA, MEXICO 71980, Phone: 011 52 94 582 1451, sunamerica@prodigy.net.mx7
Specialties: Personal and hunting knives with carved handles in oosic and ivory. Patterns: Hunters, Bowies, daggers, camp and personal knives. Technical: Grinds 440C, ATS-34 and O1. Handle materials of rosewoods, fossil mammoth ivory and oosic. Prices: $150 to $1000. Remarks: Part-time maker; first knife sold in 1983. Doing business as Sun Knife Co. Mark: SUN.

SUTTON, S RUSSELL,
4900 Cypress Shores Dr, New Bern, NC 28562, Phone: 252-637-3963, srsutton@suddenlink.net; Web: www.suttoncustomknives.com
Specialties: Straight knives and folders to customer specs and in standard patterns. Patterns: Boots, hunters, interframes, slip joints and locking liners. Technical: Grinds ATS-34, 440C and stainless Damascus. Prices: $220 to $2000. Remarks: Full-time maker; first knife sold in 1992. Provides relief engraving on bolsters and guards. Mark: Etched last name.

SWEAZA, DENNIS,
4052 Hwy 321 E, Austin, AR 72007, Phone: 501-941-1886, knives4den@aol.com

SWEENEY, COLTIN D,
1216 S 3 St W, Missoula, MT 59801, Phone: 406-721-6782

SWYHART, ART,
509 Main St, PO Box 267, Klickitat, WA 98628, Phone: 509-369-3451, swyhart@gorge.net; Web: www.knifeoutlet.com/swyhart.htm
Specialties: Traditional working and using knives of his design. Patterns: Bowies, hunters and utility/camp knives. Technical: Forges 52100, 5160 and Damascus 1084 mixed with either 15N20 or O186. Blades differentially heat-treated with visible temper line. Prices: $75 to $250; some to $350. Remarks: Part-time maker; first knife sold in 1983. Mark: First name, last initial in script.

SYLVESTER, DAVID,
465 Sweede Rd., Compton, QC, CANADA, Phone: 819-837-0304, david@swedevilleforge.com Web: swedevilleforge.com
Patterns: I hand forge all my knives and I like to make hunters and integrals

and some Bowies and fighters. I work with W2, 1084, 1095, and my damascus. Prices: $200 - $1500. Remarks: Part-time maker. ABS Journeyman Smith. Mark: D.Sylvester

SYMONDS, ALBERTO E,
Rambla M Gandhi 485, Apt 901, Montevideo, URUGUAY 11300, Phone: 011 598 27103201, Fax: 011 598 2 7103201, albertosymonds@hotmail.com
Specialties: All kinds including puukos, nice sheaths, leather and wood. Prices: $300 to $2200. Mark: AESH and current year.

SYSLO, CHUCK,
3418 South 116 Ave, Omaha, NE 68144, Phone: 402-333-0647, ciscoknives@cox.net
Specialties: Hunters, working knives, daggers & misc. Patterns: Hunters, daggers and survival knives; locking folders. Technical: Flat-grinds D2, 440C and 154CM; hand polishes only. Prices: $250 to $1000; some to $3000. Remarks: Part-time maker; first knife sold in 1978. Uses many natural materials. Mark: CISCO in logo.

SZILASKI, JOSEPH,
52 Woods Dr, Pine Plains, NY 12567, Phone: 518-398-0309, Web: www.szilaski.com
Specialties: Straight knives, folders and tomahawks of his design, to customer specs and in standard patterns. Many pieces are one-of-a-kind. Patterns: Bowies, daggers, fighters, hunters, art knives and early American-styles. Technical: Forges A2, D2, O1 and Damascus. Prices: $450 to $4000; some to $10,000. Remarks: Full-time maker; first knife sold in 1990. ABS Master Smith and voting member KMG. Mark: Snake logo.

T

TABER, DAVID E.,
51 E. 4th St., Ste. 300, Winona, MN 55987, Phone: 507-450-1918, dtaber@qwestoffice.net
Specialties: Traditional slip joints, primarily using and working knives. Technical: Blades are hollow ground on a 20" wheel, ATS-34 and some damascus steel. Remarks: Full-time orthodontist, part-time maker; first knife made in January 2011. Mark: dr.t.

TABOR, TIM,
18925 Crooked Lane, Lutz, FL 33548, Phone: 813-948-6141, taborknives.com
Specialties: Fancy folders, Damascus Bowies and hunters. Patterns: My own design folders & customer requests. Technical: ATS-34, hand forged Damascus, 1084, 15N20 mosaic Damascus, 1095, 5160 high carbon blades, flat grind, file work & jewel embellishments. Prices: $175 to $1500. Remarks: Part-time maker, sold first knife in 2003. Mark: Last name

TAKACH, ANDREW,
1390 Fallen Timber Rd., Elizabeth, PA 15037, Phone: 724-691-2271, a-takach@takachforge.com; Web: www.takachforge.com
Specialties: One-of-a-kind fixed blade working knives (own design or customer's). Mostly all fileworked. Patterns: Hunters, skinners, caping, fighters, and designs of own style. Technical: Forges mostly 5160, 1090, 01, an down pattern welded Damascus, nickle Damascus, and cable and various chain Damascus. Also do some San Mai. Prices: $100 to $350, some over $550. Remarks: Doing business as Takach Forge. First knife sold in 2004. Mark: Takach (stamped).

TAKAHASHI, MASAO,
39-3 Sekine-machi, Maebashi-shi, Gunma, JAPAN 371 0047, Phone: 81 27 234 2223, Fax: 81 27 234 2223
Specialties: Working straight knives. Patterns: Daggers, fighters, hunters, fishing knives, boots. Technical: Grinds ATS-34 and Damascus. Prices: $350 to $1000 and up. Remarks: Full-time maker; first knife sold in 1982. Mark: M. Takahashi.

TALLY, GRANT,
26961 James Ave, Flat Rock, MI 48134, Phone: 313-414-1618
Specialties: Straight knives and folders of his design. Patterns: Bowies, daggers, fighters. Technical: Grinds ATS-34, 440C and D2. Offers filework. Prices: $250 to $1000. Remarks: Part-time maker; first knife sold in 1985. Doing business as Tally Knives. Mark: Tally (last name).

TAMATSU, KUNIHIKO,
5344 Sukumo, Sukumo City, Kochi-ken, Japan 788-0000, Phone: 0880-63-3455, ktamatsu@mb.gallery.ne.jp; Web: www.knife.tamatu.net
Specialties: Loveless-style fighters, sub-hilt fighters and hunting knives. Technical: Mirror-finished ATS-34, BG-42 and CPM-S30V blades. Prices: $400 to $2,500. Remarks: Part-time maker, making knives for eight years. Mark: Electrical etching of "K. Tamatsu."

TAMBOLI, MICHAEL,
12447 N 49 Ave, Glendale, AZ 85304, Phone: 602-978-4308, mnbtamboli@gmail.com
Specialties: Miniatures, some full size. Patterns: Miniature hunting knives to fantasy art knives. Technical: Grinds ATS-34 & Damascus. Prices: $75 to $500; some to $2000. Remarks: Full time maker; first knife sold in 1978. Mark: Initials, last name, last name city and state, MT Custom Knives or Mike Tamboli in Japanese script.

TASMAN, KERLEY,
9 Avignon Retreat, Pt Kennedy, WA, AUSTRALIA 6172, Phone: 61 8 9593 0554, Fax: 61 8 9593 0554, taskerley@optusnet.com.au
Specialties: Knife/harness/sheath systems for elite military personnel and body guards. Patterns: Utility/tactical knives, hunters small game and presentation grade knives. Technical: ATS-34 and 440C, Damascus, flat and hollow grids. Prices: $200 to $1800 U.S. Remarks: Will take presentation grade commissions. Multi award winning maker and custom jeweler. Mark: Maker's initials.

TAYLOR, BILLY,
10 Temple Rd, Petal, MS 39465, Phone: 601-544-0041
Specialties: Straight knives of his design. Patterns: Bowies, skinners, hunters and utility knives. Technical: Flat-grinds 440C, ATS-34 and 154CM. Prices: $60 to $300. Remarks: Part-time maker; first knife sold in 1991. Mark: Full name, city and state.

TAYLOR, C GRAY,
560 Poteat Ln, Fall Branch, TN 37656, Phone: 423-348-8304, graysknives@aol.com; Web: www.cgraytaylor.com
Specialties: Traditonal multi-blade lobster folders, also art display Bowies and daggers. Patterns: Orange Blossom, sleeveboard and gunstocks. Technical: Grinds. Prices: Upscale. Remarks: Full-time maker; first knife sold in 1975. Mark: Name, city and state.

TAYLOR, DAVID,
113 Stewart Hills Dr., Rogersville, TN 37857, Phone: 423-293-9319, david@dtguitars.com; Web: www.dtguitars.com
Patterns: Multi-blade folders, traditional patterns. Technical: Grinds ATS-34. Prices: $400 and up. Remarks: First sold knife in 1981 at age 14. Became a member of Knifemakers Guild at age 14. Made first folder in 1983. Full-time pastor of Baptist Church and part-time knifemaker.

TAYLOR, SHANE,
42 Broken Bow Ln, Miles City, MT 59301, Phone: 406-234-7175, shane@taylorknives.com; Web: www.taylorknives.com
Specialties: One-of-a-kind fancy Damascus straight knives and folders. Patterns: Bowies, folders and fighters. Technical: Forges own mosaic and pattern welded Damascus. Prices: $450 and up. Remarks: ABS Master Smith, full-time maker; first knife sold in 1982. Mark: First name.

TEDFORD, STEVEN J.,
14238 Telephone Rd., Colborne, ON, CANADA K0K 1S0, Phone: 905-342-3696, firebornswords@yahoo.com; Web: www.steventedfordknives.com
Specialties: Handmade custom fixed blades, specialty outdoors knives. Patterns: Swept Survival Bowie, large, medium and small-size field-dressing/hunting knives, drop-point skinners, and world-class fillet knives. Technical: Exclusively using ATS-34 stainless steel, Japanese-inspired, free-hand ground, zero-point edge blade design. Prices: All knives are sold wholesale directly from the shop starting at $150 to $500+. Remarks: Tedford Knives; Function is beauty. Every knife is unconditionally guaranteed for life.

TENDICK, BEN,
798 Nadine Ave, Eugene, OR 97404, Phone: 541-912-1280, bentendick@gmail.com; Web: www.brtbladeworks.com
Specialties: Hunter/utility, tactical, bushcraft, and kitchen. Technical: Preferred steel - L6, 5160, and 15N20. Stock Removal. Prices: $130 to $700. Remarks: Part-time; has been making knives since early 90's but started seriously making knives in 2010. In business at BRT Bladeworks, no website yet but can be found on Facebook. Mark: Initials (BRT) with B backwards and T between the B and R, and also use last name.

TERRILL, STEPHEN,
16357 Goat Ranch Rd, Springville, CA 93265, Phone: 559-539-3116, slterrill@yahoo.com
Specialties: Deluxe working straight knives and folders. Patterns: Fighters, tantos, boots, locking folders and axes; traditional oriental patterns. Technical: Forges 1095, 5160, Damascus, stock removal ATS-34. Prices: $300+. Remarks: Full-time maker; first knife sold in 1972. Mark: Name, city, state in logo.

TERZUOLA, ROBERT,
10121 Eagle Rock NE, Albuquerque, NM 87122, Phone: 505-856-7077, terzuola@earthlink.net
Specialties: Working folders of his design; period pieces. Patterns: High-tech utility, defense and gentleman's folders. Technical: Grinds CPM154, Damascus, and CPM S30V. Offers titanium, carbon fiber and G10 composite for side-lock folders and tactical folders. Prices: $550 to $2000. Remarks: Full-time maker; first knife sold in 1980. Mark: Mayan dragon head, name.

TESARIK, RICHARD,
Pisecnik 87, 614 00 Brno, Czech Republic, Phone: 00420-602-834-726, rtesarik@gmail.com; Web: www.tesariknoze.cz
Specialties: Handmade art knives. Patterns: Daggers, hunters and LinerLock or back-lock folders. Technical: Grinds RWL-34, N690 and stainless or high-carbon damascus. Carves on blade, handle and other parts. I prefer fossil material and exotic wood, don't use synthetic material. Prices: $600 to $2,000. Remarks: Part-time maker, full-time hobby; first knife sold in 2009. Mark: TR.

THAYER, DANNY O,
8908S 100W, Romney, IN 47981, Phone: 765-538-3105, dot61h@juno.com
Specialties: Hunters, fighters, Bowies. Prices: $250 and up.

THEIS, TERRY,
21452 FM 2093, Harper, TX 78631, Phone: 830-864-4438
Specialties: All European and American engraving styles. Prices: $200 to $2000. Remarks: Engraver only.

THEVENOT, JEAN-PAUL,
16 Rue De La Prefecture, Dijon, FRANCE 21000
Specialties: Traditional European knives and daggers. Patterns: Hunters, utility-camp knives, daggers, historical or modern style. Technical: Forges own Damascus, 5160, 1084. Remarks: Part-time maker. ABS Master Smith. Mark: Interlocked initials in square.

THIE, BRIAN,
13250 150th St, Burlington, IA 52601, Phone: 319-850-2188, thieknives@gmail.com; Web: www.mepotelco.net/web/tknives
Specialties: Working using knives from basic to fancy. Patterns: Hunters, fighters, camp and folders. Technical: Forges blades and own Damascus. Prices: $250 and up. Remarks: ABS Journeyman Smith, part-time maker. Sole author of blades including forging, heat treat, engraving and sheath making. Mark: Last name hand engraved into the blade, JS stamped into blade.

THILL, JIM,
10242 Bear Run, Missoula, MT 59803, Phone: 406-251-5475
Specialties: Traditional working/using knives of his design. Patterns: Fighters, hunters and utility/camp knives. Technical: Grinds D2 and ATS-34; forges 10-95-85, 52100, 5160, 10 series, reg. Damascus-mosaic. Offers hand cut sheaths with rawhide lace. Prices: $145 to $350; some to $1250. Remarks: Full-time maker; first knife sold in 1962. Mark: Running bear in triangle.

THOMAS, BOB,
Sunset Forge, 3502 Bay Rd., Ferndale, WA 98248, Phone: 360-201-0160, Fax: 360-366-5723, sunsetforge@rockisland.com

THOMAS, DAVID E,
8502 Hwy 91, Lillian, AL 36549, Phone: 251-961-7574, redbluff@gulftel.com
Specialties: Bowies and hunters. Technical: Hand forged blades in 5160, 1095 and own Damascus. Prices: $400 and up. Mark: Stylized DT, maker's last name, serial number.

THOMAS, DEVIN,
PO Box 568, Panaca, NV 89042, Phone: 775-728-4363, hoss@devinthomas.com; Web: www.devinthomas.com
Specialties: Traditional straight knives and folders in standard patterns. Patterns: Bowies, fighters, hunters. Technical: Forges stainless Damascus, nickel and 1095. Uses, makes and sells mokume with brass, copper and nickel-silver. Prices: $300 to $1200. Remarks: Full-time maker; first knife sold in 1979. Mark: First and last name, city and state with anvil, or first name only.

THOMAS, KIM,
PO Box 531, Seville, OH 44273, Phone: 330-769-9906
Specialties: Fancy and traditional straight knives of his design and to customer specs; period pieces. Patterns: Boots, daggers, fighters, swords. Technical: Forges own Damascus from 5160, 1010 and nickel. Prices: $135 to $1500; some to $3000. Remarks: Part-time maker; first knife sold in 1986. Doing business as Thomas Iron Works. Mark: KT.

THOMAS, ROCKY,
1716 Waterside Blvd, Moncks Corner, SC 29461, Phone: 843-761-7761
Specialties: Traditional working knives in standard patterns. Patterns: Hunters and utility/camp knives. Technical: ATS-34 and commercial Damascus. Prices: $130 to $350. Remarks: Spare-time maker; first knife sold in 1986. Mark: First name in script and/or block.

THOMPSON, KENNETH,
4887 Glenwhite Dr, Duluth, GA 30136, Phone: 770-446-6730
Specialties: Traditional working and using knives of his design. Patterns: Hunters, Bowies and utility/camp knives. Technical: Forges 5168, O1, 1095 and 52100. Prices: $75 to $1500; some to $2500. Remarks: Part-time maker; first knife sold in 1990. Mark: P/W; or name, P/W, city and state.

THOMPSON, LEON,
45723 SW Saddleback Dr, Gaston, OR 97119, Phone: 503-357-2573
Specialties: Working knives. Patterns: Locking folders, slip-joints and liner locks. Technical: Grinds ATS-34, D2 and 440C. Prices: $450 to $1000. Remarks: Full-time maker; first knife sold in 1976. Mark: First and middle initials, last name, city and state.

THOMPSON, LLOYD,
PO Box 1664, Pagosa Springs, CO 81147, Phone: 970-264-5837
Specialties: Working and collectible straight knives and folders of his design. Patterns: Straight blades, lock back folders and slip joint folders. Technical: Hollow-grinds ATS-34, D2 and O1. Uses sambar stag and exotic woods. Prices: $150 to upscale. Remarks: Full-time maker; first knife sold in 1985. Doing business as Trapper Creek Knife Co. Remarks: Offers three-day knife-making classes. Mark: Name.

THOMPSON, TOMMY,
4015 NE Hassalo, Portland, OR 97232-2607, Phone: 503-235-5762
Specialties: Fancy and working knives; mostly liner-lock folders. Patterns: Fighters, hunters and liner locks. Technical: Grinds D2, ATS-34, CPM440V and T15. Handles are either hardwood inlaid with wood banding and stone or shell, or made of agate, jasper, petrified woods, etc. Prices: $75 to $500; some to $1000. Remarks: Part-time maker; first knife sold in 1987. Doing business as Stone Birds. Knife making temporarily stopped due to family obligations. Mark: First and last name, city and state.

THOMSEN, LOYD W,
25241 Renegade Pass, Custer, SD 57730, Phone: 605-673-2787, loydt@yahoo.com; Web: horseheadcreekknives.com
Specialties: High-art and traditional working/using straight knives and presentation pieces of his design and to customer specs; period pieces. Hand carved animals in crown of stag on handles and carved display stands. Patterns: Bowies, hunters, daggers and utility/camp knives. Technical: Forges and grinds 1095HC, 1084, L6, 15N20, 440C stainless steel, nickel 200; special restoration process on period pieces. Makes sheaths. Uses natural materials for handles. Prices: $350 to $1000. Remarks: Full-time maker; first knife sold in

1995. Doing business as Horsehead Creek Knives. Mark: Initials and last name over a horse's head.

THORBURN, ANDRE E,
P.O. Box 1748, Bela Bela, Warmbaths, LP, SOUTH AFRICA 0480, Phone: 27-82-650-1441, Fax: 27-86-750-2765, andrethorburn@gmail.com; Web: www.thorburnknives.co.za
Specialties: Working and fancy folders of own design to customer specs. Technical: Uses RWL-34, Damasteel, CPM steels, Bohler N690, and carbon and stainless damascus. Prices: Starting at $350. Remarks: Full-time maker since 1996; first knife sold in 1990. Member of South African, Italian, and German guilds. Mark: Initials and name in a double circle.

THOUROT, MICHAEL W,
T-814 Co Rd 11, Napoleon, OH 43545, Phone: 419-533-6832, Fax: 419-533-3516, mike2row@henry-net.com; Web: wwwsafariknives.com
Specialties: Working straight knives to customer specs. Designed two-handled skinning ax and limited edition engraved knife and art print set. Patterns: Fishing and fillet knives, Bowies, tantos and hunters. Technical: Grinds O1, D2, 440C and Damascus. Prices: $200 to $5000. Remarks: Part-time maker; first knife sold in 1968. Mark: Initials.

THUESEN, ED,
21211 Knolle Rd, Damon, TX 77430, Phone: 979-553-1211, Fax: 979-553-1211
Specialties: Working straight knives. Patterns: Hunters, fighters and survival knives. Technical: Grinds D2, 440C, ATS-34 and Vascowear. Prices: $150 to $275; some to $600. Remarks: Part-time maker; first knife sold in 1979. Runs knifemaker supply business. Mark: Last name in script.

TIENSVOLD, ALAN L,
PO Box 355, 3277 U.S. Hwy. 20, Rushville, NE 69360, Phone: 308-360-0613
Specialties: Working knives, tomahawks and period pieces, high end Damascus knives. Patterns: Random, ladder, twist and many more. Technical: Hand forged blades, forges own Damascus. Prices: Working knives start at $300. Remarks: Received Journeyman rating with the ABS in 2002. Does own engraving and fine work. Mark: Tiensvold hand made U.S.A. on left side, JS on right.

TIENSVOLD, JASON,
PO Box 795, Rushville, NE 69360, Phone: 308-360-2217, jasontiensvoldknives@yahoo.com
Specialties: Working and using straight knives of his design; period pieces. Gentlemen folders, art folders. Single action automatics. Patterns: Hunters, skinners, Bowies, fighters, daggers, liner locks. Technical: Forges own Damascus using 15N20 and 1084, 1095, nickel, custom file work. Prices: $200 to $4000. Remarks: Full-time maker, first knife sold in 1994; doing business under Tiensvold Custom Knives. Mark: J. Tiensvold on left side, MS on right.

TIGHE, BRIAN,
12-111 Fourth Ave, Suite 376 Ridley Square, St. Catharines, ON, CANADA L0S 1M0, Phone: 905-892-2734, Web: www.tigheknives.com
Specialties: Folding knives, bearing pivots. High tech tactical folders. Patterns: Boots, daggers and locking. Technical: BG-42, RWL-34, Damasteel, 154CM, S30V, CPM 440V and CPM 420V. Prefers natural handle material inlay; hand finishes. Prices: $450 to $4000. Remarks: Full-time maker; first knife sold in 1989. Mark: Etched signature.

TILL, CALVIN E AND RUTH,
11 Chadron Creek Trl. Ct., Chadron, NE 69337-6967, Phone: 308-432-6945
Specialties: Straight knives, hunters, Bowies; no folders Patterns: Training point, drop point hunters, Bowies. Technical: ATS-34 sub zero quench RC59, 61. Prices: $700 to $1200. Remarks: Sells only the absolute best knives they can make. Manufactures every part in their knives. Mark: RC Till. The R is for Ruth.

TILTON, JOHN,
24041 Hwy 383, Iowa, LA 70647, Phone: 337-582-6785, john@jetknives.com
Specialties: Bowies, camp knives, skinners and folders. Technical: All forged blades. Makes own Damascus. Prices: $150 and up. Remarks: ABS Journeyman Smith. Mark: Initials J.E.T.

TINDERA, GEORGE,
BURNING RIVER FORGE, 751 Hadcock Rd, Brunswick, OH 44212-2648, Phone: 330-220-6212
Specialties: Straight knives; his designs. Patterns: Personal knives; classic Bowies and fighters. Technical: Hand-forged high-carbon; his own cable and pattern welded Damascus. Prices: $125 to $600. Remarks: Spare-time maker; sold first knife in 1995. Natural handle materials.

TINGLE, DENNIS P,
19390 E Clinton Rd, Jackson, CA 95642, Phone: 209-223-4586, dtknives@earthlink.net
Specialties: Swords, fixed blades: small to medium, tomahawks. Technical: All blades forged. Remarks: ABS, JS. Mark: D. Tingle over JS.

TIPPETTS, COLTEN,
4068 W Miners Farm Dr, Hidden Springs, ID 83714, Phone: 208-229-7772, coltentippetts@gmail.com
Specialties: Fancy and working straight knives and fancy locking folders of his own design or to customer specifications. Patterns: Hunters and skinners, fighters and utility. Technical: Grinds BG-42, high-carbon 1095 and Damascus. Prices: $200 to $1000. Remarks: Part-time maker; first knife sold in 1996. Mark: Fused initials.

TODD, RICHARD C,
375th LN 46001, Chambersburg, IL 62323, Phone: 217-327-4380, ktodd45@yahoo.com
Specialties: Multi blade folders and silver sheaths. Patterns: Jewel setting and

hand engraving. Mark: RT with letter R crossing the T or R Todd.

TOICH, NEVIO,
Via Pisacane 9, Rettorgole di Caldogna, Vincenza, ITALY 36030, Phone: 0444-985065, Fax: 0444-301254
Specialties: Working/using straight knives of his design or to customer specs. Patterns: Bowies, hunters, skinners and utility/camp knives. Technical: Grinds 440C, D2 and ATS-34. Hollow-grinds all blades and uses mirror polish. Offers hand-sewn sheaths. Uses wood and horn. Prices: $120 to $300; some to $450. Remarks: Spare-time maker; first knife sold in 1989. Doing business as Custom Toich. Mark: Initials and model number punched.

TOKAR, DANIEL,
Box 1776, Shepherdstown, WV 25443
Specialties: Working knives; period pieces. Patterns: Hunters, camp knives, buckskinners, axes, swords and battle gear. Technical: Forges L6, 1095 and his Damascus; makes mokume, Japanese alloys and bronze daggers; restores old edged weapons. Prices: $25 to $800; some to $3000. Remarks: Part-time maker; first knife sold in 1979. Doing business as The Willow Forge. Mark: Arrow over rune and date.

TOLLEFSON, BARRY A,
104 Sutter Pl, PO Box 4198, Tubac, AZ 85646, Phone: 520-398-9327
Specialties: Working straight knives, some fancy. Patterns: Hunters, skinners, fighters and camp knives. Technical: Grinds 440C, ATS-34 and D2. Likes mirror-finishes; offers some fancy filework. Handles made from elk, deer and exotic hardwoods. Prices: $75 to $300; some higher. Remarks: Part-time maker; first knife sold in 1990. Mark: Stylized initials.

TOMBERLIN, BRION R,
ANVIL TOP CUSTOM KNIVES, 825 W Timberdell, Norman, OK 73072, Phone: 405-202-6832, anviltopp@aol.com
Specialties: Hand forged blades, working pieces, standard classic patterns, some swords, and customer designs. Patterns: Bowies, hunters, fighters, Persian and eastern-styles. Likes Japanese blades. Technical: Forge 1050, 1075, 1084, 1095, 5160, some forged stainless, also do some stock removal in stainless. Also makes own damascus. Prices: Start at $275 up to $2000 or higher for swords and custom pieces. Remarks: Part-time maker, Mastersmith America Bladesmith Society. Prefers natural handle materials, hand rubbed finishes. Likes temperlines. Mark: BRION with MS.

TOMES, P J,
594 High Peak Ln, Shipman, VA 22971, Phone: 434-263-8662, tomgsknives@juno.com; Web: www.tomesknives.com
Specialties: Scagel reproductions. Patterns: Front-lock folders. Technical: Forges 52100. Prices: $150 to $750. Mark: Last name, USA, MS, stamped in forged blades.

TOMEY, KATHLEEN,
146 Buford Pl, Macon, GA 31204, Phone: 478-746-8454, ktomey@tomeycustomknives.com; Web: www.tomeycustomknives.com
Specialties: Working hunters, skinners, daily users in fixed blades, plain and embellished. Tactical neck and belt carry. Japanese influenced. Bowies. Technical: Grinds O1, ATS-34, flat or hollow grind, filework, satin and mirror polish finishes. High quality leather sheaths with tooling. Kydex with tactical. Prices: $150 to $500. Remarks: Almost full-time maker. Mark: Last name in diamond.

TOMPKINS, DAN,
PO Box 398, Peotone, IL 60468, Phone: 708-258-3620
Specialties: Working knives, some deluxe, some folders. Patterns: Hunters, boots, daggers and push knives. Technical: Grinds D2, 440C, ATS-34 and 154CM. Prices: $85 to $150; some to $400. Remarks: Part-time maker; first knife sold in 1975. Mark: Last name, city, state.

TONER, ROGER,
531 Lightfoot Pl, Pickering, ON, CANADA L1V 5Z8, Phone: 905-420-5555
Specialties: Exotic sword canes. Patterns: Bowies, daggers and fighters. Technical: Grinds 440C, D2 and Damascus. Scrimshaws and engraves. Silver cast pommels and guards in animal shapes; twisted silver wire inlays. Uses semi-precious stones. Prices: $200 to $2000; some to $3000. Remarks: Part-time maker; first knife sold in 1982. Mark: Last name.

TORRES, HENRY,
2329 Moody Ave., Clovis, CA 93619, Phone: 559-297-9154, Web: www.htknives.com
Specialties: Forged high-performance hunters and working knives, Bowies, and fighters. Technical: 52100 and 5160 and makes own Damascus. Prices: $350 to $3000. Remarks: Started forging in 2004. Has mastersmith with American Bladesmith Association.

TOSHIFUMI, KURAMOTO,
3435 Higashioda, Asakura-gun, Fukuoka, JAPAN, Phone: 0946-42-4470

TOWELL, DWIGHT L,
2375 Towell Rd, Midvale, ID 83645, Phone: 208-355-2419
Specialties: Solid, elegant working knives; art knives, high quality hand engraving and gold inlay. Patterns: Hunters, Bowies, daggers and folders. Technical: Grinds 154CM, ATS-34, 440C and other maker's Damascus. Prices: Upscale. Remarks: Full-time maker. First knife sold in 1970. Member of AKI. Mark: Towell, sometimes hand engraved.

TOWNSEND, ALLEN MARK,
6 Pine Trail, Texarkana, AR 71854, Phone: 870-772-8945

TOWNSLEY, RUSSELL,
PO BOX 91, Floral, AR 72534-0091, Phone: 870-307-8069, circleTRMtownsley@yahoo.com
Specialties: Using knives of his own design. Patterns: Hunters, skinners,

folders. Technical: Hollow grinds D2 and O1. Handle material - antler, tusk, bone, exotic woods. Prices: Prices start at $125. Remarks: Arkansas knifemakers association. Sold first knife in 2009. Doing business as Circle-T knives. Mark: Encircled T.

TRACE RINALDI CUSTOM BLADES,
1470 Underpass Rd, Plummer, ID 83851, Trace@thrblades.com; Web: www.thrblades.com
Technical: Grinds S30V, 3V, A2 and talonite fixed blades. Prices: $300-$1000. Remarks: Tactical and utility for the most part. Mark: Diamond with THR inside.

TRINDLE, BARRY,
1660 Ironwood Trail, Earlham, IA 50072-8611, Phone: 515-462-1237
Specialties: Engraved folders. Patterns: Mostly small folders, classical-styles and pocket knives. Technical: 440 only. Engraves. Handles of wood or mineral material. Prices: Start at $1000. Mark: Name on tang.

TRISLER, KENNETH W,
6256 Federal 80, Rayville, LA 71269, Phone: 318-728-5541

TRITZ, JEAN JOSE,
Schopstrasse 23, Hamburg, GERMANY 20255, Phone: 040-49 78 21
Specialties: Scandinavian knives, Japanese kitchen knives, friction folders, swords. Patterns: Puukkos, Tollekniven, Hocho, friction folders, swords. Technical: Forges tool steels, carbon steels, 52100 Damascus, mokume, San Maj. Prices: $200 to $2000; some higher. Remarks: Full-time maker; first knife sold in 1989. Does own leatherwork, prefers natural materials. Sole authorship. Speaks French, German, English, Norwegian. Mark: Initials in monogram.

TROUT, GEORGE H.,
727 Champlin Rd, Wilmington, OH 45177, Phone: 937-382-2331, gandjtrout@msn.com
Specialties: Working knives, some fancy. Patterns: Hunters, drop points, Bowies and fighters. Technical: Stock removal: ATS-34, 440C Forged: 5160, W2, 1095, O1 Full integrals: 440C, A2, O1. Prices: $150 and up. Remarks: Makes own sheaths and mosaic pins. Fileworks most knives. First knife 1985. Mark: Etched name and state on stock removal. Forged: stamped name and forged.

TRUJILLO, ALBERT M B,
2035 Wasmer Cir, Bosque Farms, NM 87068, Phone: 505-869-0428, trujilloscutups@comcast.net
Specialties: Working/using straight knives of his design or to customer specs. Patterns: Hunters, skinners, fighters, working/using knives. File work offered. Technical: Grinds ATS-34, D2, 440C, S30V. Tapers tangs, all blades cryogenically treated. Prices: $75 to $500. Remarks: Part-time maker; first knife sold in 1997. Mark: First and last name under logo.

TRUNCALI, PETE,
2914 Anatole Court, Garland, TX 75043, Phone: 214-763-7127, truncaliknives@yahoo.com Web:www.truncaliknives.com
Specialties: Lockback folders, locking liner folders, automatics and fixed blades. Does business as Truncali Custom Knives.

TSCHAGER, REINHARD,
S. Maddalena di Sotto 1a, Bolzano, ITALY 39100, Phone: 0471-975005, Fax: 0471-975005, reinhardtschager@virgilio.it
Specialties: Classic, high-art, collector-grade straight knives of his design. Patterns: Jewel knife, daggers, and hunters. Technical: Grinds ATS-34, D2 and Damascus. Oval pins. Gold inlay. Offers engraving. Prices: $900 to $2000; some to $3000. Remarks: Spare-time maker; first knife sold in 1979. Mark: Gold inlay stamped with initials.

TUOMINEN, PEKKA,
Pohjois-Keiteleentie 20, Tossavanlahti, FINLAND 72930, Phone: 358405167853, puukkopekka@luukku.com; Web: www.puukkopekka.com
Specialties: Puukko knives. Patterns: Puukkos, hunters, leukus, and folders. Technical: Forges silversteel, 1085, 52100, and makes own Damascus 15N20 and 1095. Grinds RWL-34 and ATS-34. Prices: Starting at $300. Remarks: Part-time maker. Mark: PEKKA; earlier whole knife.

TURCOTTE, LARRY,
1707 Evergreen, Pampa, TX 79065, Phone: 806-665-9369, 806-669-0435
Specialties: Fancy and working/using knives of his design and to customer specs. Patterns: Hunters, skinners, utility/camp knives. Technical: Grinds 440C, D2, ATS-34. Engraves, scrimshaws, silver inlays. Prices: $150 to $350; some to $1000. Remarks: Part-time maker; first knife sold in 1977. Doing business as Knives by Turcotte. Mark: Last name.

TURECEK, JIM,
12 Elliott Rd, Ansonia, CT 06401, Phone: 203-734-8406, jturecek@sbcglobal.net
Specialties: Exotic folders, art knives and some miniatures. Patterns: Trout and bird knives with split bamboo handles and one-of-a-kind folders. Technical: Grinds and forges stainless and carbon damascus. All knives are handmade using no computer-controlled machinery. Prices: $2,000 to $10,000. Remarks: Full-time maker; first knife sold in 1983. Mark: Last initial in script, or last name.

TURNBULL, RALPH A,
14464 Linden Dr, Spring Hill, FL 34609, Phone: 352-688-7089, tbull2000@bellsouth.net; Web: www.turnbullknives.com
Specialties: Fancy folders. Patterns: Primarily gents pocket knives. Technical: Wire EDM work on bolsters. Prices: $300 and up. Remarks: Full-time maker; first knife sold in 1973. Mark: Signature or initials.

TURNER, KEVIN,
17 Hunt Ave, Montrose, NY 10548, Phone: 914-739-0535
Specialties: Working straight knives of his design and to customer specs;

period pieces. Patterns: Daggers, fighters and utility knives. Technical: Forges 5160 and 52100. Prices: $90 to $500. Remarks: Part-time maker; first knife sold in 1991. Mark: Acid-etched signed last name and year.

TURNER, MIKE,
PO BOX 194, Williams, OR 97544, Phone: 541-846-0204, mike@turnerknives.com Web: www.turnerknives.com
Specialties: Forged and stock removed full tang, hidden and thru tang knives. Patterns: Hunters, fighters, Bowies, boot knives, skinners and kitchen knives. Technical: I make my own damascus. Prices: $200 - $1,000. Remarks: Part-time maker, sold my first knife in 2008, doing business as Mike Turner Custom Knives. Mark: Name, City, & State.

TYRE, MICHAEL A,
1219 Easy St, Wickenburg, AZ 85390, Phone: 928-684-9601/602-377-8432, michaeltyre@msn.com
Specialties: Quality folding knives upscale gents folders one-of-a-kind collectable models. Patterns: Working fixed blades for hunting, kitchen and fancy Bowies. Technical: Grinds prefer hand rubbed satin finishes and use natural handle materials. Prices: $250 to $1300.

TYSER, ROSS,
1015 Hardee Court, Spartanburg, SC 29303, Phone: 864-585-7616
Specialties: Traditional working and using straight knives and folders of his design and in standard patterns. Patterns: Bowies, hunters and slip-joint folders. Technical: Grinds 440C and commercial Damascus. Mosaic pins; stone inlay. Does filework and scrimshaw. Offers engraving and cut-work and some inlay on sheaths. Prices: $45 to $125; some to $400. Remarks: Part-time maker; first knife sold in 1995. Doing business as RT Custom Knives. Mark: Stylized initials.

U

UCHIDA, CHIMATA,
977-2 Oaza Naga Shisui Ki, Kumamoto, JAPAN 861-1204

UPTON, TOM,
Little Rabbit Forge, 1414 Feast Pl., Rogers, AR 72758, Phone: 479-636-6755, Web: www.upton-knives.com
Specialties: Working fixed blades. Patterns: Hunters, utility, fighters, bowies and small hatchets. Technical: Forges 5160, 1084 and W2 blade steels, or stock removal using D2, 440C and 154CM. Performs own heat treat. Prices: $150 and up. Remarks: Part-time maker; first knife sold in 1977. Member of ABS, Arkansas Knifemakers Association and Knife Group Association. Mark: Name (Small Rabbit logo), city and state, etched or stamped.

V

VAGNINO, MICHAEL,
PO Box 67, Visalia, CA 93279, Phone: 559-636-0501; cell: 559-827-2802, mvknives@lightspeed.net; Web: www.mvknives.com
Specialties: Folders and straight knives, working and fancy. Patterns: Folders--locking liners, slip joints, lock backs, double and single action autos. Straight knives--hunters, Bowies, camp and kitchen. Technical: Forges 52100, W2, 15N20 and 1084. Grinds stainless. Makes own damascus and does engraving. Prices: $275 to $4000 and above. Remarks: Full-time maker, ABS Mastersmith. Mark: Logo, last name.

VAIL, DAVE,
554 Sloop Point Rd, Hampstead, NC 28443, Phone: 910-270-4456
Specialties: Working/using straight knives of his own design or to the customer's specs. Patterns: Hunters/skinners, camp/utility, fillet, Bowies. Technical: Grinds ATS-34, 440c, 154 CM and 1095 carbon steel. Prices: $90 to $450. Remarks: Part-time maker. Member of NC Custom Knifemakers Guild. Mark: Etched oval with "Dave Vail Hampstead NC" inside.

VALLOTTON, BUTCH AND AREY,
621 Fawn Ridge Dr, Oakland, OR 97462, Phone: 541-459-2216, Fax: 541-459-7473
Specialties: Quick opening knives w/complicated mechanisms. Patterns: Tactical, fancy, working, and some art knives. Technical: Grinds all steels, uses others' Damascus. Uses Spectrum Metal. Prices: From $350 to $4500. Remarks: Full-time maker since 1984; first knife sold in 1981. Co/designer, Appelgate Fairbarn folding w/Bill Harsey. Mark: Name w/viper head in the "V."

VALLOTTON, RAINY D,
1295 Wolf Valley Dr, Umpqua, OR 97486, Phone: 541-459-0465
Specialties: Folders, one-handed openers and art pieces. Patterns: All patterns. Technical: Stock removal all steels; uses titanium liners and bolsters; uses all finishes. Prices: $350 to $3500. Remarks: Full-time maker. Mark: Name.

VALLOTTON, SHAWN,
621 Fawn Ridge Dr, Oakland, OR 97462, Phone: 503-459-2216
Specialties: Left-hand knives. Patterns: All styles. Technical: Grinds 440C, ATS-34 and Damascus. Uses titanium. Prefers bead-blasted or anodized finishes. Prices: $250 to $1400. Remarks: Full-time maker. Mark: Name and specialty.

VALLOTTON, THOMAS,
621 Fawn Ridge Dr, Oakland, OR 97462, Phone: 541-459-2216
Specialties: Custom autos. Patterns: Tactical, fancy. Technical: File work, uses Damascus, uses Spectrum Metal. Prices: From $350 to $700. Remarks: Full-time maker. Maker of ProtŽgé 3 canoe. Mark: T and a V mingled.

VAN CLEVE, STEVE,
Box 372, Sutton, AK 99674, Phone: 907-745-3038

VAN DE MANAKKER, THIJS,
Koolweg 34, Holland, NETHERLANDS, Phone: 0493539369, www.ehijsvandemanakker.com
Specialties: Classic high-art knives. Patterns: Swords, utility/camp knives and period pieces. Technical: Forges soft iron, carbon steel and Bloomery Iron. Makes own Damascus, Bloomery Iron and patterns. Prices: $20 to $2000; some higher. Remarks: Full-time maker; first knife sold in 1969. Mark: Stylized "V."

VAN DEN BERG, NEELS,
166 Van Heerdan St., Capital Park, Pretoria, Gauteng, South Africa, Phone: +27(0)12-326-5649 or +27(0)83-451-3105, neels@blackdragonforge.com; Web: http://www.blackdragonforge.com or http://www.facebook.com/neels.vandenberg
Specialties: Handforged damascus and high-carbon steel axes, hunters, swords and art knives. Patterns: All my own designs and customer collaborations, from axes, hunters, choppers, bowies, swords and folders to one-off tactical prototypes. Technical: Flat and hollow grinding. Handforges high-carbon steels and maker's own damascus. Also works in high-carbon stainless steels. Prices: $50 to $1,000. Remarks: Part-time maker; first knife sold in Oct. 2009. Mark: Stylized capital letter "N" resembling a three-tier mountain, normally hot stamped in forged blades.

VAN DEN ELSEN, GERT,
Purcelldreef 83, Tilburg, NETHERLANDS 5012 AJ, Phone: 013-4563200, gvdelsen@home.nl
Specialties: Fancy, working/using, miniatures and integral straight knives of the maker's design or to customer specs. Patterns: Bowies, fighters, hunters and Japanese-style blades. Technical: Grinds ATS-34 and 440C; forges Damascus. Offers filework, differentially tempered blades and some mokume-gane fittings. Prices: $350 to $1000; some to $4000. Remarks: Part-time maker; first knife sold in 1982. Doing business as G-E Knives. Mark: Initials GE in lozenge shape.

VAN DER WESTHUIZEN, PETER,
PO Box 1698, Mossel Bay, SC, SOUTH AFRICA 6500, Phone: 27 446952388, pietvdw@telkomsa.net
Specialties: Working knives, folders, daggers and art knives. Patterns: Hunters, skinners, bird, trout and sidelock folders. Technical: Sandvik, 12627. Damascus indigenous wood and ivory. Prices: From $450 to $5500. Remarks: First knife sold in 1987. Full-time since 1996. Mark: Initial & surname. Handmade RSA.

VAN DIJK, RICHARD,
76 Stepney Ave Rd 2, Harwood Dunedin, NEW ZEALAND, Phone: 0064-3-4780401, Web: www.hoihoknives.com
Specialties: Damascus, Fantasy knives, sgiandubhs, dirks, swords, and hunting knives. Patterns: Mostly one-offs, anything from bird and trout to swords, no folders. Technical: Forges mainly own Damascus, some 5160, O1, 1095, L6. Prefers natural handle materials, over 40 years experience as goldsmith, handle fittings are often made from sterling silver and sometimes gold, manufactured to cap the handle, use gemstones if required. Makes own sheaths. Prices: $300 and up. Remarks: Full-time maker, first knife sold in 1980. Doing business as HOIHO KNIVES. Mark: Stylized initials RvD in triangle.

VAN EIZENGA, JERRY W,
14281 Cleveland, Nunica, MI 49448, Phone: 616-638-2275
Specialties: Hand forged blades, Scagel patterns and other styles. Patterns: Camp, hunting, bird, trout, folders, axes, miniatures. Technical: 5160, 52100, 1084. Prices: Start at $250. Remarks: Part-time maker, sole author of knife and sheath. First knife made 1970s. ABS member who believes in the beauty of simplicity. Mark: J.S. stamp.

VAN ELDIK, FRANS,
Ho Flaan 3, Loenen, NETHERLANDS 3632 BT, Phone: 0031 294 233 095, Fax: 0031 294 233 095
Specialties: Fancy collector-grade straight knives and folders of his design. Patterns: Hunters, fighters, boots and folders. Technical: Forges and grinds D2, 154CM, ATS-34 and stainless Damascus. Prices: Start at $450. Remarks: Spare-time maker; first knife sold in 1979. Knifemaker 30 years, 25 year member of Knifemakers Guild. Mark: Lion with name and Amsterdam.

VAN HEERDEN, ANDRE,
P.O. Box 905-417, Garsfontein, Pretoria, GT, SOUTH AFRICA 0042, Phone: 27 82 566 6030, andrevh@iafrica.com; Web: www.andrevanheerden.com
Specialties: Fancy and working folders of his design to customer specs. Technical: Grinds RWL34, 19C27, D2, carbon and stainless Damascus. Prices: Starting at $350. Remarks: Part-time maker, first knife sold in 2003. Mark: Initials and name in a double circle.

VAN REENEN, IAN,
6003 Harvard St, Amarillo, TX 79109, Phone: 806-236-8333, ianvanreenen@suddenlink.net Web: www.ianvanreenenknives.com
Specialties: Slipjoints, single and double blades. Patterns: Trappers, peanuts, saddle horn trappers. Technical: ATS-34 and CPM 154.Prices: $400 to $700. Remarks: Specializing in slipjoints. Mark: VAN REENEN

VAN RYSWYK, AAD,
AVR KNIVES, Werf Van Pronk 8, Vlaardingen, NETHERLANDS 3134 HE, Phone: +31 10 4742952, info@avrknives.com; Web: www.avrknives.com
Specialties: High-art interframe folders of his design. Patterns: Hunters and locking folders. Technical: Uses semi-precious stones, mammoth ivory, iron wood, etc. Prices: $550 to $3800. Remarks: Full-time maker; first knife sold in 1993.

VANCE, DAVID,
2646 Bays Bend Rd., West Liberty, KY 41472, Phone: 606-743-1465 or 606-362-6191, dtvance@mrtc.com; Web: www.facebook.com/ddcutlery
Specialties: Custom hunting or collectible knives, folders and fixed blades, also unique bullet casing handle pins and filework. Patterns: Maker's design or made to customers' specifications. Technical: Uses stock removal method on 1095 steel. Remarks: Part-time maker; first knife made in 2006. Mark: Cursive D&D.

VANDERFORD, CARL G,
2290 Knob Creek Rd, Columbia, TN 38401, Phone: 931-381-1488
Specialties: Traditional working straight knives and folders of his design. Patterns: Hunters, Bowies and locking folders. Technical: Forges and grinds 440C, O1 and wire Damascus. Prices: $60 to $125. Remarks: Part-time maker; first knife sold in 1987. Mark: Last name.

VANDERKOLFF, STEPHEN,
5 Jonathan Crescent, Mildmay, ON, CANADA N0g 2JO, Phone: 519-367-3401, steve@vanderkolffknives.com; Web: www.vanderkolffknives.com
Specialties: Fixed blades from gent's pocketknives and drop hunters to full sized Bowies and art knives. Technical: Primary blade steel 440C, Damasteel or custom made Damascus. All heat treat done by maker and all blades hardness tested. Handle material: stag, stabilized woods or MOP. Prices: $150 to $1200. Remarks: Started making knives in 1998 and sold first knife in 2000. Winner of the best of show art knife 2005 Wolverine Knife Show.

VANDEVENTER, TERRY L,
3274 Davis Rd, Terry, MS 39170-8719, Phone: 601-371-7414, tvandeventer@comcast.net
Specialties: Bowies, hunters, camp knives, friction folders. Technical: 1084, 1095, 15N20 and L6 steels. Damascus and mokume. Natural handle materials. Prices: $600 to $3000. Remarks: Sole author; makes everything here. First ABS MS from the state of Mississippi. Mark: T.L. Vandeventer (silhouette of snake underneath). MS on ricasso.

VANHOY, ED AND TANYA,
24255 N Fork River Rd, Abingdon, VA 24210, Phone: 276-944-4885, vanhoyknives@centurylink.net
Specialties: Traditional and working/using straight knives and folders and innovative locking mechanisms. Patterns: Fighters, straight knives, folders, hunters, art knives and Bowies. Technical: Grinds ATS-34 and carbon/stainless steel Damascus; forges carbon and stainless Damascus. Offers filework and engraving with hammer and chisel. Prices: $250 to $3000. Remarks: Full-time maker; first knife sold in 1977. Wife also engraves. Doing business as Van Hoy Custom Knives. Mark: Acid etched last name.

VARDAMAN, ROBERT,
2406 Mimosa Lane, Hattiesburg, MS 39402, Phone: 601-268-3889, rvx222@gmail.com
Specialties: Working straight knives of his design or to customer specs. Patterns: Bowies, hunters and integrals. Technical: Forges 52100, 5160, 1084 and 1095. Filework. Prices: $250 to $1,000. Remarks: Part-time maker. First knife sold in 2004. Mark: Last name, last name with Mississippi state logo.

VASQUEZ, JOHNNY DAVID,
1552 7th St, Wyandotte, MI 48192, Phone: 734-281-2455

VAUGHAN, IAN,
351 Doe Run Rd, Manheim, PA 17545-9368, Phone: 717-665-6949

VEIT, MICHAEL,
3289 E Fifth Rd, LaSalle, IL 61301, Phone: 815-223-3538, whitebear@starband.net
Specialties: Damascus folders. Technical: Engraver, sole author. Prices: $2500 to $6500. Remarks: Part-time maker; first knife sold in 1985. Mark: Name in script.

VELARDE, RICARDO,
7240 N Greenfield Dr, Park City, UT 84098, Phone: 435-901-1773, velardeknives@mac.com Web: www.velardeknives.com
Specialties: Investment grade integrals and interframs. Patterns: Boots, fighters and hunters; hollow grind. Technical: BG on Integrals. Prices: $1450 to $5200. Remarks: First knife sold in 1992. Mark: First initial and last name.

VELICK, SAMMY,
3457 Maplewood Ave, Los Angeles, CA 90066, Phone: 310-663-6170, metaltamer@gmail.com
Specialties: Working knives and art pieces. Patterns: Hunter, utility and fantasy. Technical: Stock removal and forges. Prices: $100 and up. Mark: Last name.

VENSILD, HENRIK,
Gl Estrup, Randersvei 4, Auning, DENMARK 8963, Phone: +45 86 48 44 48
Specialties: Classic and traditional working and using knives of his design; Scandinavian influence. Patterns: Hunters and using knives. Technical: Forges Damascus. Hand makes handles, sheaths and blades. Prices: $350 to $1000. Remarks: Part-time maker; first knife sold in 1967. Mark: Initials.

VESTAL, CHARLES,
26662 Shortsville Rd., Abingdon, VA 24210, Phone: 276-492-3262, charles@vestalknives.com; Web: www.vestalknives.com
Specialties: Hunters and double ground fighters in traditional designs and own designs. Technical: Grinds CPM-154, ATS-134, 154-CM and other steels. Prices: $300 to $1000, some higher. Remarks: First knife sold in 1995.

VIALLON, HENRI,
Les Belins, Thiers, FRANCE 63300, Phone: 04-73-80-24-03, Fax: 04 73-51-02-02
Specialties: Folders and complex Damascus Patterns: His draws. Technical: Forge. Prices: $1000 to $5000. Mark: H. Viallon.

VICKERS, DAVID,
11620 Kingford Dr., Montgomery, TX 77316, Phone: 936-537-4900, jdvickers@gmail.com
Specialties: Working/using blade knives especially for hunters. His design or to customer specs. Patterns: Hunters, skinners, camp/utility. Technical: Grinds ATS-34, 440C, and D-2. Uses stag, various woods, and micarta for handle material. Hand-stitched sheaths. Remark: Full-time maker. Prices: $125 - $350. Mark: VICKERS

VIELE, H J,
88 Lexington Ave, Westwood, NJ 07675, Phone: 201-666-2906, h.viele@verizon.net
Specialties: Folding knives of distinctive shapes. Patterns: High-tech folders and one-of-a-kind. Technical: Grinds ATS-34 and S30V. Prices: Start at $575. Remarks: Full-time maker; first knife sold in 1973. Mark: Japanese design for the god of war.

VILAR, RICARDO AUGUSTO FERREIRA,
Rua Alemada Dos Jasmins NO 243, Parque Petropolis, Mairipora, SP, BRAZIL 07600-000, Phone: 011-55-11-44-85-43-46, ricardovilar@ig.com.br.
Specialties: Traditional Brazilian-style working knives of the Sao Paulo state. Patterns: Fighters, hunters, utility, and camp knives, welcome customer design. Specialize in the "true" Brazilian camp knife "Soracabana." Technical: Forges only with sledge hammer to 100 percent shape in 5160 and 52100 and his own Damascus steels. Makes own sheaths in the "true" traditional "Paulista"-style of the state of Sao Paulo. Remark: Full-time maker. Prices: $250 to $600. Uses only natural handle materials. Mark: Special designed signature styled name R. Vilar.

VILLA, LUIZ,
R. Com. Miguel Calfat 398, Itaim Bibi, SP, BRAZIL 04537-081, Phone: 011-8290649
Specialties: One-of-a-kind straight knives and jewel knives of all designs. Patterns: Bowies, hunters, utility/camp knives and jewel knives. Technical: Grinds D6, Damascus and 440C; forges 5160. Prefers natural handle material. Prices: $70 to $200. Remarks: Part-time maker; first knife sold in 1990. Mark: Last name and serial number.

VILLAR, RICARDO,
Al. dos Jasmins 243, Mairipora, SP, BRAZIL 07600-000, Phone: 011-4851649
Specialties: Straight working knives to customer specs. Patterns: Bowies, fighters and utility/camp knives. Technical: Grinds D6, ATS-34 and 440C stainless. Prices: $80 to $200. Remarks: Part-time maker; first knife sold in 1993. Mark: Percor over sword and circle.

VILPPOLA, MARKKU,
Jaanintie 45, Turku, Finland 20540, Phone: +358 (0)50 566 1563, markku@mvforge.fi Web: www.mvforge.fi
Specialties: All kinds of swords and knives. Technical: Forges silver steel, CO, 8%, nickel, 1095, A203E, etc. Mokume (sterling silver/brass/copper). Bronze casting (sand casting, lost-wax casting). Prices: Starting at $200.

VINING, BILL,
9 Penny Lane, Methuen, MA 01844, Phone: 978-688-4729, billv@medawebs.com; Web: www.medawebs.com/knives
Specialties Liner locking folders. Slip joints & lockbacks. Patterns: Likes to make patterns of his own design. Technical: S30V, 440C, ATS-34. Damascus from various makers. Prices: $450 and up. Remarks: Part-time maker. Mark: VINING or B. Vining.

VISTE, JAMES,
EDGE WISE FORGE, 9745 Dequindre, Hamtramck, MI 48212, Phone: 313-587-8899, grumblejunky@hotmail.com
Mark: EWF touch mark.

VISTNES, TOR,
, Svelgen, NORWAY N-6930, Phone: 047-57795572
Specialties: Traditional and working knives of his design. Patterns: Hunters and utility knives. Technical: Grinds Uddeholm Elmax. Handles made of rear burls of different Nordic stabilized woods. Prices: $300 to $1100. Remarks: Part-time maker; first knife sold in 1988. Mark: Etched name and deer head.

VITALE, MACE,
925 Rt 80, Guilford, CT 06437, Phone: 203-457-5591, Web: www.laurelrockforge.com
Specialties: Hand forged blades. Patterns: Hunters, utility, chef, Bowies and fighters. Technical: W2, 1095, 1084, L6. Hand forged and finished. Prices: $100 to $1000. Remarks: American Bladesmith Society, Journeyman Smith. Full-time maker; first knife sold 2001. Mark: MACE.

VOGT, DONALD J,
9007 Hogans Bend, Tampa, FL 33647, Phone: 813-973-3245, vogtknives@verizon.net
Specialties: Art knives, folders, automatics. Technical: Uses Damascus steels for blade and bolsters, filework, hand carving on blade bolsters and handles. Other materials used: jewels, gold, mother-of-pearl, gold-lip pearl, black-lip pearl, ivory. Prices: $4,000 to $10,000. Remarks: Part-time maker; first knife sold in 1997. Mark: Last name.

VOGT, PATRIK,
Kungsvagen 83, Halmstad, SWEDEN 30270, Phone: 46-35-30977
Specialties: Working straight knives. Patterns: Bowies, hunters and fighters. Technical: Forges carbon steel and own Damascus. Prices: From $100. Remarks: Not currently making knives. Mark: Initials or last name.

custom knifemakers

VOORHIES, LES,
14511 Lk Mazaska Tr, Faribault, MN 55021, Phone: 507-332-0736, lesvor@msn.com; Web: www.lesvoorhiesknives.com
Specialties: Steels. Patterns: Liner locks & autos. Technical: ATS-34 Damascus. Prices: $250 to $1200. Mark: L. Voorhies.

VOSS, BEN,
2212 Knox Rd. E, Victoria, IL 61485-9644, Phone: 309-879-2940
Specialties: Fancy working knives of his design. Patterns: Bowies, fighters, hunters, boots and folders. Technical: Grinds 440C, ATS-34 and D2. Prices: $35 to $1200. Remarks: Part-time maker; first knife sold in 1986. Mark: Name, city and state.

VOTAW, DAVID P,
305 S State St, Pioneer, OH 43554, Phone: 419-737-2774
Specialties: Working knives; period pieces. Patterns: Hunters, Bowies, camp knives, buckskinners and tomahawks. Technical: Grinds O1 and D2. Prices: $100 to $200; some to $500. Remarks: Part-time maker; took over for the late W.K. Kneubuhler. Doing business as W-K Knives. Mark: WK with V inside anvil.

W

WACHOLZ, DOC,
95 Anne Rd, Marble, NC 28905, Phone: 828-557-1543, killdrums@aol.com; web: rackforge.com
Specialties: Forged tactical knives and tomahawks. Technical: Use 52100 and 1084 high carbon steel; make own Damascus; design and dew own sheaths. Grind up and down fashion on a 3" wheel. Prices: $300 to $800. Remarks: Part-time maker; started forging in 1999, with ABS master Charles Ochs.. Mark: Early knives stamped RACK, newer knives since 2005 stamped WACHOLZ.

WADA, YASUTAKA,
2-6-22 Fujinokidai, Nara City, Nara, JAPAN 631-0044, Phone: 0742 46-0689
Specialties: Fancy and embellished one-of-a-kind straight knives of his design. Patterns: Bowies, daggers and hunters. Technical: Grinds ATS-34. All knives hand-filed and flat grinds. Prices: $400 to $2500; some higher. Remarks: Part-time maker; first knife sold in 1990. Mark: Owl eyes with initial and last name underneath or last name.

WAGAMAN, JOHN K,
107 E Railroad St, Selma, NC 27576, Phone: 919-965-9659, Fax: 919-965-9901
Specialties: Fancy working knives. Patterns: Bowies, miniatures, hunters, fighters and boots. Technical: Grinds D2, 440C, 154CM and commercial Damascus; inlays mother-of-pearl. Prices: $110 to $2000. Remarks: Part-time maker; first knife sold in 1975. Mark: Last name.

WAIDE, RUSTY,
Triple C Knives, PO Box 499, Buffalo, MO 65622, Phone: 417-345-7231, Fax: 417-345-1911, wrrccc@yahoo.com; Web: www.tripleeknives.com
Specialties: Custom-designed hunting knives and cowboy working knives in high-carbon and damascus steels. Prices: $150 to $450. Remarks: Part-time maker; first knife sold in 2010. Mark: Name.

WAITES, RICHARD L,
PO Box 188, Broomfield, CO 80038, Phone: 303-465-9970, Fax: 303-465-9971, dickknives@aol.com
Specialties: Working fixed blade knives of all kinds including "paddle blade" skinners. Hand crafted sheaths, some upscale and unusual. Technical: Grinds 440C, ATS 34, D2. Prices: $100 to $500. Remarks: Part-time maker. First knife sold in 1998. Doing business as R.L. Waites Knives. Mark: Oval etch with first and middle initial and last name on top and city and state on bottom. Memberships; Professional Knifemakers Association and Rocky Mountain Blade Collectors Club.

WALKER, BILL,
431 Walker Rd, Stevensville, MD 21666, Phone: 410-643-5041

WALKER, DON,
2850 Halls Chapel Rd, Burnsville, NC 28714, Phone: 828-675-9716, dlwalkernc@gmail.com

WALKER, JIM,
22 Walker Ln, Morrilton, AR 72110, Phone: 501-354-3175, jwalker46@att.net
Specialties: Period pieces and working/using knives of his design and to customer specs. Patterns: Bowies, fighters, hunters, camp knives. Technical: Forges 5160, O1, L6, 52100, 1084, 1095. Prices: Start at $450. Remarks: Full-time maker; first knife sold in 1993. Mark: Three arrows with last name/MS.

WALKER, MICHAEL L,
925-A Paseo del, Pueblo Sur Taos, NM 87571, Phone: 505-751-3409, Fax: 505-751-3417, metalwerkr@msn.com
Specialties: Innovative knife designs and locking systems; titanium and SS furniture and art. Patterns: Folders from utility grade to museum quality art; others upon request. Technical: State-of-the-art materials: titanium, stainless Damascus, gold, etc. Prices: $3500 and above. Remarks: Designer/MetalCrafts; full-time professional knifemaker since 1980; four U.S. patents; invented LinerLock® and was awarded registered U.S. trademark no. 1,585,333. Mark: Early mark MW, Walker's Lockers by M.L. Walker; current M.L. Walker or Michael Walker.

WALLINGFORD JR., CHARLES W,
9024 Old Union Rd, Union, KY 41091, Phone: 859-384-4141, Web: www.cwknives.com
Specialties: 18th and 19th century styles, patch knives, rifleman knives. Technical: 1084 and 5160 forged blades. Prices: $125 to $300. Mark: CW.

WALTERS, A F,
PO Box 523, 275 Crawley Rd., TyTy, GA 31795, Phone: 229-528-6207
Specialties: Working knives, some to customer specs. Patterns: Locking folders, straight hunters, fishing and survival knives. Technical: Grinds D2, 154CM and 13C26. Prices: Start at $200. Remarks: Part-time maker. Label: "The jewel knife." Mark: "J" in diamond and knife logo.

WARD, CHUCK,
PO Box 2272, 1010 E North St, Benton, AR 72018-2272, Phone: 501-778-4329, chuckbop@aol.com
Specialties: Traditional working and using straight knives and folders of his design. Technical: Grinds 440C, D2, A2, ATS-34 and O1; uses natural and composite handle materials. Prices: $90 to $400, some higher. Remarks: Part-time maker; first knife sold in 1990. Mark: First initial, last name.

WARD, J J,
7501 S R 220, Waverly, OH 45690, Phone: 614-947-5328
Specialties: Traditional and working/using straight knives and folders of his design. Patterns: Hunters and locking folders. Technical: Grinds ATS-34, 440C and Damascus. Offers handmade sheaths. Prices: $125 to $250; some to $500. Remarks: Spare-time maker; first knife sold in 1980. Mark: Etched name.

WARD, KEN,
1125 Lee Roze Ln, Grants Pass, OR 97527, Phone: 541-956-8864
Specialties: Working knives, some to customer specs. Patterns: Straight, axes, Bowies, buckskinners and miniatures. Technical: Grinds ATS-34, Damascus. Prices: $100 to $700. Remarks: Part-time maker; first knife sold in 1977. Mark: Name.

WARD, RON,
PO BOX 21, Rose Hill, VA 24281, Phone: 276-445-4757
Specialties: Classic working and using straight knives, fantasy knives. Patterns: Bowies, hunter, fighters, and utility/camp knives. Technical: Grinds 440C, 154CM, ATS-34, uses composite and natural handle materials. Prices: $50 to $750. Remarks: Part-time maker, first knife sold in 1992. Doing business as Ron Ward Blades. Mark: RON WARD BLADES.

WARD, W C,
817 Glenn St, Clinton, TN 37716, Phone: 615-457-3568
Specialties: Working straight knives; period pieces. Patterns: Hunters, Bowies, swords and kitchen cutlery. Technical: Grinds O1. Prices: $85 to $150; some to $500. Remarks: Part-time maker; first knife sold in 1969. He styled the Tennessee Knife Maker. Mark: TKM.

WARDELL, MICK,
20 Clovelly Rd, Bideford, N Devon, ENGLAND EX39 3BU, wardellknives@hotmail.co.uk Web: www.wardellscustomknives.com
Specialties: Spring back folders and a few fixed blades. Patterns: Locking and slip-joint folders, Bowies. Technical: Grinds stainless Damascus and RWL34. Heat-treats. Prices: $300 to $2500. Remarks: Full-time maker; first knife sold in 1986. Takes limited Comissions. Mark: Wardell.

WARDEN, ROY A,
275 Tanglewood Rd, Union, MO 63084, Phone: 314-583-8813, rwarden@yhti.net
Specialties: Complex mosaic designs of "EDM wired figures" and "stack up" patterns and "lazer cut" and "torch cut" and "sawed" patterns combined. Patterns: Mostly "all mosaic" folders, automatics, fixed blades. Technical: Mosaic Damascus with all tool steel edges. Prices: $100 to $1000. Remarks: Part-time maker; first knife sold in 1987. Mark: WARDEN stamped or initials connected.

WARE, TOMMY,
158 Idlewilde, Onalaska, TX 77360, Phone: 936-646-4649
Specialties: Traditional working and using straight knives, folders and automatics of his design and to customer specs. Patterns: Hunters, automatics and locking folders. Technical: Grinds ATS-34, 440C and D2. Offers engraving and scrimshaw. Prices: $425 to $650; some to $1500. Remarks: Full-time maker; first knife sold in 1990. Doing business as Wano Knives. Mark: Last name inside oval, business name above, city and state below, year on side.

WARREN, AL,
1423 Sante Fe Circle, Roseville, CA 95678, Phone: 916-257-5904, Fax: 215-318-2945, al@warrenknives.com; Web: www.warrenknives.com
Specialties: Working straight knives and folders, some fancy. Patterns: Hunters, Bowies, fillets, lockback, folders & multi blade. Technical: Grinds ATS-34 and S30V.440V. Prices: $225 to $2,500. Remarks: Full-time maker; first knife sold in 1978. Mark: First and middle initials, last name.

WARREN, DANIEL,
571 Lovejoy Rd, Canton, NC 28716, Phone: 828-648-7351
Specialties: Using knives. Patterns: Drop point hunters. Prices: $200 to $500. Mark: Warren-Bethel NC.

WASHBURN, ARTHUR D,
ADW CUSTOM KNIVES, 211 Hinman St / PO Box 625, Pioche, NV 89043, Phone: 775-962-5463, knifeman@lcturbonet.com; Web: www.adwcustomknives.com
Specialties: Locking liner folders. Patterns: Slip joint folders (single and multiplied), lock-back folders, some fixed blades. Do own heat-treating; Rockwell test each blade. Technical: Carbon and stainless Damascus, some 1084, 1095, AEBL, 12C27, S30V. Prices: $200 to $1000 and up. Remarks: Sold first knife in 1997. Part-time maker. Mark: ADW enclosed in an oval or ADW.

WASHBURN JR., ROBERT LEE,
1929 Lava Flow Dr., St. George, UT 84790, Phone: 435-619-4432, Fax: 435-574-8554, rlwashburn@excite.com; Web: www.washburnknives.net
Specialties: Hand-forged period, Bowies, tactical, boot and hunters. Patterns: Bowies, tantos, loot hunters, tactical and folders. Prices: $100 to $2500.

Remarks: All hand forged. 52100 being his favorite steel. Mark: Washburn Knives W.

WATANABE, MELVIN,
1297 Kika St., Kailua, HI 96734, Phone: 808-261-2842, meltod808@yahoo.com
Specialties: Fancy folding knives. Some hunters. Patterns: Liner-locks and hunters. Technical: Grinds ATS-34, stainless Damascus. Prices: $350 and up. Remarks: Part-time maker, first knife sold in 1985. Mark: Name and state.

WATANABE, WAYNE,
PO Box 3563, Montebello, CA 90640, wwknives@gmail.com; Web: www.geocities.com/ww-knives
Specialties: Straight knives in Japanese-styles. One-of-a-kind designs; welcomes customer designs. Patterns: Tantos to katanas, Bowies. Technical: Flat grinds A2, O1 and ATS-34. Offers hand-rubbed finishes and wrapped handles. Prices: Start at $200. Remarks: Part-time maker. Mark: Name in characters with flower.

WATERS, GLENN,
11 Doncaster Place, Hyland Park, NSW, AUSTRALIA 2448, Phone: 172-33-8881, watersglenn@hotmail.com; Web: www.glennwaters.com
Specialties: One-of-a-kind collector-grade highly embellished art knives. Folders, fixed blades, and automatics. Patterns: Locking liner folders, automatics and fixed art knives. Technical: Grinds blades from Damasteel, and selected Damascus makers, mostly stainless. Does own engraving, gold inlaying and stone setting, filework, and carving. Gold and Japanese precious metal fabrication. Prefers exotic material, high karat gold, silver, Shyaku Dou, Shibu Ichi Gin, precious gemstones. Prices: Upscale. Remarks: Designs and makes some-of-a-kind highly embellished art knives often with fully engraved handles and blades. A jeweler by trade for 20 years before starting to make knives. Full-time since 1999, first knife sold in 1994. Mark: Glenn Waters maker Japan, G. Waters or Glen in Japanese writing.

WATSON, BERT,
9315 Meade St., Westminster, CO 80031, Phone: 303-587-3064, watsonbd21960@q.com
Specialties: Working/using straight knives of his design and to customer specs. Patterns: Hunters, utility/camp knives. Technical: Grinds O1, ATS-34, 440C, D2, A2 and others. Prices: $150 to $800. Remarks: Full-time maker. Mark: GTK and/or Bert.

WATSON, BILLY,
440 Forge Rd, Deatsville, AL 36022, Phone: 334-365-1482, billy@watsonknives.com; Web: www.watsonknives.com
Specialties: Working and using straight knives and folders of his design; period pieces. Patterns: Hunters, Bowies and utility/camp knives. Technical: Forges and grinds his own Damascus, 1095, 5160 and 52100. Prices: $40 to $1500. Remarks: Full-time maker; first knife sold in 1970. Doing business as Billy's Blacksmith Shop. Mark: Last name.

WATSON, DANIEL,
350 Jennifer Ln, Driftwood, TX 78619, Phone: 512-847-9679, info@angelsword.com; Web: http://www.angelsword.com
Specialties: One-of-a-kind knives and swords. Patterns: Hunters, daggers, swords. Technical: Hand-purify and carbonize his own high-carbon steel, pattern-welded Damascus, cable and carbon-induced crystalline Damascus. Teehno-Wootz™ Damascus steel, heat treats including cryogenic processing. European and Japanese tempering. Prices: $125 to $25,000. Remarks: Full-time maker; first knife sold in 1979. Mark: "Angel Sword" on forged pieces; "Bright Knight" for stock removal. Avatar on Techno-Wootz™ Damascus. Bumon on traditional Japanese blades.

WATSON, PETER,
66 Kielblock St, La Hoff, NW, SOUTH AFRICA 2570, Phone: 018-84942
Specialties: Traditional working and using straight knives and folders of his design. Patterns: Hunters, locking folders and utility/camp knives. Technical: Sandvik and 440C. Prices: $120 to $250; some to $1500. Remarks: Part-time maker; first knife sold in 1989. Mark: Buffalo head with name.

WATSON, TOM,
1103 Brenau Terrace, Panama City, FL 32405, Phone: 850-785-9209, tom@tomwatsonknives.com; Web: www.tomwatsonknives.com
Specialties: Utility/tactical linerlocks. Patterns: Tactical and utility. Technical: Flat grinds satin finished D2 and Damascus. Prices: Starting at $375. Remarks: Full-time maker. In business since 1978. Mark: Name and city.

WATTELET, MICHAEL A,
PO Box 649, 125 Front, Minocqua, WI 54548, Phone: 715-356-3069, redtroll@frontier.com
Specialties: Working and using straight knives of his design and to customer specs; fantasy knives. Patterns: Daggers, fighters and swords. Technical: Grinds 440C and L6; forges and grinds O1. Silversmith. Prices: $75 to $1000; some to $5000. Remarks: Full-time maker; first knife sold in 1966. Doing business as M and N Arts Ltd. Mark: First initial, last name.

WATTS, JOHNATHAN,
9560 S Hwy 36, Gatesville, TX 76528, Phone: 254-487-2866
Specialties: Traditional folders. Patterns: One and two blade folders in various blade shapes. Technical: Grinds ATS-34 and Damascus on request. Prices: $120 to $400. Remarks: Part-time maker; first knife sold in 1997. Mark: J Watts.

WATTS, WALLY,
9560 S Hwy 36, Gatesville, TX 76528, Phone: 254-223-9669
Specialties: Unique traditional folders of his design. Patterns: One- to five-blade folders and single-blade gents in various blade shapes. Technical: Grinds ATS-34; Damascus on request. Prices: $150 to $400. Remarks: Full-time maker; first

knife sold in 1986. Mark: Last name.

WEBSTER, BILL,
58144 West Clear Lake Rd, Three Rivers, MI 49093, Phone: 269-244-2873, wswebster_5@msn.com Web: www.websterknifeworks.com
Specialties: Working and using straight knives, especially for hunters. His patterns are custom designed. Patterns: Hunters, skinners, camp knives, Bowies and daggers. Technical: Hand-filed blades made of D2 steel only, unless other steel is requested. Preferred handle material is stabilized and exotic wood and stag. Sheaths are made by Green River Leather in Kentucky. Hand-sewn sheaths by Bill Dehn in Three Rivers, MI. Prices: $75 to $500. Remarks: Part-time maker, first knife sold in 1978. Mark: Originally WEB stamped on blade, at present, Webster Knifeworks Three Rivers, MI laser etched on blade.

WEEKS, RYAN,
PO Box 1101, Bountiful, UT 84001, Phone: 801-755-6789, ryan@ryanwknives.com; Web: www.ryanwknives.com
Specialties: Military and Law Enforcement applications as well as hunting and utility designs. Patterns: Fighters, bowies, hunters, and custom designs, I use man made as well as natural wood and exotic handle materials. Technical: Make via forge and stock removal methods, preferred steel includes high carbon, CPM154 CM and ATS34, Damascus and San Mai. Prices: $160 to $750. Remarks: Part-time maker; Business name is "Ryan W. Knives." First knife sold in 2009. Mark: Encircled "Ryan" beneath the crossed "W" UTAH, USA.

WEEVER, JOHN,
1162 Black Hawk Trl., Nemo, TX 76070, Phone: 254-898-9595, john.weever@gmail.com; Web: WeeverKnives.com
Specialties: Traditional hunters (fixed blade, slip joint, and lockback) and tactical. Patterns: See website. Technical: Types of steel: S30V, Damascus or customer choice. Handles in mammoth ivory, oosic, horn, sambar, stag, etc. Sheaths in exotic leathers. Prices: $400 to $1200. Remarks: Stock removal maker full-time; began making knives in 1985. Member of knifemakers guild. Mark: Tang stamp: head of charging elephant with ears extended and WEEVER curved over the top.

WEHNER, RUDY,
297 William Warren Rd, Collins, MS 39428, Phone: 601-765-4997
Specialties: Reproduction antique Bowies and contemporary Bowies in full and miniature. Patterns: Skinners, camp knives, fighters, axes and Bowies. Technical: Grinds 440C, ATS-34, 154CM and Damascus. Prices: $100 to $500; some to $850. Remarks: Full-time maker; first knife sold in 1975. Mark: Last name on Bowies and antiques; full name, city and state on skinners.

WEILAND JR., J REESE,
PO Box 2337, Riverview, FL 33568, Phone: 813-671-0661, RWPHIL413@verizon.net; Web: www.reeseweilandknives.com
Specialties: Hawk bills; tactical to fancy folders. Patterns: Hunters, tantos, Bowies, fantasy knives, spears and some swords. Technical: Grinds ATS-34, 154CM, 440C, D2, O1, A2, Damascus. Titanium hardware on locking liners and button locks. Prices: $150 to $4000. Remarks: Full-time maker, first knife sold in 1978. Knifemakers Guild member since 1988.

WEINAND, GEROME M,
14440 Harpers Bridge Rd, Missoula, MT 59808, Phone: 406-543-0845
Specialties: Working straight knives. Patterns: Bowies, fishing and camp knives, large special hunters. Technical: Grinds O1, 440C, ATS-34, 1084, L6, also stainless Damascus, Aebl and 304; makes all-tool steel Damascus; Dendritic D2 from powdered steel. Heat-treats. Prices: $30 to $100; some to $500. Remarks: Full-time maker; first knife sold in 1982. Mark: Last name.

WEINSTOCK, ROBERT,
PO Box 170028, San Francisco, CA 94117-0028, Phone: 415-731-5968, robertweinstock@att.net
Specialties: Folders, slip joins, lockbacks, autos. Patterns: Daggers, folders. Technical: Grinds A2, O1 and 440C. Chased and hand-carved blades and handles. Also using various Damascus steels from other makers. Prices: $3000 to 7000. Remarks: Full-time maker; first knife sold in 1994. Mark: Last name carved in steel.

WEISS, CHARLES L,
PO BOX 1037, Waddell, AZ 85355, Phone: 623-935-0924, weissknife@live.com
Specialties: High-art straight knives and folders; deluxe period pieces. Patterns: Daggers, fighters, boots, push knives and miniatures. Technical: Grinds 440C, 154CM and ATS-34. Prices: $300 to $1200; some to $2000. Remarks: Full-time maker; first knife sold in 1975. Mark: Name and city.

WELLING, RONALD L,
15446 Lake Ave, Grand Haven, MI 49417, Phone: 616-846-2274
Specialties: Scagel knives of his design or to customer specs. Patterns: Hunters, camp knives, miniatures, bird, trout, folders, double edged, hatchets, skinners and some art pieces. Technical: Forges Damascus 1084 and 1095. Antler, ivory and horn. Prices: $250 to $3000. Remarks: Full-time maker. ABS Journeyman maker. Mark: First initials and or name and last name. City and state. Various scagel kris (1or 2).

WELLING, WILLIAM,
Up-armored Knives, 5437 Pinecliff Dr., West Valley, NY 14171, Phone: 716-942-6031, uparmored@frontier.net; Web: www.up-armored.com
Specialties: Innovative tactical fixed blades each uniquely coated in a variety of Up-armored designed patterns and color schemes. Convexed edged bushcraft knives for the weekend camper, backpacker, or survivalist. Knives developed specifically for tactical operators. Leather- and synthetic-suede-lined

custom knifemakers

Kydex sheaths. Patterns: Modern samples of time tested designs as well as contemporary developed cutting tools. Technical: Stock removal specializing in tested 1095CV and 5160 steels. Prices: $200 to $500. Remarks: Part-time maker; first knife sold in 2010. Mark: Skull rounded up by Up-Armored USA.

WERTH, GEORGE W,
5223 Woodstock Rd, Poplar Grove, IL 61065, Phone: 815-544-4408
Specialties: Period pieces, some fancy. Patterns: Straight fighters, daggers and Bowies. Technical: Forges and grinds O1, 1095 and his Damascus, including mosaic patterns. Prices: $200 to $650; some higher. Remarks: Full-time maker. Doing business as Fox Valley Forge. Mark: Name in logo or initials connected.

WESCOTT, CODY,
5330 White Wing Rd, Las Cruces, NM 88012, Phone: 575-382-5008
Specialties: Fancy and presentation grade working knives. Patterns: Hunters, locking folders and Bowies. Technical: Hollow-grinds D2 and ATS-34; all knives file worked. Offers some engraving. Makes sheaths. Prices: $110 to $500; some to $1200. Remarks: Full-time maker; first knife sold in 1982. Mark: First initial, last name.

WEST, CHARLES A,
1315 S Pine St, Centralia, IL 62801, Phone: 618-532-2777
Specialties: Classic, fancy, high tech, period pieces, traditional and working/using straight knives and folders. Patterns: Bowies, fighters and locking folders. Technical: Grinds ATS-34, O1 and Damascus. Prefers hot blued finishes. Prices: $100 to $1000; some to $2000. Remarks: Full-time maker; first knife sold in 1963. Doing business as West Custom Knives. Mark: Name or name, city and state.

WESTBERG, LARRY,
305 S Western Hills Dr, Algona, IA 50511, Phone: 515-295-9276
Specialties: Traditional and working straight knives of his design and in standard patterns. Patterns: Bowies, hunters, fillets and folders. Technical: Grinds 440C, D2 and 1095. Heat-treats. Uses natural handle materials. Prices: $85 to $600; some to $1000. Remarks: Part-time maker; first knife sold in 1987. Mark: Last name-town and state.

WHEELER, GARY,
351 Old Hwy 48, Clarksville, TN 37040, Phone: 931-552-3092, LR22SHTR@charter.net
Specialties: Working to high end fixed blades. Patterns: Bowies, Hunters, combat knives, daggers and a few folders. Technical: Forges 5160, 1095, 52100 and his own Damascus. Prices: $125 to $2000. Remarks: Full-time maker since 2001, first knife sold in 1985 collaborates/works at B&W Blade Works. ABS Journeyman Smith 2008. Mark: Stamped last name.

WHEELER, NICK,
140 Studebaker Rd., Castle Rock, WA 98611, Phone: 360-967-2357, merckman99@yahoo.com
Specialties: Bowies, integrals, fighters, hunters and daggers. Technical: Forges W2, W1, 1095, 52100 and 1084. Makes own damascus, from random pattern to complex mosaics. Also grinds stainless and other more modern alloys. Does own heat-treating and leather work. Also commissions leather work from Paul Long. Prices: Start at $250. Remarks: Full-time maker; ABS member since 2001. Journeyman bladesmith. Mark: Last name.

WHEELER, ROBERT J,
289 S Jefferson, Bradley, IL 60915, Phone: 815-932-5854, b2btaz@brmemc.net

WHETSELL, ALEX,
PO Box 215, Haralson, GA 30229, Phone: 770-599-8012, www.KnifeKits.com
Specialties: Knifekits.com, a source for fold locking liner type and straight knife kits. These kits are industry standard for folding knife kits. Technical: Many selections of colored G10 carbon fiber and wood handle material for kits, as well as bulk sizes for the custom knifemaker, heat treated folding knife pivots, screws, bushings, etc.

WHIPPLE, WESLEY A,
1002 Shoshoni St, Thermopolis, WY 82443, Phone: 307-921-2445, wildernessknife@yahoo.com
Specialties: Working straight knives, some fancy. Patterns: Hunters, Bowies, camp knives, fighters. Technical: Forges high-carbon steels, Damascus, offers relief carving and silver wire inlay and checkering. Prices: $300 to $1400; some higher. Remarks: Full-time maker; first knife sold in 1989. A.K.A. Wilderness Knife and Forge. Mark: Last name/JS.

WHITE, BRYCE,
1415 W Col Glenn Rd, Little Rock, AR 72210, Phone: 501-821-2956
Specialties: Hunters, fighters, makes Damascus, file work, handmade only. Technical: L6, 1075, 1095, O1 steels used most. Patterns: Will do any pattern or use his own. Prices: $200 to $300. Sold first knife in 1995. Mark: White.

WHITE, DALE,
525 CR 212, Sweetwater, TX 79556, Phone: 325-798-4178, dalew@taylortel.net
Specialties: Working and using knives. Patterns: Hunters, skinners, utilities and Bowies. Technical: Grinds 440C, offers file work, fancy pins and scrimshaw by Sherry Sellers. Prices: From $45 to $300. Remarks: Sold first knife in 1975. Mark: Full name, city and state.

WHITE, GARRETT,
871 Sarijon Rd, Hartwell, GA 30643, Phone: 706-376-5944
Specialties: Gentlemen folders, fancy straight knives. Patterns: Locking liners and hunting fixed blades. Technical: Grinds 440C, S30V, and stainless Damascus. Prices: $150 to $1000. Remarks: Part-time maker. Mark: Name.

WHITE, JOHN PAUL,
231 S Bayshore, Valparaiso, FL 32580, Phone: 850-729-9174, johnwhiteknives@gmail.com
Specialties: Forged hunters, fighters, traditional Bowies and personal carry knives with handles of natural materials and fittings with detailed file work. Technical: Forges carbon steel and own Damascus. Prices: $500 to $3500 Remarks: Master Smith, American Bladesmith Society. Mark: First initial, last name.

WHITE, LOU,
7385 Red Bud Rd NE, Ranger, GA 30734, Phone: 706-334-2273

WHITE, RICHARD T,
359 Carver St, Grosse Pointe Farms, MI 48236, Phone: 313-881-4690

WHITE, ROBERT J,
RR 1 641 Knox Rd 900 N, Gilson, IL 61436, Phone: 309-289-4487
Specialties: Working knives, some deluxe. Patterns: Bird and trout knives, hunters, survival knives and locking folders. Technical: Grinds A2, D2 and 440C; commercial Damascus. Heat-treats. Prices: $125 to $250; some to $600. Remarks: Full-time maker; first knife sold in 1976. Mark: Last name in script.

WHITE JR., ROBERT J BUTCH,
RR 1, Gilson, IL 61436, Phone: 309-289-4487
Specialties: Folders of all sizes. Patterns: Hunters, fighters, boots and folders. Technical: Forges Damascus; grinds tool and stainless steel. Prices: $500 to $1800. Remarks: Spare-time maker; first knife sold in 1980. Mark: Last name in block letters.

WHITENECT, JODY,
, Halifax County, Elderbank, NS, CANADA B0N 1K0, Phone: 902-384-2511
Specialties: Fancy and embellished working/using straight knives of his design and to customer specs. Patterns: Bowies, fighters and hunters. Technical: Forges 1095 and O1; forges and grinds ATS-34. Various filework on blades and bolsters. Prices: $200 to $400; some to $800. Remarks: Part-time maker; first knife sold in 1996. Mark: Longhorn stamp or engraved.

WHITESELL, J. DALE,
P.O. Box 455, Stover, MO 65078, Phone: 573-569-0753, dalesknives@yahoo.com; Web: whitesell-knives.webs.com
Specialties: Fixed blade working knives, a nd some collector pieces. Patterns: Hunting and skinner knives, camp knives, and kitchen knives. Technical: Blades ground from O1, 1095, and 440C in hollow, flat and saber grinds. Wood, bone, deer antler, and G10 are basic handle materials. Prices: $100 to $450. Remarks: Part-time maker, first knife sold in 2003. Doing business as Dale's Knives. All knives have serial number to indicate steel (since June 2010). Mark: Whitesell on the left side of the blade.

WHITLEY, L WAYNE,
1675 Carrow Rd, Chocowinity, NC 27817-9495, Phone: 252-946-5648

WHITLEY, WELDON G,
4308 N Robin Ave, Odessa, TX 79764, Phone: 432-530-0448, Fax: 432-530-0448, wgwhitley@juno.com
Specialties: Working knives of his design or to customer specs. Patterns: Hunters, folders and various double-edged knives. Technical: Grinds 440C, 154CM and ATS-34. Prices: $150 to $1250. Mark: Name, address, road-runner logo.

WHITTAKER, ROBERT E,
PO Box 204, Mill Creek, PA 17060
Specialties: Using straight knives. Has a line of knives for buckskinners. Patterns: Hunters, skinners and Bowies. Technical: Grinds O1, A2 and D2. Offers filework. Prices: $35 to $100. Remarks: Part-time maker; first knife sold in 1980. Mark: Last initial or full initials.

WHITTAKER, WAYNE,
2900 Woodland Ct, Metamore, MI 48455, Phone: 810-797-5315, lindorwayne@yahoo.com
Specialties: Liner locks and autos. Patterns: Folders. Technical: Damascus, mammoth, ivory, and tooth. Prices: $500 to $1500. Remarks: Full-time maker. Mark: Inside of backbar.

WICK, JONATHAN P.,
300 Cole Ave., Bisbee, AZ 85603, Phone: 520-227-5228, vikingwick@aol.com Web: jpwickbladeworks.com
Specialties: Fixed blades, Bowies, hunters, neck knives, copper clad sheaths, collectibles, most handle styles and materials. Technical: Forged blades and own Damascus, along with shibuichi, mokume, lost wax casting. Prices: $250 - $1800 and up. Remarks: Full-time maker, ABS member, sold first knife in 2008. Mark: J P Wick, also on small blades a JP over a W.

WICKER, DONNIE R,
2544 E 40th Ct, Panama City, FL 32405, Phone: 904-785-9158
Specialties: Traditional working and using straight knives of his design or to customer specs. Patterns: Hunters, fighters and slip-joint folders. Technical: Grinds 440C, ATS-34, D2 and 154CM. Heat-treats and does hardness testing. Prices: $90 to $200; some to $400. Remarks: Part-time maker; first knife sold in 1975. Mark: First and middle initials, last name.

WIGGINS, BILL,
105 Kaolin Lane, Canton, NC 28716, Phone: 828-226-2551, wncbill@bellsouth.net Web: www.wigginsknives.com
Specialties: Forged working knives. Patterns: Hunters, Bowies, camp knives and utility knives of own design or will work with customer on design. Technical: Forges 1084 and 52100 as well as making own Damascus. Prices: $250 - $1500. Remarks: Part-time maker. First knife sold in 1989. ABS board member. Mark: Wiggins

WIGGINS, HORACE,
203 Herndon Box 152, Mansfield, LA 71502, Phone: 318-872-4471
Specialties: Fancy working knives. Patterns: Straight and folding hunters. Technical: Grinds O1, D2 and 440C. Prices: $90 to $275. Remarks: Part-time maker; first knife sold in 1970. Mark: Name, city and state in diamond logo.

WILBURN, AARON
2521 Hilltop Dr., #364, Redding, CA 96002, Phone: 530-227-2827, wilburnforge@yahoo.com; Web: www.wilburnforge.com
Patterns: Daggers, bowies, fighters, hunters and slip-joint folders. Technical: Forges own damascus and works with high-carbon steel. Prices: $500 to $5,000. Remarks: Full-time maker and ABS master smith. Mark: Wilburn Forge.

WILCHER, WENDELL L,
RR 6 Box 6573, Palestine, TX 75801, Phone: 903-549-2530
Specialties: Fantasy, miniatures and working/using straight knives and folders of his design and to customer specs. Patterns: Fighters, hunters, locking folders. Technical: Hand works (hand file and hand sand knives), not grind. Prices: $75 to $250; some to $600. Remarks: Part-time maker; first knife sold in 1987. Mark: Initials, year, serial number.

WILKINS, MITCHELL,
15523 Rabon Chapel Rd, Montgomery, TX 77316, Phone: 936-588-2696, mwilkins@consolidated.net

WILLEY, WG,
14210 Sugar Hill Rd, Greenwood, DE 19950, Phone: 302-349-4070, Web: www.willeyknives.com
Specialties: Fancy working straight knives. Patterns: Small game knives, Bowies and throwing knives. Technical: Grinds 440C and 154CM. Prices: $350 to $600; some to $1500. Remarks: Part-time maker; first knife sold in 1975. Owns retail store. Mark: Last name inside map logo.

WILLIAMS, JASON L,
PO Box 67, Wyoming, RI 02898, Phone: 401-539-8353, Fax: 401-539-0252
Specialties: Fancy and high tech folders of his design, co-inventor of the Axis Lock. Patterns: Fighters, locking folders, automatics and fancy pocket knives. Technical: Forges Damascus and other steels by request. Uses exotic handle materials and precious metals. Offers inlaid spines and gemstone thumb knobs. Prices: $1000 and up. Remarks: Full-time maker; first knife sold in 1989. Mark: First and last initials on pivot.

WILLIAMS, MICHAEL,
333 Cherrybark Tr., Broken Bow, OK 74728, Phone: 580-420-3051, hforge@pine-net.com
Specialties: Functional, personalized, edged weaponry. Working and collectible art. Patterns: Bowies, hunters, camp knives, daggers, others. Technical: Forges high carbon steel and own forged Damascus. Prices: $500 - $12000. Remarks: Full-time ABS Master Smith. Mark: Williams MS.

WILLIAMS, ROBERT,
15962 State Rt. 267, East Liverpool, OH 43920, Phone: 203-979-0803, wurdmeister@gmail.com; Web: www.customstraightrazors.com
Specialties: Custom straight razors with a philosophy that form must follow function, so shaving performance drives designs and aesthetics. Technical: Stock removal and forging, working with 1095, O1 and damascus. Natural handle materials and synthetics, accommodating any and all design requests and can incorporate gold inlays, scrimshaw, hand engraving and jewel setting. All work done in maker's shop, sole-source maker shipping worldwide. Remarks: Full-time maker; first straight razor in 2005. Mark: Robert Williams - Handmade, USA with a hammer separating the two lines.

WILLIAMS JR., RICHARD,
1440 Nancy Circle, Morristown, TN 37814, Phone: 615-581-0059
Specialties: Working and using straight knives of his design or to customer specs. Patterns: Hunters, dirks and utility/camp knives. Technical: Forges 5160 and uses file steel. Hand-finish is standard; offers filework. Prices: $80 to $180; some to $250. Remarks: Spare-time maker; first knife sold in 1985. Mark: Last initial or full initials.

WILLIAMSON, TONY,
Rt 3 Box 503, Siler City, NC 27344, Phone: 919-663-3551
Specialties: Flint knapping: knives made of obsidian flakes and flint with wood, antler or bone for handles. Patterns: Skinners, daggers and flake knives. Technical: Blades have width/thickness ratio of at least 4 to 1. Hafts with methods available to prehistoric man. Prices: $58 to $160. Remarks: Student of Errett Callahan. Mark: Initials and number code to identify year and number of knives made.

WILLIS, BILL,
RT 7 Box 7549, Ava, MO 65608, Phone: 417-683-4326
Specialties: Forged blades, Damascus and carbon steel. Patterns: Cable, random or ladder lamented. Technical: Professionally heat treated blades. Prices: $75 to $600. Remarks: Lifetime guarantee on all blades against breakage. All work done by maker; including leather work. Mark: WF.

WILLUMSEN, MIKKEL,
Nyrnberggade 23, S Copenhagen, DENMARK 2300, Phone: 4531176333, mw@willumsen-cph.com Web: www.wix.com/willumsen/urbantactical
Specialties: Folding knives, fixed blades, and balisongs. Also kitchen knives. Patterns: Primarily influenced by design that is function and quality based. Tactical style knives inspired by classical designs mixed with modern tactics. Technical: Uses CPM 154, RW 134, S30V, and carbon fiber titanium G10 for handles. Prices: Starting at $600.

WILSON, CURTIS M,
PO Box 383, Burleson, TX 76097, Phone: 817-295-3732, cwknifeman2026@att.net; Web: www.cwilsonknives.com
Specialties: Traditional working/using knives, fixed blade, folders, slip joint, LinerLock® and lock back knives. Art knives, presentation grade Bowies, folder repair, heat treating services. Sub-zero quench. Patterns: Hunters, camp knives, military combat, single and multi-blade folders. Dr's knives large or small or custom design knives. Technical: Grinds ATS-34, 440C 52100, D2, S30V, CPM 154, mokume gane, engraves, scrimshaw, sheaths leather of kykex heat treating and file work. Prices: $150-750. Remarks: Part-time maker since 1984. Sold first knife in 1993. Mark: Curtis Wilson in ribbon or Curtis Wilson with hand made in a half moon.

WILSON, JAMES G,
PO Box 4024, Estes Park, CO 80517, Phone: 303-586-3944
Specialties: Bronze Age knives; Medieval and Scottish-styles; tomahawks. Patterns: Bronze knives, daggers, swords, spears and battle axes; 12-inch steel Misericorde daggers, sgian dubhs, "his and her" skinners, bird and fish knives, capers, boots and daggers. Technical: Casts bronze; grinds D2, 440C and ATS-34. Prices: $49 to $400; some to $1300. Remarks: Part-time maker; first knife sold in 1975. Mark: WilsonHawk.

WILSON, MIKE,
1416 McDonald Rd, Hayesville, NC 28904, Phone: 828-389-8145
Specialties: Fancy working and using straight knives of his design or to customer specs, folders. Patterns: Hunters, Bowies, utility knives, gut hooks, skinners, fighters and miniatures. Technical: Hollow grinds 440C, L6, O1 and D2. Mirror finishes are standard. Offers filework. Prices: $50 to $600. Remarks: Full-time maker; first knife sold in 1985. Mark: Last name.

WILSON, PHILIP C,
SEAMOUNT KNIFEWORKS, PO Box 846, Mountain Ranch, CA 95246, Phone: 209-754-1990, seamount@bigplanet.com; Web: www.seamountknifeworks.com
Specialties: Working knives; emphasis on salt water fillet knives and utility hunters of his design. Patterns: Fishing knives, hunters, utility knives. Technical: Grinds CPM10V, S-90V, CPMS110V, K390, K294, CPM154, M-390, ELMAX. Heat-treats and Rockwell tests all blades. Prices: Start at $400. Remarks: First knife sold in 1985. Doing business as Sea-Mount Knife Works. Mark: Signature.

WILSON, RON,
2639 Greenwood Ave, Morro Bay, CA 93442, Phone: 805-772-3381
Specialties: Classic and fantasy straight knives of his design. Patterns: Daggers, fighters, swords and axes, mostly all miniatures. Technical: Forges and grinds Damascus and various tool steels; grinds meteorite. Uses gold, precious stones and exotic wood. Prices: Vary. Remarks: Part-time maker; first knives sold in 1995. Mark: Stamped first and last initials.

WILSON, RW,
PO Box 2012, Weirton, WV 26062, Phone: 304-723-2771, rwknives@comcast.net
Specialties: Working straight knives; period pieces. Patterns: Bowies, tomahawks and patch knives. Technical: Grinds 440C; scrimshaws. Prices: $85 to $175; some to $1000. Remarks: Part-time maker; first knife sold in 1966. Knifemaker supplier. Offers free knife-making lessons. Mark: Name in tomahawk.

WILSON, STAN,
8931 Pritcher Rd, Lithia, FL 33547, Phone: 727-461-1992, swilson@stanwilsonknives.com; Web: www.stanwilsonknives.com
Specialties: Fancy folders and automatics of his own design. Patterns: Locking liner folders, single and dual action autos, daggers. Technical: Stock removal, uses Damascus, stainless and high carbon steels, prefers ivory and pearl, Damascus with blued finishes and filework. Prices: $400 and up. Remarks: Member of Knifemakers Guild and Florida Knifemakers Association. Full-time maker will do custom orders. Mark: Name in script.

WILSON, VIC,
9130 Willow Branch Dr, Olive Branch, MS 38654, Phone: 901-233-7126, vdubjr55@earthlink.net; Web: www.knivesbyvic.com
Specialties: Classic working and using knives and folders. Patterns: Hunters, boning, utility, camp, my patterns or customers. Technical: Grinds O1 and D2. Also does own heat treating. Offer file work and decorative liners on folders. Fabricate custom leather sheaths for all knives. Prices: $150 to $400. Remarks: Part-time maker, first knife sold in 1989. Mark: Etched V over W with oval circle around it, name, Memphis, TN.

WINGO, GARY,
240 Ogeechee, Ramona, OK 74061, Phone: 918-536-1067, wingg_2000@yahoo.com; Web: www.geocities.com/wingg_2000/gary.html
Specialties: Folder specialist. Steel 44OC, D2, others on request. Handle bone-stag, others on request. Patterns: Trapper three-blade stockman, four-blade congress, single- and two-blade barlows. Prices: 150 to $400. Mark: First knife sold 1994. Steer head with Wingo Knives or Straight line Wingo Knives.

WINGO, PERRY,
22 55th St, Gulfport, MS 39507, Phone: 228-863-3193
Specialties: Traditional working straight knives. Patterns: Hunters, skinners, Bowies and fishing knives. Technical: Grinds 440C. Prices: $75 to $1000. Remarks: Full-time maker; first knife sold in 1988. Mark: Last name.

WINKLER, DANIEL,
PO Box 2166, Blowing Rock, NC 28605, Phone: 828-295-9156, danielwinkler@bellsouth.net; Web: www.winklerknives.com
Specialties: Forged cutlery styled in the tradition of an era past as well as

producing a custom-made stock removal line. Patterns: Fixed blades, friction folders, lock back folders, and axes/tomahawks. Technical: Forges, grinds, and heat treats carbon steels, specialty steels, and his own Damascus steel. Prices: $350 to $4000+. Remarks: Full-time maker since 1988. Exclusively offers leatherwork by Karen Shook. ABS Master Smith; Knifemakers Guild voting member. Mark: Hand forged: Dwinkler; Stock removal: Winkler Knives

WINN, MARVIN,
Maxcutter Custom Knives, 8711 Oakwood Ln., Frisco, TX 75035, Phone: 214-471-7012, maxcutter03@yahoo.com Web: www.maxcutterknives.com
Patterns: Hunting knives, some tactical and some miniatures. Technical: 1095, 5160, 154 CM, 12C27, CPMS30V and CPM154CM, Damascus or customer specs. Stock removal. Prices: $75 - $850. Remarks: Part-time maker. First knife made in 2002. Mark: Name, city, state.

WINN, TRAVIS A.,
558 E 3065 S, Salt Lake City, UT 84106, Phone: 801-467-5957
Specialties: Fancy working knives and knives to customer specs. Patterns: Hunters, fighters, boots, Bowies and fancy daggers, some miniatures, tantos and fantasy knives. Technical: Grinds D2 and 440C. Embellishes. Prices: $125 to $500; some higher. Remarks: Part-time maker; first knife sold in 1976. Mark: TRAV stylized.

WINSTON, DAVID,
1671 Red Holly St, Starkville, MS 39759, Phone: 601-323-1028
Specialties: Fancy and traditional knives of his design and to customer specs. Patterns: Bowies, daggers, hunters, boot knives and folders. Technical: Grinds 440C, ATS-34 and D2. Offers filework; heat-treats. Prices: $40 to $750; some higher. Remarks: Part-time maker; first knife sold in 1984. Offers lifetime sharpening for original owner. Mark: Last name.

WIRTZ, ACHIM,
Mittelstrasse 58, Wuerselen, GERMANY 52146, Phone: 0049-2405-462-486, wootz@web.de
Specialties: Medieval, Scandinavian and Middle East-style knives. Technical: Forged blades only, Damascus steel, Wootz, Mokume. Prices: Start at $200. Remarks: Part-time maker. First knife sold in 1997. Mark: Stylized initials.

WISE, DONALD,
304 Bexhill Rd, St Leonardo-On-Sea, East Sussex, ENGLAND TN3 8AL
Specialties: Fancy and embellished working straight knives to customer specs. Patterns: Hunters, Bowies and daggers. Technical: Grinds Sandvik 12C27, D2 D3 and O1. Scrimshaws. Prices: $110 to $300; some to $500. Remarks: Full-time maker; first knife sold in 1983. Mark: KNIFECRAFT.

WOLF, BILL,
4618 N 79th Ave, Phoenix, AZ 85033, Phone:623-910-3147, bwcustomknives143@gmail.com Web: billwolfcustomknives.com
Specialties: Investment grade knives. Patterns: Own designs or customer's. Technical: Grinds stainless and all steels. Prices: $400 to ? Remarks: First knife made in 1988. Mark: WOLF

WOLF JR., WILLIAM LYNN,
4006 Frank Rd, Lagrange, TX 78945, Phone: 409-247-4626

WOOD, ALAN,
Greenfield Villa, Greenhead, Brampton, ENGLAND CA8 7HH, info@alanwoodknives.com; Web: www.alanwoodknives.com
Specialties: High-tech working straight knives of his design. Patterns: Hunters, utility/camp and bushcraft knives. Technical: Grinds 12C27, RWL-34, stainless Damascus and O1. Blades are cryogenic treated. Prices: $200 to $800; some to $1,200. Remarks: Full-time maker; first knife sold in 1979. Not currently taking orders. Mark: Full name with stag tree logo.

WOOD, OWEN DALE,
6492 Garrison St, Arvada, CO 80004-3157, Phone: 303-456-2748, wood.owen@gmail.com; Web: www.owenwoodknives.net
Specialties: Folding knives and daggers. Patterns: Own Damascus, specialties in 456 composite blades. Technical: Materials: Damascus stainless steel, exotic metals, gold, rare handle materials. Prices: $1000 to $9000. Remarks: Folding knives in art deco and art noveau themes. Full-time maker from 1981. Mark: OWEN WOOD.

WOOD, WEBSTER,
22041 Shelton Trail, Atlanta, MI 49709, Phone: 989-785-2996, mainganikan@src-milp.com
Specialties: Works mainly in stainless; art knives, Bowies, hunters and folders. Remarks: Full-time maker; first knife sold in 1980. Retired guild member. All engraving done by maker. Mark: Initials inside shield and name.

WORLEY, JOEL A.,
PO BOX 64, Maplewood, OH 45340, Phone: 937-638-9518, j.a.worleyknives@woh.rr.com
Specialties: Bowies, hunters, fighters, utility/camp knives also period style friction folders. Patterns: Classic styles, recurves, his design or customer specified. Technical: Most knives are fileworked and include a custom made leather sheath. Forges 5160, W2, Cru forge V, files own Damascus of 1080 and 15N20. Prices: $250 and up. Remarks: Part-time maker. ABS member. First knife sold in 2005. Mark: First name, middle initial and last name over a shark incorporating initials.

WRIGHT, KEVIN,
671 Leland Valley Rd W, Quilcene, WA 98376-9517, Phone: 360-765-3589, kevinw@ptpc.com
Specialties: Fancy working or collector knives to customer specs. Patterns:

Hunters, boots, buckskinners, miniatures. Technical: Forges and grinds L6, 1095, 440C and his own Damascus. Prices: $75 to $500; some to $2000. Remarks: Part-time maker; first knife sold in 1978. Mark: Last initial in anvil.

WRIGHT, L T,
1523 Pershing Ave, Steubenville, OH 43952, Phone: 740-282-4947, knifemkr@sbcglobal.net; Web: www.ltwrightknives.com
Specialties: Hunting and tactical knives. Patterns: Drop point hunters, bird, trout and tactical. Technical: Grinds D2, 440C and O1. Remarks: Full-time maker.

WRIGHT, RICHARD S,
PO Box 201, 111 Hilltop Dr, Carolina, RI 02812, Phone: 401-364-3579, rswswitchblades@hotmail.com; Web: www.richardswright.com
Specialties: Bolster release switchblades, tactical automatics. Patterns: Folding fighters, gents pocket knives, one-of-a-kind high-grade automatics. Technical: Reforges and grinds various makers Damascus. Uses a variety of tool steels. Uses natural handle material such as ivory and pearl, extensive file-work on most knives. Prices: $850 and up. Remarks: Full-time knifemaker with background as a gunsmith. Made first folder in 1991. Mark: RSW on blade, all folders are serial numbered.

WRIGHT, ROBERT A,
21 Wiley Bottom Rd, savannah, GA 31411, Phone: 912-598-8239; Cell: 912-656-9085, Fax: 912-598-8239, robwright57@yahoo.com; Web: www.RobWrightKnives.com
Specialties: Fixed blade fighters, hunting and skinning, fillets, small backpacker knives.Patterns: Customer and maker designs; sculpted handles of high quality materials.Technical: All types of steel (CPMS30V, D2< 440C, Damascus, etc.).Prices: $200 and up depending on design and materialsRemarks: Full-time maker, member of the Georgia knifemakers guild. Proven high quality steel and handle materials; exotic wood and other materials. Mark: Etched maple leaf with makers name.

WRIGHT, TIMOTHY,
PO Box 3746, Sedona, AZ 86340, Phone: 928-282-4180
Specialties: High-tech folders and working knives. Patterns: Interframe locking folders, non-inlaid folders, straight hunters and kitchen knives. Technical: Grinds BG-42, AEB-L, K190 and Cowry X; works with new steels. All folders can disassemble and are furnished with tools. Prices: $150 to $1800; some to $3000. Remarks: Full-time maker; first knife sold in 1975. Mark: Last name and type of steel used.

WUERTZ, TRAVIS,
2487 E Hwy 287, Casa Grande, AZ 85222, Phone: 520-723-4432

WULF, DERRICK,
25 Sleepy Hollow Rd, Essex, VT 05452, Phone: 802-777-8766, dickwulf@yahoo.com Web: www.dicksworkshop.com
Specialties: Makes predominantly forged fixed blade knives using carbon steels and his own Damascus.Mark: "WULF".

WYATT, WILLIAM R,
Box 237, Rainelle, WV 25962, Phone: 304-438-5494
Specialties: Classic and working knives of all designs. Patterns: Hunters and utility knives. Technical: Forges and grinds saw blades, files and rasps. Prefers stag handles. Prices: $45 to $95; some to $350. Remarks: Part-time maker; first knife sold in 1990. Mark: Last name in star with knife logo.

WYLIE, TOM,
Peak Knives, 2 Maun Close, Sutton-In-Ashfield, Notts, England NG17 5JG, tom@peakknives.com
Specialties: Knives for adventure sports and hunting, mainly fixed blades. Technical: Damasteel or European stainless steel used predominantly, handle material to suit purpose, embellished as required. Work can either be all handmade or CNC machined. Prices: $450+. Remarks: Pro-Am maker. Mark: Ogram "tinne" in circle of life, sometimes with addition of maker's name.

Y

YASHINSKI, JOHN L,
207 N Platt, PO Box 1284, Red Lodge, MT 59068, Phone: 406-446-3916
Specialties: Native American beaded sheaths, painted rawhide sheaths and tack sheaths. Prices: Vary.

YEATES, JOE A,
730 Saddlewood Circle, Spring, TX 77381, Phone: 281-367-2765, joeyeates291@cs.com; Web: www.yeatesBowies.com
Specialties: Bowies and period pieces. Patterns: Bowies, toothpicks and combat knives. Technical: Grinds 440C, D2 and ATS-34. Prices: $600 to $2500. Remarks: Full-time maker; first knife sold in 1975. Mark: Last initial within outline of Texas; or last initial.

YESKOO, RICHARD C,
76 Beekman Rd, Summit, NJ 07901

YONEYAMA, CHICCHI K.,
5-19-8 Nishikicho, Tachikawa-City, Tokyo, Japan 190-0022, Phone: 081-1-9047449370, chicchi.ky1007@gmail.com; Web: https://sites.google.com/site/chicchiyoneyama/
Specialties: Folders, hollow ground, lockback and slip-joint folders with interframe handles. Patterns: Pocketknives, desk and daily-carry small folders. Technical: Stock-removal method on ATS-34, 440C, V10 and SG2/damascus blade steels. Prices: $300 to $1,000 and up. Remarks: Full-time maker; first knife sold in 1999. Mark: Saber tiger mark with logos/Chicchi K. Yoneyama.

YORK, DAVID C,
PO Box 3166, Chino Valley, AZ 86323, Phone: 928-636-1709, dmatj@msn.com
Specialties: Working straight knives and folders. Patterns: Prefers small hunters and skinners; locking folders. Technical: Grinds D2. Prices: $75 to $300; some to $600. Remarks: Part-time maker; first knife sold in 1975. Mark: Last name.

YOSHIHARA, YOSHINDO,
8-17-11 Takasago Katsushi, Tokyo, JAPAN

YOSHIKAZU, KAMADA,
540-3 Kaisaki Niuta-cho, Tokushima, JAPAN, Phone: 0886-44-2319

YOSHIO, MAEDA,
3-12-11 Chuo-cho tamashima, Kurashiki-city, Okayama, JAPAN, Phone: 086-525-2375

YOUNG, BUD,
Box 336, Port Hardy, BC, CANADA V0N 2P0, Phone: 250-949-6478
Specialties: Fixed blade, working knives, some fancy. Patterns: Drop-points to skinners. Technical: Hollow or flat grind, 5160, 440C, mostly ATS-34, satin finish. Using supplied damascus at times. Prices: $150 to $2000 CDN. Remarks: Spare-time maker; making knives since 1962; first knife sold in 1985. Not taking orders at this time, sell as produced. Mark: Name.

YOUNG, CLIFF,
Fuente De La Cibeles No 5, Atascadero, San Miguel De Allende, GJ, MEXICO 37700, Phone: 011-52-415-2-57-11
Specialties: Working knives. Patterns: Hunters, fighters and fishing knives. Technical: Grinds all; offers D2, 440C and 154CM. Prices: Start at $250. Remarks: Part-time maker; first knife sold in 1980. Mark: Name.

YOUNG, ERROL,
4826 Storey Land, Alton, IL 62002, Phone: 618-466-4707
Specialties: Traditional working straight knives and folders. Patterns: Wide range, including tantos, Bowies, miniatures and multi-blade folders. Technical: Grinds D2, 440C and ATS-34. Prices: $75 to $650; some to $800. Remarks: Part-time maker; first knife sold in 1987. Mark: Last name with arrow.

YOUNG, GEORGE,
713 Pinoak Dr, Kokomo, IN 46901, Phone: 765-457-8893
Specialties: Fancy/embellished and traditional straight knives and folders of his design and to customer specs. Patterns: Hunters, fillet/camp knives and locking folders. Technical: Grinds 440C, CPM440V, and stellite 6K. Fancy ivory, black pearl and stag for handles. Filework: all stellite construction (6K and 25 alloys). Offers engraving. Prices: $350 to $750; some $1500 to $3000. Remarks: Full-time maker; first knife sold in 1954. Doing business as Young's Knives. Mark: Last name integral inside Bowie.

YOUNG, JOHN,
483 E. 400 S, Ephraim, UT 84627, Phone: 435-340-1417 or 435-283-4555
Patterns: Fighters, hunters and bowies. Technical: Stainless steel blades, including ATS-34, 440C and CTS-40CP. Prices: $800 to $5,000. Remarks: Full-time maker since 2006; first knife sold in 1997. Mark: Name, city and state.

YOUNG, RAYMOND L,
CUTLER/BLADESMITH, 2922 Hwy 188E, Mt. Ida, AR 71957, Phone: 870-867-3947
Specialties: Cutler-Bladesmith, sharpening service. Patterns: Hunter, skinners, fighters, no guard, no ricasso, no handle. Technical: Edge tempered 1095, 516C, mosaic handles, water buffalo and exotic woods. Prices: $100 and up. Remarks: Federal contractor since 1995. Surgical steel sharpening. Mark: R.

YURCO, MICKEY,
PO Box 712, Canfield, OH 44406, Phone: 330-533-4928, shorinki@aol.com
Specialties: Working straight knives. Patterns: Hunters, utility knives, Bowies and fighters, push knives, claws and other hideouts. Technical: Grinds 440C, ATS-34 and 154CM; likes mirror and satin finishes. Prices: $20 to $500. Remarks: Part-time maker; first knife sold in 1983. Mark: Name, steel, serial number.

Z

ZACCAGNINO JR., DON,
2256 Bacom Point Rd, Pahokee, FL 33476-2622, Phone: 561-985-0303, zackknife@gmail.com Web: www.zackknives.com
Specialties: Working knives and some period pieces of their designs. Patterns: Heavy-duty hunters, axes and Bowies; a line of light-weight hunters, fillets and personal knives. Technical: Grinds 440C and 17-4 PH; highly finished in complex handle and blade treatments. Prices: $165 to $500; some to $2500. Remarks: Part-time maker; first knife sold in 1969 by Don Zaccagnino Sr. Mark: ZACK, city and state inside oval.

ZAFEIRIADIS, KONSTANTINOS,
Dionyson Street, Marathon Attiki, Greece 19005, Phone: 011-30697724-5771 or 011-30697400-6245, info@kzknives.com; Web: www.kzknives.com
Specialties: Fixed blades, one-of-a-kind swords with bronze fittings made using the lost wax method. Patterns: Ancient Greek, central Asian, Viking, bowies, hunting knives, fighters, daggers. Technical: Forges 5160, O1 and maker's own damascus. Prices: $1,100 and up. Remarks: Full-time maker; first knife sold in 2010. Mark: (backward K)ZK.

ZAHM, KURT,
488 Rio Casa, Indialantic, FL 32903, Phone: 407-777-4860
Specialties: Working straight knives of his design or to customer specs. Patterns: Daggers, fancy fighters, Bowies, hunters and utility knives. Technical: Grinds D2, 440C; likes filework. Prices: $75 to $1000. Remarks: Part-time maker; first knife sold in 1985. Mark: Last name.

ZAKABI, CARL S,
PO Box 893161, Mililani Town, HI 96789-0161, Phone: 808-626-2181
Specialties: User-grade straight knives of his design, cord wrapped and bare steel handles exclusively. Patterns: Fighters, hunters and utility/camp knives. Technical: Grinds 440C and ATS-34. Prices: $90 to $400. Remarks: Spare-time maker; first knife sold in 1988. Doing business as Zakabi's Knifeworks LLC. Mark: Last name and state inside a Hawaiian sharktooth dagger.

ZAKHAROV, GLADISTON,
Bairro Rio Comprido, Rio Comprido Jacarei, Jacaret, SP, BRAZIL 12302-070, Phone: 55 12 3958 4021, Fax: 55 12 3958 4103, arkhip@terra.com.br; Web: www.arkhip.com.br
Specialties: Using straight knives of his design. Patterns: Hunters, kitchen, utility/camp and barbecue knives. Technical: Grinds his own "secret steel." Prices: $30 to $200. Remarks: Full-time maker. Mark: Arkhip Special Knives.

ZBORIL, TERRY,
5320 CR 130, Caldwell, TX 77836, Phone: 979-535-4157, tzboril@tconline.net
Specialties: ABS Journeyman Smith.

ZEMBKO III, JOHN,
140 Wilks Pond Rd, Berlin, CT 06037, Phone: 860-828-3503, johnzembko@hotmail.com
Specialties: Working knives of his design or to customer specs. Patterns: Likes to use stabilized high-figured woods. Technical: Grinds ATS-34, A2, D2; forges O1, 1095; grinds Damascus. Prices: $50 to $400; some higher. Remarks: First knife sold in 1987. Mark: Name.

ZEMITIS, JOE,
14 Currawong Rd, Cardiff Heights, NSW, AUSTRALIA 2285, Phone: 0249549907, jjvzem@bigpond.com
Specialties: Traditional working straight knives. Patterns: Hunters, Bowies, tantos, fighters and camp knives. Technical: Grinds O1, D2, W2 and 440C; makes his own Damascus. Embellishes; offers engraving. Prices: $150 to $3000. Remarks: Full-time maker; first knife sold in 1983. Mark: First initial, last name and country, or last name.

ZERMENO, WILLIAM D.,
9131 Glenshadow Dr, Houston, TX 77088, Phone: 281-726-2459, will@wdzknives.com Web: www.wdzknives.com
Specialties: Tactical/utility folders and fixed blades. Patterns: Frame lock and liner lock folders the majority of which incorporate flippers and utility fixed blades. Technical: Grinds CPM 154, S30V, 3V and stainless Damascus. Prices: $250 - $600. Remarks: Part-time maker, first knife sold in 2008. Doing business as www.wdzknives.com. Mark: WDZ over logo.

ZIMA, MICHAEL F,
732 State St, Ft. Morgan, CO 80701, Phone: 970-867-6078, Web: http://www.zimaknives.com
Specialties: Working and collector quality straight knives and folders. Patterns: Hunters, lock backs, LinerLock®, slip joint and automatic folders. Technical: Grinds Damascus, 440C, ATS-34 and 154CM. Prices: $200 and up. Remarks: Full-time maker; first knife sold in 1982. Mark: Last name.

ZINKER, BRAD,
BZ KNIVES, 1591 NW 17 St, Homestead, FL 33030, Phone: 305-216-0404, bzknives@aol.com
Specialties: Fillets, folders and hunters. Technical: Uses ATS-34 and stainless Damascus. Prices: $200 to $600. Remarks: Voting member of Knifemakers Guild and Florida Knifemakers Association. Mark: Offset connected initials BZ.

ZIRBES, RICHARD,
Neustrasse 15, Niederkail, GERMANY 54526, Phone: 0049 6575 1371, r.zirbes@freenet.de Web: www.zirbes-knives.com www.zirbes-messer.de
Specialties: Fancy embellished knives with engraving and self-made scrimshaw (scrimshaw made by maker). High-tech working knives and high-tech hunters, boots, fighters and folders. All knives made by hand. Patterns: Boots, fighters, folders, hunters. Technical: Uses only the best steels for blade material like CPM-T 440V, CPM-T 420V, ATS-34, D2, C440, stainless Damascus or steel according to customer's desire. Prices: Working knives and hunters: $200 to $600. Fancy embellished knives with engraving and/or scrimshaw: $800 to $3000. Remarks: Part-time maker; first knife sold in 1991. Member of the German Knifemaker Guild. Mark: Zirbes or R. Zirbes.

ZOWADA, TIM,
4509 E Bear River Rd, Boyne Falls, MI 49713, Phone: 231-881-5056, tim@tzknives.com Web: www.tzknives.com
Specialties: Working knives and straight razors. Technical: Forges O1, L6, his own Damascus and smelted steel "Michi-Gane". Prices: $200 to $2500; some to $5000. Remarks: Full-time maker; first knife sold in 1980. Mark: Gothic, lower case "TZ"

ZSCHERNY, MICHAEL,
1840 Rock Island Dr, Ely, IA 52227, Phone: 319-848-3629, zschernyknives@aol.com
Specialties: Quality folding knives. Patterns: Liner-lock and lock-back folders in titanium, working straight knives. Technical: Grinds ATS-34 and commercial Damascus, prefers natural materials such as pearls and ivory. Prices: Starting at $500. Remarks: Full-time maker, first knife sold in 1978. Mark: Last name, city and state; folders, last name with stars inside folding knife.

AK

Barlow, Jana Poirier	Anchorage
Brennan, Judson	Delta Junction
Breuer, Lonnie	Wasilla
Broome, Thomas A	Kenai
Cawthorne, Christopher A	Wrangell
Chamberlin, John A	Anchorage
Cornwell, Jeffrey	Anchorage
Dempsey, Gordon S	N. Kenai
Desrosiers, Adam	Petersburg
Desrosiers, Haley	Petersburg
Dufour, Arthur J	Anchorage
England, Virgil	Anchorage
Flint, Robert	Anchorage
Gouker, Gary B	Sitka
Grebe, Gordon S	Anchor Point
Harvey, Mel	Nenana
Hibben, Westley G	Anchorage
Hook, Bob	North Pole
Kelsey, Nate	Anchorage
Knapp, Mark	Fairbanks
Lance, Bill	Eagle River
Lance, Lucas	Wasilla
Malaby, Raymond J	Juneau
Mcfarlin, Eric E	Kodiak
Miller, Nate	Fairbanks
Miller, Terry	Healy
Mirabile, David	Juneau
Moore, Marve	Willow
Parrish Iii, Gordon A	North Pole
Stegall, Keith	Wasilla
Van Cleve, Steve	Sutton

AL

Batson, James	Madison
Baxter, Dale	Trinity
Bell, Tony	Woodland
Bowles, Chris	Reform
Brothers, Dennis L.	Oneonta
Coffman, Danny	Jacksonville
Conn Jr., C T	Attalla
Daniels, Alex	Town Creek
Dark, Robert	Oxford
Daughtery, Tony	Loxley
Di Marzo, Richard	Birmingham
Durham, Kenneth	Cherokee
Elrod, Roger R	Enterprise
Gilbreath, Randall	Dora
Golden, Randy	Montgomery
Grizzard, Jim	Oxford
Hammond, Jim	Arab
Howard, Durvyn M	Hokes Bluff
Howell, Keith A.	Oxford
Howell, Len	Opelika
Howell, Ted	Wetumpka
Huckabee, Dale	Maylene
Hulsey, Hoyt	Attalla
Mccullough, Jerry	Georgiana
Mcnees, Jonathan	Northport
Militano, Tom	Jacksonville
Morris, C H	Frisco City
Pardue, Melvin M	Repton
Ploppert, Tom	Cullman
Roe Jr., Fred D	Huntsville
Russell, Tom	Jacksonville
Sinyard, Cleston S	Elberta
Smith, Lacy	Jacksonville
Thomas, David E	Lillian
Watson, Billy	Deatsville

AR

Anders, David	Center Ridge
Ardwin, Corey	North Little Rock
Barnes Jr., Cecil C.	Center Ridge
Brown, Jim	Little Rock
Browning, Steven W	Benton
Bullard, Benoni	Bradford
Bullard, Tom	Flippin
Chambers, Ronny	Beebe
Cook, James R	Nashville
Copeland, Thom	Nashville
Cox, Larry	Murfreesboro
Crawford, Pat And Wes	West Memphis
Crotts, Dan	Elm Springs
Crowell, James L	Mtn. View
Dozier, Bob	Springdale
Duvall, Fred	Benton
Echols, Rodger	Nashville
Edge, Tommy	Cash
Ferguson, Lee	Hindsville
Ferguson, Linda	Hindsville
Fisk, Jerry	Nashville
Fitch, John S	Clinton
Flournoy, Joe	El Dorado
Foster, Ronnie E	Morrilton
Foster, Timothy L	El Dorado
Frizzell, Ted	West Fork
Gadberry, Emmet	Hattieville
Greenaway, Don	Fayetteville
Herring, Morris	Dyer
Hutchinson, Alan	Conway
Kirkes, Bill	Little Rock
Lawrence, Alton	De Queen
Lemoine, David C	Mountain Home
Livesay, Newt	Siloam Springs
Lunn, Gail	Mountain Home
Lunn, Larry A	Mountain Home
Lynch, Tad	Beebe
Maringer, Tom	Springdale
Martin, Bruce E	Prescott
Martin, Hal W	Morrilton
Massey, Roger	Texarkana
Newberry, Allen	Lowell
Newton, Ron	London
Nolte, Steve	Lowell
Olive, Michael E	Leslie
Passmore, Jimmy D	Hoxie
Pearce, Logan	De Queen
Perry, Jim	Hope
Perry, John	Mayflower
Peterson, Lloyd (Pete) C	Clinton
Polk, Clifton	Van Buren
Polk, Rusty	Van Buren
Quattlebaum, Craig	Beebe
Randow, Ralph	Greenbrier
Red, Vernon	Conway
Reeves, J.R.	Texarkana
Rhea, Lin	Prattsville
Richards, Ralph (Bud)	Bauxite
Roberts, T. C. (Terry)	Fayetteville
Solomon, Marvin	Paron
Stanley, John	Crossett
Stout, Charles	Gillham
Sweaza, Dennis	Austin
Townsend, Allen Mark	Texarkana
Townsley, Russell	Floral
Upton, Tom	Rogers
Walker, Jim	Morrilton
Ward, Chuck	Benton
White, Bryce	Little Rock
Young, Raymond L	Mt. Ida

ARGENTINA

Ayarragaray, Cristian L.	Parana, Entre Rios
Bertolami, Juan Carlos	Neuquen
Gibert, Pedro	San Martin de los Andes, Neuquen
Kehiayan, Alfredo	Maschwitz, Buenos Aires
Rho, Nestor Lorenzo	Junin, Buenos Aires
Santiago, Abud	Buenos Aires

AUSTRALIA

Barnett, Bruce	Mundaring, WA
Bennett, Peter	Engadine, NSW
Brodziak, David	Albany, WA
Crawley, Bruce R	Croydon, VIC
Cross, Robert	Tamworth, NSW
Del Raso, Peter	Mt. Waverly, VIC
Gerner, Thomas	Walpole, WA
Giljevic, Branko	New South Wales
Green, William (Bill)	View Bank, VIC
Harvey, Max	Pert , WA
Hedges, Dee	Bedfordale, WA
Husiak, Myron	Altona, VIC
K B S, Knives	North Castlemaine, VIC
Maisey, Alan	Vincentia, NSW
Mcintyre, Shawn	Hawthornm, E VIC
Phillips, Alistair	Amaroo, ACT
Tasman, Kerley	Pt Kennedy, WA
Waters, Glenn	Hyland Park, NSW
Zemitis, Joe	Cardiff Heights, NSW

AZ

Ammons, David C	Tucson
Bennett, Glen C	Tucson
Birdwell, Ira Lee	Congress
Boye, David	Dolan Springs
Cheatham, Bill	Laveen
Choate, Milton	Somerton
Clark, R W	Surprise
Dawson, Barry	Prescott Valley
Dawson, Lynn	Prescott Valley
Deubel, Chester J.	Tucson
Dodd, Robert F	Camp Verde
Fuegen, Larry	Prescott
Goo, Tai	Tucson
Hancock, Tim	Scottsdale
Hoel, Steve	Pine
Holder, D'Alton	Wickenburg
Karp, Bob	Phoenix
Kiley, Mike And Jandy	Chino Valley
Kopp, Todd M	Apache Jct.
Lampson, Frank G	Chino Valley
Lee, Randy	St. Johns
Mcfall, Ken	Lakeside
Mcfarlin, J W	Lake Havasu City
Miller, Michael	Kingman
Montell, Ty	Thatcher
Mooney, Mike	Queen Creek
Newhall, Tom	Tucson
Purvis, Bob And Ellen	Tucson
Robbins, Bill	Sierra Vista
Rybar Jr., Raymond B	Came Verde
States, Joshua C	New River
Tamboli, Michael	Glendale
Tollefson, Barry A	Tubac
Tyre, Michael A	Wickenburg
Weiss, Charles L	Waddell
Wick, Jonathan P.	Bisbee
Wolf, Bill	Phoenix
Wright, Timothy	Sedona
Wuertz, Travis	Casa Grande
York, David C	Chino Valley

BELGIUM

Dox, Jan	Schoten
Monteiro, Victor	Maleves Ste Marie

BRAZIL

Bodolay, Antal — Belo Horizonte, MG
Bossaerts, Carl — Ribeirao Preto, SP
Campos, Ivan — Tatui, SP
Dorneles, Luciano Oliverira — Nova Petropolis, RS
Gaeta, Angelo — Centro Jau, SP
Gaeta, Roberto — Sao Paulo
Garcia, Mario Eiras — Caxingui, SP
Ikoma, Flavio — Presidente Prudente, SP
Lala, Paulo Ricardo P And Lala, Roberto P. — Presidente Prudente, SP
Neto Jr.,, Nelson And De Carvalho, Henrique M. — Braganca Paulista, SP
Paulo, Fernandes R — Lencois Paulista, SP
Petean, Francisco And Mauricio — Birigui, SP
Ricardo Romano, Bernardes — Itajuba MG
Sfreddo, Rodrigo Menezes — Nova Petropolis, RS
Vilar, Ricardo Augusto Ferreira — Mairipora, SP
Villa, Luiz — Itaim Bibi, SP
Villar, Ricardo — Mairipora, SP
Zakharov, Gladiston — Jacaret, SP

CA

Abegg, Arnie — Huntington Beach
Adkins, Richard L — Mission Viejo
Athey, Steve — Riverside
Barnes, Gregory — Altadena
Barron, Brian — San Mateo
Begg, Todd M. — Petaluma
Benson, Don — Escalon
Berger, Max A. — Carmichael
Biggers, Gary — Camarillo
Bolduc, Gary — Corona
Bost, Roger E — Palos Verdes
Boyd, Francis — Berkeley
Breshears, Clint — Manhattan Beach
Brooks, Buzz — Los Angles
Brous, Jason — Goleta
Browne, Rick — Upland
Bruce, Richard L. — Yankee Hill
Bruce, Richard L. — Yankee Hill
Butler, Bart — Ramona
Cabrera, Sergio B — Wilmington
Cantrell, Kitty D — Ramona
Caston, Darriel — Folsom
Caswell, Joe — Newbury
Clinco, Marcus — Venice
Coffey, Bill — Clovis
Coleman, John A — Citrus Heights
Connolly, James — Oroville
Cucchiara, Matt — Fresno
Davis, Charlie — Lakeside
De Maria Jr., Angelo — Carmel Valley
Dion, Greg — Oxnard
Dixon Jr., Ira E — Ventura
Dobratz, Eric — Laguna Hills
Doolittle, Mike — Novato
Driscoll, Mark — La Mesa
Dwyer, Duane — San Marcos
Ellis, William Dean — Sanger
Emerson, Ernest R — Harbor City
English, Jim — Jamul
Ernest, Phil (Pj) — Whittier
Essegian, Richard — Fresno
Felix, Alexander — Torrance
Ferguson, Jim — Temecula
Forrest, Brian — Descanso
Fraley, D B — Dixon
Fred, Reed Wyle — Sacramento
Freeman, Matt — Fresno
Freer, Ralph — Seal Beach

Fulton, Mickey — Willows
Girtner, Joe — Brea
Guarnera, Anthony R — Quartzhill
Hall, Jeff — Paso Robles
Hardy, Scott — Placerville
Harris, Jay — Redwood City
Harris, John — Riverside
Helton, Roy — San Diego
Herndon, Wm R "Bill" — Acton
Hink Iii, Les — Stockton
Hoy, Ken — North Fork
Humenick, Roy — Rescue
Jacks, Jim — Covina
Jackson, David — Lemoore
Jensen, John Lewis — Pasadena
Johnson, Randy — Turlock
Kazsuk, David — Perris
Kelly, Dave — Los Angeles
Keyes, Dan — Chino
Kilpatrick, Christian A — Citrus Hieghts
Koster, Steven C — Huntington Beach
Larson, Richard — Turlock
Leland, Steve — Fairfax
Lin, Marcus — Rolling Hills Estates
Lockett, Sterling — Burbank
Luchini, Bob — Palo Alto
Maccaughtry, Scott F. — Camarillo
Mackie, John — Whittier
Massey, Ron — Joshua Tree
Mata, Leonard — San Diego
Maxwell, Don — Clovis
Mcabee, William — Colfax
Mcclure, Michael — Menlo Park
Mcgrath, Patrick T — Westchester
Melin, Gordon C — La Mirada
Meloy, Sean — Lemon Grove
Montano, Gus A — San Diego
Morgan, Jeff — Santee
Moses, Steven — Santa Ana
Mutz, Jeff — Rancho Cucamonga
Naten, Greg — Bakersfield
Orton, Rich — Covina
Osborne, Donald H — Clovis
Packard, Bob — Elverta
Palm, Rik — San Diego
Panchenko, Serge — Citrus Heights
Pendleton, Lloyd — Volcano
Perry, Chris — Fresno
Pfanenstiel, Dan — Modesto
Pitt, David F — Anderson
Quesenberry, Mike — Blairsden
Randall, Patrick — Newbury Park
Rozas, Clark D — Wilmington
Schmitz, Raymond E — Valley Center
Schneider, Herman J. — Apple Valley
Schroen, Karl — Sebastopol
Sharp, David — Hesperia
Sibrian, Aaron — Ventura
Sjostrand, Kevin — Visalia
Slobodian, Scott — San Andreas
Smith, Shawn — Clouis
Sornberger, Jim — Volcano
Stapel, Chuck — Glendale
Steinberg, Al — Laguna Woods
Stimps, Jason M — Orange
Strider, Mick — San Marcos
Terrill, Stephen — Springville
Tingle, Dennis P — Jackson
Torres, Henry — Clovis
Vagnino, Michael — Visalia
Velick, Sammy — Los Angeles
Warren, Al — Roseville
Watanabe, Wayne — Montebello
Weinstock, Robert — San Francisco
Wilburn, Aaron — Redding
Wilson, Philip C — Mountain Ranch
Wilson, Ron — Morro Bay

CANADA

Arnold, Joe — London, ON
Beauchamp, Gaetan — Stoneham, QC
Beets, Marty — Williams Lake, BC
Bell, Donald — Bedford, NS
Berg, Lothar — Kitchener ON
Beshara, Brent (Besh) — NL
Boos, Ralph — Edmonton, AB
Bourbeau, Jean Yves — Ile Perrot, QC
Bradford, Garrick — Kitchener, ON
Bucharsky, Emil — Alberta
Burke, Dan — Springdale, NL
Dallyn, Kelly — Calgary, AB
Debraga, Jose C. — Trois Rivieres, QC
Debraga, Jovan — Quebec
Deringer, Christoph — Cookshire, QC
Desaulniers, Alain — Cookshire, QC
Diotte, Jeff — LaSalle, ON
Doiron, Donald — Messines, QC
Doucette, R — Brantford, ON
Doussot, Laurent — St. Bruno, QC
Downie, James T — Ontario
Frigault, Rick — Golden Lake, ON
Ganshorn, Cal — Regina, SK
Garvock, Mark W — Balderson, ON
Gilbert, Chantal — Quebec City, QC
Haslinger, Thomas — Calgary, AB
Hayes, Wally — Essex, ON
Hindmarch, Garth — Carlyle, SK
Hofer, Louis — Rose Prairie, BC
Jobin, Jacques — Levis, QC
Kaczor, Tom — Upper London, ON
Lambert, Kirby — Regina, SK
Langley, Mick — Qualicum Beach, BC
Lay, R J (Bob) — Logan Lake, BC
Leber, Heinz — Hudson's Hope, BC
Lightfoot, Greg — Kitscoty, AB
Linklater, Steve — Aurora, ON
Loerchner, Wolfgang — Bayfield, ON
Lyttle, Brian — High River, AB
Maneker, Kenneth — Galiano Island, BC
Marchand, Rick — Wheatley, ON
Marzitelli, Peter — Langley, BC
Massey, Al — Mount Uniacke, NS
Mckenzie, David Brian — Campbell River, BC
Miville-Deschenes, Alain — Quebec
Moeller, Harald — Parksville, BC
Nease, William — LaSalle, ON
Niro, Frank — Kamloops, B.C.
O'Hare, Sean — Grand Manan, NB
Olson, Rod — High River, AB
Painter, Tony — Whitehorse, YT
Patrick, Bob — S. Surrey, BC
Pepiot, Stephan — Winnipeg, MB
Piesner, Dean — Conestogo, ON
Poirier, Rick — New Brunswick E4V 2W7
Rassenti, Peter — Quebec J7P 4C2
Ridley, Rob — Sundre, AB
Roberts, George A — Whitehorse, YT
Ross, Tim — Thunder Bay, ON
Schoenfeld, Matthew A — Galiano Island, BC
Stancer, Chuck — Calgary, AB
Storch, Ed — Mannville, AB
Stuart, Steve — Gores Landing, ON
Sylvester, David — Compton, QC
Tedford, Steven J. — Colborne, ON
Tighe, Brian — St. Catharines, ON
Toner, Roger — Pickering, ON
Vanderkolff, Stephen — Mildmay, ON
Whitenect, Jody — Elderbank, NS
Young, Bud — Port Hardy, BC

directory

CO

Anderson, Mark Alan	Denver
Anderson, Mel	Hotchkiss
Booco, Gordon	Hayden
Brock, Kenneth L	Allenspark
Burrows, Chuck	Durango
Dannemann, Randy	Hotchkiss
Davis, Don	Loveland
Dennehy, John D	Loveland
Dill, Robert	Loveland
Fairly, Daniel	Bayfield
Fredeen, Graham	Colorado Springs
Fronefield, Daniel	Peyton
Hackney, Dana A.	Monument
High, Tom	Alamosa
Hockensmith, Dan	Berthoud
Hughes, Ed	Grand Junction
Hughes, Tony	Littleton
Irie, Michael L	Colorado Springs
Kitsmiller, Jerry	Montrose
Leck, Dal	Hayden
Mcwilliams, Sean	Carbondale
Miller, Don	Montrose
Miller, Hanford J	Cowdrey
Miller, M A	Northglenn
Ott, Fred	Durango
Owens, John	Nathrop
Rexford, Todd	Woodland Park
Roberts, Chuck	Golden
Rollert, Steve	Keenesburg
Ronzio, N. Jack	Fruita
Sanders, Bill	Mancos
Thompson, Lloyd	Pagosa Springs
Waites, Richard L	Broomfield
Watson, Bert	Westminster
Wilson, James G	Estes Park
Wood, Owen Dale	Arvada
Zima, Michael F	Ft. Morgan
Redd, Bill	Broomfield

CT

Buebendorf, Robert E	Monroe
Chapo, William G	Wilton
Cross, Kevin	Higganum
Framski, Walter P	Prospect
Jean, Gerry	Manchester
Loukides, David E	Cheshire
Meyer, Christopher J	Tolland
Plunkett, Richard	West Cornwall
Putnam, Donald S	Wethersfield
Rainville, Richard	Salem
Turecek, Jim	Ansonia
Vitale, Mace	Guilford
Zembko Iii, John	Berlin

Czech Republic

Tesarik, Richard	614 00 Brno

DE

Willey, Wg	Greenwood

DENMARK

Andersen, Henrik Lefolii	Fredensborg
Anso, Jens	Sporup
Henriksen, Hans J	Helsinge
Rafn, Dan C.	Hadsten
Strande, Poul	Dastrup
Vensild, Henrik	Auning
Willumsen, Mikkel	S Copenhagen

ENGLAND

Bailey, I.R.	Colkirk
Barker, Stuart	Oadby, Leicester
Boden, Harry	Derbyshire
Ducker, Brian	Colkirk
Farid, Mehr R	Kent
Harrington, Roger	East Sussex
Nowacki, Stephen R.	Southampton, Hampshire
Orford, Ben	Worcestershire
Penfold, Mick	Tremar, Cornwall
Price, Darrell Morris	Devon
Stainthorp, Guy	Stroke-on-Trent
Wardell, Mick	N Devon
Wise, Donald	East Sussex
Wood, Alan	Brampton

FINLAND

Palikko, J-T	00190 Helsinki
Ruusuvuori, Anssi	Piikkio
Tuominen, Pekka	Tossavanlahti
Vilppola, Markku	Turku

FL

Adams, Les	Hialeah
Alexander,, Oleg, And Cossack Blades	Wellington
Anders, Jerome	Miramar
Angell, Jon	Hawthorne
Atkinson, Dick	Wausau
Bacon, David R.	Bradenton
Barry Iii, James J.	West Palm Beach
Beers, Ray	Lake Wales
Benjamin Jr., George	Kissimmee
Blackwood, Neil	Lakeland
Bosworth, Dean	Key Largo
Bradley, John	Pomona Park
Bray Jr., W Lowell	New Port Richey
Brown, Harold E	Arcadia
Burris, Patrick R	Jacksonville
Butler, John	Havana
Chase, Alex	DeLand
D'Andrea, John	Citrus Springs
Davis Jr., Jim	Zephyrhills
Dietzel, Bill	Middleburg
Dintruff, Chuck	Seffner
Doggett, Bob	Brandon
Dotson, Tracy	Baker
Ellerbe, W B	Geneva
Ellis, Willy B	Tarpon Springs
Enos Iii, Thomas M	Orlando
Ferrara, Thomas	Naples
Fowler, Charles R	Ft McCoy
Gamble, Roger	Newberry
Gardner, Robert	West Palm Beach
Ghio, Paolo	Pensacola
Goers, Bruce	Lakeland
Granger, Paul J	Largo
Greene, Steve	Intercession City
Griffin Jr., Howard A	Davie
Grospitch, Ernie	Orlando
Harris, Ralph Dewey	Brandon
Heaney, John D	Haines City
Heitler, Henry	Tampa
Hodge Iii, John	Palatka
Hostetler, Larry	Fort Pierce
Humphreys, Joel	Lake Placid
Hunter, Richard D	Alachua
Hytovick, Joe "Hy"	Dunnellon
Jernigan, Steve	Milton
Johanning Custom Knives, Tom	Sarasota
Johnson, John R	Plant City
King, Bill	Tampa
Krapp, Denny	Apopka
Levengood, Bill	Tampa
Lewis, Mike	DeBary
Long, Glenn A	Dunnellon
Lovestrand, Schuyler	Vero Beach
Lozier, Don	Ocklawaha
Lyle Iii, Ernest L	Chiefland
Mandt, Joe	St. Petersburg
Mason, Bill	Hobe Sound
Mcdonald, Robert J	Loxahatchee
Miller, Ronald T	Largo
Miller, Steve	Clearwater
Mink, Dan	Crystal Beach
Newton, Larry	Jacksonville
Ochs, Charles F	Largo
Owens, Donald	Melbourne
Parker, Cliff	Zephyrhills
Partridge, Jerry D.	DeFuniak Springs
Pattay, Rudy	Citrus Springs
Pendray, Alfred H	Williston
Piergallini, Daniel E	Plant City
Randall Made Knives,	Orlando
Reed, John M	Port Orange
Renner, Terry	Palmetto
Robinson, Calvin	Pace
Robinson Iii, Rex R	Leesburg
Rodkey, Dan	Hudson
Romeis, Gordon	Fort Myers
Russ, Ron	Williston
Schwarzer, Lora Sue	Crescent City
Schwarzer, Stephen	Crescent City
Smith, Michael J	Brandon
Stapleton, William E	Merritt Island
Steck, Van R	Orange City
Stephan, Daniel	Valrico
Stipes, Dwight	Palm City
Straight, Kenneth J	Largo
Tabor, Tim	Lutz
Turnbull, Ralph A	Spring Hill
Vogt, Donald J	Tampa
Watson, Tom	Panama City
Weiland Jr., J Reese	Riverview
White, John Paul	Valparaiso
Wicker, Donnie R	Panama City
Wilson, Stan	Lithia
Zaccagnino Jr., Don	Pahokee
Zahm, Kurt	Indialantic
Zinker, Brad	Homestead

FRANCE

Bennica, Charles	Moules et Baucels
Chauzy, Alain	Seur-en-Auxios
Chomilier, Alain And Joris	Clermont-Ferrand
Doursin, Gerard	Pernes les Fontaines
Graveline, Pascal And Isabelle	Moelan-sur-Mer
Headrick, Gary	Juan Les Pins
Madrulli, Mme Joelle	Salon De Provence
Reverdy, Nicole And Pierre	Romans
Thevenot, Jean-Paul	Dijon
Viallon, Henri	Thiers

GA

Arrowood, Dale	Sharpsburg
Ashworth, Boyd	Powder Springs
Barker, John	Cumming
Barker, Robert G.	Bishop
Bentley, C L	Albany
Bish, Hal	Jonesboro
Brach, Paul	Cumming
Bradley, Dennis	Blairsville
Buckner, Jimmie H	Putney
Cambron, Henry	Dallas
Chamblin, Joel	Concord
Cole, Welborn I	Athens
Crockford, Jack	Chamblee
Daniel, Travis E	Thomaston
Davis, Steve	Powder Springs

Dunn, Charles K — Shiloh
Frost, Dewayne — Barnesville
Gaines, Buddy — Commerce
Gatlin, Steve — Leesburg
Glover, Warren D — Cleveland
Greene, David — Covington
Hammond, Hank — Leesburg
Hammond, Ray — Woodstock
Hardy, Douglas E — Franklin
Hawkins, Rade — Fayetteville
Hensley, Wayne — Conyers
Hinson And Son, R — Columbus
Hoffman, Kevin L — Savannah
Hossom, Jerry — Duluth
Jones, Franklin (Frank) W — Columbus
Kimsey, Kevin — Cartersville
King, Fred — Cartersville
Knott, Steve — Guyton
Landers, John — Newnan
Lockett, Lowell C. — Canton
Lonewolf, J Aguirre — Demorest
Mathews, Charlie And Harry — Statesboro
Mcgill, John — Blairsville
Mclendon, Hubert W — Waco
Mitchell, James A — Columbus
Moncus, Michael Steven — Smithville
Parks, John — Jefferson
Poole, Marvin O — Commerce
Powell, Robert Clark — Smarr
Prater, Mike — Flintstone
Price, Timmy — Blairsville
Pridgen Jr., Larry — Fitzgerald
Ragsdale, James D — Ellijay
Roghmans, Mark — LaGrange
Rosenfeld, Bob — Hoschton
Sculley, Peter E — Rising Fawn
Smith Jr., James B "Red" — Morven
Snow, Bill — Columbus
Sowell, Bill — Macon
Stafford, Richard — Warner Robins
Thompson, Kenneth — Duluth
Tomey, Kathleen — Macon
Walters, A F — TyTy
Whetsell, Alex — Haralson
White, Garrett — Hartwell
White, Lou — Ranger
Wright, Robert A — savannah

GERMANY

Balbach, Markus — WeilmŸnster
Becker, Franz — Marktl
Boehlke, Guenter
Borger, Wolf — Graben-Neudorf
Dell, Wolfgang — Owen-Teck
Drumm, Armin — Dornstadt
Faust, Joachim — Goldkronach
Fruhmann, Ludwig — Burghausen
Greiss, Jockl — Schenkenzell
Hehn, Richard Karl — Dorrebach
Herbst, Peter — Lauf a.d. Pegn.
Joehnk, Bernd — Kiel
Kressler, D F — D-28832 Achim
Rankl, Christian — Munchen
Rinkes, Siegfried — Markterlbach
Selzam, Frank — Bad Koenigshofen
Steinau, Jurgen — Berlin
Tritz, Jean Jose — Hamburg
Wirtz, Achim — Wuerselen
Zirbes, Richard — Niederkail

GREECE

Filippou, Ioannis-Minas — Athens
Zafeiriadis, Konstantinos — Marathon Attiki

HI

Evans, Vincent K And Grace — Keaau
Fujisaka, Stanley — Kaneohe
Gibo, George — Hilo
Lui, Ronald M — Honolulu
Mann, Tim — Honokaa
Matsuoka, Scot — Mililani
Mayo Jr., Tom — Waialua
Mitsuyuki, Ross — Honolulu
Onion, Kenneth J — Kaneohe
Ouye, Keith — Honolulu
Watanabe, Melvin — Kailua
Zakabi, Carl S — Mililani Town

IA

Brooker, Dennis — Chariton
Brower, Max — Boone
Clark, Howard F — Runnells
Cockerham, Lloyd — Denham Springs
Helscher, John W — Washington
Lainson, Tony — Council Bluffs
Lewis, Bill — Riverside
Mckiernan, Stan — Lamoni
Miller, James P — Fairbank
Thie, Brian — Burlington
Trindle, Barry — Earlham
Westberg, Larry — Algona
Zscherny, Michael — Ely

ID

Alderman, Robert — Sagle
Alverson, Tim (R.V.) — Moscow
Bloodworth Custom Knives, — Meridian
Burke, Bill — Boise
Eddy, Hugh E — Caldwell
Hawk, Grant And Gavin — Idaho City
Hogan, Thomas R — Boise
Horton, Scot — Buhl
Howe, Tori — Athol
Mann, Michael L — Spirit Lake
Metz, Greg T — Cascade
Patton, Dick And Rob — Nampa
Quarton, Barr — McCall
Reeve, Chris — Boise
Rohn, Fred — Coeur d'Alene
Sawby, Scott — Sandpoint
Sparks, Bernard — Dingle
Steiger, Monte L — Genesee
Tippetts, Colten — Hidden Springs
Towell, Dwight L — Midvale
Trace Rinaldi Custom Blades, — Plummer

IL

Bloomer, Alan T — Maquon
Camerer, Craig — Chesterfield
Cook, Louise — Ozark
Cook, Mike — Ozark
Detmer, Phillip — Breese
Dicristofano, Anthony P — Melrose Park
Eaker, Allen L — Paris
Fiorini, Bill — Grayville
Hawes, Chuck — Weldon
Heath, William — Bondville
Hill, Rick — Maryville
Knuth, Joseph E — Rockford
Kovar, Eugene — Evergreen Park
Leone, Nick — Pontoon Beach
Markley, Ken — Sparta
Meers, Andrew — Carbondale
Meier, Daryl — Carbondale
Myers, Paul — Wood River
Myers, Steve — Springfield
Nevling, Mark — Hume

Nowland, Rick — Waltonville
Pellegrin, Mike — Troy
Pritchard, Ron — Dixon
Rosenbaugh, Ron — Crystal Lake
Rossdeutscher, Robert N — Arlington Heights
Rzewnicki, Gerald — Elizabeth
Schneider, Craig M — Claremont
Smale, Charles J — Waukegan
Smith, John M — Centralia
Todd, Richard C — Chambersburg
Tompkins, Dan — Peotone
Veit, Michael — LaSalle
Voss, Ben — Victoria
Werth, George W — Poplar Grove
West, Charles A — Centralia
Wheeler, Robert — Bradley
White, Robert J — Gilson
White Jr., Robert J Butch — Gilson
Young, Errol — Alton

IN

Ball, Ken — Mooresville
Barkes, Terry — Edinburgh
Barrett, Rick L. (Toshi Hisa) — Goshen
Bose, Reese — Shelburn
Bose, Tony — Shelburn
Chaffee, Jeff L — Morris
Claiborne, Jeff — Franklin
Cramer, Brent — Wheatland
Crowl, Peter — Waterloo
Curtiss, David — Granger
Damlovac, Sava — Indianapolis
Darby, Jed — Greensburg
Fitzgerald, Dennis M — Fort Wayne
Fraps, John R — Indianapolis
Good, D.R. — Tipton
Harding, Chad — Solsberry
Hunt, Maurice — Brownsburg
Imel, Billy Mace — New Castle
Johnson, C E Gene — Chesterton
Kain, Charles — Indianapolis
Keeslar, Steven C — Hamilton
Keeton, William L — Laconia
Kinker, Mike — Greensburg
Mayville, Oscar L — Marengo
Minnick, Jim & Joyce — Middletown
Patton, Phillip — Yoder
Quakenbush, Thomas C — Ft Wayne
Robertson, Leo D — Indianapolis
Seib, Steve — Evansville
Shull, James — Rensselaer
Smock, Timothy E — Marion
Snyder, Michael Tom — Zionsville
Thayer, Danny O — Romney
Young, George — Kokomo

IRELAND

Moore, Davy — Quin, Co Clare

ISRAEL

Shadmot, Boaz — Arava

ITALY

Ameri, Mauro — Genova
Ballestra, Santino — Ventimiglia
Bertuzzi, Ettore — Bergamo
Bonassi, Franco — Pordenone
Esposito, Emmanuel — Buttigliera Alta TO
Fogarizzu, Boiteddu — Pattada
Frizzi, Leonardo — Firenze
Garau, Marcello — Oristano
Giagu, Salvatore And Deroma Maria Rosaria — Pattada (SS)

Ramondetti, Sergio (CN) — CHIUSA DI PESIO
Riboni, Claudio — Truccazzano (MI)
Scordia, Paolo — Roma
Simonella, Gianluigi — Maniago
Toich, Nevio — Vincenza
Tschager, Reinhard — Bolzano

JAPAN

Aida, Yoshihito — Tokyo
Ebisu, Hidesaku — Hiroshima
Fujikawa, Shun — Osaka
Fukuta, Tak — Gifu
Hara, Koji — Gifu
Hirayama, Harumi — Saitama
Hiroto, Fujihara — Hiroshima
Isao, Ohbuchi — Fukuoka
Ishihara, Hank — Chiba
Kagawa, Koichi — Kanagawa
Kanki, Iwao — Hyogo
Kansei, Matsuno — Gifu
Kato, Shinichi — Aichi
Katsumaro, Shishido — Hiroshima
Keisuke, Gotoh — Oita
Koyama, Captain Bunshichi — Aichi
Mae, Takao — Osaka
Makoto, Kunitomo — Hiroshima
Matsuno, Kansei — Gifu-City
Matsusaki, Takeshi — Nagasaki
Michinaka, Toshiaki — Tottori
Narasada, Mamoru — NAGANO
Ryuichi, Kuki — Saitama
Sakakibara, Masaki — Tokyo
Sugihara, Keidoh — Osaka
Sugiyama, Eddy K — Oita
Takahashi, Masao — Gunma
Tamatsu, Kunihiko — Kochi-ken
Toshifumi, Kuramoto — Fukuoka
Uchida, Chimata — Kumamoto
Wada, Yasutaka — Nara
Yoneyama, Chicchi K. — Tokyo
Yoshihara, Yoshindo — Tokyo
Yoshikazu, Kamada — Tokushima
Yoshio, Maeda — Okayama

KS

Bradburn, Gary — Wichita
Burrows, Stephen R — Humboldt
Chard, Gordon R — Iola
Craig, Roger L — Topeka
Culver, Steve — Meriden
Darpinian, Dave — Olathe
Davison, Todd A. — Lyons
Dawkins, Dudley L — Topeka
Dick, Dan — Hutchinson
Evans, Phil — Columbus
Hegwald, J L — Humboldt
Herman, Tim — Olathe
Keranen, Paul — Tacumseh
King Jr., Harvey G — Alta Vista
Kraft, Steve — Abilene
Lamb, Curtis J — Ottawa
Magee, Jim — Salina
Petersen, Dan L — Auburn
Smith, Jerry — Oberlin
Stice, Douglas W — Wichita

KY

Addison, Kyle A — Hazel
Baskett, Barbara — Eastview
Baskett, Lee Gene — Eastview
Bybee, Barry J — Cadiz
Carson, Harold J "Kit" — Vine Grove
Carter, Mike — Louisville

Downing, Larry — Bremen
Dunn, Steve — Smiths Grove
Edwards, Mitch — Glasgow
Finch, Ricky D — West Liberty
Fister, Jim — Simpsonville
France, Dan — Cawood
Frederick, Aaron — West Liberty
Greco, John — Greensburg
Hibben, Daryl — LaGrange
Hibben, Gil — LaGrange
Hibben, Joleen — LaGrange
Hoke, Thomas M — LaGrange
Holbrook, H L — Sandy Hook
Howser, John C — Frankfort
Keeslar, Joseph F — Almo
Lott, Sherry — Greensburg
Pease, W D — Ewing
Pierce, Harold L — Louisville
Rados, Jerry F — Columbia
Richerson, Ron — Greenburg
Rigney Jr., Willie — Bronston
Smith, John W — West Liberty
Soaper, Max H. — Henderson
Steier, David — Louisville
Vance, David — West Liberty
Wallingford Jr., Charles W — Union

LA

Barker, Reggie — Springhill
Blaum, Roy — Covington
Caldwell, Bill — West Monroe
Calvert Jr., Robert W (Bob) — Rayville
Capdepon, Randy — Carencro
Capdepon, Robert — Carencro
Chauvin, John — Scott
Dake, C M — New Orleans
Dake, Mary H — New Orleans
Durio, Fred — Opelousas
Faucheaux, Howard J — Loreauville
Fontenot, Gerald J — Mamou
Gorenflo, James T (Jt) — Baton Rouge
Graves, Dan — Shreveport
Johnson, Gordon A. — Choudrant
Ki, Shiva — Baton Rouge
Laurent, Kermit — LaPlace
Lemaire, Ryan M. — Abbeville
Leonard, Randy Joe — Sarepta
Mitchell, Max Dean And Ben — Leesville
Phillips, Dennis — Independence
Potier, Timothy F — Oberlin
Primos, Terry — Shreveport
Provenzano, Joseph D — Ponchatoula
Randall Jr., James W — Keithville
Reggio Jr., Sidney J — Sun
Sanders, Michael M — Ponchatoula
Tilton, John — Iowa
Trisler, Kenneth W — Rayville
Wiggins, Horace — Mansfield

MA

Banaitis, Romas — Medway
Cooper, Paul — Woburn
Dailey, G E — Seekonk
Dugdale, Daniel J. — Walpole
Entin, Robert — Boston
Gaudette, Linden L — Wilbraham
Gedraitis, Charles J — Holden
Grossman, Stewart — Clinton
Hinman, Theodore — Greenfield
Jarvis, Paul M — Cambridge
Khalsa, Jot Singh — Millis
Klein, Kevin — Boston
Kubasek, John A — Easthampton
Lapen, Charles — W. Brookfield
Little, Larry — Spencer

Martin, Randall J — Bridgewater
Mcluin, Tom — Dracut
Moore, Michael Robert — Lowell
Rebello, Indian George — New Bedford
Rizzi, Russell J — Ashfield
Rua, Gary — Fall River
Saviano, James — Douglas
Siska, Jim — Westfield
Smith, J D — Roxbury
Stuart, Mason — Mansfield
Vining, Bill — Methuen

MD

Bagley, R. Keith — White Plains
Barnes, Aubrey G. — Hagerstown
Barnes, Gary L. — New Windsor
Cohen, N J (Norm) — Baltimore
Dement, Larry — Prince Fredrick
Fuller, Jack A — New Market
Gossman, Scott — Whiteford
Hart, Bill — Pasadena
Hendrickson, E Jay — Frederick
Hendrickson, Shawn — Knoxville
Kreh, Lefty — "Cockeysville"
Mccarley, John — Taneytown
Mcgowan, Frank E — Sykesville
Merchant, Ted — White Hall
Nicholson, R. Kent — Phoenix
Nuckels, Stephen J — Hagerstown
Presti, Matt — Union Bridge
Sentz, Mark C — Taneytown
Smit, Glenn — Aberdeen
Sontheimer, G Douglas — Potomac
Spickler, Gregory Noble — Sharpsburg
St. Clair, Thomas K — Monrovia
Walker, Bill — Stevensville

ME

Bohrmann, Bruce — Yarmouth
Ceprano, Peter J. — Auburn
Coombs Jr., Lamont — Bucksport
Fogg, Don — Auburn
Gray, Daniel — Brownville
Hillman, Charles — Friendship
Leavitt Jr., Earl F — E. Boothbay
Oyster, Lowell R — Corinth
Sharrigan, Mudd — Wiscasset

MEXICO

Scheurer, Alfredo E Faes — Distrito Federal
Sunderland, Richard — Puerto Escondido, OA
Young, Cliff — San Miguel De Allende, GJ

MI

Ackerson, Robin E — Buchanan
Alcorn, Douglas A. — Chesaning
Andrews, Eric — Grand Ledge
Arms, Eric — Tustin
Behnke, William — Kingsley
Booth, Philip W — Ithaca
Buckbee, Donald M — Grayling
Carr, Tim — Muskegon
Carroll, Chad — Grant
Casey, Kevin — Hickory Corners
Cashen, Kevin R — Hubbardston
Cook, Mike A — Portland
Cousino, George — Onsted
Cowles, Don — Royal Oak
Dilluvio, Frank J — Prudenville
Ealy, Delbert — Indian River
Erickson, Walter E. — Atlanta
Gordon, Larry B — Farmington Hills

Gottage, Dante	Clinton Twp.
Gottage, Judy	Clinton Twp.
Haas, Randy	Marlette
Harm, Paul W	Attica
Harrison, Brian	Cedarville
Hartman, Arlan (Lanny)	Baldwin
Hoffman, Jay	Munising
Hughes, Daryle	Nunica
Krause, Roy W	St. Clair Shores
Lankton, Scott	Ann Arbor
Lark, David	Kingsley
Lucie, James R	Fruitport
Mankel, Kenneth	Cannonsburg
Marsh, Jeremy	Ada
Mills, Louis G	Ann Arbor
Morris, Michael S.	Yale
Noren, Douglas E	Springlake
Parker, Robert Nelson	Royal Oak
Repke, Mike	Bay City
Rose Ii, Doun T	Fife Lake
Sakmar, Mike	Howell
Sandberg, Ronald B	Brownstown
Serven, Jim	Fostoria
Tally, Grant	Flat Rock
Van Eizenga, Jerry W	Nunica
Vasquez, Johnny David	Wyandotte
Viste, James	Hamtramck
Webster, Bill	Three Rivers
Welling, Ronald L	Grand Haven
White, Richard T	Grosse Pointe Farms
Whittaker, Wayne	Metamore
Wood, Webster	Atlanta
Zowada, Tim	Boyne Falls

MN

Andersen, Karl B.	Warba
Davis, Joel	Albert Lea
Hagen, Doc	Pelican Rapids
Hansen, Robert W	Cambridge
Hebeisen, Jeff	Hopkins
Johnson, Jerry L	Worthington
Johnson, R B	Clearwater
Knipschield, Terry	Rochester
Leblanc, Gary E	Royalton
Maines, Jay	Wyoming
Metsala, Anthony	Princeton
Mickley, Tracy	North Mankato
Rydbom, Jeff	Annandale
Shadley, Eugene W	Grand Rapids
Taber, David E.	Winona
Voorhies, Les	Faribault

MO

Abernathy, Lance	Platte City
Allred, Elvan	St. Charles
Andrews, Russ	Sugar Creek
Betancourt, Antonio L.	St. Louis
Braschler, Craig W.	Zalma
Buxton, Bill	Kaiser
Chinnock, Daniel T.	Union
Cover, Jeff	Potosi
Cover, Raymond A	Mineral Point
Cox, Colin J	Raymore
Davis, W C	El Dorado Springs
Dippold, Al	Perryville
Duncan, Ron	Cairo
Eaton, Frank L Jr	Farmington
Ehrenberger, Daniel Robert	Mexico
Engle, William	Boonville
Hanson Iii, Don L.	Success
Harris, Jeffery A	Chesterfield
Harrison, Jim (Seamus)	St. Louis
Jones, John A	Holden
Kinnikin, Todd	Pacific
Knickmeyer, Hank	Cedar Hill

Knickmeyer, Kurt	Cedar Hill
Krause, Jim	Farmington
Martin, Tony	Arcadia
Mccrackin, Kevin	House Spings
Mccrackin And Son, V J	House Springs
Mosier, David	Independence
Mulkey, Gary	Branson
Muller, Jody	Goodson
Newcomb, Corbin	Moberly
Ramsey, Richard A	Neosho
Rardon, A D	Polo
Rardon, Archie F	Polo
Riepe, Richard A	Harrisonville
Robbins, Howard P	Flemington
Royer, Kyle	Mountain View
Scroggs, James A	Warrensburg
Seaton, David D	Rolla
Sonntag, Douglas W	Nixa
Sonntag, Jacob D	Robert
Sonntag, Kristopher D	Nixa
Steketee, Craig A	Billings
Stewart, Edward L	Mexico
Stormer, Bob	Dixon
Waide, Rusty	Buffalo
Warden, Roy A	Union
Whitesell, J. Dale	Stover
Willis, Bill	Ava

MS

Black, Scott	Picayune
Boleware, David	Carson
Cohea, John M	Nettleton
Davis, Jesse W	Sarah
Evans, Bruce A	Booneville
Flynt, Robert G	Gulfport
Jones, Jack P.	Ripley
Lamey, Robert M	Biloxi
Lebatard, Paul M	Vancleave
May, Charles	Aberdeen
Mayo Jr., Homer	Biloxi
Nichols, Chad	Blue Springs
Phillips, Donavon	Morton
Pickett, Terrell	Lumberton
Provost, J.C.	Laurel
Roberts, Michael	Clinton
Robinson, Chuck	Picayune
Shiffer, Steve	Leakesville
Smith, J.B.	Perkinston
Taylor, Billy	Petal
Vandeventer, Terry L	Terry
Vardaman, Robert	Hattiesburg
Wehner, Rudy	Collins
Wilson, Vic	Olive Branch
Wingo, Perry	Gulfport
Winston, David	Starkville

MT

Barnes, Jack	Whitefish
Barnes, Wendell	Clinton
Barth, J.D.	Alberton
Beam, John R.	Kalispell
Beaty, Robert B.	Missoula
Bell, Don	Lincoln
Bizzell, Robert	Butte
Brooks, Steve R	Walkerville
Caffrey, Edward J	Great Falls
Campbell, Doug	McLeod
Carlisle, Jeff	Simms
Christensen, Jon P	Stevensville
Colter, Wade	Colstrip
Conklin, George L	Ft. Benton
Crowder, Robert	Thompson Falls
Curtiss, Steve L	Eureka
Dunkerley, Rick	Lincoln
Eaton, Rick	Broadview

Ellefson, Joel	Manhattan
Fassio, Melvin G	Lolo
Forthofer, Pete	Whitefish
Fritz, Erik L	Forsyth
Gallagher, Barry	Lewistown
Harkins, J A	Conner
Hill, Howard E	Polson
Hintz, Gerald M	Helena
Hulett, Steve	West Yellowstone
Kajin, Al	Forsyth
Kauffman, Dave	Montana City
Kelly, Steven	Bigfork
Luman, James R	Anaconda
Mcguane Iv, Thomas F	Bozeman
Mckee, Neil	Stevensville
Moyer, Russ	Havre
Nedved, Dan	Kalispell
Olson, Joe	Geyser
Parsons, Pete	Helena
Patrick, Willard C	Helena
Peele, Bryan	Thompson Falls
Peterson, Eldon G	Whitefish
Pursley, Aaron	Big Sandy
Rodewald, Gary	Hamilton
Ruana Knife Works,	Bonner
Smith, Josh	Frenchtown
Sweeney, Coltin D	Missoula
Taylor, Shane	Miles City
Thill, Jim	Missoula
Weinand, Gerome M	Missoula
Yashinski, John L	Red Lodge

NC

Baker, Herb	Eden
Barefoot, Joe W.	Wilmington
Best, Ron	Stokes
Bisher, William (Bill)	Denton
Brackett, Jamin	Fallston
Britton, Tim	Bethania
Busfield, John	Roanoke Rapids
Craddock, Mike	Thomasville
Drew, Gerald	Mill Spring
Gaddy, Gary Lee	Washington
Gingrich, Justin	Wade
Goode, Brian	Shelby
Greene, Chris	Shelby
Gross, W W	Archdale
Hall, Ken	Waynesville
Johnson, Tommy	Troy
Laramie, Mark	Raeford
Livingston, Robert C	Murphy
Maynard, William N.	Fayetteville
Mcghee, E. Scott	Clarkton
Mclurkin, Andrew	Raleigh
Mcnabb, Tommy	Bethania
Mcrae, J Michael	Mint Hill
Nichols, Calvin	Raleigh
Parrish, Robert	Weaverville
Patrick, Chuck	Brasstown
Patrick, Peggy	Brasstown
Randall, Steve	Lincolnton
Rapp, Steven J	Marshall
Santini, Tom	Pikeville
Scholl, Tim	Angier
Simmons, H R	Aurora
Sterling, Murray	Mount Airy
Summers, Arthur L	Concord
Sutton, S Russell	New Bern
Vail, Dave	Hampstead
Wacholz, Doc	Marble
Wagaman, John K	Selma
Walker, Don	Burnsville
Warren, Daniel	Canton
Whitley, L Wayne	Chocowinity
Wiggins, Bill	Canton
Williamson, Tony	Siler City

Wilson, Mike — Hayesville
Winkler, Daniel — Blowing Rock

ND

Kommer, Russ — Fargo
Pitman, David — Williston

NE

Archer, Ray And Terri — Omaha
Hielscher, Guy — Alliance
Jokerst, Charles — Omaha
Marlowe, Charles — Omaha
Moore, Jon P — Aurora
Mosier, Joshua J — Deshler
Sloan, David — Diller
Suedmeier, Harlan — Nebraska City
Syslo, Chuck — Omaha
Tiensvold, Alan L — Rushville
Tiensvold, Jason — Rushville
Till, Calvin E And Ruth — Chadron

NETHERLANDS

Brouwer, Jerry — Alkmaar
Sprokholt, Rob — Gatherwood
Van De Manakker, Thijs — Holland
Van Den Elsen, Gert — Tilburg
Van Eldik, Frans — Loenen
Van Ryswyk, Aad — Vlaardingen

NEW ZEALAND

Bassett, David J. — Auckland
Gunther, Eddie — Auckland
Jansen Van Vuuren, Ludwig — Dunedin
Knapton, Chris C. — Henderson, Aukland
Pennington, C A — Kainga Christchurch
Reddiex, Bill — Palmerston North
Ross, D L — Dunedin
Sandow, Brent Edward — Auckland
Sandow, Norman E — Howick, Auckland
Sands, Scott — Christchurch 9
Van Dijk, Richard — Harwood Dunedin

NH

Hitchmough, Howard — Peterborough
Hudson, C Robbin — Rummney
Macdonald, John — Raymond
Philippe, D A — Cornish
Saindon, R Bill — Goshen

NJ

Fisher, Lance — Pompton Lakes
Grussenmeyer, Paul G — Cherry Hill
Knowles, Shawn — Great Meadows
Lesswing, Kevin — Bayonne
Licata, Steven — Boonton
Mccallen Jr., Howard H — So Seaside Park
Nadeau, Brian — Stanhope
Pressburger, Ramon — Howell
Sheets, Steven William — Mendham
Slee, Fred — Morganville
Viele, H J — Westwood
Yeskoo, Richard C — Summit

NM

Black, Tom — Albuquerque
Burnley, Lucas — Albuquerque
Chavez, Ramon — Belen
Cherry, Frank J — Albuquerque
Cordova, Joseph G — Bosque Farms
Cumming, Bob — Cedar Crest
Digangi, Joseph M — Santa Cruz

Duran, Jerry T — Albuquerque
Dyess, Eddie — Roswell
Fisher, Jay — Clovis
Garner, George — Albuquerque
Goode, Bear — Navajo Dam
Gunter, Brad — Tijeras
Hartman, Tim — Albuquerque
Hethcoat, Don — Clovis
Hume, Don — Albuquerque
Kimberley, Richard L. — Santa Fe
Leu, Pohan — Rio Rancho
Lewis, Tom R — Carlsbad
Lynn, Arthur — Galisteo
Macdonald, David — Los Lunas
Meshejian, Mardi — Santa Fe
Reid, Jim — Albuquerque
Rogers, Richard — Magdalena
Schaller, Anthony Brett — Albuquerque
Stalcup, Eddie — Gallup
Stetter, J. C. — Roswell
Terzuola, Robert — Albuquerque
Trujillo, Albert M B — Bosque Farms
Walker, Michael L — Pueblo Sur Taos
Wescott, Cody — Las Cruces

NORWAY

Bache-Wiig, Tom — Eivindvik
Sellevold, Harald — Bergen
Vistnes, Tor — Svelgen

Notts, England

Wylie, Tom — Sutton-In-Ashfield

NV

Barnett, Van — Reno
Beasley, Geneo — Wadsworth
Bingenheimer, Bruce — Spring Creek
Cameron, Ron G — Logandale
Dellana, — Reno
George, Tom — Henderson
Hrisoulas, Jim — Henderson
Kreibich, Donald L. — Reno
Nishiuchi, Melvin S — Las Vegas
Thomas, Devin — Panaca
Washburn, Arthur D — Pioche

NY

Baker, Wild Bill — Boiceville
Castellucio, Rich — Amsterdam
Davis, Barry L — Castleton
Farr, Dan — Rochester
Faust, Dick — Rochester
Gregory, Matthew M. — Glenwood
Hobart, Gene — Windsor
Johnson, Mike — Orient
Johnston, Dr. Robt — Rochester
Levin, Jack — Brooklyn
Loos, Henry C — New Hyde Park
Ludwig, Richard O — Maspeth
Lupole, Jamie G — Kirkwood
Manaro, Sal — Holbrook
Maragni, Dan — Georgetown
Mccornock, Craig — Willow
Meerdink, Kurt — Barryville
Page, Reginald — Groveland
Phillips, Scott C — Gouverneur
Rachlin, Leslie S — Elmira
Rappazzo, Richard — Cohoes
Rotella, Richard A — Niagara Falls
Scheid, Maggie — Rochester
Schippnick, Jim — Sanborn
Serafen, Steven E — New Berlin
Skiff, Steven — Broadalbin
Smith, Lenard C — Valley Cottage

Smith, Raymond L — Erin
Summers, Dan — Whitney Pt.
Szilaski, Joseph — Pine Plains
Turner, Kevin — Montrose
Welling, William — West Valley

OH

Bendik, John — Olmsted Falls
Bennett, Brett C — Kensington
Busse, Jerry — Wauseon
Coffee, Jim — Norton
Collins, Lynn M — Elyria
Coppins, Daniel — Cambridge
Cottrill, James I — Columbus
Crews, Randy — Patriot
Downing, Tom — Cuyahoga Falls
Downs, James F — Powell
Etzler, John — Grafton
Francis, John D — Ft. Loramie
Franklin, Mike — Aberdeen
Gittinger, Raymond — Tiffin
Glover, Ron — Mason
Greiner, Richard — Green Springs
Hinderer, Rick — Shreve
Hudson, Anthony B — Amanda
Humphrey, Lon — Newark
Imboden Ii, Howard L. — Dayton
Johnson, Wm. C. "Bill" — Enon
Jones, Roger Mudbone — Waverly
Kiefer, Tony — Pataskala
Longworth, Dave — Felicity
Loro, Gene — Crooksville
Maienknecht, Stanley — Sardis
Mcdonald, Rich — Hillboro
Mcgroder, Patrick J — Madison
Mercer, Mike — Lebanon
Messer, David T — Dayton
Morgan, Tom — Beloit
Munjas, Bob — Waterford
O'Machearley, Michael — Wilmington
Panak, Paul S — Andover
Potter, Billy — Dublin
Roddy, Roy "Tim" — Hubbard
Rose, Derek W — Gallipolis
Rowe, Fred — Amesville
Salley, John D — Tipp City
Schuchmann, Rick — Cincinnati
Sheely, "Butch" Forest — Grand Rapids
Shinosky, Andy — Canfield
Shoemaker, Carroll — Northup
Shoemaker, Scott — Miamisburg
Spinale, Richard — Lorain
Strong, Scott — Beavercreek
Summers, Dennis K — Springfield
Thomas, Kim — Seville
Thourot, Michael W — Napoleon
Tindera, George — Brunswick
Trout, George H. — Wilmington
Votaw, David P — Pioneer
Ward, J J — Waverly
Williams, Robert — East Liverpool
Worley, Joel A. — Maplewood
Wright, L T — Steubenville
Yurco, Mickey — Canfield
Stidham, Daniel — Gallipolis

OK

Baker, Ray — Sapulpa
Berg, Lee — Ketchum
Carrillo, Dwaine — Moore
Coye, Bill — Tulsa
Crenshaw, Al — Eufaula
Crowder, Gary L — Sallisaw
Damasteel Stainless Damascus, — Norman
Darby, David T — Cookson
Dill, Dave — Bethany

Duff, Bill — Poteau
Dunlap, Jim — Sallisaw
Gepner, Don — Norman
Heimdale, J E — Tulsa
Johns, Rob — Enid
Kennedy Jr., Bill — Yukon
Kirk, Ray — Tahlequah
Lairson Sr., Jerry — Ringold
Martin
Martin, John Alexander — Okmulgee
Mcclure, Jerry — Norman
Menefee, Ricky Bob — Blawchard
Midgley, Ben — Wister
Miller, Michael E — Chandler
Parsons, Larry — Mustang
Shropshire, Shawn — Piedmont
Spivey, Jefferson — Yukon
Stanford, Perry — Broken Arrow
Tomberlin, Brion R — Norman
Williams, Michael — Broken Bow
Wingo, Gary — Ramona

OR

Bell, Gabriel — Coquille
Bell, Michael — Coquille
Bochman, Bruce — Grants Pass
Brandt, Martin W — Springfield
Buchanan, Thad — Prineville
Buchanan, Zac — Eugene
Buchner, Bill — Idleyld Park
Busch, Steve — Oakland
Carter, Murray M — Hillsboro
Clark, Nate — Yoncalla
Coon, Raymond C — Damascus
Crowner, Jeff — Cottage Grove
Davis, Terry — Sumpter
Eirich, William — Bend
Frank, Heinrich H — Dallas
Gamble, Frank — Salem
Goddard, Wayne — Eugene
Harsey, William H — Creswell
Horn, Jess — Eugene
House, Cameron — Salem
Kelley, Gary — Aloha
Lake, Ron — Eugene
Little, Gary M — Broadbent
Magruder, Jason — Talent
Martin, Gene — Williams
Martin, Walter E — Williams
Ochs, Eric — Sherwood
Olson, Darrold E — McMinnville
Pruyn, Peter — Grants Pass
Richard, Raymond — Gresham
Richards, Chuck — Salem
Rider, David M — Eugene
Sarganis, Paul — Jacksonville
Scarrow, Wil — Gold Hill
Schoeningh, Mike — North Powder
Schrader, Robert — Bend
Sevey Custom Knife, — Gold Beach
Sheehy, Thomas J — Portland
Shoger, Mark O — Beaverton
Sibert, Shane — Gladstone
Smith, Rick — Rogue River
Tendick, Ben — Eugene
Thompson, Leon — Gaston
Thompson, Tommy — Portland
Turner, Mike — Williams
Vallotton, Butch And Arey — Oakland
Vallotton, Rainy D — Umpqua
Vallotton, Shawn — Oakland
Vallotton, Thomas — Oakland
Ward, Ken — Grants Pass

PA

Anderson, Gary D — Spring Grove
Anderson, Tom — Manchester
Appleby, Robert — Shickshinny
Besedick, Frank E — Monongahela
Blystone, Ronald L. — Creekside
Candrella, Joe — Warminster
Clark, D E (Lucky) — Johnstown
Corkum, Steve — Littlestown
Darby, Rick — Levittown
Evans, Ronald B — Middleton
Frey Jr., W Frederick — Milton
Godlesky, Bruce F. — Apollo
Goldberg, David — Ft Washington
Gottschalk, Gregory J — Carnegie
Harner Iii, "Butch" Lloyd R. — Littlestown
Heinz, John — Upper Black Eddy
Hudson, Rob — Northumberland
Johnson, John R — New Buffalo
Jones, Curtis J — Washington
Malloy, Joe — Freeland
Marlowe, Donald — Dover
Mensch, Larry C — Milton
Miller, Rick — Rockwood
Moore, Ted — Elizabethtown
Morett, Donald — Lancaster
Nealy, Bud — Stroudsburg
Neilson, J — Wyalusing
Ogden, Bill — Avis
AVIS
Ortega, Ben M — Wyoming
Parker, J E — Clarion
Root, Gary — Erie
Rose, Bob — Wagontown
Rupert, Bob — Clinton
Sass, Gary N — Sharpsville
Scimio, Bill — Spruce Creek
Sinclair, J E — Pittsburgh
Steigerwalt, Ken — Orangeville
Stroyan, Eric — Dalton
Takach, Andrew — Elizabeth
Vaughan, Ian — Manheim
Whittaker, Robert E — Mill Creek

RI

Dickison, Scott S — Portsmouth
Jacques, Alex — East Greenwich
Mchenry, William James — Wyoming
Olszewski, Stephen — Coventry
Williams, Jason L — Wyoming
Wright, Richard S — Carolina

RUSSIA

Kharlamov, Yuri — Tula

SC

Beatty, Gordon H. — Seneca
Branton, Robert — Awendaw
Brend, Walter — Ridge Springs
Cannady, Daniel L — Allendale
Cox, Sam — Gaffney
Denning, Geno — Gaston
Estabrook, Robbie — Conway
Frazier, Jim — Wagener
Gainey, Hal — Greenwood
George, Harry — Aiken
Gregory, Michael — Belton
Hendrix, Jerry — Clinton
Hendrix, Wayne — Allendale
Hucks, Jerry — Moncks Corner
Kay, J Wallace — Liberty
Knight, Jason — Harleyville
Kreger, Thomas — Lugoff

Langley, Gene H — Florence
Lutz, Greg — Greenwood
Manley, David W — Central
Miles Jr., C R "Iron Doctor" — Lugoff
Odom Jr., Victor L. — North
O'Quinn, W. Lee — Elgin
Page, Larry — Aiken
Parler, Thomas O — Charleston
Peagler, Russ — Moncks Corner
Perry, Johnny — Inman
Sears, Mick — Kershaw
Smith, Ralph L — Taylors
Thomas, Rocky — Moncks Corner
Tyser, Ross — Spartanburg

SD

Boley, Jamie — Parker
Boysen, Raymond A — Rapid Ciy
Ferrier, Gregory K — Rapid City
Thomsen, Loyd W — Custer

SLOVAKIA

Albert, Stefan — Filakovo 98604
Bojtos, Arpad — 98403 Lucenec
Kovacik, Robert — 98401 Lucenec
Laoislav, Santa-Lasky — 97637 Hrochot
Mojzis, Julius — 98511 Halic
Pulis, Vladimir — 96701 Kremnica

SOUTH AFRICA

Arm-Ko Knives, — Marble Ray , KZN
Baartman, George — Bela-Bela, LP
Bauchop, Robert — Munster, KN
Beukes, Tinus — Vereeniging, GT
Bezuidenhout, Buzz — Malvern, KZN
Boardman, Guy — New Germany, KZN
Brown, Rob E — Port Elizabeth, EC
Burger, Fred — Munster, KZN
Burger, Tiaan — Pretoria, GT
Dickerson, Gavin — Petit, GT
Grey, Piet — Naboomspruit, LP
Harvey, Heather — Belfast, MP
Harvey, Kevin — Belfast, LP
Herbst, Gawie — Akasia, GT
Herbst, Thinus — Akasia, GT
Horn, Des — Onrusrivier, WC
Klaasee, Tinus — George, WC
Kojetin, W — Germiston, GT
Lancaster, C G — Free State
Liebenberg, Andre — Randburg, GT
Mackrill, Stephen — Johannesburg, GT
Mahomedy, A R — Marble Ray, KZN
Mahomedy, Humayd A.R. — Marble Ray, KZN
Naude, Louis — Malmesbury, WC
Pienaar, Conrad — Free State
Prinsloo, Theuns — Free State
Rietveld, Bertie — Magaliesburg, GT
Russell, Mick — Port Elizabeth, EC
Schoeman, Corrie — Free State
Steyn, Peter — Freestate
Thorburn, Andre E. — Warmbaths, LP
Van Den Berg, Neels — Pretoria, Gauteng
Van Der Westhuizen, Peter — Mossel Bay, SC
Van Heerden, Andre — Pretoria, GT
Watson, Peter — La Hoff, NW

SOUTH AUSTRALIA

Edmonds, Warrick — Adelaide Hills

SPAIN

Cecchini, Gustavo T. Sao Jose Rio Preto

SWEDEN

Bergh, Roger	Bygdea
Billgren, Per	Soderfors
Eklund, Maihkel	Farila
Embretsen, Kaj	Edsbyn
Hedlund, Anders	Brastad
Henningsson, Michael	Vastra Frolunda
(Gothenburg)	
Hogstrom, Anders T	Johanneshov
Johansson, Anders	Grangesberg
Lundstrom, Jan-Ake	Dals-Langed
Lundstrom, Torbjorn (Tobbe)	Are
Nilsson, Jonny Walker	Arvidsjaur
Nordell, Ingemar	FSrila
Persson, Conny	Loos
Ryberg, Gote	Norrahammar
Styrefors, Mattias	Boden
Vogt, Patrik	Halmstad

SWITZERLAND

Roulin, Charles	Geneva
Soppera, Arthur	Ulisbach

TN

Accawi, Fuad	Clinton
Adams, Jim	Cordova
Bailey, Joseph D.	Nashville
Blanchard, G R (Gary)	Dandridge
Breed, Kim	Clarksville
Byrd, Wesley L	Evensville
Canter, Ronald E	Jackson
Casteel, Dianna	Monteagle
Casteel, Douglas	Monteagle
Claiborne, Ron	Knox
Clay, Wayne	Pelham
Conley, Bob	Jonesboro
Coogan, Robert	Smithville
Corby, Harold	Johnson City
Ewing, John H	Clinton
Hale, Lloyd	Lynnville
Harley, Larry W	Bristol
Harley, Richard	Bristol
Heflin, Christopher M	Nashville
Hughes, Dan	Spencer
Hurst, Jeff	Rutledge
Hutcheson, John	Chattanooga
Johnson, David A	Pleasant Shade
Johnson, Ryan M	Signal Mountain
Kemp, Lawrence	Ooltewah
Largin, Ken	Sevierville
Levine, Bob	Tullahoma
Marshall, Stephen R	Mt. Juliet
Mccarty, Harry	Blaine
Mcdonald, W.J. "Jerry"	Germantown
Moulton, Dusty	Loudon
Raley, R. Wayne	Collierville
Sampson, Lynn	Jonesborough
Smith, Newman L.	Gatlinburg
Taylor, C Gray	Fall Branch
Taylor, David	Rogersville
Vanderford, Carl G	Columbia
Ward, W C	Clinton
Wheeler, Gary	Clarksville
Williams Jr., Richard	Morristown

TX

Adams, William D	Burton
Alexander, Eugene	Ganado
Allen, Mike "Whiskers"	Malakoff
Aplin, Spencer	Brazoria
Appleton, Ron	Bluff Dale
Ashby, Douglas	Dallas
Baker, Tony	Allen
Barnes, Marlen R.	Atlanta
Barr, Judson C.	Irving
Batts, Keith	Hooks
Blackwell, Zane	Eden
Blum, Kenneth	Brenham
Bratcher, Brett	Plantersville
Brewer, Craig	Killeen
Broadwell, David	Wichita Falls
Brooks, Michael	Lubbock
Brown, Douglas	Fort Worth
Budell, Michael	Brenham
Bullard, Randall	Canyon
Burden, James	Burkburnett
Buzek, Stanley	Waller
Callahan, F Terry	Boerne
Carey, Peter	Lago Vista
Carpenter, Ronald W	Jasper
Carter, Fred	Wichita Falls
Champion, Robert	Amarillo
Chase, John E	Aledo
Chew, Larry	Weatherford
Childers, David	W. Spring
Churchman, T W (Tim)	Bandera
Cole, James M	Bartonville
Connor, John W	Odessa
Connor, Michael	Winters
Costa, Scott	Spicewood
Crain, Jack W	Granbury
Darcey, Chester L	College Station
Davidson, Larry	New Braunfels
Davis, Vernon M	Waco
De Mesa, John	Lewisville
Dean, Harvey J	Rockdale
Debaud, Jake	Dallas
Delong, Dick	Centerville
Dietz, Howard	New Braunfels
Dominy, Chuck	Colleyville
Dyer, David	Granbury
Eldridge, Allan	Ft. Worth
Elishewitz, Allen	New Braunfels
Epting, Richard	College Station
Eriksen, James Thorlief	Garland
Evans, Carlton	Gainesville
Fant Jr., George	Atlanta
Ferguson, Jim	San Angelo
Fisher, Josh	Murchison
Foster, Al	Magnolia
Foster, Norvell C	Marion
Fowler, Jerry	Hutto
Fritz, Jesse	Slaton
Fry, Jason	Abilene
Fuller, Bruce A	Blanco
Gann, Tommy	Canton
Garner, Larry W	Tyler
George, Les	Corpus Christi
Graham, Gordon	New Boston
Green, Bill	Sachse
Griffin, Rendon And Mark	Houston
Grimes, Mark	Bedford
Guinn, Terry	Eastland
Halfrich, Jerry	San Marcos
Halligan, Ed	San Antonio
Hamlet Jr., Johnny	Clute
Hand, Bill	Spearman
Hawkins, Buddy	Texarkana
Hawkins Jr., Charles R.	San Angelo
Hayes, Scotty	Tesarkana
Haynes, Jerry	Gunter
Hays, Mark	Austin
Hemperley, Glen	Willis
Hicks, Gary	Tuscola
Hill, Steve E	Spring Branch
Horrigan, John	Burnet
Howell, Jason G	Lake Jackson
Hudson, Robert	Humble
Hughes, Lawrence	Plainview
Jackson, Charlton R	San Antonio
Jaksik Jr., Michael	Fredericksburg
Johnson, Ruffin	Houston
Keller, Bill	San Antonio
Kern, R W	San Antonio
Kious, Joe	Kerrville
Ladd, Jim S	Deer Park
Ladd, Jimmie Lee	Deer Park
Lambert, Jarrell D	Granado
Laplante, Brett	McKinney
Lay, L J	Burkburnett
Lemcke, Jim L	Houston
Lennon, Dale	Alba
Lister Jr., Weldon E	Boerne
Love, Ed	San Antonio
Lovett, Michael	Mound
Luchak, Bob	Channelview
Luckett, Bill	Weatherford
Majors, Charlie	Montgomery
Martin, Michael W	Beckville
Mcconnell Jr., Loyd A	Marble Falls
Merz Iii, Robert L	Katy
Miller, R D	Dallas
Minchew, Ryan	Pampa
Mitchell, Wm Dean	Warren
Moen, Jerry	Dallas
Moore, James B	Ft. Stockton
Neely, Greg	Bellaire
Nolen, Steve	Keller
Oates, Lee	La Porte
O'Brien, Mike J.	San Antonio
Odgen, Randy W	Houston
Ogletree Jr., Ben R	Livingston
Osborne, Warren	Waxahachie
Ott, Ted	Elgin
Overeynder, T R	Arlington
Ownby, John C	Murphy
Packard, Ronnie	Bonham
Pardue, Joe	Hillister
Patterson, Pat	Barksdale
Pierce, Randall	Arlington
Pollock, Wallace J	Cedar Park
Polzien, Don	Lubbock
Powell, James	Texarkana
Powers, Walter R.	Lolita
Ralph, Darrel	Founcy
Ray, Alan W	Lovelady
Richardson Jr., Percy	Pollok
Roberts, Jack	Houston
Robinson, Charles (Dickie)	Vega
Rucker, Thomas	Nacogdoches
Ruple, William H	Pleasanton
Ruth, Michael G	Texarkana
Ruth, Jr., Michael	Texarkana
Self, Ernie	Dripping Springs
Shipley, Steven A	Richardson
Sloan, Shane	Newcastle
Smart, Steve	McKinney
Snody, Mike	Aransas Pass
Stokes, Ed	Hockley
Stone, Jerry	Lytle
Stout, Johnny	New Braunfels
Theis, Terry	Harper
Thuesen, Ed	Damon
Truncali, Pete	Garland
Turcotte, Larry	Pampa
Van Reenen, Ian	Amarillo
Vickers, David	Montgomery
Ware, Tommy	Onalaska
Watson, Daniel	Driftwood
Watts, Johnathan	Gatesville
Watts, Wally	Gatesville
Weever, John	Nemo
White, Dale	Sweetwater
Whitley, Weldon G	Odessa

Wilcher, Wendell L	Palestine
Wilkins, Mitchell	Montgomery
Wilson, Curtis M	Burleson
Winn, Marvin	Frisco
Wolf Jr., William Lynn	Lagrange
Yeates, Joe A	Spring
Zboril, Terry	Caldwell
Zermeno, William D.	Houston

UNITED ARAB EMIRATES

Kukulka, Wolfgang	Dubai

UNITED KINGDOM

Hague, Geoff	Quarley, Hampshire
Heasman, H G	Llandudno, N. Wales
Horne, Grace	Sheffield
Maxen, Mick	Hatfield, Herts

URUGUAY

Gonzalez, Leonardo Williams	Maldonado
Symonds, Alberto E	Montevideo

UT

Allred, Bruce F	Layton
Black, Earl	Salt Lake City
Carter, Shayne	Payson
Ence, Jim	Richfield
Ennis, Ray	Ogden
Erickson, L.M.	Ogden
Hunter, Hyrum	Aurora
Johnson, Steven R	Manti
Jorgensen, Carson	Mt Pleasant
Lang, David	Kearns
Maxfield, Lynn	Layton
Nell, Chad	St. George
Nielson, Jeff V	Monroe
Nunn, Gregory	Castle Valley
Palmer, Taylor	Blanding
Peterson, Chris	Salina
Ricks, Kurt J.	Trenton
Strickland, Dale	Monroe
Velarde, Ricardo	Park City
Washburn Jr., Robert Lee	St. George
Weeks, Ryan	Bountiful
Winn, Travis A.	Salt Lake City
Young, John	Ephraim
Jenkins, Mitch	Manti
Johnson, Jerry	Spring City

VA

Apelt, Stacy E	Norfolk
Arbuckle, James M	Yorktown
Ball, Butch	Floyd
Ballew, Dale	Bowling Green
Batley, Mark S.	Wake
Batson, Richard G.	Rixeyville
Beverly Ii, Larry H	Spotsylvania
Catoe, David R	Norfolk
Chamberlain, Charles R	Barren Springs
Davidson, Edmund	Goshen
Foster, Burt	Bristol
Goodpasture, Tom	Ashland
Harris, Cass	Bluemont
Hedrick, Don	Newport News
Hendricks, Samuel J	Maurertown
Herb, Martin	Richmond
Holloway, Paul	Norfolk
Jones, Barry M And Phillip G	Danville
Jones, Enoch	Warrenton
Kearney, Jarod	Swoope
Martin, Herb	Richmond

Mccoun, Mark	DeWitt
Metheny, H A "Whitey"	Spotsylvania
Mills, Michael	Colonial Beach
Murski, Ray	Reston
Norfleet, Ross W	Providence Forge
Parks, Blane C	Woodbridge
Pawlowski, John R	Newport News
Schlueter, David	Madison Heights
Tomes, P J	Shipman
Vanhoy, Ed And Tanya	Abingdon
Vestal, Charles	Abingdon
Ward, Ron	Rose Hill

VT

Bensinger, J. W.	Marshfield
Haggerty, George S	Jacksonville
Kelso, Jim	Worcester
Wulf, Derrick	Essex

WA

Amoureux, A W	Northport
Ber, Dave	San Juan Island
Berglin, Bruce	Mount Vernon
Boguszewski, Phil	Lakewood
Bromley, Peter	Spokane
Brothers, Robert L	Colville
Brown, Dennis G	Shoreline
Brunckhorst, Lyle	Bothell
Bump, Bruce D.	Walla Walla
Butler, John R	Shoreline
Campbell, Dick	Colville
Chamberlain, Jon A	E. Wenatchee
Conti, Jeffrey D	Bonney Lake
Conway, John	Kirkland
Crowthers, Mark F	Rolling Bay
D'Angelo, Laurence	Vancouver
Davis, John	Selah
De Wet, Kobus	Yakima
Diaz, Jose	Ellensburg
Diskin, Matt	Freeland
Erickson, Daniel	Snohomish
Ferry, Tom	Auburn
Gray, Bob	Spokane
Greenfield, G O	Everett
Hansen, Lonnie	Spanaway
House, Gary	Ephrata
Hurst, Cole	E. Wenatchee
Keyes, Geoff P.	Duvall
Lisch, David K	Seattle
Norton, Don	Port Townsend
O'Malley, Daniel	Seattle
Padilla, Gary	Bellingham
Podmajersky, Dietrich	Seatlle
Rader, Michael	Wilkeson
Roeder, David	Kennewick
Rogers, Ray	Wauconda
Sanford, Dick	Montesano
Schempp, Ed	Ephrata
Schempp, Martin	Ephrata
Stegner, Wilbur G	Rochester
Sterling, Thomas J	Coupeville
Straub, Salem F.	Tonasket
Swyhart, Art	Klickitat
Thomas, Bob	Ferndale
Wheeler, Nick	Castle Rock
Wright, Kevin	Quilcene

WI

Boyes, Tom	West Bend
Brandsey, Edward P	Janesville
Bruner Jr., Fred Bruner Blades	Fall Creek
Carr, Joseph E.	Menomonee Falls
Coats, Ken	Stevens Point
Delarosa, Jim	Janesville

Haines, Jeff	Wauzeka
Johnson, Richard	Germantown
Kanter, Michael	New Berlin
Kohls, Jerry	Princeton
Kolitz, Robert	Beaver Dam
Lary, Ed	Mosinee
Lerch, Matthew	Sussex
Maestri, Peter A	Spring Green
Martin, Peter	Waterford
Mikolajczyk, Glen	Caledonia
Millard, Fred G	Richland Center
Nelson, Ken	Racine
Niemuth, Troy	Sheboygan
Ponzio, Doug	Beloit
Rabuck, Jason	Springbrook
Revishvili, Zaza	Madison
Ricke, Dave	West Bend
Rochford, Michael R	Dresser
Roush, Scott	Washburn
Schrap, Robert G	Wauwatosa
Steinbrecher, Mark W	Pleasant Prairie
Wattelet, Michael A	Minocqua

WV

Crist, Zoe	Marlinton
Derr, Herbert	St. Albans
Drost, Jason D	French Creek
Drost, Michael B	French Creek
Elliott, Jerry	Charleston
Jeffries, Robert W	Red House
Liegey, Kenneth R	Millwood
Maynard, Larry Joe	Crab Orchard
Morris, Eric	Beckley
Pickens, Selbert	Dunbar
Reynolds, Dave	Harrisville
Small, Ed	Keyser
Steingass, T.K.	Hedgesville
Tokar, Daniel	Shepherdstown
Wilson, Rw	Weirton
Wyatt, William R	Rainelle

WY

Alexander, Darrel	Ten Sleep
Amos, Chris	Riverton
Ankrom, W.E.	Cody
Banks, David L.	Riverton
Barry, Scott	Laramie
Bartlow, John	Sheridan
Deveraux, Butch	Riverton
Draper, Audra	Riverton
Draper, Mike	Riverton
Fowler, Ed A.	Riverton
Friedly, Dennis E	Cody
Kilby, Keith	Cody
Oliver, Todd D	Cheyenne
Rexroat, Kirk	Wright
Reynolds, John C	Gillette
Rodebaugh, James L	Carpenter
Ross, Stephen	Evanston
Spragg, Wayne E	Lovell
Whipple, Wesley A	Thermopolis

ZIMBABWE

Burger, Pon	Bulawayo

Not all knifemakers are organization-types, but those listed here are in good standing with these organizations.

the knifemakers' guild

2013 membership

a Les Adams, Douglas A. Alcorn, Mike "Whiskers" Allen

b Robert K. Bagley, Tony Baker, Santino e Arlete Ballestra, Norman P. Bardsley, James J. Barry, III, John Bartlow, Barbara Baskett, Gene Baskett, Michael S. Blue, Arpad Bojtos, Philip W. Booth, Tony Bose, Dennis Bradley, Gayle Bradley, Edward Brandsey, W. Lowell Bray, Jr., George Clint Breshears, Fred Bruner, Jr., John Busfield

c Harold J. "Kit" Carson, Michael Carter, Kevin Casey, Dianna Casteel, Douglas Casteel, William Chapo, Daniel Chinnock, Wayne Clay, Kenneth R. Coats, Bob F. Conley, George Cousino, Colin J. Cox, Pat Crawford, Kevin Cross

d Charles Dake, Alex K. Daniels, Jack Davenport, Edmund Davidson, John H. Davis, William C. Davis, Herbert K. Derr, Mike Dilluvio, David Dodds, Larry Downing, Tom Downing, William Duff, Fred Durio, Will Dutton

e Jacob Elenbaas, Jim Elliott, William B. Ellis, James T. Eriksen, Carlton R. Evans

f Stephen J. Fecas, Cliff Fendley, Lee Ferguson, Robert G. Flynt, Michael H. Franklin, John R. Fraps, Stanley Fujisaka, Bruce A. Fuller

g Steve Gatlin, Warren Glover, Stefan Gobec, Richard R. Golden, Gregory J. Gottschalk, Kenneth W. Guth

h Philip (Doc) L. Hagen, Gerald Halfrich, Jim Hammond, Don L Hanson III, Koji Hara, Ralph Dewey Harris, Rade Hawkins, Earl Jay Hendrickson, Wayne Hendrix, Wayne G. Hensley, Gil Hibben, Wesley G. Hibben, R. Hinson, Steven W. Hoel, Kevin Hoffman, Desmond R. Horn, Larry Hostetler, Rob Hudson, Roy Humenick, Joseph Hytovick

i Billy Mace Imel, Michael Irie

j James T. Jacks, Brad Johnson, Jerry L. Johnson, Keith R. Johnson, Ronald B. Johnson, Steven R. Johnson, William "Bill" C. Johnson, Enoch D. Jones, Jack Jones, Lonnie L. Jones

k William L. Keeton, Bill Kennedy, Jr., Bill King, Harvey King, Terry Knipschield

l Kermit Laurent, Paul M. LeBetard, Gary E. LeBlanc, Kevin T. Lesswing, William S. Letcher, William L. Levengood, Jack Levin, Bob Levine, Wolfgang Loerchner, Schuyler Lovestrand, Don Lozier, Bill Luckett, Gail Lunn, Larry Lunn, Ernest Lyle

m Stephen Mackrill, Riccardo Mainolfi, Joe Malloy, Herbert A. Martin, Charlie B. Mathews, Harry S. Mathews, Jerry McClure, Lloyd McConnell, Mike Mercer, Ted Merchant, Robert L. Merz, III, Toshiaki Michinaka, James P. Miller, Stephen C. Miller, Dan Mink, Jerry Moen, Jeff Morgan

n Bud Nealy, Corbin Newcomb, Larry Newton, Rick Noland, Ross W Norfleet

o Clifford W. O'Dell, Charles F. Ochs, III, Ben R. Ogletree, Jr., Warren Osborne, T. R. Overeynder, John E. Owens, Clifford W. O'Dell, Sean O'Hare

p Larry Page, Cliff Parker, Jerry Partridge, John R. Pawlowski, W. D. Pease, Alfred Pendray, John W. PerMar, Daniel Piergallini, Otakar Pok, Larry Pridgen, Jr., Joseph R. Prince,

r Jason Rabuck, James D. Ragsdale, Steven Rapp, Ron F. Richard, Joseph Calvin Robinson, Michael Rochford, A.G. Russell

s Michael A. Sakmar, Scott W. Sawby, Juergen Schanz, Mike Schirmer, Mark C. Sentz, Eugene W. Shadley, John I Shore, Jim Siska, Steven C. Skiff, Scott Slobodian, Ralph Smith, Arthur Soppera, David Steier, Murray Sterling, Douglas W. Stice, Russ Sutton, Charles C. Syslo

t Robert Terzuola, Leon Thompson, Bobby L. Toole, Reinhard Tschager, Ralph Turnbull

v Aas van Rijswijk, Donald Vogt

w George A. Walker, Edward Wallace, Charles B. Ward, Tom Watson, Charles G. Weeber, John S. Weever, Zachary Whitson, Wayne Whittaker, Donnie R. Wicker, R.W. Wilson, Stan Wilson, Daniel Winkler, Marvin Winn

y George L. Young, Mike Yurco

z Brad Zinker, Michael Zscherny

abs master smith listing

a   David Anders, Jerome Anders, Gary D. Anderson, E. R. Russ Andrews II

b   Gary Barnes, Aubrey G. Barnes Sr., James L. Batson, Jimmie H. Buckner, Bruce D. Bump, Bill Burke, Bill Buxton

c   Ed Caffrey, Murray M. Carter, Kevin R. Cashen, Hsiang Lin (Jimmy) Chin, Jon Christensen, Howard F. Clark, Wade Colter, Michael Connor, James R. Cook, Joseph G. Cordova, Jim Crowell, Steve Culver

d   Sava Damlovac, Harvey J. Dean, Christoph Deringer, Adam DesRosiers, Bill Dietzel, Audra L. Draper, Rick Dunkerley, Steve Dunn, Kenneth Durham

e   Dave Ellis

f   Robert Thomas Ferry III, Jerry Fisk, John S. Fitch, Joe Flournoy, Don Fogg, Burt Foster, Ronnie E. Foster, Larry D. Fuegen, Bruce A. Fuller, Jack A. Fuller

g   Tommy Gann, Bert Gaston, Thomas Gerner, Greg Gottschalk

h   Tim Hancock, Don L. Hanson III, Heather Harvey, Kevin Harvey, Wally Hayes, E. Jay Hendrickson, Don Hethcoat, John Horrigan, Gary House, Rob Hudson

j   Jim L. Jackson

k   Joseph F. Keeslar, Keith Kilby, Ray Kirk, Hank Knickmeyer, Jason Knight, Bob Kramer

l   Jerry Lairson Sr., Mick Langley

m   J. Chris Marks, John Alexander Martin, Roger D. Massey, Victor J. McCrackin, Shawn McIntyre, Hanford J. Miller, Wm Dean Mitchell

n   Greg Neely, J. Neilson, Ron Newton, Douglas E. Noren

o   Charles F. Ochs III

p   Alfred Pendray, John L. Perry, Dan Petersen Ph.D., Timothy Potier

r   Michael Rader, J. W. Randall, Kirk Rexroat, Linden W. Rhea, Dickie Robinson, James L. Rodebaugh, Kyle Royer, Raymond B. Rybar Jr.

s   James P. Saviano, Stephen C. Schwarzer, Mark C. Sentz, Rodrigo Menezes Sfreddo, J.D. Smith, Josh Smith, Raymond L. Smith, Bill Sowell, Charles Stout, Joseph Szilaski

t   Shane Taylor, Jean-paul Thevenot, Jason Tiensvold, Brion Tomberlin, P. J. Tomes, Henry Torres

v   Michael V. Vagnino Jr., Terry L. Vandeventer

w   James L. Walker, Daniel Warren, John White, Michael L. Williams, Daniel Winkler

professional knifemaker's association

Mike Allen, Pat Ankrom, Shane Paul Atwood, Eddie J. Baca, D. Scott Barry, John Bartlow, Donald Bell, Tom Black, Justin Bridges, Kenneth L. Brock, Lucas Burnley, Tim S. Cameron, Ken Cardwell, Vance Corich, Del Corsi, Culpepper & Co., John Easter, Ray W. Ennis, Lee Ferguson, Chuck Fraley, Graham Fredeen, Bob Glassman, Bob Ham, Alford "Alf" Hanna, Wayne Hensley, Gary Hicks, Guy E. Hielscher, Jay Higgins, Mike L. Irie, Mitch Jenkins, Harvey King, Todd Kopp, Jim Krause, Tom Krein, Scott Kuntz, Tim "Chops" Lambkin, James R. Largent, Ken Linton, Arthur Lynn, Jim Magee, Jerry & Sandy McClure, Mardi Meshejian, Clayton Miller, Michael Miller, Tyree L. Montell, Mike Mooney, Steve Myers, Robert Nash, Fred A. Ott, William Pleins, James L. Poplin, Bill Post, Calvin Powell, Steve Powers, Peter Pruyn, Bill Redd, Jim Reid, Steve Rollert, David Ruana, Dennis "Bud" Ruana, Don Ruana, Walter Scherar, Terry Schreiner, M.L. "Pepper" Seaman, Eugene Solomonik, Eddie F. Stalcup, Craig Steketee, Douglas Stice, Mark Strauss, Kurt Swearingen, James D. Thrash, Ed Thuesen, Albert Trujillo, Pete Truncali, Charles Turnage, Mike Tyre, Dick Waites, James Walton, Al Warren, Rodney Watts, Hans Weinmueller, Harold J. Wheeler, Jacob Wilson, R.W. Wilson, Michael C. Young, Monte Zavatta, Russ Zima, Daniel F. Zvonek.

state/regional associations

alaska interior knifemakers association

Frank Ownby, Fred DeCicco, Bob Hook, Jenny Day, Kent Setzer, Kevin Busk, Loren Wellnite, Mark Knapp, Matthew Hanson, Mel Harvey, Nate Miller, Richard Kacsur, Ron Miller, Terry Miller, Bob LaFrance, Randy Olsen

alaska knifemakers association

A.W. Amoureux, John Arnold, Bud Aufdermauer, Robert Ball, J.D. Biggs, Lonnie Breuer, Tom Broome, Mark Bucholz, Irvin Campbell, Virgil Campbell, Raymond Cannon, Christopher Cawthorne, John Chamberlin, Bill Chatwood, George Cubic, Bob Cunningham, Gordon S. Dempsey, J.L. Devoll, James Dick, Art Dufour, Alan Eaker, Norm Grant, Gordon Grebe, Dave Highers, Alex Hunt, Dwight Jenkins, Hank Kubaiko, Bill Lance, Bob Levine, Michael Miller, John Palowski, Gordon Parrish, Mark W. Phillips, Frank Pratt, Guy Recknagle, Ron Robertson, Steve Robertson, Red Rowell, Dave Smith, Roger E. Smith, Gary R. Stafford, Keith Stegall, Wilbur Stegner, Norm Story, Robert D. Shaw, Thomas Trujillo, Ulys Whalen, Jim Whitman, Bob Willis

arizona knifemakers association

D. "Butch" Beaver, Bill Cheatham, Dan Dagget, Tom Edwards, Anthony Goddard, Steve Hoel, Ken McFall, Milford Oliver, Jerry Poletis, Merle Poteet, Mike Quinn, Elmer Sams, Jim Sornberger, Glen Stockton, Bruce Thompson, Sandy Tudor, Charles Weiss

arkansas knifemakers association

Mike Allen, David Anders, Robert Ball, Reggie Barker, James Batson, Twin Blades, Craig Braschler, Kim and Gary Breed, Wheeler, Tim Britton, Benoni Bullard, Bill Buxton, J.R. Cook, Gary Crowder, James Crowell, Steve Culver, Jesse Davis, Jim Downie, Bill Duff, Fred Durio, Rodger Echols, Shawn Ellis, Lee Ferguson, Linda Ferguson, Jerry Fisk, Joe Flournoy, Ronnie Foster, James Glisson, Gordon Graham, Bob Ham, Douglas and Gail Hardy, Gary Hicks, Alan Hutchinson, Jack Jones, Lacy Key, Harvey King, Ray Kirk, Bill Kirkes, Jim Krause, Jerry Lairson, Ken Linton, Bill Luckett, Tad Lynch, Jim Magee, Roger Massey, Jerry McClure, Rusty McDonald, W.J. McDonald, Don McIntosh, Tony Metsala, Bill Miller, Skip Miller, Ronnie Mobbs, Sidney Moon, Gary Mulkey, Keith Murr, Steve Myers, Mark Nevling, Allen Newberry, Corbin Newcomb, Ron Newton, Chad Nichols, John Perry, Paul Piccola, Rusty Polk, Bill Post, J.W. Randall, Vernon Red, Lin Rhea, Ralph Richards, Ron Richerson, Bobby Rico, Dennis Riley, T.C. Roberts, Kenny Rowe, Kyle Royer, Mike Ruth, James Scroggs, Richard Self, Tex Skow, Mike Snider, Marvin Snider, Marvin Snider, Marvin Solomon, Craig Steketee, Ed Sticker, Charles Stout, Jeff Stover, Tim Tabor, Brian Thie, Brion Tomberlin, Russell Townsley, Leon Treiber, Pete Truncali, Terry Vandeventer, Charles Vestal, Jim Walker, John White, Mike Williams

australian knifemakers guild inc.

Peter Bald, Col Barn, Bruce Barnett, Denis Barrett, Alistair Bastian, David Brodziak, Stuart Burdett, Jim Deering, Peter Del Raso, Michael Fechner, Keith Fludder, John Foxwell, Thomas Gerner, Branko Giljevic, Stephen Gregory-Jones, Peter Gordon, Barry Gunston, Mal Hannan, Rod Harris, Glenn Henke, Matt James, Peter Kenney, Joe Kiss, Robert Klitscher, Maurie McCarthy, Shawn McIntyre, John McLarty, Ray Mende, Richard Moase, Adam Parker, Jeff Peck, Mike Petersen, Alistair Philllps, Mick Ramage, Wayne Saunders, Murray Shanaughan, Andre Smith, Jim Steele, Rod Stines, Doug Timbs, Stewart Townsend, Hardy Wangermann, Brendan Ware, Ross Yeats

california knifemakers association

Stewart Anderson, Elmer Art, Anton Bosch, Roger Bost, Clint Breshears, Christian Bryant, Mike Butcher, Joe Caswell, Marcus Clinco, Clow Richard, Mike Desensi, Parker Dunbar, Frank Dunkin, Vern Edler III, Stephanie Engnath, Robert Ewing, Chad Fehmie, Alex Felix, Jim Ferguson, Bob Fitlin, Brian Forrest, Dave Gibson, Joe Girtner, Jerry Goettig, Jeanette Gonzales, Russ Green, Tim Harbert, John Harris, Wm. R. 'Bill' Herndon, Neal A. Hodges, Jerid Johnson, Lawrence Johnson, David Kahn, David Kazsuk, Paul Kelso, Steve Koster, Robert Liguori, Harold Locke, R.W. Loveless, Gerald Lundgren, Gordon Melin, Jim Merritt, Russ Moody, Gerald Morgan, Mike Murphy, Tim Musselman, Jeff Mutz, Aram Nigoghossian, Bruce Oakley, Rich Orton, Barry E. Posner, Pat Randall, E. J. Robison, Valente Rosas, Clark Rozas, H. J. Schneider, Red St. Cyr, Chris Stanko, Bill Stroman, Tyrone Swader, Reinhardt Swanson, Tony Swatton, Billy Traylor, Trugrit, Larry White, Stephen A. Williams

canadian knifemakers guild

Joe Arnold, John Benoit, Andre Benoit, Paul Bold, Guillaume Cote, Christoph Deringer, Alain Desaulniers, Sylvain Dion, Jim Downie, Eric Elson, Paul-Aime Fortier, Rick Frigault, Thomas Haslinger, Paul H. Johnston, Kirby Lambert, Greg Lightfoot, Steve Linklater, Wolfgang Loerchner, Brian Lyttle, David MacDonald, Antoine Marcal, James McGowan, Edward McRae, Mike Mossington, William Nease, Simone Raimondi, George Roberts, Paul Savage, Murray St. Amour, Stephen Stuart, David Sylvester, Brian Tighe, Stephen Vanderkolff, Craig Wheatley, Peter Wile, Elizabeth Loerchner, Fred Thynne, Rick Todd

florida knifemaker's association

Dick Atkinson, George Bachley, Mitch Baldwin, James Barry III, Dwayne Batten, Terry Betts, James H. Beusse Jr., Howard Bishop, Dennis Blaine, Dennis Blankenhem, Stephen A. Bloom, Dean Bosworth, John Boyce, W. Lowell Bray, Jr., Patrick R. Burris, Steve Butler, Norman Caesar, Tim Caldwell, Jason Clark, Lowell Cobb, William Cody, David Cole, Steve Corn, Jack Davenport, John Davis, Kenny Davis, Cary Desmon, Tim Caldwell, Jacob Elenbaas, Jim Elliot, William Ellis, Lynn Emrich, Tom Enos, Gary Esker, Frank Fischer, Todd Fischer, Mike Fisher, Travis Fletcher, Roger Gamble, Tony Garcia, James"Hoot" Gibson, Pedro Dick Gonzalez, Paul J. Granger, Ernie Grospitch, David Gruber, Chuck Harnage, Fred Harrington, R. Dewey Harris, Henry Heitler, Kevin Hoffman, Edward O. Holloway, Larry Hostetler, Stewart R. Hudson, Julie Hyman, Joe "Hy" Hytovick, Tom Johanning, Richard Johnson, Roy Kelleher, Paul Kent, Bill King, Bryan Komula, George H. Lambert, William S. Letcher, Bill Levengood, Glenn A. Long, Ernie Lyle, Bob Mancuso, Stephen Mathewson, Michael Matthews, James McNiel, Faustina Mead, Steve Miller, Dan Mink, Martin L. Murphy, Gary Nelson, Larry Newton, J. Cliff Parker, Jerry D. Partridge, John W. PerMar Jr., Larry Patterson, Dan Piergallini, Terry Lee Renner, Calvin J. Robinson, Vince Ruano, Roberto Sanchez, Russell Sauls, Dave Semones, Stuart Shaw, Ann Sheffield, Brad Shepherd, Bill Simons, Jimmie H. Smith, Fred Stern, Kent Swicegood, Timothy Tabor, , Dale Thomas, Wayne Timmerman, Michael Tison, Ralph Turnbull, Louis Vallet, Donald Vogt, Bruce Wassberg, Stan Wilson, Denny Young, Brad Zinker

georgia custom knifemakers' guild

Don R. Adams, Doug Adams, Dennis Bradley, Aaron Brewer, Mike Brown, Robert Busbee, Henry Cambron, Jim Collins, John Costa, Jerry Costin, Scott Davidson, Charles K. Dunn, Will Dutton, Emory Fennell, Stephan Fowler, Dean Gates, Warren Glover, George Hancox, Rade Hawkins, Wayne Hensley, Ronald Hewitt, Kevin Hoffman, Frank Jones, Davin Kates, Dan Masson, Charlie Mathews, Harry Mathews, Leroy Mathews, David McNeal, Dan Mink, James Mitchell, Ralph Mitchell, Sandy Morrisey, Jerry Partridge, Wes Peterson, James Poplin, Joan Poythress, Carey Quinn, Jim Ragsdale, Carl Rechsteiner, David Roberts, Andrew Roy, Joe Sangster, Jamey Saunders, Craig Schneeberger, Randy Scott, Ken Simmons, Nelson Simmons, Jim Small, Bill Snow, Don Tommey, Alex Whetsel, Mike Wilson, Patrick & Hillary Wilson, Robert A. Wright

knife group association of oklahoma

Mike "Whiskers" Allen, Ed Allgood, David Anders, Rocky Anderson, Tony and Ramona Baker, Jerry Barlow, Troy Brown, Dan Burke, Tom Buchanan, F. L. Clowdus Bill Coye, Gary Crowder, Steve Culver, Marc Cullip, David Darby, Voyne Davis, Dan Dick, Dave Dill, Lynn Drury, Bill Duff, Beau Erwin, David Etchieson, Harry Fentress, Lee Ferguson, Linda Ferguson, Daniel Fulk, Gary Gloden, Steve Hansen, Paul Happy, Calvin Harkins, Ron Hebb, Billy Helton, Ed Hites, Tim Johnston, Les Jones, Jim Keen, Bill Kennedy, Stew Killiam, Barbara Kirk, Ray Kirk, Nicholas Knack, Jerry Lairson, Sr., Al Lawrence, Ken Linton, Ron Lucus, Aidan Martin, Barbara Martin, Duncan Martin, John Martin, Jerry McClure, Sandy McClure, Rick Menefee, Ben Midgley, Michael E. Miller, Roy Miller, Ray Milligan, Duane Morganflash, Gary Mulkey, Jerald Nickels, Jerry Parkhurst, Chris Parson, Larry Parsons, Jerry Paul, Larry Paulen, Paul Piccola, Cliff Polk, Roland Quimby, Ron Reeves, Lin Rhea, Mike Ruth, Dan Schneringer, Terry Schreiner, Allen Shafer, Shawn Shropshire, Randell Sinnett, Clifford Smith, Jeremy Steely, Doug Sonntag, Perry Stanford, Mike Stegall, Gary Steinmetz, Mike Stott, Dud Hart Thomas, Brian Tomberlin, Tom Upton, Chuck Ward, Brett Wheat-Simms, Jesse Webb, Rob Weber, Joe Wheeler, Bill Wiggins, Joe Wilkie, Gary Wingo, Daniel Zvonek

knifemakers' guild of southern africa

Jeff Angelo, John Arnold, George Baartman, Francois Basson, Rob Bauchop, George Beechey, Arno Bernard, Buzz Bezuidenhout, Harucus Blomerus, Chris Booysen, Thinus Botha, Ian Bottomley, Peet Bronkhorst, Rob Brown, Fred Burger, Sharon Burger, Trevor Burger, William Burger, Brian Coetzee, Larry Connelly, Andre de Beer, André de Villiers, Melodie de Witt, Gavin Dickerson, Roy Dunseith, Mike Fellows, Leigh Fogarty, Werner Fourie, Andrew Frankland, Brian Geyer, Ettoré Gianferrari, Dale Goldschmidt, Stan Gordon, Nick Grabe, John Grey, Piet Gray, Heather Harvey, Kevin Harvey, Dries Hattingh, Gawie Herbst, Thinus Herbst, Greg Hesslewood, Des Horn, Nkosi Jubane, Billy Kojetin, Mark Kretschmer, Steven Lewis, Garry Lombard, Steve Lombard, Ken Madden, Abdur-Rasheed Mahomedy, Peter Mason, Edward Mitchell, George Muller, Günther Muller, Tom Nelson, Andries Olivier, Jan Olivier, Christo Oosthuizen, Cedric Pannell, Willie Paulsen, Nico Pelzer, Conrad Pienaar, David Pienaar, Jan Potgieter, Lourens Prinsloo, Theuns Prinsloo, Hilton Purvis, Derek Rausch, Chris Reeve, Bertie Rietveld, Melinda Rietveld, Dean Riley, John Robertson, Corrie Schoeman, Eddie Scott, Harvey Silk, Mike Skellern, Toi Skellern, Carel Smith, Ken Smythe, Graham Sparks, Peter Steyn, André Thorburn, Hennie Van Brakel, Fanie Van Der Linde, Johan van der Merwe, Van van der Merwe, Marius Van der Vyver, Louis Van der Walt, Cor Van Ellinckhuijzen, Andre van Heerden, Danie Van Wyk, Ben Venter, Willie Venter, Gert Vermaak, René Vermeulen, Erich Vosloo, Desmond, Waldeck, Albie Wantenaar, Henning Wilkinson, John Wilmot, Wollie Wolfaardt, Owen Wood

midwest knifemakers association

E.R. Andrews III, Frank Berlin, Charles Bolton, Tony Cates, Mike Chesterman, Ron Duncan, Larry Duvall, Bobby Eades, Jackie Emanuel, James Haynes, John Jones, Mickey Koval, Ron Lichlyter, George Martoncik, Gene Millard, William Miller, Corbin Newcomb, Chris Owen, A.D. Rardon, Archie Rardon, Max Smith, Ed Stewart, Charles Syslo, Melvin Williams

montana knifemaker's association

Peter C. Albert, Chet Allinson, Marvin Allinson, Tim & Sharyl Alverson, Bill Amoureux, Jan Anderson, Wendell Barnes, Jim & Kay Barth, Bob & Marian Beaty, Don Bell, Brett Bennett, Robert Bizzell, BladeGallery, Paul Bos, Daryl & Anna May Boyd, Chuck Bragg, Frederick Branch, Peter Bromley, Bruce Brown, Emil Bucharksky, Bruce & Kay Bump, Bill Burke, Alpha Knife Supply Bybee, Ed Caffrey, Jim & Kate Carroll, Murray Carter, Jon & Brenda Christensen, Norm Cotterman, Seith Coughlin, Bob Crowder, Mike Dalimata, John Davis, Maria DesJardins, Rich & Jacque Duxbury, Dan Erickson, Mel & Darlene Fassio, E.V. Ford, Eric Fritz, Dana & Sandy Hackney, Doc & Lil Hagen, Gary & Betsy Hannon, Eli Hansen, J.A. Harkins, Tedd Harris, Sam & Joy Hensen, Loren Higgins, Mickey Hines, Gerald & Pamela Hintz, Gary House, Tori Howe, Kevin Hutchins, Al Inman, Frank & Shelley Jacobs, Karl Jermunson, Keith Johnson, Don Kaschmitter, Steven Kelly, Dan & Penny Kendrick, Monte Koppes, Donald Kreuger, David Lisch, James Luman, Robert Martin, Max McCarter, Neil McKee, Larry McLaughlin, Mac & Nancy McLaughlin, Phillip Moen, Gerald Morgan, Randy Morgan, Dan & Andrea Nedved, Daniel O'Malley, Joe Olson, Collin Paterson, Willard & Mark Patrick, Jeffrey & Tyler Pearson, Brian Pender, James Poling, Chance & Kerri Priest, Richard Prusz, Greg Rabatin, Jim Raymond, Jim Rayner, Darren Reeves, John Reynolds, Ryan Robison, Gary Rodewald, Buster Ross, Ruana Knifeworks, Charles Sauer, Dean Schroeder, Michael Sheperes, Mike Smith, Gordon St. Clair, Terry Steigers, George Stemple, Dan & Judy Stucky, Art & Linda Swyhart, Jim Thill, Cary Thomas, James & Tammy Venne, Bill & Lori Waldrup, Jonathan & Doris Walther, Kenneth Ward, Michael Wattelet, Darlene Weinand, Gerome & Darlene Weinand, Daniel & Donna Westlind, Matt & Michelle Whitmus, Dave Wilkes, Mike & Sean Young

national independent cutlery association

Ron & Patsy Beck, Bob Bennett, Dave Bishop, Steve Corn, Dave Harvey, C.J. McKay, Mike Murray, Gary Parker, Rachel Schindler, Joe Tarbell

new england bladesmiths guild

Phillip Baldwin, Gary Barnes, Paul Champagne, Jimmy Fikes, Don Fogg, Larry Fuegen, Rob Hudson, Midk Langley, Louis Mills, Dan Maragni, Jim Schmidt, Wayne Valachovic and Tim Zowada

north carolina custom knifemakers' guild

Dr. James Batson, Wayne Bernauer, Tom Beverly, William "Bill" Bisher, Jamin Bracket, Mark Cary, Thomas Clegg, Ray Clontz, Travis Daniel, David Driggs, Russell Gardner, Talmage M. Hall, Koji Hara, John Hege, Curtis Iovito, Tommy Johnson, Barry and Phillip Jones, Frank Joyce, Carol Kelly, Tony Kelly, Robert Knight, Leon Lassiter, Gregory Manley, Mathew Manley, Aubrey McDonald, Tommy McNabb, Arthur McNeil, Christopher McNeil, William Morris, Van Royce Morton, Charles Ostendorf, James Poplin, Murphy Ragsdale, Kenneth Steve Randall, Bruce Ryan, Joel Sandifer, Tim Scholl, Andy Sharpe, Gene Smith, Octavio F. Soares, Arthur Summers, Russ Sutton, Bruce Turner.

ohio knifemakers association

Raymond Babcock, Van Barnett, Harold A. Collins, Larry Detty, Tom Downing, Jim Downs, Patty Ferrier, Jeff Flannery, James Fray, Bob Foster, Raymond Guess, Scott Hamrie, Rick Hinderer, Curtis Hurley, Ed Kalfayan, Michael Koval, Judy Koval, Larry Lunn, Stanley Maienknecht, Dave Marlott, Mike Mercer, David Morton, Patrick McGroder, Charles Pratt, Darrel Ralph, Roy Roddy, Carroll Shoemaker, John Smith, Clifton Smith, Art Summers, Jan Summers, Donald Tess, Dale Warther, John Wallingford, Earl Witsaman, Joanne Yurco, Mike Yurco

saskatchewan knifemakers guild

Vern Alton, Al Bakke, Marty Beets, Clarence Broeksma, Irv Brunas, Emil Bucharsky, Jim Clow, Murray Cook, Bob Crowder, Herb Davison, Ray Dilling, Kevin Donald, Brian Drayton, Dallas Dreger, Ray Fehler, Cal Ganshorn, Dale Garling, Wayne Hamilton, Robert Hazell, Bryan Hebb, Garth Hindmarch, John Hopkins, Cliff Kaufmann, Doug Kirkness, Donald Kreuger, Paul Laronge, Pat Macnamara, David McLellan, Ed McRae, Len Meeres, Arnold Miller, Robert Minnes, Ron Nelson, Morris Nesdole, Blaine Parry, Greg Penner, Barry Popick, Jim Quickfall, Ryan Reich, Rob Ridley, Marilyn Ridley, Robert Robson, Carl Sali, Eugene Schreiner, Kim Senft, Don Spasoff, Anthony Wachowicz, Ken Watt, Andy Weeks, Trevor Whitfield, David Wilkes, Merle Williams

scandinavian knifemakers guild

André Andersson, Michael Andersson, Jens Ansø, Magnus Axelson, Laszlo Balatoni, Mats Bjurman, Mike Blue, Ulf Brandt, Vladic Daniluk, Alfred Dobner, Maihkel Eklund, Tommy Eklund, Greger Forselius, Roger Fält, Johan Gustafsson, Jukka Hankala, Anders Hedlund, Stefan Hermansson, Jonas Holmberg, Michael Holmström, Anders Högström, Pasi Jaakonaho, Jano knives, Anders Johansson, RB Johnson, Tony Karlsson, Arto Liukko, Jari Liukko, Claes Löfgren, Thomas Löfgren, Anders Nilsson, Ingemar Nordell, Ulf Nygårdh, Erik Nylund, Jacob Nylund, Simon Nylund, Conny Pearson, JT Pälikkö, Teuvo Sorvari, Pekka Tuominen, Henrik Ussing, Rauno Vainionpää, Kay Vikström, Markku Vilppola, Jesper Voxnaes, Stig Wallman, Bjarne Widheden

south carolina association of knifemakers

Douglas Bailey, Ken Black, Bobby Branton, Richard Bridwell,Gordo Brooks, Dan Cannady, Rodger Cassey, John Conn, Allen Corbet, Bill Dauksch, Geno Denning, Charlie Douan, Gene Ellison, Eddy Elsmore, Robbie Estabrook Jr., Lewis Fowler, Jim Frazier, Tally Grant, Jerry Hendrix, Wayne Hendrix, Johnny Johnson, Lonnie Jones, John Keaton, Jason Knight, Col. Thomas Kreger, Gene Langley, Tommy Lee, David Manley, Bill Massey, C.R. Miles, Gene Miller, Claude Montjoy, Patrick Morgan, Barry Meyers, Paul Nystrom Jr., Lee O'Quinn, Victor Odom Jr., Larry Page, James Rabb, Ricky Rankin, Rick Rockwood, John Sarratt, Gene Scaffe, Mick Sears, Ralph Smith, David Stroud, Rocky Thomas, Allen Timmons, Justin Walker, Mickey Walker, Woody Walker, Syd Willis Jr.

tennessee knifemakers association

John Bartlow, Doug Casteel, Harold Crisp, Larry Harley, John W. Walker, Harold Woodward, Harold Wright

texas knifemakers & collectors association

Doug Arnew, Doug Ashby, Ed Barker, George Blackburn, Zane Blackwell, Garrett Blackwell, David Blair, Gayle Bradley, Craig Brewer, Nathan Burgess, Stanley Buzek, Dennis Clark, Dwain Coats, Emil Colmenares, Stewart Crawford, Chester Darcey, Wesley Davis, Rorick Davis, Brian Davis, Harvey Dean, James Drouillard II, Stan Edge, Carlton Evans, Jesse Everett Jr., Sammy Fischer, Christopher Flo, Norvell Foster, Theodore Friesenhahn, Jason Fry, Les George, Mark Grimes, Don Halter, Johnny Hamlet, Glenn Hemperley, Roy Hinds, Darrel Holmquist, Mark Hornung, Karl Jakubik, Mickey Kaehr, Bill Keller, David Kinn, Greg Ledet, Jim Lemcke, Ken Linton, Michael LoGiudice, Paul Long, Eliot Maldonado, Glenn Marshall, Newton Martin, Riley Martin, Bob Merz, Jerry Moen, Don Morrow, Ted Munson, Clifford O'Dell, Tom Overeynder, John Ownby, Ronnie Packard, Glenn Parks, Pat Patterson, Garrett Patterson, Troy Patterson, Steven Patterson, William Petersen III, Jeff Petzke, Paul Piccola, Bill and Pat Post, Gary Powell, Rusty Preston, Martin Rizo, Thomas Rucker, Bill Ruple, Merle Rush, James Schiller, Dwight Schoneweis, Richard Self, Kirby Simmons, Adam Starr, Linda Stone, Wayne Stone, Johnny Stout, Katie Stout, Luke Swenson, Leon Treiber, Larry Turcotte, Charles Turnage, Jimmy Vasquez, David Vickers, Austin Walter, John Walts, Chuck Ward, Bruce Weber, John Weever, Harold Wheeler, Marvin Winn, John Wootters

The firms listed here are special in the sense that they make or market special kinds of knives made in facilities they own or control either in the U.S. or overseas. Or they are special because they make knives of unique design or function. The second phone number listed is the fax number.

sporting cutlers

A.G. RUSSELL KNIVES INC
2900 S. 26th St
Rogers, AR 72758-8571
800-255-9034
fax 479-631-0130
ag@agrussell.com; www.agrussell.com
The oldest knife mail-order company, highest quality. Free catalog available. In these catalogs you will find the newest and the best. If you like knives, this catalog is a must

AL MAR KNIVES
PO Box 2295
Tualatin, OR 97062-2295
503-670-9080; fax 503-639-4789
www.almarknives.com
Featuring our Ultralight™ series of knives. Sere 2000™ Shrike, Sere™, Operator™, Nomad™ and Ultraligh series™

ATLANTA CUTLERY CORP.
2147 Gees Mill Rd., Box 839
Conyers, GA 30013
770-922-7500; fax 770-918-2026
www.atlantacutlery.com
Outdoor sporting and hunting knives, mail order

BARK RIVER KNIVES
6911 County Road 426 M.5 Road
Escanaba, MI 49829
906-789-1801
jacquie@barkriverknives.com
www.barkriverknifetool.com
Family-owned business producing bushcraft, hunting, Canadian, deluxe game, professional guide, search & rescue and EDC knives

BEAR & SON CUTLERY, INC.
111 Bear Blvd. SW
Jacksonville, AL 36265
256-435-2227; fax 256-435-9348
www.bearandsoncutlery.com
Bear Jaws®, three sizes of multi-tools, cutlery, hunting and pocketknives in traditional and innovative patterns and designs

BECK'S CUTLERY & SPECIALTIES
51 Highland Trace Ln.
Benson, NC 27504
919-902-9416
beckscutlery@ebarqmail.com;
www.beckscutleryonline.com

BENCHMADE KNIFE CO. INC.
300 Beavercreek Rd
Oregon City, OR 97045
800-800-7427
info@benchmade.com;
www.benchmade.com
Sports, utility, law enforcement, military, gift and semi custom

BERETTA U.S.A. CORP.
17601 Beretta Dr.
Accokeek, MD 20607
301-283-219
www.berettausa.com
Full range of hunting & specialty knives

BLACKHAWK PRODUCTS GROUP
6160 Commander Pkwy.
Norfolk, VA 23502
757-436-3101; fax 757-436-3088
cs@blackhawk.com
www.blackhawk.com
Leading manufacturer of tactical sheaths and knives

BLADE-TECH INDUSTRIES
5530 184th St. E, Ste. A
Puyallup, WA 98375
253-655-8059; fax 253-655-8066
tim@blade-tech.com
www.blade-tech.com

BLIND HORSE KNIVES
130b Warren Ln.
Wintersville, OH 43953
740-219-111
blindhorseknives@yahoo.com
www.blindhorseknives.com
Quality working knives

BLUE GRASS CUTLERY CORP.
20 E Seventh St PO Box 156
Manchester, OH 45144
937-549-2602; 937-549-2709 or 2603
sales @bluegrasscutlery.com;
www.bluegrasscutlery.com
Manufacturer of Winchester Knives, John Primble Knives and many contract lines

BOKER USA INC
1550 Balsam St.
Lakewood, CO 80214-5917
303-462-0662; 303-462-0668
sales@bokerusa.com; www.bokerusa.com
Wide range of fixed-blade and folding knives for hunting, military, tactical and general use

BROWNING
One Browning Place
Morgan, UT 84050
800-333-3504; Customer Service:
801-876-2711 or 800-333-3288
www.browning.com
Outdoor hunting & shooting products

BUCK KNIVES INC.
660 S Lochsa St
Post Falls, ID 83854-5200
800-326-2825; Fax: 800-733-2825
www.buckknives.com
Sports cutlery

BULLDOG BRAND KNIVES
6715 Heritage Business Ct
Chattanooga, TN 37421
423-894-5102; fax 423-892-9165
Fixed blade and folding knives for hunting and general use

BUSSE COMBAT KNIFE CO.
11651 Co Rd 12
Wauseon, OH 43567
419-923-6471; 419-923-2337
www.bussecombat.com
Simple & very strong straight knife designs for tactical & expedition use

CAMILLUS CUTLERY CO.
60 Round Hill Rd.
Fairfield, CT 06824
800-835-2263
info@camillusknives.com
www.camillusknives.com

CANAL STREET CUTLERY
30 Canal St.
Ellenville, NY 12428
845-647-5900
info@canalstreetcutlery.com
www.canalstreetcutlery.com
Manufacturers of pocket and hunting knives finished to heirloom quality

CAS HANWEI
650 Industrial Blvd
Sale Creek, TN 37373
800-635-9366
www.cashanwei.com
Extensive variety of fixed-blade and folding knives for hunting, diving, camping, military and general use. Japanese swords and European knives

CASE, W.R. & SONS CUTLERY CO.
50 Owens Way
Bradford, PA 16701
800-523-6350; Fax: 814-368-1736
consumer-relations@wrcase.com
www.wrcase.com
Folding pocket knives

CHRIS REEVE KNIVES
2949 S. Victory View Way
Boise, ID 83709-2946
208-375-0367; Fax: 208-375-0368
crknifo@chrisreeve.com;
www.chrisreeve.com
Makers of the Sebenza, Umnumzaan and Mnandi folding knives, the legendary Green Beret knife and other military knives

COAST CUTLERY CO
PO Box 5821
Portland, OR 97288
800-426-5858
www.coastcutlery.com
Variety of fixed-blade and folding knives and multi-tools for hunting, camping and general use

COLD STEEL INC
6060 Nicolle St.
Ventura, CA 93003
800-255-4716 or 805-642-9727
customerservice@coldsteel.com
www.coldsteel.com
Wide variety of folding lockbacks and fixed-blade hunting, fishing and neck knives, as well as bowies, kukris, tantos, throwing knives, kitchen knives and swords

COLONIAL KNIFE, A DIVISION OF COLONIAL CUTLERY INT.
PO Box 960
North Scituate, RI 02857
866-421-6500; Fax: 401-737-0054
stevep@colonialknifecorp.com

www.colonialknifecorp.com
Collectors edition specialty knives. Special promotions. Old cutler, barion, trappers, military knives. Industrial knives-electrician.

CONDOR™ TOOL & KNIFE
7557 W. Sand Lake Rd., #106
Orlando, FL 32819
407-354-3488
rtj@att.net

CRAWFORD KNIVES, LLC
205 N Center Drive
West Memphis, AR 72301
870-732-2452
www.crawfordknives.com
Folding knives for tactical and general use

CRKT
18348 SW 126th Place
Tualatin, OR 97062
800-891-3100; fax 503-682-9680
info@crkt.com; www.crkt.com
Complete line of sport, work and tactical knives

CUTCO INTERNATIONAL
POB 810
Olean, NY 14760
716-372-3111; 716-373-6155
www.cutco.com
Household cutlery / sport knives

DPX GEAR INC.
2321 Kettner Blvd.
San Diego, CA 92101
619-780-2600; fax: 619-780-2605
www.dpxgear.com
Hostile environment survival knives and tools

EMERSON KNIVES, INC.
1234 254th St.
Harbor City, CA 90710
310-539-5633; fax: 310-539-5609
www.emersonknives.com
Hard use tactical knives; folding & fixed blades

ESEE KNIVES
POB 99
Gallant, AL 35972
256-613-0372
www.eseeknives.com
Survival and tactical knives

EXTREMA RATIO
Mauro Chiostri/Maurizio Castrati
Via Tourcoing 40/p
59100 Prato
ITALY
0039 0574 584639; fax: 0039 0576 584312
info@extremaratio.com
Tactical/military knives and sheaths, blades and sheaths to customers specs

FALLKNIVEN AB
Granatvägen 8
S-961 43 Boden
SWEDEN
46-(0)-921 544 22; Fax: 46-(0)-921 544 33
info@fallkniven.se; www.fallkniven.com
High quality stainless knives

FAMARS USA
2091 Nooseneck Hill Rd., Ste. 200
Coventry, RI 02816
855-FAMARS1 (326-2771)
www.famarslama.com
FAMARS has been building guns for over 50 years. Known for innovative design, quality and craftsmanship. New lines of gentleman's knives, tactical fixed blades and folders, hunters and utility pieces.

FOX KNIVES USA
9918 162nd St. Ct. E, Ste. 14
Puyallup, WA 98375
303-263-2468
www.foxknivesusa.com
Designer, manufacturer and distributor of high-quality cutlery

FROST CUTLERY CO
PO Box 22636
Chattanooga, TN 37422
800-251-7768
www.frostcutlery.com
Wide range of fixed-blade and folding knives with a multitude of handle materials

GATCO SHARPENERS
PO Box 600
Getzville, NY 14068
716-646-5700; fax: 716-646-5775
gatco@gatcosharpeners.com;
www.gatcosharpeners.com
Manufacturer of the GATCO brand of knife sharpeners and Timberline brand of knives

GERBER LEGENDARY BLADES
14200 SW 72nd Ave
Portland, OR 97223
503-639-6161; fax: 307-857-4702
www.gerbergear.com
Knives, multi-tools, axes, saws, outdoor products

GINSU OUTDOORS
118 E. Douglas Rd.
Walnut Ridge, AR 72476
800-982-5233; fax: 870-886-9162
www.douglasquikut.com
Hunting and fishing knives

GROHMANN KNIVES
PO Box 40
116 Water St
Pictou, Nova Scotia B0K 1H0
CANADA
888-7KNIVES; Fax: 902-485-5872
www.grohmannknives.com
Fixed-blade belt knives for hunting and fishing, folding pocketknives for hunting and general use. Household cutlery.

H&B FORGE CO.
235 Geisinger Rd
Shiloh, OH 44878
419-895-1856
www.hbforge.com
Special order hawks, camp stoves, fireplace accessories, muzzleloading accroutements

HALLMARK CUTLERY
POB 220
Kodak, TN 37764
866-583-3912; fax: 901-405-0948
www.hallmarkcutlery.com
Traditional folders, tactical folders and fixed blades, multi-tools, shotgun shell knives, Bad Blood, Robert Klaas and Chief brand knives, and Super Premium care products

HISTORIC EDGED WEAPONRY
1021 Saddlebrook Dr
Hendersonville, NC 28739
828-692-0323; fax: 828-692-0600
histwpn@bellsouth.net
Antique knives from around the world; importer of puukko and other knives from Norway, Sweden, Finland and Lapland; also edged weaponry book "Travels for Daggers" by Eiler R. Cook

JOY ENTERPRISES-FURY CUTLERY
Port Commerce Center III
1862 M.L. King Jr. Blvd
Riviera Beach, FL 33404
800-500-3879; fax: 561-863-3277
mail@joyenterprises.com;
www.joyenterprises.com;
www.furycutlery.com
Fury™ Mustang™ extensive variety of fixed-blade and folding knives for hunting, fishing, diving, camping, military and general use; novelty key-ring knives. Muela Sporting Knives. KA-BAR KNIVES INC. Fury Tactical, Muela of Spain, Mustang Outdoor Adventure

KA-BAR KNIVES INC
200 Homer St
Olean, NY 14760
800-282-0130; fax: 716-790-7188
info@ka-bar.com; www.ka-bar.com

KAI USA LTD.
18600 S.W. Teton Ave.
Tualatin, OR 97062
800-325-2891; fax 503-682-7168
info@kershawknives.com
www.kershawknives.com
Manufacturer of high-quality, lifetime-guaranteed knives. Kai USA brands include Kershaw Knives for everyday carrying, hunting, fishing and other outdoor use; Zero Tolerance Knives for professional use; and Shun Cutlery, providing premium-quality kitchen knives

KATZ KNIVES, INC.
10924 Mukilteo Speedway #287
Mukilteo, WA 98275
480-786-9334; fax 480-786-9338
katzkn@aol.com; www.katzknives.com

KELLAM KNIVES WORLDWIDE
902 S Dixie Hwy
Lantana, FL 33462
800-390-6918; Fax 561-588-3186
info@kellamknives.com;
www.kellamknives.com
Largest selection of Finnish knives; handmade & production

KLOTZLI (MESSER KLOTZLI)
Hohengasse 3 CH 3400
Burgdorf
SWITZERLAND
41-(34)-422-23 78; fax 41-(34)-422-76 93
info@klotzli.com; www.klotzli.com
High-tech folding knives for tactical and general use

KNIGHTS EDGE LTD.
5696 N. Northwest Highway
Chicago, IL 60646-6136
773-775-3888; fax 773-775-3339
sales@knightsedge.com;
www.knightsedge.com
Medieval weaponry, swords, suits of armor, katanas, daggers

KNIVES OF ALASKA, INC.
Charles or Jody Allen
3100 Airport Dr
Denison, TX 75020
800-572-0980; fax 903-786-7371
info@knivesofalaska.com;
www.knivesofalaska.com
High quality hunting & outdoorsmen's knives

KNIVES PLUS
2467 40 West
Amarillo, TX 79109
800-687-6202
www.knivesplus.com
Retail cutlery and cutlery accessories since 1987; free catalog available

LAKOTA KNIFE USA
POB 626
Forest, VA 24551
800-807-1169; fax 434-237-9086
Hunting, fishing, ooutdoor, collectible knives

LEATHERMAN TOOL GROUP, INC.
PO Box 20595
Portland, OR 97294-059 0595 5
800-847-8665; fax 503-253-7830
info@leatherman.com;
www.leatherman.com
Multi-tools

LONE STAR WHOLESALE
P.O. Box 587
Amarillo, TX 79105
806-356-9540; fax 806-359-1603
robbie@lonestarwholesale.com
www.lonestarwholesale.com
Great prices, dealers only, most major brands

MANTIS KNIVES
520 Cameron St.
Placentia, CA 92870
714-996-9673
gwest@mantis.bz
www.mantisknives.com
Manufacturer of utility, karambit, fixed and folding blades, and Neccessikeys

MARBLE ARMS
420 Industrial Park
Gladstone, MI 49837
906-428-3710
info@marblearms.com
www.marblearms.com

MASTER CUTLERY INC
700 Penhorn Ave
Secaucus, NJ 07094
888-227-7229; fax 888-271-7228
www.mastercutlery.com
Largest variety in the knife industry

MEYERCO USA
4481 Exchange Service Dr.
Dallas, TX 75236
214-467-8949; fax 214-467-9241
www.meyercousa.com
Folding tactical,rescue and speed-assisted

pocketknives; fixed-blade hunting and fishing designs; multi-function camping tools and machetes

MICROTECH KNIVES
300 Chestnut Street Ext.
Bradford, PA 16701
814-363-9260; Fax: 814-362-7069
info@microtechknives.com
www.microtechknives.com
Manufacturers of the highest quality production knives

MISSION KNIVES
13771 Newhope St.
Garden Grove, CA 92843
714-638-4692; fax 714-638-4621
info@missionknives.com
www.missionknives.com
Manufacturer of titanium and steel knives and tools with over 20 years in business. Tactical, combat, military, law enforcement, EOD units, survivalist, diving, recreational straight blades, folding blades and mine probes, and more.

MOKI KNIFE COMPANY LTD.
15 Higashisenbo
Seki City GIFU
Pref JAPAN
575-22-4185; fax 575-24-5306
information@moki.co.jp
www.moki.co.jp
Pocketknives, folders, fixed-blade knives and gent's knives

MUSEUM REPLICAS LTD.
P.O. Box 840
2147 Gees Mill Rd
Conyers, GA 30012
800-883-8838; fax: 770-388-0246
www.museumreplicas.com
Historically accurate & battle-ready swords & daggers

NEMESIS KNIVES, LLC
179 Niblick Rd., #180
Paso Robles, CA 93446
562-594-4740
info@nemesis-knives.com
www.nemesis-knives.com
Semi-custom and production kinves

ONTARIO KNIFE CO.
PO Box 145
Franklinville, NY 14737
800-222-5233; fax 716-676-5535
knifesales@ontarioknife.com
www.ontarioknife.com
Fixed blades, tactical folders, military & hunting knives, machetes

OUTDOOR EDGE CUTLERY CORP.
9500 W. 49th Ave., #A-100
Wheat Ridge, CO 80033
800-447-3343; 303-530-7667
moreinfo@outdooredge.com;
www.outdooredge.com

PACIFIC SOLUTION MARKETING, INC.
1220 E. Belmont St.
Ontario, CA 91761
Tel: 877-810-4643
Fax: 909-930-5843
sales@pacificsolution.com
www.pacificsolution.com
Wide range of folding pocket knives, hunting knives, tactical knives, novelty knives, medieval armors and weapons as well as hand forged samurai sword and tantos.

PRO-TECH KNIVES LLC
17115 Alburtis Ave.
Artesia, CA 90701-2616
562-860-0678
service@protechknives.com
www.protechknives.com
Manufacturer specializing in automatic knives for police, military and discriminating collectors

QUEEN CUTLERY COMPANY
507 Chestnut St.
Titusville, PA 16354
814-827-3673; fax: 814-827-9693
jmoore@queencutlery.com
www.queencutlery.com
Pocket knives, collectibles, Schatt & Morgan, Robeson, club knives

RANDALL MADE KNIVES
4857 South Orange Blossom Trail
Orlando, FL 32839
407-855-8075; fax 407-855-9054
grandall@randallknives.com;
www.randallknives.com
Handmade fixed-blade knives for hunting, fishing, diving, military and general use

REMINGTON ARMS CO., INC.
PO Box 700
870 Remington Drive
Madison, NC 27025-0700
800-243-9700; Fax: 336-548-7801
www.remington.com

RUKO LLC.
PO Box 38
Buffalo, NY 14207-0038
716-874-2707; fax 905-826-2707
info@rukoproducts.com
www.rukoproducts.com

SANTA FE STONEWORKS
3790 Cerrillos Rd.
Santa Fe, NM 87507
800-257-7625; fax 505-471-0036
knives@rt66.com;
www.santafestoneworks.com
Gem stone handles

SARCO KNIVES LLC
449 Lane Dr
Florence AL 35630
256-766-8099; fax 256-766-7246
www.sarcoknives.com
Etching and engraving services, club knives, etc. New knives, antique-collectible knives

SARGE KNIVES
2720 E. Phillips Rd.
Greer, SC 29650
800-454-7448; fax 864-331-0752
cgaines@sargeknives.com
www.sargeknives.com
High-quality, affordable pocketknives, hunting, fishing, camping and tactical. Custom engraving for promotional knives or personalized gifts

SOG SPECIALTY KNIVES & TOOLS, INC.
6521 212th St SW
Lynnwood, WA 98036
425-771-6230; fax 425-771-7689
sogsales@sogknives.com
www.sogknives.com
SOG assisted technology, Arc-Lock, folding knives, specialized fixed blades, multi-tools

SPARTAN BLADES, LLC
POB 620
Aberdeen, NC 28315
910-757-0035
contact@spartanbladesusa.com
www.spartanbladesusa.com
Tactical, combat, fighter, survival and field knives

SPYDERCO, INC.
820 Spyderco Way
Golden, CO 80403
800-525-7770; fax 303-278-2229
sales@spyderco.com
www.spyderco.com
Knives, sharpeners and accessories

STONE RIVER GEAR
75 Manor Rd.
Red Hook, NY 12571
203-470-2526; fax 866-258-7202
info@stonerivergear.com
www.stonerivergear.com
Fighters, tactical, survival and military knives, household cutlery, hunting knives, pocketknives, folders and utility tools

SWISS ARMY BRANDS INC.
15 Corporate Dr.
Orangeburg, NY 10962
800-431-2994
customer.service@swissarmy.com

www.swissarmy.com
Folding multi-blade designs and multi-tools for hunting, fishing, camping, hiking, golfing and general use. One of the original brands (Victorinox) of Swiss Army Knives

TAYLOR BRANDS LLC
1043 Fordtown Road
Kingsport, TN 37663
800-251-0254; fax 423-247-5371
info@taylorbrandsllc.com
www.taylorbrandsllc.com
Smith & Wesson Knives, Old Timer, Uncle Henry and Schrade.

TIMBERLINE KNIVES
7223 Boston State Rd.
Boston, NY 14075
800-liv-sharp; fax 716-646-5775
www.timberlineknives.com
High technology production knives for professionals, sporting, tradesmen & kitchen use

TRU-BALANCE KNIFE CO.
PO Box 140555
Grand Rapids, MI 49514
616-647-1215
Manufacturing and sale of throwing knives

UNITED CUTLERY
475 U.S. Hwy. 319 S
Moultrie, GA 31768
800-548-0835; fax 229-551-0182
customerservice@unitedcutlery.com

www.unitedcutlery.com
Wholesale only; pocket, sportsman knives, licensed movie knives, swords, exclusive brands

WILLIAM HENRY STUDIO
3200 NE Rivergate St
McMinnville, OR 97128
503-434-9700; Fax: 503-434-9704
www.williamhenrystudio.com
Semi-production, handmade knives

WUU JAU CO. INC.
2600 S Kelly Ave
Edmond, OK 73013
800-722-5760; fax 405-340-5965
mail@wuujau.com; www.wuujau.com
Wide variety of imported fixed-blade and folding knives for hunting, fishing, camping, and general use. Wholesale to knife dealers only

XIKAR INC
PO Box 025757
Kansas City MO 64102
888-676-7380; 816-474-7555
info@xikar.com; www.xikar.com
Gentlemen's cutlery and accessories

importers

A.G. RUSSELL KNIVES INC
2900 S. 26th St.
Rogers, AR 72758-8571
800-255-9034 or 479-631-0130;
fax 479-631-8493
ag@agrussell.com; www.agrussell.com
The oldest knife mail-order company, highest quality. Free catalog available. In these catalogs you will find the newest and the best. If you like knives, this catalog is a must. Celebrating over 40 years in the industry

ADAMS INTERNATIONAL KNIFEWORKS
8710 Rosewood Hills
Edwardsville, IL 62025
Importers & foreign cutlers

AITOR-BERRIZARGO S.L.
P.I. Eitua PO Box 26
48240 Berriz Vizcaya
SPAIN
946826599; 94602250226
info@aitor.com; www.aitor.com
Sporting knives

ATLANTA CUTLERY CORP.
P.O.Box 839
Conyers, Ga 30012
800-883-0300; Fax: 770-388-0246
custserve@atlantacutlery.com;
www.atlantacutlery.com
Exotic knives from around the world

BAILEY'S
PO Box 550
Laytonville, CA 95454
800-322-4539; 707-984-8115
baileys@baileys-online.com;
www.baileys-online.com

BELTRAME, FRANCESCO
Fratelli Beltrame F&C snc Via dei Fabbri
15/B-33085 MANIAGO (PN)
ITALY
39 0427 701859
www.italianstiletto.com

BOKER USA, INC.
1550 Balsam St
Lakewood, CO 80214-5917
303-462-0662; 303-462-0668
sales@bokerusa.com; www.bokerusa.com
Ceramic blades

CAMPOS, IVAN DE ALMEIDA
R. Stelio M. Loureiro, 205
Centro, Tatui
BRAZIL
00-55-15-33056867
www.ivancampos.com

C.A.S. IBERIA, INC.
650 Industrial Blvd
Sale Creek, TN 37373
423-332-4700; 423-332-7248
info@casiberia.com; www.casiberia.com

CAS/HANWEI, MUELA
Catoctin Cutlery
PO Box 188
Smithsburg, MD 21783

CLASSIC INDUSTRIES
1325 Howard Ave, Suite 408
Burlingame, CA 94010

COAST CUTLERY CO.
8033 NE Holman St.
Portland, OR 97218
800-426-5858
staff@coastcutlery.com;
www.coastcutlery.com

COLUMBIA PRODUCTS CO.
PO Box 1333
Sialkot 51310
PAKISTAN

COLUMBIA PRODUCTS INT'L
PO Box 8243
New York, NY 10116-8243
201-854-3054; Fax: 201-854-7058
nycolumbia@aol.com;
http://www.columbiaproducts.homestead.com/cat.html
Pocket, hunting knives and swords of all kinds

COMPASS INDUSTRIES, INC.
104 E. 25th St
New York, NY 10010
800-221-9904; Fax: 212-353-0826
jeff@compassindustries.com;
www.compassindustries.com
Imported pocket knives

CONAZ COLTELLERIE
Dei F.Lli Consigli-Scarperia
Via G. Giordani, 20
50038 Scarperia (Firenze)
ITALY
36 55 846187; 39 55 846603
conaz@dada.it; www.consigliscarpeia.com
Handicraft workmanship of knives of the ancient Italian tradition. Historical and collection knives

CONSOLIDATED CUTLERY CO., INC.
696 NW Sharpe St
Port St. Lucie, FL 34983
772-878-6139

CRAZY CROW TRADING POST
PO Box 847
Pottsboro, TX 75076
800-786-6210; Fax: 903-786-9059
info@crazycrow.com; www.crazycrow.com
Solingen blades, knife making parts & supplies

DER FLEISSIGEN BEAVER
(The Busy Beaver)
Harvey Silk
PO Box 1166
64343 Griesheim
GERMANY
49 61552231; 49 6155 2433
Der.Biber@t-online.de
Retail custom knives. Knife shows in Germany & UK

EXTREMA RATIO SAS
Mauro Chiostri; Mavrizio Castrati
Via Tourcoing 40/p
59100 Prato (PO)
ITALY
0039 0574 58 4639; 0039 0574 581312
info@extremarazio.com;
www.extremaratio.com
Tactical & military knives manufacturing

FALLKNIVEN AB
Havrevagen 10
S-96142 Boden
SWEDEN
46 92154422; 46 92154433
info@fallkniven.se
www.fallkniven.com
High quality knives

FREDIANI COLTELLI FINLANDESI
Via Lago Maggiore 41
I-21038 Leggiuno
ITALY

GIESSER MESSERFABRIK GMBH, JOHANNES
Raiffeisenstr 15
D-71349 Winnenden
GERMANY
49-7195-1808-29
info@giesser.de; www.giesser.de
Professional butchers and chef's knives

HIMALAYAN IMPORTS
3495 Lakeside Dr
Reno, NV 89509
775-825-2279
unclebill@himalayan-imports.com; www.
himilayan-imports.com

IVAN DE ALMEIDA CAMPOS-KNIFE DEALER
R. Xi De Agosto
107, Centro, Tatui, Sp 18270
BRAZIL
55-15-251-8092; 55-15-251-4896
campos@bitweb.com.br
Custom knives from all Brazilian knifemakers

JOY ENTERPRISES
1862 M.L. King Blvd
Riviera Beach, FL 33404
800-500-3879; 561-863-3277
mail@joyenterprises.com;

www.joyenterprises.com
Fury™, Mustang™, Hawg Knives, Muela

KELLAM KNIVES CO.
902 S Dixie Hwy
Lantana, FL 33462
800-390-6918; 561-588-3186
info@kellamknives.com;
www.kellamknives.com
Knives from Finland; own line of knives

KNIFE IMPORTERS, INC.
11307 Conroy Ln
Manchaca, TX 78652
512-282-6860, Fax: 512-282-7504
Wholesale only

KNIGHTS EDGE
5696 N Northwest Hwy
Chicago, IL 60646
773-775-3888; 773-775-3339
www.knightsedge.com
Exclusive designers of our Rittersteel, Stagesteel and Valiant Arms and knightedge lines of weapon

LEISURE PRODUCTS CORP.
PO Box 1171
Sialkot-51310
PAKISTAN

L. C. RISTINEN
Suomi Shop
17533 Co Hwy 38
Frazee MN 56544
218-538-6633; 218-538-6633
icrist@wcta.net
Scandinavian cutlery custom antique, books and reindeer antler

LINDER, CARL NACHF.
Erholungstr. 10
D-42699 Solingen
GERMANY
212 33 0 856; Fax: 212 33 71 04
info@linder.de; www.linder.de

MARTTIINI KNIVES
PO Box 44 (Marttiinintie 3)
96101 Rovaniemi
FINLAND

MATTHEWS CUTLERY
4401 Sentry Dr, Suite K
Tucker, GA 30084-6561
770-939-6915

MESSER KLÖTZLI
PO Box 104
Hohengasse 3, Ch-3402 Burgdorf
SWITZERLAND
034 422 2378; 034 422 7693
info@klotzli.com; www.klotzli.com

MURAKAMI, ICHIRO
Knife Collectors Assn. Japan
Tokuda Nishi 4 Chome, 76 Banchi, Ginancho
Hashimagun, Gifu
JAPAN
81 58 274 1960; 81 58 273 7369
www.gix.orjp/~n-resin/

MUSEUM REPLICAS LIMITED
2147 Gees Mill Rd
Conyers, GA 30012
800-883-8838
www.museumreplicas.com

NICHOLS CO.
Pomfret Rd
South Pomfret, VT 05067
Import & distribute knives from EKA (Sweden), Helle (Norway), Brusletto (Norway), Roselli (Finland). Also market Zippo products, Snow, Nealley axes and hatchets and snow & Neally axes

NORMARK CORP.
Craig Weber
10395 Yellow Circle Dr
Minnetonka, MN 55343

PRODUCTORS AITOR, S.A.
Izelaieta 17
48260 Ermua
SPAIN
943-170850; 943-170001
info@aitor.com
Sporting knives

PROFESSIONAL CUTLERY SERVICES
9712 Washburn Rd
Downey, CA 90241
562-803-8778; 562-803-4261
Wholesale only. Full service distributor of domestic & imported brand name cutlery. Exclusive U.S. importer for both Marto Swords and Battle Ready Valiant Armory edged weapons

SCANDIA INTERNATIONAL INC.
5475 W Inscription Canyon Dr
Prescott, AZ 86305
928-442-0140; Fax: 928-442-0342
mora@cableone.net; www.frosts-scandia.com
Frosts knives of Sweden

STAR SALES CO., INC.
1803 N. Central St
Knoxville, TN 37917
800-745-6433; Fax: 865-524-4889
www.starknives.com

SVORD KNIVES
Smith Rd., RD 2
Waiuku, South Auckland
NEW ZEALAND
64 9 2358846; Fax: 64 9 2356483
www.svord.com

SWISS ARMY BRANDS LTD.
The Forschner Group, Inc.
One Research Drive
Shelton, CT 06484
203-929-6391; 203-929-3786
www.swissarmy.com

TAYLOR BRANDS, LLC
1043 Fordtown Road
Kingsport, TN 37663
800-251-0254; Fax: 423-247-5371
info@taylorbrandsllc.com;
www.taylorbrands.com
Fixed-blade and folding knives for tactical, rescue, hunting and general use. Also provides etching, engraving, scrimshaw services.

UNITED CUTLERY CORP.
1425 United Blvd
Sevierville, TN 37876
865-428-2532; 865-428-2267
order@unitedcutlery.com;
www.unitedcutlery.com
Harley-Davidson ® Colt ® , Stanley ®, U21 ®, Rigid Knives ®, Outdoor Life ®, Ford ®, hunting, camping, fishing, collectible & fantasy knives

UNIVERSAL AGENCIES INC
4690 S Old Peachtree Rd, Suite C
Norcross, GA 30071-1517
678-969-9147; Fax: 678-969-9169
info@knifecupplies.com;
www.knifesupplies.com;
www.thunderforged.com; www.uai.org
*Serving the cutlery industry with the finest
selection of India Stag, Buffalo Horn,
Thurnderforged ™ Damascus. Mother of Pearl,
Knife Kits and more*

VALOR CORP.
1001 Sawgrass Corp Pkwy
Sunrise, FL 33323
800-899-8256; Fax: 954-377-4941

www.valorcorp.com
Wide variety of imported & domestic knives

WENGER N. A.
15 Corporate Dr
Orangeburg, NY 10962
800-431-2996
www.wengerna.com
Swiss Army ™ Knives

WILD BOAR BLADES
1701 Broadway, Suite 282
Vancouver, WA 98663
888-476-4400; 360-735-0390
usakopro@aol.com;
www.wildboarblades.com

*Carries a full line of Kopromed knives and
kitchenware imported from Poland*

WORLD CLASS EXHIBITION KNIVES
Cary Desmon
941-504-2279
www.withoutequal.com
Carries an extensive line of Pius Lang knives

ZWILLING J.A. HENCKELS USA
171 Saw Mill River Rd
Hawthorne, NY 10532
800-777-4308; Fax: 914-747-1850
info@jahenckels.com;
www.jahenckels.com
*Kitchen cutlery, scissors, gadgets, flatware and
cookware*

knife making supplies

AFRICAN IMPORT CO.
Alan Zanotti
22 Goodwin Rd
Plymouth, MA 02360
508-746-8552; 508-746-0404
africanimport@aol.com
Ivory

ALABAMA DAMASCUS STEEL
PO Box 54
WELLINGTON, AL 36279
256-892-2950
sales@alabamadamacussteel.com
www.alabamadamascussteel.com
*We are a manufacturer of damascus steel
billets & blades. We also offer knife supplies.
We can custom make any blade design that
the customer wants. We can also make custom
damascus billets per customer specs.*

ALPHA KNIFE SUPPLY
425-868-5880; Fax: 425-898-7715
chuck@alphaknifesupply.com;
www.alphaknifesupply.com
Inventory of knife supplies

AMERICAN SIEPMANN CORP.
65 Pixley Industrial Parkway
Rochester, NY 14624
800-724-0919; Fax: 585-247-1883
www.siepmann.com
*CNC blade grinding equipment, grinding
wheels, production blade grinding services.
Sharpening stones and sharpening equipment*

ANKROM EXOTICS
Pat Ankrom
22900 HWY 5
Centerville, IA 52544
641-436-0235
ankromexotics@hotmail.com
www.ankromexotics.com
*Stabilized handle material; Exotic burls
and hardwoods from around the world;
Stabilizing services available*

ATLANTA CUTLERY CORP.
P.O.Box 839
Conyers, Ga 30012
800-883-0300; Fax: 770-388-0246
custserve@atlantacutlery.com;
www.atlantacutlery.com

BATAVIA ENGINEERING
20 Liberty Street
Magaliesburg, 1791

SOUTH AFRICA
27-14-5771294
bertie@batavia.co.za; www.batavia.co.za
*Contact wheels for belt grinders and surface
grinders; damascus and mokume*

BLADEMAKER, THE
Gary Kelley
17485 SW Phesant Ln
Beaverton, OR 97006
503-649-7867
garykelly@theblademaker.com;
www.theblademaker.com
*Period knife and hawk blades for hobbyists
& re-enactors and in dendritic D2 steel.
"Ferroulithic" steel-stone spear point, blades
and arrowheads*

BOONE TRADING CO., INC.
PO Box 669
562 Coyote Rd
Brinnon, WA 98320
800-423-1945; Fax: 360-796-4511
www.boonetrading.com
Ivory of all types, bone, horns

BORGER, WOLF
Benzstrasse 8
76676 Graben-Neudorf
GERMANY
wolf@messerschmied.de;
www.messerschmied.de

BOYE KNIVES
PO Box 1238
Dolan Springs, AZ 86441-1238
800-853-1617; 928-767-4273
info@boyeknives.com;
www.boyeknives.com
Dendritic steel and Dendritic cobalt

BRONK'S KNIFEWORKS
Lyle Brunckhorst
Country Village
23706 7th Ave SE, Suite B
Bothell, WA 98021
425-402-3484
bronks@bronksknifeworks.com;
www.bronksknifeworks.com
Damascus steel

CRAZY CROW TRADING POST
PO Box 847
Pottsboro, TX 75076
800-786-6210; Fax: 903-786-9059
info@crazycrow.com; www.crazycrow.com

Solingen blades, knife making parts & supplies

CULPEPPER & CO.
Joe Culpepper
P.O. Box 690
8285 Georgia Rd.
Otto, NC 28763
828-524-6842; Fax: 828-369-7809
culpepperandco@verizon.net
www.knifehandles.com http://www.
knifehandles.com
www.stingrayproducts.com <http://www.
stingrayproducts.com>
*Mother of pearl, bone, abalone, stingray, dyed
stag, blacklip, ram's horn, mammoth ivory,
coral, scrimshaw*

CUSTOM FURNACES
PO Box 353
Randvaal, 1873
SOUTH AFRICA
27 16 365-5723; 27 16 365-5738
johnlee@custom.co.za
Furnaces for hardening & tempering of knives

DAMASCUS-USA CHARLTON LTD.
149 Deans Farm Rd
Tyner, NC 27980-9607
252-221-2010
rcharlton@damascususa.com;
www.damascususa.com

DAN'S WHETSTONE CO., INC.
418 Hilltop Rd
Pearcy, AR 71964
501-767-1616; 501-767-9598
questions@danswhetstone.com;
www.danswhetstone.com
Natural abrasive Arkansas stone products

**DIAMOND MACHINING TECHNOLOGY,
INC. DMT**
85 Hayes Memorial Dr
Marlborough, MA 01752
800-666-4DMT
dmtsharp@dmtsharp.com;
www.dmtsharp.com
*Knife and tool sharpeners-diamond, ceramic
and easy edge guided sharpening kits*

DIGEM DIAMOND SUPPLIERS
7303 East Earll Drive
Scottsdale, Arizona 85251
602-620-3999
eglasser@cox.net
*#1 international diamond tool provider. Every
diamond tool you will ever need 1/16th of an*

inch to 11'x9'. BURRS, CORE DRILLS, SAW BLADES, MILLING SHAPES, AND WHEELS

DIXIE GUN WORKS, INC.
PO Box 130
Union City, TN 38281
800-238-6785; Fax: 731-885-0440
www.dixiegunworks.com
Knife and knifemaking supplies

EZE-LAP DIAMOND PRODUCTS
3572 Arrowhead Dr
Carson City, NV 89706
800-843-4815; Fax: 775-888-9555
sales@eze-lap.com; www.eze-lap.com
Diamond coated sharpening tools

FINE TURNAGE PRODUCTIONS
Charles Turnage
1210 Midnight Drive
San Antonio, TX 78260
210-352-5660
cat41259@aol.com
www.fineturnage.com
Specializing in stabilized mammoth tooth and bone, mammoth ivory, fossil brain coral, meteorite, etc.

FLITZ INTERNATIONAL, LTD.
821 Mohr Ave
Waterford, WI 53185
800-558-8611; Fax: 262-534-2991
info@flitz.com; www.flitz.com
Metal polish, buffing pads, wax

FORTUNE PRODUCTS, INC.
205 Hickory Creek Rd
Marble Falls, TX 78654-3357
830-693-6111; Fax: 830-693-6394
www.accusharp.com
AccuSharp knife sharpeners

GALLERY HARDWOODS
Larry Davis, Acworth, GA
www.galleryhardwoods.com
Stabilized exotic burls and woods

GILMER WOOD CO.
2211 NW St Helens Rd
Portland, OR 97210
503-274-1271; Fax: 503-274-9839
www.gilmerwood.com

GIRAFFEBONE KNIFE SUPPLY
3052 Isim Rd.
Norman, OK 73026
888-804-0683
sandy@giraffebone.com;
www.giraffebone.com
Exotic handle materials

GRS CORP.
D.J. Glaser
PO Box 1153
Emporia, KS 66801
800-835-3519; Fax: 620-343-9640
glendo@glendo.com; www.glendo.com
Engraving, equipment, tool sharpener, books/ videos

HALPERN TITANIUM INC.
Les and Marianne Halpern
PO Box 214
4 Springfield St
Three Rivers, MA 01080
888-283-8627; Fax: 413-289-2372
info@halperntitanium.com;
www.halperntitanium.com
Titanium, carbon fiber, G-10, fasteners; CNC milling

HAWKINS KNIVE MAKING SUPPLIES
110 Buckeye Rd
Fayetteville, GA 30214
770-964-1177; Fax: 770-306-2877
Sales@hawkinsknifemakingsupplies.com
www.HawkinsKnifeMakingSupllies.com
All styles

HILTARY-USGRC
6060 East Thomas Road
Scottsdale, AZ 85251
Office: 480-945-0700
Fax: 480-945-3333
usgrc@cox.net
Gibeon Meteorite, Recon Gems, Diamond cutting tools, Exotic natural minerals, garaffe bone. Atomic absorbtion/ spectographic analyst, precisious metal

HOUSE OF TOOLS LTD.
#54-5329 72 Ave. S.E.
Calgary, Alberta
CANADA T2C 4X
403-640-4594; Fax: 403-451-7006
www.houseoftools.net

INDIAN JEWELERS SUPPLY CO.
Mail Order: 601 E Coal Ave
Gallup, NM 87301-6005
2105 San Mateo Blvd NE
Albuquerque, NM 87110-5148
505-722-4451; 505-265-3701
orders@ijsinc.com; www.ijsinc.com
Handle materials, tools, metals

INTERAMCO INC.
5210 Exchange Dr
Flint, MI 48507
810-732-8181; 810-732-6116
solutions@interamco.com
Knife grinding and polishing

JANTZ SUPPLY / KOVAL KNIVES
PO Box 584
309 West Main
Davis, OK 73030
800-351-8900; 580-369-2316
jantz@brightok.net; www.knifemaking.com
Pre shaped blades, kit knives, complete knifemaking supply line

JMD INTERNATIONAL
2985 Gordy Pkwy., Unit 405
Marietta, GA 30066
678-969-9147; Fax: 770-640-9852
knifesupplies@gmail.com;
www.knifesupplies.com;
Serving the cutlery industry with the finest selection of India stag, buffalo horn, mother-of-pearl and smooth white bone

JOHNSON, R.B.
I.B.S. Int'l. Folder Supplies
Box 11
Clearwater, MN 55320
320-558-6128; 320-558-6128
www.foldingknifesupplies.com
Threaded pivot pins, screws, taps, etc.

JOHNSON WOOD PRODUCTS
34897 Crystal Rd
Strawberry Point, IA 52076
563-933-6504

K&G FINISHING SUPPLIES
1972 Forest Ave
Lakeside, AZ 85929
800-972-1192; 928-537-8877
csinfo@knifeandgun.com;
www.knifeandgun.com
Full service supplies

KOWAK IVORY
Roland and Kathy Quimby
(April-Sept): PO Box 350
Ester, AK 99725
907-479-9335
(Oct-March)
PO Box 693
Bristow, OK 74010
918-367-2684
sales@kowakivory.com;
www.kowakivory.com
Fossil ivories

LITTLE GIANT POWER HAMMER
Harlan "Sid" Suedmeier
420 4th Corso
Nebraska City, NE 68410
402-873-6603
www.littlegianthammer.com
Rebuilds hammers and supplies parts

LIVESAY, NEWT
3306 S Dogwood St
Siloam Springs, AR 72761
479-549-3356; 479-549-3357
Combat utility knives, titanium knives, sportsmen knives, custom made orders taken on knives and after market Kydex© sheaths for commercial or custom cutlery

LOHMAN CO., FRED
3405 NE Broadway
Portland, OR 97232
503-282-4567; Fax: 503-287-2678
lohman@katana4u.com;
www.japanese-swords.com

M MILLER ORIGINALS
Michael Miller
2960 E Carver Ave
Kingman AZ 86401
928-757-1359
mike@milleroriginals.com;
www.mmilleroriginals.com
Supplies stabilized juniper burl blocks and scales

MARKING METHODS, INC.
Sales
301 S. Raymond Ave
Alhambra, CA 91803-1531
626-282-8823; Fax: 626-576-7564
experts@markingmethods.com;
www.markingmethods.com
Knife etching equipment & service

MASECRAFT SUPPLY CO.
254 Amity St
Meriden, CT 06450
800-682-5489; Fax: 203-238-2373
info@masecraftsupply.com;
www.masecraftsupply.com
Natural & specialty synthetic handle materials & more

MEIER STEEL
Daryl Meier
75 Forge Rd
Carbondale, IL 62903
618-549-3234; Fax: 618-549-6239
www.meiersteel.com

NICO, BERNARD
PO Box 5151
Nelspruit 1200
SOUTH AFRICA
011-2713-7440099; 011-2713-7440099
bernardn@iafrica.com

NORRIS, MIKE
Rt 2 Box 242A
Tollesboro, KY 41189
606-798-1217
Damascus steel

NORTHCOAST KNIVES
17407 Puritas Ave
Cleveland, Ohio 44135
www.NorthCoastKnives.com
Tutorials and step-by-step projects. Entry level knifemaking supplies.

OSO FAMOSO
PO Box 654
Ben Lomond, CA 95005
831-336-2343
oso@osofamoso.com;
www.osofamoso.com
Mammoth ivory bark

OZARK KNIFE & GUN
3165 S Campbell Ave
Springfield, MO 65807
417-886-CUTT; 417-887-2635
danhoneycutt@sbcglobal.net
28 years in the cutlery business, Missouri's oldest cutlery firm

PARAGON INDUSTRIES, INC. L. P.
2011 South Town East Blvd
Mesquite, TX 75149-1122
800-876-4328; Fax: 972-222-0646
info@paragonweb.com;
www.paragonweb.com
Heat treating furnaces for knifemakers

POPLIN, JAMES / POP'S KNIVES & SUPPLIES
103 Oak St
Washington, GA 30673
706-678-5408; Fax: 706-678-5409
www.popsknifesupplies.com

PUGH, JIM
PO Box 711
917 Carpenter
Azle, TX 76020
817-444-2679; Fax: 817-444-5455
Rosewood and ebony Micarta blocks,rivets for Kydex sheaths, 0-80 screws for folders

RADOS, JERRY
7523E 5000 N. Rd
Grant Park, IL 60940
815-405-5061
jerry@radosknives.com;
www.radosknives.com
Damascus steel

REACTIVE METALS STUDIO, INC.
PO Box 890
Clarksdale, AZ 86324
800-876-3434; 928-634-3434; Fax: 928-634-6734
info@reactivemetals.com; www.reactivemetals.com

R. FIELDS ANCIENT IVORY
Donald Fields
790 Tamerlane St
Deltona, FL 32725
386-532-9070
donaldfields@aol.com
Selling ancient ivories; Mammoth, fossil & walrus

RICK FRIGAULT CUSTOM KNIVES
3584 Rapidsview Dr
Niagara Falls, Ontario
CANADA L2G 6C4
905-295-6695
zipcases@zipcases.com;

www.zipcases.com
Selling padded zippered knife pouches with an option to personalize the outside with the marker, purveyor, stores-address, phone number, email web-site or any other information needed. Available in black cordura, mossy oak camo in sizes 4"x2" to 20"x4.5"

RIVERSIDE MACHINE
201 W Stillwell
DeQueen, AR 71832
870-642-7643; Fax: 870-642-4023
uncleal@riversidemachine.net
www.riversidemachine.net

ROCKY MOUNTAIN KNIVES
George L. Conklin
PO Box 902, 615 Franklin
Ft. Benton, MT 59442
406-622-3268; Fax: 406-622-3410
bbgrus@ttc-cmc.net
Working knives

RUMMELL, HANK
10 Paradise Lane
Warwick, NY 10990
845-469-9172
hank@newyorkcustomknives.com
www.newyorkcustomknives.com

SAKMAR, MIKE
1451 Clovelly Ave
Rochester, MI 48307
248-852-6775; Fax: 248-852-8544
mikesakmar@yahoo.com
Mokume bar stock. Retail & wholesale

SANDPAPER, INC. OF ILLINOIS
P.O. Box 2579
Glen Ellyn, IL 60138
630-629-3320; Fax: 630-629-3324
sandinc@aol.com; www.sandpaperinc.com
Abrasive belts, rolls, sheets & discs

SCHEP'S FORGE
PO Box 395
Shelton, NE 68876-0395

SENTRY SOLUTIONS LTD.
PO Box 214
Wilton, NH 03086
800-546-8049; Fax: 603-654-3003
info@sentrysolutions.com;
www.sentrysolutions.com
Knife care products

SHEFFIELD KNIFEMAKERS SUPPLY, INC.
PO Box 741107
Orange City, FL 32774
386-775-6453
email@sheffieldsupply.com;
www.sheffieldsupply.com

SHINING WAVE METALS
PO Box 563
Snohomish, WA 98291
425-334-5569
info@shiningwave.com;
www.shiningwave.com
A full line of mokume-gane in precious and non-precious metals for knifemakers, jewelers and other artists

SMITH ABRASIVES, INC. / SMITH WHETSTONE, INC.
1700 Sleepy Valley Rd
Hot Springs, AR 71901
www.smithabrasives.com

SMOLEN FORGE, INC.
Nick Smolen
S1735 Vang Rd
Westby, WI 54667
608-634-3569; Fax: 608-634-3869
smoforge@mwt.net;

www.smolenforge.com
Damascus billets & blanks, Mokume gane billets

SOSTER SVENSTRUP BYVEJ 16
Søster Svenstrup Byvej 16
4130 Viby Sjælland
Denmark
45 46 19 43 05; Fax: 45 46 19 53 19
www.poulstrande.com

STAMASCUS KNIFEWORKS INC.
Ed VanHoy
24255 N Fork River Rd
Abingdon, VA 24210
276-944-4885; Fax: 276-944-3187
stamascus@hughes.net;
www.stamascus-knive-works.com
Blade steels

STOVER, JEFF
PO Box 43
Torrance, CA 90507
310-532-2166
edgedealer1@yahoo.com;
www.edgedealer.com
Fine custom knives, top makers

TEXAS KNIFEMAKERS SUPPLY
10649 Haddington Suite 180
Houston TX 77043
713-461-8632; Fax: 713-461-8221
sales@texasknife.com;
www.texasknife.com
Working straight knives. Hunters including upswept skinners and custom walking sticks

TRU-GRIT, INC.
760 E Francis Unit N
Ontario, CA 91761
909-923-4116; Fax: 909-923-9932
www.trugrit.com
The latest in Norton and 3/M ceramic grinding belts. Also Super Flex, Trizact, Norax and Micron belts to 3000 grit. All of the popular belt grinders. Buffers and variable speed motors. ATS-34, 440C, BG-42, CPM S-30V, 416 and Damascus steel

WASHITA MOUNTAIN WHETSTONE CO.
PO Box 20378
Hot Springs, AR 71903-0378
501-525-3914; Fax: 501-525-0816
wmw@hsnp

WEILAND, J. REESE
PO Box 2337
Riverview, FL 33568
813-671-0661; 727-595-0378
rwphil413@earthlink.net
Folders, straight knives, etc.

WILSON, R.W.
PO Box 2012
113 Kent Way
Weirton, WV 26062
304-723-2771

WOOD CARVERS SUPPLY, INC.
PO Box 7500-K
Englewood, FL 34223
800-284-6229; 941-460-0123
info@woodcarverssupply.com;
www.woodcarverssupply.com
Over 2,000 unique wood carving tools

WOOD LAB
Michael Balaskovitz
P.O. Box 222
Hudsonville, MI 49426
616-322-5846
michael@woodlab.biz;
www.woodlab.biz
Acrylic stabilizing services and materials

WOOD STABILIZING SPECIALISTS INT'L, LLC
2940 Fayette Ave
Ionia, IA 50645
800-301-9774; 641-435-4746
mike@stabilizedwood.com;
www.stabilizedwood.com
Processor of acrylic impregnated materials

ZOWADA CUSTOM KNIVES
Tim Zowada
4509 E. Bear River Rd
Boyne Falls, MI 49713
231-348-5416
tim@tzknives.com; www.tzknives.com
Damascus, pocket knives, swords, Lower case gothic tz logo

mail order sales

A.G. RUSSELL KNIVES INC
2900 S. 26th St
Rogers, AR 72758-8571
800-255-9034 or 479-631-0130;
fax 479-631-8493
ag@agrussell.com; www.agrussell.com
The oldest knife mail-order company, highest quality. Free catalog available. In these catalogs you will find the newest and the best. If you like knives, this catalog is a must

ARIZONA CUSTOM KNIVES
Julie Hyman
2225 A1A South
Suite B-5
St. Augustine, FL 32080
904-826-4178
sharptalk@arizonacustomknifes.com;
www.arizonacustomknifes.com
Color catalog $5 U.S. / $7 Foreign

ARTISAN KNIVES
Ty Young
575 Targhee Twn Rd
Alta, WY 83414
304-353-8111
ty@artisanknives.com;
www.artisanknives.com
Feature master artisan knives and makers in a unique "coffee table book" style format

ATLANTA CUTLERY CORP.
P.O.Box 839
Conyers, Ga 30012
800-883-0300; Fax: 770-388-0246
custserve@atlantacutlery.com;
www.atlantacutlery.com

ATLANTIC BLADESMITHS/PETER STEBBINS
50 Mill Rd
Littleton, MA 01460
978-952-6448
Sell, trade, buy; carefully selected handcrafted, benchmade and factory knives

BALLARD CUTLERY
1495 Brummel Ave.
Elk Grove Village, IL 60007
847-228-0070

BECK'S CUTLERY SPECIALTIES
107 S Edinburgh Dr
Cary, NC 27511
919-460-0203; Fax: 919-460-7772
beckscutlery@mindspring.com;
www.beckscutlery.com
Knives

BLADEGALLERY, INC. / EPICUREAN EDGE, THE
107 Central Way
Kirkland, WA 98033
425-889-5980; Fax: 425-889-5981
info@bladegallery.com;
www.bladegallery.com
Bladegallery.com specializes in hand-made one-of-a-kind knives from around the world. We have an emphasis on forged knives and high-end gentlemen's folders

BLUE RIDGE KNIVES
166 Adwolfe Rd
Marion, VA 24354
276-783-6143; 276-783-9298
onestop@blueridgeknives.com;
www.blueridgeknives.com
Wholesale distributor of knives

BOB NEAL CUSTOM KNIVES
PO Box 20923
Atlanta, GA 30320
770-914-7794
bob@bobnealcustomknives.com;
www.bobnealcustomknives.com
Exclusive limited edition custom knives-sets & single

BOB'S TRADING POST
308 N Main St
Hutchinson, KS 67501
620-669-9441
bobstradingpost@cox.net;
www.gunshopfinder.com
Tad custom knives with reichert custom sheaths one at a time, one of a kind

BOONE TRADING CO., INC.
PO Box 669
562 Coyote Rd
Brinnon, WA 98320
800-423-1945; Fax: 360-796-4511
www.boonetrading.com
Ivory of all types, bone, horns

CARMEL CUTLERY
Dolores & 6th
PO Box 1346
Carmel, CA 93921
831-624-6699; 831-624-6780
ccutlery@ix.netcom.com;
www.carmelcutlery.com
Quality custom and a variety of production pocket knives, swords; kitchen cutlery; personal grooming items

CUSTOM KNIFE CONSIGNMENT
PO Box 20923
Atlanta, GA 30320
770-914-7794; 770-914-7796
bob@customknifeconsignment.com; www.customknifeconsignment.com
We sell your knives

CUTLERY SHOPPE
3956 E Vantage Pointe Ln
Meridian, ID 83642-7268
800-231-1272; Fax: 208-884-4433
order@cutleryshoppe.com;
www.cutleryshoppe.com
Discount pricing on top quality brands

CUTTING EDGE, THE
2900 South 26th St
Rogers, AR 72758-8571
800-255-9034; Fax: 479-631-8493
ce_info@cuttingedge.com;
www.cuttingedge.com
After-market knives since 1968. They offer about 1,000 individual knives for sale each month. Subscription by first class mail, in U.S. $20 per year, Canada or Mexico by air mail, $25 per year. All overseas by air mail, $40 per year. The oldest and the most experienced in the business of buying and selling knives. They buy collections of any size, take knives on consignment. Every month there are 4-8 pages in color featuring the work of top makers

DENTON, JOHN W.
703 Hiawassee Estates
Hiawassee, GA 30546
706-781-8479
jwdenton@windstream.net
Loveless knives

DUNN KNIVES INC.
PO Box 204
5830 NW Carlson Rd
Rossville, KS 66533
800-245-6483
steve.greene@dunnknives.com;
www.dunnknives.com

ELLIS, DAVE
770 Sycamore Ave., Ste. 122, Box 451
Vista, CA 92083
760-945-7177
ellis@mastersmith.com;
www.exquisiteknives.com and
www.robertloveless.com

FAZALARE, ROY
PO Box 7062
Thousand Oaks, CA 91359
805-496-2002 after 7pm
ourfaz@aol.com
Handmade multiblades; older case; Fight'n Rooster; Bulldog brand & Cripple Creek

FROST CUTLERY CO.
PO Box 22636
Chattanooga, TN 37422
800-251-7768; Fax: 423-894-9576
www.frostcutlery.com

GENUINE ISSUE INC.
949 Middle Country Rd
Selden, NY 11784
631-696-3802; 631-696-3803
gicutlery@aol.com
Antique knives, swords

**GEORGE TICHBOURNE CUSTOM
KNIVES**
7035 Maxwell Rd #5
Mississauga, Ontario L5S 1R5
CANADA
905-670-0200
sales@tichbourneknives.com;
www.tichbourneknives.com
*Canadian custom knifemaker has full retail
knife store*

GODWIN, INC. G. GEDNEY
PO Box 100
Valley Forge, PA 19481
610-783-0670; Fax: 610-783-6083
sales@gggodwin.com;
www.gggodwin.com
18th century reproductions

GOLCZEWS KNIVES
Larry Golczewski, dba New Jersey Knifer
30 Quigley Rd.
Hewitt, NJ 07421
973-728-2386
*Medium- to high-priced custom and
handmade knives, some production if made
in USA, Japan, Germany, or Italy. Practical to
tactical. Consignments welcome. Also buy,
design, and appraise.*

**GRAZYNA SHAW/QUINTESSENTIAL
CUTLERY**
715 Bluff St.
Clearwater, MN 55320
201-655-4411; Fax: 320-558-6128; www.
quintcut.com
*Specializing in investment-grade custom
knives and early makers*

GUILD KNIVES
Donald Guild
320 Paani Place 1A
Paia, HI 96779
808-877-3109
don@guildknives.com;
www.guildknives.com
Purveyor of custom art knives

HOUSE OF TOOLS LTD.
#136, 8228 Macleod Tr. SE
Calgary, Alberta, Canada
T2H 2B8

**JENCO SALES, INC. / KNIFE
IMPORTERS, INC. / WHITE
LIGHTNING**
PO Box 1000
11307 Conroy Ln
Manchaca, TX 78652
303-444-2882
kris@finishlineusa.com
www.whitelightningco.com
Wholesale only

KELLAM KNIVES CO.
902 S Dixie Hwy
Lantana, FL 33462
800-390-6918; 561-588-3186
info@kellamknives.com;
www.kellamknives.com
*Largest selection of Finnish knives; own line
of folders and fixed blades*

KNIFEART.COM
13301 Pompano Dr
Little Rock AR 72211
501-221-1319; Fax: 501-221-2695
www.knifeart.com
*Large internet seller of custom knives &
upscale production knives*

KNIFEPURVEYOR.COM LLC
646-872-0476
mdonato@knifepurveyor.com; www.
knifepurveyor.com
*Owned and operated by Michael A. Donato
(full-time knife purveyor since 2002). We
buy, sell, trade, and consign fine custom
knives. We also specialize in buying and
selling valuable collections of fine custom
knives. Our goal is to make every transaction
a memorable one.*

KNIVES PLUS
2467 I 40 West
Amarillo, TX 79109
800-687-6202
salessupport@knivesplus.com; www.
knivesplus.com
*Retail cutlery and cutlery accessories since
1987*

KRIS CUTLERY
2314 Monte Verde Dr
Pinole, CA 94564
510-758-9912 Fax: 510-223-8968
kriscutlery@aol.com; www.kriscutlery.com
Japanese, medieval, Chinese & Philippine

LONE STAR WHOLESALE
2407 W Interstate 40
Amarillo, TX 79109
806-356-9540
*Wholesale only; major brands and
accessories*

MATTHEWS CUTLERY
4401 Sentry Dr
Tucker, GA 30084-6561
770-939-6915

MOORE CUTLERY
PO Box 633
Lockport, IL 60441
708-301-4201
www.knives.cx
*Owned & operated by Gary Moore since 1991
(a full-time dealer). Purveyor of high quality
custom & production knives*

MORTY THE KNIFE MAN, INC.
4 Manorhaven Blvd
Pt Washington, NY 11050
516-767-2357; 516-767-7058

MUSEUM REPLICAS LIMITED
2147 Gees Mill Rd
Conyers, GA 30012
800-883-8838
www.museumreplicas.com
*Historically accurate and battle ready swords
& daggers*

NORDIC KNIVES
1634-C Copenhagen Drive
Solvang, CA 93463
805-688-3612; Fax: 805-688-1635
info@nordicknives.com;
www.nordicknives.com
Custom and Randall knives

**PARKERS' KNIFE COLLECTOR
SERVICE**
6715 Heritage Business Court
Chattanooga, TN 37422
615-892-0448; Fax: 615-892-9165

PLAZA CUTLERY, INC.
3333 S. Bristol St., Suite 2060
South Coast Plaza
Costa Mesa, CA 92626
866-827-5292; 714-549-3932
dan@plazacutlery.com;
www.plazacutlery.com
*Largest selection of knives on the west coast.
Custom makers from beginners to the best.
All customs, William Henry, Strider, Reeves,
Randalls & others available online by phone*

RANDALL KNIFE SOCIETY
PO Box 158
Meadows of Dan, VA 24120
276-952-2500
payrks@gate.net;
www.randallknifesociety.com
*Randall, Loveless, Scagel, moran, antique
pocket knives*

ROBERTSON'S CUSTOM CUTLERY
4960 Sussex Dr
Evans, GA 30809
706-650-0252; 706-860-1623
rccedge@csranet.com; www.
robertsoncustomcutlery.com
*World class custom knives, Vanguard knives-
Limited exclusive design*

**SMOKY MOUNTAIN KNIFE WORKS,
INC.**
2320 Winfield Dunn Pkwy
PO Box 4430
Sevierville, TN 37864
800-251-9306; 865-453-5871
info@smkw.com; www.eknifeworks.com
*The world's largest knife showplace, catalog
and website*

VOYLES, BRUCE
PO Box 22007
Chattanooga, TN 37422
423-238-6753; Fax: 423-238-3960
bruce@jbrucevoyles.com;
www.jbrucevoyles.com
Knives, knife auctions

knife services

appraisers

Levine, Bernard, P.O. Box 2404, Eugene, OR, 97402, 541-484-0294, brlevine@ix.netcom.com

Russell, A.G., Knives Inc, 2900 S. 26th St., Rogers, AR 72758-8571, phone 800-255-9034 or 479-631-0130, fax 479-631-8493, ag@agrussell.com, www.agrussell.com

Vallini, Massimo, Via G. Bruno 7, 20154 Milano, ITALY, 02-33614751, massimo_vallini@yahoo.it, Knife expert

custom grinders

McGowan Manufacturing Company, 4854 N Shamrock Pl #100, Tucson, AZ, 85705, 800-342-4810, 520-219-0884, info@mcgowanmfg.com, www.mcgowanmfg.com, Knife sharpeners, hunting axes

Peele, Bryan, The Elk Rack, 215 Ferry St. P.O. Box 1363, Thompson Falls, MT, 59873

Schlott, Harald, Zingster Str. 26, 13051 Berlin, GERMANY, 049 030 9293346, harald.schlott@T-online.de, Custom grinder, custom handle artisan, display case/box maker, etcher, scrimshander

Wilson, R.W., P.O. Box 2012, Weirton, WV, 26062

custom handles

Cooper, Jim, 1221 Cook St, Ramona, CA, 92065-3214, 760-789-1097, (760) 788-7992, jamcooper@aol.com

Burrows, Chuck, dba Wild Rose Trading Co, 289 Laposta Canyon Rd, Durango, CO, 81303, 970-259-8396, chuck@wrtcleather.com, www.wrtcleather.com

Fields, Donald, 790 Tamerlane St, Deltona, FL, 32725, 386-532-9070, donaldfields@aol.com, Selling ancient ivories; mammoth & fossil walrus

Grussenmeyer, Paul G., 310 Kresson Rd, Cherry Hill, NJ, 08034, 856-428-1088, 856-428-8997, pgrussentne@comcast.net, www.pgcarvings.com

Holland, Dennis K., 4908-17th Pl., Lubbock, TX, 79416

Imboden II, Howard L., hi II Originals, 620 Deauville Dr., Dayton, OH, 45429

Kelso, Jim, 577 Collar Hill Rd, Worcester, VT, 05682, 802-229-4254, (802) 223-0595

Knack, Gary, 309 Wightman, Ashland, OR, 97520

Marlatt, David, 67622 Oldham Rd., Cambridge, OH, 43725, 740-432-7549

Mead, Dennis, 2250 E. Mercury St., Inverness, FL, 34453-0514

Myers, Ron, 6202 Marglenn Ave., Baltimore, MD, 21206, 410-866-6914

Saggio, Joe, 1450 Broadview Ave. #12, Columbus, OH, 43212, jvsag@webtv.net, www.j.v.saggio@worldnet.att.net, Handle Carver

Schlott, Harald, Zingster Str. 26, 13051 Berlin, GERMANY, 049 030 9293346, harald.schlott@T-online.de, Custom grinder, custom handle artisan, display case/box maker, etcher, scrimshander

Snell, Barry A., 4801 96th St. N., St. Petersburg, FL, 33708-3740

Vallotton, A., 621 Fawn Ridge Dr., Oakland, OR, 97462

Watson, Silvia, 350 Jennifer Lane, Driftwood, TX, 78619

Wilderness Forge, 315 North 100 East, Kanab, UT, 84741, 435-644-3674, bhatting@xpressweb.com

Williams, Gary, (GARBO), PO Box 210, Glendale, KY, 42740-2010

display cases and boxes

Bill's Custom Cases, P O Box 603, Montague, CA, 96064, 530-459-5968, billscustomcases@earthlink.net

Brooker, Dennis, Rt. 1, Box 12A, Derby, IA, 50068

Chas Clements' Custom Leathercraft, Chas, 1741 Dallas St., Aurora, CO, 80010-2018, 303-364-0403, GRYPHONS@HOME.NET, Display case/box maker, Leatherworker, Knife appraiser

Freund, Steve, Tomway LLC, 1646 Tichenor Court, Atlanta, GA, 30338, 770-393-8349, steve@tomway.com, www.tomway.com

Gimbert, Nelson, P.O. Box 787, Clemmons, NC, 27012

McLean, Lawrence, 12344 Meritage Ct, Rancho Cucamonga, CA, 91739, 714-848-5779, lmclean@charter.net

Miller, Michael K., M&M Kustom Krafts, 28510 Santiam Highway, Sweet Home, OR, 97386

Miller, Robert, P.O. Box 2722, Ormond Beach, FL, 32176

Retichek, Joseph L., W9377 Co. TK. D, Beaver Dam, WI, 53916

Robbins, Wayne, 11520 Inverway, Belvidere, IL, 61008

S&D Enterprises, 20 East Seventh St, Manchester, OH, 45144, 937-549-2602, 937-549-2602, sales@s-denterprises.com, www.s-denterprises.com, Display case/ box maker. Manufacturer of aluminum display, chipboard type displays, wood displays. Silk screening or acid etching for logos on product

Schlott, Harald, Zingster Str. 26, 13051 Berlin, GERMANY, 049 030 9293346, harald.schlott@T-online.de, Custom grinder, custom handle artisan, display case/box maker, etcher, scrimshander

engravers

Adlam, Tim, 1705 Witzel Ave., Oshkosh, WI, 54902, 920-235-4589, www.adlamengraving.com

Alcorn, Gordon, 10573 Kelly Canyon Rd., Bozeman, MT 59715, 406-586-1350, alcorncustom@yahoo.com, www.alcornengraving.com

Alfano, Sam, 45 Catalpa Trace, Covington, LA, 70433, alfano@gmail.com, www.masterengraver.com

Baron, David, Baron Technology Inc., 62 Spring Hill Rd., Trumbull, CT, 06611, 203-452-0515, bti@baronengraving.com, www.baronengraving.com, Polishing, plating, inlays, artwork

Bates, Billy, 2302 Winthrop Dr. SW, Decatur, AL, 35603, bbrn@aol.com, www.angelfire.com/al/billybates

Bettenhausen, Merle L., 8300 W. 191st St., Mokena, IL, 60448, 708-532-2179

Blair, Jim, PO Box 64, 59 Mesa Verde, Glenrock, WY, 82637, 307-436-8115, jblairengrav@msn.com, www.jimblairengraving.com

Booysen, Chris, South Africa, +27-73-284-1493, chris@cbknives.com, www.cbknives.com

Churchill, Winston G., RFD Box 29B, Proctorsville, VT 05153, www.wchurchill.com

Collins, Michael, 405-392-2273, info@michaelcollinsart.com, www.michaelcollinsart.com

Cover, Raymond A., 1206 N. Third St., Festus, MO 63028 314-808-2508 cover@sbcglobal.net, http://rcoverengraving.com

DeLorge, Ed, 6734 W Main St, Houma, LA, 70360, 985-223-0206, delorge@triparish.net, http://www.eddelorge.com/

Dickson, John W., PO Box 49914, Sarasota, FL, 34230, 941-952-1907

Dolbare, Elizabeth, PO Box 502, Dubois, WY, 82513-0502 edolbare@hotmail.com, http://www.scrimshaw-engraving.com/

Downing, Jim, PO Box 4224, Springfield, MO, 65808, 417-865-5953, handlebar@thegunengraver.com, www.thegunengraver.com, Scrimshander

Duarte, Carlos, 108 Church St., Rossville, CA, 95678, 916-782-2617 carlossilver@surewest.net, www.carlossilver.com

Dubber, Michael W., 11 S. Green River Rd., Evansville, IN, 47715, 812-454-0271, m.dubber@firearmsengraving.com, www.firearmsengraving.com

Eaton, Rick, 313 Dailey Rd., Broadview, MT 59015, 406-667-2405, rick@eatonknives.com, www.eatonknives.com

Eklund, Maihkel, Föne Stam V9, S-820 41 Färila, SWEDEN, info@art-knives.com, www.art-knives.com

Eldridge, Allan, 7731 Four Winds Dr., Ft. Worth, TX 76133, 817-370-7778

Ellis, Willy B, Willy B's Customs, 1025 Hamilton Ave., Tarpon Springs, FL, 34689, 727-942-6420, wbflashs@verizon.net, www.willyb.com

Flannery Gun Engraving, Jeff, 11034 Riddles Run Rd., Union, KY, 41091, 859-384-3127, engraving@fuse.net, www.flannerygunengraving.com

Glimm, Jerome C., 19 S. Maryland, Conrad, MT, 59425, 406-278-3574, www.gunengraver.biz

Gournet, Geoffroy, 820 Paxinosa Ave., Easton, PA, 18042, 610-559-0710, ggournet@yahoo.com, www.gournetusa.com

Halloran, Tim, 316 Fenceline Dr. Blue Grass, IA 52726 563-260-8464, vivtim@msn.com, http://halloranengraving.com

Hands, Barry Lee, 30608 Fernview Ln., Bigfork, MT 59911, 406-249-4334, barry_hands@yahoo.com, www.barryleehands.com

Holder, Pat, 18910 McNeil Ranch Rd., Wickenburg, AZ 85390, 928-684-2025 dholderknives@commspeed.net, www.dholder.com

Ingle, Ralph W., 151 Callan Dr., Rossville, GA, 30741, 706-858-0641, riengraver@aol.com, Photographer

Johns, Bill, 1716 8th St, Cody, WY, 82414, 307-587-5090, http://billjohnsengraver.com

Kelso, Jim, 577 Coller Hill Rd, Worcester, VT, 05682, 802-229-4254, kelsomaker@gmail.com, www.jimkelso.com

Koevenig, Eugene and Eve, Koevenig's Engraving Service, Rabbit Gulch, Box 55, Hill City, SD, 57745-0055

Kostelnik, Joe and Patty, RD #4, Box 323, Greensburg, PA, 15601

Kudlas, John M., 55280 Silverwolf Dr, Barnes, WI, 54873, 715-795-2031, jkudlas@cheqnet.net, Engraver, scrimshander

Lark, David, 6641 Schneider Rd., Kingsley, MI 49649, Phone: 231-342-1076 dblark58@yahoo.com

Limings Jr., Harry, 959 County Rd. 170, Marengo, OH, 43334-9625

Lindsay, Steve, 3714 West Cedar Hills Drive, Kearney, NE, 68847

Lyttle, Brian, Box 5697, High River AB CANADA, T1V 1M7

Lytton, Simon M., 19 Pinewood Gardens, Hemel Hempstead, Hertfordshire HP1 1TN, ENGLAND, 01-442-255542, simonlyttonengraver@virginmedia.com

Mason, Joe, 146 Value Rd, Brandon, MS, 39042, 601-824-9867, www.joemasonengraving.com

McCombs, Leo, 1862 White Cemetery Rd., Patriot, OH, 45658

McDonald, Dennis, 8359 Brady St., Peosta, IA, 52068

McLean, Lawrence, 12344 Meritage Ct, Rancho Cucamonga, CA, 91739, 714-848-5779, lmclean@charter.net

Meyer, Chris, 39 Bergen Ave., Wantage, NJ, 07461, 973-875-6299

Minnick, Joyce, 144 N. 7th St., Middletown, IN, 47356

Morgan, Tandie, P.O. Box 693, 30700 Hwy. 97, Nucla, CO, 81424

Morton, David A., 1110 W. 21st St., Lorain, OH, 44052

Moulton, Dusty, 135 Hillview Ln, Loudon, TN, 37774, 865-408-9779

Muller, Jody & Pat, PO Box 35, Pittsburg, MO, 65724, 417-852-4306/417-752-3260, mullerforge@hotmail.com, www.mullerforge.com

Nelida, Toniutti, via G. Pasconi 29/c, Maniago 33085 (PN), ITALY

Nilsson, Jonny Walker, Tingsstigen 11, SE-933 33 Arvidsjaur, SWEDEN, +(46) 960-13048, 0960.13048@telia.com, www.jwnknives.com

Nott, Ron, Box 281, Summerdale, PA, 17093

Parsons, Michael R., McKee Knives, 7042 McFarland Rd, Indianapolis, IN, 46227, 317-784-7943

Patterson, W.H., P.O. Drawer DK, College Station, TX, 77841

Peri, Valerio, Via Meucci 12, Gardone V.T. 25063, ITALY

Pilkington Jr., Scott, P.O. Box 97, Monteagle, TN, 37356, 931-924-3400, scott@pilkguns.com, www.pilkguns.com

Rabeno, Martin, Spook Hollow Trading Co, 530 Eagle Pass, Durango, CO, 81301

Raftis, Andrew, 2743 N. Sheffield, Chicago, IL, 60614

Roberts, J.J., 7808 Lake Dr., Manassas, VA, 20111, 703-330-0448, jjrengraver@aol.com, www.angelfire.com/va2/ engraver

Robidoux, Roland J., DMR Fine Engraving, 25 N. Federal Hwy. Studio 5, Dania, FL, 33004

Rosser, Bob, Hand Engraving, 2809 Crescent Ave Ste 20, Homewood, AL, 35209-2526, www.hand-engravers.com

Rudolph, Gil, 20922 Oak Pass Ave, Tehachapi, CA, 93561, 661-822-4949, www.gtraks@csurfers.net

Rundell, Joe, 6198 W. Frances Rd., Clio, MI, 48420

Sawby, Marian, 480 Snowberry Ln., Sandpoint, ID 83864, 208-263-4253, http://sawbycustomknives.com/

Schlott, Harald, Zingster Str. 26, 13051 Berlin, GERMANY, 049 030 9293346, 049 030 9293346, harald.schlott@T-online.de, www.gravur-kunst-atelier.de.vu, Custom grinder, custom handle artisan, display case/box maker, etcher, scrimshander

Schönert, Elke, 18 Lansdowne Pl., Central, Port Elizabeth, SOUTH AFRICA

Shaw, Bruce, P.O. Box 545, Pacific Grove, CA, 93950, 831-646-1937, 831-644-0941, shawdogs@aol.com

Simmons, Rick W., 3323 Creek Manor Dr., Kingwood, TX, 77339, 504-261-8450, exhibitiongrade@gmail.com www.exhibitionengraver.com

Slobodian, Barbara, 4101 River Ridge Dr., PO Box 1498, San Andreas, CA 95249, 209-286-1980, fax 209-286-1982, barbara@dancethetide.com. Specializes in Japanese-style engraving

Small, Jim, 2860 Athens Hwy., Madison, GA 30650, 706-818-1245, smallengrave@aol.com, www.jimsmallengraving.com

Smith, Ron, 5869 Straley, Ft. Worth, TX, 76114

Smitty's Engraving, 21320 Pioneer Circle, Hurrah, OK, 73045, 405-454-6968, smittys.engraving@prodigy.net, www.smittys-engraving.us

Spode, Peter, Tresaith Newland, Malvern, Worcestershire WR13 5AY, ENGLAND

Swartley, Robert D., 2800 Pine St., Napa, CA, 94558

Takeuchi, Shigetoshi, 21-14-1-Chome kamimuneoka Shiki shi, 353 Saitama, JAPAN

Theis, Terry, 21452 FM 2093, Harper, TX, 78631, 830-864-4438

Valade, Robert B., 931 3rd Ave., Seaside, OR, 97138, 503-738-7672, (503) 738-7672

Waldrop, Mark, 14562 SE 1st Ave. Rd., Summerfield, FL, 34491

Warenski, Julie, 590 East 500 N., Richfield, UT, 84701, 435-896-5319, julie@warenskiknives.com, www.warenskiknives.com

Warren, Kenneth W., P.O. Box 2842, Wenatchee, WA, 98807-2842, 509-663-6123, (509) 663-6123

Whitehead, James 2175 South Willow Ave. Space 22 Fresno, CA 93725 559-412-4374 jdwmks@yahoo.com

Whitmore, Jerry, 1740 Churchill Dr., Oakland, OR, 97462

Winn, Travis A., 558 E. 3065 S., Salt Lake City, UT, 84106

Zietz, Dennis, 5906 40th Ave., Kenosha, WI, 53144

Zima, Russ, 7291 Ruth Way, Denver, CO, 80221, 303-657-9378, www.rzengraving.com

etchers

Baron Technology Inc., David Baron, 62 Spring Hill Rd., Trumbull, CT, 06611

Fountain Products, 492 Prospect Ave., West Springfield, MA, 01089

Hayes, Dolores, P.O. Box 41405, Los Angeles, CA, 90041

Holland, Dennis, 4908 17th Pl., Lubbock, TX, 79416

Kelso, Jim, 577 Collar Hill Rd, Worcester, VT, 05682

Larstein, Francine, FRANCINE ETCHINGS & ETCHED KNIVES, 368 White Rd, Watsonville, CA, 95076, 800-557-1525/831-426-6046, 831-684-1949, francine@francinetchings.com, www.boyeknivesgallery.com

Lefaucheux, Jean-Victor, Saint-Denis-Le-Ferment, 27140 Gisors, FRANCE

Mead, Faustina L., 2550 E. Mercury St., Inverness, FL, 34453-0514, 352-344-4751, scrimsha@infionline.net, www.scrimshaw-by-faustina.com

Myers, Ron, 6202 Marglenn Ave., Baltimore, MD, 21206, (acid) etcher

Nilsson, Jonny Walker, Tingsstigen 11, SE-933 33 Arvidsjaur, SWEDEN, +(46) 960-13048, 0960.13048@telia.com, www. jwnknives.com

Schlott, Harald, Zingster Str. 26, 13051 Berlin, GERMANY, 049 030 9293346, harald.schlott@T-online.de, Custom grinder, custom handle artisan, display case/box maker, etcher, scrimshander

Vallotton, A., Northwest Knife Supply, 621 Fawn Ridge Dr., Oakland, OR, 97462

Watson, Silvia, 350 Jennifer Lane, Driftwood, TX, 78619

heat treaters

Bay State Metal Treating Co., 6 Jefferson Ave., Woburn, MA, 01801

Bos Heat Treating, Paul, Shop: 1900 Weld Blvd., El Cajon, CA, 92020, 619-562-2370 / 619-445-4740 Home, PaulBos@BuckKnives.com

Holt, B.R., 1238 Birchwood Drive, Sunnyvale, CA, 94089

Kazou, Okaysu, 12-2 1 Chome Higashi, Ueno, Taito-Ku, Tokyo, JAPAN, 81-33834-2323, 81-33831-3012

Metal Treating Bodycote Inc., 710 Burns St., Cincinnati, OH, 45204

O&W Heat Treat Inc., One Bidwell Rd., South Windsor, CT, 06074, 860-528-9239, (860) 291-9939, owht1@aol.com

Progressive Heat Treating Co., 2802 Charles City Rd, Richmond, VA, 23231, 804-545-0010, 804-545-0012

Texas Heat Treating Inc., 303 Texas Ave., Round Rock, TX, 78664

Texas Knifemakers Supply, 10649 Haddington, Suite 180, Houston, TX, 77043

Tinker Shop, The, 1120 Helen, Deer Park, TX, 77536

Valley Metal Treating Inc., 355 S. East End Ave., Pomona, CA, 91766

Wilderness Forge, 315 North 100 East, Kanab, UT, 84741, 435-644-3674, bhatting@xpressweb.com

Wilson, R.W., P.O. Box 2012, Weirton, WV, 26062

leather workers

Abramson, David, 116 Baker Ave, Wharton, NJ, 07885, lifter4him1@aol.com, www.liftersleather.com

Bruner, Rick, 7756 Aster Lane, Jenison, MI, 49428, 616-457-0403

Burrows, Chuck, dba Wild Rose Trading Co, 289 Laposta Canyon Rd, Durango, CO, 81303, 970-259-8396, chuck@wrtleather.com

Clements' Custom Leathercraft, Chas, 1741 Dallas St., Aurora, CO, 80010-2018

Cole, Dave, 620 Poinsetta Dr., Satellite Beach, FL 32937, 321-773-1687, www.dcknivesandleather.blademakers.com. Custom sheath services.

Cooper, Harold, 136 Winding Way, Frankfort, KY, 40601

Cooper, Jim, 1221 Cook St, Ramona, CA, 92065-3214, 760-789-1097, 760-788-7992, jamcooper@aol.com

Cow Catcher Leatherworks, 3006 Industrial Dr, Raleigh, NC, 27609

Cubic, George, GC Custom Leather Co., 10561 E. Deerfield Pl., Tucson, AZ, 85749, 520-760-0695, gcubic@aol.com

Dawkins, Dudley, 221 N. Broadmoor Ave, Topeka, KS, 66606-1254, 785-235-3871, dawkind@sbcglobal.net, ABS member/knifemaker forges straight knives

Evans, Scott V, Edge Works Mfg, 1171 Halltown Rd, Jacksonville, NC, 28546, 910-455-9834, (910) 346-5660, edgeworks@coastalnet.com, www.tacticalholsters.com

Genske, Jay, 283 Doty St, Fond du Lac, WI, 54935, 920-921-8019/Cell Phone 920-579-0144, jaygenske@hotmail.com, Custom Grinder, Custom Handle Artisan

Green River Leather, 1100 Legion Park Road, PO BOX 190, Greensburg, KY, 42743, Phone: 270-932-2212 fax: 270-299-2471 email: info@greenriverleather.com

Hawk, Ken, Rt. 1, Box 770, Ceres, VA, 24318-9630

Homyk, David N., 8047 Carriage Ln., Wichita Falls, TX, 76306

John's Custom Leather, John R. Stumpf, 523 S. Liberty St, Blairsville, PA, 15717, 724-459-6802, 724-459-5996

Kelley, Jo Ann, 52 Mourning Dove Dr., Watertown, WI 53094, 920-206-0807, ladybug@ticon.net, www.hembrookcustomknives.com. Custom leather knife sheaths $40 to $100; making sheaths since 2002.

Kravitt, Chris, HC 31 Box 6484, Rt 200, Ellsworth, ME, 04605-9805, 207-584-3000, 207-584-3000, sheathmkr@aol.com, www.treestumpleather.com, Reference: Tree Stump Leather

Larson, Richard, 549 E. Hawkeye, Turlock, CA, 95380

Layton, Jim, 2710 Gilbert Avenue, Portsmouth, OH, 45662

Lee, Randy, P.O. Box 1873, 270 N 9th West, St. Johns, AZ, 85936, 928-337-2594, 928-337-5002, randylee@randyleeknives.com, info@randyleeknives.com, Custom knifemaker; www.randyleeknives.com

Long, Paul, 108 Briarwood Ln W, Kerrville, TX, 78028, 830-367-5536, PFL@cebridge.net

Lott, Sherry, 1100 Legion Park Rd., Greenburg, KY 42743, phone 270-932-2212, fax 270-299-2471, sherrylott@alltel.net

Mason, Arne, 258 Wimer St., Ashland, OR, 97520, 541-482-2260, (541) 482-7785, www.arnemason.com

McGowan, Liz, 12629 Howard Lodge Dr., Winter Add-2023 Robin Ct Sebring FL 33870, Sykesville, MD, 21784, 410-489-4323

Metheny, H.A. "Whitey", 7750 Waterford Dr., Spotsylvania, VA, 22553, 540-582-3228 Cell 540-542-1440, 540-582-3095, nametheny@aol.com, www.methenyknives.com

Miller, Michael K., 28510 Santiam Highway, Sweet Home, OR, 97386

Mobley, Martha, 240 Alapaha River Road, Chula, GA, 31733

Morrissey, Martin, 4578 Stephens Rd., Blairsville, GA, 30512

Niedenthal, John Andre, Beadwork & Buckskin, Studio 3955 NW 103 Dr., Coral Springs, FL, 33065-1551, 954-345-0447, a_niedenthal@hotmail.com

Neilson, Tess, RR2 Box 16, Wyalusing, PA, 18853, 570-746-4944, www.mountainhollow.net, Doing business as Neilson's Mountain Hollow

Parsons, Larry, 1038 W. Kyle, Mustang, OK 73064 405-376-9408 s.m.parsons@sbcglobal.net

Parsons, Michael R., McKee Knives, 7042 McFarland Rd, Indianapolis, IN, 46227, 317-784-7943

Poag, James H., RR #1 Box 212A, Grayville, IL, 62844

Red's Custom Leather, Ed Todd, 9 Woodlawn Rd., Putnam Valley, NY, 10579, 845-528-3783

Rowe, Kenny, 3219 Hwy 29 South, Hope, AR, 71801, 870-777-8216, 870-777-0935, rowesleather@yahoo.com, www.knifeart.com or www.theedgeequipment.com

Schrap, Robert G., 7024 W. Wells St., Wauwatosa, WI, 53213-3717, 414-771-6472, (414) 479-9765, knifesheaths@aol.com, www.customsheaths.com

Strahin, Robert, 401 Center St., Elkins, WV, 26241, *Custom Knife Sheaths

Tierney, Mike, 447 Rivercrest Dr., Woodstock ON CANADA, N4S 5W5

Turner, Kevin, 17 Hunt Ave., Montrose, NY, 10548

Velasquez, Gil, 7120 Madera Dr., Goleta, CA, 93117

Walker, John, 17 Laber Circle, Little Rock, AR, 72210, 501-455-0239, john.walker@afbic.com

Watson, Bill, #1 Presidio, Wimberly, TX, 78676

Whinnery, Walt, 1947 Meadow Creek Dr., Louisville, KY, 40218

Williams, Sherman A., 1709 Wallace St., Simi Valley, CA, 93065

miscellaneous

Hendryx Design, Scott, 5997 Smokey Way, Boise, ID, 83714, 208-377-8044, www.shdsheaths@msn.com Kydex Sheath Maker

Robertson, Kathy, Impress by Design, PO Box 1367, Evans, GA, 30809-1367, 706-650-0982, (706) 860-1623, impressbydesign@comcast.net, Advertising/graphic designer

Strahin, Robert, 401 Center St., Elkins, WV, 26241, 304-636-0128, rstrahin@copper.net, *Custom Knife Sheaths

photographers

Alfano, Sam, 36180 Henery Gaines Rd., Pearl River, LA, 70452
Allen, John, Studio One, 3823 Pleasant Valley Blvd., Rockford, IL, 61114
Balance Digital, Rob Szajkowski, 261 Riverview Way, Oceanside, CA 92057, 760-815-6131, rob@balancedigital.com, www.balancedigital.com
Bilal, Mustafa, Turk's Head Productions, 908 NW 50th St., Seattle, WA, 98107-3634, 206-782-4164, (206) 783-5677, mustafa@turkshead.com, www.turkshead.com, Graphic design, marketing & advertising
Bogaerts, Jan, Regenweg 14, 5757 PI., Liessel, HOLLAND
Box Photography, Doug, 1804 W Main St, Brenham, TX, 77833-3420
Brown, Tom, 6048 Grants Ferry Rd., Brandon, MS, 39042-8136
Butman, Steve, P.O. Box 5106, Abilene, TX, 79608
Calidonna, Greg, 205 Helmwood Dr., Elizabethtown, KY, 42701
Campbell, Jim, 7935 Ranch Rd., Port Richey, FL, 34668
Cooper, Jim, Sharpbycoop.com photography, 9 Mathew Court, Norwalk, CT, 06851, jcooper@sharpbycoop.com, www.sharpbycoop.com
Courtice, Bill, P.O. Box 1776, Duarte, CA, 91010-4776
Crosby, Doug, RFD 1, Box 1111, Stockton Springs, ME, 04981
Danko, Michael, 3030 Jane Street, Pittsburgh, PA, 15203
Davis, Marshall B., P.O. Box 3048, Austin, TX, 78764
Earley, Don, 1241 Ft. Bragg Rd., Fayetteville, NC, 28305
Ehrlich, Linn M., 1850 N Clark St #1008, Chicago, IL, 60614, 312-209-2107
Etzler, John, 11200 N. Island Rd., Grafton, OH, 44044
Fahrner, Dave, 1623 Arnold St., Pittsburgh, PA, 15205
Faul, Jan W., 903 Girard St. NE, Rr. Washington, DC, 20017
Fedorak, Allan, 28 W. Nicola St., Amloops BC CANADA, V2C 1J6
Fox, Daniel, Lumina Studios, 6773 Industrial Parkway, Cleveland, OH, 44070, 440-734-2118, (440) 734-3542, lumina@en.com
Freiberg, Charley, PO Box 42, Elkins, NH, 03233, 603-526-2767, charleyfreiberg@tos.net
Gardner, Chuck, 116 Quincy Ave., Oak Ridge, TN, 37830
Gawryla, Don, 1105 Greenlawn Dr., Pittsburgh, PA, 15220
Goffe Photographic Associates, 3108 Monte Vista Blvd., NE, Albuquerque, NM, 87106
Graham, James, 7434 E Northwest Hwy, Dallas, TX, 75231, 214-341-5138, jamie@jamiephoto.com, www.jamiephoto.com, Product photographer
Graley, Gary W., RR2 Box 556, Gillett, PA, 16925
Griggs, Dennis, 118 Pleasant Pt Rd, Topsham, ME, 04086, 207-725-5689
Hanusin, John, Reames-Hanusin Studio, PO Box 931, Northbrook, IL, 60065 0931
Hodge, Tom, 7175 S US Hwy 1 Lot 36, Titusville, FL, 32780-8172, 321-267-7989, egdoht@hotmail.com
Holter, Wayne V., 125 Lakin Ave., Boonsboro, MD, 21713, 301-416-2855, mackwayne@hotmail.com
Hopkins, David W, Hopkins Photography inc, 201 S Jefferson, Iola, KS, 66744, 620-365-7443, nhoppy@netks.net
Kerns, Bob, 18723 Birdseye Dr., Germantown, MD, 20874
LaFleur, Gordon, 111 Hirst, Box 1209, Parksville BC CANADA, V0R 270
Lear, Dale, 6544 Cora Mill Rd, Gallipolis, OH, 45631, 740-245-5482, dalelear@yahoo.com, Ebay Sales
LeBlanc, Paul, No. 3 Meadowbrook Cir., Melissa, TX, 75454
Lester, Dean, 2801 Junipero Ave Suite 212, Long Beach, CA, 90806-2140
Leviton, David A., A Studio on the Move, P.O. Box 2871, Silverdale, WA, 98383, 360-697-3452
Long, Gary W., 3556 Miller's Crossroad Rd., Hillsboro, TN, 37342
Long, Jerry, 402 E. Gladden Dr., Farmington, NM, 87401
Lum, Billy, 16307 Evening Star Ct., Crosby, TX, 77532
Martin, Cory, 4249 Taylor Harbor #7, Mt. Pleasant, WI 53403,

262-352-5392, corymartin@corymartinimaging.com, www.corymartinimaging.com
McCollum, Tom, P.O. Box 933, Lilburn, GA, 30226
Mitch Lum Website and Photography, 22115 NW Imbrie Dr. #298, Hillsboro, OR 97124, mitch@mitchlum.com, www.mitchlum.com, 206-356-6813
Moake, Jim, 18 Council Ave., Aurora, IL, 60504
Moya Inc., 4212 S. Dixie Hwy., West Palm Beach, FL, 33405
Norman's Studio, 322 S. 2nd St., Vivian, LA, 71082
Owens, William T., Box 99, Williamsburg, WV, 24991
Pachi, Francesco, Loc. Pometta 1, 17046 Sassello (SV) ITALY Tel-fax: 0039 019 720086 www.pachi-photo.com
Palmer Studio, 2008 Airport Blvd., Mobile, AL, 36606
Payne, Robert G., P.O. Box 141471, Austin, TX, 78714
Pigott, John, 9095 Woodprint LN, Mason, OH, 45040
Point Seven, 6450 Weatherfield Ct., Unit 2A, Maumee, OH, 43537, 419-243-8880, 877-787-3836, www.pointsevenstudios.com
Professional Medica Concepts, Patricia Mitchell, P.O. Box 0002, Warren, TX, 77664, 409-547-2213, pm0909@wt.net
Rasmussen, Eric L., 1121 Eliason, Brigham City, UT, 84302
Rhoades, Cynthia J., Box 195, Clearmont, WY, 82835
Rice, Tim, PO Box 663, Whitefish, MT, 59937
Richardson, Kerry, 2520 Mimosa St., Santa Rosa, CA, 95405, 707-575-1875, kerry@sonic.net, www.sonic.net/~kerry
Ross, Bill, 28364 S. Western Ave. Suite 464, Rancho Palos Verdes, CA, 90275
Rubicam, Stephen, 14 Atlantic Ave., Boothbay Harbor, ME, 04538-1202
Rush, John D., 2313 Maysel, Bloomington, IL, 61701
Schreiber, Roger, 429 Boren Ave. N., Seattle, WA, 98109
Semmer, Charles, 7885 Cyd Dr., Denver, CO, 80221
Silver Images Photography, 2412 N Keystone, Flagstaff, AZ, 86004
Slobodian, Scott, 4101 River Ridge Dr., P.O. Box 1498, San Andreas, CA, 95249, 209-286-1980, (209) 286-1982, www.slobodianswords.com
Smith, Earl W., 5121 Southminster Rd., Columbus, OH, 43221
Smith, Randall, 1720 Oneco Ave., Winter Park, FL, 32789
Storm Photo, 334 Wall St., Kingston, NY, 12401
Surles, Mark, P.O. Box 147, Falcon, NC, 28342
Third Eye Photos, 140 E. Sixth Ave., Helena, MT, 59601
Thurber, David, P.O. Box 1006, Visalia, CA, 93279
Tighe, Brian, RR 1, Ridgeville ON CANADA, L0S 1M0, 905-892-2734, www.tigheknives.com
Towell, Steven L., 3720 N.W. 32nd Ave., Camas, WA, 98607, 360-834-9049, sltowell@netscape.net
Verno Studio, Jay, 3030 Jane Street, Pittsburgh, PA, 15203
Ward, Chuck, 1010 E North St, PO Box 2272, Benton, AR, 72018, 501-778-4329, chuckbop@aol.com
Weyer International, 6466 Teal Rd., Petersburgh, MI, 49270, 734-279-2464, law-weyerinternational@msn.com
Wise, Harriet, 242 Dill Ave., Frederick, MD, 21701
Worley, Holly, Worley Photography, 6360 W David Dr, Littleton, CO, 80128-5708, 303-257-8091, 720-981-2800, hsworley@aol.com, Products, Digital & Film

scrimshanders

Adlam, Tim, 1705 Witzel Ave., Oshkosh, WI, 54902, 920-235-4589, www.adlamngraving.com
Alpen, Ralph, 7 Bentley Rd., West Grove, PA, 19390, 610-869-7141
Anderson, Terry Jack, 10076 Birnamwoods Way, Riverton, UT, 84065-9073
Bailey, Mary W., 3213 Jonesboro Dr., Nashville, TN, 37214, mbscrim@aol.com, www.members.aol.com/mbscrim/ scrim.html
Baker, Duane, 2145 Alum Creek Dr., Cambridge Park Apt. #10, Columbus, OH, 43207
Barrows, Miles, 524 Parsons Ave., Chillicothe, OH, 45601
Brady, Sandra, P.O. Box 104, Monclova, OH, 43542, 419-866-0435, (419) 867-0656, sandyscrim@hotmail.com, www.knifeshows.com
Beauchamp, Gaetan, 125 de la Riviere, Stoneham, PQ, G0A 4P0, CANADA, 418-848-1914, (418) 848-6859, knives@gbeauchamp.ca, www.beauchamp.cjb.net

Bellet, Connie, PO Box 151, Palermo, ME, 04354 0151, 207-993-2327, phwhitehawk@gwl.net

Benade, Lynn, 2610 Buckhurst Dr, Beachwood, OH, 44122, 216-464-0777, llbnc17@aol.com

Bonshire, Benita, 1121 Burlington Dr., Muncie, IN, 47302

Boone Trading Co. Inc., P.O. Box 669, Brinnon, WA, 98320, 800-423-1945, ww.boonetrading.com

Bryan, Bob, 1120 Oak Hill Rd., Carthage, MO, 64836

Burger, Sharon, Cluster Box 1625, Forest Hills/KLOOF 3624, KZN, South Africa, cell: +27 83 7891675, tel/fax: +27 31 7621349, scribble@iafrica.com, www.kgsa.co.za/members/sharonburger

Byrne, Mary Gregg, 1018 15th St., Bellingham, WA, 98225-6604

Cable, Jerry, 332 Main St., Mt. Pleasant, PA, 15666

Caudill, Lyle, 7626 Lyons Rd., Georgetown, OH, 45121

Cole, Gary, PO Box 668, Naalehu, HI, 96772, 808-929-9775, 808-929-7371, www.community.webshots.com/album/11836830uqyeejirsz

Collins, Michael, Rt. 3075, Batesville Rd., Woodstock, GA, 30188

Conover, Juanita Rae, P.O. Box 70442, Eugene, OR, 97401, 541-747-1726 or 543-4851, juanitaraeconover@yahoo.com

Courtnage, Elaine, Box 473, Big Sandy, MT, 59520

Cover Jr., Raymond A., Rt. 1, Box 194, Mineral Point, MO, 63660

Cox, J. Andy, 116 Robin Hood Lane, Gaffney, SC, 29340

Dietrich, Roni, Wild Horse Studio, 1257 Cottage Dr, Harrisburg, PA, 17112, 717-469-0587, ronimd@aol

DiMarzo, Richard, 2357 Center Place, Birmingham, AL, 35205

Dolbare, Elizabeth, PO Box 502, Dubois, WY, 82513-0502

Eklund, Maihkel, Föne 1111, S-82041 Färila, SWEDEN, +46 6512 4192, maihkel.eklund@swipnet.se, www.art-knives.com

Eldridge, Allan, 1424 Kansas Lane, Gallatin, TN, 37066

Ellis, Willy b, Willy B's Customs by William B Ellis, 4941 Cardinal Trail, Palm Harbor, FL, 34683, 727-942-6420, www.willyb.com

Fisk, Dale, Box 252, Council, ID, 83612, dafisk@ctcweb.net

Foster Enterprises, Norvell Foster, P.O. Box 200343, San Antonio, TX, 78220

Fountain Products, 492 Prospect Ave., West Springfield, MA, 01089

Gill, Scott, 925 N. Armstrong St., Kokomo, IN, 46901

Halligan, Ed, 14 Meadow Way, Sharpsburg, GA, 30277, ehkiss@bellsouth.net

Hands, Barry Lee, 26192 East Shore Route, Bigfork, MT, 59911

Hargraves Sr., Charles, RR 3 Bancroft, Ontario CANADA, K0L 1C0

Harless, Star, c/o Arrow Forge, P.O. Box 845, Stoneville, NC, 27048-0845

Harrington, Fred A., Summer: 2107 W Frances Rd, Mt Morris MI 48458 8215, Winter: 3725 Citrus, St. James City, FL, 33956, Winter 239-283-0721, Summer 810-686-3008

Hergert, Bob, 12 Geer Circle, Port Orford, OR, 97465, 541-332-3010, hergert@harborside.com, www.scrimshander.com

Hielscher, Vickie, 6550 Otoe Rd, P.O. Box 992, Alliance, NE, 69301, 308-762-4318, g-hielsc@bbcwb.net

High, Tom, 5474 S. 112.8 Rd., Alamosa, CO, 81101, 719-589-2108, scrimshaw@vanion.com, www.rockymountainscrimshaw.com, Wildlife Artist

Himmelheber, David R., 11289 40th St. N., Royal Palm Beach, FL, 33411

Holland, Dennis K., 4908-17th Place, Lubbock, TX, 79416

Hutchings, Rick "Hutch", 3007 Coffe Tree Ct, Crestwood, KY, 40014, 502-241-2871, baron1@bellsouth.net

Imboden II, Howard L., 620 Deauville Dr., Dayton, OH, 45429, 937-439-1536, Guards by the "Last Wax Technic"

Johnson, Corinne, W3565 Lockington, Mindora, WI, 54644

Johnston, Kathy, W. 1134 Providence, Spokane, WA, 99205

Karst Stone, Linda, 903 Tanglewood Ln, Kerrville, TX, 78028-2945, 830-896-4678, 830-257-6117, karstone@ktc.com

Kelso, Jim, 577 Coller Hill Rd, Worcester, VT, 05682

Kirk, Susan B., 1340 Freeland Rd., Merrill, MI, 48637

Koevenig, Eugene and Eve, Koevenig's Engraving Service, Rabbit Gulch, Box 55, Hill City, SD, 57745-0055

Kostelnik, Joe and Patty, RD #4, Box 323, Greensburg, PA, 15601

Lemen, Pam, 3434 N. Iroquois Ave., Tucson, AZ, 85705

Martin, Diane, 28220 N. Lake Dr., Waterford, WI, 53185

McDonald, René Cosimini-, 14730 61 Court N., Loxahatchee, FL, 33470

McFadden, Berni, 2547 E Dalton Ave, Dalton Gardens, ID, 83815-9631

McGowan, Frank, 12629 Howard Lodge Dr., Winter Add-2023 Robin Ct Sebring FL 33870, Sykesville, MD, 21784, 863-385-1296

McGrath, Gayle, PMB 232 15201 N Cleveland Ave, N Ft Myers, FL, 33903

McLaran, Lou, 603 Powers St., Waco, TX, 76705

McWilliams, Carole, P.O. Box 693, Bayfield, CO, 81122

Mead, Faustina L., 2550 E. Mercury St., Inverness, FL, 34453-0514, 352-344-4751, scrimsha@infionline.net, www.scrimshaw-by-faustina.com

Mitchell, James, 1026 7th Ave., Columbus, GA, 31901

Moore, James B., 1707 N. Gillis, Stockton, TX, 79735

Ochonicky, Michelle "Mike", Stone Hollow Studio, 31 High Trail, Eureka, MO, 63025, 636-938-9570, www.bestofmissourihands.com

Ochs, Belle, 124 Emerald Lane, Largo, FL, 33771, 727-530-3826, chuckandbelle@juno.com, www.oxforge.com

Pachi, Mirella, Via Pometta 1, 17046 Sassello (SV), ITALY, 019 720086, WWW.PACHI-KNIVES.COM

Parish, Vaughn, 103 Cross St., Monaca, PA, 15061

Peterson, Lou, 514 S. Jackson St., Gardner, IL, 60424

Pienaar, Conrad, 19A Milner Rd., Bloemfontein 9300, SOUTH AFRICA, Phone: 027 514364180 fax: 027 514364180

Poag, James H., RR #1 Box 212A, Grayville, IL, 62844

Polk, Trena, 4625 Webber Creek Rd., Van Buren, AR, 72956

Purvis, Hilton, P.O. Box 371, Noordhoek, 7979, SOUTH AFRICA, 27 21 789 1114, hiltonp@telkomsa.net, www.kgsa.co.za/member/hiltonpurvis

Ramsey, Richard, 8525 Trout Farm Rd, Neosho, MO, 64850

Ristinen, Lori, 14256 County Hwy 45, Menahga, MN, 56464, 218-538-6608, lori@loriristinen.com, www.loriristinen.com

Roberts, J.J., 7808 Lake Dr., Manassas, VA, 22111, 703-330-0448, jjrengraver@aol.com, www.angelfire.com/va2/ engraver

Rudolph, Gil, 20922 Oak Pass Ave, Tehachapi, CA, 93561, 661-822-4949, www.gtraks@csurfers.net

Rundell, Joe, 6198 W. Frances Rd., Clio, MI, 48420

Saggio, Joe, 1450 Broadview Ave. #12, Columbus, OH, 43212, 614-481-1967, jvsaggio@earthlink.net, www.j.v.saggio@worldnet.att.net

Sahlin, Viveca, Konstvaktarevagem 9, S-772 40 Grangesberg, SWEDEN, 46 240 23204, www.scrimart.use

Satre, Robert, 518 3rd Ave. NW, Weyburn SK CANADA, S4H 1R1

Schlott, Harald, Zingster Str. 26, 13051 Berlin, 929 33 46, GERMANY, 049 030 9293346, 049 030 9293346, harald.schlott@t-online.de, www.gravur-kunst-atelier.de.vu

Schulenburg, E.W., 25 North Hill St., Carrollton, GA, 30117

Schwallie, Patricia, 4614 Old Spartanburg Rd. Apt. 47, Taylors, SC, 29687

Selent, Chuck, P.O. Box 1207, Bonners Ferry, ID, 83805

Semich, Alice, 10037 Roanoke Dr., Murfreesboro, TN, 37129

Shostle, Ben, 1121 Burlington, Muncie, IN, 47302

Smith, Peggy, 676 Glades Rd., #3, Gatlinburg, TN, 37738

Smith, Ron, 5869 Straley, Ft. Worth, TX, 76114

Stahl, John, Images In Ivory, 2049 Windsor Rd., Baldwin, NY, 11510, 516-223-5007, imivory@msn.com, www.imagesinivory.org

Steigerwalt, Jim, RD#3, Sunbury, PA, 17801

Stuart, Stephen, 15815 Acorn Circle, Tavares, FL, 32778, 352-343-8423, (352) 343-8916, inkscratch@aol.com

Talley, Mary Austin, 2499 Countrywood Parkway, Memphis, TN, 38016, matalley@midsouth.rr.com

Thompson, Larry D., 23040 Ave. 197, Strathmore, CA, 93267

Toniutti, Nelida, Via G. Pascoli, 33085 Maniago-PN, ITALY

Trout, Lauria Lovestrand, 1555 Delaney Dr, No. 1723, Talahassee, FL, 32309, 850-893-8836, mayalaurie@aol.com

Tucker, Steve, 3518 W. Linwood, Turlock, CA, 95380

Tyser, Ross, 1015 Hardee Court, Spartanburg, SC, 29303

Velasquez, Gil, Art of Scrimshaw, 7120 Madera Dr., Goleta, CA, 93117

Wilderness Forge, 475 NE Smith Rock Way, Terrebonne, OR, 97760, bhatting@xpressweb.com

Williams, Gary, PO Box 210, Glendale, KY, 42740, 270-369-6752, garywilliam@alltel.net

Winn, Travis A., 558 E. 3065 S., Salt Lake City, UT, 84106

Young, Mary, 4826 Storeyland Dr., Alton, IL, 62002

organizations

AMERICAN BLADESMITH SOCIETY
c/o Office Manager, Cindy Sheely; P. O. Box 160, Grand Rapids, Ohio 45522; cindy@americanbladesmith.com; (419) 832-0400; Web: www.americanbladesmith.com

AMERICAN KNIFE & TOOL INSTITUTE*
Jan Billeb, Comm. Coordinator, AKTI, 22 Vista View Ln., Cody, WY 82414; 307-587-8296, akti@akti.org; www. akti.org

AMERICAN KNIFE THROWERS ALLIANCE
c/o Bobby Branton; 4976 Seewee Rd; Awendaw, SC 29429; www.AKTA-USA.com

ARIZONA KNIFE COLLECTOR'S ASSOCIATION
c/o D'Alton Holder, President, 7148 W. Country Gables Dr., Peoria, AZ 85381; Web: www.akca.net

ART KNIFE COLLECTOR'S ASSOCIATION
c/o Mitch Weiss, Pres.; 2211 Lee Road, Suite 104; Winter Park, FL 32789

BAY AREA KNIFE COLLECTOR'S ASSOCIATION
Doug Isaacson, B.A.K.C.A. Membership, 36774 Magnolia, Newark, CA 94560; Web: www.bakca.org

ARKANSAS KNIFEMAKERS ASSOCIATION
David Etchieson, 60 Wendy Cove, Conway, AR 72032; Web: www.arkansasknifemakers.com

AUSTRALASIAN KNIFE COLLECTORS
PO BOX 149 CHIDLOW 6556 WESTERN AUSTRALIA TEL: (08) 9572 7255; FAX: (08) 9572 7266. International Inquiries: TEL: + 61 8 9572 7255; FAX: + 61 8 9572 7266; akc@ knivesaustralia.com.au

CALIFORNIA KNIFEMAKERS ASSOCIATION
c/o Clint Breshears, Membership Chairman; 1261 Keats St; Manhattan Beach CA 90266; 310-372-0739; breshears@ mindspring.com
Dedicated to teaching and improving knifemaking

CANADIAN KNIFEMAKERS GUILD
c/o Peter Wile; RR # 3; Bridgewater N.S. CANADA B4V 2W2; 902-543-1373; www.ckg.org

CUSTOM KNIFE COLLECTORS ASSOCIATION
c/o Kevin Jones, PO Box 5893, Glen Allen, VA 23058-5893; E-mail: customknifecollectorsassociation@yahoo.com; Web: www.customknifecollectorsassociation.com
The purpose of the CKCA is to recognize and promote the artistic significance of handmade knives, to advnace their collection and conservation, and to support the creative expression of those who make them. Open to collectors, makers purveyors, and other collectors. Has members from eight countries. Produced a calednar which features custom knives either owned or made by CKCA members.

CUTTING EDGE, THE
1920 N 26th St, Lowell, AR 72745; 479-631-0055; 479-636-4618; ce-info@cuttingedge.com
After-market knives since 1968. We offer about 1,000 individual knives each month. The oldest and the most experienced in the business of buying and selling knives. We buy collections of any size, take knives on consignment or we will trade. Web: www.cuttingedge.com

FLORIDA KNIFEMAKERS ASSOCIATION
c/o President, Dan Mink, PO Box 861, Crystal beach, Florida, 34681 (727) 786 5408; Web: www.floridaknifemakers.org

JAPANESE SWORD SOCIETY OF THE U.S.
PO Box 712; Breckenridge, TX 76424

KNIFE COLLECTORS CLUB INC, THE
1920 N 26th St; Lowell AR 72745; 479-631-0130; 479-631-8493; ag@agrussell.com; Web:www.club@k-c-c.com
The oldest and largest association of knife collectors. Issues limited edition knives, both handmade and highest quality production, in very limited numbers. The very earliest was the CM-1, Kentucky Rifle

KNIFE WORLD
PO Box 3395; Knoxville, TN 37927; 800-828-7751; 865-397-1955; 865-397-1969; knifepub@knifeworld.com
Publisher of monthly magazine for knife enthusiasts and world's largest knife/cutlery bookseller. Web: www.knifeworld.com

KNIFEMAKERS GUILD
c/o Beverly Imel, Knifemakers Guild, Box 922, New Castle, IN 47362; (765) 529-1651; Web: www.knifemakersguild.com

KNIFEMAKERS GUILD OF SOUTHERN AFRICA, THE
c/o Carel Smith; PO Box 1744; Delmars 2210; SOUTH AFRICA; carelsmith@therugby.co.za; Web:www.kgsa.co.za

KNIVES ILLUSTRATED
265 S. Anita Dr., Ste. 120; Orange, CA 92868; 714-939-9991; 714-939-9909; knivesillustrated@yahoo.com; Web:www. knivesillustrated.com
All encompassing publication focusing on factory knives, new handmades, shows and industry news, plus knifemaker features, new products, and travel pieces

MONTANA KNIFEMAKERS' ASSOCIATION, THE
14440 Harpers Bridge Rd; Missoula, MT 59808; 406-543-0845
Annual book of custom knife makers' works and directory of knife making supplies; $19.99

NATIONAL KNIFE COLLECTORS ASSOCIATION
PO Box 21070; Chattanooga, TN 37424; 423-892-5007; 423-899-9456; info@nationalknife.org; Web: www.nationalknife. org

NEO-TRIBAL METALSMITHS
PO Box 44095; Tucson, AZ 85773-4095; Web: www.neo-tribalmetalsmiths.com

NEW ENGLAND CUSTOM KNIFE ASSOCIATION
George R. Rebello, President; 686 Main Rd; Brownville, ME 04414; Web: www.knivesby.com/necka.html

NORTH CAROLINA CUSTOM KNIFEMAKERS GUILD
c/o 2112 Windy Woods Drive, Raleigh, NC 27607 (919) 834-4693; Web: www.ncknifeguild.org

NORTH STAR BLADE COLLECTORS
PO Box 20523, Bloomington, MN 55420

OHIO KNIFEMAKERS ASSOCIATION
c/o Jerry Smith, Anvils and Ink Studios, P.O. Box 7887, Columbus, Ohio 43229-7887; Web: www.geocities.com/ ohioknives/

OREGON KNIFE COLLECTORS ASSOCIATION
Web: www.oregonknifeclub.org

RANDALL KNIFE SOCIETY
PO Box 158, Meadows of Dan, VA 24120 email: payrks@gate.net; Web: www.randallknifesociety.com

ROCKY MOUNTAIN BLADE COLLECTORS ASSOCIATION
Mike Moss. Pres., P.O. Box 324, Westminster, CO 80036

RESOURCE GUIDE AND NEWSLETTER / AUTOMATIC KNIVES
2269 Chestnut St., Suite 212; San Francisco, CA 94123; 415-731-0210; Web: http://latama.net/thenewsletterpage.html

SOUTH CAROLINA ASSOCIATION OF KNIFEMAKERS
c/o Victor Odom, Jr., Post Office Box 572, North, SC 29112 (803) 247-5614; Web: www.scak.org

SOUTHERN CALIFORNIA BLADES
SC Blades, PO Box 1140, Lomita, CA 90717; Web: www.scblades.com

TEXAS KNIFEMAKERS & COLLECTORS ASSOCIATION
2254 Fritz Allen Street, Fort Worth, Texas 76114; Web: www.tkca.org

THE WILLIAM F. MORAN JR. MUSEUM & FOUNDATION
4204 Ballenger Creek Pike, Frederick, MD 21703, 301-663-6923

TRIBAL NOW!
Neo-Tribal Metalsmiths; PO Box 44095; Tucson, AZ 85733-4095; Web: www.neo-tribalmetalsmiths.com

publications

BLADE
700 E. State St., Iola, WI 54990-0001; 715-445-2214; Web: www.blademag.com, www.KnifeForums.com, www.ShopBlade.com, facebook.com/blademag
The world's No. 1 knife magazine. The most indepth knife magazine on the market, covering all aspects of the industry, from knifemaking to production knives and handmade pieces. With 13 issues per year, BLADE® boasts twice the distribution of its closest competitors.

CUTLERY NEWS JOURNAL (BLOG)
http://cutlerynewsjournal.wordpress.com
Covers significant happenings from the world of knife collecting, in addition to editorials, trends, events, auctions, shows, cutlery history, and reviews

KNIFE WORLD
PO Box 3395, Knoxville, TN 37927; www.knifeworld.com

KNIVES ILLUSTRATED
265 S. Anita Dr., Ste. 120, Orange, CA 92868; 714-939-9991; knivesillustrated@yahoo.com; Web: www.knivesillustrated.com
All encompassing publication focusing on factory knives, new handmades, shows and industry news

RESOURCE GUIDE AND NEWSLETTER / AUTOMATIC KNIVES
2269 Chestnut St., Suite 212, San Francisco, CA 94123; 415-731-0210; Web: http://latama.net/theNewsletterPage.html

TACTICAL KNIVES
Harris Publications, 1115 Broadway, New York, NY 10010; Web: www.tacticalknives.com